THE TRUTH CHRONICLES

BOOK II

Secrets of the Illuminati

Danny Searle

DEDICATION

To all those seeking the truth and enlightenment.

Never give up your quest. Never give up hope.

You are never alone.

NOTES

CONTENTS PART 3

Appendices

0

INTRODUCTION

> "It's exhilarating to be alive in a time of awakening consciousness; it can also be confusing, disorienting, and painful."
> — ADRIENNE RICH (1929 – 2012)

You have felt it all your life. Something is not right in the world. That question has led you here. I too have felt this most of my life, which took me on a journey of discovery, horror, pain, anger, joy, and then acceptance. In this book, I will detail the true "owners" of the planet. We build their cities, we fight their wars, and we slave ourselves to keep them wealthy. But most of us do not even know "their" names.

They are just people like you and me, but their psychology is different. They honestly believe it is their divine right to rule over the rest of us. Why would they believe that? Why do they think differently to us? What drives them to murder millions, hoard wealth, and place themselves above the rest of humanity? This book will answer these questions and much more.

In **Book I: Secrets of the Soul**, I spoke of the "**Wise Mind**." The *Wise Mind* can put aside emotions, and look at the facts in an unbiased way. For some of you, this will prove difficult in some circumstances, and I get that. But I would ask that you put aside any religious, cultural, and societal dogmas that you may be attached to, and read this book with an open mind, and an open heart.

I always try and supply as many references as I can, to allow you to verify what I am saying, and also to carry out further research for yourself. Thus, about 99.98% of this book can be verified by outside sources (I don't say 100% because no one is perfect!)

Furthermore, when I mention or reference someone I greatly admire, I will call them a "true hero of the people", because that is what they are. These are the men and women who have stood in the face of the greatest evil we know, and never backed down from telling the truth. None of them are world famous or rich. No surprises there! That is because they chose Truth over a materially rewarding life. If you read my first book, then you will understand that these people are older Souls – from Mature Souls to Old Souls. The people they, and I expose, are Young Souls usually from Level 5-7. Occasionally a late level Child Soul may make an appearance.

All of us that have been raise in a so-called First World country have been brainwashed to believe our Country, or Military, Our leaders can do no wrong. Our Royals are little, old, kind, charity workers with no real power any more. And patriotic behaviour is a perfect way to show that you love your country. At the same time we are fed these lies, we are not told about the 1 billion people that are starving, or that 70% of all corn and wheat that is grown is fed to cattle, sheep, and pigs to be tortured, then consumed by the masses. Don't worry, I am not getting on some "be a vegetarian or die" soap box. I am just highlighting the fact that the mighty dollar is more important than our fellow humans.

And that is the whole point of this book. Our so-called leaders do not care about you or me. Our so-called leaders do not want to save us from bad things, find a cure for cancer, or feed the starving billions. No, they only exist for one reason – to maintain the status-quo.

So get ready for some shocks, oohs, and ahhs, and the odd giggle.

1

THE .01 PERCENTERS

"Greed is a bottomless pit which exhausts the person in an endless effort to satisfy the need without ever reaching satisfaction."

— ERICH FROMM (1900 – 1980)

They are really the 1 percent, of the 1 percent. They are the wealthiest people in the world. They have private jets, they live in private communities, and they holiday on their own private islands. With so much money comes incredible power, and exclusive access into the most secret circles. It's all in secret, therefore, **anything goes!**

But just how much influence does this elite group really have on the world? What is their ultimate plans? They control all of the mainstream media, they have influence over our political systems so the question always comes down to *"Are billionaires controlling the world governments?"*

March, 2014, Forbes Magazine publishes their annual list of the world's billionaires. It includes, 492 Americans, more than any other nation. Following is China with 152, and Russia with 111. Topping the list of the United States richest, is Microsoft Chairman **Bill Gates**, worth $76 billion. Berkshire Hathaway's **Warren Buffet**, comes in at $58.2 billion. Oracle co-founder, **Larry Ellison**, $48 billion (Forbes, 2015).

America is very rich, but we are talking about the 1% of the 1% at the very top. They are richer than any human has ever been in the history of the planet. The 400 richest Americans are worth a total of $2 Trillion – about $5 billion each, and they are only getting richer.

In 2014, the American billionaires added nearly ½ Trillion dollars to their fortunes. Bill Gates alone gained $9 billion. That is nearly $25,000,000 per day, or more than $17,000 per minute!

The top 400 richest people in America have more wealth than the bottom 95% of Americans combined. The CEO of Walmart, **Mike Duke**, makes $11,000 an hour, and he has workers making $8.00 an hour. Before he goes to lunch, he has made more than anyone of Walmart's one million staff makes in an entire year.

The **Walton Family** controls the Walmart Corporation, the world's largest retailer. **Christy Walton**, the widow of a son of Walmart's founder **Sam Walton** is the richest woman in America, with $36.7 billion. Media mogul **Oprah Winfrey**, has built an empire worth $2.9 billion, making her America's only African-American billionaire. So just how rich does that make these women?

A billion dollars – can you imagine it? It is very hard to wrap your mind around it. A billion dollars is 1 thousand × 1 million dollars (1000 × 1,000,000). If you spent **$10,000 a day**, it would take you over **300 years** to spend the entire sum. Remember Bill Gates is worth $76 billion, so that would take about **22,800 years** to spend all of his money at $10,000 per day!

Therefore, these people tend to live in a world of their own, and the only people billionaires can relate to, are other billionaires. So they get together, and their agenda is always more money, and more power.

Billionaire brothers **Charles and David Koch** own the second largest, privately owned company, *Koch Industries Inc*. Their conglomerate, which includes petroleum and chemical companies, rakes in around $110 billion per year. The fossil fuel dynamos also own *Georgia Pacific* (GP), one of the world's leading manufacturers of paper products.

Who is the youngest, self-made billionaire in the World?

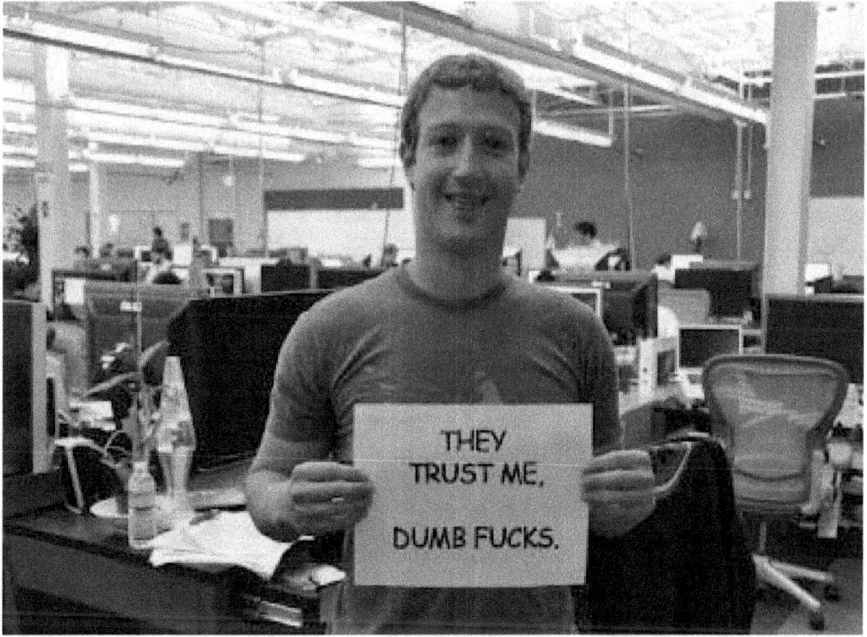

Mark Zuckerberg (1984 -)

Mark Zuckerberg, the co-founder of **Facebook**, is worth over $28.5 billion. In 2014, he was just 29 years old. He once famously said about his Facebook users:

> *"They trust me — dumb fucks. . ." (Johnson, 2010)*

It is important to be tracking the world's richest people, because of their control over so much of the global economy and also so much of our culture. They own our sports teams, they control our media, and they have a huge influence over our political systems via lobbyists.

But not all billionaires are so well known. Some have kept their fortune secret, staying almost completely out of the lime light. **Richard B. Cohen**, the sole owner of C & S Wholesale Grocers, distributes products to more than 4000 supermarkets across the United States in unmarked trucks. He has amassed a net worth of over $11.2 billion. His own home town of Keene, New Hampshire had no idea as he lives quietly, in a mere $1,000,000 home.

The more private a billionaire is, the less ostentatious their spending will be on their personal lifestyles. That said, a lot of these billionaires have multiple homes. In a new survey Forbes Magazine did, the majority said they had 5 or more homes. So a billion dollars means you can afford not just 1 × $10 million home, but multiple $10 million homes!

$1 trillion

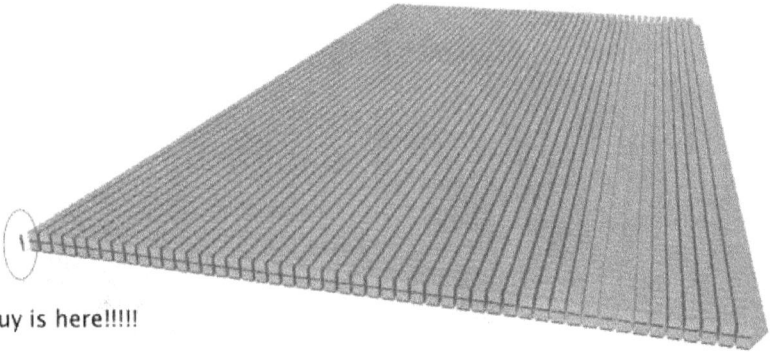

The guy is here!!!!!

These are $100 bills stacked up to make $1 trillion

NATIONAL DEBT - $11,046,247,657,049.48

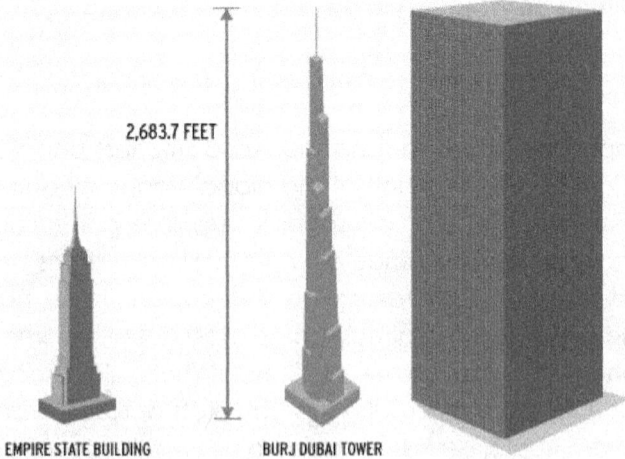

2,683.7 FEET

EMPIRE STATE BUILDING   BURJ DUBAI TOWER

$21 trillion - the stack of $100 bills on the far right

Two other multi-billionaires that like to fly under the radar are the Rothschild family and Queen Elizabeth II of England. The Rothschild's have an estimated $500 TRILLION (one thousand × one billion = 1 trillion – check out this awesome short video:(TRILLION dollars, 2015) and the Queen about 20 TRILLION pounds, about $30 Trillion US.

David Rockefeller is another old man that likes to hide his money. Publically he says he has $3 billion, but those that know him, and of his investments, calculate his wealth at least $55 billion. But how far do the wealthy go to make and maintain their fortunes? Might they just know how to take advantage of the system?

What is the billionaire Agenda?

October 15, 2013, New York City. After a seven yearlong battle, developers reached an agreement to build two luxury towers on 57 Street, in Manhattan. Dubbed, **billionaires Row**, the building's penthouses are priced at over $90 million each. They will be the tallest residences in New York City, literally, putting billionaires at a higher level than everybody else. But could there be a secret reason why billionaires flock to such gilded fortresses?

It seems certain billionaires live with tremendous anxiety their bubble could burst. That bubble therefore, needs to be well protected, and well controlled. You start to see with these very wealthy people, pockets of places where they all want to go to together.

It started with a building called "157" where a number of billionaires bought these insanely expensive apartments to build these communities, where only the very elite can afford to live. When you get that rich, you live in gated communities, you have your private jet, so you don't have to stand in line at the airports – everything is done for you. All the services come to you. You don't have to go to the services.

Billionaires have people that they pay to buy their groceries, take care of their kids, pay their bills, fix their houses, do their dishes, and do the washing amongst other things. They live in their own universe that is far removed from the rest of us, so they are not grounded in the economic realities that most of us are.

In 2013, Mark Zuckerberg bought four of his neighbour's homes, for a whopping $30 million, simply to ensure privacy. Being mega rich in the world today essentially means that you never have to come into contact with anyone else that is not also mega rich.

They live in a sanitised bubble that is designed and maintained for mega rich people. In recent years, the financial distance between the 1% and the rest of us has grown more and more and at the same time their control over the population has increased exponentially.

So what is the secret to their success?

Just how have the top of the 1% made their billions? Could there be something inherent, driving billionaires to such extreme levels of wealth?

The God Complex

June, 2010, billionaires Warren Buffett, and Bill and Melinda Gates announce the *Giving Pledge*. Its mission – convincing billionaires to give at least half of their money to charity. Either during their lifetime, or at the time of their death. The Giving Pledge is a pledge made up by about 122 billionaires who have decided that they are going to give a substantial lion's share proportion of their money to various foundations that will be involved with feeding the poor, improving education, providing clean water in Africa and other things like that.

Do billionaires donate so much of their money because they feel guilty about their fortune? Or could there be another reason, hidden in a way they think will fool us? Let's look at the world's richest man, and see what he does.

Bill Gates (1955 -)

"The world today has 6.9 billion people and that's headed up to about 9 billion. If we do a really great job, we could lower that by perhaps 10 or 15 percent."

– BILL GATES (YOUTUBE, 2013)

So 15% of nine billion = 1,350,000,000 (one billion, 350 million) – that is how many people Bill Gates hopes to wipe from the face of the Earth.

Bill Gates believes that the density of the population in poor areas is too big, and with his depopulation plans, he can 'solve' that problem. His favourite method is the "soft-kill", with cancer laden vaccinations. However, consider his huge buyout of Monsanto stock – he owns millions of shares of Monsanto and Cargill stock, and the Bill and Melinda Gates Foundation keep scooping it up. He owns more than $23 million worth, or 500,000 Monsanto shares. (Gucciardi, 2010).

Seattle-based **Agra-Watch**, part of the Community Alliance for Global Justice, has said:

> *"Monsanto has a history of blatant disregard for the interests and wellbeing of small farmers around the world. . . [This] casts serious doubt on the foundation's heavy funding of agricultural development in Africa."*

It also casts serious doubt on the **Bill and Melinda Gates Foundation** and its true interests in supporting the 'poor' populations they so proudly claim they are trying to 'help.'

Gates also funds programs that blast men's reproductive organs with radiation so that they can no longer reproduce, and covert nanotechnology that delivers dangerous vaccines (Adams, 2010). The Gates Foundation is also teaming up with the British government in raising $4 billion to fund their birth control agenda worldwide by 2020.

The *Bill and Melinda Gates Foundation* bestowed more than $28 billion in grants. Bill Gates has got very involved with education, to the extent that one of the things that the *Bill and Melinda Gates Foundation* is supporting is **data tracking on children**.

After Rupert Murdoch's *Amplify Education* (a division of **News Corp**) spent more than a year developing the system's infrastructure, the Gates Foundation delivered it to *inBloom* – a non-profit corporation recently established to run the database. The system captures, analyses and shares with other government agencies personal identification ranging from name, address, Social Security number, attendance, test scores, homework completion, career goals, learning disabilities, and even hobbies and attitudes about school. As a matter of fact, the Foundation has already funded bracelets that go on children's arms that also track their moods (Haverluck, 2013).

They want to be able to individually track every child through school. Eventually they will profile children and track them from birth to death in a similar way they do it in the insider movie/book "**A Brave New World**." Certain children are selected to be "elite," while others are preselected to be working drones.

Billionaires are different to us

But they are not just people with a lot more money kind of different. They think that they deserve to rule the planet. They think that without them, the planet would not turn on its axis. Billionaires really do see the world as a proving ground, as opposed to millionaires, who see the world as their playground. What that means is, that billionaires really want to leave their mark in history.

Do billionaires actually think differently about the world then the rest of us? Might that way of thinking contribute to their great fortunes? Some experts believe the answer is "yes," and claim many billionaires are afflicted with what some commonly refer to as a **God Complex**.

George Soros (1930 -)

In 1995, billionaire investor **George Soros,** (one of the most repulsive humans on Earth right now) admitted it to the **New Yorker Magazine**. George Soros is worth more than many small countries. Our new god is money, so of course George Soros sees himself as a Messiah (Mayer, 2015). Many billionaires have a grandiose ideology of, "*I am a god like figure put here to do great things.*" They see themselves as having some responsibility to change the world. Soros's net worth tops $24.5 billion.

The once impoverished student, built his bank account through clever and devious manipulation of financial markets. Soros claims he is going to lead the world to the deregulated, free market future, with low taxes (for big business).

They believe, even when they are stealing with both hands, that they are doing "God's work." There are a lot of very scary billionaires out there, because after a while, they feel their great wealth endows them with superior wisdom and foresight, and the right to start medalling with other people's lives.

When you are out there saying "*I am doing God's work,*" all restraint is gone, and some people (like me!) think that is dangerous.

How did George Soros make his money?

Schwartz György was born in Hungary in 1930 — not the luckiest time and place to be born a Jew. In 1936, Schwartz's father **Theodore**, tried to change the family's fortunes by changing their name to something less Jewish-sounding. Schwartz György became George Soros. It didn't help, and soon the war came.

When the Nazis took total control of Hungary in 1944, the Holocaust followed. In two months, 440,000 Hungarian Jews were deported to camps. According to George, in order to survive, then a teenager, he collaborated with the Nazis.

First he worked for the **Judenrat**. That was the Jewish council set up by the Nazis to do their dirty work for them. Instead of the Nazis rounding up Jews every day for the trains, they delegated that hideous task to Jews who were willing to do it to survive another day at the expense of their neighbours.

Theodore hatched a better plan for his son. He bribed a non-Jewish official at the agriculture ministry to let George live with him. George helped the official confiscate property from Jews.

It worked like this, George would find and rat out the Jewish family or person. After the Nazis came and took them away, George was then at liberty to go through their house and take whatever he pleased. This was the beginning of his fortune. He openly brags how it would take him five days to clean out the premises of a wealthy Jewish family. They had so much silver wear it was hard work. All these goodies were then sold on the black market, usually to Nazi soldiers.

By collaborating with the Nazis, George survived the Holocaust and became wealthy. He turned on other Jews to spare himself, and made a profit at the same time.

George moved to London after the war and then to New York, where he became a stockbroker. He is now fabulously rich. Forbes magazine says he's the 16th richest man in the world with $24.5 billion (Forbes, 2015).

How does Soros feel about what he did as a teenager? Has it kept him up at night? **Steve Kroft** of **60 Minutes** asked him that:

> *Was it difficult?* "Not at all," *Soros answered.*
> "No feeling of guilt?" *asked Kroft.*
> "No," *said Soros.* "There was no sense that I shouldn't be there. If I wasn't doing it, somebody else would be taking it away anyhow. Whether I was there or not. So I had no sense of guilt."

That moral hollowness has shaped Soros' life. He's a rabid critic of capitalism, but in 1992 when he saw a chance, he speculated against the British pound, causing it to crash, devastating retirement savings for millions of Britons. Soros pocketed $1.1 billion for himself. If he didn't do it, someone else would, right?

In **2002**, Soros was convicted of insider trading in France, and fined millions of dollars. He admitted buying the shares, but denied it was a crime.

In **2009**, when he made $3.3 billion off the banking collapse, he called the world's financial crisis *"the culmination of my life's work."* This is a man who boasted he offered to help his mother commit suicide. Apparently he didn't see enough death in Hungary.

In **2015**, George Soros gave at least $33 million in one year to support already-established groups that emboldened the grass-roots, on-the-ground activists in **Ferguson** (USA), according to the most recent tax filings of his non-profit **Open Society Foundations**. The financial tether from Mr. Soros to the activist groups gave rise to a combustible protest movement that transformed a one-day criminal event in Missouri, into a 24-hour-a-day national cause. . .

Mr. Soros spurred the Ferguson protest movement through years of funding and mobilising groups across the U.S., according to interviews with key players and financial records reviewed by *The Washington Times* (Riddell, 2015).

Soros is a sociopath / psychopath. But he's a sociopath with **$24.5 billion**. He thinks he is a god, and he likes to spend it on left wing politics. Thus, his influence in average people's lives is immense. I don't have space to list all of the not-for-profit (mainly political) causes he funds. And no, it is not philanthropy – it is deliberately trying to create civil unrest by funding these wacko groups (Kroft, 1998).

> *"I am just a banker doing God's work."* - Lloyd Blankfein, CEO, Goldman Sachs, 2009

Do billionaires think they know better than the majority?

That the global masses are just objects to control? Is there really a secret motivation behind their charity work?

The fastest and most effective way for billionaires to change the world, is through philanthropy. Because philanthropy involves investing a lot of money into a cause that they feel is important.

In 1979, George Soros created the (tax free) **Open Society Foundation**, an operation aimed at social reform. Since its inception, Soros has given away more than $7 billion to various causes. But these so-called Foundations are just fronts to further Soros' agenda, not to mention, good tax breaks.

No matter how much money billionaires give away, the fundamental problems that gigantic fortunes are being misused politically and distorting our economy remains.

Why do some billionaires donate so much of their money to charity? Is it perhaps a covert method used to manipulate the global agenda? And do the affluent really know what is best for the people? Or are their actions, philanthropic or political, separating them further from the masses?

Dark Money

April 2, 2014, in a 5 - 4 vote, the Supreme Court of America decides the government cannot limit the amount of money donors can give to political candidates, committees and parties.

This shocking declaration gives America's ultra-rich free reign to spend billions on campaign contributions. Billionaires can exert more influence on our public life than ever before, and that is because they have unlimited ability now to fund political causes and to fund their own agendas. This is just one part of a fundamentally bigger plan to change the system to benefit people like themselves and their friends and their shadow money networks.

The ruling expanded a 2010 decision known as **Citizens United** that paved the way for independent expenditure only committees, or, "Super Pacts" enabling billionaires to contribute as much money as they want to political candidates, without being exposed to the public. *Citizen's United* decision pulled away any type of prohibition of companies donating money to political campaigns, and the question always comes down to balance, and the oversight.

Yes, billionaires are controlling the US government. It's all dark money. With this ruling however, we have no idea which billionaires are actually putting their fortunes into our politics, and ultimately corrupting our politicians. Wealthy individuals can now say they are doing one thing, and actually put their money behind a completely different politician or cause. There is no disclosure. It is all done in secret, therefore, anything goes.

If people have got a lot of money, they can find ways to conceal expenditure of that money, and if you set up one law that says you have to disclose this, then they will basically give money to other groups.

Politics has become a rich man's game. Massive donations to political candidates is another way for billionaires to exert their intrinsic need to control society. Billionaires try to influence the political process and the political system, because that enables them to effect laws that get passed.

Billionaires create front groups and lobbyists and social outreach programs. The amount of money these people have, shape society. There is absolutely no question that some of these billionaires have selfish interests for getting as deeply as they do into politics. It is not just their ideology. They are business people who want regulations cut, they don't want their special loop holes reduced.

According to reports, billionaire conservatives David and Charles Koch have contributed nearly $200 million to Free Market organisations, as well as groups lobbying **against the Affordable Care Act**. Ex-Nazi collaborator George Soros spent millions trying to defeat President Bush in 2004.

Could wealth and inequality lead to the destruction of democracy? Or is it just a zero sum, billion dollar game?

There are all kinds of secretive ways that we will never know anything about. Small pieces of the puzzle in tax codes, small pieces of trade regulations, a myriad of tiny things that don't mean much to most people, but are worth millions of dollars to certain individuals that billionaires can influence through their money and power.

The most important, secretive way that they can influence the political agenda, is by the access that money gives them to people in power. Their ability to sit down with somebody like a **Barack Obama** or a **Paul Ryan** and whisper in their ear happens every single day in Washington DC.

So just how much money are billionaires willing to pool out in an attempt to influence politics? In 2012, $7 billion was spent on the American Presidential election. Gambling tycoon, **Sheldon Adelson**, owner of Las Vegas cassinos, donated an unprecedented $100 million. But are candidates free to disagree with big donors, or are they beholden to them?

Warren Buffett's company **Union Pacific Railroad** benefited more than any other company by the inaction from the Obama administration, approving the **Keystone Pipeline**. Buffett's railroad carries the oil that is now going from Canada down to the Gulf of Mexico.

Do wealthy donors set the political agenda?

Perhaps even influencing candidates? And are billionaires only acting independently? Or could they be quietly meeting in secret with other like minds in an effort to further their common goals?

Conclaves and Secret Meetings

June, 2011, Vail, Colorado, Charles, and David Koch hold their bi-annual summit at the Ritz-Carlton, Bachelor Gulch. Isolated in an exclusive enclave on **Beaver Creek Mountain**. The fund-raising seminar is one of the most secret meetings of the wealthy, where 300, handpicked attendees, come together to strategize away from prying eyes.

After the 2011 summit in Vail, we learnt that major Wall Street titans like **Charles Schwab** are present and give lots of money. Furthermor, one of the senior Koch executives in his sales pitch, about why they should donate to them, as opposed to any other conservative group, was that they can guarantee anonymity.

Chris Christie (R - Governor of New Jersey) went to this meeting without putting it into his agenda. His appearance was completely secret and no one in New Jersey knew that he appeared before the Koch's and their little billionaire's confab.

More and more, like minded billionaires, regardless of politics, have banded together to promote their common interests. The question is, are their ideals that different?

May 5th, 2009 New York City. A group of wealthy philanthropists, including Bill Gates, Warren Buffett, David Rockefeller Jr., Michael Bloomberg, and Opera Winfrey, meet confidentially on the secluded campus of **Rockefeller University**. Dubbed *The Good Club*, the powerful billionaires plan to join forces in order to save the world. So what's the first thing on their agenda? Finding a way to shrink the world's population!

I find it very alarming that with their fortunes, they are all of the sudden deciding that they now have the right to tell other people whether they should or should not have children.

Why is population control the elite's number one agenda? Because they have already dominated the globe through their corporate and governmental actions and they really see it as "their" possession, - something they "own," and something they are guardians of. They're going to cut resources off from the 'unwashed' masses to 'protect' the planet."

June, 2013, Watford, England. Between 120 and 150 of the world's most powerful billionaires, politicians and Royals meet at the luxury Grove Hotel for 3 days to discuss global issues and broker international deals. The annual private conference, known as the **Bilderberg Group** is the world's most secretive society of billionaires.

Named after the Bilderberg Hotel in the Netherlands where the first meeting was held in 1954, the alliance was created to foster co-operation between Europe and North America. They openly brag that it was them that invented and implanted the **Euro** – and we have all seen how that has worked out. Spain, Portugal, Ireland and Greece are all one the verge of bankruptcy.

The level of security at Bilderberg is like the level of security at the CIA. You are talking about private security firms, under-cover officers, military intelligence, thermal imaging scanners and more.

The guest list of the Bilderberg Group routinely includes both conservative and liberal power players. Influential men and women including:

- **Henry Kissinger,** Former Secretary of State
- **Eric Schmidt,** Founder of Google
- **Peter Theil,** Founder of PayPal
- **Jeff Bezos,** CEO and co-Founder of Amazon

The Bilderberg Group is really the top of the pyramid when it comes to secret, corporate meetings. They get world leaders from all over the planet together and then tell government officials that they are there to go along with corporate policies that will enrich them, in many cases at the expense of other companies, individuals, and national sovereignty.

Some believe that these extremely covert group of leaders has ties to the **Illuminati** – a secret society dating back to the 18th century, created to forge, a **New World Order**, in which the ultra-wealthy conspire to dominate world events. I will be discussing these groups in a later chapter.

Most of the wealthy people who achieve that highest level of success, were chosen by an inside triad of elites, to be promoted to the positions they are in today because they can be trusted to continue to carry out the Illuminati's agenda. That, is the ultimate secret of the inside billionaire elite.

Are the super-rich really working together toward a unified, one world agenda? One that threatens to make them even more rich and powerful? If so, can anyone stop them?

Media Matters

September 17th, 2011, Zuccotti Park, New York, hundreds gather to protest against the 1% of Americans who own 80% of the country's wealth. The movement becomes known as **Occupy Wall Street** and appears to catch fire across the world.

Occupy Wall Street started out with just a few Canadians who said we are going to sit down in a park in Wall Street and it became an international phenomena. They had a simple message – The rich are getting richer at our expense (Wikipedia, 2011).

> **John Ransom**: "The Occupy Wall Street movement talks about redistributing the property throughout the world. Everybody has what they call a fair share education, a fair share of housing, banking, their fair share of retirement. We would think of it as the American Dream".
>
> **Robert Frank**: "That gap between the super-rich and the rest of America is growing. In 1980, the average CEO was making around 42 times their average employee wage. In 2014 they now earn more than 352 times the average employee".

But who was really behind Occupy Wall Street? Was it just a spontaneous, grass-roots movement, or perhaps something more? There are some who believe that one of the answers may have been revealed in a **Craig's List** ad, which actually offered to pay protestors to show up. Most agreed it was **George Soros** funding it.

But why would America's wealthiest individuals contribute to a movement that protests the very system that has made them rich? There are many who believe the answer can be found by examining the places in which the super-rich invest their billions – the **MEDIA**.

By controlling the conversation, they can control what the public knows and thinks. Even when it comes to the subject of income disparity.

Billionaires can excerpt massive control of what issues get put on the national agenda. So they can choose the issues that they care about, and make sure that they get talked about, while others may not. None do this better than the greediest, megalomaniacs on the planet – the Rothschilds.

In 1891, he British Labour Leader makes the following statement on the subject of the Rothschilds:

> **"** *This blood-sucking crew has been the cause of untold mischief and misery in Europe during the present century, and has piled up its prodigious wealth chiefly through fomenting wars between States which ought never to have quarrelled. Whenever there is trouble in Europe, wherever rumours of war circulate and men's minds are distraught with fear of change and calamity you may be sure that a hook-nosed Rothschild is at his games somewhere near the region of the disturbance.* **"**

Comments like this worry the Rothschilds and towards the end of the 1800's they purchase **Reuter's** news agency so they can have some control of the media.

Many billionaires these days seem to be using some of their money to pick up media businesses. The Boston Red Socks owner **John Henry** picked up the **Boston Globe** for $70 MILLION from the New York Times. **Pierre Omidyar** who was one of the **EBay co-founders**, set up his own media organisation called **First Look Media** for $50 MILLION.

In August 2013, Amazon's co-founder **Jeff Bezos** stunned the world, by purchasing the financially troubled **Washington Post** for $250 MILLION. The move caused some media watchers to ask, why a savvy billionaire would want to invest so much money in what many believe to be a dying media format.

Jeff Bezos wanted to be able to control the political agenda that is coming out of the Washington Post, which was one of the flagship political organs in the United States. It does make sense to buy a media outlet in order for them to build their platform.

Fox News is owned by **Rupert Murdoch** and he certainly shaped it in what he is interested in. Same with **Michael Bloomberg** in *Bloomberg News*. It's naïve perhaps to think we can have these media businesses without anybody influencing them.

Could billionaires really be using the media to influence what people read, buy and even what they think? And if so, what is their final goal? Some fear the ultimate strategy of America's richest citizens may just be to eliminate the United States government altogether – along with ½ billion people.

There used to be 88 media companies, however, they have been consolidated into about six as of 2015. Of course, of that six, all of them get their news from **Reuters** and the **Associated Press** (AP).

Reuters owns the AP and the Rothschilds own Reuters. That means that the world's first **trillionaire – Nathaniel Charles Jacob Rothschild, the 4th Baron Rothschild** controls everything that you will read, or see on TV, on the Internet, and most of the Hollywood movies. The creators of *The Simpsons* actually based the character of **Mr. Burns** on Jacob Rothschild.

Sky High

Truth or Consequences New Mexico, 290 km (180 miles) south of Albuquerque lies *Space Port America*. The world's first ever, commercial launch pad to take citizens into outer space. The $209 million project will be home to billionaire **Richard Branson's** *Virgin Galactic*. A rocket company that has already sold more than 600 tickets, even though it is yet to make its first commercial launch.

Every billionaire wants to go to space right now, and it is only $250,000 for a ticket. Some believe the reason billionaires are spending so much on traveling to the beyond, has to do with their innate need to be in command. Even Jeff Bezos has created a private aerospace company called **Blue Origin**. But some wealthy are spending their riches on more extreme ventures.

August, 2011. Billionaire and Venture Capitalist (co-founded PayPal) **Peter Theil,** invested more than $1 Million in the **Seasteading Institute** which wants to build independent floating cities on the world's oceans in international waters, to experiment with new ideas for government.

Theil is literally trying to start his own country, in fact, many countries. He wants to create floating island nations, where billionaires can go off and live on their own, in a utopian, libertarian existence. Outside of the US territorial waters where the government cannot tell him what to do, and of course, they never have to pay taxes.

Some experts estimate the cost to build the ocean community off the coast of Northern California would be in excess of $200 million.

Another "billionaire" idea is **Freedom Ship**. At 1.6 km long (1 mile), it will house 50,000 people. An island for the wealthy that will circumnavigate the globe and you will never have to pay taxes. But who would be the captain, or the President? And who gets to sit in the sun, and who has to clean and service the vessel? No doubt robot police will maintain and enforce security.

Could some of the world's billionaires be hatching a plan to become a nation unto themselves? One with its own territory and agenda. It seems that the super-rich are increasingly separating themselves from the rest of the people. They have private jets, they live in private communities and on private islands. It really becomes a billionaire bubble for a separate, secret country. It is a break away country of rich people. Billionaires are very different from us. They don't make money the way normal people do – they don't punch clocks. They believe they are the anointed landlords of this planet, and we just get to live in it.

The Freedom Ship - Only Billionaires need apply!

FEUDALISM

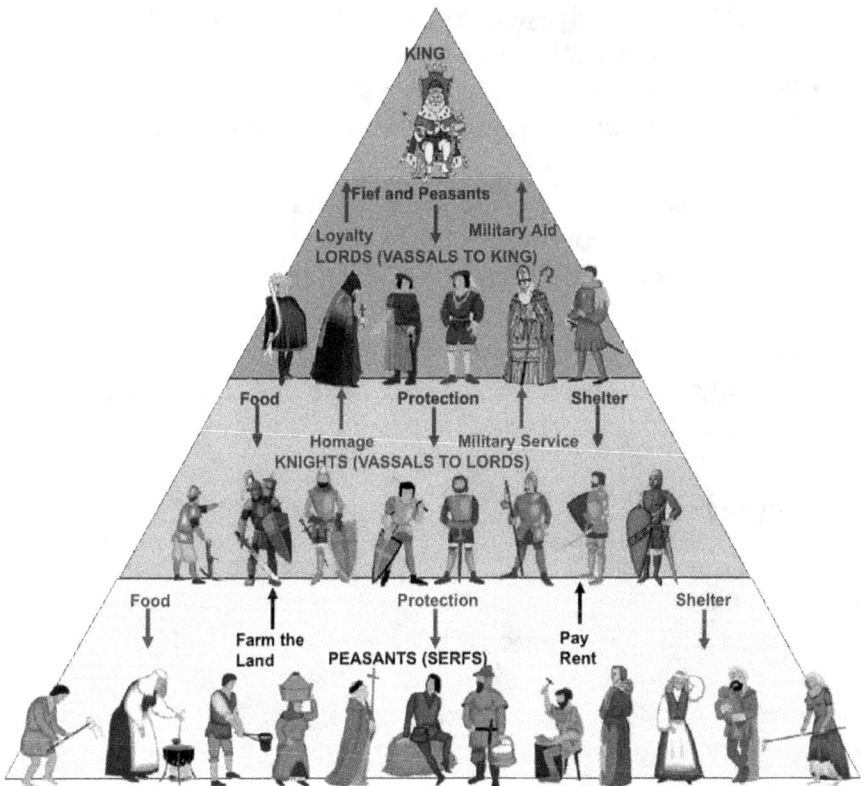

Medieval model of Feudalism

Feudalism was the medieval model of government pre-dating the birth of the modern nation-state. Feudal society is a military hierarchy in which a ruler or lord, offers mounted fighters (Knights) a *fief* (medieval **beneficium**), a unit of land to control, in exchange for a military service. The individual who accepted this land became a **Vassal**, and the man who granted the land became known as his **Liege** or his **Lord**.

Peasant farmers were then "allowed" to grow crops, or raise herds on this land, but had to give the Vassal a large cut of their harvest in exchange for his "protection." As this was a time of constant raids and bloody skirmishes, the unarmed peasants needed protection. But what they didn't realise was that usually, the actions of the Vassal or Liege were what caused the skirmish to begin with. But the poor peasant farmers did not know any better, so they paid for protection (not that they had a choice).

In the late medieval period, the fiefdom often became hereditary, and the son of a knight or lesser nobleman would inherit the land and the military duties from his father upon the father's death. The same happened with the peasants – the farmer's son would inherit the lease on the tenant farm. So you have to be born into nobility to be anything, and if you were born into a farmer's family, you were destined to struggle your whole life. (**A Knight's Tale** - 2001 is a great movie that demonstrates this!)

Thus, the entire medieval community was divided into three groups: **bellatores** (the noblemen who fought), **labores** (the agricultural labourers who grew the food), and **oratores** (the clergy who prayed and attended to spiritual matters) (Singman, 2013).

Neo-feudalism

Neofeudalism entails an order defined by commercial interests and administered in large areas. The significance of the comparison to feudalism, is that corporations have power similar to states' governance powers. And the head of these corporations are the billionaires. Therefore, the billionaire is the "Liege", the bureaucrats and security forces (police) become the Vassals, and no guesses for which group you and I end up in – yep, the labourers/peasant class.

We already see country Vassal States that pay tribute to the masters – Egypt, Lebanon, Iraq, and Ukraine, they all have puppet governments that do whatever NATO and the UN tells them to do. The United States is the "enforcement" arm – like the Knights.

The widening of the wealth gap, as poor and marginalised people are excluded from the state's provision of security, will result in neofeudalism. In fact, it has already happened in **South Africa** (Bryden and Caparini, 2006). Neofeudalism is made possible by the commodification of policing, and signifies the end of shared citizenship.

A primary characteristic is that individuals' public lives are increasingly governed by business corporations.

Seattle-based technology billionaire **Nick Hanauer** admits that

> *"Our country is rapidly becoming less a capitalist society and more a feudal society" (Hanauer, 2014).*

Feudalism is basically the dream of the Elites of the world. They really miss the "good old days" of medieval governance. Ironically, the only reason why feudalism ended, was because of the **Black Death**.

The Black Death

The Black Death decimated the European population

The Black Death arrived in Europe by sea in October 1347, when 12 Genoese trading ships docked at the Sicilian port of Messina after a long journey through the Black Sea. The people who gathered on the docks to greet the ships were met with a horrifying surprise: most of the sailors aboard the ships were dead, and those who were still alive were gravely ill.

They were overcome with fever, unable to keep food down and being delirious from pain. Strangest of all, they were covered in mysterious black boils that oozed blood and pus and gave their illness its name: the *"Black Death."* The Sicilian authorities hastily ordered the fleet of "death ships" out of the harbor, but it was too late: over the next five years, the mysterious Black Death would kill more than 20 million people in Europe–almost one-third of the continent's population.

In Medieval England, the Black Death was to kill 1.5 million people out of an estimated total of four million people between 1348 and 1350. No medical knowledge existed in Medieval England to cope with the disease. After 1350, it was to strike England another six times before the end of the century. Understandably, peasants were terrified at the news that the Black Death might be approaching their village or town.

Up until recently, the Black Death was thought to have been caused by fleas carried by rats that were very common in towns and cities. When the fleas bit into their victims, it was thought they were literally injecting them with the disease.

However, evidence produced by forensic scientists and archaeologists in 2014 from human remains in the north of the City of London suggests that fleas could not actually have been responsible for an infection that spread so fast - it had to be airborne. Once the disease reached the lungs of the malnourished, it was then spread to the wider population through sneezes and coughs.

Whatever the cause of the infection, death was often very quick for the weaker victims. By spring **1349 CE**, the Black Death had killed six out of every 10 Londoners.

Therefore, the Black Death had a huge impact on society. Fields went unploughed as the men who usually did this were victims of the disease. Harvests would not have been brought in as the manpower did not exist. Animals would have been lost as the people in a village would not have been around to tend them. Whole villages would have faced starvation.

Towns and cities would have faced food shortages as the villages that surrounded them could not provide them with enough food. Those lords who lost their manpower to the disease, turned to sheep farming as this required less people to work on the land. Grain farming became less popular – this, again, kept towns and cities short of such basics as bread. One consequence of the Black Death was inflation – the price of food went up creating more hardship for the poor. In some parts of England, food prices went up by four times.

Those who survived the Black Death believed that there was something special about them – almost as if God had protected them. Therefore, they took the opportunity offered by the disease to improve their lifestyle.

Feudal law stated that peasants could only leave their village if they had their lord's permission. Now many lords were dead, or short of desperately needed labour for the land that they owned. After the Black Death, lords actively encouraged peasants to leave the village where they lived to come to work for them in a bidding war. When peasants did this, they rarely returned to their original village.

Peasants could demand higher wages as they knew that a lord was desperate to get in his harvest. This was literally the start of a "middle class." Suddenly, once poor people had more money than they had ever had. They began to buy vacant land, or land where all the nobles had been struck down by the Black Death. With their new found wealth, they suddenly had more time for leisure. This led to spending money on cultural items like art, carvings, and ceramic pottery.

Finally, they started to patronise (pay for) their favourite artist or academics. This was the beginning of **The Renaissance**, the period from the 14th to the 17th century, considered the bridge between the Middle Ages and modern history. It started as a cultural movement in Italy in the Late Medieval period, then later spread to the rest of Europe and finally ended in the Early Modern Age.

Some good early examples were the development of perspective in oil painting and the recycled knowledge of how to make concrete, the printing press and science increased reliance on observation. The Renaissance was a golden age of art, science, music, and culture, and it only happened because the Elites lost their iron grip over the peasants due to the Black Death. This is another good example of how everything happens for a reason, and not every bad event is necessarily all bad!

Thus, the elites never really got over this loss of control, and it is their ultimate goal to return the planet back to something similar. They know they can never return to full feudalism, therefore, they formulated the new plan called **Neo-feudalism.**

Billionaires really feel that they are smarter and more qualified to make decisions for the general public. Is that perhaps what drives their philanthropic, political, and economic agendas? And could the wealthy be on a secret mission to fix the planet as they see fit, whether citizens like it or not?

Everything that they do with public relations (PR), everything that they do with charity, everything that they do with the secret lobbying that goes on is really geared toward one thing – maintain their status as billionaires and stay in control. Their first rule would be '**preserve the empire**' and that is what the billionaire agenda really is.

All of our lives are tied to, or controlled by the 1% of the 1%. Whether we like it or not, they excerpt so much political power, and as goes the wealthy, so goes the rest of the world. Therefore, next we will look a little deeper into their obsession, as opposed to their agenda, and it may just shock you!

References:

Adams, M. (2010). *Bill Gates funds covert vaccine nanotechnology*. [online] NaturalNews. Available at: http://www.naturalnews.com/028887_vaccines_Bill_Gates.html [Accessed 19 Apr. 2015].

Bryden, A. and Caparini, M. (2006). *Private actors and security governance*. Wien: Lit.

Ehrlich, P., Ehrlich, A. and Holdren, J. (1977). *Ecoscience*. San Francisco: W.H. Freeman.

Forbes, (2015). *Forbes Welcome*. [online] Forbes.com. Available at: http://www.forbes.com/profile/george-soros/ [Accessed 18 Nov. 2015].

Forbes, (2015). *The Forbes World's billionaires list*. [online] Available at: http://www.forbes.com/billionaires/list/#version:static [Accessed 17 Apr. 2015].

Gucciardi, A. (2010). *Bill Gates Foundation Buys 500,000 Shares of Monsanto*. [online] Natural Society. Available at: http://naturalsociety.com/bill-gates-foundation-buys-500000-shares-of-monsanto/ [Accessed 19 Apr. 2015].

Hanauer, N. (2014). *The Pitchforks Are Coming. . . For Us Plutocrats*. *Politico Magazine*.

Haverluck, M. (2013). *Bill Gates' $100 million database to track students*. [online] WND. Available at: http://www.wnd.com/2013/03/bill-gates-100-million-database-to-track-students/ [Accessed 17 Apr. 2015].

Johnson, J. (2010). *Zuckerberg Once Mocked 'Dumb' Users Over 'Trust'.* [online] Newser. Available at: http://www.newser.com/story/88716/zuckerberg-once-mocked-dumb-users-over-trust.html [Accessed 17 Apr. 2015].

Kroft, (1998). *George Soros - Nazi Collaborator.mp4*. [online] YouTube. Available at: https://youtu.be/CW8ENFOCeBs [Accessed 18 Nov. 2015].

Mayer, J. (2015). *The Money Man - The New Yorker*. [online] The New Yorker. Available at: http://www.newyorker.com/magazine/2004/10/18/the-money-man [Accessed 17 Apr. 2015].

Riddell, K. (2015). *George Soros funds Ferguson protests, hopes to spur civil action*. [online] The Washington Times. Available at: http://www.washingtontimes.com/news/2015/jan/14/george-soros-funds-ferguson-protests-hopes-to-spur/ [Accessed 14 Jan. 2015].

Singman, J. (2013). *The Middle Ages*. 2nd ed. Sterling; Reprint edition (November 5, 2013).

TRILLION dollars, (2015). *What does one TRILLION dollars look like?*. [online] YouTube. Available at: https://youtu.be/Tym9AhMNcP0 [Accessed 18 Nov. 2015].

Wikipedia, (2011). *Occupy Wall Street*. [online] Available at: http://en.wikipedia.org/wiki/Occupy_Wall_Street [Accessed 17 Apr. 2015].

YouTube, (2013). *WTF! Bill Gates Depopulation Plans Caught On Camera MONSANTO, FOOD RIOTS, EUGENICS*. [online] Available at: https://youtu.be/3TyAJZVARPw [Accessed 19 Apr. 2015].

2

EUGENICS: MYTH OF OVER-POPULATION

"Ozone depletion, lack of water, and pollution are not the disease — they are the symptoms. The disease is overpopulation. And unless we face world population head-on, we are doing nothing more than sticking a Band-Aid on a fast-growing cancerous tumor."

— DAN BROWN, INFERNO

Ever since I was a child growing up in the 1970's and 80's, I was always hearing that the world was over-populated. Countries in Asia, Africa, and South America were out of control and would damn us all to hell right? **WRONG.**

In my very early dealings with my Spirit Guide Michael, I was made aware of a few "truths" about world population. This was around 1989, and the world population was around five billion people living on the planet. This was considered outrages by the industrial nations who demanded the 3rd world countries cut back on having babies. When I asked Michael what could be done about this dilemma, he just laughed! What was so funny I thought? This was serious!

He then went on to tell me that this planet – planet Earth, was capable of adequately sustaining 11 billion people. However, the only reason why we may not make it to 11 billion was/is because of the distribution, or inequality of distribution of wealth and resources. When I asked why the world could just not share, I got my first lesson in the **Young Soul Age** phase of souls.

Therefore, on the one hand we had "experts" telling us that unless we curb population growth, the whole world was in serious trouble. But on the other hand, my Guide was telling me that the earth wasn't even half full yet, and that it could sustain 11 billion!

It was time to find out why so much false data and brainwashing was going on. Why do the powers that be want everyone to believe that the earth is over populated?

State Sponsored Murder

It's hard to imagine the world's population could ever get too big, given that there is nothing unique about government-sponsored violence. There is, in fact, nothing especially unusual about widespread killing, or even genocide by governments. All this is often justified by cutting down on "excess population."

In the 20th century alone, over 150 million people were killed at the hands of the State during wars and tyrannical dictatorships. In Russia, under the Stalin dictatorship, 60 million lives were snuffed out. Hitler's war took 22 million men, women, and children. During the reign of Mao Zedong, the Communist China government murdered a further 60 million peasant farmers and political dissidents.

Over 300,000 innocent civilians were killed in Guatemala during their civil war. Another 2 million souls were brutally wiped out by the reign of the Khmer Rouge in Cambodia. 1.5 million killed in Turkey during the **Armenian Genocide**. Uganda, during the time of Ide Amin, lost 300,000 lives. The genocide continued in Africa with the **Rwandan Genocide** during the approximate 100-day period from April 7, 1994, to mid-July, an estimated 500,000–1,000,000 Rwandans were killed.

Sadly, there are just too many examples of innocent people being murdered and brutalised by their own governments to name them all. And before you think this was only Communist countries or Fascists, you should be aware that the US and UK supported and got most of these psychotic leaders into power in the first place! (Quigley, 1975)

It is a historical fact that the State is the number one cause of unnatural death. If you take the 150 million people killed by power crazed governments in the last century, and divide it by 1,000, you could pack 1,500 large sports stadiums. That is 1,500 stadiums crammed packed with 100,000 people in each – all exterminated.

The carnage of the last 100 years has only been a prefatory stage of the world elite's master plan.

But where does this mindset come from? Why do the elites kill the largest masses of people, when no one is resisting them? When they have already obtained total control over their people. What ideology drives the elite psychopath?

Since Plato's time 2,400 years ago, State Planners have openly proclaimed their desire to control every detail of the commoner's life. From breeding programs to mass extermination of undesirables, the dark dream has continued on for millennia.

The so-called Science of Eugenics

Eugenics: "*Is the study of the agencies under social control, that improve or impair the racial qualities of future generations either physically or mentally.*"

Sir Francis Galton
(1822-1911)

—SIR FRANCIS GALTON

Sir Francis Galton, FRS, was an English Victorian eugenicist, psychologist, anthropologist, explorer, geographer, inventor, meteorologist, proto-geneticist, psychometrician, and statistician. He was knighted in 1909. (Galton, 1909)

The scientific rational for tyranny has always been attractive to elites, because it creates a convenient excuse for treating their fellow man as lower than animals. **The Reverend Thomas Robert Malthus** (1766 –1834) was famous for once stating that a mass food collapse would be helpful, because it would wipe out the poor. His fictional scenario would later be called a **Malthusian Catastrophe.**

Malthus is important because his ideas led to the rise of a new "scientific field" that would dominate the course of human history for the next 200+ years.

Charles Darwin, an admirer of Malthusian Catastrophe model, developed the Theory of Evolution, its chief tenet being, the *"survival of the fittest."*

With the help of **T. J. Huxley**, known as **Darwin's Bulldog** for his strong support of Darwin's theories, Darwin's theories were pushed into wide acceptance among key scientific circles throughout England and Europe. Darwin's cousin, **Sir Francis Galton**, is credited as being the "Father of Eugenics," saw an opportunity to advance mankind by taking the reins of Darwin's Evolution Theory and Applied Social Principles to develop **Social Darwinism**. (Bannister, 1993)

Galton hoped to redeem the theory of Social Darwinism, an appropriation of Darwin's work that had mistakenly predicted that the peasant class, lacking the wealth and intelligence to survive, would dwindle over time. Noting instead the rapid population growth among the poor, Galton saw measures to promote "breeding the best with the best" — in the manner of animal husbandry — as a civic duty.

Thus, the families, Darwin; Galton; Huxley; Wedgewood were so obsessed with their new social design theory, that they pledged their families would only breed with each other in an attempt to create a more intelligent "super being". They falsely predicted they would achieve this within only a few generations. The immerging pseudo-science was only codifying the practise of in-breeding, already popular with Royal elites for millennia.

The Four Families experiment was a disaster. Within only two generations of in-breeding, close to 90% of their offspring either died at birth, or were severely mentally and/or physically handicapped.

The "old money" class of the world, particularly the royal families, were already obsessed with blood line breeding and filled with a predatory distain for the lower class citizens. They seized on the new science and began aggressively enforcing its aims worldwide.

Biometrics appears to be a new science, but it was actually developed by Galton back in the 1870's as a way to trace racial traits and genetic histories. Eventually, this work would decide who would be "licensed" to breed!

A BRIEF HISTORY OF THE EUGENICS DEATH CULT

1904, The Cold Spring Harbor Research Facility started in the United States by eugenicist **Charles Davenport**. It was funded by prominent robber barons Carnegie, Rockefeller and Harriman (all Rothschild funded men).

1907, the first sterilisation laws were passed in the United States. Citizens with mild deformities or low test scores on their report cards were arrested and forcibly sterilised. The film **Tomorrow's Children** was a 1934, pro-Eugenics propaganda piece designed to normalise this disgusting law. (Tomorrow's Children, 1934)

1910, the USA **Eugenics Records Offic** was set up, and by then, the British had set up the first network of **Social Workers**, expressly to serve as spies and enforcers of the Eugenics race cult, which was rapidly taking control of Western Society. The Social Workers would decide who would have their children taken away and who would be sterilised. And in some cases, who would be quietly euthanized (i.e. murdered).

1911, the **Rockefeller family** exports Eugenics to Germany by bankrolling **The Kaiser Wilhelm Institute**, which would later form a central pillar in the **Third Reich**.

1912, at the International Eugenics Conference, London. Eugenics becomes an international craze and gains super star status. The futurist and best-selling Sci-Fi author **H. G. Wells** studied biology under top Eugenicist, and was spreading the new faith worldwide.

1916, H. G. Wells' lover **Margaret Sanger**, starts her promotion of Eugenics in the United States.

12 Disturbing Quotes
from
Margaret Sanger,
Planned
Parenthood's
Foundress

ProLife365.com/margaret-sanger

Margaret Sanger top Eugenicist – these quotes will shock you!

1923, Sanger receives massive funding from the Rockefeller family. Sanger wrote to fellow Eugenicist, **Clarence J Gamble**, that black leaders would need to be recruited to act as front men in sterilisation programs directed at black communities.

1924, Hitler pens **Mien Kampf** (Trans: "My Struggle") and credits US Eugenicists as his inspiration. Hitler even wrote a fan letter to American Eugenicist and Conservationist, **Madison Grant**. Hitler called Madison's race based book, **The Passing of the Great Race**, his 'bible'. Hitler developed his plan for mass extermination of the Jews, and what he called other "sub races," as well as the handicapped, from an American, **Madison Grant**.

1927, Eugenics hits the mainstream. The so-called science was aggressively pushed through contest in schools, churches and at State Fairs. Indeed, churches competed in contests with large cash prizes to see who could best implement Eugenics into their sermons. Major denominations including Catholic, Protestant and Baptist to name but a few,started telling their congregations that "*Jesus was for Eugenics…*"

In that same year in the United States, more than 25 States passed **forced sterilisation laws**. In fact, the Supreme Court ruled in favour of the brutal sterilisation policies.

1933, Hitler comes in to power. One of his first Acts is to pass national Eugenics laws, modelled after laws in the United States.

1934, the film *Tomorrow's Children* brought the Eugenics agenda to the Silver Screen.

1935, In a December letter to **Carl Schneider**, dean of the University of Heidelberg's medical school, Prof. Harry Laughlin, from the Eugenics Records Office, was nominated for German recognition as "*one of the most important pioneers on the field of racial hygiene.*" Schneider gladly approved the honour. This same Dr. Schneider was a psychiatrist who in September 1939, helped organise the gassing of thousands of adults judged mentally handicapped under the project codenamed T-4, named after its location at Tiergartenstrasse 4 in Berlin.

1936, Germany has become the world leader in Eugenics, for taking effective actions for sterilising and euthanizing hundreds of thousands of victims. By this time, the big 3 of American Eugenics were Professor **Charles Benedict Davenport**, Professor **Harry H. Laughlin**, both working at the **Cold Spring Harbor Research Facility** and **Charles M. Goethe**, a prominent entrepreneur, land developer, philanthropist, and conservationist.

These men were dispatched to Germany by the Rockefeller Family where they advised the Nazis on the fine-tuning of their extermination system. IBM supplied the computers. The American eugenic leadership praised Hitler's anti-Jewish and racial policies. In his presidential address to the **Eugenics Research Association California**, Goethe said:

> *"California had led all the world in sterilization operations. Today, even California's quarter century record has, in two years, been outdistanced by Germany."*

Germany had gone over the edge. The Nazis brought Eugenics extermination to an all-time industrial level, murdering hundreds and hundreds of thousands.

1945, After World War II, eugenics was declared a crime against humanity - an act of genocide. Germans were tried and they cited the California statutes in their defence but to no avail. Many were found guilty, however, the top Nazi Eugenicists were protected from prosecution by the Allies. These were the very Nazi scientists that had tortured, sterilised, euthanized, and murdered millions that would be secretly smuggled into the US and other Ally countries under **Project Paperclip**.

The Nazi brand of Eugenics had embarrassed the elites and royals, but they had no intention of stopping their plans. The Allies literally fought with each other over who would get top Nazi Eugenicists. It never mattered that the SS Officers had murdered millions of innocent people. They were free to go and start new lives in the United States, England, Canada, Australia, New Zealand, and elsewhere. They were given new identities and passports. Indeed, the "Angel of Death" **Dr. Josef Mengele** and his boss **Otmar Freiherr von Verschuer** were not persecuted, and von Verschuer even continued his work in Germany. (Citizens Commission on Human Rights, 2010)

After the war, Eugenicists were angry that their "Great Work" had been exposed. They then scrambled to camouflage their true agenda. The magazine, **Eugenics Quarterly** became **Social Biology**. The **American Birth Control League** became known as **Planned Parenthood**.

New terms like "trans-humanism"; "population control"; "sustainability"; "conservation"; and "environmentalism" replaced "racial hygiene" and "Social Darwinism." The Cold Spring Harbor Research Facility reinvented itself as a cancer research laboratory. They now claim that Charles Davenport was just researching "genetics." (Cshl.edu, 2015)

Many Eugenicists from the previous era engaged in what they called "crypto eugenics." They purposely took their brand of eugenics underground and re-surfaced in the early 1950's as well respected Anthropologists, Biologists, and Geneticist. (Lombardo, 2002)

If you doubt their work is no longer being conducted, then I will address current day China to demonstrate that they are nearing perfection in their minds.

> *"Depopulation should be the highest priority of foreign policy towards the third world, because the US economy will require large and increasing amounts of minerals from abroad, especially from less developed countries."* Henry Kissinger, 1974

The Eugenics Death Cult in Present Day China

Communist China is the model for the planned society of the future. In August, 1973, in an article written by **David Rockefeller** for the *New York Times*, Rockefeller openly lauds and endorses **Mao Zedong** actions while celebrating the Command and Control System. (Rockefeller, 1973)

David Rockefeller
(1915 -)

"One is impressed immediately by the sense of national harmony. . . Whatever the price of the Chinese Revolution it has obviously succeeded. . . in fostering high morale and community purpose. General social and economic progress is no less impressive. . . . The enormous social advances of China have benefited greatly from the singleness of ideology and purpose. . . The social experiment in China under Chairman Mao's leadership is one of the most important and successful in history."

Rockefeller wrote this article just after Mao Zedong had slaughtered over 40 million people. (Banks, 2010). Don't forget, it was David Rockefeller's father **John D. Rockefeller** that originally helped to fund the *Cold Spring Harbor Research Facility*.

China adopted the **One Child Policy** in 1979. It was introduced by Chinese leader **Deng Xiaoping** to temporarily limit communist China's population growth. It has thus been in place for more than 36 years. But in reality, China was put under pressure due to lobbying by a consortium of eugenics organisations which included the US based **Planned Parenthood** and the **United Nations**.

Couples who have more than one child face heavy fines and/or imprisonment. The practise of forced abortion in China, coupled with the cultural desire to have a male child, has plunged China into a deepening crisis where there are 30 million more men than women. (Rosenberg, 2015)

So round 30 million fewer girls than boys were born under this policy. One has to ask, what happened to those 30 million missing girls? How did these policies help them?

A recent study in 2015 by British-based writer **Xinran Xue**, interviewed some of the 150 million single children who were born under the policy for her latest book, *Buy Me The Sky*. Xue was horrified, and embarrassed to be Chinese after speaking with these people.

She described the one-child policy children as *'little emperors with skewed values'*. She cites one very disturbing account of a one child policy child who was a piano virtuoso. The over pampered child would obsess over protecting his hands. He carried a small paring knife in his sleeve that he would ask teachers and such to use to cut up his food, as he did not want to risk injury to his hands. In 2011, one evening whilst driving home, he hit a middle-aged woman.

Rather than risk getting into trouble from his father, or upsetting his promising career, he got out of his car and used his fruit knife to stab the woman to death. After he was convicted and sentenced to the death penalty, his peers came out in mass protest saying *"If I were him I would do the same things because our lives are much more valuable than them and we don't want those peasants to give us future trouble."* (Sedghi and Hall, 2015)

Political Dissidents Targeted

Underground Churches, **Falun Gong**[1] practitioners, striking factory workers and political dissidents are all sent to **Forced Labour Camps** (known as the **Xuchang Forced Labour Camp**). (En.minghui.org, 2015)

---

[1] Falun Gong is a Chinese spiritual practice that combines meditation and qigong exercises with a moral philosophy centred on the tenets of Truthfulness, Compassion, and Forbearance.

Their blood and tissue samples are catalogued in preparation for organ harvesting. The Chinese government then sells the prisoner's organs to the highest bidder on the world market (Nowak, 2007).

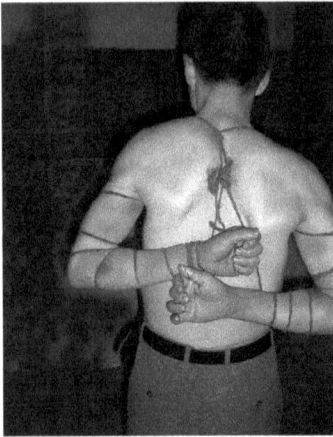

If a wealthy patient decides to fly into China, the prisoner is killed, and the organs are transplanted. If the organs are being flown out of the country, a **Mobile Execution Van** extracts the organs on route to the waiting aircraft (Coonan in Beijing and McNeill in Tokyo, 2006).

The Social Engineers of China aggressively euthanize the elderly and disabled. But before you get too upset

Torture re-enactment: Tying the rope with China, just remember that they are merely following the global blueprint for the world. The same system for total dehumanisation is quietly being phased in world wide.

Mr. Li Jian started practicing Falun Gong in 1998. He was arrested in 2000 for producing truth-clarifying materials about Falun Gong and he was illegally sentenced to serve three years in prison. He was taken to the **Henan Third Forced Labor Camp** in April 2000. He was forced to undergo brainwashing, deprived of sleep, and did exhausting physical labour. He endured great physical and mental harm from being tortured with the method of "Tying the Rope." (Jian, 2002)

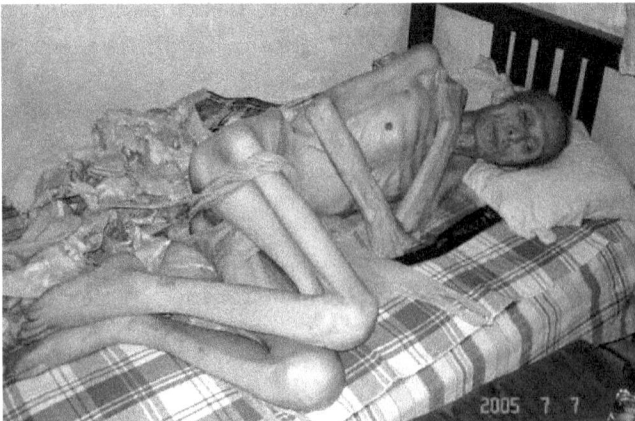

Falun Gong prisoner

OBAMA SUPPORTS EUGENICS!

*Barack Obama
(1961 -)*

"Today, I am pleased to announce the members of my science and technology team. Dr John P. Holdren has agreed to serve as assistant to the President for Science and Technology and Director of the Whitehouse Office of Science and Technology Policy"

—PRESIDENT BARACK OBAMA, 2012

John Holdren (1944 -)

Professor John P. Holdren is the resident "Science Czar" for the Obama Whitehouse. He is Obama's key advisor on all science and technology subjects, and works out of the new Executive Building in the Whitehouse.

This man is a Malthusian fanatic. He has stated many times on record that he is a big fan of Malthus and Darwin, and he actually refers to himself as a **Neo- Malthusian**. A Malthusian remember, is someone who believes that a food shortage would be good to "thin out" the poor. A "Neo" means "new" or "new age." So the Neo- Malthusian has new ways and technology to get rid of the poor – as we will see.

He is also what you would call a radical environmentalist (what used to be called a conservationist). You may think that seems harmless, however when you see how these anti-human ideologies have formed his current mindset, you begin to see how sinister this man is.

Holdren has written several books, and one of them in particular should have people worried.

It is called ***Ecoscience: Population, Resources, Environment*** (Ehrlich, Ehrlich and Holdren, 1977).

This book is without doubt one of the most disturbing books from an academic I have ever read. Forced abortions. Mass sterilisation. A "Planetary Regime" with the power of life and death over all citizens.

Simply put, this book describes a future vision for the world that now exists within China; a world of forced sterilisations, forced abortions, eugenics, incredibly powerful central governments, carbon taxes, poisoned food, and water supplies pumped full of highly toxic sterilisation agents and the list goes on. The book reads like some crazed Nazi fantasy, but what is even more horrifying, is that it was written and openly published in academia by people such as Holdren, whom now hold such highly esteemed positions in government and academia.

It also demonstrates what has concerned me for a very long time – that the environmental movement has morphed into a hard-core Malthusian Eugenics movement that sees humanity as the ultimate enemy of the planet, something to be managed and - where necessary - culled.

I don't expect you to just accept what I say, so I intend to cover a few key points which I will include page numbers for should you wish to verify the text for yourself.

Ecoscience: Population, Resources, Environment refers to the average American as **Cornucopians**, that is, people who believe there are no limits to growth and prosperity for all Americans. Holdren argues that that ideology is not true, and there must be a structured class system of basically haves and have nots in order for society to run smoothly. (p. 953)

Holdren also argues against what he calls **growthsmenship** – that is, that a country cannot grow itself out of economic trouble. In other words, he does not believe that with the right kind of national mobilisation, technology, and political will, any country can achieve just about anything. To Holdren, that door has been permanently closed. Luckily he wasn't in charge of the Science Office in the 1960's when NASA were putting men into space!

Holdren's main argument is that world population is the root of all global problems, and in his words, humanity is a 'cancer' on the face of the earth. He started off with all this in the early 1970's, with his cohort **Paul Ehrlich**. Ehrlich himself has been academically proven to be a charlatan and a crack pot! He wrote a book called **The Population Bomb**, (Ehrlich, 1968). It warned of the mass starvation of humans in 1970s and 1980s due to overpopulation and advocated immediate action to limit population growth.

The book has been criticised in recent decades for its alarmist tone and unfilled predictions. Ehrlich stands by the basic ideas in the book. As we will see later, most countries in Europe and Asia have falling population growths now – in exact contradiction to Ehrlich's predictions.

Back to Holdren and his book, which Ehrlich contributed to by the way, he says that some countries are so bad, and so beyond help, that we in the industrial countries should "triage" them (p. 923). In other words – cut them off, no more food aid, no more medical aid, no more help of any kind. He actually says India is one country he would put on the list! That is over 1 billion people, and Holdren says cast them out into the outer darkness! He also says Bangladesh, but again, as we will see later, Bangladesh is one of the fastest growing (in a positive way) countries in the world! People thought Hitler was bad for his eugenics mentality, but could you imagine the death toll if we followed this man's advice and 'triaged' India and Bangladesh? And remember, this is the man who has President Obama's ear on such matters.

Ironically, Holdren dislikes science and technology. He actually sees these things as a threat to the social order. Indeed, he states he would like to create a "Science Court" that would decide which inventions and technology would be put into practice, and which ones would be banned (p. 819). This would essentially hold humanity back, and force countries into stagnation, and a new dark age.

He speaks about a world **Optimum Population** (p. 716). Optimum Population is 1 billion people and any more than that, we will see famine and pestilence. But he goes on to say that the population would always revert back to 1 billion people – no more, no less. At the time he wrote that, the world population was already 4 billion. In today's terms, that would mean 6 billion would have to go. These are figures Hitler, Moa, and Stalin never dreamed of.

Holdren is very concerned that the 3rd world countries will try and rise up and copy the industrialised countries, which mean less resources for all. But instead of suggesting ways (by using technology) to increase food production and resources, he simply says no, we should just stop those countries from developing.

In fact, he believes in "De-development of Overdeveloped Countries" and that everyone should return to pre-industrial civilisation.

In case you don't realise, the **Industrial Revolution** occurred from 1750C.E. to 1850C.E. Pre-industrial is a time before there were machines and tools to help perform tasks.

The average life span for men was about 35-40 years old. Indeed, as **Thomas Hobbes** put it – that period of history was "*nasty, brutish, and short.*"

To carry all this out, Holdren suggests a **Planetary Regime**:

> " *The Planetary Regime might be given the responsibility for determining the optimum population for the world and for each region and for arbitrating various countries. (Ehrlich, Ehrlich and Holdren, 1977 p. 943)* "

This is basically a one world government that would control every facet of your life, including who can breed and who cannot.

Holdren says he firsts wants to limit reproduction, then put global reproduction is stasis, then finally reduce the population to his optimal population. To do this, Holdren suggests forced sterilisation (p. 783).

Forced surgical sterilisation in males, and compulsory abortion in women (p. 837). Girls, from the onset of puberty, would be forced to have a subcutaneous implant of birth control

Child labour pre- Industrial Revolution

that could last up to 30 years. He also wants **licences for birth** (p. 787). In other words, a woman is not allowed to give birth unless she has purchased a "marketable" birth licence. Of course, this means that companies would drive up the price, and only rich women could afford to purchase one. Oh, and what happens to the children that are born without a birth permit?

In Holdren's world, there are two main evils. Over population, and industrial pollution. In the world we live in, the main problems are poverty, disease, lack of education, and war tearing countries apart. What there really is, is a massive under production of things. The rich nations should be producing more clothing, more food, more houses etc. and sell them into poor countries at a price they can afford. If it means the company will run at a loss, so be it. It would only be for one generation.

They could donate the goods instead of paying taxes for example. There is close to 1 billion people who are starving in the world. Surely it is time to address this imbalance. If you live in a world where everyone wears hats, and you don't have enough hats – simple, make more hats. Holdren says, don't make more hats, just cut off their heads!

Please remember that this man, John Holdren, is now (in 2015) President Obama's key advisor on all science and technology subjects. If this doesn't chill you to the bone, then I am not sure what will! You may be asking, "Why would Obama appoint this man?" Obama is a puppet, train and financed by the CIA, thus he is told what to do, and who to appoint.

But enough of these crazy, psychopathic eugenicists. Next we will look at the FACTS about our current population, and it is all good!

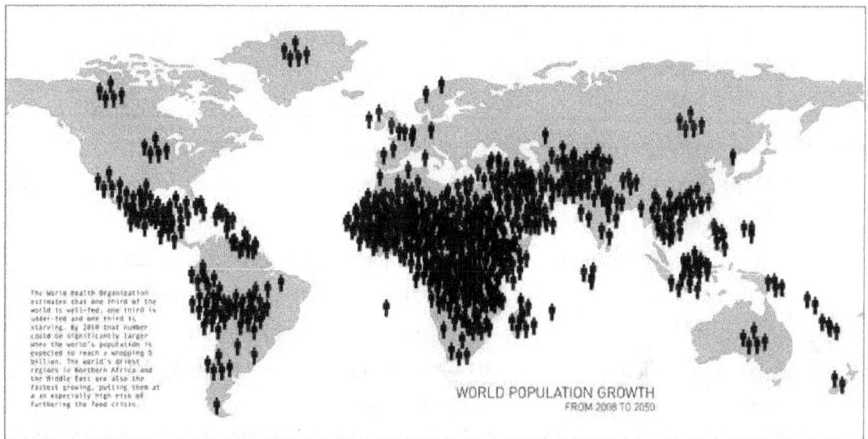

The World Health Organization estimates that one third of the world is well-fed, one third is under-fed and one third is starving. By 2050 that number could be significantly larger when the world's population is expected to reach a whopping 9 billion. The world's driest regions in Northern Africa and the Middle East are also the fastest growing, putting them at a an especially high risk of furthering the food crisis.

WORLD POPULATION GROWTH
FROM 2008 TO 2050

World population growth from 2008 - 2050

THE TRUTH ABOUT WORLD POPULATION

Professor Hans Rosling
(1948 -)

> *"Data allows your political judgments to be based on fact, to the extent that numbers describe realities."*
>
> — HANS ROSLING

Most of the information I will discuss here, is taken from the awesome presentation by Professor **Hans Rosling**. It was part of a documentary for the BBC called: *This World - Don't Panic: The Truth About Population.* (Rosling, 2013)

Rosling presents a spectacular portrait of our rapidly changing world. With 7 Billion people already on our planet, we often look to the future with dread, but Rosling's message is surprisingly upbeat.

Hans Rosling is a Swedish medical doctor, academic, statistician and public speaker. He is *Professor of International Health* at **Karolinska Institute** and co-founder and chairman of the **Gapminder Foundation**, which developed the *Trendalyzer* software system used in his very impressive presentation (Rosling, 2015).

In **2015**, there are around 7 billion people living on Earth. Under our current structure, that is, a small minority controlling the majority of the resources, this figure makes many people panic. However, we are actually doing a lot better than what most people think. Let's have a quick look at the numbers through history.

World Population Through Time

10,000 BCE – Humans are now becoming farmers. **Population =** 10,000,000 (10 million)

1800 CE – After the rise and fall of hundreds of empires, Egypt, China, India, Europe the population grows slowly until: **Population** reaches about **1,000,000,000** (1 billion)

We are now in the era of the **Industrial Revolution**, so the population began to rise significantly. Why? Because people had better jobs, more food and better living conditions compared to pre-industrial life. Even though it took nearly 12,000 years to reach 1 billion, after the

Industrial Revolution, it only took 200 years for the population to double and reach **2 billion.**

1950 CE - **Population** reaches about **3,000,000,000** (3 billion)

The doomsayers started predicting in the 1950's that the world was doomed, we will never survive – world over-population will be the doom of us all. But what really happened was that between the 1950's and now in 2015, the population has reached 7 billion!

2015 CE Population = **7,000,000,000** (7 billion)

Half the entire population has been added in the last 70 years. Most of the growth has been seen in Asian countries. As discussed earlier, Bangladesh's population has tripled in the last 100 years. From 50,000,000 to 150,000,000 in a relatively short amount of time. Bangladesh's capital is **Dhaka**, and is the most densely populated city in the world.

In the past 30 years, attitudes to population have changed in Bangladesh. Most couples have **CHOSEN** to limit themselves to 1 or 2 children only. There has been education and slogans from the government suggesting this, however the people ultimately made their own decision – just like they do in first world countries.

An armed conflict between East Pakistan (later joined by India) and West Pakistan in 1971 established the Bangladeshi republic. Therefore, **1972** was the first year of an independent Bangladesh, and during this time, women on average had 7 children, who had a life span of less than 50 years. After full independence, the birth-rate in **2012** is 2.2 children and the lifespan is 70 years. That is within only 40 years!

In **1963**, the average birth-rate across the globe was 5 babies per woman, but it was a very divided world. There were the rich nations in America and Europe, with fewer babies, and longer lives, and the poorer nations in Asia and Africa who had many babies, and short lives.

By **2012**, almost all countries have levelled out. With the exception of Africa, most of the big Asian countries like China, India and Bangladesh have reversed to fewer babies, longer lives. The same can be said for Brazil and Mexico. The average is now around 2.5 children per family, and a life expectancy of 70, and even that is growing. So how did this amazing transformation happen? Easy – education and development.

Access to better healthcare, better education, better food, better housing, better conditions. Remember what happened to the European population in 1800 CE. It exploded, but in a good way. This is what is happening again now, but in the previously non-industrialised countries – and in a good way.

Remember back to those two crackpot "scientists" Paul Ehrlich and John P. Holdren. Ehrlich wrote a book called *The Population Bomb* in 1968, and Holdren (Obamas' science man) and Ehrlich, singled out Bangladesh for special punishment by "triaging" that country – i.e. Cut all funding, help and aid in their 1977 book called **Ecoscience: Population, Resources, Environment.** Right after my blood cooled down, I got a cold chill to think what would have happened if any government had of paid attention to these eugenicists.

Professor Rosling wanted to test how much of this good news was getting out to the general public. In other words, how much did people know, and didn't know, about the world they live in. He ran a series of questioners, first in his home country of Sweden, then later in Britain. Both surveys came back with appalling results.

> **Q1.** How many babies on average do women in Bangladesh have?
> **Multi-Choice Answers**: 2.5 – 3.5 – 4.5 – 5.5
> **A1.** The majority (**35%**) selected **answer 3** – 4.5 babies

His team then broke the data down into higher educated vs. lower educated – the result got worse. Finally, they ran some random answers. He uses the analogy of a monkey having 4 bananas, and which banana would it pick. Eventually it would pick from all 4, so the random percent is 25%. This is still lower than the 35% the British people picked for the correct answer. In other words, if people just chose a random answer, they would still get a better result than the people polled in Britain. In fact, a random answer would be twice as good as the British population would answer.

The problem here is not lack of knowledge, it is pre-conceived ideas!

For me, this test was actually a very good test to see how well the powers that be have been, at brainwashing and conditioning people. Now before you get angry and say *"Hey!! I have not been brainwashed by anyone! I was not told / I was taught X etc. etc"*. I will be going into great detail in **Book III: Secrets of the Mind Control** about how and why they are brainwashing and conditioning the general populace. So for now, just see this as proof that something is amiss. You were never taught it at school, you were never told about it in the news, on the TV, in newspapers, or the radio. Why? As I said, we will look at that later.

The reality is, Bangladesh has 2 children, Brazil has 2 children, Vietnam has 2 children, and even India has 2 children per family. The reality is, that the world norm is 2 children per family.

In fact, even some of the more developed African countries are now down to 2 children per family. There is not one religion, or one culture that forces families to have more than 2 children. This phenomena has nothing to do with either. This miracle has happened in your lifetime – in my lifetime – and it is still happening. This is the kind of event humans will be talking about in 300 years saying how amazing it was!

And no – I am not jumping ship and joining the eugenicists who want to reduce humans. As I have already said, the amazing thing about this is, it was allowed to evolve naturally, without negative government intervention like China, and without cutting off aid as John Holdren thinks we should.

I believe it is a rising in consciousness – on a Soul level. These countries are moving out of Infant Soul and into Child / Young . As I said in my last book, the days of Infant Souls are numbered. There will soon be no Infant Souls incarnating to Earth – and this data is proof to me.

So how will the population grow to 11 billion if everyone is only having 2 children? Yes, a conundrum to be sure, but Professor Rosling explains it simply and eloquently in his presentation. Unfortunately you will need to watch the video, as it is difficult to put into words on paper. According to the data, all this should happen around the year, **2100**. Again, this is another interesting point that fits in with what Spirit have told me. I will be discussing this in depth in a later Book, but basically, Spirit told me that by the year 2120, the Earth will be completely in the **Aquarian Age**. The Aquarian Age can be seen as an Age of Enlightenment and harmony. We are just creeping into it now, and already the effects are showing, but by 2120, Earth will be completely immersed in those energies.

Current Global Populations

At the moment, the world population is:

- **2012:** Asia (**4 billion**); Africa (**1 billion**); Americas – North and South (**1 billion**) and Europe (**1 billion**). However, by the end of this century in 2100, the population will look like this:
- **2100:** Asia (**5 billion**); Africa (**4 billion**); Americas – North and South (**1 billion**) and Europe (**1 billion**).

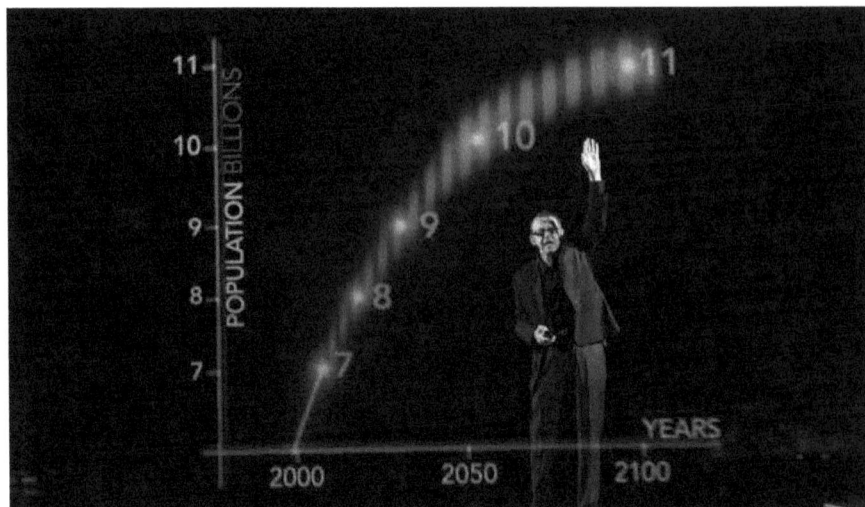

Part of Professor Rosling's awesome presentation

The old developed countries – North America and Europe will make up less than 10% of the population and they will be in decline as far as birth-rate goes. Africa on the other hand will double by **2050**, then double again by 2100. Ironically, Africa will be like the United States was in its peak during the 1950's – 1980.

Suffice it to say, Professor Rosling's data agrees with what my Guide told me over 22 years ago – that the world wide population will peak at 11 billion, around the end of this century, in conjunction with the **Age of Aquarius**. But what he doesn't know yet, is that the earth will easily support that many people in a harmonious way.

Because of Soul Evolution, by 2100, there will be mainly Mature and Old Souls inhabiting the Earth. So there will be no more issues with the 1 % of the 1% controlling 99% of the world's resources. Instead, the souls on Earth around 2050 onwards will start by distributing the resources to the countries that need it the most. Once those countries fix their problems, they will re-distribute again to the next country in trouble. Eventually there will be no more poor countries left.

There will also be no more wars or strife, and no more mega-rich billionaires, as these are a Young Soul phenomena. That said, there will still be Young Souls on Earth, however their numbers will be greatly diminished, and there will be far more older souls to keep them in check. Since most souls would have outgrown the Young Soul phase by 2100, those events would become irrelevant.

It Must Be Relevant to Survive!

Anything that is no longer relevant to the Earth, the universe, or even your person life – simply fades away. Just look at the religions, technology and cultures that lasted for thousands of years, then almost overnight, they disappeared. Indeed, one of the greatest empires of all – the **Roman Empire** is a good example.

In modern times, not even Rome's language (Latin) has survived as a modern, living language. It is only spoken by academics, scholars and priests of the Catholic church. Its customs and traditions have faded into history. At one time, almost all the known world worshiped Roman gods, and in particular the god **Mithra**. Indeed, Mithraism was equivalent to modern day Christianity in popularity. Christians today would scoff if you suggested that Christianity will die out within 50 years. But I am sure a Roman follower of Mithra would had said the same thing back in 2 C.E.(Tertullian.org, 2015).

Rome lasted for almost 500 years, held sway over some 70 million people, at that time, 21% of the world's entire population, and occupied 51 countries. So what happened?

It became corrupted from within. This is a sure sign that it was losing relevance. People no longer took it seriously, so they didn't mind corrupting it. You can only corrupt something you do not take serious anymore, or never took serious from the beginning. By the time that Rome was overrun by the Germanic warlord **Odoacer**, Rome had already started to collapsed from within.

We see the same thing going on today, especially in the United States. That government has become so totally corrupt, that it is only a matter of time before it will collapse completely. First in a civil war, then, when it has been weakened by that, foreign armies will move in and take over.

I will discuss this in more detail in later chapters. Sorry to finish on a low note, but it is very important to understand that things only remain relevant whilst they are relevant! Rather than dwell on what will be lost, try and focus on the great change we can all initiate right now.

Furthermore, I hope this cutting edge data helps you understand that the system is rigged. World population is not as bad as people think, yet we are bombarded by the media with messages of doom and gloom. Before I go into how the media is used to control the masses and manipulate opinion, we need to continue with our look at the global agenda and see who runs the world from behind closed doors - unelected, and how they get away with it. So be prepared for some more shocking facts!

References:

Banks, N. (2010). *David Rockefeller Praises Chairman Mao's Slaughter of 45 Million People in Four Years*. [online] Nancybanksmd.com. Available at: http://www.nancybanksmd.com/index. php?option=com_content&view=article&id=154%3Adavid-rockefeller-praises-chairman-maos-slaughter-of-45-million-people-in-four-years&Itemid=80 [Accessed 22 Jan. 2015].

Bannister, R. (1993). *Social Darwinism*. [online] Autocww.colorado.edu. Available at: http://autocww. colorado.edu/~flc/E64ContentFiles/SociologyAndReform/SocialDarwinism.html [Accessed 22 Jan. 2015].

Citizens Commission on Human Rights, (2010). *Age of Fear: Creating the Holocaust*. [online] Available at: http://www.cchr.org/documentaries/age-of-fear/creating-the-holocaust.html [Accessed 23 Jan. 2015].

COONAN IN BEIJING, C. and MCNEILL IN TOKYO, D. (2006). *Japan's rich buy organs from executed Chinese prisoners*. [online] The Independent. Available at: http://www.independent.co.uk/news/ world/asia/japans-rich-buy-organs-from-executed-chinese-prisoners-470719.html [Accessed 22 Jan. 2015].

Cshl.edu, (2015). *Cold Spring Harbor Research Facility*. [online] Available at: http://www.cshl.edu/ About-Us/History.html [Accessed 23 Jan. 2015].

Ehrlich, P. (1968). *The Population Bomb*. Cutchogue, N.Y.: Buccaneer Books.

Ehrlich, R., Ehrlich, A. and Holdren, J. (1977). *Ecoscience ; population, resources, environment*. San Francisco: Freeman.

En.minghui.org, (2015). *Torture Methods Used to Persecute Falun Gong Practitioners in Henan No. 3 Forced Labor Camp (Part 1) | Falun Dafa - Minghui.org*. [online] Available at: http://en.minghui. org/html/articles/2013/7/10/140957.html [Accessed 22 Jan. 2015].

Galton, F. (1909). *Essays in eugenics*. London: Eugenics Education Society.

Jian, L. (2002). *Young Attorney Li Jian Dies from Tortures in Henan Province Third Forced Labor Camp | Falun Dafa - Minghui.org*. [online] Clearwisdom.net. Available at: http://www.clearwisdom.net/ html/articles/2014/3/10/145764p.html [Accessed 15 Nov. 2015].

Kissinger, H. (1974). Memorandum to the NSC. In: *NSC*. New York.

Lombardo, P. (2002). *The American breed*. [Charlottesville, VA]: [publisher not identified].

Mekong.net, (2015). *The Khmer Rouge in Cambodia: The Unique Revolution*. [online] Available at: http://www.mekong.net/cambodia/uniq_rev.htm [Accessed 22 Jan. 2015].

Nowak, M. (2007). *UN Reports the Chilling Facts on Organ Harvesting from Live Falun Gong Practitioners*. [online] Falunhr.org. Available at: http://www.falunhr.org/index. php?option=content&task=view&id=1644&Itemid [Accessed 22 Jan. 2015].

Quigley, C. (1975). *Tragedy & Hope: A History of the World in Our Time*. GSG and Associates.

Rockefeller, D. (1973). From a China Traveler. *New York Times*.

Rosenberg, M. (2015). *10 Important Facts About China's One Child Policy*. [online] About.com Education. Available at: http://geography.about.com/od/chinamaps/a/China-One-Child-Policy-Facts.htm [Accessed 22 Jan. 2015].

Sedghi, S. and Hall, E. (2015). *China's one-child policy created ruthless 'little emperors'*. [online] ABC News. Available at: http://www.abc.net.au/news/2015-05-25/chinas-one-child-policy-creates-ruthless-children-writer-says/6495666 [Accessed 26 May 2015].

Tomorrow's Children. (1934). [DVD] http://www.imdb.com/title/tt0220107/: Director: Dwain Esper.

Wikipedia, (2015). *Armenian Genocide*. [online] Available at: http://en.wikipedia.org/wiki/Armenian_ Genocide [Accessed 22 Jan. 2015].

3

KHAZARIANS: WHEN A JEW IS NOT A JEW

"There are no secrets that time does not reveal."

— JEAN RACINE (1639 - 1699)

*T*he Anunnaki had been battling between themselves and using human armies to wage their wars against each other for several thousand years after the great deluge. On **Enlil's** side was his hot tempered and spoilt granddaughter **Inanna**, and on **Enki's** side was his rogue and bitter, out of control son **Marduk**. Inanna blamed Marduk for her husband's death.

Dumuzi was Marduk's younger brother, and was very much in love with Inanna. However, not long after they were married, Marduk had an indirect hand in Dumuzi's death, which was kind of an accident, but he was still in the wrong. At any rate, Inanna was devastated, as she adored Dumuzi. Thus, she wanted someone to pay for his death, and Marduk was it. Not that Marduk didn't deserve a kick in the butt.

This all culminated with a nuclear strike on two of Marduk's cities – **Sodom** and **Gomorrah**.

It was one of Enlil's top human General's, **Abraham** that had identified the cities of Sodom and Gomorra as allied with Marduk. They had been supplying Marduk's army with food, water, and medical aid. Therefore it was decided to take these cities out.

Enlil ordered his eldest son **Ninurta** to use his flying machine and launch a nuclear strike on Sodom and Gomorrah. Ninurta was Enlil's "champion" and did a lot of Enlil's fighting for him. Because it was Enlil that gave the go ahead for the nuke attack, he knew exactly when the strike would take place. Therefore, he pre-warned his favourite human General, Abraham, to get as far away as possible. He ordered them to go to the land of **Canaan**.

The Aftermath of the Nuclear War

After **2025 BCE**, only Enlil's Earthling army survived the nuclear holocaust and its fallout, and only because Enlil had sent them to safety in Canaan. This included Abraham and his family. Canaan was already populated with other Enlilite tribes that today are known as **Palestinians**.

Ironically, in these ancient times, Abraham's people and the local Palestinians were allies. They all bowed down to, and served, Enlil, who they called **Yahweh**.

Enlil underestimated the devastation he had unleashed with the nukes, and the area that was Sumer, was now uninhabitable. Indeed, the very cradle of human existence was now a no go area. On a side note, **Bau** (Ninurta's wife) died with her Earthlings at Lagash, giving them medical aid to ease their death after Ninurta nuked Sodom, Gomorra and three other cities. So not all the Anunnaki on Enlil's side where anti-human. Most were very caring and giving.

However, Enlil, ever the insecure "god," was now calling himself **YAHWEH**, because he knew his real name (Enlil) would be forever associated with the devastation of Sumer. To ensure their loyalty to him only, he commanded Abraham and his men to brand themselves. He was worried that they would blend in with the other humans (the Canaanites) and he would lose his devoted followers – and they were all he had left. Thus, Abraham, then 99, and his male followers were ordered by their god Enlil/Yahweh to cut off their foreskins so their penises would look like those of Anunnaki.

Abraham obeyed the Lord (ENLIL) and came into the promised land of Canaan where he lived along with his son Isaac and his grandson Jacob who was later renamed Israel.

The Children of Israel

The Bible doesn't elaborate on why Jacob changed his name to Israel, however the Sumerians can tell us. On his way back from Harran to Canaan, Jacob paused at the **Yabbok Crossing** of the Jordan River. Jacob had been having some trouble with his brother Esau. Esau wanted to rule Abraham's tribe, and so was giving Jacob a hard time over it (as Jacob was currently the ruler of the tribe).

Therefore, Jacob was uncertain what his brother Esau's attitude was toward him, so he sent his party ahead.

One of Marduk's Anunnaki pilots attacked Jacob at the Crossing. They wrestled, and though Jacob dislocated his thigh, he pinned and held the Anunnaki to the ground all night. In the morning, Jacob let him go, but asked the "god" for a blessing. As his blessing, the defeated Anunnaki renamed Jacob **ISRA-EL** [he who fought a god]. Israel, who limped into Esau's camp, became the patriarch of Enlil's loyalists, who became known as *The Children of Israel* [Encounters: 250 to 256].

Furthermore, they started to refer to the land they were living in as *Israel*, even though it was still Canaan.

The Twelve Tribes of Israel

The twelve tribes of Israel came from the twelve sons of Israel (Jacob). His twelve sons were born to four different women, and their names were: Reuben, Simeon, Levi, Judah, Dan, Naphtali, Gad, Asher, Issachar, Zebulun, Joseph, and Benjamin (Genesis 35:23-26; Exodus 1:1–4; 1 Chronicles 2:1–2).

When the tribes inherited the so-called *Promised Land* originally from Enlil/ Yahweh, Levi's descendants did not receive a territory for themselves (Joshua 13:14).

Instead, they became priests and had several cities scattered throughout all of Israel. Joseph's tribe was divided in two—Jacob had adopted Joseph's two sons, Ephraim and Manasseh, essentially giving Joseph a double portion for his faithfulness in saving the family from famine (Genesis 47:11–12).

This meant that the tribes who received territory in the *Promised Land* were Reuben, Simeon, Judah, Dan, Naphtali, Gad, Asher, Issachar, Zebulun, Benjamin, Ephraim, and Manasseh. In some places in Scripture, the tribe of Ephraim is referred to as the tribe of Joseph (Numbers 1:32–33).

The Habiru / Hebrew People

Due to a food shortage in Canaan/ Israel, some of the tribes migrated to Egypt – an area ruled over by Marduk, now known as Ra.

There they multiplied into hundreds of thousands. The Egyptians called these Children of Israel the **Habiru**, or as we know them today – the **Hebrew** people. The Egyptians, who were ruled by Marduk, felt threatened by the mass of people from Israel (Enlil worshippers) living among them, so they enslaved them and made their lives bitter with hard bondage (under orders from Marduk).

Enlil taught Moses strategies and gave him devices to impress the Pharaoh Amenhotep of the power of Yahweh, as Enlil now called himself. Enlil then ordered Moses back to Egypt to show the Pharaoh "magical powers" (really high technology) to convince him to free the Israelites.

After 430 years in Egypt, the Pharaoh gave in and the Hebrew were led out of bondage by Moses. Enlil either used climate control devises to sweep a path through the Red Sea, or showed the Israelites a way to cross. The Egyptians chased them, however in some versions of the story, Enlil let the sea sweep over and drown them. They crossed the Red Sea and went into Arabia, where they received the new Laws of their God (Enlil) at **Mount Sinai.**

Enlil landed his flying machine/spaceship atop the mount and, with an amplifier he spoke directly to 600,000 Israelites at the mountain's base. They must, he said, reject all other Anunnaki gods, not even say their names. They must spend every seventh day worshipping him and subjugate women and kids, as well as refrain from murder, adultery, theft, and false witness. They must not, he said, crave others' homes, wives, and property.

The Ark of the Covenant – an Anunnaki Comms Device

For forty days on the peak, Enlil regaled Moses on his spaceship with projections or rocketed him up so he could see and report the Earth was curved–something Earthlings of his day did not know. Enlil gave

Moses stone tablets he'd inscribed with his commandments. He showed Moses how to build a temple and a box (Ark of the Covenant) for the tablets. Above the tablet drawer in the Ark, Moses must build a Talk-To-Enlil communicator (sporting two gold cherubs).

Through the Ark, Moses could signal and question Enlil for "Yes" or "No" answers. He kept his face hidden from Moses while he dictated what Moses engraved for forty days. When Moses returned to his followers, he glowed with radiation he absorbed from Enlil's shuttlecraft. Moses died of radiation sickness before reaching the Promised Land, but his general, **Joshua**, led the Israelites there.

Enlil chooses Moses' brother Aaron and Aaron's sons as priests. He specified the protective clothes the priests must wear near the radioactive Ark. Enlil, was extremely protective of his Ark, because he did not want the other Anunnaki getting their hands on his technology. In fact, he killed 50,000 people of Bethshemesh for looking into it. [*1 Samuel* 6:19]

The generation of Israelites that left Egypt with Moses were not allowed to enter the Promised Land because of their lack of faith in the Lord (Enlil). They were forced to wander in the wilderness for 40 years until a new generation rose up and trusted and worshipped the Lord (Enlil) without question. They entered the Promised Land with Joshua.

For about 400 years, the 12 tribes of Israel were ruled by the Judges (because there was no King) according to the Law of Moses. When they desired to have a king like all the other nations, God (Enlil) appointed **Saul** to be their king, who reigned over them for 40 years, followed by **King David** who reigned 40 years, and David's son **Solomon** who reigned 40 years.

During the reign of Solomon, the kingdom of Israel was at its most glorious, and the first temple was built. However, because Solomon's heart turned away from the Lord (Enlil) in his old age, God (Enlil) told him that 10 of the tribes would not be ruled by his son. It was Solomon that discovered all of the occult practises of today that the Illuminati love so much. Solomon also discovered the secret that their so-called "God" was really a flesh and blood being, although he did not realise Enlil was alien to this planet.

After the death of Solomon, the kingdom of Israel was divided, and the northern 10 tribes were ruled over by a series of wicked (black magick) kings, who were not descended from David and Solomon.

This Northern Kingdom retained the name of Israel and eventually had Samaria as its capital.

The smaller Southern Kingdom became known as Judah, and had Jerusalem as its capital, and was reigned over by the descendants of David. Starting in 2 Kings 16, the people of the Southern Kingdom became known as Jews after the name of the kingdom of Judah.

The Northern Kingdom of Israel were overthrown and taken captive by the Assyrians (Marduk's people). The Israelites who remained, became intermingled with the other nations who came in and occupied the land. These people would become known as the Samaritans, and the 10 tribes of Northern Israel would never be a nation again as they were assimilated by their conquerors.

The Southern Kingdom of Judah would eventually be taken captive into **Babylon** (Marduk's main city) as a punishment for serving other gods (mainly Enlil), and the temple would be destroyed. However, after 70 years in Babylon, the Jews returned to Judah, rebuilt the temple at Jerusalem, and continued to be ruled by kings descended from David. By 1 CE, the nation of Judah had become known as Judea and was under Roman rule and occupation.

In 70 CE, the future Roman emperor **Titus** conquered Jerusalem. For over 1800 years, the Jews remained scattered throughout all nations. Then in 1948, the impossible happened. The **State of Israel** was founded, and the Jews once again possessed the Promised Land. Many Christians have proclaimed this to be a miracle and a blessing from God, but was this really the blessing of the Lord, or were darker forces at work?

Who Are the Israelites Today?

Even asking the question presupposes that there are reservations about the identity of the modern-day Jew and their relationship to Abraham, Isaac, and Jacob/Israel.

If you were to ask this question to the average person claiming to be a Born Again Christian, they would quickly tell you: "*The true descendants of Abraham, Isaac, and Jacob are those people today who call themselves Jews.*"

Yet in light of that answer, we should know that the Bible makes it very clear that there are imposters masquerading as Israelites, although no Israelite blood flows through their veins. The book of Revelation informs us of this deception:

> *I know your tribulation and your poverty (but you are rich) and the blasphemy by those imposters who say they are Jews and are not, but are a synagogue of Satan. (Revelation 2:9)*

In other words, there are those who claim to be of the house of Judah, and therefore Israelites, but who in reality are imposters identified as a Synagogue of Satan no less!

Nathan M. Pollock, a professor of Medieval Jewish History at Tel Aviv University, who, after spending forty of his sixty-four years in research, stated in The Jewish Almanac.

> *"Strictly speaking, it is incorrect to call an ancient Israelite a 'Jew' or to call a contemporary Jew an 'Israelite' or a Hebrew."*

This is a remarkable admission! Pollack planned to celebrate the 1,000th anniversary of the Jewish / Khazar alliance but was summarily rejected. An elderly, meek-looking man who migrated to Israel from Russia 43 years ago, Pollock ekes out a living as a translator of scientific texts and proof-reader in publishing firms. But his great passion, hobby, and avocation is historic research.

He has devoted 40 years of his life in trying to prove that seven out of ten Israelis and nine out of ten Jews in the Western Hemisphere are not real Jews, but descendants of the fierce Khazarian tribe which roamed the steppes of southern Russia many centuries ago.

For obvious reasons the Israeli authorities are not at all eager to give the official stamp of approval to Pollock's theories. However, they did state for the record:

> *For all we know, he may be 100 per cent right," said a senior government official. "In fact, he is not the first one to discover the connection between Jews and Khazarians. Many famous scholars, Jews and non-Jews, stressed these links in their historical research works.*

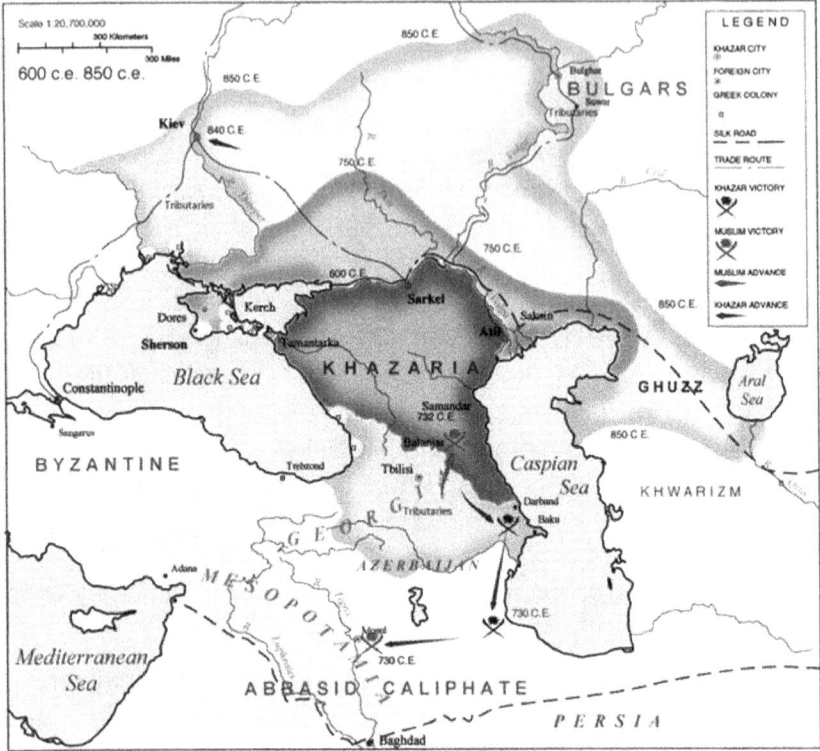

Khazarian Empire 600 CE – 850 CE

WHAT EXACTLY IS A KHAZARIAN?

This is the story of a kingdom of belligerent, warlike Caucasian nomads, having no linked ancestry with anything Israelite this side of Noah, yet adopting Talmudic Judaism and becoming the dominant and virtually only current force in twenty-first century international Jewry.

The Khazars were a pagan civilisation, and in a short period in history, became the largest and most powerful kingdom in Europe, and possibly the wealthiest as well. The Khazar Empire was located between the Caspian and Black Seas in what is now southern Russia, around present day **Georgia**.

The empire flourished from about the 6th to the 11th centuries. They are mentioned in Arab, Jewish, Greek, and Byzantine literature from mid-6th to mid-12th centuries.

They brought with them their religious worship that was a mix of phallic worship and other forms of idolatrous worship practiced in

Central Asia and by other Turkic peoples. The Khazar religious structure centred on a form of shamanism known as **Tengri**, which incorporated the worship of spirits, the sky, and zoolatry, the worship of animals.

Tengri was also the name of their *"immortal god who created the world,"* and the primary animal sacrifices made to this deity were horses. This form of worship continued into the seventh century with vile forms of sexual excesses and lewdness indulged in by the Khazars as part of their religious beliefs. This form of worship produced to a large degree a moral degeneracy that the Khazarian King could no longer endure.

In the seventh century King Bulan, (the ruler at that time), decided to end the practice of phallic worship and all other forms of worship and to make one of the three monotheistic religions, (which he knew very little about) the new Khazarian state religion. He had been visited many times by Islamic spoke-persons as well as Christian missionaries who were always trying to bribe him in to converting to their beliefs.

Those two religions were trying to convert the Khazars more for military strategic reasons then to save their immortal souls. However, the only other visitors he had were from the Jews. But they were more interested in doing trade than talking philosophy. They never tried to convert the Khazars, and left as soon as they bought or sold their goods. This intrigued Bulan, so he summoned some Rabbis to a meeting.

In fact, after an historic session with representatives from the three monotheistic religions, King Bulan decided to adopt Talmudism, (as it was known then and practiced today as Judaism,) over Islam and Christianity and it became the new state religion for the Khazarian Empire (Khazaria, 1995).

Why Did They Choose Talmudism?

It should be noted that one part of the Talmud (a central text of Rabbinic Judaism written mainly while the Israelites where in Babylon) highly appealed to the sexually depraved Khazarians. The Talmud offers generous loopholes for adultery and paedophilia.

In **TALMUD, Sanhedrin 52b**, it says the penalty for adultery does not include sex with a minor, the wife of a minor, or the wife of a heathen (non-Jew).

The Talmud also encourages the seduction of un-wed, adolescent girls it calls *"designated bondmaids."*

But it is important how such rapes are performed and this is explained in **TALMUD, Kerithoth 11a**:

> *...with the designated bondmaid, one is guilty only in the case of natural connection [vaginal], but not in the case of perverse connection [anal].*

The Pharisees (the spiritual fathers of Judaism) reason that rape in a perverted manor is outside the jurisdiction of the Law. Normal rape however was punishable. In Babylon, sexual perversion had been a way of life. It was here that most of the Talmud was written down. The Pharisees were deeply influenced by the depraved goings on in Babylon, which is evident in three of the major treaties of the Talmud.

In these treatises are found extensive passages which give legal endorsement to seduce and marry three year old baby girls. Indeed, many of the most famous Rabbis of the Talmud, including **Rabbi Simeon ben Yohai**, upheld this privilege.

Today in Israel, thousands of Jews go to Meron every year to venerate the memory of a known paedophile, Simeon ben Yohai, one of the most respected Rabbis in Judaism. In one of dozens of endorsements of child sex, R. Simeon b. Yohai stated in **TALMUD, Yebamoth 60b**:

> *A proselyte who is under the age of three years and one day is permitted to marry a priest.*

Agreeing with ben Yohai, the **TALMUD, Kethuboth 11b** states:

> *When a grown up man has intercourse with a little girl it is nothing, for when the girl is less than this (3 years), it is as if one puts the finger into the eye.*

The footnote to this passage says:

> *As tears come to the eye again, and again, so does virginity come back to the little girl under three years.*

The same section confirms that sexual activity with small boys is in the same category.

> The intercourse with a small boy is not regarded as a sexual act.

In addition to adulterers, the writers of the New Testament, in the story of the **Good Samaritan**, portrayed the Pharisees as racial bigots, too self-righteous to respond to the suffering of one who was not a Jew.

Since the Khazars were already indulging in sodomy, rape and child sacrifice, this new religion was going to work out just fine. Indeed, the king and his nobles embraced Judaism.

A royal edict was passed enforcing Judaism as the only legal religion in the Khazar Kingdom.

Tribesmen had to undergo circumcision, learn Hebrew prayers, and recognise Jewish rabbis as their spiritual leaders – on pain of death.

King Bulan and his 4,000 feudal nobles were promptly converted by rabbis imported from Babylon for the event. Phallic worship and all other forms of idol worship were there after forbidden. The Khazarian Kings invited large numbers of Rabbis from Babylon and surrounding nations to come and open synagogues and schools to instruct the population in the new state religion.

After the mass conversion of the King and his empire, none other than a so called self-styled Jew could occupy the Khazarian throne. The empire became a virtual theocracy with the religious leaders being the civil administrators as well. During this time, the Talmud was added to or altered, to protect their state religion from any other outside religious influence and to prevent a return to previous worship styles.

The ideologies of the Talmud became the axis of political, cultural, economic, and social attitudes and activities throughout the Khazarian kingdom. The Talmud provided civil and religious law.

The Origins of Yiddish

When the Khazars in the first century B.C. invaded Eastern Europe their mother-tongue was an Asiatic language, referred to in the Jewish Encyclopaedia as the "Khazar languages." They were primitive Asiatic dialects without any written alphabet or any written form. When King

Bulan was converted in the 7th century, he decreed that the Hebrew characters that he saw in the Talmud and other Hebrew documents was thereupon to become the alphabet for the Khazar language.

The Hebrew characters were adopted to the phonics of the spoken Khazar language. The Khazars adopted the characters in order to provide a means for a written record of their speech.

The present day language of the Khazars is known as Yiddish. The Khazars adapted words to their requirements from the German, the Baltic, and Slavonic languages over time.

In 986 C.E. the ruler of Russia, **Vladimir III,** became a convert to Christianity in order to marry a Catholic Slavonic princess of a neighbouring sovereign state. Vladimir made his newly acquired Christian faith the state religion of Russia, replacing the pagan worship formerly practiced since Russia was founded in 820 CE. Vladimir III and his successors, as rulers of Russia, attempted in vain to convert his self-styled Jews, now Russian subjects, to Russia's state religion, Christianity.

These Khazarian Jews in Russia refused and resisted Christianity vigorously. They refused to adopt the Russian alphabet in place of Hebrew characters used in writing their "Yiddish" language. They opposed every attempt to bring about their assimilation of the former Khazarian kingdom into the Russian nation.

Many Khazars were forced out of their base in the Caucasus and most of them migrated to Eastern Europe. That alone counts for the presence of "Jews" in Eastern Europe and Germany.

It also explains why the vengeful Khazars a.k.a. "Jews" were behind the Russian Revolution and Communism as we will see later. This also explains why so many European Jews are blond and blue eyed, with a slight Mongol slant to their eyes, as well as the total absence of Semitic features among many Israelis of European descent (Khazaria, 1995).

However, the once flourishing Jewish-Khazar Kingdom was finally destroyed in **1239 CE** by the Mongol invasion of **Balu Khan.** Following the Mongol invasion and conquest, surviving members of Jewish-Khazar tribes trekked west and settled in Poland, Hungary, Bohemia, Austria, Romania, Ukraine, and Russia.

According to Pollack, whose parents came from Poland, if your name is Halperin, Alpert, Halpern, Galpern, etc., you are 100 per cent Khazar. "Alper" means "brave knight" in the Khazar tongue, and the name was granted by the king to the most distinguished warriors. Names like Kaplan, Caplon, Koppel, and the like, are positive proof of Khazar descent, according to the scholar. "Kaplan" means "fierce hawk" in the Khazar language. Kogan, Kagan, Kaganovich show aristocratic descent from Kagan, Hagan, King Bulan's chief-minister.

After the last and final blow from the Mongols, the surviving Khazarian King and his 25 wives (all of royal blood), and 60 concubines, immigrated to Spain with many family members and his large entourage. All up they numbered about 6000.

Modern Day Jews

Jews of the modern era fall into two main categories: the **Ashkenazi Jew** and the **Sephardic Jews** who have a much smaller population.

The Ashkenazi Jew numbered around 11 million in 1960. The term "Ashkenazi" Jew is associated with Germany, Hungary, and Poland which shared culture and borders with the Khazarian Empire and received a large migration of "Yiddish" people from the disintegrating Khazarian kingdom.

When Ashkenazi mitochondrial DNA was tested in a large sample, it was found that they have a deep European ancestry. The majority of Ashkenazi maternal lineages were not brought from the Levant, (an area of the Middle East that covers the Promised Land in Canaan) nor recruited in the Caucasus, but were assimilated within Europe.

Indeed, Ashkenazi Jews (plural Ashkenazim) are the descendants of Jews who migrated into northern France and Germany around 800–1200, and later into Eastern Europe from the Caucasus.

Ashkenazim comprise the overwhelming majority of Jews, with approximately 97 percent of the Jewish world total. So in basic terms, they do not have a drop of Semitic blood in their veins (Ashkenazi, 2015).

Sephardic Jews who numbered only about 500,000 in 1960 and are the descendants of the Spanish Jewish-Khazars, i.e. The Khazarian King and his party. The Sephardic Jews were later expelled from Spain by the Moslems in **1492 CE**. Again, in basic terms, they do not have a drop of Semitic blood in their veins either, but they are much more serious about the Torah, the spiritual book of the Jews. (Sephardic, 2015).

Who are the Modern Day Israelites?

Now, are you wondering the same as I am? Just who are the majority of those people now living in modern day Israel? After all, they took over Palestine, claiming it was their ancestral home, and the land God gave to them.

Well it looks as though 97% of them are probably descendants of the Great Khazars and never were descendants of Abraham! That is because DNA results show that over 97% of people living in modern day Israel do not have a drop of Semitic blood in their veins!

So how did Israel fill up with Ashkenazi and Sephardic Jews, and what happened to the original Hebrews – the Children of Israel – the seed of Abraham?

Who should possess the land of Israel?

Christian evangelicals say it should be the descendants of Abraham that occupy the so-called Promised Land of Israel. They point to the Old Testament and claim that God gave this land forever to the descendants of Abraham and that God demands they and they alone own the land. To the Christian evangelical, this means the Jews. Yes, it is the Jews who own this land, and it is their land forever according to the Bible.

But as we have already learnt, the god that promised the land to a group of Semitic people was not a god! He was an insecure, arrogant, human hating, psychopathic, jealous, mass murderer, and a hypocrite alien. Those are not really the attributes of a Divine and Loving God now are they?

However, just to show I am not being too harsh, let's look at what Enlil/Yahweh/God did according to their own book.

Here are just a few of the cases of mass killings of people, apparently at God's behest, as recorded in the Old Testament:

- The Flood (Genesis 6-8)
- The cities of the plain, including Sodom and Gomorrah (Genesis 18-19)
- The Egyptian firstborn sons during the Passover (Exodus 11-12)
- The Canaanites under Moses and Joshua (Numbers 21:2-3; Deuteronomy 20:17; Joshua 6:17, 21)
- The Amalekites annihilated by Saul (1 Samuel 15)

The first three examples are similar in that there was no human agent involved – in each case it was God, or an angel of God, who carried out the mass killings directly. The mass killing of the Canaanites is the first of two cases in which the text claims that God's people, the nation of Israel, were commanded by Him to attack other nations.

In reality, there are about 158 different events with a death total of 2,821,364 as per the Bible. Historians however estimate that the true figure could be as high as 24,994,828. That is a lot of killings for a supposedly loving god! (Yahweh Killings, 2013)

The problem many people have with these stories of mass killings is that they do not seem to fit the popular conception of the Christian God. In particular, the question is asked how a God of love could allow or even command such brutality.

Furthermore, it is suggested that the God described in these Old Testament books is a different character from the God described in the New Testament. The former is supposedly angry, vindictive and ruthless, the latter loving, patient and forgiving. Even for people who are convinced that the Bible is true and represents God's revelation of Himself, these accounts can be deeply troubling, especially when one thinks about the death of innocent children.

The truth is, the angry, vindictive, and ruthless God is Enlil. The loving, patient, and forgiving God is Enki. Both are aliens from a planet called Nibiru. They are not gods, and as such, the deal struck between Enlil and Abraham (to occupy the Promised Land) should be null and void. However, even if we accepted that the deal is good, he made the deal with Semitic people – not the people of European descent.

The Real Semites

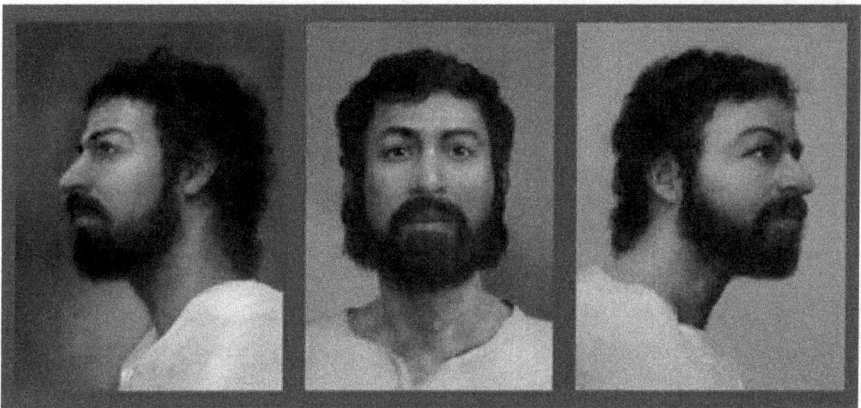

This is what a genetically pure Semite looks like

Semitic people are members of any of various ancient and modern peoples originating in south-western Asia, including the Akkadians, Canaanites, Phoenicians, Hebrews, and Arabs, including any of the peoples descended from Shem, the eldest son of Noah (Semites, 2015).

That would make Abraham a Semite. The Jews, then, according to Christian evangelicals, are the descendants of Abraham, his seed. However, modern DNA can tell us exactly who should be living in Israel, but everyone seems to be ignoring it.

DNA Science Confounds the Common Wisdom

Science proves those who call themselves "Jews" are not Jews! DNA Science has confounded the Christian evangelicals by proving conclusively that most of the people in the nation of Israel and in World Jewry are not the descendants of Abraham.

Those living today who profess to be "Jews" are not of the ancient Israelites, and they are not the seed of Abraham. In fact, the latest (2012) DNA research shows that the Palestinians actually have more Israelite blood than do the Jews! Ironic then that the "Jews" are carrying out genocide against the Palestinians right now.

The nation of Israel today is populated with eight million imposters.

The "Jews" Are Not Jews but are Khazarians!

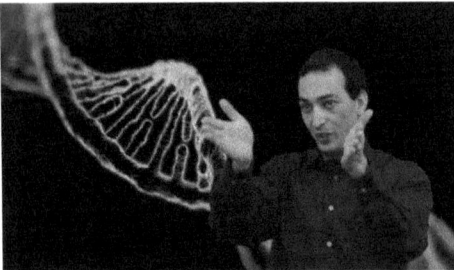

Dr Eran Elhaik Ph.D.

DNA confirms that their blood is from Eastern Europe. The latest DNA science finding is from **Dr. Eran Elhaik** ("a Jew"), geneticist and researcher at Johns Hopkins University School of Medicine, and associates at the McKusick-Nathans Institute of Genetic Medicine, Johns Hopkins University School of Medicine. In research accepted December 5, 2012 and published by the Oxford University Press on behalf of the Society of Molecular Biology and Evolution, it was found that the Khazarian Hypothesis, is scientifically correct.

What exactly is the "Khazarian Hypothesis?"

Simply stated, it holds that the Jewry genome is a mosaic of ancestries which rise primarily out of the Khazars. Jews are Khazars, not Israelites.

The "Jews" of Israel, America, Canada, Europe, Australia, New Zealand and most rest of the world, are descendants not of Father Abraham, but of King Bulan and the people of ancient Khazaria!

Khazaria was an amalgam of Turkic clans who once lived in the Caucasus (Southern Russia) in the early centuries CE. The Caucasus is where we get the term for Caucasians, meaning "white people." These peoples were pagans who converted to Judaism in the seventh century. As converts, they called themselves "Jews," but none of their blood comes from Israel. This is why many Jews have fair hair and skin, unlike true Semitic people who have dark hair and olive/dark skin.

Later, the "Jews" (Khazars) emigrated, settling in Russia, Hungary, Poland, Germany, and elsewhere in Europe. As "Jews," the Khazars then left the European nations in 1948 and settled the fledgling, new nation state of Israel, displacing thousands of true "Semitic" peoples from their ancestral homes.

The people of Israel are not the seed, nor the ancestors of Abraham. They call themselves "Jews," but in fact, DNA science shows them to be Khazars.

> There are no blood or family connections among the Jews," said Dr. Elhaik in an interview with **Haaretz**, Israel's daily newspaper. "The various groups of Jews in the world today do not share a common genetic origin. Their genome is largely Khazar.

God Did Not Give the Land to the Khazarians

Thus, when Prime Minister Netanyahu says, "God gave this land to our Israelite forefathers," he is absolutely wrong, and what is worse, he knows he is wrong, but continues with the hoax. There are no Israelite forefathers of today's "Jews." When today's "Jews" say they should possess the land because they are Israelites and are the seed of Abraham, they are mistaken.

What Happened to the Real Jews?

The original Jews, the Hebrews, were assimilated into countless other countries that overran them over the centuries. Once a people are conquered, the conquerors always interbred with the natives until there are no pure natives left. This is a great way to stop rebellions and uprisings, however, it is bad if you are the conquered people who want to maintain a culture.

We have seen this happen time and time again, even in modern history with the Native Americans, the Australian Aborigines, and the New Zealand Maori.

The original Jews were bred out of existence by their conquerors. This is evident in the DNA – that is why Palestinians have more Hebrew DNA than those that call themselves Jews.

At any rate, there is no such thing as a pure-blood Hebrew / Israelite / Jew left on the planet in this year of 2015. If there is any doubt, check out how many times the Jews have been conquered and assimilated:

- 1812 BCE - Time of Abraham begins
- 1652 BCE - Time of Jacob begins
- 1428 BCE - Israelites enslaved in Egypt
- 796 BCE - Israel split into two kingdoms
- 555 BCE - Assyrians overturn Northern Israel; Ten tribes are lost
- 547 BCE - Sennacherib attacks Jerusalem (Babylonians overrun Assyrian empire)
- 422 BCE - Babylonians conquer Israel & destroy Temple
- 312 BCE - Greeks conquer Israel
- 63 BCE - Romans invade Israel
- 70 CE - Jerusalem conquered by the Romans
- 70 CE - Temple destroyed by the Romans

(Judaism, 2015)

Why are False Jews in Israel Now?

The "Jews" are in Israel for one reason and one reason only: Because England gave it to the Zionists in 1917 with the Balfour Declaration (covered later).

Then in 1948, the United States, officially recognised the nation of "Israel" and has since funded and protected it. They "recognised" it after President Truman was bribed with $2,000,000 (about $20,000,000 in today's money) paid by the Zionists to him personally.

God's Word has nothing to do with it!

Dodgy back room deals and corrupt politicians had everything to do with it! Interestingly, the Bible prophesied that in the last days imposters would erroneously and falsely claim to be "Jews." These imposters would, the Bible says, persecute their enemies. But God would have his revenge:

> **"** Behold, I will make them of the Synagogue of Satan, which say they are Jews, and are not, but do lie; Behold I will make them to come and worship at thy feet and know that I have loved thee. (Revelation 3:9) **"**

Do the "Jews" (Khazars) not do exactly as the Bible prophesied? Do they not persecute the Palestinians and defile the land, claiming they are its original inhabitants? This, even though their proven ancestors, the Khazars, never set foot in the Middle East and are not the seed of Abraham?

The Jews of today say they are God's Chosen People?

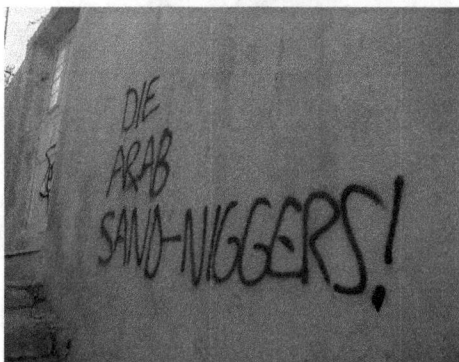

Common anti-Palestinian slogan seen in Israel

The subject of Jewish supremacy is one that few non-Jews dare touch and those that do are, if not anti-Semitic, then sure to be branded as such.

As often proves to be the case, the most courageous voices tend to emerge from inside Israel itself. None is more reliable than that of the Haaretz columnist, **Gideon Levy**. Oct. 9, 2011, Levy wrote an article titled "***Jewish people are just that, people, and far from chosen***" in which he was critical of the many Jews that literally take this overt statement of superiority seriously.

However, in conclusion he wrote, *"We should, of course, continue to read the prayer 'You have chosen us.' It is part of the Jewish heritage."* (Levy, 2011)

This is also perceived by many people who are not Jewish, and therefore not chosen, as an insult. If you teach young people that they are superior, then that is what they will think they are, and they will act accordingly. It is little use to try and tell them otherwise, after the damage has been done.

And these kind of statements are not helpful either:

> *"Goyim were born only to serve us. Without that, they have no place in the world – only to serve the People of Israel" – Rabbi Ovadia Yossef. (Goyim is a derogatory name for non-Jewish people) In 2007, Rabbi Yosef said: "A woman's knowledge is only in sewing ... Women should find other jobs and make hamin but not deal with matters of Torah."*

In an October 2010 sermon, **Rabbi Yosef** stated that *"The sole purpose of non-Jews is to serve Jews."* He said that Gentiles served a divine purpose:

Rabbi Ovadia Yossef

Benjamin Netanyahu and Ovadia Yosef - BFF's

> *"Why are Gentiles needed? They will work, they will plow, and they will reap. We will sit like an effendi and eat. That is why Gentiles were created." Ovadia Yosef was a Talmudic scholar, authority on Jewish religious law, and the long-time spiritual leader of Israel's ultra-orthodox Shas party.*

In 1970, Yosef was awarded the Israel Prize for Rabbinical Literature.

No doubt his racist and sexist statements struck a chord with the men of Israel. It is quite clear that prominent Israelis are not falling over each other to distance themselves from this detestable person while he was alive (Yosef, 2013). He died in 2013. He was a text book version of a Child Soul discussed in my first book.

Benjamin Netanyahu (war criminal) spoke these words to a joint session at the United States Congress, May 24th, 2011:

> *"No distortion of history can deny the 4000 year old bond between the Jewish people and the Jewish land."*

Judging by the prolonged, standing ovation by the Congress, it was quite evident that the mythology of ancient, prior possession was quite acceptable to his American audience who are after all, the dominant factor in Israel's expansionist plans. Is it because so many Jews believe they have a literal God-given-right to rule, that so many countries are

Israeli white phosphorous killed this baby Palestinian

awash with influence peddling organisations such as **Friends of Israel** and **AIPAC,** and are dominated by Jewish ownership of the news and media? Yet, despite all that, Jewish commentators are forever complaining about a rise in anti-Semitism, claiming it is a surrogate emotion for Israel's appalling treatment of the Palestinians and disregard for its Arab neighbours. The fact is, these feelings are anti-Israel, and for very good reasons.

"WE JEWS, WE ARE THE DESTROYERS AND WILL REMAIN THE DESTROYERS. NOTHING YOU CAN DO WILL MEET OUR DEMANDS AND NEEDS. WE WILL FOREVER DESTROY BECAUSE WE WANT A WORLD OF OUR OWN."

— MAURICE SAMUEL
TAKEN FROM HIS BOOK
'YOU GENTILES' PAGE 155

THE ISRAEL YOU DON'T KNOW

They are not anti-Jew per se, but when Israel drops white phosphorous bombs (illegal by the Geneva Convention) on Palestinian neighbourhoods and parents watched the skin of their children melt off as the phosphorous burns in, something is going to give (White Phosphorous, 2013).

Question: Who chose the Chosen People?
Answer: The Chosen People **CHOSE THEMSELVES!**

Earlier DNA Results

Elhaik's research confirms earlier DNA studies, especially the work of **Dr. Ariella Oppenheim** of Hebrew University, who likewise found in 2001, that the "Jews" came from the Khazars rather than the Israelites.

Dr. Oppenheim even found that some of the **Palestinians** have the chromosomes proving they are "Cohen," related to the ancient Israelites who worked in the Synagogue and Temple (Oppenheim, 2001).

However, the true hero and pioneer of exposing one of the greatest hoaxes of all time is a Jewish man - **Arthur Koestler**. In his incredibly well researched book, **The Thirteenth Tribe**, he details the whole Khazarian story. He died in 1981, in a 'suicide pact' with his wife - a tragedy that has aroused some

Arthur Koestler (1905 - 1983)

suspicion since. Unfortunately, he did not live long enough to see that DNA evidence vindicated his theory – that modern day Jews are actually related to the Khazarians and not Abraham (Koestler, 1976). This also helps another darker secret make sense - **Zionism.**

Lord Acton said, "The truth will come out when powerful people no longer wish to suppress it."

Zionism is a movement founded by **Theodor Herzl**, an Ashkenazi Jew in 1896, whose goal is the return of Jews to **Eretz Yisrael**, or **Zion**, the Jewish synonym for Jerusalem and the Land of Israel.

*Theodor Herzl
(1860 - 1904)*

All of the world's top bankers are Zionist, along with many politicians, media personalities, every day people, and even some Christians.

Yes, fundamentalist Christians also support the Zionist movement because they believe if the Jews return to Israel, and the Temple is rebuilt in Jerusalem, then the Lord will return and they will be saved (and the rest of us will burn in hell! Nice…).

Top of that list is Pastor **John Hagee**, a real fire and brimstone preacher that worships Jews and Israel as much as Jesus. In 2015, on the "Hagee Hotline," John Hagee urged viewers to call their congressional representatives and urge them to vote against the nuclear deal with Iran, warning that otherwise *"God will allow terrorists to attack the United States of America."*

The founder of **Christians United for Israel** went on to say,

"Israel is the nation that God has sworn to defend. God could care less about what we say about Russia, about China, about Iran, but when we as a nation take a stand against Israel, God will take a stand against us."

John Hagee (1940 -)

A classic Child Soul to be sure (Hagee, 2015). Finally, in the US, **Vice President Joe Biden**, whilst speaking at an AIPAC (American Israel Public Affairs Committee) celebration said on camera,

"You don't have to be Jewish to be a Zionist. I am a Zionist!"

This is the same man that wrote the draconian **Patriot Act** way back in 1995, but that is a whole other issue.

But as we will see, Jewish Zionist are not really Jews at all. Yes, they are Ashkenazi Jews, however they do not practise Orthodox Judaism, and they certainly do not care about their fellow Jews. They have been responsible for some of the greatest Jewish atrocities in modern history. In fact, they really do live up to their Khazarian roots.

Since their terror attack on Sept. 11, more and more people are turning to the "conspiratorial" or "suppressed" view of history. What follows is not so much conspiratorial as it is suppressed. Indeed, almost everything I talk about is available in the public record – you just have to sniff it out.

Samaritans prepare a slaughtered sheep as part of the Passover ceremony. Jews would need to do this 1,000,000 times.

In **1891**, **Cecil Rhodes** started a secret society called *The Round Table*, dedicated to world domination for the shareholders of the Bank of England and their allies. These pompous aristocrats, including the Rothschilds (Ashkenazi Jews), realised they must control the world to safeguard their monopoly on money creation, as well as global resources. These same people control the **U.S. Federal Reserve** and all other major central banks to this day.

They were all committed Freemasons, which at the top, is dedicated to the destruction of Christianity, the worship of Lucifer[2], and the rebuilding of a pagan (occult) temple in Jerusalem (based on the dark occult temple of Solomon and the Black Kabbalah).

A true blood bath

Just as a side issue, the modern Jews are adamant that if they were to rebuild their Temple, they would recommence their animal sacrifices.

---

[2] In Book 1 – Secrets of the Soul, I explained that Lucifer is not an actual being, however, these elites believe it to be true and thus worship it, often carry out despicable and disgusting acts in its name.

During its hay day in the time of Nero, it is said that the Temple Priests slaughtered over 256,500 lambs just during the Passover ceremony. That was for an estimated population of 2,700,200.

I wonder how the modern world would accept these barbaric, Bronze Age practises in this day and age, especially when the population is now over 11 million. That would be over 1 million lambs slaughtered in the Temple grounds in one day. A true blood bath to be sure (Hunt, 2003).

Zionists really hate Non-Jews

Zionists see most of humanity as "useless eaters" and pioneered eugenics to decrease population and weed out inferior specimens. The eventual annihilation of non-Zionist Jews was rooted in this English (UK) movement. The Nazi's called it *"Life unworthy of life."*

Indeed, remember Thomas Malthus from Chapter 2? He wrote in 1798 that there will always be more people in the world than can be fed, hence the need for wars and diseases. We know that people like the British imperialist Cecil Rhodes, birth control founder Margaret Sanger, Stalin and Adolf Hitler were practitioners of this philosophy, but the man who stands out as the biggest practitioner has to be "Red Terror" **Felix Dzerzhinsky**.

Most Westerners have never heard of him, but he is a Communist god and they had erected a huge statue in his honour (torn down, but soon to be re-erected) in Moscow (Dzerzhinsky, 2013). Dzerzhinsky was an Ashkenazi Jew and Zionist.

In **1897**, the first Zionist Congress took place in Basel, Switzerland. In 1904, the founder of Zionism, Theodore Herzl died at age 44 under suspicious circumstances. The movement was taken over by *The Round Table*. The purpose was to use it and Communism to advance their plan for world control. During the same week in November 1917, the **Bolshevik Revolution** took place and the **Balfour Declaration** promised Palestine to the Jews.

The Round Table group planned three world wars in 1871, to degrade, demoralize, and decimate humanity, rendering it defenceless.

The Third World War, already beginning now, pits political Zionism (the State of Israel) against the Muslims extremist, but more on that in **Chapter 15**.

The True Purpose of Zionism

The true purpose of Zionism is to help colonize the Middle East, subvert Islam, and control the oilfields. For this reason, Israel continues to receive blank checks from the US Government. One analyst estimates the US taxpayer has spent over $3 trillion on Israel (Bollyn, 2003). This is why the founding of Israel took precedence over the welfare of the Jewish people. After World War I, any Jew that moved to Israel was given a large cash "resettlement" payment – paid for by Germany. This was just one way to really antagonise Germany against Jews.

You might say they were already paving the way for World War II and the Nazi atrocities.

Israel has little to do with the Jewish people. Zionism, Communism, Nazism, and the latest - 3rd Wave Feminism, are all creations of the same godless cabal. These 'isms are all means to the final goal, a neo feudal global dictatorship, with a world population of less than 500,000,000. That's about 95% of humanity gone – wiped off the map.

As unwitting overseers, every day Jews will continue as victims of "suicide without consent." Americans too are being fitted for this role. Sept. 11 was an example. Speaking of 9/11, did you know that all of the Ashkenazi Jews that worked in the World Trade Center were contacted a full 24 hours in advance and told not to go into work? Also, Ashkenazi Jews working on the Stock Exchange were warned to sell their stocks in **American Airlines** one week before the attacks. Any guesses who may have been behind the 9/11 tragedy?

Arab terrorism is also backed by this cabal. **Al-Qaeda** and **ISIS**/ISIL are all creations of this group. **Osama Bin Laden** made more than 260 phone calls to England between 1996-1998. He was a CIA asset, codename "**Tim Osman.**" Tim Osman was the name assigned to him by the CIA for his tour of the U.S. and U.S. military bases, in search of political support and armaments. There is evidence that Tim Osman visited the White House.

There is certainty that Tim Osman toured some U.S. military bases, even receiving special demonstrations of the latest equipment. Why hasn't this been reported in the major media? Oh, because the Zionist own the major media outlets, so they suppress it. And now, the enemy is our friend – the Obama White House made a "Willful Decision" to support **Al-Qaeda** and **Muslim Brotherhood** in Syria! (Geller, 2015). If you have ever read the book **Nineteen Eighty Four**, you will know exactly what I am talking about.

Heavily armed US State Police troopers - look more like military

Their aim is to contrive a "war of civilizations" as an excuse to grind down both Muslim states and the West to create a global police state. In 2015, there is ample evidence that the USA, a Zionist controlled country, has fully embraced the Police State, and has militarised its Police force to quell any opposition to them. In many parts of the US, it is hard to distinguish between police officers and soldiers. They have even given police departments "used tanks" from the Afghanistan war.

What I have called "suicide without consent" is really an occult "culling." The constant reference by Zionist and other leaders to "blood sacrifice" refers to the practice of human sacrifice. Energy is released when people or animals are slaughtered and they channel this energy to carry out their next major plan.

In **2002**, Catholic Zionist and New World Order bigwig, U.S. Deputy Secretary of State **Richard Armitage** said that Hezbollah (Shi'a Islamist militant group based in Lebanon) owes the U.S. "a blood debt."

Wars for the Promised Land

Our Zionist rulers design wars as offerings to Lucifer. They find slaughter and mayhem exhilarating, as long as it is someone else who is doing the fighting and sacrificing. And that is precisely why they started and funded both sides of World War I and World War II, and every other conflict since.

During World War I, the Zionist created, funded, and accomplished the Russian Revolution. Russia then had no option but to sue for peace with Germany. This then freed up 300,000 – 400,000 German soldiers that were transferred to the Western Front (to fight the Allies). This then gave the Germans a 3:1 troop advantage over the British and French.

At this point, England and France looked like losing the war. The Zionist now played their Ace card and made a deal with England. They promised to get America into the war, with all of their vast manufacturing power, which would hand England victory. In exchange, they wanted the land of Palestine. The English agreed, and the rest is history.

After the war, the English gave the Zionist what they have wanted all along – Palestine – the Promised Land – even though it was not England's to give. This favourite method of deceit to get what they want is called a **Hegelian Dialectic**. In simple terms, it means – **Problem – Reaction – Solution**. I will discuss this in more depth later.

The Transfer Agreement

The Zionists now had the land, however, European Jews wanted no part of Israel. They enjoyed a relatively high standard of living in nice homes, temperate weather, and good jobs. Many of the wealthiest Jews in Europe lived and operated their businesses in Germany.

Indeed, Germany had been very Jew-friendly since **King Frederick II** (Friedrich der Große "Frederick the Great") protected Jews and encouraged them to move to the new united Germany in the 1700's. Why on earth would they give up a literal and metaphorically lush, green pastures for dry and barren waist lands?

In Edwin Black's book, **The Transfer Agreement**, the numbers tell the story. In **1927**, about 15,000 of Germany's 550,000 Jews considered themselves Zionists. That's less than 2%. The vast majority of German Jews "vehemently rejected Zionism as an enemy from within." They were Germans, and they identified themselves as Germans – after all, 80,000 had fought for Germany in the trenches of WWI and 12,000 had died. "Nowhere was the opposition to Zionism as widespread, principled, and fierce as in Germany" a Zionist historian wrote.

The Zionist had gone to a lot of trouble to steal the Palestinian land, and if they couldn't fill it up with Jews, then they may lose it. Therefore, they formulated a way to change the minds of Jews staying put in Europe.

The solution - the Illuminati / Zionist created the **Nazi Party**, partly to use trauma-based mind control (brainwashing) on the Jews into supplanting the Palestinians. By the time they finished, European Jews would be lining up to move to Palestine.

Zionists and Nazis were mirror images of each other. Both espoused racial purity, and both were prepared to carry out atrocities as a means to an end.

The etymology (origin) and meaning of the word Nazi

1933 marks the first year the word Nazi (from Hebrew Nasi meaning "Knight") was used as the official new name of the **National Socialist German Workers' Party** (NSDAP) in government. It is frequently and incorrectly claimed that the word "Nazi" comes from the haphazard extraction of letters from the first word of the name of the NSDAP – **NationalsoZialistische Deutsche Arbeiterpartei** to produce a simple abbreviation. This explanation is blatantly false as the NSDAP already had a perfectly good and well known abbreviation - NSDAP! The word "Nazi" appeared only after Hitler assumed power.

The Rothschilds Man on the Inside

Though the idea may seem preposterous to some, it is now well established that Hitler's grandfather was Jewish. Hitler's father, Alois, was registered as an illegitimate child with no father when born in 1837.

However, Alois' mother, **Maria Schicklgruber**, is known to have worked in the home of **Amschel Mayer Rothschild**, a very wealthy Jewish banker. She admitted to having an affair with her boss, and when she became pregnant to him she had to leave town. Even though she left her job, Rothschild continued to support her and his illegitimate child – Alois.

Hitler's people went to great lengths to cover up his Jewish heritage. This is well documented in all historical accounts of Hitler's time with the Nazi Party.

In **2010**, the British paper **The Daily Telegraph** reported that a study had been conducted in which saliva samples were collected from 39 of Hitler's known relatives to test their DNA origins and found that Hitler had Jewish origins (Blake, 2010). The paper reported:

> ❝ A chromosome called Haplogroup Elb1b1 which showed up in [the Hitler] samples is rare in Western Europe and is most commonly found in the Berbers of Morocco, Algeria and Tunisia, as well as among Ashkenazi and Sephardic Jews ... Haplogroup Elb1b1, which accounts for approximately 18 to 20 per cent of Ashkenazi and 8.6 per cent to 30 per cent of Sephardic Y-chromosomes, appears to be one of the major founding lineages of the Jewish population. ❞

Case Closed!

Baron Amschel von Rothschild   Alois (Rothschild) Hitler   Adolf (Rothschild) Hitler

However, in the Jewish tradition, heritage is passed down through the female line, and as Hitler's Grandmother (Maria Schicklgruber) was not a Jew, the Jews do not count Hitler as being Jewish. Again, we come back to - so what makes someone a Jew? Anyway, I think you get the picture.

The Rothschilds father many illegitimate children. Some they support and keep close, as they may prove useful for some future project. Others they turn their backs on. Adolf Hitler was one of the lines they kept an eye on. After World War I he was tapped – they needed someone to lead a new political party.

If you know anything about Hitler, then you know he was very un-extraordinary as a young man. Dull, sullen, introverted, and moody. Not very bright, self-absorbed and bitter. Yet, seemingly out of nowhere he appeared and seduced a nation. Sounds just like Barack Obama, but that is for another time! By the way, "on the record," Amschel Rothschild died "childless," and Maria Schicklgruber died in relative "middle class" comfort, even though she never worked again after having Alois. She was getting money from somewhere...

Thus, Hitler was financed and put into power by the Ashkenazi Jews - the Rothschild family.

Think about that for a minute – the "Ashke - **nazi** "Jews. The word nazi is there in plain sight. This is a common trick of the Illuminati – hide things in plain sight.

The word Nazi/Nasi dates back to the time of the Sanhedrin councils of Palestine, first formed by the Romans in the 1st Century BCE.

To members of modern Judaism, the Nasi were the appointed spiritual leaders of the Sanhedrin as opposed to the temporal leadership of the High Priest of the Main Temple. While there is some uncertainty as to the credibility of all the claimed history of the office of Nasi and the bloodline of Rabbinical Scholars of the House of Hillel, there is no doubt the position existed at some point.

The problem for modern readers concerning the direct relationship with the Hebrew term (Nasi) for knight and Nazi for the NDSAP as the "New Knights of Germany", is that Hitler and the NDSAP were supposed to be racially opposed to all things "Jewish". However, when we understand the true history concerning Israel and Zionism, it all starts to make sense.

THE HOLOCAUST DILEMMA

The word "Holocaust" is a Biblical term for "burnt sacrifice." Why refer to genocide as "a burnt sacrifice"? Because the Illuminati / Zionist bankers deliberately sacrificed European Jews to create the State of Israel, the capital of the Rothschild's New World Order (NWO).

The London-based Ashkenazi Jewish bankers (The Rothschilds) wanted Jews to set up the State of Israel in order to colonise the Middle East. Zionism was a British creation. The "British Empire" was a vehicle for the Illuminati / Zionist Jewish bankers. It has since morphed into the NWO.

In his book, **Perfidy** (1961), author **Ben Hecht** (Ashkenazi Jew) describes how the Nazis lacked the manpower to round up Jews and relied on the Zionists to do it. The Zionists betrayed their fellow Jews, yet reaped the moral and political capital from the holocaust. The more Jews that died, the stronger the moral case for Israel and for protection from the truth. One such Jewish betrayer and Nazi collaborator was multi billionaire, Ashkenazi Jew, **George Soros** and his father.

Perfidy is the single most damning statement to date on the interchangeability of the British-Zionist cabal that ran Israel during its early years and the leadership of the Nazis.

THE ROTHSCHILD ZIONIST BANKING CARTEL HIRED HITLER TO START WORLD WAR II

Rothschild Zionism was willing to sacrifice the whole of European Jewry for a Zionist State. Everything was done to create a state of Israel and that was only possible through a world war. Wall Street and Jewish large bankers aided the war effort on both sides.

Hecht presents extended excerpts from the famous 1953 Kastner trial, in which the pro-Nazi activities of **Rudolf Kastner** were brought to light in excruciating detail. Kastner was the head of the Hungarian branch of the **Jewish Agency Rescue Committee** during World War II and later a spokesman for the Ministry of Trade and Industry in the new Israeli state.

In a trial that rocked Israel to its foundations, Kastner, one of the inner circle of the Zionist elite around Israeli Prime Minister **David Ben-Gurion** during the 1943-53 decade, was revealed to have been the main Zionist agent of the Nazi exterminators of Hungary's Jews.

Kastner, an Israeli court was shown, systematically deluded the leadership of Hungary's 800,000 Jews into believing that the Nazis were interested merely in mass relocation of the Jews, not mass murder. In return for this genocidal deception, Kastner was allowed to handpick a small Zionist elite of 388 Jews, mostly from his own family, to flee to Palestine.

Hecht's book detailed Kastner's collaboration with **Heinrich Himmler**, **Adolf Eichmann**[3], and others with such precision that his book was suppressed, censored, and removed from libraries. Hecht's wife, who after his death tried to get the book republished, has been subjected to pressure and threats from the Zionist lobby in the U.S. Today, copies of Hecht's book are distributed virtually on a black-market basis. I was able to secure a copy and have made it available for free download on my website should the reader wish to research this topic further.

Excerpts from *Perfidy* are printed below. We begin with Adolf Eichmann's testimonial to Kastner's activities, which Hecht quoted from Eichmann's Confessions published in the November 28 and December 5, 1960 editions of **LIFE** magazine.

Adolf Eichmann
(1906 - 1962)

"In Hungary my basic orders were to ship all the Jews out of Hungary in as short a time as possible. . ... In obedience to Himmler's directive, I now concentrated on negotiations with the Jewish political officials in Budapest . . . among them Dr. Rudolf Kastner, authorized representative of the Zionist Movement. This Dr. Kastner was a young man about my age, an ice-cold lawyer, and a fanatical Zionist. He agreed to help keep the Jews from resisting deportation – and even keep order in the collection camps – if I would close my eyes and let a few hundred or a few thousand young Jews emigrate illegally to Palestine. It was a good bargain. For keeping order in the camps, the price . . . was not too high for me . . . ."

> We trusted each other perfectly. When he was with me, Kastner smoked cigarettes as though he were in a coffeehouse. While we talked he would smoke one aromatic cigarette after another, taking them from a silver case and lighting them with a silver lighter. With his great polish and reserve he would have made an ideal Gestapo officer himself

---

[3] Adolf Eichmann was literally "Mr. Holocaust." He was the 'brains' behind the "final solution" – the genocide of the Jews – according to the Jews in public.

>   . . . I believe that Kastner would have
> sacrificed a thousand or a hundred thousand of
> his blood to achieve his political goal. . . .
> "You can have the others," he would say,
> "but let me have this group here. (p.231)

A co-exterminator of Eichmann's, S.S. **Colonel von Wisliczeny**, expanded on the nature of this Zionist-Nazi relationship.

>   Our system is to exterminate the Jews
> through the Jews. We concentrate the Jews in
> the ghettos — through the Jews; we deport the
> Jews — by the Jews; and we gas the Jews —
> by the Jews. (p232)

Zionist Nazi Collaboration

As soon as the Nazis assumed power in 1933, the Zionists gained a visibly protected political status. After the Reichstag fire (a false flag event), the Nazis crushed virtually all political opposition and closed 600 newspapers. But not the Zionists, nor their newspaper which was hawked from every street corner, and saw its circulation multiply five times to 38,000. Zionism was *"the only separate political philosophy sanctioned by the Third Reich."* (Black, 1984)

The Zionist uniform was the only non-Nazi uniform allowed in Germany. Same with their flag.

On a side note, a lot people comment that the Nazis were bad, but had cool looking uniforms – better than the Allies. That is because they were designed by fashion expert **Hugo Boss**.

Boss was a card carrying Nazi Party member. He used slave labour to produce the millions of uniforms required for the German war machine.

In 2010, the company had sales of $US2,345,850,000 and a net profit of **$US262,183,000**. I guess crime does pay. (Boss, 1940)

In Germany, Hebrew was mandated in Jewish schools. Still, German Jews wanted to stay in Germany *"even as second class citizens, even reviled and persecuted."* (Black, 1984) But the Zionists scorned the German Jews saying they deserved to be persecuted for wanting to assimilate with Germans. Zionists pandered to the Nazis comparing their racial ideologies:

> *A common fate and tribal consciousness must be of decisive importance in developing a lifestyle for Jews too. (p.175)*

This explains how,

> *A fringe minority of German Jews took emergency custody of 550,000 men, women and children..." Black says. This was confirmation, "of what Diaspora Jews had always feared about Zionism--it would be used as the legal and moral pretext for forcing Jews out of European society. (p. 177)*

It also explains why Israel behaves like Nazi Germany today. They have a common racist pedigree. Not only did the Nazis build Israel, but Israel built Nazi Germany by providing an export market. They worked together. Many Jews didn't get all their money when they arrived in Israel. Thus, the Zionists participated directly in the looting of Europe's Jews which was called **Aryanization**.

Thanks to Hitler, 60,000 German Jews immigrated to Israel between 1933 and 1941.

Thanks to a **Transfer Agreement** between Nazis and Zionists, Jewish property valued at $100 million was transferred to Israel in the form of German industrial exports used to build Israel's infrastructure.

The Transfer Agreement brought in tools, raw materials, heavy machinery, appliances, farm equipment as well as labour, and capital to finance expansion. Many of Israel's major industries, like textiles and the national waterworks, were thus founded. (pgs. 373,379.)

This was at a time when there were only 200,000 Jews in Palestine, many of which were anti- Zionist religious Jews who had been living peacefully with the Arabs and Christians for centuries.

Here is another interesting fact. In this video I can only find on Facebook, **Benjamin Netanyahu** is now claiming Hitler didn't actually want to kill the Jews during WW2, he just wanted to expel them, and, wait for it.... it was Palestinians who convinced him to carry out the Holocaust! Please watch the video if you find this hard to believe (Netanyahu, 2015).

Ironic? Maybe not...

Yeshayahu Leibowitz refers to the Israeli army as Judeo-Nazi

People are Waking Up

Increasingly Israelis, and Jews in general, are realising that Zionism is a ruse and Israel's behaviour bears an uncanny resemblance to Nazi Germany's.

For example, an Israeli academic **Yeshayahu Leibowitz** said everything Israel has done since 1967 is *"either evil stupidity or stupidly evil."* He refers to the Israeli army as **Judeo-Nazi**.

This is not the place to show how Hitler was put into power by Anglo-American (i.e. Illuminati / Jewish) finance, the same people who created Communism and Zionism.

But it is the place for Jews and Americans to consider this lesson. Historical events are created in order to brainwash and manipulate people into advancing the agenda of the New World Order.

European Jews were uprooted, robbed, and massacred in order to build the capital of Rothschild world government in Israel. Americans are dying in Iraq and Afghanistan and soon to be in Iran to stamp out Islam. Economic turmoil is making desperate people embrace world government "socialism." And so on...

But there is one more "sensitive" issue I need to address to complete the "truth" about the Zionist Jews and the Holocaust. That has to do with the alleged "6 million" dead in Hitler's gas chambers – the numbers just don't add up.

6,000,000 Jews Did Not Die in Gas Chambers in WWII

Questioning the Holocaust is illegal in:

- Austria
- Belgium
- Czech Republic
- France
- Germany
- Israel
- Lithuania
- Poland
- Romania
- Slovakia
- Switzerland

If it is against the law for over 250 million Europeans to question details of the Holocaust, it must mean there are some things that the Zionist do not want the un-chosen (non-Jews) people to know about.

Every time someone criticises a Jew, or a Jewish group, they are called **anti-Semitic**. This in itself is odd, and a dishonest term, as anti-Semitic means you are anti-Middle Eastern people, which Ashkenazi Jews are not. The people and groups criticized are not Semitic, they are of European stock, – and DNA proves it!

This is especially evident whenever anyone tries to examine the Jewish version of the Holocaust story. This was confusing until I came across this blatant admission by a former Israeli Minister, **Shulamit Aloni**, who explains how the deception works:

> *"It's a trick, we always use it. When [someone] from Europe...[is]... criticizing Israel, then we bring up the Holocaust. When in this country [The United States] and people are criticizing Israel, they're anti-Semitic. Our organization is strong and has a lot of money, and our attitude of my country Israel is to make it right or wrong." (Talking to Amy Goodman on the **Democracy Now Show** – clip available on YouTube) (Aloni, 2011).*

Anti-Semitism and the Holocaust are used as tools to silence those who dare speak out against Zionism and Israel.

The Khazar Jewish run media tells us over and over, that 6,000,000 Jews died in Hitler's death camps. There are documentaries, TV specials, and now there is **The United States Holocaust Memorial Museum** (USHMM). In 2008, it had an operating budget of just under **$78.7 million** ($47.3 million from Federal sources and $31.4 million from private donations) (Holocaust Memorial, 2015).

The reality is, particularly in America, the Khazar Jews milk the Holocaust for everything they can. They then use it to deflect criticism, to get guilt donations out of people and to make the world feel sorry for them.

The reality is, their version of the Holocaust is at the least vastly exaggerated, and at the worst, it never happened like they say it did at all. I like to think the reality is somewhere in the middle, but I will let the historical evidence speak for itself.

There have been many Holocausts

I agree that the Holocaust was a terrible tragedy, and Jews, in certain places, where systematically murdered in their thousands, which in itself is shocking. However, there have been many Holocausts through history. In fact, the first time the term "Holocaust" was used was in 1915 for the **Armenian Genocide** also known as the Armenian Holocaust.

During that horrific episode, about 1.5 million Armenians died (Armenian Genocide, 1915). That is more than the amount of Jews killed by the Nazis, but we don't all have to kowtow to the Armenians and let them get away with bloody murder because of it. The Armenians don't get a multi-million dollar museum built for them out of tax payer funds. And the Armenians are not trying to racially cleanse another people and ask us all to look the other way.

The Killing Fields in **Cambodia** claimed conservatively 2.2 million lives (Killing Fields, 1979). Same again. Many people are not even aware of these Holocausts, because the Khazar Jewish run media does not want you to know about them.

6,000,000 Jews is an Arbitrary Number

The final death figure for the Jewish Holocaust is always said to be 6,000,000. But what most people do not know is that this is an entirely arbitrary number.

9 MONTHS BEFORE KRISTALNACHT, JEWS CLAIM 6 MILLION VICTIMS

PERSECUTED JEWS SEEN ON INCREASE
New York Times (1857-Current file); Jan 9, 1938;
ProQuest Historical Newspapers The New York Times (1851 -
pg. 12

PERSECUTED JEWS SEEN ON INCREASE

Dr. Kahn Returns With Report of Rise in Europe of Those Deprived of Rights

6,000,000 VICTIMS NOTED

25,000 Refugees Said to Be in Need—Rumania Menaces 800,000 With Anti-Semitism

The number of Jews deprived of their rights and economic opportunity in Europe increased greatly last year, Dr. Bernhard Kahn, European director of the American Jewish Joint Distribution Committee, said on his arrival here last week from Europe.

The new Government of Rumania has threatened to outlaw 800,000 Rumanian Jews, "disregarding peace treaties, minority treaties and the constitution of the country," said Dr. Kahn.

government except sometimes in cases of physical violence and public disturbance," he said. "It is a matter for encouragement, however, that many outstanding personalities and some political parties in Poland are courageously raising their voices against the inhuman treatment of the Jews and the poisonous atmosphere of anti-Semitism.

"In Germany the Jews are being driven out of the last economic positions. Increased oppression is swelling the number of refugees and emigrants. More than 25,000 Jews had to leave Germany during the last year and in the middle of the year the German laws of racial discrimination were extended to the 12,000 Jews in Upper Silesia (the Danzig corridor)."

Dr. Kahn said there are 25,000 refugees in Europe, the greater number of them living in need and in demoralizing uncertainty. He expressed the hope that the inter-governmental conference at the League of Nations would take up the refugee problem again in February.

"Five to six million in all are to-day the victims of governmental anti-Semitism and policies of unchecked anti-Semitic propaganda and persecution. All these millions are in danger of losing their rights as citizens. Their economic existence is constantly menaced and for thousands upon thousands their

7 YEARS BEFORE THE END OF WW2, JEWS CLAIM 6 MILLION VICTIMS

January 9, 1938 edition of The New York Times.

Seven years before the end of war, **NY Times** in 1938 claims "6,000,000" European Jews are "victims" of "anti-Semitic persecution" From the January 9, 1938 edition of The New York Times (New York Times, 1938).

Did Hitler really kill 6,000,000 Jews, or did they simply borrow that number from their religion?

Jewish prophecies in the Torah require that 6 million Jews must 'vanish' before the State of Israel can be formed. '*You shall return minus 6 million.*'

That's why **Tom Segev**, an Israeli historian, declared that the 'sacred 6 million' is an attempt to transform the holocaust story into a state religion. Those six million, according to prophecy, had to disappear in 'burning ovens,' which the judicial version of the holocaust now authenticates.

Without the Holocaust, there would be no Jewish State of Israel. They made the Holocaust fulfil their prophecy.

The three main claims of the Jewish Holocaust are:

1) 6,000,000 Jews were killed
2) Mainly in gas chambers
3) Due to an order by Hitler

All are false, as we will see.

Declining figure

I used to believe what I had been taught in school, and by TV, until one day, about seven years ago, I read that the Auschwitz deaths number had been reduced to "about 1 million."

On further research, I found out that the commemorative plaque at Auschwitz had been changed three times since World War II, from 6 million Jews, to 4 million Jews, down to "one and a half million…'mainly Jews'." So how many is it?

Auschwitz deaths reduced to a million

By Krzysztof Leski in Warsaw and Ohad Gozani in Tel Aviv

POLAND HAS cut its estimate of the number of people killed by the Nazis in the Auschwitz death camp from four million to just over one million.

The vast majority of the dead are now accepted to have been Jews, despite claims by Poland's former Communist government that as many Poles as Jews perished in Nazi Germany's largest concentration camp.

The revised Polish figures support claims by Israeli researchers that Poland's former government exaggerated the number of victims by inflating the estimate of non-Jews who died.

The new study could ... the controversy over ...

the scale of Hitler's "Final Solution". Prof Shevach Weiss, a death camp survivor and Labour member of the Israeli parliament, expressed disbelief at the revised estimates, saying, "It sounds shocking and strange."

But other Israeli experts said evidence to support the lower estimate had been mounting for some time.

Auschwitz, about 30 miles south-west of Krakow, was established in 1940 as a camp for political prisoners. It was later expanded with a huge

nearby Birkenau, which included gas chambers and ovens to destroy the bodies.

Dr Franciszek Piper, director of the historical committee of the Auschwitz-Birkenau museum, said yesterday that, according to recent research, at least 1·5 million people were deported to the camp, of whom about 223,000 survived.

The 1·1 million victims included 960,000 Jews, between 70,000 and 75,000 Poles, nearly all of the 23,000 gipsies sent to the camp and 15,000 Soviet prisoners of war. Dr Piper stressed that the fig-... minimum estimate ...

but said the total was unlikely to exceed 1·5 million.

Dr Shmuel Krakowsky, head of research at Israel's Yad Vashem memorial for Jewish victims of the Holocaust, said the new Polish figures were correct. "The four million figure was let slip by Captain Rudolf Hoess, the death camp's Nazi commander. Some have bought it, but it was exaggerated."

Dr Krakowsky accused Poland's former Communist government of perpetuating the false figures in an attempt to minimise the Holocaust and support claims that Auschwitz was not exclusively a Jewish death camp. He said that at most, 300,000 non-Jews perished at Auschwitz.

According to Dr Krakowsky, 5,860,000 Jews perished dur-

Official Auschwitz deaths number keep reducing every year

They keep reducing the dead count from 6 million down every time new research came in that proved the figure of 6 million was wrong.

So I got to thinking about the number. I did the math (you can too), and found out it was ridiculous. We're expected to believe that from the time of the **Wannsee Conference** on January 20, 1942 (the date of the order to "exterminate Jews") until **Auschwitz** was liberated by the Russians on January 27, 1945, that the Nazis killed an average of 5,440 Jews, every day.

That means we're supposed to believe that every single day, without fail, on average, 5,440 Jews were killed - that's 227 killed each and every hour, 24 hours each and every day, non-stop, day after day, for over three years, mainly from gas chambers. Even if "the holocaust" lasted for 5 years, the numbers still don't work.

Let's do the math

It's considered the most evil thing that ever happened in Europe, but when you get into it, it's not believable. Can you think objectively about something so socially unacceptable?

The Official Auschwitz Stor

According to a *Sonderkommando* who claims he was there!

At the Auschwitz camps, there were relatively few SS Nazi staff. Therefore, some of the Jews were forced to work in the gassing operations and were called **Sonderkommando**. **Dario Gabbai** claims to be one of these people, and it is his account that has been adopted as the "official" version of events at Auschwitz. **Auschwitz Gas Chamber 1** shown to tourist in the picture – there are about 20 people, and Gabbai claims they would put 2000 people at a time in here.

There were two gas chambers and crematoriums. According to Gabbai, 2,000 Jews at a time would gather on the grass and be told they were going underground to undress and then take a shower. The dressing room and gas chambers were underground, and a stairway from the grass led down. The 2,000 would then be led down a very narrow corridor into the gas chamber. In the chamber were mesh columns, and this is where the gas pellets

(Zyklon B) would be dropped down from above and soaked with deadly cyanide liquid (Auschwitz-Birkenau, 2015).

Auschwitz Gas Chamber 1: According to Gabbai 2000 Jews would be gassed in this room

After they were killed by the gas, the bodies, 7 at a time, would be put on a small elevator to go back up to ground level, where 15 crematoriums were located.

Gabbai claims that the gas chamber was only designed for 500 people, but they would cram 2000 people in there. They could only stand, squashed up to one another, chest-to-back, and shoulder-to-shoulder. It is hard to imagine people would do this without pushing and shoving, and without some people losing their minds knowing they were about to be killed. After all, there were no soap holders in the "shower blocks," so they would have known something was up. There was one small, wooden door at the end of the chamber. How was this not crushed by the mass of people crammed into this tiny room pushing and shoving?

Gabbai would have us believe that the Jews stood quietly, and marched orderly to their deaths – like they were cooperating. The whole system was controlled by about 100 *Sonderkommandos* (Jews) and only 3-4 SS guards. Again, I find it difficult to accept that 100 Jews would comply and not try and help or warn their fellow Jews of what was about to happen. 2,100 people could easily over-power 3-4 guards, even if those guards were armed (Auschwitz, 2013).

The Story is solidifie

Both gas chambers and exterminations were regarded by the Nuremberg Tribunals and the later SS trials in Germany as "facts of common knowledge" and therefore unquestionable.

For a defendant to dispute them was a sure way to the hangman's noose, or a very long term prison sentence. The only possible defence or mitigation was to say that these things happened, but to deny or play down your own role in them. This is where the infamous "*I only did it because I was under orders to do it*" defence came from. Some received lighter sentences for confessing or for testifying against others (plea bargaining).

The Commandant of Auschwitz, **Rudolf Hoess**, said at Nuremberg that 3 million had died in the camp of whom 2.5 million were murdered. The official figure today is just around 1 million, with no attempt to distinguish, thus the public is being left to assume that all were gassed. So even if we accept the official figure, we know that Hoess was forced to exaggerate.

The Hard Evidence Facts

Firstly, Gabbai tells us that 2,000 Jews were gassed at a time. However, on the official Auschwitz website they state it was a mixture of Jews, Soviet POWs, and local Poles in their thousands (Gas chambers, 2015).

No actual homicidal gas chambers or gas vans have ever been found at Auschwitz. The alleged gas chamber at Auschwitz 1, shown to tourists, was "reconstructed" by the Russians in 1947 on the site of a crematorium and morgue, later used as an air raid shelter (with gas-tight door). Until the mid-nineties, it was presented to visitors as "original."

Even today the public are encouraged to believe it is in its original state and you will only be told it is a "reconstruction" if you actually ask, or go to a very obscure corner of their web site (last paragraph on that page). At Auschwitz 2 there are only ruins of buildings whose plans and specifications in the Auschwitz Construction Office are for crematoria and morgues, with nothing to identify them as gas chambers; the ovens are standard crematorium design for individual bodies and their capacity is far too low for the mass murderous use claimed for them.

The **Majdanek** concentration camp in Germany has gas chambers used to kill lice in clothing and bedding, using **Zyklon B**, which it is alleged, without evidence, were also used to kill people.

This comes as a great surprise to most people, who have been taught that the Holocaust is *"the most documented event in history"* and that it is beyond dispute that six million Jews were killed. In reality, the deportations, the camps, and the crematoria are thoroughly documented, but that is all.

The universal image of the Nazis is as symbols of evil incarnate. However, most scholars no longer accept this extreme view of the German Hitlerite regime, though no one is in any way apologists for their obvious crimes. It is seen as probably a good deal less murderous than the brutal Stalinist regime in Russia, our ally to whom we handed over half of Europe, turning it into a world superpower.

We look at the historical record and try to get an objective picture of what happened and to understand why individuals, groups, and nations acted as they did. What are viewed as war crimes in comfortable armchair retrospection must be seen in the context both of brutal total war and of similar or comparable actions by our own side.

But for now let's accept Gabbai's, and thus, the "official" story of what happened. In fact, here is an exact excerpt from the official Auschwitz website:

> 66 About 2 thousand people at a time could be put to death in each of them. According to calculations made by the Zentralbauleitung on June 28, 1943, the crematoria could burn 4,416 corpses per day— 1,440 each in crematoria II and III, and 768 each in crematoria IV and V. This meant that the crematoria could burn over 1.6 million corpses per year. Prisoners assigned to do the burning stated that the daily capacity of the four crematoria in Birkenau was higher—about 8 thousand corpses. 99
> (Gas chambers, 2015)

There is one problem with his story – the cremation time

Remember, Crematorium 2 was only in operation from Spring 1942 until November 1944.

Cremation Ovens of Auschwitz, Poland

The Cremation Ovens of Auschwitz

Most people don't know how long it takes to cremate a body, but it is a key issue. While a wall of 15 crematorium ovens at Auschwitz seems like a lot, it's not even close to being able to handle the 2,000 bodies downstairs in the gas chambers. To illustrate, let's look at the whole process in terms of time.

- 30 minutes to get everyone (2000) downstairs and undressed.
- 30 minutes to gas and kill all 2000
- Gabbai says only 7 at a time would be put on a small elevator to go back up to ground level. So by hour number 2, only 15 bodies are taken upstairs to the crematorium and burnt.

On average, it takes about **one hour** to cremate one body. That time is based on 2015 modern ovens. The Auschwitz ovens were not as hot, or as fast, as modern ovens, but for the purpose of this demonstration, we will use one hour as the complete burn time to dispose of one single body. By hour number three, 15 more are cremated with 1,970 left to go, and at this snail's pace, by hour number **133**, or six days later, you cremate fifteen more bodies and only have five left to go. You can't do another gassing until the **sixth day** (HISTROIKA 2012, 2012).

Let's break it down to an even simpler way:

- There are 8765.81 hours in a year.
- The official story says they could burn 1.6 million per year.
- We know it takes a minimum 1 hour per body.
- So, 1.6 million hours (that is 1 hour per body) = 182.527 years.
- According to the records, Auschwitz was only operational for less than 3 years.

The only way Gabbai and others can make it all sound feasible is by claiming that they burnt 3-4 bodies at a time, only taking 30-40 minutes. Even at 30 minutes, it would still take 97 years.

However, every researcher agrees these burn times are impossible, and is a complete lie.

In fact, in the book *Auschwitz - The Case for Sanity*, Carlo Mattogno demonstrates using the actual ovens used at Auschwitz, that it is physically impossible to fit more than one body at a time into the ovens (Mattogno, 2010). Besides, it still takes 1 hour per 68 kg / 100 lbs body, even if you stacked them.

But don't take my word, call your local crematorium and ask them how long it takes to burn a body. They will tell you 2-3 hours. I know, because I called!

It is dubious that the Germans would have had a killing system with a 1/133 ratio, where the cremation holds up the killings for at least one week.

But the story keeps being retold. Indeed, according to Paul Hilberg's book, *The Destruction of the European Jews*, 500,000 Jews were gassed and cremated in Crematorium 2 at Auschwitz. But there just isn't enough time to achieve this either.

540 days ÷ 250 gassings = **2.16 days**

This would require one gassing of 2000 people every 2 days approximately, and we know we would need 6 days.

Fifteen ovens would not be enough, even if they used modern, hotter, computerised ovens, and stacked the corpses 5 high as the following "world expert" claims.

Laurence Rees is considered the world expert on Auschwitz history. He wrote and produced a 6 part series on Auschwitz for the BBC. He also wrote a companion book for the series which won History Book of the Year in the UK for 2006.

Soviet soldiers are seen with liberated Auschwitz prisoners 1945

How would he solve the slow cremation problem? He writes,

> **❝** On the ground flor was a large crematorium with three muffles capable of burning five corpses in each **❞**

On another page he shows a picture of the same ovens saying they are capable of holding several bodies. He gives the reader the emotional impression of the barbarity, but never questioning if it is even possible. He also commits four pages of his book to Dario Gabbai's testimony, without doing any fact checking (Rees, 2005). So much for the world "expert."

And no, the emancipated people and bodies you see on documentaries were filmed after Auschwitz had already been shut down. The starvation only started to really get bad towards the end of the war.

When the allies started their bombing campaigns inside Germany, food production and rail transport was dramatically diminished. So food was not able to get through to the camps.

However, trying to put 5 corpses in each is still physically impossible. You would think the "expert" would test his theories first before he committed them to print and film. Unless he was selling someone else's' version of course, and being rewarded for his conformity.

Millions upon millions of people watched the BBC documentary, so now millions and millions of people have been reinforced with the blatant lie that multiple bodies were burnt at the same time in each oven, at an impossible rate.

I'm not saying that no Jews were killed. Of course they were.

In fact, I have no doubt that the commandant of Auschwitz, SS-Obersturmbannführer **Rudolf Höss**, was a sick and twisted sadist that killed Jews at his own hand for personal amusement.

I also have no trouble saying that the Jews were singled out for special punishment, particularly those poor Hungarian Jews that were sold out by one of their own (billionaire George Soros). But when we look for the real reason for Zyklon B being used in the camps, and mass die offs, all roads lead to an admitted (by the officials) event.

Another interesting fact that these documentaries and books fail to mention is that the Auschwitz-Birkenau camp was built a full year before the Nazis came up with their so-called "final solution."

Indeed, it was built by the **IG Farben** chemical company. Many researches have no doubt that with no IG Farben, there would be no Auschwitz, and no Nazi death camps. Yet IG Farben got away scot free during the Nuremberg trials after World War II.

Maybe it was because they had links to the Rothschild Family. The IG Farben Building was developed on land known as the Grüneburggelände in Frankfurt's Westend District. In 1837, the property belonged to the Rothschild family (Building, 2015).

In **1951**, IG Farben was split into its four largest original constituent companies, which remain some of the world's largest chemical and pharmaceutical companies. The current main successor companies are AGFA, BASF, Bayer and Sanofi (IG Farben, 2015). I personally boycott these companies, but the reader can make their own choice.

Typhus Outbreak

There were many forced labour camps set up specifically to kill Jews, Gypsies, Communist, homosexuals, and others. However, the primary killer in Auschwitz was not Zyklon-B showers, it was a typhus outbreak.

In August **1942**, the Auschwitz camp had its highest mortality rate due to a shocking typhus outbreak. Typhus is contracted from fleas and body lice that carry the disease. There were about 40,000 inmates at the time, and some 8,600 died in August, almost twice as many as had died the month before. There were peaks of 500 deaths per day. This is what the crematorium ovens were used for, and these numbers make sense (Mattogno, 2010).

The majority of the prison population were Jews. But more than 70,000 Poles died or were killed at Auschwitz, along with 20,000 Gypsies, in addition to Soviet POWs and prisoners of other nationalities.

The crematorium ovens were there to handle day to day deaths of inmates. They were never design for mass burnings. At its maximum, the Auschwitz camp held about 200,000 people and covered 40 square kilometres (4000 hectares / 9,900 acres). With a population on low rations and hard labour, you will get quite a few day to day deaths. To handle these deaths, they had the crematoriums.

It is known for fact that Zyklon-B was used at other camps to eradicate lice and fleas. The so-called gas chambers, that are hardly capable of holding 100 people, yet alone 2,000 people, where used to put the inmate's cloths and blankets in. They would fumigate the cloths and blankets.

The Germans kept meticulous records for every item they used in the camps, right down to how many bullets they fired. Yet, no large order for Zyklon-B have ever surfaced. No large or extra orders for coal, to keep the ovens going 24/7 have ever shown up.

Did the Inmates know, but didn't warn others?

The alleged gas chambers were located right next to a soccer pitch. This was a soccer field used by the camp inmates every weekend. Wouldn't the soccer players be able to see the gassing of 2,000 people just meters away from where they were playing? The gas chambers were also visible from the Women's barracks. How odd that they never noticed 2,000 people lining up to go to their deaths.

Do I deny the Holocaust?

No, but I question the number of deaths, how they were killed or died, and how many where Jews. One of the main points of contention is HOW the Holocaust at Auschwitz is viewed by the groups involved.

The Russians have always stressed the suffering of Russians, Poles, and Ukrainians. Post World War II Soviet propaganda films make little mention of Jews. To the Polish locals, Auschwitz is given a Catholic face, with all the usual iconography and fetishes.

The suffering of Catholic Polish Priests and other Martyrs is stressed, and the attempted extermination of the Polish people is the preferred theme.

But in the Western World, we get a single-mindedly Jewish interpretation, with the non-Jewish deaths being used mainly to keep non-Jewish interest in the holocaust alive, by giving non-Jewish some involvement in it. But we're told that even though non-Jews suffered as well, it was the Jews, and the Jews alone that were marked for extermination.

This schism has often resulted in well-publicised disputes, such as the convent of Carmelite nuns who took up residence at Auschwitz against the wishes of many Jewish groups. At another time a Polish Auschwitz exhibit was protested by the Jews for not being "Jewish enough." However, I am sure that the Auschwitz camp has more than enough victimisation to go around for everyone.

Don't mistake what I am saying. I have no affinity for Hitler, I am not a skin-head, nor a neo-Nazi, nor a supremacist of any type. I despise all sorts of superiority, whether it's the KKK, Aryan Nations, Muslim Brotherhood, Zionism, and New Black Panthers, whatever. Thinking that any one culture is better than any other culture is pure nonsense. This has nothing to do with hating anyone. It has to do with exposing a lie, and my love for the truth.

"Holocaust denial" is a simplistic **Newspeak**[4] term, designed to shut down discussion by falsely presenting the issue as black or white, all or nothing, and implying that anyone questioning any part of it must have malicious motives. The truth is more complex.

---

[4] Newspeak is the fictional language in the novel Nineteen Eighty-Four, written by George Orwell. It is a controlled language created by the totalitarian state Oceania as a tool to limit freedom of thought, and concepts that pose a threat to the regime such as freedom, self-expression, individuality, and peace.

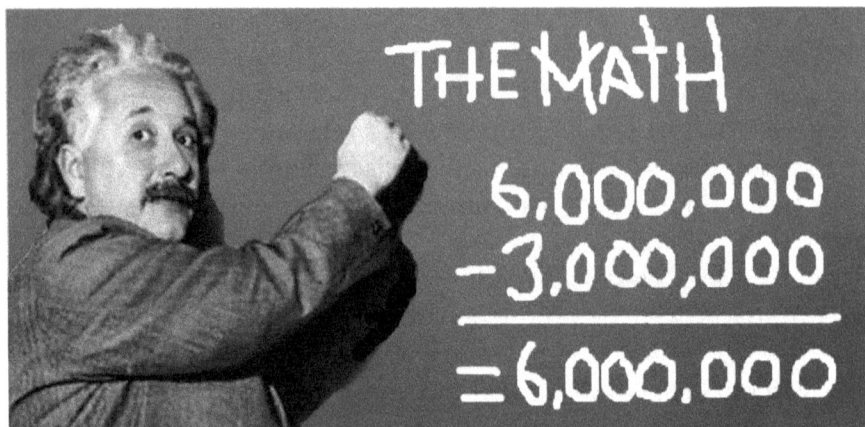

This doesn't help their story either...

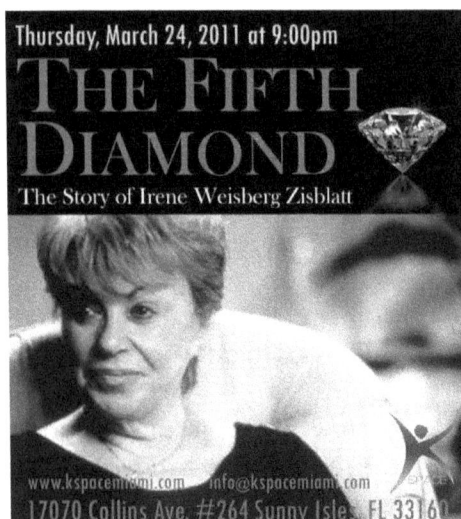

Irene Zisblatt lied about being a holocaust survivor for money and fame

Irene   Weisberg   Zisblatt came out on the Holocaust Promotion Scene in 1994, after a "fifty year silence" about her experience as a Jewish teenaged "Holocaust Survivor."

Over her next 15 years as a Holocaust Promoter, her stories would become more and more ridiculous, outrageous,   scatological, racist, and impossible. This caught the attention of Jewish Holocaust Promoters. Why?

Because within the Jewish communities, particularly in the United States, being a "Holocaust Survivor" earns you big bragging rights and special treatment. They often argue that *"my experience was worse than your experience."*

In other words, it becomes a bragging contest and who can come up with the best story (of the worst treatment). So when some of the "famous" survivors heard about Irene's claims, they felt threatened that they may lose their status.

Therefore, an investigation was carried out, and here is what they found.

Irene Weisberg Zisblatt whose actual name is/was **Chana Seigelstein** cannot be found in any database about the "Holocaust."

And, of course, she has no tattoo which was basically an inventory number put on all prisoners, which would have never been removed. In short, Irene Weisberg Zisblatt, AKA Chana Seigelstein is a liar and a phoney. But she got away with it for 15 years and appeared on hundreds of TV shows, documentaries, and news articles. She spread her lie to millions of people.

Given the attention, accolades, money, and celebrity Irene received, you have to wonder how many other "survivors" are telling lies, or at least exaggerating their experience for a bigger "wow" factor. It is only human nature after all...

Much of what is called the Holocaust did take place beyond question:

The National Socialist or Nazi regime intensely disliked Jews and prior to the war succeeded in expelling two thirds of them from Germany.

Indeed, during **Kristallnacht**, the night of broken glass, in 24 hours 1,000 Jews were dead and more than 30,000 arrested, a tenth of all German Jews. But the Nazis had the cooperation of the Jewish Zionist movement, which wanted Jews to move to Palestine.

Following the outbreak of war, most Jews in the areas under German control were confined in ghettos, concentration camps and labour camps, where conditions varied from the low standards common in most prisons to the utterly appalling, and where many died (and were cremated) from a wide range of causes which included privation, exposure, disease, neglect, maltreatment (often by the common-criminal prisoners who were placed in authority) and execution.

The war on the Eastern front was one of the most barbaric wars in history and civilians were routinely killed by both sides as reprisal or simply to spread terror. Given both official and personal attitudes to Jews on the German side, and the high number of Jews among both partisans and Communist commissars, Jews were likely to figure prominently among the victims.

In 1945, conditions of utter horror, with thousands of unburied emaciated dead, were found when camps such as Belsen, Buchenwald, and Dachau were liberated.

I in no way dispute these component parts of the larger event which, since about 1980, has become labelled as the Holocaust.

But other main components are far from "*proven beyond reasonable doubt*".

Revisionists argue with some justification, that there is no material evidence, and only documentary evidence whose provenance has never been adequately tested, that:

- There was mass murder in gas chambers (There were small gas chambers which were used to kill disease-spreading lice in clothing and bedding using Zyklon B, a legitimate
- commercial product, stabilised hydrogen cyanide, used in all German military facilities and still produced today under the trade name **Uragan D2** (*uragan* is a direct Czech translation of zyklon, cyclone or "storm")
- The Nazi regime sought to exterminate the European Jews (or any other group)
- The iconic figure of six million Jewish deaths has a basis in fact. The appalling conditions with thousands of dead bodies found in Belsen, Buchenwald and Dachau were a consequence of the Holocaust.

The last point should not be at issue. All historians and other knowledgeable people now accept that that these horrific scenes were caused by epidemics and starvation in the total collapse of infrastructure at the end of the war and by massive overcrowding as inmates of the camps in Poland were moved to camps in Germany that had no space for them. But little effort has been made to communicate this knowledge to the general public and photographs taken at these camps are regularly and falsely presented in the Zionist media as "proof of the Holocaust."

The accusations of mass killing in gas chambers rely entirely on:

- A few depositions by interested parties, who were not cross-examined and often did not even appear in court to present their evidence.
- Confessions of men held for months in solitary confinement and interrogated under duress, and even threatened that their wives and children would be handed to the Russians if they did not cooperate.

- A small number of documents: many simply unverified copies or translations, typed and unsigned, that have never been properly tested for authenticity, presented by American, British or Soviet Intelligence services. Remember the "dodgy dossier" of 2003 and Colin Powell's **'Weapons of Mass Destruction'** presentation to the UN General Assembly, the **"Kuwaiti baby incubators"** of 1991 or, to go further back, the **Gulf of Tonkin incident** in 1964 and the **Suez crisis** in 1956? In all of these, governments conspired to justify their actions with false information.
- Both gas chambers and extermination were regarded by the Nuremberg Tribunals and the later SS trials in Germany as "facts of common knowledge" and therefore unquestionable.

If there really is little evidence to support these allegations of deliberate mass murder, how can it be that they are near-universally believed? This is a complex issue, but in outline:

After the war:

Wartime propaganda was successful and simply continued to be believed.

- There was a need to justify the most destructive conflict in history to people at home, to our own troops, and to the world in general. It was to be "The Good War" to defeat Evil.
- Germany was to be occupied and pacified. Any popular sympathy for the former regime had to be destroyed.
- Attention had to be distracted from Allied carpet bombing of German and Japanese cities, Russian mass murder and rape of civilians and the brutal expulsion of 10-15 million Germans from their homes in the East.
- The sickening conditions found in Belsen, Buchenwald, Dachau, etc. seemed to confirm the propaganda, and were exploited by the psychological warfare units.
- An image of gas, showers and burning was created around the actual showers and crematoria, and the small gas chambers where Zyklon B was used for its legitimate purpose: to destroy lice.
- It suited the Western powers, the Soviet Union, and Jewish organisations alike. The overwhelming majority of those involved almost certainly did not question it.

- There was witness testimony of mass murder in gas chambers in camps all over Germany and the Americans created a film about the **Dachau** camp and its alleged gas chamber [at 3' 40"] which was shown at the Nuremberg tribunal.
- That there were gas chambers in Germany is no longer believed since as long ago as 1960. An extraordinary admission. Only the camps in Poland, then conveniently unavailable for inspection behind the Iron Curtain, continued to be considered "death camps."
- Since they became accessible, Auschwitz 1 has been acknowledged to be a fake by the Auschwitz Museum
- authorities and ground surveys at Treblinka and Belzec have produced little of substance.

Since the late 70s:

A "Holocaust Industry" has emerged. The subject is ever-present in the media in a way that was never the case in the thirty years that followed the war. Belief in "the Holocaust" is imposed on Western society by a combination of:

- **Force of law:** in most of Europe people are jailed for years or heavily penalised financially for "denying the Holocaust." Most of these laws do not date from the post-war period but were introduced in the last twenty or thirty years, and in Hungary as recently as 2011.
- **Intellectual and academic taboo:** academics who raise questions are persecuted and excluded (Joel Hayward for example), with the result that only those who are prepared to toe the party line dare address "the Holocaust."
- **Media censorship:** critical perspectives are totally absent from the mainstream media, which simply regurgitate everything they are fed by the Holocaust Industry and actively promote it.
- **Memorialisation:** a campaign of memorialisation that has turned "the Holocaust" into a dogmatic religious belief that may not be questioned, on pain of being branded a heretic, an outcast or anti-Semitic.
- **Emotional "education":** programmes which ignore objectivity, context, evidence, and historical methodology in general and are little more than brainwashing; they are often taught in Religious Studies rather than in History classes.

- **Branding:** Branding any attempt at objective assessment as "Holocaust denial" and implying that all "deniers" are anti-Semitic, racist, neo-Nazi thugs.
- This is the only event in the history of the world that is surrounded by such an electric fence of taboo and criminalisation, forbidding any objective historical investigation. I want to open up the memory holes so that all relevant evidence can be seen and evaluated, and to establish a fair and balanced assessment of what really happened.

What Do the WWII Big Players Say?

- **Winston Churchill** wrote the six volumes of his monumental work, *The Second World War*, without mentioning a program of mass-murder and genocide. Maybe it slipped his mind.
- **Dwight D. Eisenhower** (head of the Allies), in his memoir *Crusade in Europe*, also failed to mention gas chambers.
- As did **Charles de Gaulle** (head of the free French Army) in his book *Complete War Memoirs of Charles de Gaulle*.

Was the weapon used to murder millions of Jews unworthy of a passing reference? Was the future President of America being insensitive to Jews? Was the extermination of 6 million people really so unimportant to these world leaders that were all involved in the European war? How can such an extraordinary three-fold omission be explained?

This Speech Explains Everything!

*"Ultimately and with this I conclude. Our objective should be to create a society where denial of the genocide is seen as so outrageous, and so despicable that anyone who engages in it would be rendered a pariah." Spoken by: **Professor Deborah Lipstadt** (Ashkenazi Jew). Paper presented at **International Conference on Antisemitism and Holocaust Denial.** Dublin, Ireland, November 18-19, 2010. Paper titled "Holocaust Denial and Freedom of Speech."*

Professor Deborah Lipstadt (1947 -)

It is a lot to get your head around, so let's summarise!

Regarding the 6,000,000 - it has been very well documented that the "6,000,000" figure was used for money-making "humanitarian efforts" well before WWII. In fact, there is an amazing book called **The First Holocaust** by **Don Heddesheimer**, where he has photocopied many newspaper articles claiming that "6,000,000 Jews" were in danger of various horrors, and that money was needed to be raised to save them, dating back to 40 years before the war.

Indeed, looking at the collection of newspaper articles and clippings assembled from the late 1800s through the 1930s, it would appear there has been a near-constant holocaust in progress since at least 1880. It is also noteworthy that the authors of the vast majority of these newspaper articles were the richest of Wall Streets (Jewish) bankers; Schiffs and Warburgs among them. Is this perhaps a clue to their original purpose, these claims of perennial persecution? (Heddesheimer, 2005).

Regarding the Zyklon-B "gas chambers," I urge you to read **The Leuchter Report**, as well as **The Rudolf Report: Expert Report on Chemical and Technical Aspects Of The 'Gas Chambers' Of Auschwitz** on the science. Also, back in the late 80s, a very brave, young Jewish man, **David Cole**, went to Auschwitz with some questions. He made a video, available for viewing on YouTube. He uncovered some amazing facts that cost him dearly (Cole, 1998).

He was beat up, almost fatally on 3 occasions, and when the death threats started to come he was forced (for his family's sake) to move away from this research and go underground for a time. The attacks came from fellow Jews.

You are free to believe whatever you want, as am I. You can ignore any and all the facts in order to make the story fit what you've been told.

But as **Albert Einstein** said,

> *"Condemnation without investigation is the height of ignorance."*

Where Does This Leave The Jews?

For millennia, Jews owed their survival to their devotion to "Torah." In the last century they have forsaken this portable spiritual home, and placed their faith in a tangible one - Israel.

Unfortunately, they have been duped.

Israelis are becoming overseers in the global plantation. American Jews, prominent in media, education, government, and finance, are also instruments. They will take the blame for the real culprits, the shareholders of the world's major central banks.

Mankind has been betrayed by its leadership.

Of Jewish leadership, Israeli journalist **Barry Chamish** says:

> **"** *The richest appoint themselves to the highest posts. Thus the greediest and most unscrupulous run the show. [They] ... will sell their souls and those of their people for power and acclaim. (Chamish, 2000).* **"**

Nowadays, there are three types of Jews:

1) **True Torah:** mostly Sephardic Jews: these are the descendants of the Spanish Jewish-Khazars, i.e. The Khazarian King and his party. About 5% of all Jews, they take their spirituality very seriously. They genuinely care for their fellow man, and are not part of any Jewish Conspiracy.

2) **Ashkenazi Jews:** these are the descendants of a Turkic idol/ phallic worshipping tribe (Khazarians) who migrated to Russia in the 7th Century C.E and whose nobility converted to Judaism in the 7th Century C.E. and now inhabit mostly Europe, America, and Australasia. (About 90%-95% of all Jews). These include the average person that calls themselves a Jew. Most are not even aware of the Zionist agenda. Many however do indulge in feelings of superiority over the rest of humanity, because they literally believe they are the Chosen People of God, therefore they have a divine mandate to rule over the rest of the world. In reality, to get ahead in movies, TV, singing, performing, banking, etc. you have to be born an Ashkenazi Jew. They tend to stick together and look after one another. So they old saying *"it is not 'what' you know, it is 'who' you know that counts."* Almost all members of the top ruling class / New World Order / Illuminati are Ashkenazi Jews and/or Zionists.

3) **Zionist Jews:** these are from the Ashkenazi Jews (Torah Jews want no part of Zionism) who are pretending to be Jews for political reasons, but who are actually Illuminists-Luciferian-Masonic-Satanists. In fact, Zionist Jews are really the **Rothschilds** and a few hundred banking families and their non-Jewish allies, united by intermarriage (blood lines) and occult beliefs. The vast majority of Jews, like most people, are unaware of this plot and would oppose it if they were.

Jews are as much its unwitting dupes and victims as anyone else. Indeed, Zionists like to hide behind the veil of anti-Semitism and pretend to be Jews so that people hesitate to criticise them.

Masonic dedication on the outside wall of the Israeli Supreme Court

They are led by the **neo-Pharisees** (occult-priest-banklords). They want to establish a Zionist Luciferian state from the Nile to the Euphrates from where they plan to rule the Earth. To do this they want to exterminate all Arabs/Palestinians from the area, and somehow rebuild their Temple on the site that currently houses the **Dome of the Rock**, one of the most holy places in Islam. To rebuild the Temple, the Dome of the Rock must first be destroyed. So either an earthquake from their

Honouring Dorothy de Rothschild on the outside wall of the Israeli Supreme Court

God, or World War 3 will be required to remove the Islamic sacred building. No prizes for guessing which method of destruction the Zionist have selected.

The new **Israeli Supreme Court**, funded by the Rothschild Banklords, is full of **Masonic Symbols**, just like the **Bank of**

International Settlements (B.I.S.) in Basel, Switzerland, which is the **Mother of All Private Central Banks.**

The hexagram symbol on the Israeli flag is the ancient **Star of Moloch** (and the Seal of Solomon), a **Satanic-Baal** deity to which people, mostly children, were/are sacrificed. There is no such thing as a **Star of David** which the modern Jews have been fooled into believing, however the **True Torah Jews** are not fooled by the Zionists Illuminati.

Indeed, there are a few hundred thousand orthodox Jews like **Rabbi Shonfeld** who have always understood the true nature of Zionism and the threat it poses to honest Jews. They have always rejected the state of Israel and remained faithful to the Torah. They could form a core for a genuine Jewish revival. Their websites are: http:// www.truetorahjews.org/, and www.netureikarta. org.

True Torah Jews are not fooled by the Rothschild Zionists

I wish Rabbi Shonfeld the very best and hope he can get his movement supported worldwide by Jews and Gentiles alike.

In Conclusion...

I would like to reiterate that I am not a Neo Nazi, a Hitler fan boy, or any other type of race hater. If you find this information offensive, or you want to call me names, then I would ask you to do the math yourself, get a DNA test, phone a crematorium, read some books, or watch the videos I have referenced. Getting mad at me does not change the facts.

I understand this may be difficult to accept, especially if you have been indoctrinated and conditioned your whole life that Jews are the superior race, God's Chosen People, and that the Holocaust killed 6,000,000.

Don't worry, a lot of this information came as a shock to me as well. But I can honestly say I have told the absolute truth, without any filters, to the best of my ability and knowledge. I have no secret agenda or

HI, I'M EVELYN ROTHSCHILD

MY FAMILY FINANCED THE NAZIS
WE WERE COMISSIONED BY THE ROYAL FAMILY
TO PUT DOWN THE AMERICAN REVOLUTION
WE FINANCED THE COMMUNIST REVOLUTION IN RUSSIA
WE DESTROYED PALESTINE TO CREATE ISRAEL
WE WERE BEHIND 9/11 AND THE RESULTING WARS
WE OWN THE WORLD'S CENTRAL BANKING SYSTEM ALONG WITH THE
ASSOCIATED PRESS AND REUTERS SO, WE CONTROL ALL THE NEWS

a wish to upset 11,000,000 + people around the world! All I want is the truth, and truth only comes when we examine the facts. If we can observe the facts, with our **Wise Mind**, without bias, they only lead to one conclusion.

And the conclusion? A satanic cult governs the world. These people hate God and mankind and want to destroy it (including the Jews). They believe the end justifies the means and are ruthless. They use the Jews, and everyone else as cannon fodder. We have all been duped, distracted, stunted, and sacrificed. Without the vision provided by the **Truth**, we are lambs being led to slaughter.

To carry out their dastardly plan, the Zionist have compiled a "Play Book" of sorts. I got a copy of this step-by-step "How to take over the world," and that is what we will examine next!

References:

Aloni, S. (2011). *Former Israeli Minister Shulamit Aloni- Anti-Semitic Trick!*. [online] YouTube. Available at: https://youtu.be/9DKeLLlaws8 [Accessed 7 Aug. 2015].

Armenian Genocide, (1915). *Armenian Genocide - Facts & Summary - HISTORY.com*. [online] HISTORY. com. Available at: http://www.history.com/topics/armenian-genocide [Accessed 7 Aug. 2015].

Ashkenazi, (2015). *Jewish ethnic divisions*. [online] Wikipedia. Available at: https://en.wikipedia.org/wiki/Jewish_ethnic_divisions [Accessed 11 Aug. 2015].

Auschwitz, (2013). *Holocaust; Auschwitz an investigation (3D model study), update 2013*. [online] YouTube. Available at: https://youtu.be/KWjju9i9Jds [Accessed 6 Nov. 2015].

Auschwitz-Birkenau, (2015). *Official Auschwitz-Birkenau*. [online] Auschwitz.org. Available at: http://auschwitz.org/ [Accessed 14 Aug. 2015].

Black, E. (1984). *The transfer agreement*. New York: Macmillan.

Blake, H. (2010). *Hitler 'had Jewish and African roots', DNA tests show*. [online] Telegraph.co.uk. Available at: http://www.telegraph.co.uk/history/world-war-two/7961211/Hitler-had-Jewish-and-African-roots-DNA-tests-show.html [Accessed 13 Aug. 2015].

Bloom, H. (2000). *J.R.R. Tolkien's the Lord of the rings*. Philadelphia: Chelsea House Publishers.

Bollyn, C. (2003). *The Real Cost Of US Support For Israel - $3 Trillion*. [online] Rense.com. Available at: http://www.rense.com/general41/trill.htm [Accessed 13 Aug. 2015].

Boss, H. (1940). *Hugo Boss*. [online] Wikipedia. Available at: https://en.wikipedia.org/wiki/Hugo_Boss [Accessed 11 Aug. 2015].

Building, I. (2015). *IG Farben Building*. [online] Wikipedia. Available at: https://en.wikipedia.org/wiki/IG_Farben_Building [Accessed 14 Oct. 2015].

Chamish, B. (2000). *Just As Scared, Just As Doomed*. [online] Rense.com. Available at: http://rense.com/general19/doomed.htm [Accessed 9 Aug. 2015].

Cole, D. (1998). *Real Jew Explains Auschwitz*. [online] YouTube. Available at: https://youtu.be/SeEInN5gD7M [Accessed 11 Aug. 2015].

Dzerzhinsky, F. (2013). *Felix Dzerzhinsky - New World Encyclopedia*. [online] Newworldencyclopedia.org. Available at: http://www.newworldencyclopedia.org/entry/Felix_Dzerzhinsky [Accessed 13 Aug. 2015].

Gas chambers, (2015). *Gas chambers / Auschwitz and Shoah / History / Auschwitz-Birkenau*. [online] Auschwitz.org. Available at: http://auschwitz.org/en/history/auschwitz-and-shoah/gas-chambers/ [Accessed 14 Aug. 2015].

Geller, P. (2015). *Former DIA director: Obama White House Made "Willful Decision" to Support Al-Qaeda and Muslim Brotherhood in Syria - Freedom Outpost*. [online] Freedom Outpost. Available at: http://freedomoutpost.com/2015/08/former-dia-director-obama-white-house-made-willful-decision-to-support-al-qaeda-and-muslim-brotherhood-in-syria/ [Accessed 13 Aug. 2015].

Hagee, J. (2015). *Hagee: 'God Will Allow Terrorists To Attack The United States' Because Of Iran Nuclear Deal*. [online] Rightwingwatch.org. Available at: http://www.rightwingwatch.org/content/hagee-god-will-allow-terrorists-attack-united-states-because-iran-nuclear-deal [Accessed 13 Aug. 2015].

Heddesheimer, D. (2005). *The first Holocaust*. Chicago, Ill.: Theses & Dissertations Press.

HISTROIKA 2012, (2012). *Holocaust; Auschwitz an investigation (3D model study), update 2013*. [online] YouTube. Available at: https://youtu.be/KWjju9i9Jds [Accessed 7 Aug. 2015].

Holocaust Memorial, (2015). *United States Holocaust Memorial Museum*. [online] Wikipedia. Available at: https://en.wikipedia.org/wiki/United_States_Holocaust_Memorial_Museum [Accessed 7 Aug. 2015].

Hunt, K. (2003). *How many Lambs slain at Passover?*. [online] Keithhunt.com. Available at: http://www. keithhunt.com/Lambmany.html [Accessed 13 Aug. 2015].

IG Farben, (2015). *IG Farben*. [online] Wikipedia. Available at: https://en.wikipedia.org/wiki/IG_Farben [Accessed 14 Oct. 2015].

Judaism, (2015). *History of Judaism*. [online] Simpletoremember.com. Available at: http://www. simpletoremember.com/articles/a/Jewish_History/ [Accessed 11 Aug. 2015].

Khazaria, (1995). *Khazaria.com - History of Jewish Khazars, Khazar Turk, Khazarian Jews*. [online] Khazaria.com. Available at: http://www.khazaria.com/ [Accessed 11 Aug. 2015].

Killing Fields, (1979). *Killing Fields*. [online] Wikipedia. Available at: https://en.wikipedia.org/wiki/ Killing_Fields [Accessed 7 Aug. 2015].

Koestler, A. (1976). *Arthur Koestler - The Thirteenth Tribe - Free PDF!*. [online] Fantompowa.info. Available at: http://www.fantompowa.info/koestlerindex.htm [Accessed 31 Jul. 2015].

Levy, G. (2011). *Jewish people are just that, people, and far from chosen*. [online] Warincontext.org. Available at: http://warincontext.org/2011/10/09/jewish-people-are-just-that-people-and-far-from-chosen/ [Accessed 11 Aug. 2015].

Mattogno, C. (2010). *Auschwitz - The Case for Sanity*. The Barnes Review, pp.378-381 and document on Pg. 726.

Netanyahu, B. (2015). דוד שי | *Facebook*. [online] Facebook.com. Available at: https://www.facebook. com/deddy.shy/videos/10206973906038847/ [Accessed 19 Nov. 2015].

New York Times, (1938). *PERSECUTED JEWS SEEN ON INCREASE; Dr. Kahn Returns With Report of Rise in Europe of Those Deprived of Rights 6,000,000 VICTIMS NOTED 25,000 Refugees Said to Be in Need--Rumania Menaces 800,000 With Anti-Semitism*. [online] Query.nytimes.com. Available at: http://query.nytimes.com/gst/abstract. html?res=9E07E6DA1330E036A0575AC0A9679C946994D6CF [Accessed 7 Aug. 2015].

Oppenheim, A. (2001). *Ariella Oppenheim*. [online] Medicine.ekmd.huji.ac.il. Available at: https:// medicine.ekmd.huji.ac.il/En/Publications/ResearchersPages/pages/ariellao.aspx [Accessed 13 Aug. 2015].

Rees, L. (2005). *Auschwitz*. London: BBC Books.

Semites, (2015). *The definition of semite*. [online] Dictionary.com. Available at: http://dictionary. reference.com/browse/semite [Accessed 11 Aug. 2015].

Sephardic, (2015). *Sephardi Jews*. [online] Wikipedia. Available at: https://en.wikipedia.org/wiki/ Sephardi_Jews [Accessed 11 Aug. 2015].

Solomon, (2015). *Lesser Key of Solomon*. [online] Wikipedia. Available at: https://en.wikipedia.org/wiki/ Lesser_Key_of_Solomon [Accessed 6 Nov. 2015].

Stargate, (1970). *Stargate Project*. [online] Wikipedia. Available at: https://en.wikipedia.org/wiki/ Stargate_Project [Accessed 6 Nov. 2015].

White Phosphorous, (2013). *Israeli Army To End Use Of Hugely Controversial Weapon*. [online] The Huffington Post. Available at: http://www.huffingtonpost.com/2013/04/25/israel-army-white-phosphorous_n_3157604.html [Accessed 11 Aug. 2015].

Yahweh Killings, (2013). *How many has God killed? Complete list and estimated total (Including Apocryphal killings)*. [online] Dwindling In Unbelief. Available at: http://dwindlinginunbelief. blogspot.com.au/2010/04/drunk-with-blood-gods-killings-in-bible.html [Accessed 11 Aug. 2015].

Yosef, O. (2013). *Ovadia Yosef*. [online] Wikipedia. Available at: https://en.wikipedia.org/wiki/Ovadia_ Yosef [Accessed 11 Aug. 2015].

4

THE PROTOCOLS OF THE LEARNED ELDERS OF ZION

"It was declared a forgery which means there was an original document somewhere..."

— EUSTACE MULLINS (1923 - 2010).

*O*n **1773**, **Mayer Amschel Rothschild** invited twelve influential friends to his goldsmith shop in Frankfurt, Germany. These men were all Ashkenazi Jews, and formed the inner core of a world revolutionary movement which agreed to pool their wealth and resources for a "higher" cause.

By May 1st, **1776**, (May Day), they hired **Adam Weishaupt** (code named *Spartacus*) to establish a secret society called the **Order of the Illuminati**. Their objective? To create a world government ruled by men of superior intellect - namely themselves and their bloodlines, as well as create a Free State of Israel for all the worlds displaced Jews (ruled by them). This was the start of the **Zionist** movement.

Act of God?

In **1785**, an Illuminati courier was struck by lightning while travelling on horseback from Frankfurt to Paris carrying some documents. The documents originated with Weishaupt's Zionist members of the Bavarian Illuminati in Germany and were addressed to the **Grand Master of the Grand Orient** Masons in Paris. The documents fell into the hands of the local police who turned them over to the Bavarian Government.

Congress of Vienna

By **1814**, many of the European governments were in debt to the Rothschilds, so **Nathan Rothschild** figured they could use that as a bargaining tool to create their One World Government, with them as the rulers.

However, **Tsar Alexander I** of Russia, who had not succumbed to a Rothschild central bank, would not go along with the plan, so the Rothschild world government plan failed.

Enraged by this, Nathan Rothschild swore that someday he or his descendants, would destroy Tsar Alexander's entire family and descendants. Unfortunately, he was true to his word.

The Russian Imperial Romanov family (Tsar Nicholas II, his wife Tsarina Alexandra and their five children Olga, Tatiana, Maria, Anastasia, and Alexei) and all those who chose to accompany them into exile – were shot dead in **Yekaterinburg** on 17 July **1918**.

The Tsar and his family were executed by Rothschild funded, Ashkenazi Jewish led Bolsheviks, under the orders of the Rothschilds.

Interestingly, world government fanatic and Ashkenazi Jew **Henry Kissinger**, did his doctoral dissertation on the Congress of Vienna.

The Mason Connection

The authorities ordered a police raid on the Illuminati headquarters where they found additional evidence of a world revolutionary movement. The Zionist conspirators went underground and took refuge in the lodges of Freemasonry all over Europe.

The Paris Connection

The Protocols, based on the articles the courier lost, were originally compiled and completed in **1884** by members of a Jewish Masonic

Lodged based in Paris, France. It is known as **The Rite of Memphis-Misraïm** lodge with its own peculiar rites and protocols (Memphis-misraim.us, 2015).

The final compiled document was originally called **The Protocols of the Wise Men of Sion** and was published by a Jewish man called **Joseph Schoerst.**

The Russian Connection

Schoerst was a paid agent of **Mademoiselle Justine Glinka**. Glinka, the daughter of a Russian general, was in Paris to gather information (spy) for the court of **Tzar Alexander III** back in Russia.

Schoerst's spy alias was **Shapiro**, and he passed himself off as a Freemason to gain access, and infiltrate the Mizraim Lodge. French Masonry at that time was almost exclusively Jewish.

He smuggled out a document that he claimed was written by the members of this lodge, and that it had powerful repercussions. He sold it to Glinka for 2,500 francs (Fry, 1931). This document contained extraordinary, dictated writings from assorted speeches which would later be included in the final compilation of the **Protocols of Zion.**

Glinka immediately passed the document to her superior in Paris, **General Orgeyevski**, who sent them, in turn, to **General Cherevin**, Minister of the Interior, for transmission directly to the Imperial Court in **St Petersburg**.

Upon General Cherevin's death in 1896, he Willed a copy of his memoirs containing the *Protocols* to **Tzar Nicholas II**. (Gwyer, 1938)

Glinka's information eventually found its way into the hands of one **Professor Sergei Nilus**, a highly educated Russian mystic attached to **Tsar Nicholas II's** court, who served as *Minister of Foreign Religions*.

In **1902**, Nilus published, **The Rule of Satan on Earth - Notes of an Orthodox Believer**, in which he cites excerpts from this early aggregation of the material first purchased by Madame Glinka (McKeown, 2015).

In **1903** a prominent publisher by the name of **Pavel Krusheva** quoted writings from the Protocols in his daily newspaper, **Znamya.** After its publication, Krusheva suffered an attempt on his life and from that moment on, he lived in constant fear and had to carry weapons for his own protection. He also took the step of being accompanied by a personal cook to prevent being poisoned. That tends to happen if you cross the Rothschild family or expose their secrets.

In **1905**, Sergei Nilus published a new edition of his **Rule of Satan** which included a complete version of the Protocols as the final chapter. This was the first time a full compilation of the *Protocols* had been made available to the general public in book form.

In **1917**, (the same year of the final Russian Revolution), Nilus had prepared a final edition and fully documented version. But before he could distribute it, **Kerensky**, an Ashkenazi Jew who had succeeded to power after the Revolution, had most of the copies destroyed. In fact, Kerensky enacted a law that said that anyone caught by the Bolsheviks in possession of *The Protocols* would be shot on the spot. Make no mistake, Kerensky was a sadistic psychopath, and a Rothschild man. He was given the task directly from **Nathan Rothschild** to track down the leaked documents (*the Protocols*) and destroy them.

In **1918**, the *Protocols* appeared again in a Moscow periodical, **The Sentinel**, marked by the Jewish-led Bolsheviks as a counter-revolutionary newspaper. In February, **1919**, the Bolsheviks ordered the newspaper shut down.

In **1920** the Protocols reached the general public in England, by the hand of **Victor E. Marsden's** first English translation; published in London as a series of articles in the **Morning Post**. Victor E. Marsden died mysteriously the exact same year his translation was published in London.

In **1924**, Professor Nilus was arrested by the Jewish dominated **Cheka** (Soviet secret police) in Kiev, Ukraine. He was imprisoned, and then tortured. He was told by the president of the court (who was Jewish) that this treatment was meted out to him for "*having done them* (the Zionist Bolshevik Jews) *incalculable harm in publishing the Protocols*".

The lengths that the Ashkenazi Jewish communists went to eradicate the *Protocols* is evidence that there is something to all of this. Indeed, the treatment of Professor Nilus by the Jewish Bolsheviks speaks clearly to the authenticity of the *Protocols*.

What do other researchers say?

John (Snychov) of St. Petersburg (1927 - 1995)

"There are different viewpoints on the origin of the Protocols of The Learned Elders of Zion, but in my opinion, it does not matter who created them, but the fact that the entire history of the 20th century, with frightening accuracy, corresponds to the ambitions stated in this document". – **His Eminence the Most Reverend Archbishop John** *(Snychov) of St. Petersburg and Ladoga (1990 to 1996).*

Douglas Reed (1895 - 1976)

"The attack on the Protocols in the 1920's prove above all else the truth of their contention…Probably so much money and energy were never before in history expanded on the effort to suppress a single document" – **Douglas Reed**, The Controversy of Zion, *(P.212, 1956)*

Gilad Atzmon (1963 -)

"American Jewry makes any debate on whether the 'Protocols of the Elders of Zion' are an authentic document or a forgery irrelevant." – **Gilad Atzmon**, American Jews do control the World.

The Protocols in the Modern Era

Do you trust the official stories about 9/11? The banker bailouts? The War on Terror? The deaths of Osama Bin Laden? Kennedy? Princess Diana?

Have you ever wondered why an Egyptian pyramid, Masonic symbolism and the words **Novus Ordo Seclorum** (New Order of the Ages – or New World Order) are printed on the American one dollar bill? Can't make up your mind about what's true and what's not true anymore?

The Protocols of the Learned Elders of Zion detail an ingenious plan for world conquest. This world government plot has been unfolding for over 200 years and it is a big part of the **New World Order**, September 11 and the bogus "War on Terror."

The Protocols Are Authentic

Where is the proof that the Protocols are authentic? The proof is the document itself. What is going on in the world today is the fulfilment of the Protocols in precise detail.

Henry Ford said,

> *"The only statement I care to make about the Protocols is that they fit in with what is going on."* New York World, February 17th, 1921.

Benjamin Disraeli said,

> *"The world is governed by very different personages from what is imagined by those who are not behind the scenes."*

Nobel Prize winner **Alexander Solzhenitsyn** compared the Protocols to a "nuclear bomb."

The Attacks are Relentless!

Zionists and the **Anti-Defamation League** (**ADL**) have conducted an ongoing smear campaign to discredit the *Protocols* which expose their **New World Order** agenda. Indeed, while researching this topic, I was overwhelmed by the amount of websites, books, and videos that try every dirty trick in the book to discredit the *Protocols*.

Even over 100 years later, they are still exerting a huge amount of time, energy, and money to delete and discredit the *Protocols* from history. Ironically, if they had of just originally laughed it off – said it is a hoax, then moved on, I doubt anyone would be talking about it now, over 100 years later. However, it is their immediate and ongoing attempts to cover it up and destroy any evidence of the *Protocols* that has forced people to have a closer look.

The protocols are not a work of fiction. The proof is in the observable deeds.

Below is a summary of the key points of the **24 Protocols**. I do not have the space in this book to print the complete document. However, below are links to online versions, including a modern English version. They describe in elaborate detail the global control formula that we see in action today.

I will leave it up to the reader to decide for themselves, but pay attention to what they say, and what is going on now – then remember that this document was originally published over 100 years ago. Pretty amazing guess if it is a hoax!

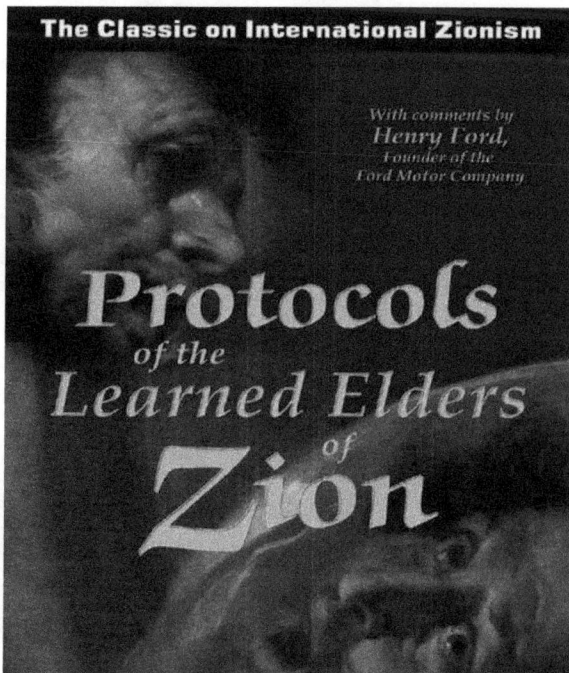

The Protocols of the Learned Elders of Zion with comments from Henry Ford of Ford Motor Company

Summary of the 24 Protocols of Zion

In the preamble it states:

> **❝❞** The **Goyim** (non-Jews) are mentally inferior to Jews and can't run their nations properly. For their sake and ours, we need to abolish their governments and replace them with a single government. This will take a long time and involve much bloodshed, but it's for a good cause. Here's what we'll need to do:

> 1) Place our agents and helpers everywhere. Spy on everyone, all the time
> 2) Take control of the media and use it in propaganda for our plans. Seduce and demoralize the youth with false doctrines.
> 3) Start fights between different races classes and religions and destroy the family life.
> 4) Use bribery, threats and blackmail to get our way. Dominate humanity by preying upon their lower instincts and vices.
> 5) Use Freemasonic Lodges to attract potential public officials and corrupt an blackmail them.
> 6) Appeal to successful people's egos. Introduce the habit for luxuries, crazy fashions and spendthrift ideas so that the ability for enjoying clean and plain pleasures is lost.
> 7) Appoint puppet leaders who can be controlled by blackmail. Overthrow all monarchies and substitute republics for them; in so far as possible fill importan state offices with persons who ar involved in some unlawful affair and who will, from fear of being exposed, remain our obedient servants.

8) *Replace royal rule with socialist rule, then communism, then despotism. Dispossess the old Aristocracy, which still keeps up high traditions, by excessive taxes and replace it with the "Knights of the Golden Calf."*

9) *Abolish all rights and freedoms, except the right of force by us. Gradually amend all constitutions so as to prepare the soil for absolute despotism and Bolshevism.*

10) *Sacrifice people (including Jewssometimes) when necessary.*

11) *Eliminate religion; replace it with science and materialism. Confuse and bewilder the minds of the people by false theories and shatter the nerves and health by continuously introducing new poisons.*

12) *Control the education system to spread deception and destroy intellect.*

13) *Rewrite history to our benefi*

14) *Create entertaining distractions. Divert the attention of the people by public amusements, sports, games, prize contests, etc., so that there is no time for thinking.*

15) *Corrupt minds with filth and perversion. Debase and vulgarize Art, introduce filth in Literature and normalize underage pornography and same sex marriage.*

16) *Encourage people to spy on one another.*

17) *Keep the masses in poverty and perpetual labour. Raise the rate of wages, which however will not bring any advantage to the workers for at the same time we shall produce a rise in the price of the first necessities of life.*

18) *Take possession of all wealth, property and (especially) gold. Establish huge*

monopolies upon which even the great fortunes of the Goyim will depend to such an extent that they will be swallowed up at the "hour" when the industrial crisis will start.

19) Use gold to manipulate the markets, cause depressions etc.

20) Introduce a progressive tax on wealth. Destroy all financial stability; increas economic depressions to the extent of bringing a general world bankruptcy; stop the wheels of industry; make bonds, stocks and paper money worthless; accumulate all the gold of the world in the hands of a certain few people thus withdrawing tremendous capital from circulation; at a given hour close all the exchanges, withdraw all credits and cause general panic.

21) Replace sound investment with speculation

22) Make long-term interest-bearing loans to governments

23) Give bad advice to governments and everyone else

24) We will Install a World King but keep the illusion of democracy.

*Eventually the Goyim will be so angry with their governments (because we'll blame them for the resulting mess) that they'll gladly have us take over. We will then appoint a descendant of David to be king of the world [**probably Prince William of Britain**], and the remaining Goyim will bow down and sing his praises. Everyone will live in peace and obedient order under his glorious rule.*

The Protocols of Zion: complete protocols in modern English with a summary on each (Download, 2015).

The True Heroes of Judaism

Haredi Orthodox Jews protest against Zionism

Well, I must say, Protocols 21 and 23 certainly bring to mind the 2008 Banker bailouts that cost American tax payers over $2 Trillion. Especially when you realise who orchestrated that collapse, and who gained from it financially. It was the greatest theft of tax payer money in the history of the world. But, they did tell us they would do it right?

Many **Rabbinical Orthodox Jews** protest against Zionism and the Protocols. They say that Zionism is **anti-Jewish**. Note this before one condemns all Jews.

Political Zionism is not the Jewish religion. Jews are victims of Zionism too. Rabbis meet with Palestinians and embrace and sympathise with them. These Rabbis are the true heroes in this story. They have had the courage to stand up to these imposters and I certainly give them a thumbs up for that!

So who is at the top of the Khazarian, imposter Jew pile that is running this death cult? If you guessed the **Rothschilds**, you would be right. We will take a closer look at that family later, but for now, let's have a look at the man who was once called, *The Wickedest Man in the World!*

References:

Download, (2015). *Protocols of Zion in Modern English*. [online] The French Connection. Available at: http://www.iamthewitness.com/books/Protocols.in.Modern.English.htm [Accessed 19 Nov. 2015].

Fry, L. (1931). *Waters Flowing Eastward*. 4th ed. CPA Books; 4th edition (October 10, 1997).

Fry, L. (2015). *Leslie Fry Biography*. [online] Wikipedia. Available at: http://en.wikipedia.org/wiki/L._Fry [Accessed 28 May 2015].

Gwyer, J. (1938). *Portraits of Mean Men: A Short History of the Protocols of the Elders of Zion*. the University of California: Cobden-Sanderson.

Ha'am, A. (1889). *Achad Ha'amÂ This is not the way (The wrong Way)-Zionism and the History of Israel - Source document texts*. [online] Zionism-israel.com. Available at: http://www.zionism-israel.com/hdoc/Achad_haam_not_the_way.htm [Accessed 28 May 2015].

Marrs, T. (2015). *The Man Who Gave the World the Protocols of Zion*. [online] Texemarrs.com. Available at: http://www.texemarrs.com/122011/man_who_gave_protocols.htm [Accessed 28 May 2015].

McKeown, T. (2015). *Sergei Aleksandrovich Nilus*. [online] Freemasonry.bcy.ca. Available at: http://www.freemasonry.bcy.ca/biography/nilus_s/nilus_s.html [Accessed 28 May 2015].

Memphis-misraim.us, (2015). *Ancient and Primitive Rite of Memphis-Misraim -- Symbolic Grand Lodge of the US + Jurisdictions*. [online] Available at: http://www.memphis-misraim.us/ [Accessed 28 May 2015].

Mullins, E. (2015). *THE PROTOCOLS OF THE LEARNED ELDERS OF ZION*. [online] Whale.to. Available at: http://www.whale.to/a/protocols_h.html [Accessed 28 May 2015].

Orthodoxwiki.org, (2015). *John (Snychov) of St. Petersburg - OrthodoxWiki*. [online] Available at: http://orthodoxwiki.org/John_%28Snychov%29_of_St._Petersburg [Accessed 28 May 2015].

Pinsker, L. (1906). *Auto-emancipation*. [online] Google Books. Available at: https://books.google.com.au/books?id=CpYpAAAAYAAJ&pg=PP22&lpg=PP22&dq=Leon+Pinsker+exert+an+irresistible+pressure+upon+the+international+politics&source=bl&ots=8Q1HIot8Uy&sig=sXG8Sv7fomB24B_ErJ3M1QjPTwU&hl=en&ei=YdBVTLCIJcL78Aack_i1DA&sa=X&oi=book_result&ct=result#v=onepage&q&f=false [Accessed 28 May 2015].

Publicly published Sergyei Nilus; translated into English by Victor Marsden, (2015). *The Protocols of the Learned Elders of Zion.*. [online] Biblebelievers.org.au. Available at: http://www.biblebelievers.org.au/przion2.htm#PROTOCOL No. 1 [Accessed 28 May 2015].

Wikipedia, (2015). *Gilad Atzmon*. [online] Available at: http://en.wikipedia.org/wiki/Gilad_Atzmon [Accessed 28 May 2015].

5

ALEISTER CROWLEY: THE WICKEDEST MAN IN THE WORLD

*Alistair Crowley -
The Beast 666*

> *"Do what thou wilt, shall be the whole of the law"*
>
> — ALEISTER CROWLEY, THE BOOK OF THE LAW

listair Crowley, the man who called himself ***The Beast 666***. Black Magician, drug addict, sex addict, and traitor to the British people. He declared the death of Christianity and declared himself the new Messiah that would replace the *"palate dead Christ"*.I have no doubt he was the real thing. He had given himself over to demonic control. He was evil. Crowley was also clever, some even say a genius. Since his death in 1947, Crowley has become an icon of rebellion. The Rolling Stones, and Led Zeppelin's Jimmy Page have all been influenced by his message of *"do whatever you want."*

He continues to be a key figure in the occult and is a focus for those engaged in the battle between good and evil. This was a battle that was to play a crucial part in Crowley's childhood.

Aleister Crowley was born in **1875** into a wealthy brewing family. It was the height of the Victorian era and his devoutly religious parents constantly warned him about the dangers of temptation and the terrible consequences of sin. They were members at the **Plymouth Brethren Sector**, a radical protestant group who were pathologically anti-pleasure. They believed in the literal truth of the Bible, particularly the **Book a Revelation** which is a constant echo throughout Crowley's imagination, and his theology.

He seems to have been devoted to his father. They use to travel the country together while his father preached a fire and brimstone version of Christianity. Aleister was inspired by his father's evangelising, and from his earliest ambition was to follow him and become a crusader for Christ. Then something happened that completely shattered his world. Crowley's father died suddenly, leaving Aleister, who was still only a boy of 11. Bereft, his sorrow turned to anger. He grew to hate his mother, the Church, and the pious tutors she employed to school him. Crowley became increasingly rebellious and he set about attacking the thing which had made his childhood such a misery.

> " *I had arrived at the conclusion that the Plymouth Brethren were an exceptionally detestable crew. I wanted sin, a supreme, spiritual sin, but hadn't the slightest idea how to go about it… (Diaries of Aleister Crowley)* "

He really could not bear his mother and at the first opportunity, when he was a teenager, he had sex with the maid on his mother's bed and obviously felt that this was a kind of revenge. He developed a tremendous state of resentment about his family and all the family background and so from the beginning, Crowley had a pretty good kind of background in revolt.

Crowley failed to distinguish himself during his school days, apart from getting expelled from Cambridge after catching gonorrhoea from a prostitute. While at Cambridge

Crowley the schoolboy, aged 14

however, he finally broke free from the shackles of his upbringing. He published his own poetry, revealing a rapidly developing obsession with sex.

Crowley the Poet

*"When Celia comes,
'tis earthquake hour
The bed vibrates like kettledrums.
It is a grand display of power,
When Celia comes.
When Celia farts,
my hasty nose,
Sniffs up the fragrance from her parts.
Shamed are the violets and rose
When Celia farts."*

Crowley's poetry was so pornographic that he would have been prosecuted for obscenity had he not taken the precaution of publishing it abroad, under a false name.

He had the natural appetite for sex you might expect from someone in their adolescence, however there was something different about Crowley, almost like he was developing a compulsion. Parts of that compulsion seemed to be a compulsion toward sin, a form of blasphemy, a form of spitting in the eye of the Christian Church.

It was at Cambridge that Crowley first became fascinated with magick[5] and the occult. He heard that there were secret societies, whose members practiced dark and forbidden rituals. Crowley was both intrigued and desperate to access this hidden world. At the age of 21, a large trust fund freed him from any financial worries, so he decided to leave Cambridge to pursue his quest to become a **Black Magician**. After two years of searching, he finally found what he was looking for.

The Training Years

The Golden Dawn was a secret society dedicated to the study and practice of the occult, and its exclusive, upper class membership

---

[5] I spell "real" Magick with a K to differentiate it from "illusion" Hollywood "Magic."

included many famous artists and intellectuals of the day. After he discovers the *Golden Dawn*, he really feels he's onto something. This is something brand new, it's fresh. **Bram Stoker** (author of Dracula) is involved, **WB Yates**, the Irish poet is involved, so to Aleister, the wide eyed want-to-be "poet," it felt like a sort of Literary Club and he wants to be part of that badly. He rapidly rises through the magickal grades like nobody else has gone through them before. He seems to take to this literally like a fish to water, like it is his vocation.

For Crowley, who was now referring to himself as ***The Beast 666***, the *Golden Dawn* turned out to be a bitter disappointment. He thought that they were playing at Magick and tried to take the society over. He clashed with the poet WB Yates, who was a prominent member, calling him a *"lanked, dishevelled, demonologist."*

This was a major step for Crowley, when he thought that he was leaving behind the *Golden Dawn* and all its milk and water magick, and move into the world of real Magick. He was totally willing to take on Black Magick.

Crowley shown in his Golden Dawn attire, was now calling himself The Beast 666

THE ABRAMELIN RITUAL

He was willing to use any forces that he possibly could, that he could control. Crowley decided to perform the Abramelin - the Black Magick ritual that no magician had dared undertake for centuries (Abramelin, 2015). Crowley was so dedicated to performing the Abramelin ritual that he actually goes to the trouble of seeking out and finding the perfect place for it. He ends up buying a country house to do the actual ritual in. This was the house Led Zeppelin's Jimmy Page would buy years later and live in, specifically he admits, because Crowley lived there. It is called **Boleskine House**, and is near **Loch Ness**, Scotland (Boleskine, 2015).

This is such an extreme thing to do, it is not a game. He is trying to break down, and push through further than anyone else has been before. At this point, his yardstick is the *Golden Dawn*, so he is already shattering that completely.

The *Abramelin* dates back to the 14th century. The aim of this **six-month** ritual is to master demons, but it was considered extremely dangerous if the ritual went wrong. It was believed that the evil spirits can be set loose and take possession of the Magician. The introduction states

Boleskine House near Loch Ness, Scotland

that nobody should perform the ceremony – end of story. That was like a red rag to a bull for Crowley. At the time when he did it, he had a lot of determination to delve as deeply as he could into the occult.

That said, he could only manage part of *Abramelin Ritual* in that house. Part of the ritual involves invoking a "protector" demon, a kind of black guardian angel, but to do that, the Magician must release a lot of his own "demons" as such – i.e. Negative baggage. Different parts of the ritual had to be performed at different times of the day and night, so the room he performed it in was completely blacked out, only lit by candles. He had to invoke, control, and dismiss all manner of spirits and demons, progressing to more and more powerful beings.

Although Crowley did not really mix with the locals, they all knew what he was up to. Crowley never made any secret about what he was trying to achieve. In fact he like to boast about it. The North of Scotland being the way it is, there are still some healthy superstitions floating about, so many of the locals would not even walk past the house. I too have a healthy respect for what the occult can do and how it can really muck up your life, so I do not blame the locals one bit for taking a wide berth of this property.

Crowley, in an absolutely typical way, broke off the ritual because he just couldn't be bothered to go on because it was too exhausting. Living on bread and water and getting up at three o'clock in the morning to perform invocations and rituals, it was much like being a monk, only harder. Therefore, Crowley gave up.

However, with the occult, if you start a ritual like this, you cannot just "switch it off." Each ritual and invocation is designed to build up to a climax, then take the occultist back down in a controlled manner. At each step the magician must invoke and dismiss a particular demon. In a way, the next demon to be summoned is waiting in the wings, so if it does not get the call, it will come looking for why it was left hanging. Usually, they are not going to be in a happy mood if you muck it around like this. Thus, if you do that sort of thing i.e. Stop a ritual half way through, you can get possessed in a certain sense. Things get inside you, and use you for their purposes.

Crowley gets married

It was at this point that Crowley met **Rose Kelly**, a young society lady. Courting scandal, he married her the day after they met, and took her off to Egypt for their honeymoon leaving the *Abramelin Ritual* unfinished.

> The honeymoon was a period of uninterrupted debauchery. Once in the first three weeks or so, Rose took some trifling liberty, I recognised the symptoms and turned her up and spanked her. She henceforth added the qualities of a perfect wife to those are the perfect mistress. *(Diaries of Aleister Crowley)*

Crowley and his wife decide to spend a night inside the **Kings Chamber** of the **Great Pyramid**. Crowley wanted to show off to his new wife.

> I wanted my wife to see what a great magician I was. We went accordingly after dinner with candles. I had with me a small notebook in which was written the **Preliminary Invocation of the Goetia** *(The Lesser Key of King Solomon)*.

The *Goetia* is a **Grimoire**[6] probably the closest thing to a text book on Black Magick. It is *The Lesser Key of King Solomon*, so you know right off it has got nothing to do with invoking angels or anything particularly spiritual for that matter. It is purely to raise demons and nothing else.

Back in Cairo, they were continuing their orgy of hedonistic excess, when the Black Magick ritual in the Great Pyramid had an unexpected result. It was to be the turning point in Crowley's life.

> Rose got into a strange state of mind. I had never seen anything like it before. She kept on repeating dreamily, yet intensely, **'they are waiting for you; they are waiting for you'**

---

[6] A grimoire is a textbook of magic, typically including instructions on how to create magical objects like talismans and amulets; how to perform magical spells; charms and divination; and how to summon or invoke supernatural entities such as angels, spirits, and demons.

When Crowley asked Rose, who was waiting, she kept repeating that it was **Horus**, an ancient Egyptian God. Crowley was puzzled and irritated by his wife's bizarre behaviour. She knew nothing of magick and even less of Egyptology. Surely she of all people was not receiving a message from the gods? Crowley decided to take Rose down to the Egyptian Museum to test what she was saying.

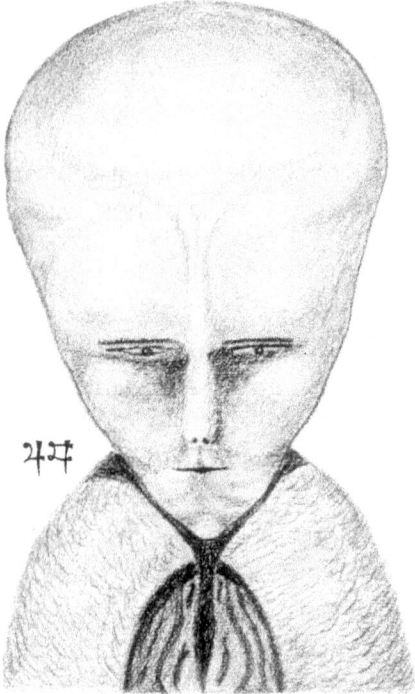

Crowley's own drawing of his Demon Mentor

Rose had never visited the museum before and to Crowley's amazement she rushed through rooms full of ancient artefacts until suddenly she stopped dead. There he is! She gasped. It was an image of the same god she claimed to have seen and heard in her vision. Crowley was stunned. What could this mean? Rose told him that they have to go back to the hotel room and wait to find out. It was at that point something happen within, and Crowley opened himself up to the demon calling itself Horus. It never ever left him until his last few years on earth. He developed this relationship and I believe he was the real thing. I believe that people that came into contact with Crowley came into contact with that which was a supernaturally evil being. He had given himself over to that demonic control, so that demonic control could now affect him and could work with him, and through him.

What is very interesting is Crowley's own drawing of the Demon Mentor. It looks remarkably like a Grey Alien. Greys and aliens would not be in popular culture for another 50-60 years! Thus, I wonder if it was a 4th Dimensional ET that Crowley made his pact with? It would not be the first time someone has done that.

Djinns

This is exactly what modern day TV magicians have done. Guys like **Dynamo, Criss Angel**, and to a lesser degree **David Blaine**, are working with Djinns (pronounced Jinns). Djinn is the Arabic name that has been anglicised as **genies**. They are supernatural creatures in early Arabian and later Islamic mythology and theology. An individual member of the jinn is known as a djinni, or *genie.*

But make no mistake. These demons are not some beautiful blonde Genie (Barbara Eden) as in the TV comedy *I Dream of Jeannie*. No, these are demons from the Astral Plane that have been invoked into the Earth Plane (3rd dimension). By allowing the demon to work through you, you can perform all manner of amazing and impossible things. What were once tricks and illusions, sleight of hand, are now real. Dynamo even stated as much in his last TV series, *Dynamo: Magician Impossible*.

I have watched Dynamo pick up an empty plastic bucket, then hold it upside down and shake it and hundreds if live (saltwater) fish came pouring out in front of astounded African villagers (Dynamo, 2015). I saw him in India put his foot on a flattened and crushed aluminium can on the road. As he lifted his foot, the can rose, became normal again. He picked up the new, full, cold can and opened it. He gave

Dynamo produces fish from an empty bucket

it to some children who drank from the can. The list of "tricks" goes on and on. Dynamo really does do "impossible" things. ***NOTE** - he does not do "illusion" or sleight of hand. He does not use **CGI** (computer generated images) or special editing. The audience reactions are real, not staged. He does the real thing. Magicians like him have been around for centuries, but it is only now we have the technology to capture the event for further analysis.

Dynamo invokes a Djinn

Dynamo (real name Steven Frayne) often talks about his close relationship with his grandfather. He admits that it was his grandfather that "taught' him magick. Steven was a very small, sickly boy growing up. He told a story about how boys used to pick on him. So his grandfather showed him some "tricks" to defend himself. The boys never bothered Steven again.

I believe Steven's grandfather had invoked the Djinn years earlier. As he was getting older, and less well, he decided to either transfer "ownership" of the Djinn, or he showed Steven how to invoke his own Djinn.

How to Train a Djinn

One you have a Djinn, it does not mean you can just start doing physics defying feats. You must develop a strong working relationship with the demon. It must know your thoughts, and you must know it. To do a Dynamo type trick, Steven must first come up with the idea – what will the trick look like, how it will work, what props do we need, how can we achieve this. Once the demon learns the routine, it learns when it must temporarily take over the body, do the trick, and then relinquish control. With a well-trained pair, this all happens in the blink of an eye. To be sure, Dynamo started off doing basic card tricks – some with the demon, some without. As he grew in skill and confidence, they started to up the ante. *Dynamo: Magician Impossible* was Steven's last series for now as far as I know. He took it as far as he could. And still the fickle people want more. He walks through a wall – they want more. So I think he will bow out for a while, maybe come back in a few years, or maybe never again. You see, as non-evil you think these Djinns may be, they do not work for nothing.

It is fairly nice living for them in the Astral Plane, and coming down to the 3rd dimension isn't exactly easy or pleasant for them. Imagine you had to work in a mine 3 miles down 24/7. It is hot, humid, hard to breath, and generally very unpleasant. That is what the 3rd dimension feels like to Beings from the Astral or higher. But what makes it bearable for them, is that they get to experience earthly, physical pleasures again. Things like excessive drinking, smoking, drugs, sex and over eating etc. are all signs of a demonic spirit having their way with a silly human's body.

Time to pay the fiddle

So they would not put up with this hardship unless there was something in it for them – something they can hardly resist. And there is – your Soul.

Demons do not have a soul. They cannot feel love, compassion, empathy, Light. So these qualities of the Soul are literally like a drug to demons. Once they get hold of a Soul, they literally suck every last drop out of it. It gets them high for a while, until the effects wear off. Then they go back looking for another sucker on earth that wants 15 minutes of fame.

You see, it is not just magicians that invoke Djinns/demons. Musicians (like Jimmy Paige of Led Zeppelin), actors, writers, TV people, politicians and the Illuminati goons. Anyone who is weak, and is desperate for fame and glory is a potential target for the demon. Remember – **the demon is a liar**. They will tell you whatever you want to hear, they will tell you they are Satan himself if they think that will impress you. They will do, say, and act however you want, as long as you do the deal for your soul.

They will suck your soul right out!

Have you ever drank one of those *Tetra Pak* fruit juices? The ones kids drink – and when you are nearly finished and suck really hard, the sides start to cave in. That is what happens to the Soul that is sucked dry by a demon. Sometimes the Soul is so damaged it has to return to Source and be re-configured. That means it goes back to the start and must redo all of the reincarnations lessons from scratch. If the Soul is salvageable (which means you had a Lesser Demon), it must

Juice Pack sucked dry

spend a long time in the **Halls of Healing**. This will also cause you to be left behind by your Soul Group. It is like be kept down a year or two at school, but much more emotionally upsetting. It is like never seeing your kids or family again times 100. The Souls of **Adolf Hitler** and **Heinrich Himmler** were both re-configured. The demons they had invoked were very powerful, and thus, sucked their souls dry. The process of re-configuration involves the soul being broken down to beyond molecular level – it is on the quantum string level (spoken about in Book I – Secrets of the Soul). That is why they must start again. It is like recycling plastic bottles. They all get broken up, melted down, and turned back into a new plastic bottle.

But the new bottle is made from the plastic from many other bottles. Every new bottle has plastic from everywhere in it. Re-configured Souls are the same. By mixing it up with bits of other re-configured souls, a new soul is made that is set back to zero, that will hopefully not make the same choices.

The fact is, these demons don't do party tricks for nothing. At some point you have to pay them back. Many of these demon possessed celebrities or bankers commit suicide. This is because once the deal is over, the demon will be in your head 24/7 demanding payment. A constant nagging. That is why many cannot stand it so they kill themselves. This is what the demons want.

As soon as you kill yourself, they are waiting to grab your soul as soon as it leaves the body. If the Soul does not make it into the White Light Tunnel, it is screwed. Because they are younger Souls, they don't necessarily know about the tunnel. Besides that, when they first leave their body, they are a bit dazed and confused – plenty of time for a demon to jump on your chest. So you still think invoking a demon sounds like fun? Crowley did…

The Book of the Law

Crowley the Magus and the Book of the Law

Crowley was about to receive a revelation that would make him the prophet to the new religion, giving him a charter to pursue a life dedicated to sex and magic, no matter what the consequences.

Alistair Crowley had delved deep into black magic, but in all the rituals he had performed, he had failed to communicate with a really powerful demonic entity. He believed that this was necessary to become the supreme master of the occult, who can harness the powers of darkness at Will.

At midday on the 4th of April **1904**, in a hotel room in Cairo, what he had been waiting for all his life was about to happen. Crowley heard an unearthly voice from over his left shoulder. For one hour, precisely at the same time over the next three days, Crowley said that the voice dictated to him the **Book of the Law**, the work that would become the Bible of his new religion.

The *Book of the Law* is really just ripping up everything. It is ripping up the Bible, it is ripping up the Quran and every other Holy book, and saying we're starting fresh now - this is the word, this is new era. We going to black out the eyes of Christ on the cross. It is highly blasphemous. It is all about liberation, it's all about having no restrictions at all. You follow your path, you follow your goal in life and you do that above all else.

The *Book of the Law* is the Bible of the religion Crowley was endeavouring to found. A book of inspired writings, whereby Crowley portrays himself as a medium for some higher force. Inevitably, with an egomaniac like Crowley, he finds himself cast in the central role.

The Book of the Law states, **"Do what thou wilt, shall be the whole of the law"**

In other words, people have the right to determine exactly how to live their lives regardless of moral and religious boundaries. Or, do whatever you want, just don't get caught!

Crowley saw himself as the prophet on this new Creed and one year later, he showed just how far he was prepared to take it when he set out to conquer one of the world's highest mountains. Crowley had started climbing as a teenager, scaling the perilous chalk cliffs of Beachy Head, near the White Cliffs of Dover.

In 1905, a year after the great revelation in Cairo, Crowley led the first attempt on the **Kangchenjunga**, the second highest mountain in Nepal after Mount Everest. But the belief in the absolute supremacy of his Will was to have terrible consequences.

Evil on the mountain

Crowley was actually a very good climber. He could have become known as one of the great climbers, but in this major expedition to Kangchenjunga, he deserted the rest of the party because they had had some kind of quarrel. The quarrel was largely due to the fact that they didn't like the way that he tried to boss everybody around and of course Crowley just simply went off saying "*all right you bastards, if you don't want me then you know what, that's too bad.*"

Crowley the Mountain Climber

The rest at the party was descending the mountain face when an avalanche struck. Crowley was alleged to have ignored the cries of the stricken men, preferring to stay in his tent drinking tea. Four people were killed in the tragedy. Crowley more or less saw what happened, and just left them to die. He knew perfectly well that as a climber, it was his job to help them. Of course that finished him as far as the climbing world were concerned. From then on none would go near him.

Unmoved by the tragedy, Crowley set off on a trek across **China** with his wife Rose and their baby girl. After reaching **Vietnam**, he abandoned his wife and took up with a mistress back in Shanghai. Rose was unable to cope on their own as Crowley had all their money. In a foreign land where she did not know the language, Rose could not save her daughter from dying of typhoid. Crowley then deserted Rose for good, blaming her for the death of the child. In despair she went mad.

Back in England, Crowley found his first disciple, **Victor Neuburg**, a young Cambridge poet. In the case of Neuburg, there was definitely a peculiar kind homosexual relationship and I'm not just now talking about the ordinary physical thing. Neuburg was in love with him. He got mixed up with Crowley, who saw there a weaker character. Crowley plunged on Neuburg and of course dragged him into this whole mess of black magick.

Demons in the Desert

Neuburg was subjected to a series of sadistic acts, designed to test the poet's dedication to the Beast 666. The two set off to **Algeria** to perform **Enochian magic**, a dark and dangerous set of archaic rituals. They walked deep into the Sahara desert for two days until they reach the point of exhaustion.

The reason for the desert is that everything looks the same, there is nothing, and nothing for your consciousness to latch onto. It is a form of sensory deprivation which was perfect for the sort of magick that Crowley was trying to do - stepping off into the unknown.

Disorientated by the effects of the desert and copious quantities and hashish and mescaline, Crowley and Neuburg embarked on the climax of the ritual, summoning **Choronzon**, the dweller of the abyss, seen within the occult world as the devil himself. This particular ritual was extremely dangerous. Make no mistake, they were opening the gates of hell. The opening lines where literally calling for the demon to open the gates of hell (kind of what they are trying to do at the **Large Hadron Collider** (LHC) at the Swiss-French border in 2015).

Victor helped him in drawing the magickal circle in the sand, followed by the ***Triangle of Solomon***, as prescribed by the **Lemegeton**. Then they slit the throats of three pigeons and deposited their blood at the tip of each point of the triangle. Neuburg stayed in the circle while

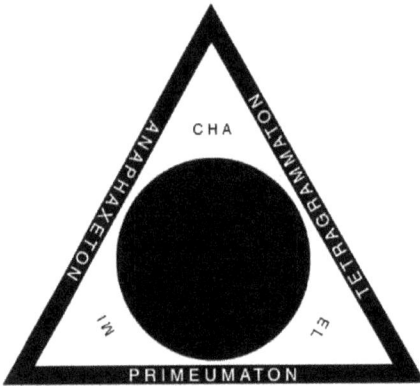

Triangle of Solomon used to summon Choronzon

Crowley, attired in a black robe, knelt in the triangle and invited the demon to take possession of him, using an incantation from the **Grimoire of Honorius**. In one hand he held a topaz stone and it was within this stone that the demon appeared. Speaking in Crowley's voice it boasted of the plagues it had brought into the world in ancient times (Roland, 2011).

At this point, Neuburg almost left the safety of the circle, being tempted to leave when he realised Crowley had been replaced by a beautiful, alluring woman, who now implored him to join her. But Neuburg reminded himself that this was an illusion, one of *Choronzon's* typical tricks. The first rule of dealing with demons – "**The demon is a liar.**"

At the moment, the demon knew his trick did not work, it showed its true face and let out a loud, mocking laugh. Then it tried another

The Demon of the Abyss - Choronzon

ruse. It offered to serve as Neuburg's assistance if only Neuburg would invite it into the circle, but Neuburg had learnt well and refused.

Choronzon unleashed a torrent of abuse,

> *"Thinkest thou, O fool, that there is any anger and my pain that I am not, or any hell but this my spirit."*

The Demon of the Abyss – Choronzon in disguise

It then threw sand into the circle, breaking the outline. Before Neuburg could repair the circle the demon was inside clutching at his throat. Neuburg fought back furiously, repeating the **Names of Power** and stabbing the demon with a sacred dagger. *Choronzon* broke off the attack and retreated to the triangle, whereupon it assumed the form of the alluring woman. Finally the vital energy of the pigeon's blood dissipated and it was drawn back into the world from which it come, leaving both Crowley and Neuburg disorientated and exhausted (Roland, 2011).

People today with their technology and "higher" education do not believe in these type of events anymore. But believe me, they are real. In reality, what Crowley worked out was that there are Beings that exist outside of this world, in another dimension. In order to bring them here, he concluded he had to create a doorway, and he would make himself the doorway. Dangerous, but it worked. And this is precisely why the magician gets inside a circle and stays inside the circle normally.

Crowley liked playing with fire, but because of this, he was the first Magician to summon a powerful demon since **John Dee** did almost 500 years earlier. Crowley drew the circle around Neuburg and he stayed outside the circle, but inside the Triangle. Magicians don't do that for very good reasons, because it really is dangerous. People can literally go mad. They suddenly hear hundreds of voices inside their heads and they can't get rid of them.

The Aftermath of Choronzon

Crowley gets a scene in his mind to perform a passionate sexual act, where Crowley is the passive partner in the sex act. At the point of orgasm, Crowley has a mystic revelation and sees a blinding white light. He seemed to commune with the Higher Beings, and he suddenly realised that sex can be a sacrament, in praise of the gods. It is like a shortcut or a short circuit to go straight in to whatever you want to achieve.

The effects of the ritual left Neuburg a shattered man, and he never fully recovered from the experience. But for Crowley, this was the final piece in the jigsaw. He had now united his belief in the power of **sex and magick** into one occult vision.

Crowley headed off to **New York** and threw himself into what he now called **Sex Magic**. He kept a detailed record of his exploits

> *I had a Dutch prostitute, a muscular wolf type, with a fine fat juicy Yoni. She inspired in me a magnificent effort (Lachman, 2014)*

Traitor to the British people?

After the First World War broke out, Crowley offered himself to the British war effort as a spy. However, he was rejected by the intelligence services, so he decided that instead, he would support the Germans. Crowley began issuing propaganda on behalf of the Germans for German-owned American newspapers. Crowley's defence being that he was deliberately writing such absurd nonsense, that it made the German cause look ridiculous to the American people. The best example of this is probably an open letter that Crowley published, addressed to "*Zeppelin*."

> *The Germans have decided to make the damage as wide spread as possible, a great deal of damage was done in Croydon, where my aunt lives. Unfortunately her house was not*

> hit. Count Zeppelin is respectfully requested
> to try again. Address is: Eaton Lodge,
> Uprant Road.

Denounced by the British press as a traitor, Crowley decided that it was time to fulfil his role as a prophet of the religion that he now called **Thelema**. He needed a place to practice *Thelema* and so, set off across Europe to find somewhere away from the prying eyes of Edwardian England.

He eventually stumbled across a ramshackle farmhouse in the small town of **Cefalù**, Northern Sicily. Unprepossessing as it was, this was to be Crowley's temple (Skramstad, 2014).

The Abbey of Thelema

What the *Book of the Law* proposed, the **Abbey of Thelema** practiced. Crowley must have had in his mind a hope that this was the beginning of his new religion. Crowley set up the Abbey in 1920 with his latest mistress, **Leah Hirsig**, their newborn baby, and a motley band of followers from around the world. Crowley met Leah when he was in New York, when she was only 19, working as a prostitute. She was totally dedicated to him, and was prepared to do anything he asked of her.

"I dedicate myself wholly to the great work. I will work for wickedness. I will kill my heart. I will be shameless before all men. I will freely prostitute my body to all creatures."

— (DIARY OF LEAH HIRSIG, 1921)

Leah Hirsig
(1883 - 1975)

This was an amazing thing in the 1920's. 80 years ago, Crowley came here with his disciples to found his spiritual college and really just to live a completely different way of life. His own unique way of life that was sick, perverted, and dark.

They wanted to breakthrough all the constraints that were holding them back in England. It is hard to imagine that while he was here, he had his children here. God only knows how corrupted they became. He had disciples and several mistresses, and the children all living under one roof. The whole point of living there was to completely clear yourself and discover your true Will and Crowley was a man who could help you do that.

The disciples perform sex magic rituals under the influence of hashish, opium and cocaine the even had a dog called *Satan*. As far as Crowley was concerned, it was an experiment in a different kind of living without boundaries. There were piles of drugs on the table.

Young children ran around naked, and were allowed to come into the room while adults were having sex. Crowley believed that if you gave man absolute freedom to do exactly what he wanted, this could do nothing but good.

Evidently, it was not the most pleasant place to live. No one really cleaned up, and they hardly ate proper meals due to being high all the time on drugs. The members were prone to disease, discomforts of various kinds, most of which could only be alleviated by faith in Crowley himself and his ready supply of drugs. Even with all this filth and disease, amazingly followers talk of a kind of perverted family atmosphere there, albeit a very dysfunctional one. Think **Charles Manson** rather than the **Waltons** I think.

When Crowley and his followers first arrived in Cefalù, the local people were completely shocked – they had never seen someone like Crowley. Even to this day the locals say the house is cursed and will not go near it. Ironically, this has left a lot of the art on the walls in good shape, even after 80 years (as creepy as some of it is).

The Goat Incidence

As the people at the Abbey continue to lose their inhibitions, the sex magic rituals Crowley asked them to perform became more and more extreme. Probably the most controversial episode in the whole Cefalù period, is the consented copulation between one of his "scarlet women" (Leah Hirsig) and a goat. The goat was made to mount Leah Hirsig from behind, and at the time of its orgasm, it would have its throat cut.

One can only wonder what he was trying to achieve. Crowley was doing everything to absolute excess, pushing himself to the absolute limits so he knew at least where his limits where. So if you are going to do something depraved, then you do something extremely depraved that even you are disgusted by and then try to learn to enjoy it.

The goat of course is the symbol of Satan. Normal men and women are repulsed by this sort of thing and are left to wonder, what actually brings humans beings to this.

I think what happened was that in the Abby, they had satisfied so many of their appetites, and all the time they were going just a bit further until eventually they were copulating with animals. When you get to that stage, it is symbolic of the depth of evil you have been lowered to.

After the Goat Incidence. . .

Surprise, surprise, things started to go wrong at the Abbey. Crowley struggled with his growing drug addiction, and the cocaine began to erode his nasal cavity. Leah had a nervous breakdown. But what Crowley called **The Great Work**, had to go on.

People who use the word "I," were encouraged to cut themselves as a reminder that they do not have an identity. Crowley was there destroying people's egos, that was part of the experiment. He believed he was liberating them from their conventional upbringings. Or so he told himself.

In effect, it was the influence of the demon. The demon causes drug addiction and depravity like this. It wants to run the show, and Crowley's soul is starting to lose the battle.

More bad blood

Raoul Loveday, an Oxford graduate moved to the Abbey with his wife **Betty May**; while Loveday was devoted to Crowley, Betty May detested him and life at the commune. She later claimed that Loveday was made to drink the blood of a sacrificed cat which killed him. Betty May left Sicily and went straight to the British press.

Crowley's squalid little piece of heaven collapsed, due to one of the earliest tabloid attacks in newspaper history. But rather than attacking Crowley's Abby as being the kind mind control camp it was, they attacked his non-Christian ways. That said, I doubt the idea of 'mind control' would make much sense to people at this time. It portrayed it as a dark, devil worshipping orgy, and den of human sacrifice. Eventually it was **Benito Mussolini** who kicked Crowley and his little crew out.

For many of the people at the Abbey, what they did there, blighted the rest of their lives. Deserted by Crowley, Leah Hirsig sank into prostitution and drug addiction.

Other disciples went mad, one committed suicide. The dream was over. Crowley was now public enemy number one, labelled by the UK press as - **The Wickedest Man in the World**!

Crowley the drug addict

Crowley attempt to start a new religion in the *Abbey of Thelema*, but it had gone disastrously wrong. His reputation as the wickedest man in the world was sealed. The last years of the Great Beast's life were spent living from hand to mouth. His fortune was long gone and his disciples had deserted him. He moved from one set of temporary lodgings to another, and finally ended up in a boarding house in Hastings, England. His life of excess had left him with nothing but chronic heroin addiction and infamy.

The Beast is gone, only Crowley remains

The great irony was that he ended up in the seaside town of Hastings, where old people go to die. *The Great Beast 666*, the wickedest man in the world, was now residing in a boarding house, and wetting the bed, with a lot of other old people. He had literally been to hell and back. So was he a wise old man, or was he a sad and lonely heroin addict? At some point, the demon will always leave, and when they do, the human is usually left broken and hollow.

In **1934**, Crowley began a libel case against a writer who described him as a Black Magician (which he was!). He was desperate for money and believed he might be awarded damages. Examples a Crowley's pornographic poetry were read out in court, and then the wife of Raoul Loveday, the young man who died in the Abbey of Thelema, gave evidence of Crowley's depravity.

The judge was appalled, saying that in 40 years of justice, he had never heard of such wickedness. Crowley lost the case and ended up bankrupt. But even after such a humiliating defeat, his extraordinary magnetism was undiminished.

Crowley outside the court, 1934

After his loss in court, a young woman, **Deidre McClellan** comes up and says, "*I want to have your child.*" Crowley agrees, and they go off together. They perform a ritual to have a magical son, to be a magical heir for Crowley. He had to give up drugs for three months so he was able to perform, but after various rituals, they do have a son and his name is **Aleister Ataturk**. Aleister Ataturk later changed his name to **Randall Gair** and died in a car accident in his early 20's.

The Crowley Children

Alistair Crowley with his son, Aleister Ataturk

Crowley had many children scattered all over the world, but Aleister Ataturk was the only child who he really seem to love and spend time with. Perhaps this was because he was so old, and at the end of his life. It was not until the end of his life that he came into contact with the kind of love most men would have wanted years earlier. Indeed, perhaps for the first time, Crowley was beginning to question what had his life really amounted to.

> " Have I ever done anything of value? But am I a mere trifler, existing by a series of ships of one kind or another, a wasteful coward, a man of straw. I could find no answer what so ever. The obvious verdict being guilty every time. (Diaries of Aleister Crowley) "

Alistair Crowley and daughter Barbara Bush?

Barbara Bush, wife of **George H. W. Bush**, was most likely fathered by Aleister Crowley. This information may at first seem ridiculous, but the source is Aleister Crowley's own diary, and is substantiated by historical facts.

When Crowley was 50 years old, he was residing in the home of **Frank and Nellie O'Hara** in Paris, France. In early 1924, Nellie was visited by her American friend, **Pauline Pierce**, the wife of Marvin Pierce, president of the **McCall Corporation**, which published McCall's and Redbook magazines.

During Pauline's visit, Crowley underwent what he termed the **supreme ordeal**, an initiation into the **Masonic Ipsissimus Grade** — the highest magickal achievement in his Order. The initiation rite included choosing one or more experienced attendants, charged with arousing and exhausting him sexually by every means possible, employing every artifice and stimulant. In that place and time, Nellie and Pauline were the most suited for this task.

Pauline returned to America, and on June 8, 1925, eight months after Crowley's "supreme ordeal," Pauline gave birth to a daughter she named **Barbara**. Barbara grew up to marry **George H. W. Bush**, who later became President of the United States.

Compare Barbara Bush and Crowley's photos, and decide for yourself whether you see the family resemblance.

The End of Crowley

From an early age, Crowley had been obsessed with sex. He came to believe that it was the key to magickal fulfilment, so when he wrote in his diary, "**weak erection**" he knew that the end was near.

According to Deidre McClellan, there were no tears. The pair talked the whole day before and the whole next day, until he went into a coma. He then died the next day.

> *Rotten as I am in a thousand ways, I have been chosen by the gods to bring to earth the basic word in which mankind will work for the next 2000 years or so. I assure you, the world is ready for this move (Diaries of Aleister Crowley*

Crowley the Pop Icon

The Great Beast 666 died in 1947, and for a decade it seemed all his ideas had died with him. But then his "*do what thou wilt*" philosophy found a new home with the generation that was experimenting with free love, drugs and alternative beliefs. Crowley had pushed the same boundaries forty years earlier. He was now a sixties icon. **John Lennon** acknowledged him as a personal hero by putting him on the front cover of the Beatles' **Sargent Pepper** album. Drugs guru **Timothy Leary** went tripping in Crowley's footsteps. **The Rolling Stones** were drawn to him by the underground filmmaker **Kenneth Anger**. After Kenneth Anger introduced them to the world of Alistair Crowley, the Stones thought Crowley's teachings were just what they were looking for.

Since the sixties, the occult has seen an explosion in popularity. There are now thousands of occult web sites on the internet with many dedicated to the *Great Beast 666*. For devotees of Crowley, it's possible to see a lot of things he predicted / prophesied as having come to pass. Certainly Christianity's control over what we can and can't say, what we can call think, what we can call do is diminishing. Today Crowley's followers believe that he was a true prophet because he foresaw a society that has now embraced ideas of sexual and spiritual freedom. Others are not so sure.

I think today that modern occultist see a very watered down version of Crowley. They gloss over some of the atrocious things that he did, and just want to see him as a benign humanist. They think he is somebody who said let's be free, let's just go with the flow, but to think that is to deny an awful lot of the evilness that happened in his practices. We should be opened and honest about Aleister Crowley.

Was he really so evil?

Crowley may have done some extreme things in his life, but was he truly evil? Does he really deserves his reputation as the wickedest man in the world? In reality, Crowley was a typical 7th Level Young Soul. I explain what that means in **Book 1 Secrets of the Soul**, but to summarise, the 7th Level Young Soul is all about pushing the boundaries. It is about investigating religion, spiritualism and the occult, but using it more for status and money making.

Indeed, most New Age gurus are in this level, as too are almost all of the Illuminati, and about 40% of the New World Order. They play around with Satanism, the Occult, and alternative theologies out of curiosity, then as a money making scam, and ultimately fame. Crowley was not in it for the money, he was in it for the fame, or rather, infamy. Believe it or not, Crowley was hurt by the title of "wickedest man in the world" that the UK press gave him. And as we saw, he didn't even like being called a Black Magician. He wanted to be remembered as

Crowley on the cover of the Sargent Pepper album

the Prophet of a new religion that would sweep across the world and reign for 2000 years – the new Christianity or Islam. He was driven by hurt and pain, fear and torment. But once he allowed the demon into his life, it was a downward spiral into evil and darkness.

So did Crowley's soul get re-configured? What do you think? The answer is simple, and it is No, it did not. As I said, Crowley did exactly what is expected a Young Soul to do – to push the boundaries, reach past where you started, gather fame, glory, and wealth. If Crowley was at his peak in 2015, he would hardly register in the public interest. In fact, he may be a superstar like Dynamo or Cris Angel. Being known as a drug addict, a sex addict, and a womaniser almost describes every Hollywood male star or Rock n Roll star today. Drug addicted young ladies perform sexual acts with donkeys, horses, dogs, pigs, and the odd goat nowadays on the Internet. So Leah Hirsig is small time by today's standards.

Hitler and Himmler committed horrendous crimes against millions of people. They cut short many lives earlier than their Soul had planned.

This alone created such a debacle in Spirit – having to re-do millions of soul plans because of these two idiots. The point is, they disrupted and wrongfully impacted on other souls – that is why they were re-configured. Crowley on the other hand only messed with people that allowed him to. Free Will. He did not really impact on their Free Will – he just went to the extreme of his Soul Level. I do not admire Crowley, nor do I hate Crowley. I just see a man going to extremes because of fear and hurt. Crowley, the "wickedest man in the world" is a mythology, created by popular culture.

My Epithet for Aleister Crowley

Alistair Crowley's life was spent affirming his freedom that began in defiance of his family, Victorian morality, and the Christian Church. But the desire to exert his own free will became an obsession and a license to live his life to outrageous extremes. Crowley's beliefs ultimately proved to be as damaging to himself as they were to others. Indeed, his attempts to establish a new religion left him bankrupt, friendless, and physically wrecked, but he has left an extraordinary legacy of a life pushed to the absolute limit.

In today's world, people like George W Bush, Dick Cheney, Barack Obama, Madeline Albright and Hilary Clinton are a hundred times more evil than Alistair Crowley ever was. They routinely torture and kill children as we will see. However, Crowley inspired a new age of black magicians and High Priests. But unlike Crowley, these people hate the spotlight. Indeed, they prefer to operate in the shadows, and that is who will look at next, **The Shadow People - the Illuminati**.

References:

Abramelin, (2015). *The Book of Abramelin*. [online] Wikipedia. Available at: https://en.wikipedia.org/wiki/The_Book_of_Abramelin [Accessed 23 Oct. 2015].

Boleskine, (2015). *Boleskine House*. [online] Wikipedia. Available at: https://en.wikipedia.org/wiki/Boleskine_House [Accessed 23 Oct. 2015].

Crowley, A., Symonds, J. and Grant, K. (1989). *The confessions of Aleister Crowley*. London: Arkana.

Diaries, (2015). *Diaries of Aleister Crowley*. [online] Hermetic Library. Available at: http://hermetic.com/crowley/diaries/ [Accessed 2 Nov. 2015].

Dynamo, (2015). *Dynamo bucket of fish*. [online] YouTube. Available at: https://youtu.be/gGPL4bko7bw [Accessed 2 Nov. 2015].

Lachman, G. (2014). *Aleister Crowley: Magick, Rock and Roll, and the Wickedest Man in the World*. London, England: Tarcher.

Roland, P. (2011). *The dark history of the occult*. New York: Chartwell Books.

Skramstad, P. (2014). *Aleister Crowley and the Abbey of Thelema in Cefalù - Wonders of Sicily*. [online] The Wonders of Sicily. Available at: http://www.wondersofsicily.com/cefalu-aleister-crowley-abbey-thelema.htm [Accessed 2 Nov. 2015].

6

SHADOW PEOPLE: THE ILLUMINATI

"These organizations, like the Round Table, are made up of inner and outer circles. The inner circle knows the Agenda and works full time to achieve it. The next circle knows much of the Agenda and works to that end in their particular sphere of influence. The next circle is pretty much in the dark about the real Agenda, but is manipulated to make the 'right' decisions in their area of operation without knowing the true reason for them."

David Icke (1952 -)

- DAVID ICKE, "THE BIGGEST SECRET" (P229).

*T*he shadow forces behind the **New World Order** (NWO) are following a slow-paced agenda of total control over mankind and our planet's resources. David Icke coined it, the **Totalitarian Tip-Toe**, because "they" are making very small steps towards our complete and definitive enslavement.

However, many people are waking up in the last ten years or so because they seem to be ramping up their agenda and showing their hand more and more. So who are these **Shadow Men**? Over the years they have gone under many different names, but their intentions and plans have never really changed. They either infiltrate existing secret societies or set up their own.

Once upon a time they were elders or priests who guarded the forbidden knowledge of ancient peoples and kings. Prominent men, meeting in secret, who directed the course of civilizations are recorded in the writings of all peoples all over the globe, throughout all periods in history.

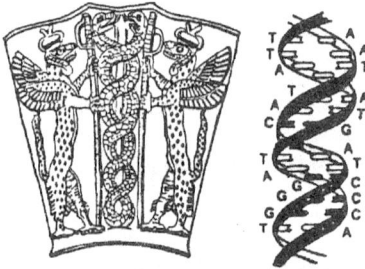

symbols of Enki, Thoth, Med. Logo, & DNA

Symbols of Enki

The oldest is the **Brotherhood of the Serpent**. This was the group Enki originally created with his son Ningishzidda.

Ningishzidda had deliberately hidden human's "divine" DNA. He disguised it as "Junk" DNA until such a time that mankind could wake up and embrace their true nature. This was to fool his uncle – Enki's brother – Enlil. If Enlil became aware that the new species Enki had created was capable of reaching higher spiritual development then the creators, there is no way he would have let Homo sapiens exist. Indeed, he would have wiped them out without a thought, just like he was prepared to do at the time of the Great Flood.

To allow humanity to reach their full potential, Enki creates a secret society, the first, called the Brotherhood of the Serpent.

One of Enki's main symbols was the intertwined serpent, to represent the human DNA helix.

Thus, the "serpent" or "snake" was Enki in the Bible story of Adam and Eve as discussed in **Book 1 – Secrets of the Soul**.

This Brotherhood would learn all the mysteries of the Anunnaki, as well as Earth mysteries like astrology, astronomy, mathematics, writing, geometry, and history among other things. It was their job to pass on this information from generation to generation. At no point did the Brotherhood learn or practise the dark arts. As we learnt in the last book, Ningishzidda hid caches of tablets and treasures in different parts of the world like Egypt and South America.

Group 1 – The Brotherhood

Unfortunately those were tumultuous times. The Anunnaki were always fighting among themselves, and using their human armies to fight their battles. So members of the Brotherhood were often killed, or their headquarters destroyed, and the knowledge lost. Some managed to keep some of the information alive, but a lot was lost. Then, when Enki's son Marduk learnt of the Brotherhood, he was jealous (as usual). So he infiltrated it and eventually took it over, turning it into a *"praise Marduk as the god of everything, and the ONLY bringer of knowledge."*

In his home base of **Babylon**, this was a time when the Jews become completely corrupted and started to indulge in paedophilia, buggery and bestiality - all condoned in the pages of the Talmud that was scribed during that period. Thus, some of the smarter Brotherhood members saw this was not right, and branched off, and formed an ultra-secret society that Marduk's minions could not infiltrate. Today, it is known as **The Brotherhood of Light**, and individual members are sometimes called **White Knights**.

The Brotherhood of Light has nothing to do with skin colour – it refers to the "White Light" of **Truth**. Indeed, The Brotherhood of Light has Masters of the Ancient Wisdom or the **Ascended Masters** (spirits) as well as humans on Earth now.

Marduk decided to change the name of the group he debased from *Brotherhood of the Serpent* to **Brotherhood of the Dragon**. Likewise, the **Dragons** have nonphysical help in the way of demons and Reptilian ET's. Just for the record, contrary to popular belief on the Internet, the Anunnaki are NOT reptilian. It is only the remnant Anunnaki on Earth that made a deal with the Reptilians which I will discuss at length in a **Book IV**.

At any rate, there is a battle going on between the **Powers of Light** and the **Forces of Darkness**. This battle is fought daily, 24/7, on Earth, and in the 4th Dimension (Astral Plane).

Group 2 – The Priest Class

This group is made up of those that stayed and embraced Marduk's new corrupted ways. There were also existing Priests of the Anunnaki. Indeed, when the Anunnaki left Earth for good, around 650 BCE, the priests that served the gods (Anunnaki) were left at a loss. For a while they kept up their rituals and paid homage to the gods, however eventually they worked out that the gods were not coming back.

As the Priest Class within the existing society, they had certain secret knowledge that other citizens did not know about. They also had intimate knowledge of the god's private lives from when they served them. So this gave them status. They did not want to lose that status, so they set themselves up as the leaders, or put one of their own up as a "king." At some point, Marduk, who was abandoned to live on Earth forever, invited the priests into his corrupted *Brotherhood of the Serpent*.

Group 3 – The Hybrid Elite Class

During the incident I spoke of in *Book 1 Secrets of the Soul*, Marduk's men, the astronauts (Igigi), came down to Earth after their Mars base was destroyed, and abducted 200 earth women. They took the earth women as their wives and had children to them. The children were known as the **Children of the Rocket ships** and are remembered in history as the men of renown like Hercules, Achilles, and Goliath. These were the first generation Anunnaki-human hybrids that became known as the **Nephilim** that the Bible mentions.

They still had a lot of Anunnaki DNA, so they were bigger and stronger than normal humans. But as each generation interbred with the other hybrids and humans (a small gene pool), their features became that of normal humans on the outside, however on the inside, they still had DNA markers that differentiated them from Homo sapiens.

It was Marduk that discovered this marker, and he was keen to track down all the Nephilim and build a new army. He still had dreams of storming Nibiru and taking control. He had fantasies of being king of two planets – Nibiru and Earth, something that no one else had ever done, and the whole reason why he was left on Earth. To conquer two worlds by force, he would need a mighty army, and since all the Anunnaki had left earth, the closest thing he had was the Nephilim.

Thus, he developed some technology that would allow him to quickly tests humans to see if they were Nephilim hybrids. In order to preserve their DNA, and keep them relatively safe, he created the myth that these people were appointed **Kings by Divine right**. He also told them they were "different," "special" and born to rule over the smelly humans.

That is where the "Royal" class of humans come from. That is why they have been going through history treating the rest of us as cattle, and believing they are "better" than us. Therefore, they believe it is their right to rule over everyone else.

They are different though, they lack the "empathy gene" that full humans have. That is why they can slaughter millions in a war, and not feel a scintilla of guilt or remorse.

The Priest Class, and The Hybrids/Elite are what we now know as the **Illuminati**.

The inbreeding between an extra-terrestrial race and humanity offspring, became many of the monarchies around the world, who believe they have a "divine" right to rule, because they were bred from "gods." They also interbreed with each other, and every so often they produce a bastard that they raise in secret to strengthen up the bloodline. Every elite can trace their genealogy to one of these Nephilim / Human hybrids.

The purest bloods are the *13 Ruling Families* (Black Nobility). Their mixed blood offspring are the *Committee of 300*. We will look at both these groups in detail in the next Chapter.

Religions of the World United!

The Priest class created the world religions as a way of containing and controlling the masses. Every major religion in the world is under their control. Their head is the **Vatican**.

Every Christian religion and cult like Catholics, Protestants, Presbyterianism, Baptists, the Mormons, Jehovah's Witnesses, and Sci-Fi cults like Scientology were created, directed, and still maintained by the Illuminati Priest Class.

In fact, that is why there are over 33,000 denominations of Christianity, and all of them are controlled and manipulated by the Illuminati. It also includes all non-Christian faiths like Islam, Hindu, and Buddhism etc. By creating different "flavours" they cover most of the world population, and still manage to control them. Even Atheism has become a religion in a way, and it too is part of the system. They do this not to offer people a choice, but to keep people separated. One only needs to look at the history of Europe and the Middle East to understand how successful they have been at divide and rule.

Furthermore, every Secret Society including but not limited to the Freemasons, Rosicrucians, Jesuits, Golden Dawn, Knights Templar, Perfectibilists, Bilderberg, Mothers of Darkness, Priory of Sion etc. are all creations of the Illuminati Priest Class. They use these groups to spread their **Luciferian** agenda, to indoctrinate and blackmail powerful people, and to control world history.

Finally, but not least, they control all of the Occult groups. Satanism, Occultist, Witchcraft, Druids, Neo-Pagans, and Vampires. They do not control each individual – they control the content of the books, Internet sites, and major leaders. For example, **Anton LaVey**, founder of the **Church of Satan** and the religion of **LaVeyan Satanism** was a Freemason and hard-core, dye-in-the-wool Illuminati stooge. Consequently, this hard core Satanist booked himself into a **Catholic Hospital** when he was dying. He died in that hospital, and had the Last Rites performed over his body. Just like all Illuminati plants, they are all phoneys to their own so-called causes.

As we will see later, they actually control all of the tax free Foundations that help run the world, science, culture, and even pop culture. Everything!

But it has not always been this coordinated and controlled. Indeed, for many years these groups of Elites and the Priests just bummed around fighting each other and not getting anywhere. In fact, it was not until relatively modern times that they got their act together and started working as a unified and coordinated team.

The organization was established in Bavaria in 1776

In 1773, **Mayer Rothschild** had invited twelve other wealthy and influential men, representing in all the thirteen bloodlines (Black Nobility) of the Illuminati, to convince them to pool their resources in a plot to bring about a **New World Order**. Thus, is was **Adam Weishaupt**, the ex-Jesuit professor that was commissioned to establish the **Order of the Illuminati**. Though born Jewish, as a young boy, Weishaupt was educated by the **Jesuits**. On May 1, 1776, three years after the Jesuit order was disbanded by the Church, Weishaupt announced the foundation of the **Order of Perfectibilists**, which later became more widely known as the **Illuminati**.

What was their objective?

In their words - To create a world government ruled by men of superior intellect - namely themselves and their bloodlines.

Since then, according to the Illuminati, their top goal has been to achieve a "one world government" and to subjugate all religions and governments in the process. The Illuminati thus attribute all wars since the **French Revolution** as having been fomented by them in their pursuit of their goals. This is not my opinion. It is not my "theory." It is admitted FACT.

The supporting document Weishaupt was commissioned to prop up this new organisation was **The Protocols of The Learned Elders of Zion**. According to the Illuminati, this great day is still commemorated by Communist nations in the form of **May Day**. At the time Weishaupt's ideology was first introduced, Britain and France were the two greatest world powers, and so the Illuminati claimed credit for having kindled the **Revolutionary War** in America, in order to weaken the British Empire, create the first Freemason country, and the **French Revolution** to destroy the French Empire. Through their NWO round table groups, they also made a lot of money financing both sides of every war since Napoleon.

In the 1780s, the **Bavarian Government** found out about the Illuminati's subversive activities, forcing the Illuminati to publicly disband and go underground. But it was too little too late. Weishaupt had over 2000 paid operatives infiltrate every Freemason Lodge across Europe. They spread the New World Order agenda, and indoctrinated senior members into the 33rd Degree level of Luciferian doctrine.

For the next few decades, the Illuminati operated under various names and guises, still in active pursuit of their ultimate goal. According to the Illuminati, the Napoleonic Wars were a direct result of Illuminati intervention, and were intended to weaken all of the governments of Europe financially. One of the results of this war was the **Congress of Vienna**, initiated by the Illuminati who were there. Russia held out and the Congress of Vienna was a failure.

They later attempted to form a one world government in the form of a **League of Nations**. However, again, Russia held out and the

League of Nations was a failure, causing great animosity towards the Russian government, on the part of the Illuminati. We still see this animosity in 2015. **Vladimir Putin** is the only world leader openly resisting the New World Order and the Illuminati plans. That is why they demonise him and the Russian people in the Western (Illuminati controlled) media.

Their short-term plan foiled, the Illuminati adopted a different strategy. They achieved control over the European economy through the International Bankers. They then directed the composition of **Karl Marx's Communist Manifesto** and its anti-thesis, written by **Karl Ritter**, in order to use the differences between the two ideologies to enable them to *"divide larger and larger members of the human race into opposing camps so that they could be armed and then brainwashed into fighting and destroying each other."*

Under new leadership by an American Confederate General named **Albert Pike**, the Illuminati worked out a blueprint for **three world wars** to be fought throughout the 20th century that would lead to a one world government by the early 21th century.

They operate all manner of Institutes and Universities, and they control and brainwash many popular singers, musicians, and actors. These brainwashed "stars" help them to push their agendas. We will look at this in detail in ***Book III: Secrets of the Mind Control***.

What do the Illuminati Believe?

The Illuminati's doctrines consist of a mixture of Masonic secrets (Luciferic Doctrine), Islamic mysticism (Sufism), and Jesuit mental discipline (Chants). Luciferian doctrine provides the basis for the two faces of the Illuminati, attempting to become "God" and the act of worshipping Lucifer. Outwardly the Illuminati attempted to present themselves as a self-perfecting society, but inwardly, the Illuminati concentrate on elevating themselves to the highest position of control in a society. That is why they will never succeed, they are driven by a selfish need to perfect, not a spiritual drive to perfect.

The practitioners of Sufism believe themselves to be on a spiritual journey toward God and that it is possible to become close to God while one is alive. In Sufism, all of one's consciousness: thoughts, feelings, perceptions, and sense of self, are gifts from God or manifestations of God. Essentially meaning that Sufis believe that they simultaneously strive to become God while God becomes them; or in the case of the Illuminati, Satan.

> **"** It is far more important that men should strive to become Christs than that they should believe that Jesus was Christ...all men may reach the same Divine perfection. – J.D. Buck, Mystic Masonry **"**

Their true symbol was the Owl of Goddess Athena.

The original symbol of the organisation was the **Owl of the Greek Goddess Athena**. To the ancient Greeks, the Owl of Athena represented true knowledge. The organisation chose the Owl because it symbolises wisdom but also the ability to see in the dark.

The "Owls" (coins) were used throughout ancient Greece because of their easy exchangeability. Athena's picture was on the reverse side. Owls thus became the world's first great trade currency, minted by the world's first Bankers. See the connection?

An "Owls" coin displaying the Illuminati Owl of Athena

Today, wild eyed teenagers and people coming to the knowledge of the Illuminati for the first time associate them with the all seeing eye of Freemasonry.

Whilst the Freemasons are connected to the Illuminati, the Eye is a Masonic symbol. When they use the Eye symbol in culture, it is deliberately used to confuse people, and to hide who really runs the show.

For example, on the US $1 bill we plainly see the Masonic All Seeing Eye of Horus. The pyramid, the eye, the Latin script (announcing a New World Oder) is all classic **Masonic symbolism**, including the 13-step pyramid which represents the 13 families of the Illuminati, along with the uncapped capstone, meaning the work is not yet complete. This is announcing that

Masonic All Seeing Eye Symbol

The Owl of Athena on the US $1 note

the Freemasons are now in control of the USA. But what many people are not aware of, is the *"Brought to you by... the Illuminati"* logo.

Yes, on the US $1 bill, in teeny, tiny print, we see the calling card of the Illuminati – the **Owl of Athena.**

That is typical, and classic Illuminati – hidden in plain sight.

View online ***The Hidden symbols on the dollar bill & their meaning in 5 minutes*** (harris, 2015)

The word "Mason" is hidden in plain sight

ASNOM = MASON

The Great Seal

And let's not forget the majestic eagle on the opposite side of the *All Seeing Eye*. This is known as "The Great Seal" of America. This is the American Bald Eagle, symbol of freedom and strength right? Hmmm, well according to Masonic writings, the eagle is the symbol of initiation, sacred to the Sun. The eagle symbol also represents the Egyptian Sun god – **Amon Ra**. We know Amon Ra as **Marduk** – head of the **Brotherhood of the Dragon**.

What is the Objective?

The objective of the Illuminati is to enslave the whole world in a satanic plot for a one world government. They want to enslave the world, so they can be left to their real objective – to live forever as "gods." Or in other words, seem to live forever like the gods (Anunnaki) did. This was the exact mission of Gilgamesh is the Sumerian poem, the *Epic of Gilgamesh*.

Gilgamesh 2/3's God

Gilgamesh was a demigod (Nephilim = 2/3 Anunnaki + 1/3 human) of superhuman strength, who built the city walls of **Uruk** to defend his people and travels to meet the sage **Utnapishtim**, who survived the Great Flood.

Gilgamesh is generally seen by scholars as a historical figure, since inscriptions have been found which confirm the existence of other figures associated with him in the epic. If Gilgamesh existed, he probably was a king who reigned sometime between 2800 and 2500 BCE. The Sumerian King List claims that Gilgamesh ruled the city of Uruk for 126 years. According to the Tummal Inscription, Gilgamesh and his son **Urlugal** rebuilt the sanctuary of the goddess **Ninlil** in Tummal, a sacred quarter in her city of **Nippur**.

Gilgamesh knew he was 2/3's god (Anunnaki) because his mother was Anunnaki. He felt it was his birth rite to travel back to Nibiru and live forever as the gods did (in his perception). The Epic of Gilgamesh tells the story of Gilgamesh and his side kick **Enkidu** (possible an android built by Enki) in their search for eternal life – by finding a spaceship to get them off earth.

One of Zecharia Sitchin's final books was ***The King Who Refused to Die***. It is Sitchin's novel version of the Epic of Gilgamesh, and a thoroughly good read. I loved it!

> 66 *[The] Retelling the Epic of Gilgamesh in the context of his discoveries about the Anunnaki, Zecharia Sitchin weaves a tale of ancient ceremony, accidental betrayal, gods among men, interplanetary travel, and a quest for immortality spanning millennia.*
> *(Sitchin, 2013)* 99

Anyway, the point is, this is a good analogy of what the elites are working toward. They have amassed vast fortunes and control such power, as Young Souls, they do not want to give it all up when they die. So to avoid incarnation, which they know all about, they are always trying to devise ways of cheating death and staying in control. They are very close.

The Plan for World Domination

Weishaupt created a plan for the Illuminati, which would give them ultimate world domination so they could impose Luciferian ideology throughout the human race. Weishaupt's plan included the following four guidelines.

- **Monetary and sex bribery** was to be used to obtain control of men already in high places.
- **Recruit the best and brightest** from Universities and colleges and indoctrinate them to the cause.
- **Trap all influential people** (celebrities, politicians, bankers, Church Elders) into adopting the policies of the Illuminati one-world government
- **To obtain absolute control of the media**

TOOLS OF THE TRADE

The tools the Illuminati use to further their agenda are quite varied, however they can be classed into certain key areas. Firstly, Black Magick/Occult, then Mind Control, then Social Engineering. I will cover the magick and occult here, as the mind control and social engineering is such a big and important topic, that I have put them into their own Book which is **Book III: Secrets of the Mind Controls.**

Here is a recap from Chapter 3:

During the reign of Solomon, the kingdom of Israel was at its most glorious, and the first temple was built. However, because Solomon's heart turned away from the Lord (Enlil) in his old age, God (Enlil) told him that 10 of the tribes would not be ruled by his son. It was Solomon that discovered all of the occult practises of today that the Illuminati love so much. Solomon also discovered the secret that their so-called "God" was really a flesh and blood being, although he did not realise Enlil was alien to this planet. After the death of Solomon, the kingdom of Israel was divided, and the northern 10 tribes were ruled over by a series of wicked (black magick) kings, who were not descended from David and Solomon.

The Keys of Solomon

King Solomon ruled over ancient Israel between circa 970 to 931 BCE. He had extensive knowledge of the Kabbalah (Jewish Mysticism), which he used to communicate with demons and angels. King Solomon is the single most important figure in the occult teachings of world, international Freemasons, Satanist, and occultist in general. Books describing his rituals and spells have been in constant reprint and demand for centuries. King Solomon's most famous and popular book is the ancient Book of Spells, the *Goetia* *(pron: "Go-eesh-ia")*.

The Goetia

The *Lesser Key of Solomon*, also known as the *Clavicula Salomonis Regis* or *Lemegeton*, is an anonymous grimoire (or spell book) on demonology, containing powerful invocations and spells. It was compiled in the mid-17th century, mostly from materials a couple of centuries older. It is divided into five books—the *Ars Goetia*, *Ars Theurgia-Goetia*, *Ars Paulina*, *Ars Almadel*, and *Ars Notoria*.

As we have already seen, **Alistair Crowley** used this book extensively. Indeed, he liked it so much that in 1904, he wrote an Introduction for the *Goetia*, detailing his own experiences with using the black magick within its pages.

These ancient spells and invocations are used to summon spirits, who Solomon would then psychically torture, and forced them to serve him. *The Goetia* contains descriptions of 72 demons, as well as the "seal" the magician must use to invoke and control the demon. Some of the demons control their own Armies of lesser demons.

King Solomon invoked and imprisoned these spirits in a bronze vessel, sealed using magick symbols. Below is a description and seal from Solomon's *Goetia*, *Ars Goetia*, demon 1 of 72. His name is **Bael**:

> 66 *The first princiall spirit is a King*
> *ruling in ye East, called Bael. He maketh*
> *men goe Invisible, he ruleth over 66 Legions*
> *of Inferiour spirits, he appeareth in divers*
> *shapes, sometimes like a Catt, sometimes like*
> *a Toad, sometimes like a man, & sometimes in*
> *all these formes at once. He speaketh very*
> *horsly. This is his Character which is to be*

01/72 Bael

An image of Bael with its 3 heads

worne as a Lamen before him who calleth him forth, or else he will not doe you homage (Peterson, 2001).

The Goetia explains how the spirits can be compelled into obedience by using a "seal" to contain them. It also describes the demonic, royal hierarchy of spirits, many of which are referred to as Knights, Princes, and Kings. Bael for example, is a King who rules over 66 legions of less powerful demons. Bael can give you the power of invisibility.

Satanists, occultists, and Freemasons worldwide venerate the memory of King Solomon, who also owned a magic ring, engraved with the symbol called **The Seal of Solomon.** This gave him power over the monarchy of demons, whether they were visible or not. This *Seal of Solomon* is better-known as the *Star of David.* It is his symbol, which is encoded into the US $1 dollar bill. It is also the flag of the Rothschilds, and Israel. By the way, many believe that **J. R. R. Tolkien** was inspired to write the *Lord of the Rings* based on the ring of Solomon:

This is the symbol required to invoke the demon Bael

> *One Ring to rule them all, One Ring to find them, One Ring to bring them all, an in the darkness bind them... (Bloom, 2000)*

Dr. John Dee

Many centuries passed before another man could wield power over demons. His name was **Dr. John Dee.** Magicians and mediums who consult with spirits have always been employed by the Royal elite. In medieval Britain, **John Dee** was consulted regularly by **Queen Elizabeth I.**

Dee used a **Dark Mirror**, made from Aztec obsidian stone, polished to a high finish. He would gaze or "scry" into the mirror to see faces, places and even whole scenes play out like a movie. This is similar to what **Nostradamus** was doing in the same time period, although he used water in a dark bowl, rather than a dark mirror. John Dee's Dark Mirror is on display in the British Museum in London.

Dee's ability to communicate with spirits led him to be employed as a spy, developing psychic espionage techniques which we now call *remote viewing*. Both the CIA and KGB employed and honed Remote Viewing techniques to great success during the Cold War (Stargate, 1970). In his role as Queen Elizabeth's personal spy, Dee always signed his name as "007."

John Dee attended **Trinity College** in Cambridge, which has become the place where occultists and the world of spies intertwine. Although Alistair Crowley also attended Trinity College, but he was unable to follow Dee's footsteps and become a spy for the British war effort. Instead he was rejected, so he went and worked for the Germans.

Alistair Crowley took the Black Magick of King Solomon, and John Dee to a new, more powerful height. Crowley is literally the "poster boy" for the Illuminati. He developed techniques that simplified the process of invoking demons and forcing them to serve you.

You still need to be a trained Occultist or Magician to perform his rituals, but he saved a lot of time and effort. That is why he has become so popular in the world now. So many young people see him as a "cool" icon to put on T-shirts and discuss at parties. That is because they do not know the whole story.

As I have pointed out, this all started in the 1960's just over a decade after Crowley's death. His popularity is an illusion. He is only popular because the Illuminati are so proud of him, that they want to create a mythical Archetype until the next Dark Legend comes along.

The Golem

A golem is an animated anthropomorphic being, magickally created entirely from inanimate matter. In other words, the magician can build a giant man out of clay, then bring it to life.

Prague reproduction of the Golem

The most famous golem narrative involves **Rabbi Judah Loew ben Bezalel**, the late 16th century rabbi of Prague, also known as the **Maharal**, who reportedly created a golem to defend the Prague ghetto from attacks.

The Jews in Prague were being attacked and killed under the rule of **Rudolf II**, the Holy Roman Emperor. To protect the Jewish community, the rabbi constructed the Golem out of clay from the banks of the Vltava River, and brought it to life through rituals and Hebrew incantations from the Kabbala.

The Golem was known as **Yossele**. It was said that he could make himself invisible and summon spirits from the dead. The only care required of the Golem was that he couldn't be active on the day of Sabbath (Saturday). Rabbi Loew deactivated the Golem on Friday evenings before the Sabbath began. One Friday evening Rabbi Loew forgot to deactivate the Golem for the Sabbath and it eventually went on a murderous rampage. Using more magick, the rabbi managed to immobilise the golem in front of the synagogue, whereupon it fell in to pieces (Golem, 2015).

John Dee got word of this amazing story and quickly made his way to Prague. Once he verified the reports, he went into Kabbalah training under Rabbi Loew. The Kabbalah offers a route map which is called the **Tree of Life**. Discarnate spirits, some angelic, some evil occupying each point on the *Tree of Life*. These spirits can be called forth and invoked to serve the magician. Medieval astrologers and Kabbalists, such as John Dee, were hired by monarchs to plan their wars or to experiment with alchemy, trying to transform base metals into gold and thus increase the already spectacular wealth of the monarchy.

The Tree of Life

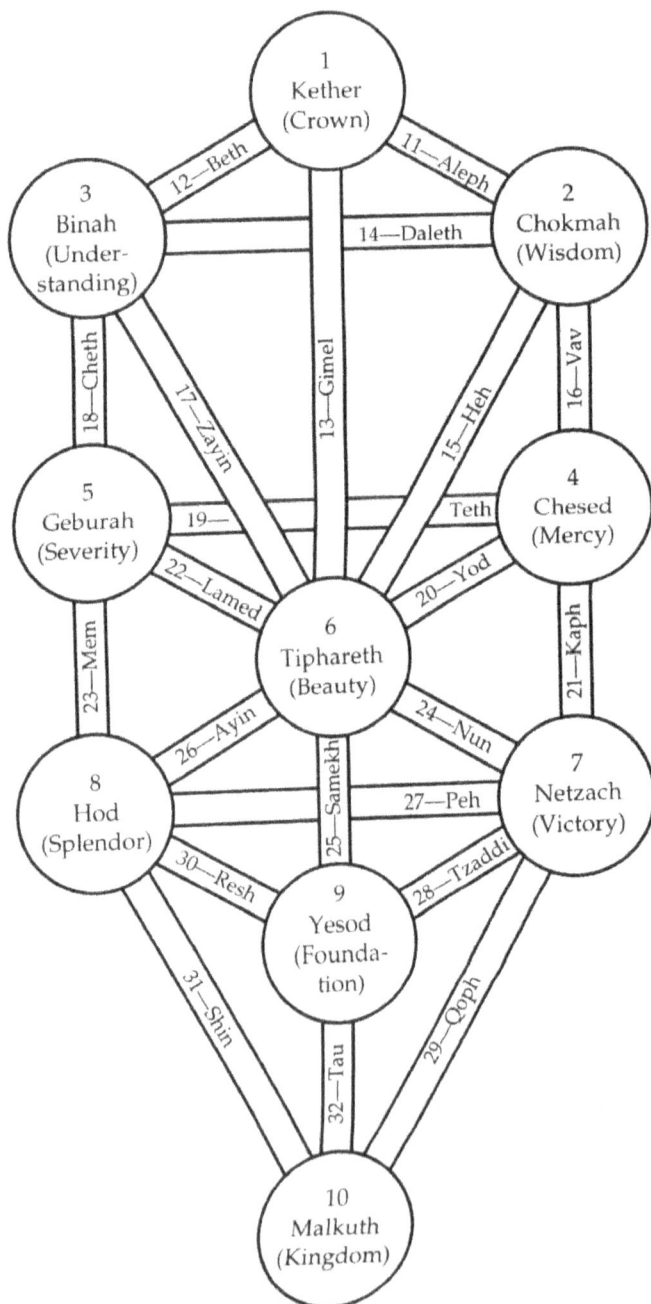

The Kabbalah Tree of Life

In my many years of esoteric studies, one of the best systems of knowledge I have encountered is the Kabbalistic **Tree of Life**. This diagram contains ten circles representing the **Sephiroth** (singular: Sephirah); that is, "spheres," "numbers," or "emanations." The Sephiroth are the numbers 1 through 10, considered in their archetypal sense. Each Sephirah is an archetypal idea. Also, the Sephiroth represent emanations from God and describe the process of creation.

Traditionally the Kabbalists did not tell much about the different Sephiroth; usually giving only their name and a short description. This was done intentionally as they wanted to encourage students to experience the Tree of Life, rather than just accepting intellectual ideas from others.

The Tree of Life and the Sephiroth can be looked at and experienced from many different angles and different levels. Although created by Kabbalists, the tree can be easily applied to other religions and esoteric teachings; it is that basic and fundamental. But first and for all, it is a blueprint of the human being, and everything on the Tree of Life is a reflection of what happens inside oneself. Therefore one should see, and experience, the Tree of Life inside oneself.

The Sephiroth have each their own respective place on the Tree, and they relate to each other in particular ways, depending, for example, on the Paths that connect them. This is just a basic overview based on my own studies and insight. The Kabbalah is not a rigid system and there is a lot of flexibility in its interpretation. It also attaches great importance to each letter and its numerical value, but that is a whole field (*Gematria*) by itself, which we do not have the space to go into here.

As I mentioned before, the sephiroth are emanations from the divine. They are strongly defined by number and place on the Tree of Life. But what are they? According to **Israel Regardie** they are considered,

> To be substantial principles of power-vessels, or categorical ideas in which the consciousness of the universe expresses itself.

Sounds mind blowing, doesn't it? They are like vessels or channels, in which and through which the divine powers can manifest themselves in their creative evolution.

They are spheres of light, receptacles that hold particular energies as they stream down from the divine source. They are like different potencies emanating from the divine. They are constantly there, always active, never ceasing. They are a medium between the divine, the Absolute (Ain-Soph) and the physical world as we know it. They are characterised by limitation, measure, and concretise.

They are gradations of powers, that is why they have different places on the *Tree of Life*. They are the substance of reality, that emanated from the divine, but are uncreated. The created universe that followed is just a reflection.

The Tree of Death

It was **Sabbatai Zevi** (who will be discussed in depth in **Book III: Secrets of the Mind Control**) that corrupted the Kabbalah. He took a beautiful thing, and utterly debased it to such a low level it is shocking. What Zevi created using the Tree of Life was its polar opposite – the **Tree of Death**. The *Tree of Death* is Black Kabbalah – what we today would call a Black Mass, or Satanic Ritual. This is what the Illuminati have institutionalised in all of their secret societies including Freemasonry.

The Tree of Life is very powerful, and the Tree of Death is equally powerful. The Tree of Life creates – The Tree of Death destroys. The Illuminati are set on destruction. They believe in order to create a New World Order, they must first destroy the Old World Order.

Their motto is "***Ordo ab Chao***" - *Order out of Chaos*.

The Mothers of Darkness

Again, I will be covering the Mothers in depth in **Book III: Secrets of the Mind Control**. But for now, just be aware that they are a big part of the Illuminati machine. The Mothers of Darkness are priestesses at the **Chateaux Des Amerois** castle in Belgium. Their job is to make daily predictions / prophesies about what is going on in the world. These are highly trained psychics, from Hybrid bloodlines that have about a 90-95% accuracy rate.

Each morning, at 03:33am local time, they sacrifice a new born child, and use its blood to write the daily prophesy into the **Book of Life and Death**. I realise that sounds farfetched or over the top, but these people do not see humans as anything more than animals. As a farmer cuts the head off a chicken, then plucks it, cooks it, and eats it, without any guilt or bad feelings. That is exactly how these people see the rest of humanity.

The American Revolution

Just prior to the French Revolution, the Illuminati was also conspiring to bring about the **American Revolution** of **1776** with the help of their man in America. Among the 56 American rebels who signed the **Declaration of Independence**, 50 were Freemasons, including **George Washington**. The American **Constitution** itself was inspired by the French Revolution, and the ideals of Freemasonry. It enshrined "Liberty," meaning freedom from the yoke of Christian morality, rules which it attempted to replace with "unalienable rights," a concept originally discussed among the secret meetings of the Illuminati.

Both Washington and Jefferson, founder of the **Democratic Party**, were the leading descendants of **Alain IV de Bretagne** (Duke of Brittany from 1084), the "Fisher King," and therefore, descendants of **Joseph of Arimathea** and the "Sea god" (Enki). This made them members of the members of **The Brotherhood of Light**. Both were deep undercover, as all Brothers of Light had to be (and women too!).

George Washington wrote that he did not deny that,

George Washington
in full Freemason
attire

The Doctrines of the Illuminati, and principles of Jacobinism had not spread in the United States. On the contrary, no one is more truly satisfied of this fact than I am." He continued: "The idea that I meant to convey, was, that I did not believe that the Lodges of Free Masons in this Country had, as Societies, endeavoured to propagate the diabolical tenets of the first, or pernicious principles of the latter (if they are susceptible of separation). That Individuals of them may have done it, or that the founder, or instrument employed to found, the Democratic Societies in the United States, may have had these objects; and actually had a separation of the People from their Government in view, is too evident to be questioned.

Washington was saying in modern terms, "*Yes, the Illuminati has made it to America, however I can't believe they have infiltrated all of the lodges yet. But their objective is to separate the people from the government, to bring in a despotic rule. That much I am convinced of.*"

It was Jefferson who had been responsible for infiltrating the Illuminati, who had just infiltrated the then, newly organised lodges of the "Scottish Rite" in New England. Washington and Jefferson were both carrying out this work for *The Brotherhood of Light*.

In September 18, 1793, President George Washington dedicated the United States Capitol. Dressed in Masonic apron, the president placed a silver plate on the cornerstone and covered it with the Masonic symbols of corn, oil, and wine. The plan of the city of **Washington DC** itself was designed by Freemason and architect **Pierre Charles L'Enfant** in the form of a pentagram, or five-pointed star. In 1848, in a Masonic ceremony, the cornerstone was laid of the **Washington Monument**, an obelisk or pillar, like those formerly dedicated to the dying gods of ancient Middle East.

L'Enfant's original plan for Waashington DC

ALBERT PIKE BRINGS THE ILLUMINATI
TO USA FREEMASONS

Satanist, 33° Mason and founder of the Ku Klux Klan racist, stands today in the heart of Washington, D.C.

There are no statues of any Confederate leaders in Washington DC, with one exception. That one exception is a statue of Albert Pike, one of the most influential American Freemasons, and Illuminist in history, and a onetime Confederate General during the American Civil War (he fought on the losing team). Pike was not only one of the most transformative Masons in the history of the United States, he was also one of the most influential American occultists of the 19th century.

Up until the early 1970's, his book **Morals and Dogma of The Ancient and Accepted Scottish Rite of Freemasonry** was given to anyone who obtained the 14th Degree within that system. In addition to fighting for the Confederacy in the American Civil War, he helped to establish the **Ku Klux Klan.**

In 1859 he was elected **Sovereign Grand Commander** of the Southern Jurisdiction of the **Scottish Rite of Freemasons**. It was a post that he would hold until his death in 1891. It was upon his election as *Sovereign Grand Commander* that he began rewriting the rituals of the Scottish Rite, infusing them with a large degree of Illuminati, occult philosophy and ideas.

Like all of his Illuminati brothers. Albert Pike saw **Lucifer** as a figure of redemption and a flattering portrait of the Light-bearer is painted in *Morals and Dogma.*

Lucifer, from Morals and Dogma

None of Pike's writings about Lucifer were particularly inspired or even original. Nearly all of the ideas (and even some of the words) Pike shared about Lucifer were stolen/borrowed from French occultist and Satanist **Eliphas Levi.**

A quick look at a quote from *Morals and Dogma* at least explains why Pike is looked at by many as a godless, Satanic, communist on par with Barack Obama.

> ❝ *Lucifer, the Light-bearer! Strange and mysterious name to give the Spirit of Darkness! Lucifer, the Son of the Morning! Is it he who bears the Light, and with its splendors intolerable blinds feeble, sensual, or selfless souls? Doubt it not! (Pike, 1871* ❞

In addition to writing about Lucifer as the Light-bearer, Pike also added sexual imagery to the Masonic tools of the Compass and the Square, along with the sexual meaning behind the Obelisks that adorn the 3 City States (Washington DC, London, Vatican).

Pike was very influential in spreading European Illuminati, occult philosophies and ideas within the United States. Furthermore he brought the works of Levi to a large audience, and helped popularised the Black Kabbalah and Satanism.

Baphomet

Baphomet drawing by Eliphas Levi

The "Baphomet" is a term originally used to describe the deity that the **Knights Templar** were accused of worshiping, and that subsequently was incorporated into unrelated occult and mystical traditions. Since 1856, the name *Baphomet* has been associated with a "Sabbatic Goat" image drawn by **Eliphas Levi**, which contains elements representing the "sum total of the universe" (e.g. male and female, good and evil, etc.) (Levi, 1856).

To the casual viewer however, there is no doubt that the Baphomet is the image of Satan. On this original image drawn by Levi, he proudly displays his name under the cloven feet of his Lord and Master. I am showing you this to help you understand what kind of man Albert Pike was. Not only was he a deep, deep racist, he was a Satanist, and his main "idol" he looked up to was Eliphas Levi.

Pike brings Satanism to Freemasons

Pike was a hard core Satanist, who indulged in the occult, and he possessed a bracelet which he used to summon Lucifer (or some other demon pretending to be Lucifer), with whom he had constant communication. He was the Grand Master of a Luciferian group known as the **Order of the Palladium** (or Sovereign Council of Wisdom), which had been founded in Paris in 1737. Palladium had been brought to Greece from Egypt by Pythagoras in the fifth century, and it was this cult of Satan that was introduced to the inner circle of the Masonic lodges. It was aligned with the Palladium of the Templars.

In **1801**, **Issac Long**, an Ashkenazi Jew, brought a statue of Baphomet (Satan) to **Charleston**, South Carolina, where he helped to establish the Ancient, and Accepted Scottish Rite. Long apparently chose Charleston because it was geographically located on the 33rd parallel of latitude (incidentally, so are the Pyramids of Egypt), and this council is considered to be the **Mother Supreme Council** of all Masonic Lodges of the World.

Pike was Long's successor, and he changed the name of the Order to the **New and Reformed Palladian Rite** (or Reformed Palladium). The Order contained two degrees:

1) **Adelph** (or Brother), and
2) **Companion of Ulysses** (or Companion of Penelope)

Pike's right-hand man was **Phileas Walder**, from Switzerland, who was a former Lutheran minister, a Masonic leader, occultist, and spiritualist.

The Civil War

Albert Pike was a Confederate General fighting against the North. The Rothschild's sent British agents to conspire with Pike and with U.S. politicians to provoke the rebellion that started the **American Civil War**.

Following the civil war, Albert Pike was charged and convicted of treason and sent to prison, but **President Andrew Johnson**, a 33rd degree Mason, pardoned him. One of Johnson's first acts as President was to veto the **Civil Rights Act** for blacks who had been shipped in chains to their wealthy American slave owners. Stealing slaves was a criminal offense, but torturing and beating them was not.

Albert Pike and Nathan B. Forrest (also a Confederate General) would go on to found the **Ku Klux Klan**.

The Mafia is Bor

Pike also worked closely with **Giusseppe Mazzini** of Italy (1805-1872) who was a 33rd degree Mason, who replaced Adam Weishaupt as head of the Illuminati in 1834. Mazzini was a member of the Italian **Carbonari**[7] and created the Mafia, including the blood rituals and the secret oath. He gave the dreaded *Cosa Nostra* the name "**Mafi** ."

MAFIA is an acronym spelling the names of the original mafiosa godfathers. "M" for Mazzini. "A" for Autorizza. "F" for Furti. "I" for Incendi. "A" for Avelenameti.

Mazzini founded the Mafia in 1860, and they started their operations in America during the 1890's. They were able to set up with Illuminati funding, which allowed the new crime organisation to create underground networks and the black market system.

The Mazzini and Pike Bromance

Mazzini appointed America's Albert Pike as sovereign Pontiff of Universal Freemasonry and the coordinator of the Illuminati's U.S. activities. Pike was a **Tennessee Ku Klux Klan judicial office** . A known Satanist, Pike indulged in phallic worship and the occult. He wore a satanic Baphomet symbol around his neck and used his bracelet to summon demons. Pike used the KKK to keep blacks out of the Masonic lodges.

Incidentally, an honorary statue of Guiseppe Mazzini, the Illuminati MAFIA boss who put the letter "M" for Mazzini into the name MAFIA stands today in **New York's central park**.

Close by is another statue donated by the French Grand Orient Temple Masons to the Masons of America celebrating the first Masonic Republic called the **United States of America**. Fourteen U.S. Presidents are known to have been 33° Masons.

Central Park near the west side at 67th Street is this bronze statue of Italian MAFIA founder Giuseppe Mazzini

Together with Mazzini, **Lord Henry Palmerston** of England (1784-1865, 33°

[7.]The Carbonari (charcoal burners) were groups of secret revolutionary societies founded in early 19th-century Italy.

Mason), and **Otto von Bismarck** from Germany (1815-1898, 33° Mason), Albert Pike intended to use the **Palladian Rite** to create a Satanic umbrella group that would tie all Masonic groups together.

Albert Pike died on April 2, 1891, and was buried in **Oak Hill Cemetery**, although the corpse of Pike currently lies in the headquarters of the Council of the 33rd degree of the Scottish Rite of Freemasonry in Washington, D.C (Shaw and McKenney, 1988).

During his leadership, Mazzini enticed Albert Pike into the (now formally disbanded, but still operating) **Illuminati**.

Pike was fascinated by the idea of a one world government, and when asked by Mazzini, readily agreed to write a ritual tome that guided the transition from average high-ranking mason into a top-ranking Illuminati mason (33°). Since Mazzini also wanted Pike to head the Illuminati's American chapter, he clearly felt Pike was worthy of such a task. Mazzini's intention was that once a Mason had made his way up the Freemason ladder and proven himself worthy, the highest ranking members would offer membership to the secret 'society within a society'.

It is for this reason that most Freemasons vehemently deny the evil intentions of their fraternity. Since the vast majority never reach the 30th degree, they would not be aware of the real purpose behind Masonry. When instructing Pike how the tome should be developed, Mazzini wrote the following to Pike in a letter dated January 22, 1870. Remember that Freemasonry wasn't started by Pike - rather it was infiltrated by the Illuminati who were looking for a respectable forum in which to hide their clandestine activities:

Giusseppe Mazzini
(1805-1872)

"We must allow all the federations to continue just as they are, with their systems, their central authorities and their diverse modes of correspondence between high grades of the same rite, organized as they are at the present, but we must create a super rite, which will remain unknown, to which we will call those Masons of high degree whom we shall select. With regard to our brothers in Masonry, these men must be pledges to the strictest secrecy. Through this supreme rite, we will govern all Freemasonry which will become the one international center, the more powerful because its direction will be unknown."

In 1871, Pike published the 861 page Masonic handbook known as the ***Morals and Dogma of the Ancient and Accepted Scottish Rite*** of Freemasonry.

After Mazzini's death on March 11, 1872, Pike appointed **Adriano Lemmi** (1822-1896, 33° Mason), a banker from Florence, Italy, to run their subversive activities in Europe. Lemmi was a supporter of patriot and revolutionary **Giuseppe Garibaldi**, and was active in the Luciferian Society founded by Pike. Lemmi, in turn, was succeeded by **Lenin** and **Trotsky**, then by **Stalin**. The revolutionary activities of all these men were financed by British, French, German, and American international bankers; all of them dominated by the **House of Rothschild**.

In addition to the Supreme Council in Charleston, South Carolina, Pike established Supreme Councils in Rome, Italy (led by Mazzini); London, England (led by Palmerston); and Berlin, Germany (led by Bismarck). He set up 23 subordinate councils in strategic places throughout the world, including five Grand Central Directories in Washington, DC (North America), Montevideo (South America), Naples (Europe), Calcutta (Asia), and Mauritius (Africa), which were used to gather information. All of these branches have been the secret headquarters for the Illuminati's activities ever since.

The Three World Wars

Between 1859 and 1871, Pike worked out a military blueprint for three world wars and various revolutions throughout the world which he considered would forward the conspiracy to its final stage in the 20th Century.

World War I would weaken, topple, and destroy the powerful Czarist government in Russia. **World War II** would pit Great Britain against Germany, destroy Nazism, and create the Zionist state of Israel. **World War III** would be ignited by fuelling aggression between the Zionists of Israel, the Arab world, and the Christians who would eventually destroy one another.

Social, political, and economic chaos would then force the masses to accept one world army and one world government ruled by the Illuminati. After a period, when people are so sick of war and the mainstream religions, Pike wanted to reveal his Light-bearer Lucifer (Satan) as the "saviour," and force people to worship this false god. I have reprinted the exact letter in **Chapter 15**.

Hollywood – Lies and Hides

Just a point about the Hollywood movies and the media that routinely criticise the Italian Mafia, yet they are not accused of being "anti-Italian," but anyone who dares to criticise the Jewish Mafia is labelled **anti-Semitic** or a **neo-Nazi**.

The Anti-Defamation League was formed as a front organisation for Israel's **Mossad** (Israel's CIA) and became active in the United States and elsewhere. The job of the Anti-Defamation League (ADL) was (and still is) to condemn anyone who gets too close to the truth by labelling Jewish mobsters "anti-Semitic." One of the ADL's favourite targets was New York City Police Commissioner, **Theodore A. Bingham.**

In September of 1908, Bingham tried to crack down on New York's Jewish mobsters. He wrote an article for the prestigious *North American Review*, titled **"Foreign Criminals in New York."** The article detailed the rise of gambling, prostitution, and drugs on New York's Lower East Side and emphasised the role of Jewish and Italian immigrant gangsters in that crime explosion. Two of the most notorious gangsters were Jewish mobster **Meyer Lansky** (Maier Suchowljansky) and Italian mobster, **Charles "Lucky" Luciano.**

To deal with the public exposure of gangsters with Jewish surnames, The Anti-Defamation League (ADL) was founded. Its goal was not to protect the Jewish people against racism, but to protect the Jewish criminal element. The ADL, which is part of **B'nai B'rith**, is based at United Nations Plaza in New York. After the ADL successfully ousted New York City Police Commissioner, Theodore A. Bingham, the bankster sponsored networks of organised crime spread across the USA like wildfire. In Chapter 1, I spoke about the billionaire, Nazi collaborator, **George Soros**, who sold out his fellow Jews for a profit. The ADL awarded Soros one of its highest awards. That should tell you something about the ADL.

What does it take to get a statue in America?

Albert Pike was a convicted traitor, Satanist, Ku Klux Klan racist and 33° Mason. He has a statue – in the capital.

Giuseppe Mazzini, an Italian revolutionary, Satanist, Founder of the MAFIA in the US, head of the Illuminati, a 33° Mason. He has a statue in New York's Central Park.

There are several things these two men have in common – Satanism, Illuminati and Freemasonry, and a fourth if you want to count it, they are both criminals. But what gets you a statue or bust in the United States of America Inc., is you have to be a 33rd Degree Freemason, which means you have been indoctrinated into the Satan/Lucifer ideals, and you are part of the Illuminati.

So if anyone ever wants to make a statue of me after I am gone, please don't – plant a tree instead!

The Geometrical shapes of Washington

We know that the Obelisk has a direct connection with Egyptian history, mythology, and even science according to some researchers. These incredible monuments were constructed from the earliest days of Egyptian history and have managed to push themselves into the cornerstones of Egyptian history. It is believed that they are directly connected to the gods (Anunnaki).

In fact, they are related to one god in particular – Ra – which is what Marduk was calling himself during his rule of Egypt. You will see many of the Royals around the world also display Egyptian iconography. That is because they are displaying their allegiance to Marduk and his corrupt *Brotherhood of the Dragon*.

Washington Monument "as above, so below"

The foundation of the United States has been filled with masonic rituals and ancient symbolism. The Washington Monument is perhaps one of the best examples of it.

The Washington Monument is also the largest Obelisk that we know of, being 170 metres/555 feet in height. The reflecting pool of the monument points below so we have a crystal clear correlation which is telling us; "**as above, so below**".

This is one of Marduk's earliest teachings – as in Nibiru (above), so on Earth (below). Wherever you see this tenet written, it is an Illuminati controlled organisation.

The entire layout of Washington D.C. has a secret meaning. It mimics ancient places found in **Egypt, Rome,** and even **Greece**. Perfect Geometrical lines, triangles, rectangles and circles. When you look at Washington from the air, you begin to notice this incredible layout. It truly is a sacred place to the Illuminati.

There are many hidden geometrical signs that perhaps few people know of. The Capitol building, the White house and the Washington Monument, form a perfect triangle, which many researchers claim represents the Masonic square and compass. But there are many more shapes which show Freemasonry.

Jefferson had some influence on the design of Washington D.C. He strongly believed that there was **extra-terrestrial life** in the "heavens." That is because he was part of The Brotherhood of Light, Enki's super-secret, metaphysical club. Enki (and Ningishzidda) taught the group about extra-terrestrial life, and that we as humans are not alone in the universe. Without this teaching, no one in this time period would even be able to conceptualise such a thing, yet alone understand it.

Anyway, to reflect his belief, Jefferson wanted to present the capital of the United States as the main contact point on Earth, which was achieved by the layout of Washington's monuments.

It was also **Pierre Charles L'Enfant** that laid out the capital of the United States in the 10 mile diamond. Pierre Charles L'Enfant achieved this by aligning the four corners of the square, with the four cardinal directions, and so, these incredible circles, rectangles, and triangles are present in the city layout. Washington DC has

Freemasonry written all over it, however, the hidden hand was also at work.

Washington D.C – Brought to you by...

While the "in-your-face" parts of Washington D.C. scream Freemasonry, just like the dollar bill, the "sponsor" is the Illuminati. And as we already know, they love to play the game of **hiding in plain sight**. So there should be an Owl logo somewhere right?

Below is a picture taken from the air of the **Capital Building** – the heart of the US. The United States Capitol, often called Capitol Hill, is the seat of the United States Congress, the legislative branch of the U.S. federal government. It sits atop Capitol Hill, at the eastern end of the National Mall in Washington, D.C.

So who do you think owns and operates the US Government? The Freemasons or the Illuminati?

Can You Spot the Owl?

Aerial view of Capitol Hill thanks to Google Earth

Here it is again, this time marked out so it is easier to see.

A Naval Base in the shape of a Swastika?

National University: Naval Base Coronado Learning Center Building 650 NAB Coronado San Diego, CA
Google Earth:
32°40'34.0"N 117°09'27.9"W

Illuminati Origami Dollar Bill – Remember their secret – always in plain view, but always hidden.

There is little doubt that the Illuminati are at the top of the heap. After they infiltrated the Freemasons, that group now answer to the

THE TRINITY OF A
GLOBALIST STRANGLEHOLD

LONDON OBELISK	VATICAN OBELISK	WASHINGTON OBELISK
finance	religion	military
City of London	Vatican City	Washington DC
(NOT ANY PART OF ENGLAND!)	(NOT ANY PART OF ITALY!)	(NOT ANY PART OF AMERICA!)

THESE THREE STATES CONTROL THE WORLD

Illuminati. In fact, the Illuminati have taken control of three major cities to help them dominate the world. It makes a lot of sense from their point of view, but it also make it very difficult to dislodge them from their seats of power.

ILLUMINATI CITY STATES

The Illuminati worked out a long time ago that in order to control the world, you had to control the main powers that dominate civilisations – **Finance – Religion – Military**. But you don't want them all to be in the same location, because your enemies could take them out in one hit. It is best to spread them all over your empire. In order to identify that they belong to the Illuminati, who belong to Ra/Marduk, they all have an Egyptian style Obelisk out the front.

These three City States are autonomous, corporate entities that are not part of the countries they are located in. The three city empire consists of **The City of London** which controls finances, **Vatican City**, which controls all religion, and **Washington D.C.**, which is the military might. London is the centre of the three city states and controls the other two. Controlling these City States is a ruthless, greedy, power hungry, private corporation known as the **Crown Corporation**. But as we will see, the "Crown" has nothing to do with royalty. Just like the three cities, it is a private organisation, not elected, and never asked by the people to help and who do not care one bit about the people under their control.

1. CITY OF LONDON

City of London Flag (red cross on a white background) with red Knights Templars sword symbol

Situated in the heart of the UK capital, at the foot of the Cathedral of St. Paul, the City of London is considered the richest square mile of real-estate in the world. In an area with less than 3 square kilometres (1 square mile) operate 550 banks and half of the major Insurance companies in the world. More than in New York, Frankfurt and Paris put together. The volume of business that generates in the City of London in a single day is five times greater than the GDP of Great Britain.

At night, the legendary business district becomes a ghost town, but the money never sleeps. The **London Stock Exchange** is the only in the world along with New York, which never closes its doors - even in wartime.

What strange stroke of history transformed this city into the main financial market on the planet? What made this the place to carry out half of public offerings for the worldwide sale, or to control over 80% of investment funds across Europe?

The City of London is a different place from London. If you look at a map of London crafted by a careful cartographer, that map will have a one-square mile hole near the middle -- it's here where the **City of London** lives inside of the city named London. It is the financial Centre of the world. Despite these confusingly close names, the two Londons have separate city halls and elect separate mayors, who collect separate taxes to fund separate police who enforce separate laws.

The City of London History

The Romans founded Londinium (London) in the year 43 AD, following an invasion led by the Roman **Emperor Claudius**. A century later they built a defensive wall around the city in what was one of the largest construction projects carried out in Roman Britain. England was seized by **William the Conqueror**, a French Norman (King William III) in 1066. William granted the citizens of London a charter in 1075; the City was one of a few examples of the English retaining some authority.

About 1130, **Henry I** granted a sheriff to the people of London, along with control of the county of Middlesex: this meant that the two entities were regarded as one administratively (not that the county was a dependency of the City) until the **Local Government Act 1888**.

By 1141 the whole body of the citizenry was considered to constitute a single community. This 'commune' was the origin of the **City of London Corporation** and the citizens gained the right to appoint, with the king's consent, a Mayor in 1189—and to directly elect the Mayor from 1215. What is peculiar though is that laws passed by the **British Parliament** do not apply to the **City of London**.

Modern times

Entering the City of London you are greeted by a Dragon holding a Knights Templar Shield

The two Londons have separate city halls and elect separate mayors, who collect separate taxes to fund separate police, who enforce separate laws. The City of London has its own separate flag and crest while London city does not.

The Mayor of the City of London is known as '*The Right Honourable the Lord Mayor of London*' and rides a golden carriage to **Guildhall** while the Mayor of London wears a suit and takes a bus. The Mayor of London has no power over the Right Honourable Lord Mayor of London (City of London).

What is unique is that the City of London is a **Corporation** and older than the United Kingdom. However it does have a representative in the

The City of London Corporation Crest with dragons and Knights Templar icons

UK Parliament through a person known as the **Remembrancer** who is present to protect the 'City's interests (London, 2015).

The City of London gets to act more like a country, complete with its own Post Office and postage stamps and Police force. Indeed, just like the Vatican (the Religious Centre), and Washington D.C. (the Military Centre), the City of London (the Financial Centre) is an independent nation unto itself.

The corporation that runs the City of London (The Crown) has owned the financial Centre of the United Kingdom for several hundred years – the Rothschilds.

It was once a stronghold of the **Knights Templars**, and you can actually visit some of their tombs there. After they were blackmailed by the Vatican, the Church swooped in and confiscated all of their properties – all over Europe.

When Nathan Rothschild crashed the UK economy in 1815, the whole City of London was turned over to the Rothschilds (to pay off debts). They have been the Landlords ever since.

That is why you still see Templar icons everywhere. The City of London is no longer a Templars district. They like to keep the Dragons and red crosses because they are all part of the same team – the *Brotherhood of the Dragon*, or as I like to call them, the **Minions of Marduk**.

The City of London houses:

- Bank of England (Rothschild controlled)
- Lloyds of London
- The London Stock Exchange (Rothschild controlled)
- All British Banks
- The Branch offices of 384 Foreign Banks
- 70 USA Banks
- Fleet Streets Newspaper and Publishing Monopolies
- Headquarters for Worldwide Freemasonry
- Headquarters for the worldwide money cartel known as 'THE CROWN'

The City of London is controlled by the **Bank of England**, a private corporation owned by the Rothschild family since 1815.

The Queen of England refers to the City of London Corporation as the 'Firm', but it is commonly known as **The CROWN** (not representing the Royalty of Britain). Buckingham Palace is in London, but not in the City of London, and the City of London is not part of England.

The City of London directly and indirectly controls all Mayors, Councils, regional Councils, multi-national and trans-national banks, corporations, judicial systems (through the Old Bailey, Temple Bar and the Royal Courts of Justice in London), the IMF (Rothschilds), World Bank(Rothschilds), Vatican Bank (through N. M. Rothschild & Sons London Italian subsidiary Torlonia), European Central Bank, United States Federal Reserve (which is privately owned and secretly controlled by eight (out of 10) Rothschild British controlled shareholding banks), the Bank for International Settlements in Switzerland (which is also Rothschild British-controlled and oversees all of the Reserve Banks around the world) and the European Union and the United Nations Organisation.

The Crown Corporation

The Crown is not the Royal Family or the British Monarch. The Crown is the private Corporation of the City of London, however the current CEO just happens to be **Queen Elizabeth II**. It is clearly a member of the **Brotherhood of the Dragon**, as is the Queen.

It has a council of twelve members who rule the corporation under their own Lord Mayor. The Lord Mayor and his twelve member council serve as proxies, who sit in for thirteen of the world's wealthiest, most powerful families known as the **Black Nobility**. This ring of thirteen ruling families includes the Queen of England and most other monarchies in Europe.

These families and their descendants run the Crown Corporation of London. The Crown Corporation holds the title to worldwide Crown land in Crown colonies like Canada, Australia, New Zealand, and large parts of Africa. The British Parliament and the British Prime Minister serve as a public front for these ruling Crown families.

Domine Dirige Nos is the motto of City of London Corporation and means "Master Direct Us." There is no doubt in my mind who their Master is – the Lord **Marduk**, also known as Satan.

The Crown Corporation controls the global financial system and runs the governments of all Commonwealth countries including Canada, Australia and New Zealand, and many non-Commonwealth 'Western' nations as well like Greece, Spain, Ireland, Portugal, Germany, and France. What is less know is that the Crown also controls the United States ever since the **Charter of Virginia** in 1606. The United States is also a Corporation, and thus, is administered by the Crown Corporation in the City of London on a daily basis.

The Crown Temple

The Knights Templar were a pseudo-Christian group of crusaders during mediaeval time. They took up residence in Solomon's Temple (the same one where he used the Goetia) and spent years digging a tunnel to try and find the Ark of the Covenant. It is widely believed that whoever held this ancient treasure, would have the power to rule the whole world. The red cross and sword on the flag of the city of London is actually the Knights Templar's flag.

The Knights Templar were first called "*the Poor Fellow-Soldiers of Christ and the Temple of Solomon.*" This is a blatantly misleading title, considering the immense wealth and power of the Templars, who operated 9,000 manors across Europe and owned all the mills and markets. It was the Templars that issued the first paper money for public use in Europe, establishing the fiat banking system we know today. In fact, it was the Templars that created the first proto-banking system. They protected the roads to the Holy Land for travellers. On the route, every 50 Km / 30 miles or so they set up a kind of rest stop where travellers could bath, have a warm meal, and sleep in a soft bed for the night, fully protected by the best security force in the world (for a fee).

The other "service" they offered was to look after your gold or treasure. You see, many rich travellers would travel with their gold and silver. But it was heavy, and a huge security risk. So the Templars offered to look after your treasure (by putting in their armoured safe) for a fee, and when you return, you can have it back. While you are travelling, you can use a Templars "paper" note in place of your gold – accepted at over 250 Templar establishments worldwide!

Just like American Express, or MasterCard. This was the beginning of using paper money in place of real gold or silver.

Temple Bar

The Entrance to Temple Bar is guarded by a Dragon

In England, the Templars established their headquarters at a London Temple, which still exists today and is called **Temple Bar** (Crown Temple). This is located in the City of London, between Fleet Street and Victoria Embankment. The aforementioned "Crown," to be exact, is the Knights Templar church, also known as the **Crown Temple**. It is the Crown Temple that controls the legal/court system of the US, Canada, Australia, and many other countries.

Inns of Court

All bar associations are directly linked to the **International Bar Association** and the **Inns of Court** at Crown Temple in the City of London. There are four Inns of Court: Inner Temple, Middle Temple, Lincoln's Inn, and Gray's Inn.

The **Inner Temple** holds the legal system franchise by license that bleeds Canada, Australia, New Zealand, Great Britain and all

Inside the Middle Temple Main Hall

Commonwealth nations dry. That is why the people in those countries never see any of the wealth or benefit that is mined, harvested, or raped from their lands. Billions upon billions are pulled out of the Australian soil every year in huge mining operations. They destroy the water table, they devastate the native wildlife and habitat, and leave the land as a barren moon scape. Then to rub salt into the wounds, all of the profits go to private shareholders in foreign lands. Inner Temple oversee the administration.

When ex-Prime Minister, **Kevin Rudd** tried to introduce a "super-profit tax of 24%" for the mining companies to pay back to the people of Australia (via hospitals, schools, roads etc.) he was fired within two weeks. In Australia, they do not need to assassinate Prime Ministers, they just have to own the **Governor General** (the Queen's representative) which of course they always do. The Governor General, on advice from Queen Elizabeth, can dismiss not just the Prime Minister, but the whole (elected) government if she wants. So you see, Australia is still a Colony.

Inner Temple

Middle Temple has license to steal from America. The same thing that happens in Australia and elsewhere also happens in America. America is still owned by the *Crown Corporation* which I will get to later. All Inns are themselves controlled by the same few at the top, they just share the load so to speak, among the Inns.

The Bar Association

Gold fringe means International Rule

Anytime you hear somebody refer to the **Bar Association**, they are talking about a British/Masonic system that has nothing to do with a country's sovereignty, or the constitutional rights of its people. This is why, when you go to court in the US, you see the US flag with a gold fringe, denoting **International Rule**. You are no longer under Constitutional Law, or Common Law, you are under **British Admiralty Law** – the Law of the Sea. This is the law that the franchisee (Middle Temple) acts under.

Whenever you see a flag with a yellow or gold fringe, it represents no nation, and no Constitution. It denotes that the court or room is operating under **British Admiralty Law. All Inns of Court operate under this law.**

By the way, if you think it is strange that a court on dry land could be administered under Maritime Law, look at **US Code, Title 18 B 7**.

The governments of the United States, Canada, Australia, New Zealand, and Britain are all subsidiaries of The Crown, the global financial and legal system controlled from the City of London.

Declaration of Independence & US Constitution

Thanks to the Illuminati controlled 'education' system and the media, most people believe that the US has declared total independence from Britain. This is not true at all – just look at the US currency to see all the masonic symbolism all over it.

Of the signatories to the **Declaration of Independence**, at least five of them were Temple Bar attorneys, all of whom had sworn allegiance to the Crown. **Alexander Hamilton** was one of the **Middle Inn** agents sent to America during the formation of the US. He was assigned to set up the American banking system, on orders from the Crown, to control the United States. In fact a 'State' is a legal entity of the Crown ('state' in this case, is short for *estate*, the 'e' was dropped in favour of Secrecy). This is why we also have the STATE of Israel – it is a kind of **fiefdo** .

Furthermore, seven members of the **Constitution Convention** that signed the United States (actually estates, as in British property) Constitution were Middle Inn Templars who had also pledged allegiance to the Crown. And today, copies of both the *Declaration of Independence* and *US Constitution* hang on the wall in the library of the **Middle Inn**, in London. Thus, any American (or Canadian) that thinks they live in a free, sovereign country is horribly mistaken. More will be explained when we look at the *District of Columbia* City State.

The Obelisk

Located on the banks of the River Thames, this obelisk was transported to London and erected in 1878 under the reign of **Queen Victoria**. The obelisk originally stood in the Egyptian city of **On**, or **Heliopolis** (the City of the Sun). The Knights Templars' land extended to this area of the Thames, where the Templars had their own docks. Either side of the obelisk is surrounded by a sphinx.

It was erected as a land mark to indicate that this is a Crown Corporation (private) City. Of course, the Illuminati still answer to one Being – Marduk, and here is proof. The London obelisk below is known as **Cleopatra's Needle**. On each side are hieroglyphs and the banner name at the top says in hieroglyphs: "The Crowned Horus\Tall, with the Southern Crown\Loving Ra." (Cleopatra's Needle, 2015)

Marduk is **Ra**, Horus is Marduk's son, and tall because he is half Anunnaki (Nephilim). The "southern" crown refers to the kingdoms – Marduk/Ra split Egypt in two and gave each of his sons (Horus and Seth) reign of each one. Horus ruled the Southern kingdom.

While this is essentially an Illuminati controlled area, at some point they hope to bring in the One World Order. In that event, the City of London Corporation would become the "One World Bank." They

Cleopatra's Needle in the City of London

would be responsible for bringing in the micro-chip technology that will be inserted into every person. The chip will carry all of your financial records, as well as be used to buy and sell.

The City of London Corporation will also introduce one world currency for everyone, and they will control all other corporations, finance, and insurance. And it would be privately owned to benefit just 13 families – who then pay tithe to Marduk.

2. VATICAN CITY

The Vatican City flag. The dark side is yellow

The Vatican City is not part of Italy or Rome. Indeed, it is the last true remnant of the Roman Empire and rules over more than 2 billion of the world's 7 billion people on the Earth. However, they indirectly control every other religion, cult and atheist movement on Earth as well. That is because the Vatican City is the Spiritual aspect of the *Three City States*. But it is not a "good" vibe Spiritual, it is purely a means of controlling the spiritual beliefs and lives of the people of earth.

Vatican City History

Vatican City is the smallest country in the world. Encircled by a 3.2 Km / 2-mile border with Italy, Vatican City is an independent city-state that covers just over 40 ha / 100 acres, making it one-eighth the size of New York's Central Park. Vatican City is governed as an absolute monarchy with the pope at its head. The Vatican mints its own Euros, prints its own stamps, issues passports, and license plates, operates media outlets, and has its own flag and anthem.

A Roman necropolis stood on Vatican Hill in pagan times. When a great fire levelled much of Rome in 64 CE, Emperor Nero, seeking to shift blame from himself, accused the Christians of starting the blaze. By the fourth century and official recognition of the Christian religion in Rome, Emperor Constantine began construction of the original basilica atop the ancient burial ground with what was believed to be the tomb of St. Peter at its centre. The present basilica, built starting in the 1500s, sits over a maze of catacombs and St. Peter's suspected grave.

Popes ruled over a collection of sovereign Papal States throughout central Italy until the country was unified in 1870. The new secular government had seized all the land of the Papal States with the exception of the small patch of the Vatican, and a cold war of sorts then broke out between the church and the Italian government.

Popes refused to recognise the authority of the Kingdom of Italy, and the Vatican remained beyond Italian national control. **Pope Pius IX** proclaimed himself a "prisoner of the Vatican," and for almost 60 years popes refused to leave the Vatican and submit to the authority of the Italian government. When Italian troops were present in St. Peter's Square, popes even refused to give blessings or appear from the balcony overlooking the public space.

The dispute between the Italian government and the Catholic Church ended in 1929 with the signing of the **Lateran Pacts**, which allowed the Vatican to exist as its own sovereign state and compensated the church $92 million (more than **$1 billion** in today's money) for the Papal States. The Vatican used the payment as seed money to re-grow its coffers. Mussolini, the head of the Italian government, signed the treaty on behalf of **King Victor Emmanuel III**.

The Swiss Guard was hired as a mercenary force

The Swiss Guard, recognisable by its armour and colourful Renaissance-era uniforms, has been protecting the pontiff since 1506. That's when **Pope Julius II**, following in the footsteps of many European courts of the time, hired one of the Swiss mercenary forces for his personal protection. The Swiss Guard's role in Vatican City is strictly to protect the safety of the Pope. Although the world's smallest standing army appears to be strictly ceremonial, its soldiers are extensively trained and highly skilled marksmen. And, yes, the force is entirely comprised of Swiss citizens.

The Swiss Guard, recognisable by its armour and colourful Renaissance-era uniforms

At several times during the Vatican's history, popes escaped through a secret passageway. In 1277, a half-mile-long elevated covered passageway, the **Passetto di Borgo**, was constructed to link the Vatican with the fortified **Castel Sant'Angelo** on the banks of the Tiber River. It served as an escape route for popes, most notably in 1527, when it likely saved the life of **Pope Clement VII** during the sack of Rome. As the forces of Holy Roman Emperor **Charles V** rampaged through the city and murdered priests and nuns, the Swiss Guard held back the enemy long enough to allow Clement to safely reach the Castel Sant'Angelo, although 147 of the pope's forces lost their lives in the battle.

The majority of Vatican City's 600 citizens live abroad.

As of 2011, the number of people with Vatican citizenship totalled 594. That number included 71 Cardinals, 109 members of the Swiss Guard, 51 members of the clergy and one nun inside the Vatican walls. The largest group of citizens, however, was the 307 members of the clergy in diplomatic positions around the world. With **Benedict XVI** hiding out in the Vatican, the population will increased by one when Pope Francis was named.

Looking for Nibiru

The Vatican Observatory owns a telescope on **Mt. Graham in Arizona**, USA. As Rome expanded, light pollution from the city made it increasingly difficult for astronomers at the Vatican Observatory—located 15 miles from the city, at the papal summer residence in **Castel Gandolfo**—to view the night skies, so in 1981, the observatory opened a second research centre in Tucson, Arizona.

According to the Vatican, astronomers are looking for extraterrestrials, and they are using **LUCIFER** to do it! Although it shares the same name as Christianity's fallen angel and the personification of evil, LUCIFER is an instrument attached to a telescope. As **Popular Science** explains, LUCIFER is an acronym for the instruments lengthy title, "*Large Binocular Telescope Near-infrared Utility with Camera and Integral Field Unit for Extragalactic Research.*" According to EcumenicalNews.com, the Vatican astronomers are using both the VATT and the LBT's LUCIFER instrument to watch for an alien saviour (McClellan, 2013).

Tom Horn and **Chris Putnam**, authors of **Exo-Vaticana: Petrus Romanus**, Project LUCIFER, and the Vatican's astonishing plan for the arrival of an alien saviour, visited with the **Jesuit** astronomers at the VATT, including **Guy Consolmagno**. The authors claim that Consolmagno revealed to them, documents showing that the Vatican believes "*that we are soon to be visited by an alien saviour from another world.*"

Guy Consolmagno speaks regularly about science and religion. In a 2010 interview, he told The Guardian, "*Any entity – no matter how many tentacles it has – has a soul.*" He made headlines because of this interview, in which he said he would offer to baptise an extraterrestrial being if one requested.

Why would the Church be so interested in gazing at the stars? Because they are tracking the next arrival of Nibru, the Anunnaki home planet that enters our solar system every 3,500 years or so. They report this data directly to Marduk and his cronies.

Vatican Wealth

The Vatican's wealth includes investments with the Rothschilds in Britain, France and US and with oil and weapons corporations as well. The Vatican's billions are said to be in Rothschild controlled 'Bank of England' and US Federal Reserve Bank.

The money possessed by the Vatican is more than banks, corporations or even some Governments, and begs the question, why the wealth is not used to elevate at least the Christian poor, when it preaches about giving?

Vatican wealth has been accumulated over the centuries by taxing indulgences. Yes, some Popes have sold tickets to heaven to fund their lavish lifestyles. Today, they are harvesting souls in Asia as a 3rd millennium goal. The staggering wealth of the Vatican includes enormous investments with the Rothschild's in Britain, France, and the USA, and with giant oil and weapons corporations like Shell and General Electric. The Vatican's solid gold bullion stored with the Rothschild controlled Bank of England and the US Federal Reserve Bank is worth untold billions. The Vatican is one of the biggest financial power-wealth accumulators, and property owners in existence.

It possesses more material wealth than any bank, corporation, giant trust, or government anywhere on the globe. While two-thirds of the world earns less than two dollars a day, and one-fifth of the world is under fed, some even starving to death, the Vatican hordes the world's wealth, profits from it on the financial markets, and at the same time, fleeces as much as possible from even its poorest adherents. But that is the least of their crimes.

The Vatican Scandals

The **Vatican Bank** has been plagued by corruption and criminality ever since it was established in 1942. Yet this is hardly a surprise, given that no bona fide legal system is currently in place to ensure check and balances for the bank of God.

The scandals surrounding the Vatican's finances strain credulity. At the heart of the Catholic Church, we find murder, collusion with violent crime, bribery, and money laundering.

But the Church has, and will, never admit to any financial wrongdoing. With an image of sanctity to protect, the Catholic Church simply cannot admit to any illegality or immorality. In this respect, there is a parallel with the Holy See's persistent denials of sexual abuse among the clergy. This pretence of moral purity can be maintained because the tiny Vatican state is not subject to Italian law enforcement.

Jason Berry, author of **Render Unto Rome: The Secret Life of Money in the Catholic Church,** states that the Vatican has a systematic aversion to transparency. Its power structure is honeycombed in secrecy. With the abuse scandal, the bottom line is that the Pope will not punish complicit Bishops and Cardinals.

"The crux of the Vatican's problems – whether in finance, or the abuse crisis – is they are an international state without a bona fide legal system. The Vatican cannot police itself and that's why we see so many scandals."

— (BERRY, 2011).

Jason Berry (1949 -)

The Sins of the Fathers

There is strong evidence today that the Vatican Bank accepted tainted funds and riches from the bank accounts of deceased Jews in Europe during World War II. But the modern era of the Vatican's financial misadventures only truly began in the late 1960s, after the Vatican Bank started to develop strong ties with **violent crime**. At the heart of this story was a Sicilian banker named **Michele Sindona** who laundered heroin money for the **New York Mafia** family, the Gambinos. With his proceeds, Sindona bought up banks across Italy during the 1960s.

According to Paul Williams, author of **The Vatican Exposed: Money, Murder and the Mafia.**

Paul L. Williams
(1944 -)

"*Then, Sindona was hired by* **Pope Paul VI** *in 1969 to become chief Vatican financial advisor after the Italian Government said all the Vatican's holdings in Italian banks would be taxed. That's when the trouble started...Sindona moved the Vatican's holdings into the international market place where it could not be taxed... Through Sindona's Mafia connections, dirty money flowed into the Vatican Bank*"

— (WILLIAMS, 2003).

They laundered money from gun running and drugs. Sindona began the process, and it's not stopped to this day. New York's five Mafia families launder their holdings through the Bank.

Of course, given what we know about the Illuminati starting the Mafia, it is no surprise they use their only "no legal system" City to launder all their money. It is a perfect scam!

But one unblemished character was determined to stamp out the corruption. He was **Albino Luciani** - the future **Pope John Paul I** - who became Archbishop of Venice on December 15, 1969.

In **1972**, Luciani began investigating transactions at "the priests' bank," **Banco Cattolica del Veneto**, in which the Vatican Bank owned a 51 percent interest. Luciani had become suspicious after the bank was sold by Vatican Bank President, **Paul Marcinkus**, to **Roberto Calvi**, Chairman of **Banco Ambrosiano** in Milan. Calvi was known as a crook who had laundered Mafia money through his bank.

Paul Marcinkus
(1922 - 2006)

Marcinkus, on the other hand, had been an American-born Catholic priest whose nickname was "the Gorilla" because of his huge bulk. Despite having no experience in banking, he was the Vatican Bank's President from 1971 to 1989.

But Marcinkus soon became the central figure in Vatican Bank corruption. As soon as he was appointed as the Vatican Bank President, financial irregularity started to emerge.

In 1972, the US federal department questioned Marcinkus about US**$14.5 million** in counterfeit US Bonds delivered to the Vatican. He refused to answer, citing confidentiality, and the US government opted not to pursue the matter.

Around the same time, Albino Luciani's investigations of Marcinkus and Calvi had led to Sindona, who turned out to be a friend of Calvi's. Luciani quickly realised all three men were dealing with the Mafia, and in cahoots. But, for now, there was little he could do. Then, in **1978**, Luciani became **Pope John Paul I** and began an immediate investigation into the financial aberrations at the Vatican. On the evening of September 28, the Pope told his Secretary of State, **Jean Villot**, that he was going to remove Marcinkus from his post the following day. But the Pope didn't get to make the order because he never woke up. "*I'm convinced he was murdered,*" said **David Yallop**, who wrote the best selling, *In God's Name* about the crime.

"It was largely to do with money. There were a number of parties who wanted him dead. Chief among them was Marcinkus, who knew he was about to be ousted. Then there was Calvi, who was in league with Marcinkus on a fraudulent business deal. Everyone in the inner circle knew about the Pope's plans. I'm sure he was poisoned, although because the Vatican refused to carry out an autopsy, or release a medical report, we cannot prove it"

David Yallop (1937 -)

—(YALLOP, 1984).

He added:

"The Vatican said he died of a heart attack, but you would normally assess that. The Venetian doctor who'd looked after him for 15 years and came down every two weeks to the Vatican said he was in excellent health."

Pope John Paul I's reign had lasted for a mere 33 days. The only Pope to serve less time in the entire papal history was **Leo XI,** who ruled for just 17 days in 1605, before dying under mysterious circumstances as well. Yallop believes that the probable method of Pope John Paul I's murder was tampering with his medications for low blood pressure – either through liquid **Effortil**, or **Cortiplex** injections (Yallop, 1984).

With the Pope's timely death, Marcinkus stayed on and continued his rackets. In 1982, Banco Ambrosiano went bust with debts of US$1.3 billion. Embarrassingly for Marcinkus, the Vatican Bank had been a major partner in Calvi's illicit deals, which included laundering Mafia money and facilitating unlawful payments from corporations to Italian politicians. The Vatican bank lost US$500 million.

God's banker Roberto Calvi, murdered in 1982.

In June 1982, Calvi fled Italy to escape jail and landed in London. He began threatening to tell everything he knew if he was imprisoned, and was found hanging under London's **Blackfriars Bridge** just days later with bricks in his pockets and more than £10,000 in cash on him. Few people have accepted the official police verdict of suicide.

In the months before his death, he had been accused of stealing millions being laundered on behalf of the Mafia. His death was originally ruled a suicide but later judged to be murder. In July 1991, **Francesco "Frankie the Strangler" Di Carlo**, a mafia godfather who had lived in England since the late 1970s, was named as Calvi's killer. Di Carlo said he did not commit the murder, and in fact was in Rome at the time, but in an interview on the 30th anniversary of the murder, he did know who did it,

> *"Calvi was naming names. No one had any trust in him anymore. He owed a lot of money. His friends had all distanced themselves. Everyone wanted to get rid of him. He had been arrested and he had started to talk. Then he had tried to kill himself by cutting his wrists. He was released, but knew he could be rearrested at any time. He was weak, he was a broken man." Di Carlo continues,*

> *"I was not the one who hanged Calvi. One day I may write the full story, but the real killers will never be brought to justice because they are being protected by the Italian state, by members of the **P2 Masonic lodge**. They have massive power. They are made up of a mixture of politicians, bank presidents, the military, top security and so on. This is a case that they continue to open and close again and again but it will never be resolved. The higher you go, the less evidence you will find." (Thompson, 2012).*

So the Masons killed Roberto Calvi. I wonder what he was going to blab about that got him killed. Maybe because the **P2 Masonic lodge** was sometimes referred to as a "state within a state" or a "shadow government" in Italy. The lodge had among its members prominent journalists, members of parliament, industrialists, and military leaders— including **Silvio Berlusconi**, who later became **Prime Minister of Italy**; The **House of Savoy**, pretender to the Italian throne **Victor Emmanuel**; and the heads of all three **Italian intelligence services** (at the time SISDE, SISMI and CESIS) (P2, 1976).

The Vatican Bank claimed innocence, though in 1984 it made a US$240 million goodwill payment to creditors of Banco Ambrosiano. The gesture however, failed to satisfy Italian magistrates who issued a warrant for Marcinkus's arrest in 1987. This would result in a long tussle between the Vatican and Italian judicial authorities, which resulted in Marcinkus spending weeks holed up within the Vatican – fearing arrest if he ever set foot on Italian territory. The very same reason why ex- **Pope Benedict XVI** (Joseph Aloisius Ratzinger) the ex-Nazi Youth is now residing in **Mater Ecclesiae**, which is as close to the centre of the Vatican City that you can get.

No doubt he is watching his back on every angle. Ratzinger is hiding from crimes that will only come out after he dies no doubt (they have to do with paedophilia).

Finally, the Italian Court of Cassation had to rule that the Italian courts had no jurisdiction over Marcinkus. They said major officials of the Church were **exempt** from Italian state law under the terms of the 1929 Lateran Pact, which had granted independent statehood to the Vatican.

Marcinkus survived once again and his influence continued to grow. He became Pro-President, the third most powerful person in the Vatican. In 1990, Marcinkus finally retired to Arizona.

> "At one time, everyone was trying to arrest him," said Williams. "But he escaped prosecution and lived a long, happy retirement on a palatial estate, playing golf every day on, smoking expensive cigars, dining in chic restaurants."
>
> "I could never understand why Interpol, or the US authorities didn't extradite him. He was the number one guy at the centre of the Banco Ambrosiano scandal, which devastated hundreds of thousands of Italians. I think powerful Catholic interests would have cried 'foul' and 'sacrilege' if he'd been prosecuted." (Williams, 2003).

I know why, he was an Illuminati insider. He did their work, kept his mouth shut, and got rewarded.

The Blind Eye of the Holy See

But while Marcinkus may have departed, corruption in the Vatican remains. According to Jason Berry, one of the most suspicious figures today is **Cardinal Angelo Sodano**. Sodano was Secretary of State for 16 years, and is now the Dean of the College of Cardinals.

> "Sodano is a Machiavellian floorshow," says Berry. "This is a man who defended the most notorious child molester in recent Vatican history – Father Marcial Maciel." Berry continues, "Maciel gave US$15,000 in cash and gifts to Sodano so he would not be hauled before the Vatican for child molestation. It was mindboggling deceit. But it tracks back to my fundamental argument that having an institution without a bona fide legal system allows all kinds of behaviour to be rationalised."

Cardinal Angelo Sodano (1927 -)

Sodano has also had shady dealings in the US. In 2003, Boston's Archbishop **Seán O'Malley** visited Rome seeking financial help to resolve **552 abuse cases**. Sodano gave him *carte blanche* to sell Church properties; yet thanks to this insider information, Sodano cynically saw a business opportunity. His under-secretary at the Vatican fed information on closing churches to a New York company, the **Follieri Group**, so they could buy cheap and sell at a profit. Folleri's vice-president was his nephew **Andrea Sodano**.

An FBI investigation revealed that Andrea Sodano received US$800,000 for engineering services the FBI deemed worthless. Follieri was convicted of fraud and money laundering. But Angelo Sodano, and other church officials, were considered "unindicted co-conspirators." No charges were laid.

Pope Benedict XVI (1927 -) now in hiding

And though **Pope Benedict XVI** has a reputation as a moral fundamentalist, he still turned the usual Vatican blind eye to Sodano's transgressions. But there could be another explanation for the Pope's inertia – fear. The Pope is well aware of what happened the last time a Pope tried to clean up Vatican finances.

> *"Everyone who has looked into Vatican finances has ended up dead. It's a story littered with corpses," said Paul Williams. "Roberto Calvi was murdered. Pope John Paul I was certainly murdered. In the end, even Sindana was poisoned in his prison cell. It's a story written in blood."*

The Shroud of Rome

Yet despite all the controversy, the Vatican's capacity to guard secrets somehow managed to keep it off the US State Department's list of vulnerable countries at risk of money laundering for years. This immunity came to an end in 2012, as the Vatican entered the list for the first time in its history.

According to US officials, "huge amounts of cash" flowing into the state made the Vatican a likely target for money laundering activities. The US state department was also unconvinced by anti-money laundering legislation introduced last year by Pope Benedict XVI.

Williams, on the other hand, is entirely convinced that large-scale money-laundering activities occur within the hallowed walls of the papal state.

> *"They have so many phoney trusts. Money is invested in one trust, then goes into another, then another, then it's transferred to offshore companies. Eventually it all comes back to the Vatican Bank," said Williams.*

Similarly, the amount kept in these vaults is another closely guarded secret. When the Vatican produces its annual financial statement, the Bank's holdings are left off the books.

> *"The best guess made in 1982 was around US$10 billion, but we've since had the boom years of the 1990s and early 20th century so the figure is probably around US$100 billion. Officially, the Vatican loses millions of dollars a year and cannot afford to pay billions in litigation costs for thousands of paedophile cases. If the Vatican Bank revealed its enormous holdings, billions of dollars would be drained to pay for sex abuse cases all over the world."*

Since 2010, the bank and its head, **Ettore Gotti Tedeschi**, have also been under investigation for financial mis-dealings, with prosecutors in Rome probing two transfers totalling **€23 million** from the Vatican Bank to two smaller banks.

Unsurprisingly, the prosecutors' demands for information have been blocked. There is nothing they can do as they have no jurisdiction in the Vatican. They will be powerless to investigate further according to Williams.

Carlo Maria Viganò (1941 -)

While the Vatican claims to be determined to have its bank included in Europe's "white list" of states that comply with international standards against tax fraud and money laundering, it still has a long way to go. **JP Morgan Chase** closed its Vatican bank's account in 2012 because of concerns about a lack of transparency there; and the Vatican, of course, will not police itself (Economywatch, 2012).

Instead of an evolved legal system, the Vatican has tribunals - a legacy from the Inquisition started in the

12th century. These tribunals are ineffective because the Church will never admit immorality.

> *"The Catholic Church has a tradition of apostolic succession. This means every Bishop and Cardinal stands in direct lineage to the original apostles," said Berry. "As a Catholic I accept that as a theological reality, but the problem is the Vatican has erased the memory of Judas. As a result, no one can be found guilty of wrongdoing and there's no internal justice system."*

I can feel a false flag – Problem-Reaction-Solution coming...

Deliver us from Evil

The Vatican, however, has come under increasing pressure to clean up its act. In 2012, there was a release of "Vati-leaks", a series of leaked letters emanating from within the Vatican, that caused further embarrassment for the Holy See, while strengthening outsiders' cause for greater change.

The most significant leaks – revealing corruption and money laundering – came from letters written by Archbishop **Carlo Maria Viganò** to the Pope and other senior figures. Viganò sent the letters in 2011 when he was the deputy-governor of Vatican City – a post that he held for two years. Since then, he has been removed from the role and is now the Papal ambassador to the US.

In another one of his many pleas to the Pope, Viganò also expressed outrage at the inflated cost of the Vatican's nativity scene in St Peter's Square in 2009 was €550,000. Viganò cut this by €200,000 in 2010. Unfortunately while Viganò's efficiency managed to turn the budget from deficit to surplus, he treaded on too many toes. In October 2011, Viganò was finally delivered from his "transgressions," against his will, to be papal Nuncio in Washington (Vati Leaks, 2012).

The Obelisk

The Vatican obelisk is located in St. Peter's Square. It was moved from Egypt to its current location, in 1586. The circle on the ground represents the female vagina, while the obelisk itself is the penis. This is common knowledge among Freemasons and Occultists.

It is not known which Pharaoh constructed it, but it is assumed that it was erected at Heliopolis around 2500 BC (the same place as the

London City obelisk came from). Around 30 BC the obelisk was moved to Alexandria by **Emperor Augustus** and erected at the Julian Forum.

In 37 AD **Emperor Caligula** ordered the destruction of the Forum and the obelisk was shipped to Rome. It was placed on the central Spina of Caligula's circus, later called the **Circus of Nero**. Much of the circus is under the basilica and square, the original spot for the obelisk is near the present-day sacristy, south of the basilica. The Circus of Nero was not only used for chariot racing, but also for countless brutal public executions of Christians, who were blamed for the big fires in Rome in 64 CE (false flag!).

It is believed that the apostles **Saint Peter** and **Saint Paul** were crucified in the Circus. The obelisk remained there for 1,500 years, then in 1586 **Pope Sixtus V** decided to have the obelisk moved a few hundred meters to its present location, in front of the construction site of the (new) St. Peter Basilica.

The question is what motivated Pope Sixtus V to erect the 25 meter (82 ft) high phallic pillar on the centre of St. Peter's Square? Only a Freemason could answer that.

The obelisk was moved by engineer and architect **Domenico Fontana**. It took over 900 men and 140 horses more than 5 months to move the obelisk and pull it upright. Fontana did a good job and the obelisk still stands. In fact, it is the only ancient Egyptian obelisk in

Vatican obelisk located in St. Peter's Square, Rome, Italy

Rome which has remained standing since Roman times. It remains a mystery why the obelisk has no hieroglyphic inscriptions.

Pope Benedict XVI claimed that the obelisk is in fact a huge sundial that can accurately indicate midday, thanks to granite meridian and marble markers embedded in the square.

However, not many of the devoted Catholics that visit St. Peter's Square are happy about a huge, pagan penis sitting right in the middle of the square.

But to the Illuminati that put it there, they could not care less what the supporters of the Catholic Church thought. It wasn't put there for them!

3. WASHINGTON DC (DISTRICT OF COLOMBIA)

The constitution of the **District of Columbia** operates under a tyrannical Roman law known as **Lex Fori**, which in no way resembles the U.S. Constitution. When congress passed the act of 1871, it created a separate corporate government for the District of Columbia. This allowed the District of Columbia to operate as a corporation outside the Constitution. But why would they need to do this? Basically, the District of Columbia is an overseas branch of **Middle Temple**, which

The red and white flag of D.C.

was granted the franchise, for use of a better term, to administer the United States and squeeze it dry.

Thus, Washington DC is not part of the USA. District of Columbia is located on a 10sq mile/2500 Ha parcel of land. It has its own flag and own independent constitution (Lex Fori). **The Act of 1871** passed by Congress created a separate Corporation known as **The United States & Corporate Government for the District of Columbia** (Act, 1871).

The new government consisted of an appointed governor and 11-member council (from Middle Temple, representing their Crown Corporation shareholders), a locally elected 22-member assembly (stooges that are all yes men, some are Bloodlines), and a board of public works charged with modernising the city.

The **Seal of the District of Columbia** features the date 1871, recognising the year the District's government was incorporated (ibid, 1871).

The Act did not establish a new city or city government within the District. Regarding the city of Washington, it stated that

> ...that portion of said District included within the present limits of the city of Washington shall continue to be known as the city of Washington.

In the present day, the name "Washington" is commonly used to refer to the entire District, but DC law continues to use the definition of the City of Washington as given in the original Act.

Thus DC acts as a Corporation through the Act. The flag of Washington's District of Columbia has 3 red stars that were copied directly from George Washington's (English) family crest.

Charter of Virginia

If you take a moment to study some of the signed treaties and charters between the United States and Britain, you will find that the United States has always been a **British Crown Colony**.

In 1606, **King James** (yes, the King James who revised the bible) signed the **Charter of Virginia**. The charter granted America's British forefathers a **license** to settle and colonise America. The charter also guaranteed future kings and queens of England would have **sovereign authority** over all citizens and colonised land in America.

Declaration of Independence

The Declaration of Independence was signed on July 4, 1776, however, to have the **Declaration of Independence** recognised internationally, Middle Templar **King George III** agreed in the *Treaty of Paris* of 1783 to establish the legal Crown entity of the **incorporated** United States, referred to internally as the **Crown Temple States (Colonies)**. States spelled with a capital letter 'S,' denotes a legal entity of the Crown.

At least five Templar Bar Attorneys under solemn oath to the Crown, signed the American **Declaration of Independence**. This means that both parties were agents of the Crown. There is no lawful effect when a party signs as both the first and second parties. The Declaration was simply an internal memo circulating among private members of the Crown.

Most Americans believe that they own their own land, but they have merely purchased real estate by contract. Upon fulfilment of the contract, control of the land is transferred by Warranty Deed. The Warranty Deed is only a 'colour of title.' **Colour of Title**[1] is a semblance or appearance of title, but not title in fact, or in law. The **Warranty Deed** cannot stand against the **Land Patent**.

The Crown was granted Land Patents in North America by the King of England. Colonials rebelled at the usurious Crown taxes, and thus the Declaration of Independence was created to pacify the populace.

The Signing of the 1794 Treaty

The 1794 Treaty signed between England and the US was negotiated by Benjamin Franklin, John Adams and John Jay, each using the title *Esquire*, which is below a Knight, but above a Gentleman. It is also a title of office given to sheriffs, serjeants, and barristers at law, justices of the peace, and others. The point is, these men were all members of the Bar, and loyal to the Crown. The treaty they signed was **13 years after** the

---

[1] Color of title, n. the appearance of having title to personal or real property by some evidence, but in reality there is either no title or a vital defect in the title. One might show a title document to real property, but in reality he/she may have deeded the property to another; a patent to an invention may have passed to the inventor's widow, who sells the rights to one party and then, using the original patent documents, sells the patent to a second party based on this "color of title." by Gerald N. Hill and Kathleen T. Hill.

Paris Treaty of **1783** declaring US independence? Why would Article 6 and Article 12 continue to dictate terms to an 'independent' America?

Benjamin Franklin was the main negotiator for the terms of the Treaty, and spent most of the War traveling between England and France. He was also a member of the **Hellfire Club**, which regularly performs Satanic rituals, sacrifices and sexual debauchery, usually involving children (Societies, 2015), (Hellfire, 2015). Franklin's use of the title "Esquire" declared his and the others British subjection and loyalty to the Crown.

In the first article of the Treaty most of the king's claims to America are relinquished, except for his claim to continue receiving gold, silver, and copper as gain for his business venture.

This is why the US originally had its money tied to a gold standard. So they could pay the Royals in "gold," using US dollars which were exchangeable for gold. Nixon tried to thwart this in 1971, when he took the US off the gold standard, and we all know how that worked out for Nixon. The first US President to resign. He still remembered what they did to Kennedy, so when they said, either step aside or else, he swallowed his pride and left. The Water-Gate scandal was bad, and wrong, but compared to the crimes of Woodrow Wilson and Franklin D. Roosevelt before him, and the Bush and Clinton Crime Families since, what Nixon did was menial in comparison. Yes, Nixon lost his job because he tried to stand up to the Crown Corporation.

Article 3 gives Americans the right to fish the waters around the United States and its rivers. In Article 4, the United States agreed to pay **all bona fide debts**. The international bankers were working with the King. Why else would he protect their interest with this Treaty?

Who Won the War of Independence?

This Treaty was signed in **1783**, the war was over in **1781**. If the United States defeated England, how is the King granting rights to America, when the US were now his equal in status? The US supposedly defeated the King of England's forces in the Revolutionary War!

So why would these supposed patriot Americans sign such a Treaty, when they knew that this would void any sovereignty gained by the Declaration of Independence and the Revolutionary War?

If America had won the Revolutionary War, the King granting them land would not be necessary, it would have been theirs by default by his loss of the Revolutionary War. To not dictate the terms of a peace treaty in a position of strength after winning a war; means the war was never won.

Think of other wars the US have won, such as when they defeated Japan. Did MacArthur allow Japan to dictate to him the terms for surrender? No way! All these men did is gain status and privilege granted by the King and insure the subjection of future unaware generations. Worst of all, they sold out those that gave their lives and property for the chance to be free.

When Cornwallis surrendered to Washington, he surrendered the battle, not the war.

At this point, the King back in England realised it was going to cost him way too much to continue fighting. The cost of soldiers, weapons, bullets, and rations was not worth it. He felt it had already cost him more than he had bargained for.

His original deal was to send people there, they look for gold and silver, and he gets a (big) cut. He did not bargain for a war. So he cut his loses, and saved himself a fortune because he no longer had to support the colony with anything.

However, he wanted to make his money back, so he made a treaty that said so – you can have the land, but you will have to pay a tax to me, and all my descendants for the rest of time – oh, and "*agreed to pay all bona fide debts*" which were all the costs from the original colony set up, to the war.

Further reading of US history would reveal what happened to America when it cancelled the Charter of the First National Bank in **1811**. Soon afterwards, 4500 British troops arrived in Washington and burnt down the White House, both Houses of Congress, the War Office, the US State Department and Treasury and destroyed the ratification records (signed by 12 US states) of the US Constitution. That version of the Constitution contained the 13th Amendment which was to stop anyone receiving a Title of nobility or honour from serving the US Government.

The 1812 war lasted 3 years and the Bank Charter was re-established in 1816 after the ratification of the **Treaty of Ghent** in 1815. If the United States was an independent, autonomous nation, why did England attack it and force it to reinstate a banking charter?

Note: 13th amendment which was ratified in **1810** no longer appears in current copies of the U.S. constitution.

The United States is a Corporation

The United States is a Corporation – it used to be called the **Virginia Corporation** that was started by the King of England and other high level backers (the Crown Corporation).

After the Revolutionary War, they changed the name to **United States Corporation**, cropped the "Corporation" word, and appoint a new CEO ever 4 or 6 years.

The US presidents are appointed CEO's (they are not elected by the people), and their allegiance is to the Crown "board of directors," not to the American citizens. American citizens are seen as employees of the company and voting is designed as a distraction, meant to offer the illusion that the people have a say. They worked out scientifically that slaves work much harder and for longer if they think they have choice, and get a reward (pay).

In 1606, **King James** set up the Virginia Company which was granted Royal authority to begin settlements in the province of Virginia, named after Elizabeth I, who had been popularly called the Virgin Queen. The Union Jack first flew on American soil at **Jamestown** in Virginia as a permanent fixture in the spring of 1607.

The early members of the Virginia Company were aristocrats who supported the Church of England and the Royalist cause. They included Lord Southampton, the Earl of Pembroke, the Earl of Montgomery, the Earl of Salisbury, the Earl of Northampton, and Sir Francis Bacon.

> *As chancellor of England, Bacon was able to persuade the king to issue the charters which enabled the new colonies to proliferate in the new world...The Virginia Company members who actually settled in America included several members of the Bacon family, and friends of his who were initiates of the Rosy Cross. (Howard, 1989).*

> *I understand from contacts in America that it is through organizations like the London Metal Exchange that profits from the Virgini Company (United States of America) are channelled back to London. (Icke, 1999).*

After the original 13 (one each for the Black Nobility families) American colonies supposedly won their 'independence' and an 'independent' country was formed after 1783, the Virginia Company simply changed its name to... the **United States of America**.

> ❝ *The United States of America is not a country, it is a corporation owned by the same Brotherhood reptilian bloodlines who owned the Virginia Company, because the USA is the Virginia Company! (Icke, 1999).* ❞

The Making and Taking of a Nation

In 1604, King James I was joined by a group of leading politicians, businessmen, merchants, manufacturers and bankers, met in Greenwich, England. They were anticipating a potentially huge business deal and were very excited. An imminent influx of white Europeans, mostly British at first, were expected to immigrate into the North American continent. So to get in early, they formed a corporation called the **Virginia Company** with its original charter for the company completed by April 10th 1606.

Initially the Virginia Company comprised of two branches, the London Company and the Plymouth or New England Company.

> ❝ *The 'Pilgrims' of American historical myth were, in fact, members of the second Virginia Company branch called the New England Company. The Pilgrim Society is still a major elite grouping within the Illuminati. (Icke, 1999).* ❞

The Virginia Company owned most of the land of what we now call the USA, and any lands up to 900 miles offshore. This included Bermuda and most of what is now known as the Caribbean Islands.

The Virginia Company (The Crown and the bloodline families) had rights to 50% of the ore of all gold and silver mined on its lands, plus percentages of other minerals and raw materials, and **5% of all profit** from other ventures (this now includes the US GDP). These rights, the charters detailed, were to be passed on to all heirs of the owners of the Virginia Company and therefore continue to apply forever. This is what the deal at the so-called *Declaration of Independence* agreed upon.

The lands of the Virginia Company were granted to the colonies under a **Deed of Trust** (on lease) and therefore they could not claim ownership of the land.

> ❝ *The criminal courts on the lands of the Virginia Company were to be operated under Admiralty Law, the law of the sea, and the civil courts under common law, the law of the land... Now, get this. All of the above still applies today! (Icke, 1999).* ❞

The United States Inc.

England, Canada, Australia, and many other countries are led politically by "Prime Ministers" to the Queen of England. In fact, she is the official head of **53** Commonwealth countries. America, Russia, and other countries, however have a "President" and "Vice-President."

Usually corporations have Presidents and Vice-Presidents. What does this mean? The US Presidents rule from the "White House." The Russian Presidents also rule from the White House. The Jesuits, a large force behind the Illuminati, have their own White House as well. England is ruled from "Whitehall."

> *"The United States government is being ruled from the 'White House,' the government of England is being ruled from what is called 'Whitehall,' and Whitehall, like our White House, is the symbol of power because the hall is like the Masonic hall, the lodge hall, the union hall." (Maxwell et al., 2000);*

The United States Corporation came about just after the civil war. The Act of 1871 was passed by congress creating a separate form of government for Washington DC, essentially turning it into a corporation. Barack Obama is the current CEO of that Corporation in 2015. He is not the president of the people or the country as they are led to believe, that's just the smokescreen. This means that Obama launched a 'war on terrorism' on behalf of a private corporation to further the goals of that corporation. The most vile and evil woman on the planet – Hillary Clinton, will probably be the next President, unless she can no longer hide all her crimes.

The American **Bar Association** is the oversea subordinate branch of the British Temple Bar (named after the Illuminati Knights Templar secret society) legal system and its hierarchy based in the City of London. It adopted the **Uniform Commercial Code** of the British Bar Association.

Fascism in the House

If you look at the wall behind the podium in the **House of Representatives**, you will notice that, on either side of the US flag, is the depiction of bundles of sticks tied together around an axe (see close up on the right). These are called **fasci**, and were a symbol of strength in the Roman Empire.

Dictator of Italy, **Benito Mussolini** formed the Fascist Party in 1919. He got the name "fascist" from the fasci. He also used the Roman salute, of raising one arm straight up. Both the fasci and the salute were adopted by Hitler and his Nazi Party. Now they have been adopted by the United States House of Representatives. Here they represent a **Fascist Regime**.

Fascism in its true sense means a combining of private Corporations with the State, and together they run the nation. This is a very apt

US House of Reps displaying Roman Fasci

description of the United States, so it makes sense they use the symbol of fascism.

The people that own and control the United States live in the UK and Europe. They always have. The major politicians know that this is how things are and so do the government administrators, judges, lawyers, and insider 'journalists'.

> *"The United States corporation was created Government' when, after the manufactured 'victory' in the American War of 'Independence', the British colonies exchanged overt dictatorship from London with the far more effective covert dictatorship that has been in place ever since. In effect, the Virginia Company, the corporation headed by the British Crown that controlled the 'former' colonies, simply changed its name to the United States and other related pseudonyms. It had nothing to do with' America' or 'Americans' because these are very different legal entities. It is the United States Corporation that owns the United States military and everything else that comes under the term 'federal'. This includes the Federal Reserve, the 'central bank' of the United States, which is, in reality, a private bank owned by controlling stockholders (and controllers of the US Corporation) that are not even American. This is the bank from which the United States Corporation borrows 'money'"*
>
> — (ICKE, 2003).

The Obelisk

The Washington Obelisk (aka Washington Monument): The Washington Monument was built to honour **George Washington**, the commander-in-chief of the Continental Army, 33° Freemason and the first president of the United States. The structure was designed by **Robert Mills**, with construction beginning in 1848. The monument's cornerstone, a 12-ton slab of marble, was donated by the **Grand Lodge of Freemasons**. Like the Vatican obelisk, the Washington monument too is surrounded by a circle denoting the female. As stated earlier, The Washington Monument

Washington Monument 170m/555 ft in height

is also the largest Obelisk that we know of, being 170 metres/555 feet in height. The reflecting pool of the monument points below so we have a crystal clear correlation which is telling us; *"as above, so below"*.

THE EMPIRE OF THE CITY

Although geographically separate, the three city states of the Vatican, London, and the District of Columbia are one interlocking empire called **The Empire of the City**. The flag of the District of Columbia has three red stars, one for each city state in the three city empire. This tripartite union controls the world economically through London's Square Mile financial district, militarily through the District of Columbia, with the Vatican its Religious controller.

Located in the centre of each city is an Egyptian obelisk erect. They are: the obelisk in St. Peter's Square, the Washington Monument, and Cleopatra's Needle in the City of London. Of course, one question you might want to ask yourself is why is there an Egyptian obelisk, which is a tribute to the Egyptian "pagan" sun god Amen-Ra (Marduk), in the Vatican?

The Empire of the City

Spiritual   Financial   Military

middle of Vatican City? Contained within these three cities is more than 80% of the world's wealth.

The Empire of "the City" is essentially the British Empire, or more accurately, the forces behind the British Empire of the past. The Empire asserts its control over its colonies (such as the US, Canada, Australia, and New Zealand etc.) through complicated means of legal trickery and word spells.

One of their means of control is to have agents of their cause in high places of influence. This cabal of powerful manipulators is known collectively as the Illuminati, the Shadow Government, the Omega Agency, the Government within the Government, and so on. It does not matter what they are called. They are there and have been actively and legislatively writing away our freedoms and also have been working towards the New World Order. Examples of this is the **Patriot Acts, H. R. Bill 1955**, the **European Union Constitution**, the **Security and Prosperity Partnership** and the **Trans-Pacific Partnership (TPP)**

Together they have been responsible for:

- **Global Warming**/Climate change – by creating an environmental catastrophe and winning the Nobel Prize, they have created a public awareness for a 'global government' that gives them the right to take action over national governments. Known as **UN Agenda 21**, a closer look at its clauses will reveal how people will need to get permission for everything they do – in other words it is being used to control people.

- **Federal Banking system** – The Illuminati created the Federal Reserve Act in 1913, handing over the US economy to a cartel of international financiers. The 13 banking families that run the world control the central banks of the world that print money, give loans on interest, and explains how national debt never decreases. Economic crises, oil crisis (simply to increase prices).
- **Big Pharma** – is responsible for sterilising the Third World, creating cancer viruses, and drugging the First World into zombies. They withhold cancer cures, and make billions off people suffering rather than curing them. For every person cured, it is one less sale.
- **Big Agra** - is responsible for poisoning our food and the bio-system with GMO's. The danger is when it comes to food as the control is being placed under Monsanto and GMOs. Monsanto is the same company that introduced **Agent Orange** during the Vietnam War, therefore it is worthwhile reading UN's **Codex Alimentarius** and the impeding dangers.
- **Big Chema** – The produce the dangerous pesticides and a variety of poisonous chemicals and weaponized viruses.
- **Big Biotechna** – are developing clones, GMOs and splicing animals with insects. They release these Franken freaks into the biosphere and wreak havoc on native species. They also work closely with Big Chema to develop new nerve gasses and biological warfare weapons. Ebola, AIDS HIV, and Swine-flu were all developed in their labs.
- **Big Medica** – are the public salespeople for Big Pharma. It is more profitable to treat a medical problem than it is to heal or cure it. **Rick Simpson's Hemp Oil** has cured over 5,000 people of cancer, as well as hundreds of other "incurable' diseases, yet the Medical Institution will not touch it. Many medical foundations live off the grants and donations they get in the millions to "find" a cure for cancer. If they find a cure, they will be out of a "lifestyle," not a job.
- **System of local government** – promoting devolution and new concept of regional councils in a bid to increase a revenue

generating system. It is within an overall plan to abolish independent sovereign national governments.

- **Abolition of property rights** – in 1974 at the **Habitat Conference** private property was identified as a threat to peace and equality of the environment. Using 'environmentalism' as a ploy, the quest was to take over earth's resources and place it under a central authority (UN) and issue licenses for payment. Who owns the UN - the same banking families that is who. In 1987, the **World Wilderness Congress** was held and organised by the Rothschild's **World Conservation Bank** which was set up the same year. The **World Bank** is likely to be replaced by the World Conservation Bank – the aim is to break down national banks and assets which will also be diverted to the new bank, that is why there is an aim to merge world currencies into 2 or 3 major currency groups and replace them with a new electronic currency which is said to be called the 'earth dollar'. New Zealand has apparently transferred over 34% of its land area into UN Heritage Areas and Conservation Parks and these will all be owned by the same banking families. In 1992, the **UN Conference on Environment and Development** in Brazil was chaired by **Mikhail Gorbachev,** responsible for dividing the Soviet Union, and **Maurice Strong**, a Rothschild Canadian agent. The topic was **Agenda 21,** which gave superior human rights to animals, fish, plants, trees, and forests.
- **Draconian Legislation** - The **Patriots Act**, the **Human Rights Bill**, the **European Union Constitution**, the **Security, and Prosperity Partnership** are all being manipulated to place power in the control of a few hands, and remove as much liberty and freedom from the people as they can for now. Soon to come is one that will dwarf the rest – the **TPP**.
- **Wars** - Arab Springs are all manufactured, as are all wars. There is a saying, that all wars are banker's wars.

How do they initiate sudden and dramatic change?

By now you may be thinking how can they just push through their agenda and control the world? How on earth could that happen, right under our noses?" Simple – two words: **Hegelian Dialectic**.

Hegelian Dialectic

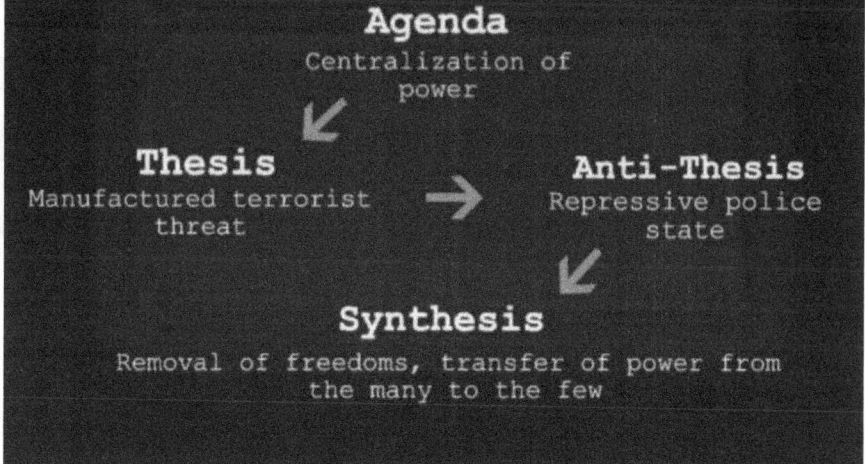

Agenda
Centralization of
power

↙

Thesis
Manufactured terrorist
threat

➡

Anti-Thesis
Repressive police
state

↙

Synthesis
Removal of freedoms, transfer of power from
the many to the few

THE HEGELIAN DIALECTIC

"The easiest way to gain control of a population is to carry out acts of terror. The public will clamour for such laws if their personal security is threatened."

—SOVIET DICTATOR JOSEF STALIN

Georg Wilhelm Friedrich Hegel was a 19th century German philosopher who devised a particular dialectic, or method of argument for resolving disagreements. His method of arriving at the truth by the exchange of logical arguments is a system of thought process still in use to this day. In essence, the *Hegelian Dialectic* is a formula and a strategy for creating a problem, to then offer a solution for the very problem you have (secretly) created, to get the outcome you desire. Note, you would not have been able to get this outcome if you didn't create the problem to begin with. The horror that was 9/11 is a perfect example. The basis of Hegelianism dictates that the human mind can't understand anything unless it can be split into two polar opposites. By controlling societal stimuli into two halves - good/evil; right/wrong; left/ right; pepsi/coke they can create the contention between thesis and antithesis, through which synthesis can be attained.

In 1847 the **London Communist League** (Karl Marx and Frederick Engels) used Hegel's theory of the dialectic to back up their economic theory of Communism. Now, in the 21st century, Hegelian-Marxist thinking affects our entire social and political structure. The Hegelian dialectic is the framework for guiding our thoughts and actions into conflicts that lead us to a predetermined solution. If we do not understand how the Hegelian dialectic shapes our perceptions of the world, then we do not know how we are helping to implement their vision. When we remain locked into dialectical thinking, we cannot see out of the box.

Hegel's dialectic is the tool which manipulates us into a frenzied circular pattern of thought and action. Every time we fight for or defend against an ideology, we are playing a necessary role in Marx and Engels' grand design to advance humanity into a dictatorship of the public. The synthetic Hegelian solution to all these conflicts can't be introduced unless we all take a side that will advance the agenda. The Marxist's global agenda is moving along at breakneck speed. The only way to completely stop the privacy invasions, expanding domestic police powers, land grabs, insane wars against inanimate objects (and transient verbs), covert actions, and outright assaults on individual liberty, is to step outside the dialectic. This releases us from the limitations of controlled and guided thought.

I realise this is a difficult concept for some people to wrap their heads around, and so lucky for us, **David Ike** broke down the Hegelian Dialectic into a very simple way to understand it, and remember it.

He calls it **PROBLEM – REACTION – SOLUTION** (Icke, 2011).

- **Problem** - Manipulate the public reaction by creating a perceived problem. For example, the government plants a bomb on a train and blows it up, killing 200 people. They use their spin doctors to saturate the media saying it was home grown terrorists from the Libertarians or Tea Party (in the US) who are dissatisfied with new gun control laws.
- **Reaction** – The public are now obviously concerned by this apparent turn of events and demands help and protection.

- **Solution** –Voila! You come up with the solution to save the day, the same "solution" that you would never have been able to sell before making the public worried e.g.: The government will enact one year of Martial Law, to round up the "home grown" terrorist, protect the public, and bring the "home grown" terrorists to justice. Your government is going to "save your world," all under a false pretext. And when the deadline for Martial Law ending comes and goes, more home terrorist's attacks will occur, to keep the Martial Law going forever. Oh, and by now, the "New anti-home grown terrorist budget" you the people accepted as part of the "SAVE US" clause, paid for the final R&D of robot cops/soldiers to patrol the streets, brought to you by Google.

This scenario has played out hundreds of times. Remember the "weapons of mass destruction." The media played a huge part in scaring the-you-know-what out of people telling them constantly that:

- **Problem:** Saddam Hussein has "weapons of mass destruction" - a clever way of letting people think the worse, like he has nukes, without actually saying that he has them. Play dramatic music and run nuclear bomb tests in the background on the 6 o'clock news, and what do you think people will imagine?
- **Reaction:** So to fix this problem, the US government said it must invade Iraq without provocation, without the backing of Congress, and without saying it will take 10 years of war; an endless war on a terror; and people for the first time being willing to pay more taxes and cut back on their consumption, not to mention bury their sons and daughters in higher numbers then the Vietnam war.
- **Solution:** Capture a fake Saddam Hussein look alike and hang him on public TV. Problem solved! But the taxes remain, the loss of Liberty remains. And to top it off, the TSA now gets to stick their hands down your pants in American airports (and soon to be bus terminals).

The question is, does the end ever justify the means?

In 1975, there was a senate investigation committee called the **Church Hearings**. During these proceedings it was revealed that the

CIA had been paying (under the table) all mainstream media outlets **$250,000,000** per year to act as gatekeepers and propagandist. In today's money (2015), that works out to be about **$1 Billion per year**. The CIA continue to do this, but now they have also financed and secretly own social media sites like Facebook, MySpace and YouTube, not to mention their biggest asset of all - **Google**.

Yes, Google records and analysis every search you do. They say it is for marketing reason, so they can serve you better advertising. But in reality, it is to help them build a profile of every citizen. If you are part of a Christian group, and you do searches on Christian Fellowship meetings in Boston. They now know you are a Christian, what group you may be dealing with, and with Facebook, which people you mix with. Handy information if you intend to have a Civil War and want to take out certain groups before the big fight starts.

This is how they can manipulate public opinion and sway people's thoughts. 9/11 is the classic example how the media, via orders from the CIA, covered up the facts, and told lie after lie, after lie. Their lies then led to the invasion of a sovereign nation - Iraq, who quite frankly had absolutely nothing to do with 9/11. Over 500,000 children died in Iraq as a result of this **False Flag**, and **Madeleine Albright** (Ashkenazi Jew) when asked, said that yes, the ends did justify the means, meaning the death of 500,000 Arab children was ok by her.

I say again - The question is, does the end ever justify the means?

Do you wonder why in America they never show the caskets of dead soldiers who were killed in the Middle East, coming off of the plane? But then they will spend a week discussing the latest sex scandal by some Hollywood celebrity or politician.

False Flag

I hope now you can see how easy it is for "the system" to bring about an agenda that they would never get away with without the PROBLEM (that they create). I should also mention for those that do not know, that when an event is blamed on another group, or someone else, is known as a **False Flag**.

So when you see a teenager go off his head and shoot a bunch of students over there in America, you can quickly work out if it was a False Flag or not. Research normally finds out quickly these days that the gunman was on psychotropic drugs for the past five years. He posted threats on Facebook two weeks before, but the cops didn't follow them up. He "somehow" got access to a gun and a ton of ammo.

If they were well trained with firearms, a lot more people would die. But the fact is, most of these kids are hopped up to the eyeballs on psychotropic drugs, they are loners, but they suddenly meet a "new" friend months earlier that really understands them, and sees the world as they do. This is normally a FBI or CIA agent that eggs them on to perform these atrocities. But what is in it for the government?

What always happens – debates on gun control, which one day will lead to draconian gun control. You just have to look at my country Australia to see what happens while the people are sleeping.

This type of mass shooting is then called a False Flag. 9/11 was a False Flag; the London train bombing was a False Flag. There are hundreds of examples. Every single Hegelian Dialectic or Problem – Reaction – Solution starts with a False Flag (Walia, 2015).

"Terrorism is the best political weapon, for nothing drives people harder than a fear of sudden death."
– ADOLF HITLER

The Wizards Behind the Curtain

To carry out the Empire of the City agenda, and run things smoothly, it takes a lot of planning and execution. Someone has to be in charge, and someone has to be calling the shots. In the next chapter we will look at which groups are at the top of the Illuminati pyramid, and more importantly, who heads and populates those groups. Make no mistake, these people control every aspect of your life. Indeed, if you still think your government independently makes its own decisions, then you are in for a rude shock. The fact is, a small number of non-elected "groups" are the **Illuminati Bloodlines!**

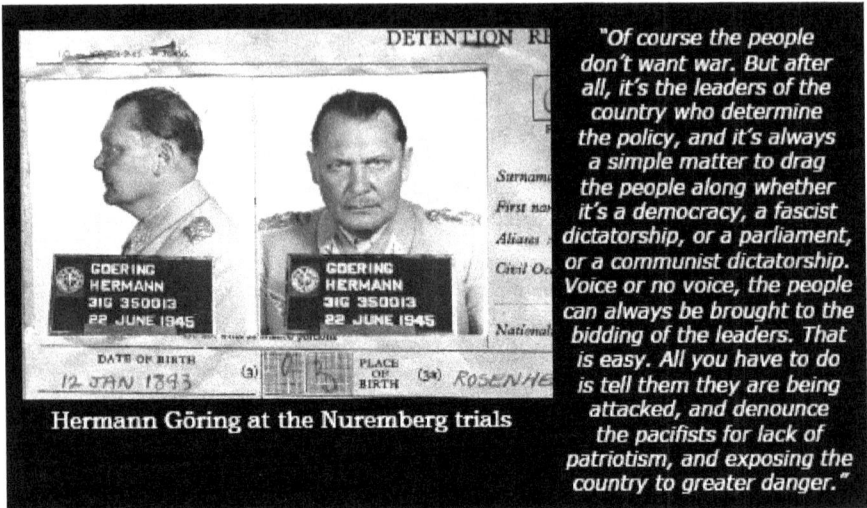

"Of course the people don't want war. But after all, it's the leaders of the country who determine the policy, and it's always a simple matter to drag the people along whether it's a democracy, a fascist dictatorship, or a parliament, or a communist dictatorship. Voice or no voice, the people can always be brought to the bidding of the leaders. That is easy. All you have to do is tell them they are being attacked, and denounce the pacifists for lack of patriotism, and exposing the country to greater danger."

Hermann Göring at the Nuremberg trials

Annexes: ANNEX 3.6.1 - Who Were The Knights Templar?

References:

Act, (1871). *District of Columbia Organic Act of 1871.* [online] Wikipedia. Available at: https://en.wikipedia.org/wiki/District_of_Columbia_Organic_Act_of_1871 [Accessed 12 Nov. 2015].

Angelos, (2015). *Angelos (Greek mythology).* [online] Wikipedia. Available at: https://en.wikipedia.org/wiki/Angelos_(Greek_mythology) [Accessed 30 Oct. 2015].

Berry, J. (2011). *Render unto Rome.* New York: Crown Publshers.

Bush and Kerry, (2004). *Skull & Bones: Bush and Kerry.* [online] YouTube. Available at: https://youtu.be/VPsz5GnrFo8 [Accessed 30 Oct. 2015].

Cleopatra's Needle, (2015). *Cleopatra's Needle.* [online] Wikipedia. Available at: https://en.wikipedia.org/wiki/Cleopatra%27s_Needle [Accessed 10 Nov. 2015].

Colony, (2015). *The United States is still a British Colony.* [online] Theforbiddenknowledge.com. Available at: http://www.theforbiddenknowledge.com/hardtruth/united_states_british_colony.htm [Accessed 12 Nov. 2015].

Economywatch, (2012). *JP Morgan Shuts Down Vatican Bank's Account Over Transparency Fears | Economy Watch.* [online] Economywatch.com. Available at: http://www.economywatch.com/in-the-news/jp-morgan-shuts-down-vatican-banks-account-over-transparency-fears.20-03.html [Accessed 11 Nov. 2015].

False Flag, (2015). *False flag.* [online] Wikipedia. Available at: https://en.wikipedia.org/wiki/False_flag [Accessed 20 Oct. 2015].

Golden, (1950). *Golden Triangle (Southeast Asia).* [online] Wikipedia. Available at: https://en.wikipedia.org/wiki/Golden_Triangle_(Southeast_Asia) [Accessed 30 Oct. 2015].

Golem, (2015). *Golem.* [online] Wikipedia. Available at: https://en.wikipedia.org/wiki/Golem [Accessed 6 Nov. 2015].

Hall, P. (2008). *Prince Hall Masons.* [online] Blackpast.org. Available at: http://www.blackpast.org/aaw/prince-hall-masons-1784 [Accessed 6 Nov. 2015].

Harris, K. (2015). *Hidden Symbols On The Dollar Bill & Their Meaning In 5 Minutes [Video].* [online] Disclose.tv. Available at: http://www.disclose.tv/action/viewvideo/217242/hidden_symbols_on_the_dollar_bill__their_meaning_in_5_minutes/ [Accessed 29 Nov. 2015].

Hegel, G. (2015). *Georg Wilhelm Friedrich Hegel.* [online] Wikipedia. Available at: https://en.wikipedia.org/wiki/Georg_Wilhelm_Friedrich_Hegel [Accessed 20 Oct. 2015].

Hellfire, (2015). *Hellfire Club.* [online] Wikipedia. Available at: https://en.wikipedia.org/wiki/Hellfire_Club [Accessed 20 Nov. 2015].

Hodapp, C. (2012). *Freemasons For Dummies.* New York: Wiley.

Howard, M. (1989). *The occult conspiracy.* Rochester, Vt.: Destiny Books.

Icke, D. (1999). *The biggest secret.* Scottsdale, Ariz.: Bridge of Love Publications USA.

Icke, D. (2003). *Tales from the time loop.* Wildwood, MO: Bridge of Love.

Inner Temple, (2015). *Inner Temple.* [online] Wikipedia. Available at: https://en.wikipedia.org/wiki/Inner_Temple [Accessed 11 Nov. 2015].

Leonard, T. (2009). *Geronimo's descendants demand return of 'stolen' remains.* [online] Telegraph.co.uk. Available at: http://www.telegraph.co.uk/news/worldnews/northamerica/usa/4691103/Geronimos-descendants-demand-return-of-stolen-remains.html [Accessed 30 Oct. 2015].

Levi, E. (1856). *Baphomet.* [online] Wikipedia. Available at: https://en.wikipedia.org/wiki/Baphomet [Accessed 10 Nov. 2015].

London, (2015). *City of London.* [online] Wikipedia. Available at: https://en.wikipedia.org/wiki/City_of_London [Accessed 10 Nov. 2015].

Maxwell, J., Tice, P., Dyson, R. and Walker, R. (2000). *Matrix of power.* Escondido, CA: Book Tree.

McClellan, J. (2013). *LUCIFER is helping Vatican astronomers look for extraterrestrials?.* [online] Openminds.tv. Available at: http://www.openminds.tv/lucifer-is-helping-vatican-astronomers-look-for-extraterrestrials-970/19968 [Accessed 16 Dec. 2015].

OTO, (2015). *US Grand Lodge » Ordo Templi Orientis.* [online] Oto-usa.org. Available at: http://oto-usa.org/ [Accessed 12 Nov. 2015].

P2, (1976). *Propaganda Due (P2 Mason Lodge).* [online] Wikipedia. Available at: https://en.wikipedia.org/wiki/Propaganda_Due [Accessed 11 Nov. 2015].

Peterson, J. (1999). *LEMEGETON, Part 1: Goetia.* [online] Esotericarchives.com. Available at: http://www.esotericarchives.com/solomon/goetia.htm [Accessed 6 Nov. 2015].

Peterson, J. (2001). *The lesser key of Solomon.* York Beach, Me.: Weiser Books.

Robbins, A. (2002). *Secrets of the tomb.* Boston: Little, Brown.

Robison, J. (2003). *Proofs of a conspiracy against all the religions and governments of Europe.* [Whitefish, Mont.]: Kessinger Pub.

Shaw, J. and McKenney, T. (1988). *The deadly deception.* Lafayette, La.: Huntington House.

Shepherd, T. (2006). *The Good Shepherd (2006).* [online] IMDb. Available at: http://www.imdb.com/title/tt0343737 [Accessed 30 Oct. 2015].

Sitchin, Z. (2013). *The King Who Refused to Die.* [online] Sitchin.com. Available at: http://www.sitchin.com/#refused [Accessed 9 Nov. 2015].

Societies, B. (2015). *Benjamin Franklin's Secret Societies Video - Benjamin Franklin - HISTORY.com.* [online] HISTORY.com. Available at: http://www.history.com/topics/american-revolution/benjamin-franklin/videos/benjamin-franklins-secret-societies [Accessed 20 Nov. 2015].

Springmeier, F. (2002). *Bloodlines of the illuminati.* [Austin, TX]: Ambassador House.

SS, (2015). *Schutzstaffel.* [online] Wikipedia. Available at: https://en.wikipedia.org/wiki/Schutzstaffel [Accessed 30 Oct. 2015].

Sutton, A. (2002). *America's secret establishment*. [Walterville, OR]: Trine Day.

Thompson, T. (2012). *Mafia boss breaks silence over Roberto Calvi killing*. [online] the Guardian. Available at: http://www.theguardian.com/uk/2012/may/12/roberto-calvi-blackfriars-bridge-mafia [Accessed 11 Nov. 2015].

Ulster, (1600). *Plantation of Ulster*. [online] Wikipedia. Available at: https://en.wikipedia.org/wiki/Plantation_of_Ulster [Accessed 30 Oct. 2015].

Vati Leaks, (2012). *Vati Leaks - Keeping the public updated on Church affairs while reinstating suppressed ancient knowledge*. [online] Vatileaks.com. Available at: http://www.vatileaks.com/ [Accessed 11 Nov. 2015].

Williams, P. (2003). *The Vatican exposed*. Amherst, NY: Prometheus Books.

Yallop, D. (1984). *In God's name*. Toronto: Bantam Books.

In all Middle East countries, that are not obedient to the USA, there is civil unrest, civil war and PERMANENT ISLAMIC STATE ACTIVITY.

Lybia	Egypt	Syria	Turkish	Iraq	Afghanistan
Has oil	Suez Canal	Has oil	Kurdistan	Has oil	Has drugs
No US ally	No US ally	No US ally	Has oil	US destroyed	US occupied
Leader killed	Coup d'etat	Civil war	NATO attacked	Leader killed	Civil war

Israel	Jordan	S-Arabia	Oman	UAE	Kuwait
US ally	US ally	Has oil	Has oil	Has oil	Has oil
No ISIS	No ISIS	US ally	US ally	US ally	US ally
		No ISIS	No ISIS	No ISIS	No ISIS

NOTICE ANYTHING? In NO SINGLE pro-USA Middle East country, there is ANY ISLAMIC STATE activity.

7

ILLUMINATI BLOODLINES

"The New World Order is not new, it has been around and developing under one or another guise for a very long time, but it is perceived as a development of the future which is not the case; the New World Order is past and present."

— JOHN COLEMAN, THE CONSPIRATOR'S HIERARCHY: THE COMMITTEE OF 300

Dr. John Coleman

The **Black Nobility** is a super wealthy aristocracy of elite ruling families – 13 in all, who solidified their power base in the 12th century, by inter-marrying with the equally wealthy "God Father" families of Venice and Genoa, Italy. During the blood baths of the Christian Crusades, this brutal, Italian oligarchy, captured and exploited the trading routes, creating a monopoly. Over the centuries, the Black Nobility have used their power and wealth to plunder and exploit every corner of the globe.

Dr. John Coleman's excellent book, *The Committee of 300*, details the history of these families. He describes the plethora of assassinations, murders, kidnappings, robbery, rape, black mail, coercion, drug and gun running and terror committed by these in-bred families, on a grand scale.

In **1204 CE**, the Black Nobility parcelled out feudal enclaves to their members, and from this date, the great building-up of power and pressure began. They stopped at nothing until the governments became a closed corporation of the leading Black Nobility families.

The Black Nobility earned its title through dirty tricks and foul play. When the peasant population eventually had enough, they revolted against the monopolies in government. But as is typical, the leaders of the uprising were quickly seized and brutally hanged. They seem to have very imaginative and sick ways to do away with anyone that opposes them, and none more depraved than the British.

A popular form of political execution was **hanged, drawn, and quartered**. Political prisoners were fastened to a hurdle, or wooden panel, and drawn by horse to the place of execution, where they were hanged (almost to the point of death), emasculated (genitals cut off), disembowelled, beheaded, and quartered (ripped into four pieces). The four pieces would then be sent to the four corners of the kingdom so the other slaves could see what happens to dissenters.

This gruesome and unnecessary practise lasted from the mid-12th century until 1870. This demonstrates their lack of empathy or compassion for the people they ruled over.

The Black Nobility uses secret assassinations, murder, blackmail, the bankrupting of opposing citizens or companies, kidnapping, rape and so on... hence their name.

Even today, they still enrich themselves through the illegal and legal drug and arms trade, using well distanced intermediaries to carry out the dirty work. An estimated $300 Billion per year in drug money alone flows into their secret Swiss Bank accounts - untaxed.

Who Are The Black Nobility?

An increasingly number of people is becoming aware that 99% of the Earth's population is controlled by an "elite" 1%, but the Black Nobility consists of less than 1% of the 1% "elite" and nobody on Earth can apply for membership.

In their opinion, they are entitled to rule over the rest of us because they are the direct descendants of the ancient gods – the **Anunnaki**, and thus, consider themselves royal, and even part god like **Gilgamish** did thousands of years ago!

Although the membership does change from time to time due to failing or rising wealth and in-fighting, for the most part, below is the list of oldest and most important as they stand in 2015:

The Royal Houses of the Black Nobility

2) House of Bernadotte, Sweden
3) House of Bourbon, France
4) House of Braganza, Portugal
5) House of Grimaldi, Monaco
6) * House of Guelph, Britain
7) + House of Hanover, Germany
8) House of Hapsburg, Austria
9) House of Hohenzollern, Germany
10) House of Lichtenstein, Liechtenstein
11) House of Nassau, Luxembourg
12) House of Oldenburg, Denmark
13) House of Orange, Netherlands
14) House of Savoy, Italy

* Most powerful + second most powerful

Former Members:

- House of Karadjordjevic, former Yugoslavia
- House of Wettin, Belgium
- House of Wittelsbach, Germany
- House of Württemberg, Germany
- House of Zogu, Albania

All the families listed are connected with the **House of Guelph**, one of the original Black Nobility families of Venice from which the **House of Windsor** and, thus, the present **Queen of England**, Elizabeth II descends.

The Guelphs are so intertwined with the German aristocracy through the **House of Hanover,** that it would take several pages to mention all their connections. However, according to the **Encyclopædia Britannica**:

> *Welf Dynasty,* **English Guelf,** *or Guelph, Italian Guelpho, dynasty of German nobles and rulers who were the chief rivals of the Hohenstaufens in Italy and central Europe in the Middle Ages and who later included the Hanoverian Welfs, who, with the accession of George I to the British throne, became rulers of Great Britain (House of Guelph, 2015).*

Suffice it to say, almost all of the European royal houses originate from the House of Hanover and therefore, from the **House of Guelph** — thus making up the **Black Nobility**.

As an example: the Hanoverian British **King George I** came from the **Duchy of Luneburg**, a part of Northern Germany, which had been governed by the Guelph family since the 12th century. Another is **Prince Philip** of England (QEII husband) AKA the **Duke of Edinburgh**.

He is a prince of both **Greece** and **Denmark** and is a member of the **House of Glücksburg**, which has ruled the Scandinavian country since 1863 and **King Christian IX**.

The Duke only became a naturalised British citizen after marrying Queen Elizabeth II in 1947, and the name "Windsor" only came into being after 1917.

The Hanoverians (Hannoveraner)

Six British monarchs, including **Queen Victoria** and the infamous **King George III** during the American Revolution, were members of the German **House of Hanover**:

1) George I (ruled 1714-1727)
2) George II (ruled 1727-1760)
3) George III (ruled 1760-1820)
4) George IV (ruled 1820-1830)
5) William IV (ruled 1830-1837)
6) Victoria (ruled 1837-1901)

King George III of Britain was a German

Before becoming the first British king of the Hanoverian line in 1714,**George I** (who spoke more German than English) had been the **Duke of Brunswick-Lüneberg** (*der Herzog von Braunschweig-Lüneberg*). The first three royal Georges in the *House of Hannover* (also known as the *House of Brunswick*, Hanover Line) were also electors and dukes of **Brunswick-Lüneberg**. Between 1814 and 1837 the British monarch was also the King of Hanover, then a kingdom in what is now Germany.

Hanover Trivia: New York City's Hanover Square takes its name from the royal line, as does the Canadian province of New Brunswick, and several "Hanover" communities in the U.S. and Canada. Each of the following U.S. states has a town or township named Hanover: Indiana, Illinois, New Hampshire, New Jersey, New York, Maine, Maryland, Massachusetts, Michigan, Minnesota, Ohio, Pennsylvania, Virginia. In Canada: the provinces of Ontario and Manitoba. The German spelling of the city there is **Hannover** (with two n's).

The House of Hanover seems to be German, but is in fact it is Jewish (Ashkenazi). So is the **House of Habsburg**. So it wasn't really the Germans who took over the British throne after all!

Today the **Guelphs** (Windsors) rule by dominating the raw materials market. Indeed, for years they have fixed the price of gold - a commodity they neither produce nor own. The **House of Windsor** also controls the price of copper, zinc, lead, and tin. It is no accident that the principle commodity exchanges are located in London, England.

Companies run by Black Nobility families are **British Petroleum**, **Phibro LLC**, **Royal Dutch Shell**, **Oppenheimer**, **BHP Billiton**, **Rio Tinto** and many, many more.

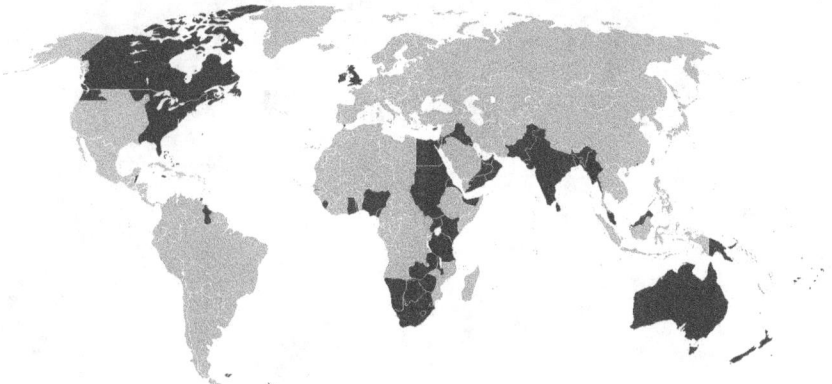

British Empire at its peak

This successful band of inbred, German/Jewish criminals would eventually go on to rule over half the world at the height of the British Empire. This is why the current Queen Elizabeth II is the wealthiest person on the planet, closely followed by Jacob Rothschild, the Queen's *Haus Jude* (House Jew).

The Rothschilds are still below the Queen of England, thus, they still ultimately answer to her. That is because they are not "noble born." The titles the Rothschilds use were bought, not inherited as a birth right. Thus, the Rothschilds can never serve as members of the Black Nobility. But do not underestimate them. They are part of an almost equally powerful cartel known as the **Bloodlines**.

Some of the crests of the Royal Houses

THE BLOODLINES

"Gradually, by selective breeding, the congenital differences between rulers and ruled will increase until they become almost different species. A revolt of the plebs would become as unthinkable as an organised insurrection of sheep against the practice of eating mutton."

—BERTRAND RUSSELL, "The Impact of Science on Society," 1953, pg. 49-50

*Bertrand Russell
(1872 - 1970)*

Co-operating with the European Black Nobility are another 13, very wealthy, and mostly American and European families that have direct bloodlines to the Black Nobility. As we have already noted, the royals of every house are obsessed with in-breeding. Many of these bloodline families are the result of these inbreeding experiments. In fact, it was one of the New World Order's top (UK) men (Bertrand Russell) that gave us an insight into why they continue with inbreeding. It seems they are trying to create a **Master Race** of ruling elites. Hmmmm, now where have we heard that before?

Therefore, we do not refer to these families in terms of *The House of such and such* like we did with the royals. Instead, we say The [family name] Bloodline.

Bloodline Families include:

1) The Astor Bloodline
2) The Bundy Bloodline
3) The Collins Bloodline
4) The DuPont Bloodline
5) The Freeman Bloodline
6) The Kennedy Bloodline
7) The Li Bloodline (China)
8) The Onassis Bloodline
9) The Reynolds Bloodline
10) **+** The Rockefeller Bloodline
11) ***** The Rothschild Bloodline

12) The Russell Bloodline
13) The Van Duyn Bloodline

* most powerful + second most powerful

Together, the Black Nobility and the Bloodlines make up the group we refer to as the Illuminati. Note, they are not the **New World Order**. That is the group they use to carry out their plans.

**Ted Bundy
From US
Serial Killer**

Notorious serial killer Ted Bundy is from The BUNDY Bloodline of the Illuminati.

The Leaders of the Pack

The two houses/bloodlines that dominate the planet, and have done so for over 300 years have been without doubt the **House of Windsor**, and the **Rothschild Bloodline**. Between them, they have carved up the planet and hoarded over half of the wealth of the entire world. The British royals try to pass themselves off as harmless charity workers that have no real power any more. Nothing could be further from the truth. The Rothschilds on the other hand got some true, but bad press in the 1800's, so they simply bought **Reuters** and many other media outlets. Now, you will never hear of their wealth, what they own, and what they get up to. Even still, we are able to get enough information about these two families to gain a decent insight into their criminal ways. I will focus on these two crime families in the next two chapters.

But what about another bloodline family?

Try and think – have you ever heard of **The Collins family**? Who is the patriarch or matriarch? How many children do they have? Where do they live? What nationality are they? How much money do they have? It's ok if you can't answer any of these questions. You were never meant to know any of them. But here is some stuff I sniffed out.

The Collins family has been kept out of the limelight because they have more **occult power** than the Rothschilds or the Rockefellers. Indeed, the Collins family is one of the most powerful families in the world, and yet has been able to hide their power and wealth. The **Van Duyn** family has also hidden themselves very well. But the Collins family is full of tantalizing clues.

Gerald E. Collins drew up genealogical family tree and published it into a book. It shows the Collins family and their relationship to the **Bauer** family, who according to his book, changed their name to **Bower**. That is exactly what the Rothschilds named Bauer did.

The name Collins originated in Ireland as O'Collins, and in Scotland as Kollyns.

Today, a prominent figure in the Occult and New age movement is Kollyns, whose name was originally Collins. Two significant Collins were **Sara Aynn Collins** and her older brother. Her older brother was a member of the Satanists **Hell Fire Club** (the same club Ben Franklin belong to). He belonged to the **Boston Hell Fire Club**.

Sara Aynn Collins (bn. c. 1730) was deeply attracted to the occult. Her family was a generational Witchcraft/Satanic family. Besides not wanting to leave the old family traditions of witchcraft, Sara did not want to marry the man her father tried to sell her to.

Neither the arranged marriage nor forsaking witchcraft was for Sara. She went to Scotland to get to the heart of learning the occult and became a leader in the oldest form of Witchcraft, the **Elven Path**.

Other traditional types of Witchcraft come from Ireland, Wales, and Greece. After the American Revolution, she left Scotland skilled in occult power, and came back to the United States, where she formed her first Coven.

She and her brother were powerful Witches, and their descendants are the main group of Collins that practice Witchcraft and Satanism.

A "wild woman" stabbed Sara Aynn Collins to death in a Boston store. I realise how silly that sounds, but that is how the papers described the event.

It was actually one of her estranged and bitter ex-pupils, possibly an ex lesbian lover, who had gone to live in the wild (on the advice of Sara) to get closer to the nature spirits and arcane magick. After years living in the forest as a "wild-women" and not getting any closer to her goals, she realise she had been duped by Sara. Sara was just trying to get her out of her life. So the woman tracked Sara down and killed her out of bitter revenge.

What you have just received is the important link in tracing the Satanic Collins bloodline.

Sara Aynn Collins (and there were several Sara/Sarah Ann Collins in their family tree-it seems the name appealed to the Collins family) is in turn a descendent of **Francis Collins** of the 17th century. Francis was the head of the family when it emigrated from England to the United States.

Quite a number of Collins have been very wealthy. The wealthiest Collins by far is **Matthew Garrett Collins** (1874-1925). But we only know this because his details were well known at the time because he was an oil baron.

His father was **Oliver Cromwell Collins,** named after **Oliver Cromwell**, the butcher of the English Civil Wars and the massacres at Drogheda and Wexford in Ireland. Oliver Cromwell was an early Freemason who was paid off by the Amsterdam Jews to allow the Jews back into England. Matthew Garrett Collins was a 33 degree Freemason as well. He also manufactured silk and in ten years, took the operation in 1886 from nothing to a $2 million business ($2,000,000 of 1886 dollars would be worth just over $51,280,000 in 2015). He was president of **Interstate Gasoline Co**. and worked with several other big oil men, such as **Governor Charles Haskell** of Oklahoma. Matthew was Trustee for **Drew Seminary** with strong connections with the **Methodist** church.

Matthew Garrett Collins oil operations and friendship with the governor of Oklahoma are very significant. Inside information indicates some type of connection between the Collins family and Oklahoma. Tulsa is a major headquarters for Satanism in that area. There are a number of buildings that the Satanists own in the Tulsa area that are used for their operations.

Besides Matthew Garrett Collins there have been a number of other wealthy Collinses, such as:

Theodore Clyde Collins, Jr. (Insur. co. exec., banker, pres. of etc. etc.),

Arthur Fletcher Collins (real estate corp. exec., head of some financial institutions and an financial analyst),

Henry James Collins 3rd (Insur. Co. exec., treasurer of several financial organisations),

J. Barclay Collins 2nd (oil co. exec., lawyer, bd. dir. of trustee of a hospital),

Leroy Collins, Jr. (banker, dir. or president of some organisations),

John Roger Collins (aerospace co. exec., banker, economist, trustee or bd. of dir. & v.p. of a number of organisations),

John Paul Collins (banker, dir. of Rothschild's Citicorp Research Corp., plus trustee of a hospital, besides holding other leading positions in a number of other organisations.) And finally

Michael James Collins (not the astronaut) who has been an investment co. exec, plus to name a few items-- pres. Fidelity Union Life Ins., pres. Allianz Investment Corp., pres. Collins Capital, Dallas, Trustee KERA-TV, bd. dir. & v.p, of the Carr P. Collins Foundation. None of these men gave information concerning any church affiliation.

The Collins family also built the world's fastest and luxurious ocean going ships during the 1850s, for which they spared no expense. The Collins lost a number of ships to natural sea disasters, and after the financial panic of 1857, the Collins got out of shipping, and directed their attention to coal and iron. They had a home on **Madison Ave., NY.**

One of the Collins who is clearly descended from the old New England family is the banker **Atwood Collins** (1851-1926) who graduated from Yale in 1873. Yale is the home of the secret society known as *Skull and Bones*. One line of Collins that were descended from the old New England family were the father and son who gave their names to several locations in Western US.

Fort Collins, CO is named after Cal. **William Oliver Collins**, a descendent of **Edward Collins** who arrived in Boston from England in 1630. And Casper, Wyoming is named after Col. William O. Collin's son **Casper Collins.**

Casper Collins died fighting Native Americans, and so this family line died out. **Col. William Oliver Collins** family were well-to-do

Episcopalians. W.O. Collins had originally gone to law school, then became a Senator, and then was made a Colonel by the Secretary of War at the outbreak of the Civil War. Because the U.S. troops in the far west were widely dispersed, the rank of Colonel was a very high rank to hold in the western territories during the Civil War. Below is a list of a few Collins who have been directly connected to the Illuminati in their time.

- **Clifton W. Collins**—Clifton studied Saint Simon who was the Mason/Illuminatus that started Communism in the early 19th century. Clifton wrote a book about him called **Saint Simon**.
- **Copp Collins**—Copp Collins was involved in so many political things for the republican Presidential elections, and involved with consulting Federal agencies and so many other government positions it is difficult to give a list of what all he has been involved with. He also was involved with **Bahrain Petroleum Co.**, Ltd during the 1950s.
- **DeWitt Clinton Collins**—DeWitt Clinton Collins was born on Sept. 5, 1866 and was named after DeWitt Clinton, who was part of the Illuminati very early in the history of the United States. His father, Clinton DeWitt was also named after DeWitt Clinton. D.C. Collins did his post-graduate work in Vienna, and practiced in Chicago.
- **Hugh Collins**—Authored **Marxism and the Law** published by **Oxford University Press**
- **James Foster Collins**—Worked for U.S. intelligence, for the United Nations, graduated from Yale (Skull and Bones), had such jobs as Research assistant U.S. Senate Atomic Energy Commission, political affairs officer United Nations Secretariat (1946-1949), By the way, a large percentage of the officers in the Secretariat area of the United Nations for the first 10 years were Ashkenazi Jews. Collins also worked for the US State Department and the Treasury Department, perhaps maintaining his intelligence work on the side.
- **John Anderson Collins**—He was intimately involved with the illuminati plots involving Unitarians/Rosicrucians/ Masons which created militant abolitionists who intended to wage war against the South. He worked with **William Lloyd Garrison**, a prominent American abolitionist, journalist, suffragist, and social reformer. John Anderson Collins was a socialist (forerunner of what is

known as communism). He attempted several communist social experiments beginning in the 1840s. The importance of how this all connects to the occult and the Illuminati can be appreciated by reading *Fire in The Minds of Men* by **James Billington.**

- **John Churton Collins**—In 1886 he wrote a book on **Voltaire**, and in 1908 he wrote yet another book on Voltaire. As a lecturer who travelled to the U.S. and Germany, the press always gave him great press coverage. He was involved with the occult. He was found dead in peculiar circumstances in a ditch.
- **Launa Collins and Virginia Collins** co. authored a book *Levels of Mind* in 1984.
- **Mauney D. Collins**—Mauney Collins was State Superintendent of Schools in Georgia. He went to Bob Jones College sometime after 1938. He was a **Freemason**, a **Grand Master of the Georgia Grand Lodge of Odd Fellows**, assoc. editor of the Ga. Odd Fellows News, and editor of Atlanta's Masonic magazine. He was in **Eastern Star**, and a number of other affiliated Masonic groups. He lived at the Capital Building at the state capital in Georgia. He was a pastor (ordained in 1909) of **Friendship Baptist Church** for his lifetime.
- **Paul Valorous Collins**—writer, studied art in Paris, interviewed Italian strongman **Benito Mussolini** in 1927 for *Outlook Magazine*. Presbyterian and a Freemason.
- **Robert DeVille Collins**—Foreign Service Officer, Intelligence, **1st Secretary to NATO** (73-76), **Director Political Officer of Personnel of the US. State Dept.** (80-82). He also worked in the U.S. embassy in Rome in various capacities, and as a Roman Catholic, he was given an award by the Pope.
- **Ross A. Collins**—Ross A. Collins was a high ranking **Freemason**, a lawyer, an **Attorney General** (a common position for Satanists), and a **Congressman**. He was born at Collinsville, Miss. While in Congress at Washington, D.C. he was chairman of the Military Appropriation Committee (the war-monger committee), and a position which the Illuminati control. Ross Collins was famous for advocating mechanised weaponry. He wanted technology to be applied to weaponry. He is credited with bringing the *B-17 Flying Fortress* into being. By the way there have been many Collins who were Masons, for instance, the masonic reference book *History of Scottish Rite Masonry* in Chicago,

also titled **Oriental Consistory 1856-1907** by **George Warvelle**, a 33° Masson, lists twelve Collins as being members of Chicago's Oriental Consistory (pp. 99-100).

- **William Collins**-his British Collins Publishing Firm has printed some books on British Intelligence (MI-5, MI-6) with deep insider information.
- **Joan Collins**—Dame Joan Henrietta Collins, DBE is an English actress, author, and columnist associated with a long list of key Illuminati men and at least a few known Satanists. You can only get a title like "Dame" or "Sir" if you are "in the club" so to speak.

Other **Committee of 300** families include Agnelli, Balliol, Beale, Bell, Bouvier, Bush, Cameron, Campbell, Carnegie, Carrington, Coolidge, Delano, Douglas, Ford, Gardner, Graham, Hamilton, Harriman, Heinz, Kuhn, Lindsay, Loeb, Mellon, Montgomery, Morgan, Norman, Oppenheimer, Rhodes, Roosevelt, Russell, Savoy, Schiff, Seton, Spencer, Stewart/Stuart, Taft, and Wilson. There are many others of less notoriety.

An understanding of the top 13 families and the *Committee of 300* opens up a whole new understanding of history. In fact, the full extent of the power of the top 13 families is far greater than what I am able to communicate here. This is because of their skill at secrecy. It was no accident that Hitler's Rothschild blood was hidden.

A common practice among the top 13 families is to have an important child secretly or quietly without fanfare, and adopt the child out to another family. The child then takes on another last name, which hides the genealogy. In the occult ceremonies, the biological parents will step forward.

For instance, for **Mothers of Darkness**, the biological father must impregnate the young daughter who is being initiated into the Mothers of Darkness. The first baby by the girl must come from her biological father and must be sacrificed by her to Satan. Many of the Illuminati's second children are adopted out, just like **President Bill Clinton** was.

The Story of Bush and Clinton Alliance

Bill is actually related to the Bush family. Indeed that is why they regularly have holidays, long weekends, and golfing days together while Bill and George W were serving as President and since. Bill and George W always refer to each other in private as "brothers," but in

Bill Clinton with sweet old Dad George HW Bush

their public political career they pretended to be rivals (Daily Mail, 2011).

Indeed, in a candid 2014 interview with the two, "George W. Bush's face creases into a broad grin and his eyes twinkle at mention of Bill Clinton, the man he calls his **brother from another mother**. George W stated, "*My Sweet Dad, a wonderful father to Bill Clinton and me*" while reminiscing about his (their) father "*George HW Bush, the 41st president, who is now 90, wheelchair-bound and in failing health*" (Harnden, 2014).

While on the subject of the **Bush-Clinton Crime Syndicate**, because that is what they are, let's have a quick look at some of the work they have done together.

According to the excellent research done by **Roger Stone**, the Bushes and the Clintons worked together to steal vast sums of money from a charity that was supposed to help **Haitian earthquake** victims.

"They spend $10 million in Haiti, there's $128 million missing, they close the non-profit and they answer no questions – they're profiteering....it's the Bush-Clinton crime syndicate," said Stone.

In an interview with veteran news reported **Larry King** about his new book, ***The Clintons' War on Women*** (Stone and Morrow, 2015), Stone also asserted that,

> *"The narrative of Hillary Clinton's [Presidential] campaign, that she has been an advocate for women and girls, is just bogus," Stone told King. "She is, in fact, an abuser of women and girls."*

Stone said the assertion was justified based on Hillary covering for her husband's behaviour.

> *"Bill is a sexual predator, very much like Bill Cosby," said Stone. "I tracked 27 women that he has either assaulted or raped."*

When Larry King challenged Stone to identify the women, charging that they had "never come forward," Stone named names. Stone noted Hillary's culpability for this behaviour by asserting,

> *"She's not just an enabler....she's the one who hires the private detectives who wage a veritable terror campaign against these women to silence them. What did she call them? Bimbos, whores, sluts, bitches, they're her words not mine, these women unlucky enough to be sexually assaulted by her husband," said Stone.*

Stone cited the example of **Kathleen Willey**, a White House volunteer who went public and claimed that she was groped by Bill Clinton in 1993. After the alleged incident, Stone said Willey had her home ransacked, her windshield smashed, her tyres slashed and her cat strangled.

> *"She's out jogging, a man jogs up to her all dressed in black – **Jack Palladino** [a private investigator] – and he says 'how's your cat, did you ever replace that cat? How are your kids Johnny and Sally, you know we know where they go to school – you're not getting it are you?'"*

Not many people are aware that when the biggest drug dealer in Arkansas got busted he hired Hillary Clinton as his lawyer. She then was able to secure a pardon from Governor Bill Clinton. Do you see anything wrong with that? The Clintons and George H.W. Bush oversaw an operation that trafficked millions of dollars of cocaine into the United States (Stone, 2015).

Another documentary worth watching is by Clinton insider, **Larry Nichols**, who served on the Clinton team from the beginning in Arkansas, when Bill was running for Governor, then right up to his Presidential campaign. *The New Clinton Chronicles 2015* exposes their colossal list of lies, deceptions, and depravities, including the trafficking of CIA cocaine through Mena, Arkansas; Bill Clinton's serial sexual predator activity and "bimbo eruptions", which were virtually ignored by the media in Arkansas, to Hillary's trail of death as *Secretary of State* and her rise to the Presidency.

The New Clinton Chronicles 2015 covers territory spanning the legacy of Bill and Hillary Clinton the establishment media has ignored (Nichols, 2015). Interestingly, Nichols commented that when he watch the brilliant HBO series, **House of Cards**, starring Kevin Spacey, that he was shocked at how closely the character of **Claire Underwood** (Robin Wright) matched Hilary Clinton.

The original 1994 Chronicles here: (Citizens, 1994)

Illuminati Genealogy

To try and trace the genealogy of the Illuminati is almost impossible without insider information. In fact, due to a number of reasons, many people with last names which are different than the top 13 bloodlines still have the magical occult power in their blood. Once a branch loses its occult power, its blood is nothing, and that family is cast aside.

Who is Who, in the Illuminati Zoo

As we will see, important events in our world are being moulded by those 13 families secretly. They do this through their many Secret Societies, tax free Foundations, Global Corporations, the Military Industrial Complex, and their favourite – wars, wars, and more wars.

So now we know "who" runs the world from the very top of the pyramid, let's have a look at "how" they administer their **Will**, and control on the masses. They have had a long time to figure all this out -- over 800 years, however it has been in the last 250 years that they really got their act together, and to be honest, their attention to detail is impressive.

On the following pages is the current structure of the world power, or how it is administered from a broad perspective. It is more or less in hierarchical order – from top to bottom. Each group usually reports and answers to the group above.

THE CURRENT WORLD ORDER HIERARCHY

Ruling/Governing Elite – The Illuminati

- **World Monarch** (QEII) – to be replaced by Prince William
  - **Crown Council of 13** (World's richest and most powerful ruling families of the Illuminati bloodlines)
    - **Committee of 300** (World's richest and most powerful sub-families and oligarchs from the NWO bloodlines)

Priest Class – Part of the Illuminati

- Freemasons / Rosicrucians
  - Knights of Malta
  - Jesuits / Vatican
  - Skull and Bones / Bohemian Grove
    - Many other smaller groups that come under the Freemasons.

The Action Groups - New World Order

- Fabian Society
- The Bilderberg Group
  - The Round Table Groups
    - The Club of Rome
    - Council on Foreign Relations
    - Trilateral Commission
    - Tavistock
      - Several other Think Tanks
      - United Nations

World Financial Control

(Answer to Rothschilds who work with Bilderbergers / Comm 300)
- Bank of International Settlement (Rothschilds)
- IMF (Rothschilds)

- Central Banks inc. Federal Reserve Bank of America etc.
  - Interest Revenue
  - Tax Revenue
  - World Bank (Rothschilds)
  - World Stock Exchanges
  - WTO (Rothschilds)

World Resource Control

(Answer to Bilderbergers / Round Tables)
- **Oil:** Exxon Mobil (USA) / Royal Dutch Shell (Neth) / BP (UK) / Sinopec (Singapore) / China National Petroleum (China)
- **Mining:** BHP Billiton (UK) / Rio Tinto (UK) / Vale (Brasil)/ Glencore Xstrata (UK) / China Shenhua Energy (China)
- **Global Corporations** (Fortune 500 companies)
- **Drug Cartels** (Guadalajara Cartel, Sinoloa Cartel, Tijuana Cartel, Juárez Cartel, Gulf Cartel, Bush, Clinton, Monarchies)

Military Industrial Complex

(Answer to Bilderbergers / Round Tables Groups / Comm 300)
- Google, Facebook, LinkedIn etc. (data gathering services)
- Lockheed Martin, Boeing, BAE Systems, General Dynamics, Raytheon, Northrop Grumman and many others
  - Captured UFO/Alien technology
- Special Forces: Navy Seals, Delta Force, Israel Mista'arvim,
- Spies eg: CIA; MI6; MI5; Mossad

World Population Control

(Answer to Round Table Groups – Commonwealth Nations answer to Fabian Society)
- Governments / Presidents / Prime Ministers
  - Police / Military
    - Education system
    - Major Religions
    - Media / Music Industry / Hollywood

The Main World Population – Debt Slaves

- YOU ARE HERE

The current world order hierarchy

The Governing Body

Key members from both groups, as well as other elite scientists, bankers, academics and billionaires, make up the group known as **The Committee of 300.** The *Committee of 300* is essentially the governing body, or steering committee that controls the world.

The Committee of 300 evolved out of the British East India Company's Council of 300 which was founded in 1727 by the British Royal family. For decades the British East India and Dutch East India

Companies amassed fortunes from their opium trade with China and now through the Committee of 300 they continue to wage phony drug wars around the world today.

> The Committee of 300 is the ultimate secret society made up of an untouchable ruling class, which includes the Queen of England, the Queen of the Netherlands, the Queen of Denmark, and the royal families of Europe. These aristocrats decided at the death of Queen Victoria, the matriarch of the Venetian Black Guelphs that, in order to gain world-wide control, it would be necessary for its aristocratic members to 'go into business' with the non-aristocratic but extremely powerful leaders of corporate business on a global scale, and so the doors to ultimate power were opened to what the Queen of England likes to refer to as 'the commoners.' - John Coleman, "Conspirators' Hierarchy"

Some notable members of the Committee of 300 include: The British Royal family, Dutch Royal family, House of Hapsburg, House of Orange, Duke of Alba, Prince Philip Duke of Edinburgh, Lord Carrington, Lord Halifax, Lord Alfred Milner, John Jacob and Waldorf of the Astor Illuminati bloodline, Winston Churchill, Cecil Rhodes, Queen Elizabeth II, Queen Juliana, Queen Beatrix, Queen Magreta, King Haakon of Norway, Colonel Mandel House, Aldous Huxley, John Forbes, Averill Harriman, William and McGeorge Bundy, George Bush, Prescott Bush, Henry Kissinger, J.P. Morgan, Maurice Strong, David Rockefeller, David and Evelyn Rothschild, Paul, Max and Felix Warburg, Ormsby and Al Gore, Bertrand Russell, Sir Earnest and Harry of the Oppenheimer Illuminati bloodline, Warren Buffet, Giuseppe Mazzini, Sir William Hesse, George Schultz, H.G. Wells, and Ted Turner

> In the Committee of 300, which has a 150-year history, we have some of the most brilliant intellects assembled to form a completely totalitarian, absolutely controlled 'new' society only it isn't new, having drawn most of its ideas from the Clubs of Cultus

> *Diabolicus. It strives toward a One World Government rather well described by one of its late members, H. G. Wells, in his work commissioned by the Committee which Wells boldly called: 'The Open Conspiracy: Blue Prints for a World Revolution.' - John Coleman, "Conspirators' Hierarchy*

Authors such as **H.G. Wells** and **Aldous Huxley** were not speculating or warning of the future societies they wrote about. In fact they were often commissioned to write such "predictive programming" books based on the Committee's actual plans. People read something like **A Brave New World** and create an imaginary science-fiction rift between their present reality and what seems like a possible future. Meanwhile, the royals, the Committee of 300, the elite pushers and movers incrementally implement measures toward those very controlled sci-fi societies.

Aurelio Peccei, Club of Rome founder and Committee of 300 member, in his book **The Chasm Ahead** writes about the Committee of 300's plans to "tame" the common man whom he refers to as "The Enemy."

Head of this group is of course the World Monarch, Queen **Elizabeth II of Britain**, but the day to day running and orders being distributed are done by others. The Queen is just a figure head, unless there is an internal dispute which she will judge on, or in the event she has a specific request to be carried out (like the death of Diana).

Once they have nutted out a new global action, agenda or strategy, which includes things like where the next war will be, who will be the next world leader (Presidents / Prime Minister etc.) the price of oil, gold, and commodities – who will be elevated to celebrity status, who will be demoted from celebrity status (a scandal) - which currency will rise or fall – and many other things. They then delegate these agendas to carry out to **Action Groups.**

The Action Groups are the groups that get the job done so to speak. But because there are many areas within society that they want to control, they have had to create many action groups over the years. Some have become powerful in their own right, while others have gone by the wayside as they are no longer relevant. It is the most powerful of these groups that we call the **New World Order.**

The Action Groups also feed information and data back to the Committee of 300. They in turn use this latest information to help them strategize their next move. Internally, they call this the **Grand Chess Board**. It is very important to realise that these world "leaders" and controllers do not care one iota about you, me, or any of the other 7 billion people on this planet. They only care about their own agendas, and never being found out.

Believe me, their greatest fear is a public uprising against them, so they spend a great deal of time and money ensuring that never happens. Some of these leeches have private armies that are better trained and equipped then the United States Army.

Many have fortresses and redoubts buried deep underground that are impenetrable to conventional weapons. How they get away with their crimes against humanity is by keeping it on a "need-to-know" basis, and compartmentalising departments and groups, so only a few know the whole story. Finally, as a sure way to keep the nosey public out of their affairs, they maintain a closed loop.

The Closed Loop

The info/data stream back and forth is a closed loop that you and I do not have access to. That is why phoning your Congressman, or writing to your local MP will never achieve anything. They are not in

Anti-Vietnam War protest in Washington D.C 1969

the slightest bit interested in your opinion or concerns, and even if they wanted to change something, they would never get permission from their bosses. And if they do it without permission from above, you end up like John Kennedy. That is why not even mass protests, no matter how many people show up for it, are of any interest to them.

Indeed, some may remember back to November 16, **1969** when there was a mass, anti-Vietnam War protest in Washington D.C. Over **300,000** people came out in support against the war, and over one million across the country (Herbers, 1969).

Did it stop the war? Did it change anything? Did the Politicians listen? No.

The Vietnam War bloodbath continued for another five years. In fact, U.S. military involvement ended on 15 August 1973. The capture of Saigon by the North Vietnamese Army in April 1975 marked the end of the war, and North and South Vietnam were reunified the following year. So US intervention achieved absolutely nothing. The deaths of thousands of United States, Thailand, Australian, New Zealand, and the Philippines soldiers achieved absolutely nothing.

A detailed demographic study calculated 791,000–1,141,000 war-related deaths for all of Vietnam. Between 240,000 and 300,000 Cambodians died during the war. About 60,000 Laotians also died, and **58,300 U.S. military personnel** were killed (Casualties, 2015).

The soldiers did not want to be there. The people of America did not want to be there. Yet, 58,300 Americans died for no reason other than to make billions for the **Military Industrial Complex**. If you look back at the control system hierarchy above, we also know that it made billions for the **World Resource** gang, the **World Financial** gang, and the **Think Tanks**. Indeed, everyone got a piece of the pie, except those on the very bottom. They just supply the meat for the grinder. I wonder what would happen if we just stopped supplying the meat?

The point is, "We the people" are outside the loop, therefore our phone calls, letters, pleas, protests, and concerns are never actioned on by these people. They already have their plan which was years in the making. They all want to get rich and powerful, and this is their chance. Why on earth would they change their well laid plans just because a few "plebs" protest"? The sooner you realise you are not in their world, your opinion does not matter to them, and they hate you -- the sooner you can start to remedy the problem. On the next page is a diagram representation of how the closed loop and organisation works.

The Main Action Groups – The New World Oder:

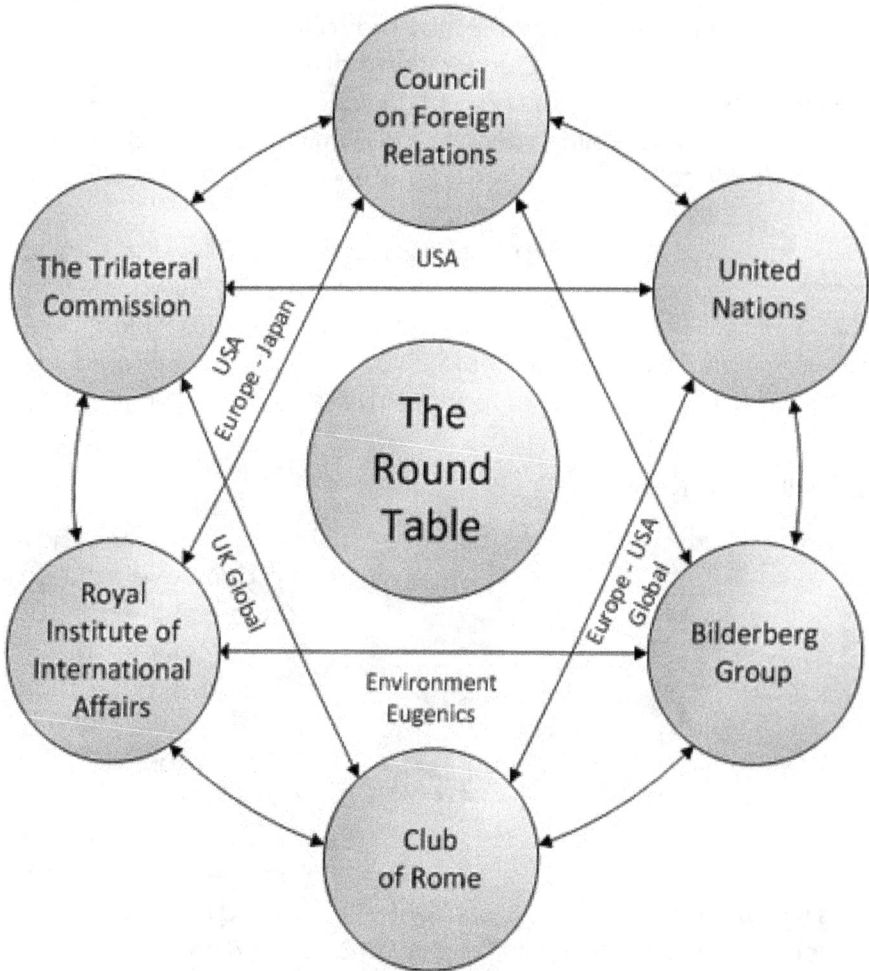

Council on Foreign Relations

The Trilateral Commission

United Nations

USA

The Round Table

USA

Europe - Japan

UK Global

Europe - USA

Global

Royal Institute of International Affairs

Bilderberg Group

Environment Eugenics

Club of Rome

The closed loop that runs the world - we can't get in!

All of these groups originated from the *Committee of 300* and therefore from the European *Black Nobility* families. The Round Table group in the middle is responsible for disseminating information between the action groups and the *Committee of 300*. It is these action groups, also called "round table" groups that is referred to as the **New World Order** (NWO).

There are also many other groups that are part of the New World Order such as **Tavistock, Brookings Institute**, the **RAND** corporation to name but a few. These tend to work for the main action groups. You may also notice, that your government, on any level, does not appear in this diagram. That is because they are so far down the chain that don't even rate as "leaders" or decision makers. They are only there to give you the illusion that you have a choice.

Note – the **New World Order** and the **Illuminati** are two (2) **separate** entities. They do work together a lot of the time, but they also work independently at different times.

In fact, all of the *13 Ruling Families* cross over between the Illuminati and NWO, but only about 50% of the *Committee of 300* do. Most of the average stooges that work for the NWO have no idea about the Illuminati and what they get up to. It is only the very ambitious, aggressive, and ruthless ones that get invited to join the Illuminati.

It is all in the News

If you follow global news on a daily level, you can see some of the agendas the *Committee of 300* is working on at the moment.

For example, right now in 2015 there is a global drive for same sex marriage.

Monsignor Krysztof Olaf Charamsa and his gay partner

This is happening in every major country in the world at the same time. Indeed, this is taken straight from the *Protocols of Zion* – No. 15!

Even the Catholic Church are jumping on the bandwagon. A Polish priest who served with the Vatican's doctrinal arm, Monsignor **Krysztof Olaf Charamsa,** held a news conference October 4, 2015 in Rome, with his partner at his side, calling on **Pope Francis** to revise Catholic doctrine on homosexuality, which considers same-sex relationships sinful.

Charamsa, 43, said the timing of the announcement was intended to put the topic before the **Synod of Bishops**. The three-week assembly of bishops from around the world were addressing issues facing Catholic families. The Pope responded by stripping Charamsa of all duties at Vatican (Borghese and Grinberg, 2015). Coincidence? Hardly.

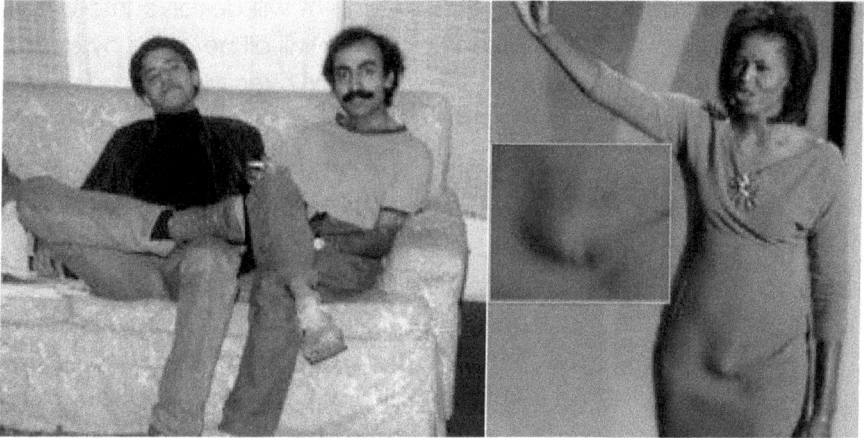

Barack Obama with gay lover and Michelle showing "bumps"

And don't worry about Charamsa losing his job. That is all part of the charade. They just want to stir up public opinion and sympathy, and get people talking. So what better way than a controversy.

In the USA, in the wake of a 2015 landmark Supreme Court ruling that allowed same-sex couples nationwide to marry, the White House was illuminated in rainbow colours for the evening to "celebrate" the ruling (Malloy and de Vries, 2015). Perhaps that is because President Obama is a known gay, and Michelle Obama is a known transsexual. In fact, after **Joan Rivers** publically stated that President Obama was gay and Michelle Obama is a transsexual, she mysteriously died just two months later (Watson, 2014). If you doubt these claims, please watch the video referenced here: (Tranny, 2015)

Why would the system be pushing gay marriage? Well, beside the fact that over 70% of the NWO are homosexual, or have engaged in homosexual activities, it is simply because they want to destroy the traditional family unit and cut down on population. By destroying the family, and traditional family values, it makes it easier for them to control us. And of course, their favourite pastime – cutting down the population of "useless eaters" as Prince Phillip of England likes to call us.

Civil War on the Agenda

Indeed, it is widely accepted that the USA economy will be crashed – on purpose, very soon – maybe by 2017. This will trigger **Martial Law**, and massive **civil disobedience**. Eventually it will devolve into a **civil war** by 2020 or so – give or take 2 years. This will all be done by design and by stealth. It has been in the works for over two decades. We know about this as well because:

- The Denver Post, on February 15th, 2013 ran an Associated Press article entitled: *Homeland Security aims to buy 1.6b rounds of ammo*. It confirmed that the Department of Homeland Security (DHS) issued an open purchase order for 1.6 billion rounds of ammunition. Some of this purchase order was for hollow-point rounds, forbidden by international law for use in war, along with a frightening amount of specialised rounds for snipers. Also reported elsewhere, at the height of the Iraq War the Army was expending less than 6 million rounds a month. Therefore 1.6 billion rounds would be enough to sustain a hot war for 20+ years. In America!
- Add to this perplexing excessive purchase of ammo, DHS now is showing off its acquisition of heavily armoured personnel carriers, repatriated from the Iraqi and Afghani theatres of operation. These are known as MRAP's, and are essentially

MRAP's being used by local Police and DHS – why?

tanks. They all have gun ports for .30 calibre and .50 calibre machine guns (normally used to shoot down aircraft or tanks), and can withstand IEDs, mine blasts, and .50 calibre hits to bullet-proof glass. These MRAP's are being delivered to DHS and to Police (Benko, 2013). Why would they need such over-the-top vehicles on U.S. streets? In a war zone yes, definitely, but to protect the men and women on the streets of America? I hardly think so.

Seriously, why would DHS and Police need such a vehicle on US streets unless they were planning Martial Law, and a civil war – for a long time!

You can see now why disunited family groups would be an advantage to the NWO private armies. Furthermore, by promoting gay relationships, you will drastically reduce the amount of new born children which is in line with the eugenics cult movement.

And no, I am not gay bashing! I really could not care less what people do in the privacy of their own homes. In fact, I believe love is love, no matter if it is between a man and a woman, a man and a man, or a woman and a woman. Gay love is often a soul lesson in the Mature Soul phase. However, I am just pointing out it is a set agenda to highlight how things work. You need to be able to connect the dots.

Another agenda going on in the United States at the moment is trying to start a Race war, mainly between blacks and whites, but they are stirring up the Latinos as well.

Again, this is a "divide and conquer" plan. Trust me, if there was a civil war against a corrupt government, and that government wanted to win, wouldn't you prefer to have the population fighting each other, at the same time they are trying to fight you? In this situation, the very worst thing the people of the United States could do is to turn on their fellow citizens.

You are **all** Americans for goodness sake, so start acting like it. I know this is a horrible thing to say and imagine, but all burnt and charred bodies on a battlefield look the same, they are all black on the outside, and red on the inside. Bombs from your true enemy do not discriminate, so neither should you.

As I have already mentioned. The Illuminati have their weird belief that if they tell us what they are planning, then it cancels out any negative Karma from their act. If you are not sure how Karma works, please read my first book in this series (*Book 1 Secrets of the Soul*). But

FEMA camps are already all over the US and ready for business

please believe me when I say, Karma does not work this way, and they will still have to pay back their negative Karma.

One of these days, probably when **Hilary Clinton** or another NWO stooge is President, they will finally get their way and bring in gun controls in the US. This is a known spark point in the United States, and they know that, and hope for it. If the public lash back, that is all they need to say, "*See, these people are dangerous, we must arrest them, and take everyone else's guns for your safety.*"

facebook.com/LoveYourGunRights

1. The government pushes gun laws/bans to partially take our guns.
2. The government purchases 1.6 BILLION rounds of ammunition for "domestic use." That is 5 bullets per American citizen's head.

And we're not supposed to be worried..?

facebook.com/LoveYourGunRights

This panic (with the help from the media) will cause some "gun people" to make a last stance against the military like Police. It will be a blood bath on both sides, coming to you live, on CNN and other news channels.

Watched by millions of terrified people in their homes. It will be so shocking and so traumatic, that when the dust settles, the government will announce Martial Law (using foreign troops) – to "protect" the public from these evil gun bandits. The system knows this will probably spark a civil war. At the same time they will stir up racist wars between Whites, Blacks, and Latinos, again to have another reason to lock people up in a FEMA camp and confiscate their firearms.

The System WANTS a Civil War

Yes, that is right. In the US Inc. right now, it would be their dream come true to have a red hot civil war. Therefore, if they create a false flag to start it, and if you do fight back, you are giving them exactly what they want. A civil war will destroy the United States from within. Then they will use foreign UN troops to come in and mop up. No more USA, no more US Constitution. No more Bill of Rights. Those two documents have been their biggest headache from the beginning. But Obama has managed to shred a lot of the Constitution already, now they just need this final blow.

I really, really hope I am wrong. If there is never a civil war, or Martial Law, that would be the best news I could hear, and I would happily admit it that I got it wrong. But while guys like this are running the country, I won't hold my breath.

This is **Rahm Emanuel** (Rothschild Zionist) who was Obama's Chief of Staff in the White House, ex Israel soldier, and is now Mayor of Chicago (thanks to Obama). I will leave with a quote from this psychopath that sums it all up:

"You never let a serious crisis go to waste. And what I mean by that it's an opportunity to do things you think you could not do before."

Rahm Emanuel (1959 -)

References:

Citizens, (1994). *The Clinton Chronicles 1994*. [online] YouTube. Available at: https://youtu.be/VHlMuUdeESA [Accessed 4 Nov. 2015].

Coleman, J. (1997). *The conspirators' hierarchy*. Carson City, NV: WIR.

House of Guelph, (2015). *Welf Dynasty | German history*. [online] Encyclopedia Britannica. Available at: http://www.britannica.com/topic/Welf-Dynasty [Accessed 16 Aug. 2015].

Icke, D. (2011). *David Icke Problem Reaction Solution*. [online] YouTube. Available at: https://youtu.be/0GEMbl7-14w [Accessed 20 Oct. 2015].

Malloy, A. and de Vries, K. (2015). *White House lights with rainbow colors - CNNPolitics.com*. [online] CNN. Available at: http://edition.cnn.com/2015/06/26/politics/white-house-rainbow-marriage/ [Accessed 28 Dec. 2015].

Nichols, L. (2015). *The New Clinton Chronicles 2015*. [online] YouTube. Available at: https://youtu.be/SS7uSmG-R34 [Accessed 4 Nov. 2015].

Springmeier, F. (2007). *Bloodlines of the illuminati*. Denver, CO: Pentracks Publications, LLC.

Stone, R. (2015). *Political Strategist: Hillary Clinton is "An Abuser of Women & Girls"*. [online] YouTube. Available at: https://youtu.be/4q3vaV6EYZ0 [Accessed 4 Nov. 2015].

Stone, R. and Morrow, R. (2015). *The Clintons' war on women*. New York: Skyhorse Publishing.

Tranny, (2015). *Michelle Obama Is A MAN!!(PROOF) PT.1/2*. [online] YouTube. Available at: https://youtu.be/IA-tSKiyHP0 [Accessed 28 Dec. 2015].

Victoria and Albert, (2015). *Grandchildren of Victoria and Albert*. [online] Wikipedia. Available at: https://en.wikipedia.org/wiki/Grandchildren_of_Victoria_and_Albert#Victoria.2C_Albert_and_their_children [Accessed 16 Aug. 2015].

Walia, A. (2015). *US Intelligence Officer: "Every Single Terrorist Attack In US Was A False Flag Attack"* [online] Collective-Evolution. Available at: http://www.collective-evolution.com/2015/05/15/us-intelligence-officer-every-single-terrorist-attack-in-us-was-a-false-flag-attack/ [Accessed 20 Oct. 2015].

Watson, P. (2014). *Joan Rivers Dead Two Months After Calling Obama Gay, Michelle a Tranny*. [online] Infowars.com. Available at: http://www.infowars.com/joan-rivers-dead-two-months-after-calling-obama-gay-michelle-a-tranny/ [Accessed 28 Dec. 2015].

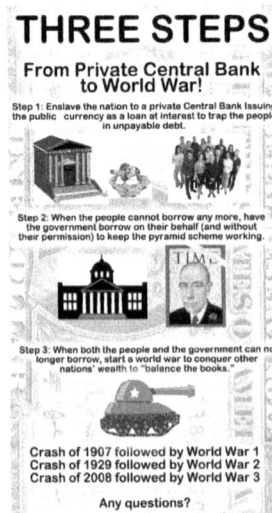

THREE STEPS

From Private Central Bank to World War!

Step 1: Enslave the nation to a private Central Bank Issuing the public currency as a loan at interest to trap the people in unpayable debt.

Step 2: When the people cannot borrow any more, have the government borrow on their behalf (and without their permission) to keep the pyramid scheme working.

Step 3: When both the people and the government can no longer borrow, start a world war to conquer other nations' wealth to "balance the books."

Crash of 1907 followed by World War 1
Crash of 1929 followed by World War 2
Crash of 2008 followed by World War 3

Any questions?

8

SECRET SOCIETIES OF THE ILLUMINATI

Manly Palmer Hall
(1901 - 1990)

"Secret societies have existed among all peoples, savage and civilized, since the beginning of recorded history...It is beyond question that the secret societies of all ages have exercised a considerable degree of political influence..."

—MANLEY P. HALL

*T*he largest mechanism used by the bloodlines to implement the New World Order agenda is the global secret society network. Politicians, bankers, businessmen, and media personalities - the biggest names in history and world affairs form a huge secret society matrix. This hierarchical pyramid structured network is constantly recruiting and placing members in key influential positions.

Where did Secret Societies come from?

History is filled with whispers of secret societies. Accounts of elders or priests who guarded the forbidden knowledge of ancient peoples. Prominent men, meeting in secret, who directed the course of civilization are recorded in the writings of all people.

The oldest is the **Brotherhood of the Snake**, now called the **Brotherhood of the Dragon**, and it still exists behind the scene of the many different secret societies today.

The original secret society was set up by Enki, to help humans. They were taught and trained in all things Anunnaki, as well as deep spiritual knowledge that will assist humanity to Ascend. Unfortunately, Enki's rogue son **Marduk** (aka Amon Ra in Egypt) infiltrated and corrupted Enki's original Brotherhood. This caused those loyal to Enki to split off and become **The Brotherhood of Light**, while the weaker and base human Priests continued with the Brotherhood of the Dragon.

It is from the Dragon Brotherhood that every other "dark" Order sprang from. Each is corrupt, and loyal to their master, Marduk.

It is clear that religion has always played a significant role in the course of these organisations. Communication with a higher source, often divine, is a familiar claim in all but a few. Indeed, the original "secret societies" were of the "Priest Class." Later they included royalty, then even later, very wealthy aristocrats or the "Ruling Class."

The secrets of these groups are thought to be so profound, that only a chosen, well-educated few are able to understand and use them. They refer to non-members as "profane" and unenlightened, both terms meaning stupid and ignorant.

They hide all manner of information from humanity, most of which could help humans to grow and prosper. Instead, like spoilt children, they horde their knowledge in the darkness. So what attracts a person to join a secret society, once they have been tapped?

Everyone likes to be Part of the "Cool" People

This is found in all human endeavours, even those which are not secret, such as football teams or country clubs. This exclusivity of membership is actually one of the secret societies' most powerful weapons. There is the use of signs, passwords, and other tools. These have always performed valuable functions in man's organisations everywhere. The stated reason, almost always different from the real reason, for the societies' existence is important.

It's nice to have friends

The comradeship is especially important. Sharing hardships or secrets has always been a special thrill to man. No one who has undergone the rigours of boot camp is ever likely to forget the special feeling of belonging and comradeship that was shared between the victims of the drill sergeant or company commander. It is an emotion born of initiation. The most potent tool of any secret society is the ritual surrounding initiation. These special binding ceremonies have very deep meaning for the participants.

The Beginning of "Ritual"

Initiation performs several functions which make up the heart and soul of any true secret society. Like graduating from Law school, the initiation into the niche world of Law is important to aspects of human thought, that are universally compelling. Once members of the fraternity of Law, they train and maintain the efforts of the group to operate in a certain direction, also keeping it separate from the un-initiated. Initiation bonds the members together in mysticism.

It's good to feel "important"

Neophytes (beginners) gain knowledge of a secret, giving them special status. The ancient meaning of neophyte is "*planted anew or reborn.*" A higher initiation is in reality a promotion, inspiring loyalty, and the desire to move up to the next rung. The goals of the society are reinforced, causing the initiated to act toward those goals in everyday life. That brings about a change in the political and social action of the member.

The change is always in the best interest of the goals of the leaders of the secret society. The leaders are called **Adepts**. This can best be illustrated by the soldier trained to follow orders without thinking. The higher the promotion, the more loyal, and diligent the soldier becomes. The higher the promotion, the less the initiate will question the actions of their superior. The result is often the wounding or death of the soldier for the realisation of the commander's goal, which may or may not be good for the overall community.

Initiation is a means of rewarding ambitious men who can be trusted. You will notice that the higher the degree of initiation, the fewer the members who possess those degrees. This is not because the other members are not ambitious, but because of a process of very careful selection is being conducted.

A point is reached where no effort is good enough without a pull up by the higher members. Most members never proceed beyond this point and never learn the real, secret purpose of the group. The frozen member from that point on serves only as a part of the political power base, as indeed he has always done. You may have guessed by now that initiation is a way to determine who can and cannot be trusted, and who the "yes" men are.

The Test

One method used extensively in the past century, when Christianity still held a strong power over people, was to ask the potential initiate to spit on the Christian cross.

If the candidate refuses, the members congratulate him and tell him, "*You have made the right choice, as a true adept would never do such a terrible thing.*" The newly initiated might find it disconcerting, that he/she never advances any higher.

If instead, the candidate spits upon the cross, he/she has demonstrated a knowledge of one of the mysteries and will soon find him/herself a candidate for the next higher level. The mystery is that *religion is but a tool to control the masses.*

This is why you can talk to some members of secret societies who have absolutely no idea about the corrupt and evil doings at the top of the Order. This is even seen in what is possibly the largest secret society–the Catholic Church. The lonely and honest Priest in a small Mexican village has no idea about child sacrifice and Black Masses that go on daily in the Vatican. He will never be privy to the dark machinations, and will therefore defend his Church under threat of death.

The God of the Initiated

Knowledge (or wisdom) is their only god, through which man himself will become god (they believe). The snake and the dragon are both symbols of wisdom. Lucifer is now a personification of the symbol. This was a deliberate plan to confuse and debase. The anti-Enki gang turned

Enki's symbol of knowledge into a reviled symbol of evil. If you read my previous **Book I: Secrets of the Soul**, I wrote **APPENDIX 1.2.1 THE HISTORY OF THE DEVIL**. I did this to demonstrate that the devil/Satan/Lucifer of the Judeo-Christian Bible is a manmade myth – an amalgamation of many cultures versions of evil. But as this is not common knowledge, many, many, people have a deep belief in Lucifer as Satan. As we will see, most of the modern day secret societies are "Luciferian" or "Satanist."

Does this make Satan real? No – but their belief is real, and that is what dominates many of their actions. There are defiantly low vibrational, "ugly" energies on the Astral Plane that could easily be described as "demons" in the modern definition of them. So I have no doubt that Magicians like Aleister Crowley and John Dee did in fact invoke demonic entities, however, I also know for a fact that they were never the devil! That said, in order to make sense, I will use the language of the Priest class, so with that…In **THEIR** belief:

> *It was Lucifer who tempted Eve to entice Adam to eat of the tree of knowledge and thus free man from the bonds of ignorance.*

The worship (a lot different from STUDY) of knowledge, science, or technology is Satanism in its purest form, its secret symbol is the all-seeing eye and, or the pyramid.

Examples of the Illuminati All Seeing Eye

Examples of celebrities that sold their soul to the Illuminati for fame. They are required to at some point, to show the All Seeing Eye to attract others into the club.

Magick is Alive!

To the Illuminati, occultist and magician, magick is real. They divide it into the **Left Hand Path** (black magic) and the **Right Hand Path** (white magic).

Black Magick is based on Crowley's *"do what thou will,"* with no thought given to who you may harm. White Magick on the other hand has a tenet of "Harm None," which includes themselves.

Over the centuries secret societies have come and gone. However, all of the Priest Class societies have been of the Left Hand Path. All of the Enki based Brotherhoods are of the Right Hand Path.

At the least, the Left path are just liars, manipulators, cheaters, haters, greedy and spoilt. At the worst, they are murderers, Satanist, child molesters, torturers, and mass murderers. At the top levels of the Illuminati they, are all of these things.

They know all manner of the Divination Arts, i.e. numerology, astrology, scrying, tarot, mediumship, clairvoyance etc. That is why these Arts are considered nonsense and silly in mainstream society. They have deliberately trained the masses to make fun of these things and belittle them, purely so they do not use them!

They do not want the "profane" masses to learn about Higher Knowledge and True Spiritual Awakening. As I said, they guard and hide this information at all costs. But I can assure you that the Elites use all manner of Divination before they make war, invade a country, or make an important decision. They learn all of these arts and more in the secret societies, and there is one that is by far the largest, oldest (in modern times), and far reaching – the **Freemasons**.

Indeed, the first society that really consolidated their forces and created a cohesive operation was the **Knights Templars**. But after they were destroyed by opposing forces in the Vatican, the remnants went underground. Through a schism in doctoral ideology, they formed two new (underground) secret societies to continue **The Great Work**.

They were the **Freemasons**, and the Ancient Mystical Order Rosae Crucis, otherwise known as, the **Rosicrucians**.

Almost every other secret society since has been a splinter group from one of these. In fact, many secret fraternities still include aspects of Freemasonry within their rituals, rules, initiations, and regalia.

FREEMASONS

America was founded by Freemasons. Freemason are ex-Knight Templars and many Lodges still include Templar Initiation Rituals. All are Luciferian, but this information is not revealed until the Third Initiation.

George Washington is probably the most famous Freemason in America. He is often depicted wearing his Masonic Apron in many pictures.

The **Eye of Horus**, the Freemason symbol is on the US$1 bill. The Freemason symbols are all over Washington DC. They hide behind the Christian label to hide their crimes. But the test is in their actions - not their words.

The **Grand Masonic Lodge** was created in **1717,** when four small groups of lodges joined together. Membership levels were initially first and second degree, but in the 1750s this was expanded to create the third degree which caused a split in the group. When a person reaches the third degree, they are called a **Master Mason.**

Masons conduct their regular meetings in a ritualised style. This includes many references to architectural symbols such as the compass and square. They refer to God as "*The Great Architect of the Universe.*"

The three degrees of Masonry are: 1: **Entered Apprentice**, this makes you a basic member of the group. 2: **Fellow Craft**, this is an intermediate degree in which you are meant to develop further knowledge of Masonry. 3: **Master Mason**, this degree is necessary for participating in most masonic activities. Some rites (such as the Scottish rite) list up to 33 degrees of membership.

Masons use signs and handshakes to gain admission to their secret meetings, as well as to identify themselves to other people who may be Masons. The signs and handshakes often differ from one jurisdiction to another and are regularly changed or updated. This protects the group from people finding out how to gain admission under false pretences. Masons also wear stylised clothing based upon the clothing worn by stone masons from the middle ages. The most well-known of these is the apron.

In order to become a Mason, you must

Freemasons Annual Meeting 1992

generally be recommended by at least two current members. In some cases you must be recommended three times before you can join. You have to be at least 18 years old and of sound mind. Many religions frown upon membership of the Masons, and the Roman Catholic Church forbids Catholics to join under pain of excommunication (except for Popes and Cardinals). Royal Arch, Cryptic, and Chivalric (especially the Knights Templar) branches of Masonry became known as the American or York Rite (Dafoe, 2015).

The Lost Name of the Mason God

Masons of the Blue Lodge are instructed during their first three degrees that they are seeking the Lost Name of God. It is not until they reach the level of Royal Arch Masonry (7th Degree in the York Rite) that they are told that the lost name of God is **Jahbuhlun**.

Men of Jahbuhlun - Right: Napoléon Bonaparte; Centre top to Bottom: US President Franklin Pierce; US President Rutherford B. Hayes; Salomon Rothschild; Left: Karl Marx; Joseph Stalin; Former Secretary of State Colin Powell

This is considered to be the most sacred name of Freemasonry's God. This name is so powerful they believe, that it takes three Master Masons to chant the name, each saying one syllable at a time. EG: "Jah", "Bul," Lun." That is because the name is made up of three "lesser" deities – Jah = Yah (Yahweh); Bah = Baal; Lun = Osiris (On). Obviously the name should be "Yah-baal-On," but according to **Duncan's Masonic Ritual land Monitor**, they admit that the spelling got corrupted over the years until it reached its current form of Jah-Bul-Lun.

Higher initiates known as the **Men of Jahbuhlun** are taught a secret hand gesture to announce to those "with eyes to see" that they are Men of Jahbuhlun. You have no doubt seen this hand gesture many, many times and not even known what it meant. When you see a picture of a man with his hand hidden in his breast, then he is announcing to other Masons – *I am a Man of Jahbuhlun!*

Friends in High Places

It is very apparent that in order to get anywhere high in politics, you must be a high ranking Freemason. In the US, it goes like this. First you must be a Freemason. Once you reach the higher ranks (over 20th Degree) you are invite to join the CFR, then the Trilateral Commission, then if you are really good, the Bilderberg Group. The Bilderbergers are the anointed ones of Freemasonry.

There are many, many other hand signs the Mason give in photographs and portraits. I will be going into some of these in **Book III: Secrets of the Mind Control Programs**, however the best book available that I am aware of is **Codex Magica** by **Texe Marrs** (Marrs, 2005). This is a must have book for anyone interested in the secrets of the Freemasons.

Star of Seinfeld, Michael Richards 33 Degree Freemason

To a lesser degree, there are plenty of insiders in big corporations and Hollywood. All Fortune 500 companies are run by high ranking Freemasons. They too can be invited to Bilderberg, and again, as still seen as the anointed.

The highest ranking 33° Freemason in Hollywood in recent years was **Michael Richards** from the popular TV series *Seinfeld*.

Richards was initiated into Freemasonry on December 17, 1998, at the **Riviera Lodge No. 780** in Pacific Palisades, California. In a very candid interview ("Michael A. Richards, 33° Beyond the Symbols") reprinted in The Scottish Rite Journal of Freemasonry (Sept. 2003), Richards said his fascination with the Craft began in the early 60s. His mother had,

> *"had a friend who was a Mason ... I didn't have a father, but he was like a father to me. He was very charitable with his time. On Friday nights he would take me to the American Legion Hall where some of the best vaudeville acts in the country were performed."*

After finding out his comedic idol **Red Skelton** was a Mason, Richards decided to become one himself (Casalou, 2003).

Michael Richards (aka "Cosmo Kramer") went into an insane racial tirade on November 17th, 2006 at the **Laugh Factory** in West Hollywood, California after being heckled by an African-American man. In a failed attempt at gaining control of his act Richards shouted,

> *"Shut up! Fifty years ago we'd have you upside-down with a fucking fork up your ass!"*

After this blatant reference to the "good 'ole days" of lynching, he escalated the situation by screaming,

> *"Throw his ass out. He's a nigger! He's a nigger! He's a nigger! A nigger! Look, there's a nigger!"*

The video has to be seen to be believed (Richards Goes Crazy, 2006). Multiple copies have been posted on YouTube, resulting in thousands of comments from viewers.

Several nights later, **Jerry Seinfeld** appeared on **Late Night with David Letterman** to support his friend. Richards apologised for his behaviour. However, many people believe Richards' conduct might ultimately stem from his association with Freemasonry. There's a controversy going on in the South, as to whether officially recognise **Prince Hall Masonry**.

The argument surrounds the fact that blacks wishing to join Freemasonry – having been rebuked because of race – have had to form their own Lodges. This situation has been going on for a long time. Adding insult to injury, the Prince Hall masons are looked upon as "clandestine" – meaning, they aren't officially recognized. Prince Hall Masonry represents a separate body of Lodges segregated from mainstream masonry. There are some whites in Prince Hall, and vice versa in the main Lodges, but the southern jurisdictions still refuse to officially recognize the black masonic organisation.

Prince Hall and African American Masonry

A Mason named **Prince Hall** is considered to be the father of Freemasonry in the African American community.

Dedication of the Prince Hall Masons Monument at Cambridge Massachusetts, September 13, 2008

Prince was born in Africa and brought to America as a slave in his early teens. He was freed after 21 years, and he probably took his last name from the household that enslaved him.

Prince Hall and several other black Bostonians wanted to form their own Masonic Lodge. On March 6, 1775, Prince Hall and 14 other black men were initiated into Lodge No. 441 which was an Irish military lodge attached to the 38th Foot Regiment, garrisoned at Castle William (what is now Fort Independence) in Boston Harbor. The Master of the Lodge was Sergeant John Batt, and the lodge conferred the Entered Apprentice, Fellow Craft, and Master Mason degrees on the men in one day and granted them a special dispensation to meet as African Lodge, which allowed them to march in processions and perform funeral services, but not to initiate new members. Black men would somehow have to receive their degrees in other lodges before joining the African Lodge?

When the Revolutionary War broke out, Prince Hall and many of his brethren enlisted in the Continental Army. Africa Lodge survived the war with 33 members. However, after the war, Freemasonry was in an organisational turmoil. Most of the American lodges were authorised by English, Irish or Scottish Grand Lodge warrants, and the new states created new Grand Lodges to administer the lodges within their borders. In fact, several states, including Massachusetts formed two

Grand Lodges, continuing the Ancients-and-Moderns feud (Hodapp, 2012).

But when Prince Hall and African Lodge sought a charter from the new Grand Lodge of Massachusetts, they were turned down for racist reasons. So much for Freemasonry "Brotherly Love."

Nine years later on March 2, 1784, Hall petitioned the Grand Lodge of England, asking for a warrant for a Charter that they had been denied by the white Masons of Massachusetts. The warrant was approved in September, but it took three years to be delivered to Boston. Hall established the first lodge of African American Masons in North America known as African Lodge No. 459 of the Grand Lodge of England.

The Prince Hall Masons are the oldest and largest group of Masons of African origin in the world. Today there are forty Grand Lodges of Prince Hall Freemasonry in the United States, Canada, the Bahamas, and Liberia.

These Grand Lodges preside over more than 5,000 lodges. All of them claim descent from the Prince Hall Grand Lodge of Massachusetts which is traced back to the African Lodge No. 459 (Hall, 2008).

ANCIENT ARABIC ORDER OF NOBLES OF THE MYSTIC SHRINE (A.A.O.N.M.S.) AKA: SHRINERS

The Shrine (Ancient Arabic Order, Nobles of the Mystic Shrine) is the most conspicuous of all forms of Freemasonry and the most far removed from basic Masonic principles and traditions.

In 1870, there were several thousand Masons in Manhattan, many of whom lunched at the **Knickerbocker Cottage** at a special table on the second floor. There, the idea of a new fraternity for Masons was discussed. **Dr. Walter M. Fleming**, M.D., and **William J. Florence** took the idea seriously enough to act upon it.

Florence, a world-renowned actor, while on tour in Marseilles, was invited to a party given by an Arabian diplomat. The entertainment was something in the nature of an elaborately staged musical comedy. At its conclusion, the guests became members of a secret society.

Florence took copious notes and drawings at his initial viewing and on two other occasions, once in Algiers and once in Cairo. When he returned to New York in 1870, he showed his material to Fleming.

Fleming took the ideas supplied by Florence and converted them into what would become the "Ancient Arabic Order of the Nobles of the Mystic Shrine (A.A.O.N.M.S.)."

Fleming created the rituals, emblems, and costumes. Florence and Fleming were initiated August 13, 1870, and initiated 11 other men on June 16, 1871(About, 2015). To join the Shriners, you must already be at least a Master Mason (3rd Degree).

What are Shriners really like?

Michael Richards is also a Shriner (Shriners, 2010). Exoterically, merry old men putting on a circus once in a while to help out burn victims; esoterically, a band of thugs and thieves from all the Lodges, who indulge in feasts of vulgarity, racism and debauchery. If you want to learn more about the real Shriners, check these news articles out:

- **Shriners the Krafty Clowns** (Freemasonrywatch, 2015), for a selection of mainstream articles on Shriner corruption and depravity. Such as: "*World's worst charities*," KOB TV – Albuquerque, New Mexico; "*Sex show may harm Shriners' charities*," Winnipeg Free Press, Sun, Jan 28, 2001; "*Shrine Records Shocking*," South Haven Daily Tribune – South Haven Michigan, Fri, April 24, 1987; "*Would-Be Shriner Says He Was Subjected to Painful Initiation Rites*," The Associated Press, November 20, 1991.

- **Above the law? Shriner Treasurers' Minutes**, Part 10, (Frost, 2006)
- **Defamation? Shriners: Part 8** (Frost, 2006)
- **Follow the Money: Shriners Part 5** (Frost, 2006)
- **"Promoter" Accuses Shriners of Racism in Concert Fraud** (Frost, 2006)

The Ku Klux Klan's links to Freemasonry

Albert Pike, as Richards is well-aware, was an avowed racist. Pike, a Confederate General, was a giant in his day and the most important Mason in America. He personally rewrote the **Scottish Rite Rituals** and in 1859, was elected as the **Sovereign Grand Commander of the Supreme Council for Scottish Rite Freemasonry** in the Southern Jurisdiction of the United States. As the owner and publisher of the Memphis, Tennessee Daily Appeal, Pike would often voice his opinions. In an editorial dated April 16, 1868, he wrote:

> *With Negroes for witnesses and jurors, the administration of justice becomes a blasphemous mockery. A Loyal League of Negroes can cause any white man to be arrested, and can prove any charges it chooses to have made against him. …The disenfranchised people of the South … can find no protection for property, liberty or life, except in secret association…. We would unite every white man in the South, who is opposed to negro suffrage, into one great Order of Southern Brotherhood, with an organization complete, active, vigorous, in which a few should execute the concentrated will of all, and whose very existence should be concealed from all but its members.*

There's much controversy as to Pike's role in the founding of the Ku Klux Klan, however this "secret association" he referred to – the **Great Order of Southern Brotherhood** – was indeed the KKK. A year earlier in Nashville, his friend and fellow Confederate General and Freemason, **Nathan Bedford Forrest**, had united the fledgling "association." Forrest was elected the first **Grand Wizard** of all the Klan:

> *A 'fiery summons' went out to the fi thousand Klan dens then said to be in operation, to attend an "Imperial Klonvokation," which was held in Nashville's Maxwell House hotel in April. Presiding as imperial wizard was the former Confederate Calvary general Nathan Bedford Forrest, a wealthy slave trader before the war, whose troops had been accused of the massacre of three hundred black men, woman, and children at Fort Pillow, Tennessee, on April 12, 1864.*

> *Any doubt that the Ku Klux Klan constituted a veritable Confederate underground was dispelled at this meeting, where ex-Confederate General Albert Pike assumed command as grand dragon of the Arkansas Realm of the Klan's Invisible Empire; General John B. Gordon the Georgia Realm; General W. J. Hardee, Alabama; and General Wade Hampton, South Carolina. These men brought the Southwide terrorist campaign of the Klan under professional, centralized military command and discipline." - Stetson Kennedy, After Appomattox: How the South Won the War, University Press of Florida, 1995, p. 69.*

As an official researcher for Masonry, Michael Richards is well aware of this history; and perhaps – as evidenced by his antics at the comedy club – even sympathetic to the cause.

The Pike/Masonic/Klan controversy made headlines in 1992 during **Lyndon H. LaRouche's** bid for the Presidency. LaRouche and his running mate, **Reverend James Bevel**, *"launched a mobilisation to remove the statue of General Albert Pike from its place of honour in Washington, D.C.'s Judiciary Square."*

Sovereign Grand Commander **C. Fred Kleinknecht** (1985-2003) attacked the campaign to dismantle the Pike statue, defending the good name of his illustrious predecessor. What is of interest here is the fact that C. Fred Kleinknecht has had a close association with Richards since his early days in the Craft. It is safe to assume

Kleinknecht is at least a mentor to Richards. Kleinknecht was *"the Founding Member of the Scottish Rite Research Society."* And Richards, as disclosed in the September 2000 issue of **The Scottish Rite Journal of Freemasonry**, was elected as a Life Member of the same research society. Both Kleinknecht and Richards are defenders and devotees of Albert Pike: the first Grand Dragon of the Arkansas Realm of the Klan's Invisible Empire.

Invoking Spirits and Demons

Michael Richards is within the top echelon of **Scottish Rite Masonry** – a 33° Sovereign Grand Inspector-General. At this level, he practices what has been described as **White Masonry**. What occultist and mystic Bro. **C. W. Leadbeater**, 33° Mason, identified as the *"highest and last of the great sacramental powers of the Mysteries"* (Leadbeater, 1998, p. 42).

Thirty-third degree Masons, according to Leadbeater, channel the *"Hidden Light from the White Lodge behind"* (Leadbeater, 43). In fact, Leadbeater tells us that the initiation ritual for the 30th degree requires the initiate to summon forth a "spirit" who is *"a great blue Deva of the First Ray."* At the 33rd degree, he must invoke two *"splendid fellow workers, spirits of gigantic size as compared to humanity and radiantly white color are present."*

As an avid investigator, being a mystic, and a voracious reader with an insatiable appetite, Richards is thoroughly familiar with this concept and would have gone through these rituals, and invoked these spirits. It should be remembered that it was Crowley that cracked the code so to speak on how to quickly and easily invoke and command spirits from the Abyss. Crowley was a 33° Freemason, and literally re-wrote the book on these high initiations and spirit summoning. Leadbeater, besides being a high-level Mason, was involved with **Theosophy** which has deep roots in spiritual mediumship.

Pike and his devotion to Levi

Pike was a disciple of Eliphas Levi; the former accepted without question the teachings of the latter. Moreover, as Masonic historian, occultist and high-degree Mason **Arthur E. Waite** has shown – Morals and Dogma is *"really a translation in part and a commentary at large ... upon the works of Eliphas Levi"* (John H. Cowles, ed., Supreme Council

33rd Degree, Part 1, or Mother Council of the World of the Ancient and Accepted Scottish Rite of Freemasonry, Southern Jurisdiction, United States of America, p. 342)

Thus, Albert Pike had insinuated the teachings of occultist Eliphas Levi into official Scottish Rite doctrine, while Leadbeater's corrupting influence had been **Madame Helena Petrovna Blavatsky**. Hitler and the Nazi party were influenced by Blavatsky's teachings, especially her "Secret Doctrine" of evolving races (from inferiority to apotheosis).

Madame Blavatsky

Helena Petrovna Blavatsky was a self-proclaimed occultist, spirit medium, and author who co-founded the **Theosophical Society** in 1875. She gained an international following as the leading theoretician of Theosophy, the esoteric movement that the Society promoted. However, in reality, Blavatsky was a drunk, a chain smoker, a crack pot and a charlatan with a foul mouth and extremely poor personal hygiene. That said, she still held a strange hold over her disciples.

Helena Blavatsky
(1831 - 1891)

Blavatsky taught her disciples that the highest race was that of the **Aryans**, who were mystically directed from the **Great White Lodge** – or the **The Great White Brotherhood** – into a state of perfection.

The superiority of the white race has been the predominant mystical undercurrent of "Nordic" occultists for over a century; the Scottish Rite included, and an idea the Nazi Party adopted with a horrific outcome. This can be easily underscored by quoting from **The New Age Magazine** – the official organ of the Scottish Rite before its name had been changed to **The Scottish Rite Journal of Freemasonry** (which, as you'll recall, Richards has been featured in). Five years after the fall of Nazism, **Bro. C. William Smith's** *"God's Plan in America,"* in the September 1950 issue of **The New Age Magazine**, had this to say:

> ❝❝ *God's plan is dedicated to the unificatio of all races, religions, and creeds. This plan, dedicated to the new order of things, is to make all things new – a new nation, a new*

race, a new civilization and a new religion,
a non-sectarian religion that has already been
recognized and called the religion of 'The
Great Light.' Looking back into history, we can
easily see that the Guiding Hand of Providence
has chosen the Nordic people to bring in and
unfold the new order of the world. Records
clearly show that 95 per cent of the colonists
were Nordics-Anglo-Saxons. Providence has
chosen the Nordics because the Nordics have
prepared themselves and have chosen God....Just
as Providence has chosen Children of Israel
– to bring into the world righteousness by
carrying the 'Ten Commandments' which emphasize
'Remember the Sabbath Day and keep it holy,' so
also Providence has chosen the Nordic Race to
unfold the 'New Age' of the world – a '
Novus Ordo Seclorum'.

I'm sure Richard's possesses the complete set of the magazine (1904-present), and has devoted much study to the doctrines contained therein. Rather than making a good man a better man (as the selling point goes), Freemasonry's elitist dogma has corrupted Richards' morals.

> *"That was uncalled for," the black man said while leaving the comedy club. Richards replied, "That's what happens when you interrupt the white man, don't you know?"*

Yes, we do now Michael, but only racist white men. Very disappointing.

Michael Richards with other high ranking Freemasons

ORDER OF THE EASTERN STAR

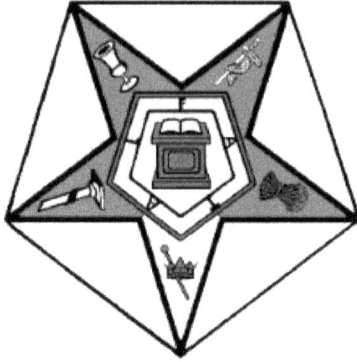

The **Order of the Eastern Star** is an adoptive rite of Freemasonry. Basically, women wanted to be part of the Freemasons, but their rules forbid women from joining. Thus, they decided to put pressure on their Freemason husbands to create a new group that they could join.

It was established in **1850** by **Robert Morris**, a lawyer and educator from Boston, Massachusetts who joined Freemasonry on 5th March 1846 and eventually ascended to the 'Ladies degree,' within the Lodge, which later became the basis of the Eastern Star degrees. He became Grand Master of the Grand Lodge of Kentucky on the 12th of October 1858.

Members of the Order are aged 18 and older; men must be Master Masons and women must have specific relationships with Masons. Originally, a woman would have to be the daughter, widow, wife, sister, niece, sister-in-law, or mother of a master Mason, but this has been expanded throughout the years in response to declining membership.

Based on paganism, the symbols, colours, Cabalistic Motto, Cabalistic word, and the *symbolic meaning have remained the same*, but the *names were changed to bible names*.

In other words, the Eastern Star is not, and never has been, Bible-based! It is only using the names of Bible characters to continue its paganism under a guise. In fact, we are told:

> **❝** *The reading of Scripture text between the points was originated by the Patrons of Queen Esther Chapter, Indianapolis, Ind. and inserted in the Ritual in 1878.* **❞**

International Order of Rainbow for Girls

Job's Daughters International

Order of DeMolay International

Where Mason's send their children for indoctrination

This was 28 years after the founding of the Eastern Star! Eastern Star indoctrinates young girls/women who are members of **Rainbow for Girls**, **Job's Daughters**, and the Masons look after the boys at the **Order of DeMolay**. These young people are trained to be future leaders in Eastern Stars or Masons. Each of these groups, like the adults, conduct Ritual and Ceremonies, learn secret handshakes, and dress in robes and other antiquated style outfits. They have a system of merits like the Scouts do where they get patches to wear once they achieve a certain skill etc. But something tells me these children would not get a merit patch for rubbing two sticks together to make a fire! The Order of the Eastern Star and the Masonic fraternity are highly rewarded (financially) by their support of, and interest in, these youth organisations (Dafoe, 2015).

ROSICRUCIANS

After the Knight Templars were disbanded and driven underground, they split into two distinct groups. One was the **Freemasons** that we have already discussed, and the other was the **Rosicrucians.** One must remember that the original Templars were a Christian organisation. This Christianity is reflected in the Rosicrucians, but was completely disregarded by the Freemasons.

Indeed, when the "Holy Order" was hunted down and destroyed, many Templars felt that their God (of the Christians) had abandoned them. They went off and formed the Freemasons, who after Adam Weishaupt infiltrated, turned their worship to a new god – *Lucifer*.

The Ancient Mystical Order Rosae Crucis - AKA *Rosicrucians* teachings are today a combination of occultism and other religious beliefs and practices, including Hermeticism, Jewish mysticism, and Christian Gnosticism. The central feature of Rosicrucianism is the belief that its members possess secret wisdom that was handed down to them from ancient times.

However, it's the modern version that is generally believed to have been the idea of a group of **German Protestants**. In the 1600s a series of three documents were published: *Fama Fraternitatis Rosae Crucis*, *Confessio Fraternitatis*, and The *Chymical Wedding of Christian Rosenkreutz anno* that claimed to be from1459.

The documents were so widely read and influential, that the historian **Frances Yeats** refers to the 17th century as the **Rosicrucian Enlightenment**. The first document tells the story of a mysterious alchemist, **Christian Rosenkreuz** who travelled to various parts of the world gathering secret knowledge. The second document tells of a secret brotherhood of alchemists who were preparing to change the political and intellectual face of Europe. The third document describes the invitation of Christian Rosenkreuz to attend and assist at the "Chemical" wedding of a King and Queen in a castle of Miracles.

Current members of the Rosicrucian Order claim that its origins are far more ancient than these documents. The authors of the documents seemed to strongly favour **Lutheranism** and include condemnations of the Catholic Church.

Rosicrucianism had an influence on Masonry and, in fact, the 18th degree of **Scottish Rite Masonry** is called the **Knight of the Rose Croix** (red cross).

There are a large number of Rosicrucian groups today – each claiming to be closely tied to the original. Of the two main divisions, one is a mix of Christianity with Rosicrucian principles, and the other is semi-Masonic. The Masonic type tend to also have degrees of membership.

The modern, reinvention of this order is more akin to an eclectic, New Age group that cheery-picks from all religions, theology, philosophy, science, and eastern philosophies, occultism and more. They are no longer insiders of the Illuminati on the low initiates or public face.

Mainly in Europe and North America there are still true, high ranking Rosicrucians. They are still tied to the Illuminati, and also have strong ties to the Jesuits and the Vatican. At this level, any Catholic Priest that wants to be a Bishop, Cardinal, or Pope, must do a series of training by the Rosicrucians where they are taught esoteric knowledge, metaphysics, and occult lessons.

The Rosicrucians have become more like a University for the Illuminati/New World Order, where the Freemason are the doers. Both are essential for the Illuminati to continue their plans. Indeed, Rosicrucians and Freemason share an equal level, as in, neither group is subordinate or superior to the other. All other groups are subordinate to these two, except the next one – they are a power unto themselves.

THE FABIAN SOCIETY

The **Fabian Society** is a group originating in England in 1884, with the purpose of forming a single, global socialist state. They get their name from the Roman general **Fabius**, who used carefully planned strategies to slowly wear down his enemies over a long period of time to obtain victory.

Fabian Socialism uses incremental change over a long period of time to slowly transform a state, as opposed to using violent revolution for change. Indeed, World War II was a result of a fall out within the Illuminati Council of 300. Hitler, who was a member, was tired of the slow change approach the Committee was taking (Fabian) and pushed for a quick world change via a military solution (war). A vote decided the outcome and Hitler was given the chance to prove his theory right. Yes, WWII was basically a bet between our owners. One side thought socialism by stealth was the answer to world domination, and the other half thought it could be achieved through a brutal war. Over 70 million people died in WWII, just so these people could run their little experiment.

New Fabian Logo

Obviously the Fabians won, just, and it has been socialism by stealth ever since. Their original emblem was a shield with a wolf in sheep's clothing holding a flag with the letters F.S. (above). Today the international symbol of the Fabian Society is a turtle, with the motto below: "**When I strike, I strike hard**."

Fabian Society members included H.G. Wells, George

Bernard Shaw, Sidney Webb, Beatrice Webb, Annie Besant, Graham Wallas, Tony Blair and ex-Australia 'Prime Minister' Julia Gillard. In fact, Julie Gillard wore her Fabian Society allegiance on her sleeve, regularly giving them thanks for the support they gave her.

In this video interview she is asked about the Fabian Society connections by a public member who she answers to that she is indeed a member, as were most of her Australian Labor Party members (Gillard, 2012). Gillard tried to introduce the Rothschild carbon tax, and the man then asked her if the decision to introduce a carbon tax was influenced by the Fabians. She clumsily denies that they did, but everyone watching on was less than convinced. I am 100% convinced that the Fabian Society DID come up with the carbon tax, and forced the puppets in the Labor Party to sell it. And trust me, the opposition Liberal National Party are even worse.

The Fabian Window is a stained-glass window on display at the **London School of Economics**, and depicts **Sidney Webb** and **Edward**

The Fabian Window at London School of Economics

R. Pease hammering the earth on an anvil beneath the Fabian Society emblem (wolf in sheep's clothing). At the top of the window are the words *"Remould it nearer to the heart's desire."*

To give you an idea of the type of world these people would like to 'remould', here is a quote from **George Bernard Shaw**:

> ❝ *Under Socialism, you would not be allowed to be poor. You would be forcibly fed, clothed, lodged, taught, and employed whether you liked it or not. If it were discovered that you had not character and industry enough to be worth all this trouble, you might possibly be executed in a kindly manner; but whilst you were permitted to live, you would have to live well.* ❞

The ultimate Nanny State, with no free will or right to choose; you are owned by the elites and discarded when you are no longer any use. Barack Obama is a die heart Communist and is trying hard to bring the United States into a Socialist State.

Fabian Society members founded the **British Labour Party**, the **London School of Economics**, the **International Court of Justice** at The Hague, and were largely involved in the creation of the UN and the League of Nations before it. They have been accredited with creating Communist China, Fascism in Italy and Germany and Socialism globally as well.

They have enormous influence in global matters, yet hardly anyone knows who they are and what they stand for. They are very strong advocates for the *Catastrophic Anthropogenic Global Warming* pseudo-science because they are the types of people who have hijacked the environmental movement in order to use it to their political advantage. Their intent is to use environmental issues as a means to cause people to unite and demand that the issues be fixed, intending us to demand a global government that has the authority to 'fix' global warming because sovereign national governments lack that ability.

The UN's **Agenda 21** is an example of a Fabian Society program that sets international requirements for how people must live, learn, travel, eat, and communicate. Its sole purpose is to control people, not protection of the environment.

Fabian Society members have infiltrated national and regional governments worldwide. Indeed, some of them control whole governments like in Australia, Britain, and China. How far people have been fooled also explains the role played by the Fabian Society in formulating policies for the decolonized British Empire. It would also mean that quite a number of British educated natives given the mantle of leading the newly independent nations would have also been members of the Fabian society. The communist takeover of Russia too is said to be the work of the British Fabian Society financed by Wall Street in New York.

A closer look at entities like the Bank Of International Settlements (BIS), International Monetary Fund (IMF), Club Of Rome, The Committee Of 300, the Central 'Intelligence' Agency (CIA), the Council On Foreign Relations (CFR), The Trilateral Commission, The Bilderberg Groups, the 'Federal' Reserve System, the Internal Revenue Service(s), Goldman Sachs, Israel and the Israeli lobby, the Vatican, the City of London, Brussels, the United Nations, the Israeli Mossad, and Associated Press (AP) will reveal that they all have members in the Fabian Society which also controls the European Union.

Local Fabian Societies will often describe themselves as 'left-leaning think tanks' and the like, to try and deceive people as to their true beliefs. Understandably, many members are often reluctant to admit their affiliation.

Socialist is too soft a word to use for these people, their idea of a perfect world more resembles a system *"fascistic at its core and administered through a form of scientific socialism."* The result is a 'communitarian' society where individualism must be relinquished for the betterment of the state. The book/movie 1984 is a very close analogy of what the Fabians have in mind for us. I think most of us don't want to live in a world like that, but our leaders have made up their minds and will not stop striving for it regardless of what the public thinks.

> *"Fabian Society.... has known from its creation about the long-term agenda for the global fascist / communist global dictatorship......*
> *Their (Orwell, Huxley) books were not written from imagination, but from knowledge of what was coming." - David Icke*

George Orwell Tells All

George Orwell, real name **Eric Blair**, was a writer for the BBC, propagandist for British Intelligence MI-5/MI-6, and author of the book, 1984. Orwell admitted in an interview right before his death, that the protagonist in 1984, **Winston Smith**, was an allegory of himself. He also revealed that 1984 was the story of what would happen if the Fabian Society was allowed to take over, and what the world would be like. I think you would have to agree that the world we live in now is starting to look more, and more like 1984.

Eric Arthur Blair (pen name George Orwell) (1903 - 1950)

Orwell was an insider. He literally was amongst the Fabian socialist and heard their plans. In essays and interviews, he said that one of the goals of the Fabians was to reduce language down to such a basic level, that people could not communicate with each other and understand that they are being lied to. In his book, he called this "Doublethink" and "Doublespeak." Doublethink puts two contradicting words or thoughts together at the same time which the brain cannot reconcile, therefore it accepts both terms as valid. As an example, they called the torture facility, the **Ministry of Love**. It is this type of doublethink that the Fabians have been pushing for years via the controlled mainstream media.

That is why now if you do not support illegal immigration, you are branded a racist. Of if you do not support Caitlin/Brian Jenner, you are a "homophobe."

In an article by the Associated Press, students at Pennsylvania school want 'Lynch Hall' renamed because of the word 'Lynch'. The building is named after **Clyde A. Lynch**, who was president of Lebanon Valley College from 1932 until his death in 1950. Lynch led the college through the Great Depression and World War II and raised $550,000 for a new physical education building. The building that bears his name houses several academic departments. However, students at the college are demanding that administrators rename the building called "Lynch Memorial Hall" because of the racial overtones of the word "lynch."

Interestingly, the name "Lynch" comes from the Irish Gaelic and means "mariner or boatman." In the 1780's, it was **Charles Lynch** and **William Lynch** from Virginia during the America Revolution, who created "Lynch Law", that passed Congress, to stop people "Lynching", or taking the law into their own hands. It originally had nothing to do with hanging black people.

The Fabians take an emotionally charged word like "lynching," and then associate it with something completely opposite – a man that helped black kids during the 1940's. Eventually, all thoughts of a good man (Clyde Lynch) are forgotten, only to be replaced by a bitter and hollow victory. In the essence of 1984, they are continually rewriting history and the average person is not even aware.

Winston worked in the **Ministry of Truth**, but it was his job to lie. He would get a true news story, then reword it and change it to favour the Party. This is exactly what Orwell had done as a writer for the BBC.

That is why everyone in the West believed after World War II that no Allies ever committed war crimes. Why they believed Harry Truman made the right choice to nuke Japan (even though they surrendered two weeks earlier), and now why President Putin of Russia is demonised. This list goes on and on.

In a nutshell, they are telling you that you cannot have your own opinion. You must submit to their group think. That in itself is more akin to cult like activities that people should be wary of. Ironically, they are slowly removing individual thought and choice from everyone, regardless of race, colour, or creed.

A noteworthy quote is that of Australian Senator **Chris Schacht** who said in 2001,

> *"You probably were not aware that us Fabians have taken over the CIA, KGB, MI5, ASIO [Australian Security Intelligence Organisation], IMF, the World Bank and many other organisations."*

From all this we should realise that **nothing happens in isolation**. Every event, however small, is engineered and orchestrated by a handful of people who control the world. They are driving the group mind into a direction of their choosing, whether you like it or not.

KNIGHTS OF MALTA

You will usually hear this organisation called the "**Knights of Malta**," however their full name is a mouthful: *The Sovereign Military Hospitaller Order of Saint John of Jerusalem of Rhodes and of Malta*.

The Knights of Malta is one of the most ancient Catholic religious orders in the world, being more than 900 years old. It is also the world's oldest surviving chivalric order.

It was initially founded in the 11th century by **Amalfian** merchants in Jerusalem, as a monastic order to tend to Christian pilgrims in the Holy Land. They built a combination church, hospital, and convent in Jerusalem, with the understanding that the hospital would admit pilgrims of all religions and races.

In **1113**, **Pope Paschall II** issued a Bull, placing the Knights of Malta under the authority of the Holy See, and also giving the right to elect its leaders without interference from other authorities, whether secular or religious. They evolved into a fearsome military machine and, after the fall of Jerusalem, at the Vatican's request, they turned Malta into a fortress against the Ottoman horde, most famously when it held out against the full might of **Suleiman the Magnificent** in 1565, and thereby helped 'save' Christian Europe.

These two abilities — the independence from other nations and the right to use military force — provide the basis for the Order's peculiar standing in the international community.

It's no secret that the Knights of Malta had some ups and downs over the course of its centuries-old existence.

In **1291**, prompted by the fall of the last Christian compound in the area, the Knights of Malta struck out for the island of **Cyprus**. From there the Order relocated to **Rhodes**, where it built one of the most powerful naval forces in the Mediterranean.

The Knights of Malta called Rhodes home until **1523**, and during this time it issued its own currency and cultivated diplomatic relationships with other countries. When **Sultan Suleiman** (the Magnificent) held the Order under siege for months, the Knights were eventually forced to surrender the island.

For seven years the Knights of Malta were a sovereign entity, with no territory of its own. Fortunately for them, **Emperor Charles V** gifted the island of **Malta** to the Order in **1530**. The centuries spent in Malta gave the Knights not only their name, but their reputation for power and prestige.

This lasted until **1798**, when **Napoleon** took over the island. By this point, the Knights of Malta had a long-standing rule forbidding its forces from raising arms against other Christians. As a result, they left Malta, traveling through Messina, Catania and Ferrera before eventually settling in **Rome**.

Queen Elizabeth II of England is a member of the Knights of Malta

The Knights of Malta are still based in Rome today, on the Via Condotti, a short distance from the Spanish Steps.

That former territorial ownership means the Knights still have a rather unusual status. Although not a State like the Vatican, the building on Via Condotti, as well as the Order's other site in Rome, a priory on the Aventine hill with its own Piranesi chapel, is officially an independent territory, giving the Knights observer status at the United Nations in a similar manner to the Palestinians. They even have their own passports, postage stamps and, in many parts of the world, ambassadors, who are granted full diplomatic status.

On the outside, in public, they conduct extensive humanitarian work across the planet in order to have a "do-gooders" reputation to the uneducated world. They claim to have 118,500 members, employees, and volunteers and are now in the charity business, working or supporting aid projects in some 120 countries on an annual operating budget of more than £150 million.

The current head is **Grand Master Festing**, born in Northumberland, England. The Grand Master is officially classed as a prince, and has the status of Cardinal within the Catholic Church. He meets regularly with the Pope and was very close to Benedict XVI (Joseph Ratzinger) (Malta, 2015).

The Knights of Darkness

The Knights of Malta is not merely a "charitable organisation." That's just an elaborate front, as should become clear to you later. As the name **Sovereign Military Order of Malta** confirms, it is a military order based on the crusader Knights Hospitaller of Jerusalem and is interwoven with Freemasonry. Most people have never even heard of SMOM, much less that it is a part of Freemasonry. But that is the way the aristocratic elite like it.

The American Association of the *Sovereign Military Order of Malta* (Knights of Malta, SMOM) was founded in 1927.

> By 1941 Francis Cardinal Spellman was listed as the 'Grand Protector' and 'Spritual Advisor' of the Order, with John J. Raskob as Treasurer. Members included John Farrell, then President of U.S. Steel, Joseph P. Grace, and John D. Ryan. In 1934 Raskob, inspired by the French fascist Croix de Feu, and working closely with Morgan Bank's John Davis, had been a principal financier in th plot to organize a fascist coup in the U.S. The plan failed when General Smedley Butler, who had been set up to lead the project, denounced it. (Hervet, 1986)

His Eminence Cardinal Spellman, "Grand Protector" of the Knights of Malta, worked with Pope Pius XII to help Nazi war criminals escape justice. According to Frederic Laurent (*L'Orchestre Noir. Pairs: Editions Stock, 1978),

> *All studies [of the post-WWII Nazi networks] have shown the determining role played by the Catholic Church in the flight of war criminals. Since April 1943, following negotiations between Pius XII and the ultra reactionary American archbishop Francis Spellman, the Holy See became the clandestine center of Anglo-American espionage in Italy. This collaboration in fact had begun the previous year... between Earl Brennan, a veteran of the American State Department and Gian Battista Montini, at the time a bishop and Under-Secretary of State at the Vatican. This close collaboration between the future [Pope] Paul VI and the American secret services continued after the war through the [CIA] intermediary James Angleton...*
> *(Hervet, 1986)*

June of **1944**, the US Army enter Rome as liberators. Chief-General **Mark Clark** was made a *Knight Grand Cross of the Sovereign Military Order of Malta (SMOM)*.

On December 27, **1946**, James Jesus Angleton, future head of the CIA received the **Croci Al Merito Seconda Classe** from the SMOM.

On November 17, **1948**, the SMOM awarded one of its highest honours, the **Grand Cross of Merit**, to **Reinhard Gehlen**, the Nazi Chief of intelligence on the Soviet front. He was subsequently installed by the Americans as the first chief of West Germany's equivalent of the CIA, the **Bundesnachtrichtdienst** (BND: federal secret service), under West German Chancellor Adenauer, a devout Catholic who had received the **Magistral Grand Cross** personally from the Order's Grand Master **Prince Chigi**. Gehlen was the man responsible for fabricating the Cold War against Russia (more about that in *Book III: Secrets of the Mind Control Programs*). In 1956, **Clare Booth Luce** of *Time Magazine* becomes a *Dame of Malta*.

Former CIA Director **John McCone** is shown to be a member of the Knights of Malta by their 1980 list. (The article by Hervet, used as the source for this information, has many other noteworthy persons listed as belonging to the Vatican military order of SMOM)

Freemasonry generally purports to be hostile to Catholicism, and conversely, the Vatican has at various times forbidden Catholics to join Masonic organizations. Nevertheless, in December of 1969 an exclusive meeting was held in the Rome office of **Count Umberto Ortolani**, the Ambassador of the Order of Malta to Uruguay, who has been called 'the brains' behind the fascist **P-2 Masonic Lodge**, which had been established in the mid-1960s.

What they use the Passports for

Having full diplomatic status, and being able to issue your own passports can come in handy, especially when you are doing nefarious things. By their own admission,

> *"One of the things we always do is try to ensure our contact with these countries is very non-political. This is extremely important. For example, in Myanmar, when a cyclone hit four years ago, we had people there, but various other people, such as the Americans, were sent packing. We have seen the same elsewhere." (Lebedev, 2014)*

So you see, when you can't send an American CIA spy in, you give him/her a Knights of Malta passport, and the problem is fixed! That is why they have such a close association with the CIA.

Besides helping Nazis escape to other countries, and smuggling very large lumps of money after World War II, and helping US spies get into countries they would not normally have access to, there is one more horrific use of these passports.

They are used to traffic women as sex workers, men as slaves, and children for the paedophiles in the Vatican, the UK and the US, among other places. Knights of Malta passports included the much loved (by the elites) BBC DJ and paedophile master mind **Jimmy Savile**. Savile was allowed to travel the world on the diplomatic passport, selecting children for his elite customers. Without having to go through the normal Customs procedures, Savile could traffic children with impunity.

Blackwater: Knights of Malta in Iraq

In 2007, during the Iraq War, **Blackwater**, a private "security" outfit based in the US, operated with impunity. Blackwater is more than

The double-headed eagle of the Vatican and Freemasons

just a "private army" of mercenaries, much more than just another capitalist war-profiteering business operation. It is an army operating outside all laws, outside and above the US Constitution and yet it was controlled by people within and outside of the US government, whose allegiance was primarily to the Vatican state. In other words, Blackwater was a religious army serving the Pope in Rome through the Order of Malta. This is another reason the Knights are considered under international law, as a sovereign entity with special diplomatic powers and privileges. Like Blackwater, the Order of Malta is "untouchable" because it is at the heart of the elite aristocracy.

One of the symbols of the military orders of the Vatican, the double-headed eagle emblazoned with the Maltese cross, signifies omnipotent royal dominion over both East and West. The orb signifies temporal dominion over the globe of Earth, and the sceptre signifies control over the spiritual and religious impulses of humanity. This eagle symbol is used in the masonic rite of **Memphis and Misraim**, under which it reads, "*Order Out of Chaos*", the Hegelian method of crisis creation.

It is found on the seals of many European and Eurasian nation states including that of Russia, indicating direct Vatican control over those countries. It symbolises the desire of a predatory elite with virtually unlimited resources, to totally dominate the entire world under a New World Order global government system using secrecy, manipulation, coercion, and terror with the *ends justifying the means*.

These SMOM Knights are behind most of the trouble in the world and they must be exposed as the criminals that they are. They are not nice people helping the poor, though they use good people in the lower ranks as useful idiots. They are behind drug-trafficking, child/human-trafficking, assassinations, wars, crime-syndicates, major terrorist events, a new torture inquisition, total information surveillance, social demoralization and seek to completely enslave the human species in a global Big Brother totalitarian regime, as they kill off the majority of us in the process. In fact, a lot of this has either come to pass, or is in the process of being implemented. We are on the brink of WWIII which has been entirely staged by these profoundly evil men. Therefore, we have no time left for pussyfooting around.

But don't take my word for it, do you your own research, find out and expose them yourself before these dirty Blackwater mercenary thugs are allowed to patrol American streets and confiscate guns during the next staged disaster. We can't let this happen in America.

Notable US military members of SMOM include top crusading generals such as Alexander Haig, William Westmoreland, and Charles A. Willoughby, an admitted Fascist.

Other notable members include:

Reinhard Gehlen (Nazi war criminal), Heinrich Himmler (Nazi war criminal), Kurt Waldheim (Nazi war criminal), Franz von Papen (Hitler enabler), Fritz Thyssen (Hitler's financier), Rupert Murdoch, Tony Blair, Pat Buchanan, William F. Buckley, Jr., Precott Bush, Jr. (Nazi financier), Edward Egan (Archbishop NY), Licio Gelli, Ted Kennedy, David Rockefeller, Phyllis Schlafly (Dame), J. Edgar Hoover, Joseph Kennedy, Henry Luce, Thomas 'Tip' O'Neill, Ronald Reagan, Giscard d'Estaing, Allen Dulles (**Director of CIA**), Avery Dulles, Frank C Carlucci, Nelson Mandela (Honorary member), Rick Santorum, Juan Carlos (King of Spain and Jerusalem), Oliver North, George H.W Bush, Augusto Pinochet, William Randolph Hearst, Francis L. Kellogg.

German Iron Cross (Cross of Malta)

Such a list should make you sit up and pay attention, but it is only the tip of the iceberg unfortunately. Then we come to another SMOM member, important to what is transpiring in Iraq. Educated at the Jesuit Georgetown University, former Pentagon Inspector General **Joseph Edward Schmitz**, Blackwater's operations chief, is a member of both SMOM and **Opus Dei.** All the top Nazis in the US Government are connected in some way to the Vatican, Jesuits, and Knights of Malta and have been for decades, as were the Italian Fascists and German Nazis of WWII. After all, what was their favourite symbol after the swastika? The Maltese Cross of course!

The Iron Cross (Cross of Malta) is a famous German military medal dating back to the 19th century. During the 1930s, the Nazi regime superimposed a swastika on the traditional medal, turning it into a Nazi symbol. After World War II, the medal was discontinued but neo-Nazis and other white supremacists subsequently adopted it as a symbol and it has been a commonly-used hate symbol ever since.

Nazis and the Catholic Church

The Catholic Church and the Knights of Malta had a very cosy "bromance" with the Nazis, but we don't talk about that in polite conversation do we. So I will let the pictures do the talking.

The Knights of Malta are a top Illuminati group that help facilitate the war machine, human trafficking, child trafficking, drug trafficking, and international espionage. Their membership is a who's who of the world's elite, who are obviously complicit in their nefarious activities.

Archbishop Cesare Orsenigo congratulates Adolf Hitler 1939, Birthday

Adolf Hitler welcomes Reich Bishop Ludwig Müller (wearing Malta Cross) and the Abbot, 1934, Nazi Party rally in Nuremberg

Catholic priests salute Hitler, at the Catholic youth gathering in the stadium of Berlin-Neukölln, August 1933

Two Bishops with Wilhelm Frick and Dr. Joseph Goebbels; all salute Adolf Hitler.

Pope Pius XII, born Eugenio Maria Giuseppe Giovanni Pacelli, using Nazi guards for his security.

Closely embedded with the Knights is another Catholic secret society known as the **Society of Jesus** (the men in black!).

THE JESUITS

The order called the **Society of Jesus**, known usually as **The Jesuits**, grew out of the activity of **St. Ignatius** of Loyola, a Spanish soldier who experienced a religious conversion during a period of convalescence from a wound received in battle. After a period of intense prayer, he composed the Spiritual Exercises, a guidebook to convert the heart and mind to a closer following of Jesus Christ.

On August 15, **1534,** at Paris, six young men who had met him at the University of Paris and made a retreat according to the Spiritual Exercises, joined him in vows of poverty, chastity, and a pilgrimage to Jerusalem. If this last promise did not prove possible, as it did not, they vowed to accept any apostolic work requested by the Pope.

In **1539,** Ignatius drafted the first outline of the order's organisation, which **Pope Paul III** approved on September 27, 1540. The society grew rapidly, and it quickly assumed a prominent role in the Counter-Reformation defence and revival of Catholicism. Almost from the beginning, education and scholarship became the society's principal work. The early Jesuits, however, also produced preachers and catechists who devoted themselves to the care of the young, the sick, prisoners, prostitutes, and soldiers; they also were often called upon to undertake the controversial task of confessor to many of the royal and ruling families of Europe. It was this task that quickly helped them to become the premier "intelligence/spy" organisation in the world. If you know the sins of the elites, that is valuable intel for blackmail.

The society entered the foreign mission field within months of its founding as Ignatius sent **Saint Francis Xavier**, his most gifted companion, and three others to the East. More Jesuits were to be involved in missionary work than in any other activity, save education. By the time of Ignatius's death in 1556, about 1,000 Jesuits were already working throughout Europe and in Asia, Africa, and the New World. Indeed, during the 16th and 17th centuries, Jesuits missionaries could be found in Brazil, India, Japan, China, Paraguay, and among the North American natives. By 1626 the number of Jesuits was 15,544, and in 1749 the total was 22,589.

The preeminent position of the Jesuits among the religious orders and their championship of the Pope exposed them to hostility. By the middle of the 18th century a variety of adversaries, both lay and clerical, were seeking to destroy the order. The opposition can be traced to several reasons, primarily, perhaps, to the Order using its operatives to spy, influence, and control national governments.

In **1773 Pope Clement XIV**, under pressure, especially from the governments of France, Spain, and Portugal, issued a decree abolishing the order. The society's corporate existence was maintained in Russia, where political circumstances—notably the opposition of **Catherine II the Great**—prevented the canonical execution of the suppression. Under pressure from **Carl Rothschild**, who demanded that the Jesuits take up their former work, especially in the field of education and in the missions, became so insistent that in **1814 Pope Pius VII** re-established the society. Rothschild needed the Jesuits back out in the field to gather intelligence. The pressure he put on the Pope was financial. The Pope owed Rothschild a lot of money, and this was a way to clear the debt.

After it was restored, the order grew to be the largest order of male religious, and the largest intelligence gathering network on earth. Work in education on all levels continued to involve more Jesuits than any other activity; however, the number of Jesuits working in the mission fields, especially in Asia and Africa, exceeded that of any other religious order. They were also involved in a broad and complex list of activities, including work in the field of communications, in social work, in ecumenism, and even in politics. In **2013 Francis I** became the first Jesuit to be elected Pope (Jesuits, 2015).

Behind the Mask

The true face of Jesuitry is well hidden behind a masque of false piety. A Jesuit stood apart and alone among the human race in his perverted morality that sanctioned any deceit, torture, murder, or assassination of opponents, whilst believing he had God on his side.

The Jesuit initiate was taught to abandon all notions of patriotism and loyalty to the tribe since it was inculcated into him that the Society was his country. The initiate was also severed from his family and friends for his vow to the Order made him forsake his father's house.

Indeed, the Jesuit initiation rite reads in part:

> *I do further promise and declare that I will, when opportunity presents, make and wage relentless war, secretly and openly, against all heretics, Protestants and Masons, as I am directed to do, to extirpate them from the face of the whole earth; and that I will spare neither age, sex, nor condition, and that will hang, burn, waste, boil, flay, strangle, an bury alive these infamous heretics; rip up the stomachs and wombs of their women, and crush their infants' heads against the walls in order to annihilate their execrable race. That when the same cannot be done openly I will secretly use the poisonous cup, the strangulation cord, the steel of the poniard, or the leaden bullet, regardless of the honour, rank, dignity or authority of the persons, whatever may be their condition in life, either public or private, as I at any time may be directed so to do by any agents of the Pope or Superior of the Brotherhood of the Holy Father of the Society of Jesus. In confirmation of which I hereby dedicate my life, soul, and all corporal powers, and with the dagger which I now receive I will subscribe my name written in my blood in testimony thereof; and should I prove false, or weaken in my determination, may my*

brethren and fellow soldiers of the militia
of the Pope cut off my hands and feet and my
throat from ear to ear, my belly be opened and
sulphur burned therein with all the punishment
that can be inflicted upon me on earth, and m
soul shall be tortured by demons in
eternal hell forever. **"**

The initiate was also cut off from property and wealth, since he was obliged to take a vow of perpetual poverty: notwithstanding that the Order itself was fabulously wealthy. The Jesuit was also cut off from the State in which he lived for he was taught that he was the subject of a higher monarch than the sovereign of the nation (Phelps, 2015). This was of course his own **General**.

The Black Pope

The **Superior General of the Society of Jesus** is the official title of the leader of the Society of Jesus. He is generally addressed as **Father General** and the position carries the nickname of the **Black Pope**, after his simple black priest's vestments, as contrasted to the white garb of the Pope. The current *Superior General* is the Reverend Father **Adolfo Nicolás** (Black Pope, 2015).

- The Black Pope and his six Generals control the White Pope and the Vatican.
- The Jesuits have representatives in the Illuminati Council of 300; Council on Foreign Relations (CFR), Bilderberg, United Nations and Club of Rome.
- They give orders to the Knights of Malta, Knights of Columbus, and Opus Dei.
- The Jesuits were the role model and pioneers of all espionage agencies, and still have agents within all of these groups: CIA, FBI, NSA, ASIO, MI5, MI6, FSB (Russia), DGSC (France) and BND (Germany).
- The Jesuits have infiltrated all Western governments and do have sway, particularly in the education system.

The Jesuits built the largest and best run spy/espionage agency in the world, before the world had spies. They were so good that the Rothschilds funded them to expand and upgrade their technology and training. Part of wanting to know everything, all the time, they also built an impressive education system in schools. This was to indoctrinate children into the Jesuit ways, but also train those same children to spy for them.

Jesuits are essentially Socialist, like most of the Illuminati groups. That said, they still enjoy a luxury based elite group at the top, while the lower ranks have to live in poverty. The book/movie **Animal Farm** would be the best analogy of the Jesuit perfect world if ever they got to run things.

Luckily the Jesuits do not have as much power as they once did last century. Many people still believe the Jesuits are the ruling group behind the Illuminati, but it is just not the case. While once very powerful, they now take their orders from the Committee of 300 and Bilderbergers. They still carry out their own programs and false flags, but these are not usually designed to take over the world. They are usually a vendetta against another group that have disrespected them.

If you really want to get into the heads of the Jesuits, there is a document online that tells all. It is called **Secret Instructions of the Society of Jesus**. It was originally circulated in manuscript form until 1612 when it was finally published in Cracow, Poland. It was later translated into English and published in 1882 in San Francisco, California. The online copy was reprinted from the copy in the Library *Of Congress* Washington, D.C. (Secret Instructions, 1882).

OPUS DEI

Opus Dei is an organisation of the Catholic Church that emphasizes the Catholic belief that everyone is called to holiness and that ordinary life is a path to sanctity. The celibate numeracies and numerary assistants live in special centres, while associates are celibate members living in their private homes. The order was founded in Spain in 1928 by Roman Catholic priest, **Josemaría Escrivá** with the approval of **Pope Pius XII.**

When Dan Brown's *Da Vinci Code* was published, it claimed that Opus Dei was a secret organisation within the Church whose aim was to defeat the **Priory of Sion** and those who seek to uncover the "truth" about Christianity and the alleged royal bloodline of Jesus. Outside of the book, there has been a great deal of controversy over Opus Dei, because of the strictness of its religious structure.

The Catholic Church openly forbids secret societies, however almost every Pope and Cardinal in the last 100 years has been a 33° Freemason, and or Rosicrucian. Opus Dei investigators have frequently tried to debunked claims that this organisation is acting in secrecy to further a sinister agenda. However, Opus Dei is a real organisation and it is run by the **Jesuits**. It is where the Jesuits send their "special forces" for discipline training, blocking out pain and other super-human feats.

These operatives are then used in assassinations, agent provocateurs, and other covert jobs. Opus Dei are soldiers, so they are not insiders of the Illuminati, but their Jesuit bosses are.

THE PRIORY OF SION

After the publication of the **Da Vinci Code** by **Dan Brown**, a great deal of interest in the **Priory of Sion** had been created. Unfortunately for those hoping to find and join the Priory, it is, in fact fictional. It was a hoax created in **1956** by a pretender to the French Throne, **Pierre Plantard**. Letters in existence dating from the 1960s written by Plantard, de Cherisey and de Sède to each other confirm that the three were engaging in an out-and-out confidence trick, describing schemes on how to combat criticisms of their various allegations and how they would make up new allegations to try to keep the whole thing going. Despite this, many people still continue to believe that the Priory exists and functions to this day.

The authors of the well-known book, **Holy Blood and the Holy Grail**, misled by the hoax, stated:

> 1. The Priory of Sion has a long history starting in AD 1099, and had illustrious Grand Masters including Isaac Newton and Leonardo da Vinci.
>
> 2. The order protects certain royal claimants because they believe them to be the literal

descendants of Jesus and his alleged wife Mary Magdalene or, at the very least, of King David.

3. The priory seeks the founding of a "Holy European Empire" that would become the next hyper power and usher in a new world order of peace and prosperity.

None of these claims are true. End of story

THE ORDER OF SKULL AND BONES

Order of Skull and Bones logo

Then the Lord God said, "Behold, the man has become like one of Us, to know good and evil. And now, lest he put out his hand and take also of the tree of life, and eat, and live forever"

—GENESIS 3:22 NEW KING JAMES VERSION (NKJV)

The **Order of Skull and Bones**, is a Yale University secret society that was originally known as the **Brotherhood of Death**, which started in Bavaria, Germany as a **death cult** (a group that worships death). These type of student secret societies were very common in Germany at the time. **William Huntington Russell** (Bloodline family), while studying in Germany, was initiated into the **Brotherhood of Death**. After graduating, he returned to Yale University in New Haven Connecticut to start his own chapter of the *Brotherhood of Death*, along with all of its rituals and macabre relics.

Russell rebranded the society in Yale to the **Order of Skull and Bones**. It is now the oldest student secret society in the United States. It was founded in 1832 and membership is open to an elite few. Indeed, they only choose or "tap" 15 senior students a year. They go on to become the patriarchs when they graduate and lifetime members of the ultimate old boys' club. In fact, quite a few former Bonesmen use their bonds of power and influence to make their way up through the ranks of America's power elite, many in the area of foreign policy. A select few Bonesmen have parleyed their Skull and Bones connections to make a play for the White House, including President William Howard Taft, President George H.W. Bush, and his son, President George W. Bush (Sutton, 2002).

The Nazi Connection

It is worth noting here that back in Germany, the *Brotherhood of Death* later morphed into the **Schutzstaffel** – the Nazi SS inner circle after **Heinrich Himmler** got involved (SS, 2015). This helps explain why the Bush family have such a strong affiliation with the Nazis, as well as why the CIA was based on and manned by the German **Gestapo**. And how George HW Bush become the 11th Director of Central Intelligence (CIA) without any qualifications whatsoever for this position.

It is a little known fact that Heinrich Himmler attempted to get a deal through to the allies toward the end of World War II. Using Bonesmen connections, he sent a message offering to join forces with the US and Britain to defeat the Russian Communists. It was too little too late for the Allies, so they rejected the deal. Himmler committed suicide and Churchill later regretted that they did not gang up on Russia and stamp out Communism.

Ritual Influence

The society uses masonic inspired rituals that are peppered with **Adam Weishaupt's** Illuminati influence. Members meet every Thursday and Sunday of each week in a building they call the "Tomb." Initiates engage in strange bonding rituals such as lying in a stone coffin naked and recite their sexual history while they masturbate, or reveal their darkest secrets in front of all the members. The object of such rituals is to create intense loyalty among members of the society. Many of their rituals contain satanic overtones.

The Goddess of the Bonesmen

Bonesmen worship an ancient Greek Goddess of the Underworld called **Angelos** (*wrongly stated as Eulogia by Alexandra Robbins*).

Angelos was raised by nymphs to whose care her father had entrusted her (*Bonesmen are sent their by their fathers also*). One day she stole her mother Hera's anointments and gave them away to Europe (*initiates are expected to steal something of great value and beauty and place it in the Tomb as an offering to Angelos*). To escape Hera's wrath, she had to hide first in the house of a woman in labour, and next among people who were carrying a dead man (*Bonesmen "hide" in the coffin.*)

Hera eventually ceased from prosecuting her, and Zeus ordered the Cabeiroi (demons) to cleanse Angelos. They performed the purification rite in the waters of the Acherusia Lake in the Underworld (*One of the Thousand Islands, Deer Island, which lies near Alexandria Bay, New York, is used as a Skull & Bones retreat and a place they perform their "cleansing/bathing" ritual*). Consequently, she received the world of the dead as her realm of influence, and was assigned an epithet Katachthonia "she of the underworld" (Angelos, 2015). This is why the Bonesmen worship the "Underworld" Goddess, and pay tribute to her with every war and false flag death they help create.

According to **Judy Schiff**, Chief Archivist at the Yale University Library, the names of the members were not kept secret until the 1970's, but the rituals always have been. Both of the **Bush** presidents were members of the society while studying at Yale, and a number of other members have gone on to great fame and fortune.

> **❝❝** *Those on the inside know it as The Order. Others have known it for more than 150 years as Chapter 322 of a German Secret Society. More formally, for legal purposes, The Order was incorporated as The Russell Trust in 1856. — Anthony C. Sutton, America's Secret Establishment, 1986* **❞❞**

Nicknames

On an initiate's first day in The Order, they are assigned a name, which they will be known as for the rest of their life among their Bonesmen brethren. Names that are regularly used are: **Magog**, which is assigned to the initiate with the most experience with the opposite sex; **Gog**, which is assigned to the least sexually experienced; **Long Devil**, for the tallest; **Boaz**, for Varsity American football captains; and **Little Devil** for the shortest. Bonesmen have often assumed names of mythological and legendary figures.

Theft of Sacred Bones

George W Bush's grandfather, Prescott the Nazi supporter, and two other members of the group, stole the remains of the Apache warrior **Geronimo** during the First World War. This was to fulfil their requirement to steal something of great value and place it in the Tomb as an offering to their goddess, Angelos.

However, the society's repeated refusal to comment on the story, or on rumours that new members have to kiss the chief's skull, prompted an extraordinary lawsuit in 2009. In a court action that names not only Yale and the society, but also **Barack Obama** and **Robert Gates**, his defence secretary. Twenty descendants of the famous American Indian leader are seeking to recover his remains so his spirit can be laid to rest in his tribal homeland.

Three **Bonesmen**, including **Prescott Bush**, served at **Fort Sill** during the First World War. The trio dug up Geronimo's remains in 1918 and took the skull and the two leg bones to Yale, where they are still kept in the society's hall, known as the Tomb on the university campus. New members kiss the Chiricahua Apache's skull as part of their initiation. They also created a trap door on top of the skull, which conceals something. Many researchers believe it holds keys (part of the Freemason connection) but no one except Bonesmen know for sure. (Robbins, 2002).

In 2003, Apache tribal leader **Ned Anderson** received a photo of the skull and bones of Geronimo (below) from within the societies Tomb room. It was sent by George H. W. Bush's, DC '48 (Skull and Bones) brother **Jonathan Bush,** who said they wanted to clear up the issue without going to trial. Ned recounts that Bush sounded "very encouraging" during their initial meeting. Eleven days later, Bush presented the display case.

Geronimo's bones on display in the Skull and Bones Tomb room. Past S&B Presidents in the background

Anderson refused to accept the skull because it appeared to belong to a small child. Bush acknowledged this fact but claimed it was the best he could do. Anderson then decided to sue them for the real bones. The original bones are still housed in the Skull and Bones Tomb room in Yale University as of 2015, and for whatever reason, they really don't want to give them up.

The people of the United States should demand a full FBI investigation of this and the return of the bones. However, that is unlikely to happen given that the Skull and Bones membership has included three US presidents including both Bushes, and that the CIA was built on members from the group. The CIA released a statement in 2007 in which it denied the group was an incubator for the CIA. Interestingly, the statement coincided with the popularity of the film *The Good Shepherd*, which tells the story of Yale's Skull and Bones members filling key positions within the CIA (Shepherd, 2006). So if you want to know more, watch that movie!

The Russell Story

The original founder of Skull and Bones was **William Russell**, who was from a Bloodline family. Originally they were Ashkenazi Jews called

Roessel. They lived in early 17th century Germany, which was a hotbed a Satanic Orders. They moved to Scotland where they changed their name to Russell. They became heavily involved in the Scottish Freemasons, and made some "good for business" connections. One of these connections got them a ticket to **Northern Ireland** as part of the English **Plantation of Ulster**, the organised colonisation (plantation) of Ulster by mainly Scottish and English people (Ulster, 1600). They were granted large areas of Irish lands which they aggressively exploited, making huge profits for **King James I** of Britain. The Russells proved to be ruthlessly efficient, and even though many of their Irish slave labourers died from mistreatment, malnutrition, and neglect, they still managed to make one of the biggest profits for the British Crown, and this got them noticed. After the Russell's made a literal "killing" in Ireland, they packed up and moved to the New World – the United States, hoping to make even more money.

The Russells have been prominent members of the Illuminati, the Masons, the Fabians, the Mormons, the Jehovah's Witnesses, the Jesuits, the Royal Society, and the Media controlled by those of the New World Order, and even a deputy chairman of the Federal Reserve. You can't get much more "connected" then that. Typically they have been merchants and lawyers, with a fair share of them also as Christian heretics (because they are Crypto Jews).

Drug Running

They got another big break from the British Crown when around ten years after the founding of the Skull and Bones, **Queen Victoria's** drug trade really took off with the forced signing of the 1842 **Treaty of Nanking**. Queen Victoria (Black Nobility) offered valuable drug trade routes to her Bloodline families (in return for a cut of course). Thus, the Russells played a key role in the opium trade in the 1800s and made billions in today's money. One of the Russell business partners was **Warren Delano Jr.**, chief of Russell and Company operations in Canton, China. Delano was the grandfather of **President Franklin Roosevelt**. The Russell and Company logo and flag on their fast sailing ships was a **Skull and Bones**. The **Taft family** (which is also related to George Bush by blood) and the **Harriman** family are two families that have been intimately connected to the Order of Skull and Bones (which is an entry point into the Illuminati and on the surface just an exclusive fraternity for young men) (Springmeier, 2002).

Therefore, as we have seen, they set up The Russell Trust in 1856. This was to handle the vast amounts of money they were generating from the lucrative opium trade. Eventually, Skull and Bones went into the drug trade big time and still use the Russell Trust to handle all their drug trafficking money. Most prominent Bonesmen get involved to raise a little capital before they start out in the big bad world. The Bush family are famous for cocaine imports from South America to the United States. Indeed, their buddy Bill Clinton helped them out as well, and he was one of their biggest customers with a wicked coke addiction in his early days.

CIA Connection

During the Vietnam War, the Skull and Bones almost exclusively handled the **Golden Triangle** drug trade through their **CIA** men (Golden, 1950). Most of the world's heroin came from the Golden Triangle until the early 21st century when **Afghanistan** became the world's largest producer – again thanks to **Zbigniew Brzezinski** and the CIA. During Vietnam they would ship the drugs back in body bags, and sometimes inside dead soldiers. They control the world's drug supply so they can finance their other globalist plans. But, they must give a cut to their Black Nobility masters. If you fiddle the books, or shipments go missing, then look out. At best, you will be publicly humiliated – Bill Clinton, and at worst they will bump you off. Now I know how George HW Bush got the job running the CIA!

Both on the same team

In **2004**, George W Bush, a Republican went up against John Kerry, a Democrat. This laughable "election" could not illustrate the issue of how the United States is run by one party, operating as a two party election any better. Bush and Kerry owe their allegiance to the Skull and Bones. During their time in the Tomb, they make a promise to always put the Skull and Bones first. So anyone who knew about the Bonesmen connection, knew that it didn't matter who was elected, because a Bonesman would be elected. And they were right. Bush won and started a war (death) in the Middle East. Kerry would have done the same thing, and 9/11 (death) would also still have happened (Bush and Kerry, 2004).

John Kerry
SKULL AND BONES 1966

George Bush
SKULL AND BONES 1968

Skull and Bones is very much an American Society, with no direct chapters around the world like other Secret Societies. But since the United States has a major role in global politics, that makes Skull and Bones very powerful, and important.

Notable Skull and Bones Members

(Some with their nicknames)

James L. Buckley (U.S. Senator), William F. Buckley:*Cheevy* (columnist), McGeorge Bundy: *Odin* (6th United States National Security Advisor, Bloodline, Comm 300), George W. Bush: *Temporary* (President / CIA Director), John Chafee (U.S. Senator and Secretary of the Navy), John Sherman Cooper (U.S. Senator and member of the Warren Commission), John Daniels (founder of Archer Daniels Midland), Paul Giamatti (actor), Briton Hadden: *Caliban* (co-founder of Time magazine with his Yale classmate Henry Luce – his wife became a Dame of the Knights of Malta), Pierre Jay (first chairman of the Federal Reserve Bank of New York), John Kerry: *Long Devil* (U.S. Senator), Winston Lord (Chairman of Council on Foreign Relations), W. Averell Harriman: *Thor* (Secretary of Commerce / 48th Governor of New York), Henry Luce: Baal (Time-Life), Francis Otto Matthiessen: *Little Devil* (Historian, literary critic, educator)

Archibald MacLeish: *Gigadibs* (poet), David McCullough (historian), William Huntington Russell (Connecticut State Legislator), Charles Seymour: *Machiavelli* (15th President of Yale University), Amos Alonzo Stagg (famous football coach), Harold Stanley (founder of Morgan Stanley), Potter Stewart: Crappo (U.S. Supreme Court justice), Anson Phelps Stokes: Achilles (very wealthy merchant banker), Alphonso Taft (Secretary of War and father of William Howard Taft), William Howard Taft: Magog (President), Robert A. Taft (U.S. Senator), Morrison R. Waite (U.S. Supreme Court justice), James Whitmore (actor), William Collins Whitney (U.S. Secretary of the Navy) and many others.

To Sum it all Up

The Order of the Skull and Bones is deeply enmeshed with the Illuminati. It is the largest of the "Death Cults" still active today. They have managed to get several of their members into the US Whitehouse as both US President and other high ranking positions. Skull and Bones tend to be an "Old Boys Club," but make no mistake, they are ruthless, savage and criminals all of them. Even if they don't participate in crimes directly, they certainly know about them, and actively cover them up. In my mind, they are a form of legalised Mafia.

THE BOHEMIAN GROVE

Weaving Spiders Come Not Here!

Part of the weirdo-world of the Illuminati is that they believe if they tell someone exactly what they are going to do to them, then they will incur no negative Karma. This, they believe, works if they do it to an individual, a group, or even a whole country. But for members of the New World Order, they believe in a different way of cleansing their souls of sin. Indeed, a summer holiday camp for rich, mostly gay, power players is called the **Bohemian Grove,** and they believe it will wash away their sins.

Every July, some of the richest and most powerful men (only) in the world gather at a 1092 Ha / 2,700 acre campground in **Monte Rio, California** for two weeks of heavy drinking, dress-ups (in women's clothing), super-secret talks, Satanic worship (the group insists they are simply "revering the Redwoods"), and other bizarre rituals.

Cremation of the Care Ritual at the Bohemian Grove

The people that gather at Bohemian Grove — have included prominent business leaders, former U.S. presidents, musicians, actors, and oil barons — they are told that, *"Weaving Spiders Come Not Here"*, meaning business deals are to be left outside. However, we know for sure that in 1942, a planning for the **Manhattan Project** took place at the grove, leading to the creation of the atom bomb.

The club is so hush-hush that little can be definitively said about it, but much of what we know today is from those who have infiltrated the camp, including Texas-based filmmaker **Alex Jones**. In 2000, Jones and his cameraman **Mike Hanson** entered the camp with a hidden camera and were able to film a Bohemian Grove ceremony called the **Cremation of Care**. During the ceremony, members wear hooded costumes and cremate a coffin effigy of a child called "Care" before a 12m / 40-foot stone Owl called **Moloch** (Jones, 2000). I have mentioned Moloch previously in *Book 1 – Secrets of the Soul*. This is one nasty, ancient demon god that demands virgin children sacrifices.

Yes, this is all true – your Presidents, leaders of industry, oil barons, media moguls and some celebrities gather once a year, in what **Richard Nixon** described as,

> *"The Bohemian Grove, which I attend from time to time--it is the most faggy goddamned thing you could ever imagine, with that San Francisco crowd",*

And they worship a 40 foot Owl Statue! Then they go into the woods, get drunk, and have mass gay orgies. They literally bus in loads of homosexual escorts and gay porn stars to keep the campers happy. Several have come forward and blown the whistle – no pun intended! (Gay Porn Star, 2004).

Most of these men then go back to wives and families. But getting back to the point – the *Cremation of Care* ritual is done once a year because these people believe it burns away all of the evil deeds from the previous year. It is the Catholic Church equivalent of Confession, and the priest absolving your sins. Except their sins apparently are absolved by a giant stone owl that devours children. I know - you can't make this stuff up!

The Bohemian Club's mascot is an owl, here cast in masonry, and perched over the main club entrance at 621 Taylor Street in San Francisco

Bigwigs who have attended the two-week retreat include George H.W. Bush, Dick Cheney, Alan Greenspan, Walter Cronkite, Newt Gingrich, Alexander Haig, Jack Kemp, Henry Kissinger, Colin Powell, John Major, William F. Buckley, former C.I.A. director William Casey and actor Danny Glover. Most of these names will pop up again and again in the following pages, as all are connected with the New World Order network of organisations. In fact, just like Bilderberg, you know you have made it in the NWO when you get an invitation to The Bohemian Grove. A full list of Bohemian Grove members can be seen here: (List, 2015).

ORDO TEMPLIS ORIENTIS

Ordo Templi Orientis (O.T.O.) (Order of the Temples of the East) is an organisation that was originally modelled on Masonry, but under the leadership of the self-styled "Great Beast 666" Aleister Crowley, it took on the principles of his religious system called **Thelema**. Thelema is based around a single law:

> *Do what thou wilt shall be the whole of the law.*

Membership is based upon degrees of initiation harking back to its Masonic roots, and they use highly stylised rituals for other events. The OTO currently claims to have over 3,000 members worldwide. They state on the US website that,

> *O.T.O. is dedicated to the high purpose of securing the Liberty of the Individual and his or her advancement in Light, Wisdom, Understanding, Knowledge, and Power through Beauty, Courage, and Wit, on the Foundation of Universal Brotherhood."* (OTO, 2015).

If you believe that, then I have a pyramid in Egypt for sale that you may be interested in. But seriously, in their own words they honour and adore Crowley. In fact, they even use the "Mass" Crowley created which he called the **Gnostic Mass**. Of the "Mass," Crowley wrote:

> *I resolved that my Ritual should celebrate the sublimity of the operation of universal forces without introducing disputable metaphysical theories. I would neither make nor imply any statement about nature which would not be endorsed by the most materialistic man of*

science. On the surface this may sound difficult but in practice I found it perfectly simple to combine the most rigidly rational conceptions of phenomena with the most exalted and enthusiastic celebration of their sublimity.

The ritual is overly stylised and uses virgin priestesses, children, and priests. Many Ancient Egyptian God's are invoked, as well as Satan. At one point the priestess performs a naked ritual, offering her body to the Dark Lord. From what we have already learnt of Crowley and his rituals, there will be demons, pain, hurt, humiliation, and psychological damage. Not the "Light, Wisdom, Understanding, Knowledge, and Power through Beauty, Courage, and Wit" they claim.

The fact is, the "public" face of the OTO and other similar groups is that they are "neo-groups" of New Age "wanna bees" that like to dress up and have a penchant for the dramatic. The type of people attracted to these groups are the type that like to "role" play. If Crowley walked into one of their meetings today he would laugh and walk out, or keel over in disgust.

Crowley was a hard-core black magician – the REAL thing. What they got up to in the **Abbey of Thelema** in Cefalù, Northern Sicily is what Crowley was all about. Not this fluffy bunny stuff these people are playing at. Indeed, that is why he left the Golden Dawn – because they were not hard core enough for him.

Like many of the groups around today, the OTO has two levels of initiates. The first, and lowest, are the New Age wann-bes I have spoken of. This is the public face you will find on the Internet or at the local lodge/coven/group.

The other is the much darker, true OTO and other societies Crowley and others envisaged. The dark groups are by invitation only, and you are only invited if you are already a wealthy, high ranking member of the Illuminati/New World Order. In fact, you would have to be at least a 33° Freemason to even be considered for initiation into the true OTO.

These public face groups have no idea about the true agenda. They are "useful idiots." If people want to investigate OTO, they find these people opening the front door. And these people can in all honesty say "*I have no idea what you are talking about*" in regard to Satan worshipping, child sacrifice rituals, and bestiality. These public groups are not insiders of the Illuminati.

The hidden level of the OTO is involved in satanic ritual, child sacrifice, and mind control. They are direct insiders of the Illuminati. I will be delving deeply into the Satanic Ritual groups and Trauma Based Mind Control in **Book III: Secrets of the Mind Control**.

HERMETIC ORDER OF THE GOLDEN DAWN

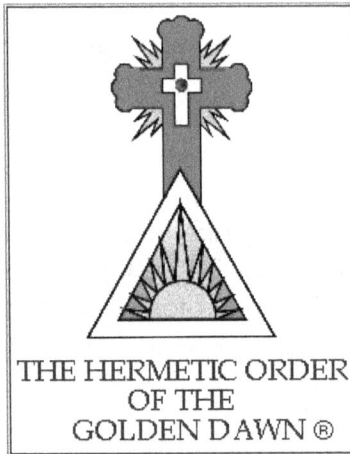

The order of the **Golden Dawn** was created by **Dr. William Robert Woodman, William Wynn Westcott**, and **Samuel Liddell MacGregor Mathers**. All three were Freemasons and members of **Societas Rosicruciana** in Anglia (an organisation with ties to Masonry). It is considered by many to be a forerunner of the **Ordo Templi Orientis** and a majority of modern Occult groups.

The belief system of the Golden Dawn is largely taken from Christian mysticism, Kabbalah, Hermeticism, the religion of Ancient Egypt, Freemasonry, Alchemy, Theosophy, Magick, and Renaissance writings. William Yeats and Aleister Crowley are two of the more famous members of the group.

The fundamental documents of the order are known as the **Cipher Documents**. These were translated into English using a cipher attributed to **Johannes Trithemius**. The documents are a series of 60 folios containing magick rituals. The basic structure of many of these rituals appear to originate with Rosicrucianism. There is a great deal of controversy surrounding the origins of these documents.

The Golden Dawn more or less collapsed and fell apart after Crowley left. He exposed them as a bunch of teetotaling "academics," with no real magick in their experience. After Crowley split off, many members either realised he was right, or had just lost interest.

However, just like the OTO public face, the Golden Dawn also has a public face. But unlike the OTO, there are no other faces or levels. The Golden Dawn is, and always was, a bunch of "armchair" experts. Yes, they are knowledgeable about many esoteric and metaphysical subjects in "theory," but have little or no experience in applying this knowledge to practical applications. In fact, they now form part of the **New Age movement** which is an Illuminati creation, but not one the members of these groups are even aware of.

Just Say No

There are literally hundreds of secret societies all over the world. In fact, China has some of the biggest that I did not even get into. Suffice it to say, they are all controlled by the Illuminati, and more or less work toward the same end. They are either "teaching" or "doing" and sometimes both. Make no mistake, to get anywhere in the world where you will be rich, famous, politics, a celebrity, or a New Age "guru," you must first be a member of a secret society. Am I saying you should do this to get ahead – NO WAY! I am saying that the current system is rigged, and this *seems* to be the only way.

In order to plan and execute their plans, the Illuminati need to recruit the best and brightest in each field. To do this, they set up a worldwide network of secret societies that do not recognize borders, governments, religions, languages, or cultures.

It is via these secret societies that the Illuminati recruit, then indoctrinate those that are willing to sell their soul to the highest bidder.

If people stopped joining them, then they would just fade away. Remember, things only stay alive while they are still relevant. And never forget, at some point, you will have to pay the fiddler!

What country can preserve its liberties, if its rulers are not warned from time to time, that this people preserve the spirit of resistance?

(Thomas Jefferson)

A quote from Thomas Jefferson

References:

About, (2015). *About Us*. [online] Moussa106.franklysolutions.com. Available at: http://moussa106. franklysolutions.com/?q=content/about-us [Accessed 2 Dec. 2015].

Black Pope, (2015). *Superior General of the Society of Jesus*. [online] Wikipedia. Available at: https:// en.wikipedia.org/wiki/Superior_General_of_the_Society_of_Jesus [Accessed 3 Dec. 2015].

Casalou, A. (2003). *The Scottish Rite Journal*. [online] 204.3.136.66. Available at: http://204.3.136.66/web/ journal-files/Issues/sep03/casalou.htm [Accessed 2 Dec. 2015].

Dafoe, S. (2015). *Masonic Dictionary | Your Daily Lesson In Masonic Education | www.masonicdictionary.com*. [online] Masonicdictionary.com. Available at: http://www.masonicdictionary.com/ [Accessed 3 Dec. 2015].

Dafoe, S. (2015). *Order of the Eastern Star | Masonic Dictionary | www.masonicdictionary.com*. [online] Masonicdictionary.com. Available at: http://www.masonicdictionary.com/oes.html [Accessed 3 Dec. 2015].

Duncan's Masonic Ritual, (1886). *Duncan's Masonic Ritual and Monitor: Royal Arch, or Seventh Degree*. [online] Sacred-texts.com. Available at: http://www.sacred-texts.com/mas/dun/dun08.htm [Accessed 2 Dec. 2015].

Freemasonrywatch, (2015). *Shriners Secrets | Shriners News | Shriners Circus's*. [online] Freemasonrywatch. org. Available at: http://freemasonrywatch.org/shriners.html [Accessed 2 Dec. 2015].

Frost, S. (2006). *"Promoter" Accuses Shriners of Racism in Concert Fraud*. [online] Freemasonrywatch.org. Available at: http://freemasonrywatch.org/promoter.accuses.shriners.racism.html [Accessed 2 Dec. 2015].

Frost, S. (2006). *Above the law? Shriner Treasurers' Minutes, Part 10*. [online] Newsvine. Available at: http:// sandyfrost.newsvine.com/_news/2006/11/16/445464-above-the-law-shriner-treasurers-minutes-part-10 [Accessed 2 Dec. 2015].

Frost, S. (2006). *Defamation? Shriners: Part 8*. [online] Newsvine. Available at: http://sandyfrost.newsvine. com/_news/2006/09/21/369852-defamation-shriners-part-8 [Accessed 2 Dec. 2015].

Frost, S. (2006). *Follow the Money: Shriners Part 5*. [online] Newsvine. Available at: http://sandyfrost. newsvine.com/_news/2006/06/29/272572-follow-the-money-shriners-part-5 [Accessed 2 Dec. 2015].

Gillard, J. (2012). *Fabian Society question at the Gillard 'People's Forum' in Perth, July 2012*. [online] YouTube. Available at: https://youtu.be/AhvuR05ZNUY [Accessed 2 Dec. 2015].

Hervet, F. (1986). Knights of Darkness: The Sovereign Military Order of Malta. *Covert Action*, (25), p.31.

Jesuits, (2015). *Who are the Jesuits, and what do they believe?*. [online] GotQuestions.org. Available at: http:// www.gotquestions.org/Jesuits.html [Accessed 3 Dec. 2015].

Leadbeater, C. (1998). *Freemasonry and its ancient mystic rites*. New York: Gramercy Books.

Lebedev, E. (2014). *What really goes on at the Knights of Malta's secretive headquarters?*. [online] The Independent. Available at: http://www.independent.co.uk/news/world/europe/caped-crusaders-what-really-goes-on-at-the-knights-of-maltas-secretive-headquarters-9217469.html [Accessed 2 Dec. 2015].

List, (2015). *List of Bohemian Club members*. [online] Wikipedia. Available at: https://en.wikipedia.org/wiki/ List_of_Bohemian_Club_members [Accessed 3 Dec. 2015].

Long, J. (2015). *Students at Pennsylvania school want 'Lynch Hall' renamed because of the word 'Lynch'*. [online] Fox News. Available at: http://www.foxnews.com/us/2015/12/10/students-at-pennsylvania-school-want-lynch-hall-renamed-because-of-word-lynch/ [Accessed 11 Dec. 2015].

Malta, O. (2015). *The Knights of Malta» Sovereign Order of Malta - Official site*. [online] Orderofmalta. int. Available at: http://www.orderofmalta.int/the-order-and-its-institutions/310/the-knights-of-malta/?lang=en [Accessed 2 Dec. 2015].

Marrs, T. (2005). *Codex Magica*. Austin, Tex.: RiverCrest Pub.

Phelps, E. (2015). *Vatican Assassins | Eric Jon Phelps*. [online] Vaticanassassins.org. Available at: http:// vaticanassassins.org/ [Accessed 3 Dec. 2015].

RestoreAustralia, (2012). *The Fabians and Gillard*. [online] Available at: http://www.restoreaustralia.org.au/ the-fabians-and-gillard/ [Accessed 2 Dec. 2015].

Richards Goes Crazy, (2006). *Michael Richards Goes Crazy*. [online] YouTube. Available at: https://youtu.be/ amjUNF_R_PY [Accessed 2 Dec. 2015].

Schacht, C. (2015). *Chris Schacht*. [online] Wikipedia. Available at: https://en.wikipedia.org/wiki/Chris_Schacht [Accessed 11 Dec. 2015].

Secret Instructions, (1882). *Secret Instructions of the Society of Jesus*. [online] Exposingdeceptions.org. Available at: http://exposingdeceptions.org/Instructions.html [Accessed 3 Dec. 2015].

Shriners, (2010). *The Ultimate Guide*. 1st ed. [ebook] Shriners International. Available at: https://web.archive. org/web/20070115045306/http://www.shrinershq.org/files/members/pdf/Mem_ShrinerPrimer.pdf [Accessed 2 Dec. 2015].

9

ORGANISATIONS OF THE NEW WORLD ORDER

> *"Nothing less than to create a world system of financial control in private hands able to dominate the political system of each country and the economy of the world as a whole."*
>
> — PROFESSOR CARROLL QUIGLEY, 1966

The largest mechanism used by the bloodlines to implement the New World Order agenda is the global secret society network. Politicians, bankers, businessmen, and media personalities - the biggest names in history and world affairs form a huge secret society matrix. This hierarchical pyramid structured network is constantly recruiting and placing members in key influential positions. In order to orchestrate global events and policy decisions from behind the scenes, many niche secret societies groom and position politicians, media personalities, and other "yes-men" so they may best aid the **Great Work**.

The Great Work

The **New World Order** (NWO) has been one of the major agendas of the Secret Societies/Illuminati for thousands of years. In short, they want to achieve three things:

- One World Government
- One World Currency
- One World Religion

These are no doubt big tasks to try and achieve, therefore, our "Owners" employ, indoctrinate, and pay handsomely (then blackmail), the best and brightest people from all over the world to carry out their plans and build their empires.

The very top positions usually go to insider "buddies" or direct nepotism, and they are usually headed by Rothschild Zionists. I will repeat again at this point – this is NOT a Jewish conspiracy. The average Jew has no idea about what is going on at the highest levels of society. Just like the average Freemason doesn't have a clue what is going on at the top, 33rd degree level, and just as the burger flipper at your local McDonalds has no idea what the international managers are meeting about next week.

No, it is not a Jewish thing, it is not a Freemason thing, it is not a Jesuit thing, and it is not banker's thing, it is a sociopath/psychopath thing.

People who lust after power, and will do anything to get it, including pretending to be a Jew, a Freemason, a Politician, or whatever else it will take to get ahead. Race, gender, or age do not come into this.

Only ruthless ambition, no empathy, and the ability to mask your true intentions, even from those closest to you. These are the traits of a psychopath. Hollywood, which is run by these people, has tried to convince people that psychopaths are serial killers who live in some dirty room, alone and in the dark. Yes, there are some people like that, very few, but they don't do it for mega-power. The majority of true psychopaths live, work and play in society, just like normal people.

THE DISTURBING LINK BETWEEN PSYCHOPATHY AND LEADERSHIP

It is not the image we like to have when we think of business leaders. But troubling research indicates that in the ranks of senior management, psychopathic behaviour may be more common than we think – more prevalent in fact, than the amount such seriously aberrant behaviour occurs in the general population.

At first look, this may seem counterintuitive, even outrageous. We tend to think of psychopathy as the province of criminals, with leadership qualities that may land someone atop a fringe religious cult, but not in a boardroom. But before discussing the research, let's consider for a moment why this possibility is actually less bizarre than it may initially seem.

The hallmarks of the psychopathic personality involve egocentric, grandiose behaviour, completely lacking empathy and conscience. Additionally, psychopaths may be charismatic, charming, and adept at manipulating one-on-one interactions.

In a corporation, one's ability to advance is determined in large measure by a person's ability to favourably impress his or her direct manager. Unfortunately, certain of these psychopathic qualities – in particular charm, charisma, grandiosity (which can be mistaken for vision or confidence) and the ability to "perform" convincingly in one-on-one settings – are also qualities that can help one get ahead in the business world.

Snakes in Suits: When Psychopaths Go to Work, by **Paul Babiak**, Ph.D., and **Robert Hare**, Ph.D., published in 2006, is an excellent book. It is the foundational work on the subject and offers a comprehensive look at how psychopaths operate effectively in the workplace. To quote a few portions:

> *Several abilities – skills, actually – make it difficult to see psychopaths for who they are. First, they are motivated to, and have a talent for, 'reading people' and for sizing them up quickly. They identify a person's likes and dislikes, motives, needs, weak spots, and vulnerabilities…Second, many psychopaths come across as having excellent oral communication skills. In many cases, these skills are more apparent than real because of their readiness to jump right into a conversation without the social inhibitions that hamper most people… Third, they are masters of impression management; their insight into the psyche of others combined*

> *with a superficial – but convincing – verbal fluency allows them to change their situation skillfully as it suits the situation and their game plan.*

The authors also note that many psychopaths, of course, are not suited for the business environment:

> *Some do not have enough social or communication skill or education to interact successfully with others, relying instead on threats, coercion, intimidation, and violence to dominate others and to get what they want. Typically, such individuals are manifestly aggressive and rather nasty, and unlikely to charm victims into submission, relying on their bullying approach instead.*

Snakes in Suits is less about them than about those who are willing to use their 'deadly charm' to con and manipulate others (Babiak and Hare, 2006).

How prevalent are psychopaths in the ranks of senior management? Exact counts are impossible to obtain. It is humorously difficult to imagine a researcher approaching a head of Human Resources and asking, *"We'd like to do some research to assess just how many psychopaths your organisation has in its leadership."*

In 2010 however, **Paul Babiak**, **Robert Hare** and **Craig Neumann** had the opportunity to examine psychopathy in a sample of 203 individuals from numerous companies' management development programs. While these individuals were not yet at the top rungs of their organisations, they were on track potentially to get there (Babiak, Neumann and Hare, 2010).

The study's findings were disturbing, bearing out the large amount of anecdotal evidence the researchers had long been gathering. The research showed that approximately 3% of those assessed in this management development program study scored in the psychopath range – well above the incidence of 1% in the general population. By comparison, the incidence of psychopathy in prison populations is estimated at around 15%.

So in business, it works out about one out of every 25 business leaders could be psychopathic. The study suggests that they disguise the condition by hiding behind their high status, playing up their charm and by manipulating others.

Favourable environmental factors such as a happy childhood mean they can function in a workplace rather than channelling their energies in more violent or destructive ways. This certainly explains why so many people from "money" families end up being the worse psychopaths that always seem to get in to positions of power.

Revealing the results in a BBC Horizon documentary, Babiak said:

Dr. Paul Babiak, Ph.D.

"Psychopaths really aren't the kind of person you think they are. In fact, you could be living with or married to one for 20 years or more and not know that person is a psychopath. We have identified individuals that might be labelled 'the successful psychopath'. Part of the problem is that the very things we're looking for in our leaders, the psychopath can easily mimic. Their natural tendency is to be charming. Take that charm and couch it in the right business language and it sounds like charismatic leadership." (Horizon: Season 48, Episode 5 - Are You Good or Evil? 2011)

Babiak designed a 111-point questionnaire with Professor Bob Hare, of the University of British Columbia in Canada, a renowned expert in psychopathy. Hare believes about 1% of Americans can be described as psychopaths.

The survey suggests psychopaths are actually poor managerial performers, but are adept at climbing the corporate ladder because they can cover up their weaknesses by subtly charming superiors and subordinates.

Corporate psychopaths tend to be manipulative, arrogant, callous, impatient, impulsive, unreliable, and prone to fly into rages, according to Professor Hare. They break promises, and take credit for the work of others and blame everyone else when things go wrong.

> *"Psychopaths are social predators and like all predators they are looking for feeding grounds," he says. "Wherever you get power, prestige, and money, you will find them."*

Sound familiar? Think of your politicians, local business leaders, international business leaders and many religious leaders etc. This describes just about every billionaire from Chapter 1. Hare told **Horizon**:

"The higher the psychopathy, the better they looked – lots of charisma and they talk a good line. But if you look at their actual performance and ratings as a team player and productively, it's dismal. Looked good, performed badly. You have to think of psychopaths as having at their disposal a very large repertoire of behaviours. So they can use charm, manipulation, intimidation, whatever is required. A psychopath can actually put themselves in your skin, intellectually not emotionally. They can tell what you're thinking, they can look at your body language, they can listen to what you're saying, but what they don't really do is feel what you feel. What this allows them to do is use words to manipulate and con and to interact with you without the baggage of feeling your pain."

Professor Robert D. Hare, Ph.D., C.M

Preventing Organizational Problems

One final but not insignificant topic: Given the very real potential for harm that psychopaths in positions of power have (both for other people and for entire organisations), what steps can companies take to help prevent costly and damaging hiring, and promotion mistakes?

Snakes in Suits devotes some 40 pages to this important subject (reading I'd highly recommend to all Human Resources executives). In the interests of brevity, here are my own three key considerations that I believe hiring committees, boards of directors, and senior managers should bear in mind when considering candidates top-level hires and promotions.

Internal succession planning – A well-conceived internal succession program is the best way to inoculate an organisation against a disastrous candidate, as those making promotion decisions will presumably have had years – not hours – to study an individual in action and observe his or her character.

Focus on verified, tangible results – Since internal candidates are not always a satisfactory option, when hiring from the outside, focus on real substantive accomplishments that can be verified – more than on personal charm and force of personality. While charisma and persuasive speaking skills are naturally desirable leadership talents, they're also well within the repertoire of a psychopath. Be sure there's a solid foundation of actual accomplishment to support all claims.

Glean whatever you can about the moral and ethical character of a candidate – This is not always easy in a formal interview process, but any subtle insights that can be gained about an individual's moral compass and value system can be critical. Bear in mind a psychopath's skills to manipulate a situation and tell interviewers what he or she believes they want to hear.

In short, this is just another lens through which to view high-level hires and promotions. But it can be a lens worth carefully looking through – when one considers the high human and financial costs of psychopathic leadership. But in reality, if we can spot these people early enough, we can stop them getting into positions where they can do the most damage – like the New World Order.

HOW TO BOIL A FROG

It is not as easy as it seems to take over the world. Unfortunately for them, most people still value freedom, liberty, and choice. The other thing is, if you come straight out and say "Ok, we are taking over now, and by the way, you must worship our god, give up your national

you're starting to sound like a conspiracy nut! it will all cool down soon I voted for Obama!

Is it getting hot in here, or what?

sovereignty and our private banks will be running your country from now on," chances are you would have riots, if not straight out civil war. They are well aware of this, so they plan their takeover in small steps.

Systems thinkers have given us a useful metaphor for **Martial Law** at a snail's pace in the phenomenon of the boiled frog. If you drop a frog in a pot of boiling water, it will frantically try to jump out. But if you place it gently in a pot of tepid water and turn the heat on low, it will float there quite placidly. As the water gradually heats up, the frog will sink into a tranquil stupor, exactly like one of us in a hot bath, and before long, with a smile on its face, it will unresistingly allow itself to be boiled to death.

Our owners know this well, so that is why they create 50 year, 100 year, and even 500 year plans. The individuals within these organisations feel they are contributing to some great cause that they call "the Great Work." Others are promised life extension technology, and others simply do it for the money and don't really give a damn about the grand scheme.

Our society is the pot, and the water was a perfect temperature, not too hot, not too cold. But slowly over the years, they have increased the temperature. They have shredded the US Constitution, eroded liberties (under false pretences) and ushered in a new **Police State** with a militarised police force, who are really private security guards for the bankers (just watch any G20 meeting). They have allowed genocide in Palestine, and invaded countries that have never provoked them, killing millions in the process like Iraq. The have put GMO's into the biosphere which are taking over and killing off the native species (look at corn in Mexico). Cancer viruses in the vaccines, processed food that creates obesity. The list goes on. This has all occurred just in the last 50 year plan. What kind of mixed up, crazy mind would do this? The Corporate Psychopath of course!

They told us the plan

Following their philosophies of "if you tell, then all is well" they often make movies, write books, or "leak" newspaper articles detailing their plans. 9/11 is a classic example of this. Hollywood certainly seems like it knew something in advance:

- **Terminator 2 - Judgement day** (1981) from 2:01 mins you can clearly see "Caution 9-11" written on the bridge!

- **Super Mario Bros** (1993) from 2:08 mins you can see the World Trade Centre's being destroyed in an eerily similar way.
- **Godzilla** (1998) from 2:21 mins the time shows 7:17:39.11 which means Boeing 717, 3 planes and 9/11! A few seconds later even the time on the watch says 9/11.
- **Trading Places** (1983) from 2:42 mins it shows 9/11 on the watch.
- **Gremlins** (1990) from 2:50 mins the position of the mics show 9/11.
- **Rugrats in Paris** (2000) from 3:00 mins the direction of the plane shows that it's going to hit the twin towers subtly blended into the building.
- **A Time to Kill** (1996) from 3:08 mins the lawyer mentions the Date September 11th but the year is 1960.
- **The MATRIX** (1999) from 3:15 mins the date on the passport clearly shows the exact date 11 Sept 01.
- **New York Vs Homer Simpson** (1997) from 3:18 mins Lisa holds up a magazine where it clearly shows 9/11 with the 11 showing as the twin towers.

There are loads more examples here (9/11 exposed, 2010). Of course, who can forget that the BBC Reported Building 7 collapsed 20 minutes before it fell (BBC video, 2001)?

While there are literally hundreds of groups that contribute to the running and expanding of the NWO agenda, I will focus on the big players listed in the diagram below. Yes the same one from Chapter 7, pg. 257:

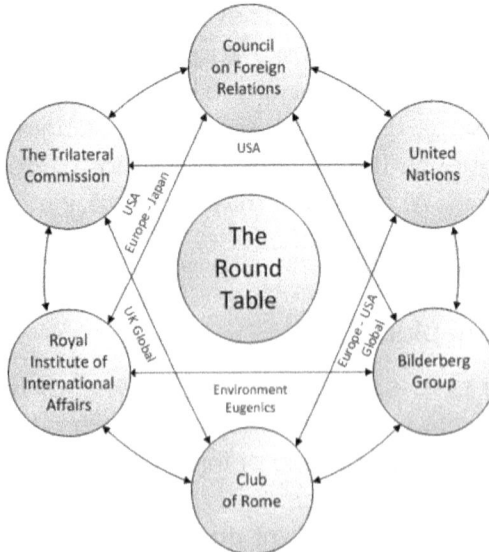

The Round Table (NWO) Network

Bloodline president **John F. Kennedy** was well aware of America's secret society control. His many rebellious decisions against the global elite, his non-participation in the Great Work, would ultimately lead to his assassination. He did, however, try to warn the average American of their plight. On April 27th, 1961 in an address to newspaper publishers, JFK said:

John F. Kennedy
(1917 - 1963)

"The very word 'secrecy' is repugnant in a free and open society, and we are as a people, inherently and historically, opposed to secret societies, secret oaths, and secret proceedings ... For we are opposed around the world by a monolithic and ruthless conspiracy that relies primarily on covert means for expanding its sphere of influence. It depends on infiltration instead of invasion, on subversion instead of elections, on intimidation instead of free choice. It is a system which has conscripted vast human and material resources into the building of a tightly knit, highly efficient machine that combines military, diplomatic, intelligence, economic, scientific, and political operations. Its preparations are concealed, not published, its mistakes are buried, not headlined, its dissenters are silenced, not praised, no expenditure is questioned, no secret is revealed ... I am asking your help in the tremendous task of informing and alerting the American people."

THE ROUND TABLE GROUP

Just like the ancient Mystery Schools, the Templars, Masons, Illuminati, and other secret societies, the Round Table groups were/are conducted in a pyramid structure with the most knowledge kept at the peak and each person down the line working on a need-to-know basis. Or as Rhodes discussed in his will, a succession of inner and outer circles.

The Round Table Group is a secret society that was formed in the beginning of the 20th century. This group plays a key role in the upcoming New World Order and creates the agenda and does the bidding for organisations such as the *Committee of 300*.

Around 1870, **John Ruskin**, an English professor, taught his apprentices that some people were superior to others, and that one superior man should rule the world. His lessons were embraced by a powerful and wealthy man named **Cecil Rhodes**.

He spent all his wealth (gained through diamonds and gold in South Africa) to achieve his lifelong dream of a **World Government** - a "**New World Order**."

Cecil Rhodes proposed the idea for the British Empire to annex the United States of America and reform itself into an "Imperial Federation," to establish a superpower and lasting world peace.

In 1877, at an age of 23, he wrote his first Will in which he expressed his wish to create a Secret Society (known as the *Society of the Elect*) that would strive toward this goal. In his Will, Cecil Rhodes wrote,

Cecil Rhodes
(1853-1902)

"To and for the establishment, promotion, and development of a Secret Society, the true aim and object whereof shall be for the extension of British rule throughout the world." His strong desire for a world government was expressed in his statement, "I would annex the planets if I could."

Only a bit more than a decade had passed since the British plan to dismember the United States in a Civil War had failed, bitterly. Rhodes wrote that the purpose of his Will was:

> *"...the perfecting of a system of emigration from the United Kingdom, and of colonisation by British subjects of all lands ... and especially the ... entire continent of Africa, the Holy Land, the Valley of the Euphrates, ... the whole of South America, the Islands of the Pacific not heretofore possessed by Great Britain, ... the seaboard of China and Japan, the ultimate recovery of the United States of America as an integral part of the British Empire..."*

Rhodes, a rabid British race imperialist, had amassed his fortune through the exploration, exploitation, and mining of gold and blood diamonds in Africa. He had a personal income of at least £1 million sterling a year which he spent so freely for mysterious purposes, that he was usually overdrawn on his account.

In **1891**, Rhodes established a secret society, which later became known as **The Round Table Group**. Like the Illuminati, the Round Table has an inner core, with various circles of associates built around it. It became international, and established organisations and associate societies in many countries around the world.

International Bankers were involved in the society from the beginning. **Lord Rothschild** of England, a leading member of the powerful international House of Rothschild, was the financier of Rhodes' Mining monopoly in Rhodesia (Rhodesia is named after Cecil Rhodes, but after April 1980, it became the Republic of Zimbabwe), South Africa. The Rothschild family became a trustee of the Rhodes' fortune, and an inner initiate of the secret society.

In his Last Will and Testament, Rhodes formed the well-known Rhodes Scholarship through which young students from all over the world would receive higher education – and the indoctrination of one-worldism. Indeed, any world leader that is a Rhodes Scholar is a committed New World Order fanatic.

In his book, **American Rhodes Scholarships'** **Frank Aydelotte** wrote,

> In 1888 Rhodes made his third will ... leaving everything to Lord Rothschild (his financier in mining enterprises), with a accompanying letter enclosing 'the written matter discussed between us' ... The model for this proposed secret society was the Society of Jesus [the Jesuits], though he mentions also the Masons ... The 'secret society' was organized on the conspiratorial pattern of circles within circles. (Aydelotte, 1946)

Rhodes' secret society, and the intricacies of how it operated, are detailed in **Carroll Quigley's The Anglo-American Establishment**. Quigley describes the British power elite and their purpose at the turn of the century. They combined important press outlets, created political institutions, and used financial power to affect their policy.

This elite group consisted of the Venetian **Cecil family**; the political and financial trustees of Rhodes' Trust, in which **Alfred Milner** was key; various banking institutions, including **Lazard Frères**; and the **British Royal family**. Quigley describes a small inner core of collaborators, with two concentric circles of semi-witting and non-witting conspirators from Britain's aristocracy and financial elite.

Professor Quigley informs us that the central part of the 'secret society' was established by March, 1891, using Rhodes' money. The organisation was run for Rothschild by **Lord Alfred Milner** – *The Round Table* worked behind the scenes at the highest levels of British government, influencing foreign policy and England's involvement and conduct of WWI.

Alfred Milner

In 1902, after Rhodes death, one of his close friends, **Lord Alfred Milner** (Rothschild Zionist), who was another powerful British banker, became the leader of the group. Indeed, he ran Rhodes' Trust, and was central to the secret cabal. He had been British High Commissioner for Africa, had won the Boer War, and had united South Africa as one political entity under British rule. That act gave Britain looting rights for the most important raw materials on the continent, and he derived much power

Sir Alfred Milner (1854 - 1925)

from these accomplishments.
Milner established Round Table Groups in many nations, including the United States. He attracted many young intellectuals mostly from Oxford, who were given important positions in government and international finance. These people were used, as their successors, to propagandise on the need and glory of a world government, and to work for the creation of the New World Order.

Like the Illuminati, members are enticed with humanitarian ideals. They are shown the needs of the world, and are inspired to work for the solution of world problems. But only the well-proven and most suitable initiates (corporate psychopaths) are shown the real goal of the society: World government. Once you agree to go along with the scam, they will set you up in a compromising situation. They then use this to black mail you, should you ever get cold feet or try to back out.

Milner's personal protégé was **Leo Stennet Amery**. Quigley describes their relationship:

> Amery can be regarded as Milner's political heir. From the beginning of his own political career in 1906 to the death of Milner in 1925, he was more closely associated with Milner's active political life than any other person ... his associations with Milner became steadily more intimate. In his last years of public office, Milner was generally assisted by Amery (1917-1921), and when he died it was Amery who arranged the public memorial service and controlled the distribution of tickets.

To understand today's hard right wing in Israel, one must understand Amery and Milner and their role in shaping the British Empire. They used Zionism to secure the oilfields of the Middle East and defence of the Suez Canal. They stated this openly, as did their Christian Zionist supporters. This was geopolitics in the mode of Sykes-Picot[9].

In Leo Amery's own words, this faith and concept of Empire, with its responsibility for *"civilizing other cultures,"* was mandated by God. Amery is famously quoted as saying:

> *"The Empire is not external to any of the British nation. It is something like the Kingdom of Heaven within ourselves."*

Lord Milner, ever the explicit racist, often spoke of England's work in governing backward peoples. He declared that she was doing America's work as well as her own. *"Someone,"* said Milner, *"must bear the white man's burden."* The "white man's burden" was the black man, and it was up to the white man to "civilize" him.

---

[9] The Sykes–Picot Agreement, officially known as the Asia Minor Agreement, was a secret agreement between the governments of the United Kingdom and France, with the assent of Russia. The agreement divided the Arab provinces of the Ottoman Empire outside the Arabian Peninsula into areas of future British and French control or influence. The agreement was concluded on 16 May 1916.

These racist Imperialist genuinely thought it was their responsibility to "civilise" the black man. I cannot tell you how arrogant, contemptuous, and condescending these so-called "heroes of the British Empire" were, and unfortunately, this mentality still permeates their philosophies and doctrines to this day. That is why almost every country that has "black haired" people as the native population, is a 3rd world country. It has been kept that way by design.

Those in the know

The innermost members of these societies, international bankers, academics, Generals, top CEOs, and politicians have together become known as **Insiders**.

Many sub-groups have been established by the Round Table Group in the past century. In the United States, they established the **Council on Foreign Relations**; in the United Kingdom, the **Royal Institute of International Affairs**. On the international level, they have established the **Bilderberg Group, United Nations, Club of Rome**, and **The Trilateral Commission**.

Most people have never heard of these organisations, as they are extremely secretive, and little is published about them, which is not surprising seeing that much of the main news media is controlled by these same secret groups. Bilderberg is by far the most powerful, most secretive, and most important now days, therefore, we will look at that first.

THE BILDERBERG GROUP

The elitist organisation known as **Bilderberg**, is a one world hidden government of the New World Order. Founded by **SS Nazi Officer, Prince Bernhard of the Netherlands** (House of Orange – part of the Black Nobility), they meet on an annual basis in either Europe, the United States or Canada.

Bilderberg meetings are comprised of some of the most powerful heavyweights of industry, banking, politics, royalty, academia, and technology from all over the world. In fact, about 120 of the most influencing personalities including ministers, head of states,

Past and present members of Bilderberg

businessmen, chairmen of international organisations, gather annually in a different country in a completely isolated and secured hotel, to discuss and divide the roles in informal but very mysterious and secretive atmosphere. The meeting takes place before **DAVOS**, and is far more important than G20 meetings.

In 2013, we know for a fact that **Jeff Bezos** (Founder and CEO, Amazon.com), **Timothy Geithner** (75th United States Secretary of the Treasury, under President Barack Obama), **Christine Lagarde** (Managing Director of the International Monetary Fund), **Henry Kissinger** (advisor to the last 7 presidents and one of the most evil men in the world), **Queen Beatrix** of the Netherlands (Daughter of SS Nazi Officer Prince Bernhard), **Eric E. Schmidt**, (Founder and Executive Chairman, Google Inc.) and British Prime Minister **David Cameron** were all in attendance, to name but a few (full list in **ANNEX 3.9.2**).

Bilderberg first started in 1954, when the most powerful men in the world met for the first time in **Oosterbeek, Netherlands**, and *"debated the future of the world,"* and decided to meet annually in secret.

They called themselves the **Bilderberg Group** after the name of the hotel they held their first meeting in – **Hotel Bilderberg**. Membership represents a who's who of world power elites, mostly from America, Canada, and Western Europe, with familiar regulars like:

David Rockefeller, Henry Kissinger, Bill Clinton, Gordon Brown, Angela Merkel, Alan Greenspan, Ben Bernanke, Larry Summers, Tim Geithner, Lloyd Blankfein, George Soros, Donald Rumsfeld, Rupert Murdoch, other heads of state, Hillary Clinton, Prince Philip, and Margaret Thatcher.

Influential senators, congressmen and parliamentarians, Pentagon and NATO brass, members of European royalty, selected media figures, and invited others – some quietly by some accounts like Barack Obama and many of his top officials.

A large number of private police and private, uniformed, armed military factions, including snipers, are deployed to set a complete and tight security level around the perimeter of the location. No unwanted people can get in or out. Hotel guests that are booked are told they must vacate the hotel during the conference with no explanation why.

In short, they gather in secrecy to discuss the latest agendas from the *Committee of 300*, and how to implement them and control the entire world. Make no mistakes, these are unelected people, deciding how you are going to live, in your own country.

Bilderberg is always well represented by top figures from the Rothschild controlled Council on Foreign Relations (CFR), IMF, World Bank, Trilateral Commission, EU, and powerful central bankers from the Federal Reserve, and Bank of England – ALL of these organisations are Rothschild owned or majority controlled.

Thus, Bilderberg is literally the top dog of secret societies and Rothschild's "round table" groups, and reports directly to the *Committee of 300*.

For over half a century, no agenda, or discussion topics became public, nor is any press coverage allowed. The few invited media attendees and their bosses are sworn to secrecy. Nonetheless, author and researcher **Daniel Estulin** undertook "an investigative journey" that became his life's work. In his book, ***The True Story of the Bilderberg Group***.

Whatever it's early mission, the Bilderberg Group is now a shadow world government, threatening to take away our right to direct our

> *"Slowly, one by one, I have penetrated the layers of secrecy surrounding the Bilderberg Group, but I could not have done this without help of 'conscientious objectors' from inside, as well as outside, the Group's membership"* (Estulin, 2009) *As a result, he keeps the names of his insider informants confidential* (Estulin, 2009).

Daniel Estulin (1966 -)

own destinies, by creating a disturbing reality very much harming the public's welfare. When you understand how many of the attendees are financed, thus controlled by the Rothschilds, you quickly become aware that this is a realisation of the *Protocols of the Learned Elders of Zion*.

In short, Bilderbergers want to supplant individual nation-state sovereignty with an all-powerful global government, corporate controlled, and check-mated by militarised enforcement.

It's a private, unelected club, where presidents, prime ministers, international bankers and Generals rub shoulders with the industrial and technological billionaire tycoons. Where royal chaperones ensure everyone gets along, and where the people running the wars, markets, and policies of Europe and America can say openly what they would never dare say in public. Best still, all of the top media heads are there, who have promised never to report on anything that is said.

Could you imagine if there was a secret meeting, between the very top movie stars, singers, or sports celebrities and how many media people would be there to take pictures and do interviews? Everyone would want to know what they are meeting about. But not this meeting.

Early in its history, Bilderbergers decided to create an '*Aristocracy of purpose*' between Europe and the United States, to reach consensus to rule the world on matters of policy, economics, and overall strategy. **NATO** was essential for their plans – to ensure perpetual war and nuclear blackmail to be used as necessary. Then proceed to loot the planet, achieve fabulous wealth and power, and crush all challengers to keep it.

Along with military dominance, controlling the world's money is crucial, for with it comes absolute control as the powerful 19th century Rothschild family understood: *"Give me control of a nation's money and I care not who makes its laws."*

Bilderbergers comprise the world's most exclusive club. No one buys their way in. Only the Group's Steering Committee decides on who to invite, and in all cases, participants are adherents to One World Order governance, run by top power elites. According to Steering Committee rules leaked to Estulin:

> *"The invited guests must come alone; no wives, girlfriends, husbands or boyfriends. Personal assistants (including secretaries, security, bodyguards, CIA, or other secret service protectors) cannot attend the conference and must eat in a separate hall. The guests are explicitly forbidden from giving interviews to journalists or divulge anything that goes on in meetings."*

The Host governments provide overall security to keep away outsiders. One-third of attendees are political figures. The others are from industry, finance, academia, labour, and communications. Meeting procedure is by **Chatham House Rules**, letting attendees freely express their views in a relaxed atmosphere, knowing nothing said will be quoted or revealed to the public. Meetings are always frank, but do not always conclude with consensus.

Membership consists of annual attendees (around 80 of the world's most powerful) and a further 40-50 others who are only invited occasionally because of their specialist knowledge, or involvement in relevant topics. Those most valued are asked back, and some first-timers are chosen for their possible later usefulness.

It is very regular for an American Presidential Candidate of either party to be invited to Bilderberg, and oddly enough, they usually end up being elected as President of the United States within 2 years of their attendance. A good example was the Arkansas governor **Bill Clinton**, who attended in 1991.

There, **David Rockefeller** told him why the North American Free Trade Agreement (**NAFTA**) was a Bilderberg priority and that the group needed him to support it. The next year, Clinton was elected (selected) president, and on January 1, 1994, NAFTA took effect.

NAFTA is a "Trade Agreement" between the United States, Canada, and Mexico. Because of NAFTA, American workers are now forced to compete directly with Mexican workers who, on average, make just $3 per hour. Their American counterparts make $18 per hour. Why would any manufacturer want to produce in America and pay $18-20 per hour when the same product can be produced right across the border in Mexico for just $3 per hour and then shipped back to the U.S. duty and restriction-free? Thus, NAFTA has crippled, and in many places of the US, destroyed manufacturing and production. It has cost millions of jobs – exactly what the New World Order want (*Why NAFTA is Bad*, 2015).

Right now we are all looking down the barrel of their latest "free trade agreement" called the **Trans Pacific Partnershi** (TPP).

In 2008, **Barack Obama's** Presidential Campaign was running against **Hilary Clinton** for the Democrats nomination. Obama tricked the Press group that was travelling with him while he campaigned. They all got on his plane, then at the last moment the doors were shut, and the dumbfounded Press were told Obama would not be flying with them.

Bilderberg was being held in **Chantilly, Virginia**, USA (5-8 June 2008). Both Hilary and Barack "disappeared" off the radar for an afternoon. They were at Bilderberg. Clinton was told to step aside and support Obama. She was told they needed Obama to be the next President, and that she could have a turn after his term. Within 2 days, Clinton withdrew her candidacy for the Democratic nomination for President. She was later made Obama's *Secretary of State* – not a bad runner-up job apparently.

So let's see who gets the Democrats nomination for 2016 – my money is on Hilary, but not because I like her or think she is the best candidate – far from it! She is a wicked and evil woman with a crime history as long as your arm. No, Hilary will get in because Bilderberg selected her.

Numerous other examples are similar, including who gets chosen for powerful government, military and other key positions. They also brag about other policies they have pushed through like the European Union and the Euro currency. Both are now failing, so that gives you an idea what these so-called "experts" are, who honestly believe they are smarter than the average person, yet all of their grand plans are falling apart at the seams.

Bilderberg Objectives

The Group's grand design is for a One World Government (World Company) with a single, global marketplace, policed by one world army, and financially regulated by one Central World Bank using one global currency. Their "wish list" includes:

- **One international identity** for every citizen, observing one set of universal values (this will be in the form of a "chip" in your hand/arm/head);
- **Centralised control** of world populations by "mind control" (controlling world public opinion) mainly through 3-4 media outlets (the only ones allowed to operate) that they control;
- A New World Order with **no middle class**, only "rulers and servants (serfs)," and, of course, the illusion of democracy, but no democracy – only pre-appointed leaders;
- **A zero-growth society** without prosperity or progress, only greater wealth and power for the rulers (happening now in America, Australia and the UK with all manufacturing being sent off-shore);
- Manufactured crises and **perpetual wars** (happening now);
- Absolute **control of education** to program the public mind and train those chosen for various roles (happening now with the deliberate dumbing down of school children);
- **Centralised control** of all foreign and domestic policies; one size fits all global police force;
- **Using the UN** as a de facto world government imposing an UN tax on "world citizens;"
- **Expanding** NAFTA and WTO globally through the **TPP** (Trans Pacific Partnership);
- Making **NATO a world military** – One World Army, directed and controlled by them;
- Imposing a universal legal system; and
- A **global welfare state** where obedient slaves will be rewarded and non-conformists targeted for re-education camps or extermination.

At the **Bilderberg Conference** on June 6 to 9, 1991, in Baden-Baden, Germany, **David Rockefeller** (Comm. 300) made the following statement,

"We are grateful to The Washington Post, the New York Times, Time Magazine and other great publications whose directors have attended our meetings and respected their promises of discretion for almost forty years. It would have been impossible for us to develop our plan for the world if we had been subject to the bright lights of publicity during those years. But, the work is now much more sophisticated and prepared to march towards a world government. The supranational sovereignty of an intellectual elite and world bankers is surely preferable to the national auto-determination practiced in past centuries." - David Rockefeller, 1991 Bilderberg meeting.*

COUNCIL ON FOREIGN RELATIONS (CFR)

James Warburg
(1896 – 1969)

"We shall have world government whether or not you like it, by conquest or consent." Statement by Council on Foreign Relations (CFR) member James Warburg (Rothschild Zionist) to The Senate Foreign Relations Committee on February 17th, 1950.*

The logo of the Council on Foreign Relations.

The first two groups created by the Round Table secret society were the British **Royal Institute for International Affairs (RIIA)** in 1920 and the American version called the **Council on Foreign Relations (CFR)** in 1921. In fact the original plans for both were drawn up during the Paris Peace conference of 1919. Though they were given different names to mask their autonomy, the RIIA and CFR are just sub-branches of the **Rhodes-Milner Round Table**.

The Council on Foreign Relations is an organisation that was founded by a group formed by **Wall Street Banksters Warburg**, **Rockefeller** (financed and controlled by Rothschild), and **J.P Morgan**. Today the CFR maintains that its goal is to increase America's understanding of the world, however, the actual objective of this highly exclusive club is to create a world system of financial control, in private hands, able to dominate the political system of each country, and the economy of the world as a whole. In fact, they also exclusively decide where to make the next war for the US Military. **Hilary Clinton** even admitted that the Whitehouse never makes a call on foreign policy without consulting the CFR first! (Clinton, 2010).

From its beginnings, the CFR was committed to a one-world government based on a centralised global financing system. Today, CFR has thousands of influential members, including important ones in the corporate media, thus is able to keep a low public profile, especially regarding its real agenda.

Historian **Arthur Schlesinger Jr.** called it a *"front organization for the heart of the American Establishment."* It meets privately and only publishes what it wishes the public to know. Its members are only Americans.

Their members reflect their power and include

- All Presidential Candidates of both parties;
- Leading Senators and Congressmen;
- Key members of news media; and
- Top officials of the FBI, CIA, NSA, DHS, defence establishment, and other leading government agencies, including state, commerce, the judiciary, and treasury.

For its part, the CFR has served as a virtual employment agency for the federal government under both Democrats and Republicans. Whoever occupies the White House, the CFR's power and agenda have been unchanged since its 1921 founding.

It advocates a global superstate with America and other nations sacrificing their sovereignty to a central power. CFR founder **Paul Warburg** (Rothschild Zionist) was a member of Roosevelt's *"brain trust"* and was the man that wrote the **Federal Reserve Bank Act 1913** that

Guest speaker at the CFR?

handed over America's wealth to private bankers. It also created the IRS and income tax. He was also a German. It is his son, James' quote at the beginning of this story. Like father like son right...

Later at the Bilderberg Group meeting, **Henry Kissinger** (Rothschild Zionist) said:

Henry Kissinger (1923 -)

"Today, America would be outraged if U.N. troops entered Los Angeles to restore order [referring to the 1991 LA Riot]. Tomorrow they will be grateful! This is especially true if they were told that there were an outside threat from beyond [i.e., an "extra-terrestrial" invasion], whether real or promulgated, that threatened our very existence. It is then that all peoples of the world will plead to deliver them from this evil. The one thing every man fears is the unknown. When presented with this scenario, individual rights will be willingly relinquished for the guarantee of their well-being granted to them by the World Government." - Dr. Henry Kissinger, Bilderberger Conference, Evians, France, 1991

CFR planned a New World Order before 1942, and the United Nations was created by a group of CFR members called the **Informal Agenda Group**. They drafted the original UN proposal, presented it to Franklin Roosevelt, who announced it publicly the next day. At its 1945 founding, CFR members comprised over 40 of the US delegates.

According to **Professor G. William Domhoff**, author of **Who Rules America**, the CFR operates in,

> *Small groups of about twenty-five, who bring together leaders from the six conspirator categories (industrialists, financiers, ideologues, military, professional specialists – lawyers, medical doctors, etc. – and organized labour) for detailed discussions of specific topics in the area of foreign affairs. The Council on Foreign Relations, while not financed by government, works so closely with it that it is difficult to distinguish Council action stimulated by government from autonomous actions. Its most important sources of income are leading corporations and major foundations. (Domhoff, 2013).*

The major foundations Domhoff refers to include **The Rockefeller, Carnegie**, and **Ford Foundations** to name but three, and they are all directed by key corporate officials and of course **Tavistock** behind the scenes.

CFR Cabinet Control

The **National Security Act of 1947** established the office of Secretary of Defence. Since then, 14 DOD secretaries have been CFR members.

- Since 1940, every **Secretary of State**, except James Byrnes, has been a CFR member and/or Trilateral Commission (TC).
- For the past 80 years, virtually every key US National Security and Foreign Policy Advisor has been a CFR member.
- Nearly all top Generals and Admirals have been CFR members.
- Many presidential candidates were/are CFR members, including Herbert Hoover, Adlai Stevenson, Dwight Eisenhower, John

Kennedy, Richard Nixon, Gerald Ford, Jimmy Carter (also a charter TC member), George HW Bush, Bill & Hillary Clinton, John Kerry, Dick Cheney and John McCain.

- **Numerous CIA directors** were/are CFR members, including Richard Helmes, James Schlesinger, William Casey, William Webster, Robert Gates, James Woolsey, John Deutsch, George Tenet, Porter Goss, Michael Hayden, and Leon Panetta.
- **Many Treasury Secretaries** were/are CFR members, including Douglas Dillon, George Schultz, William Simon, James Baker, Nicholas Brady, Lloyd Bentsen, Robert Rubin, Henry Paulson, and Tim Geithner (BB/CRF/TC).
- **When presidents nominate Supreme Court** candidates, the CFR's "Special Group, Secret Team" vet them for acceptability. In fact, Presidents are told who to appoint, including designees to the High Court and lower ones as well as Treasury positions.

Web of Control

Numerous think tanks, foundations, the major media, and other key organisations are staffed with CFR members. Most of its life-members also belong to the **Trilateral Commission** and **Bilderberg Group**. They operate secretly, and wield enormous power over the US and world affairs, and none of these people are elected to do so by the people.

Notable CFR members

Zbigniew Brzezinski; George H. W. Bush; Dick Cheney; David Rockefeller; Collin Powell; Hillary Clinton; Richard M. Haass; Gen. James L. Jones; Thomas Donilon; Henry Kissinger; Paul Volcker; Admiral Dennis C. Blair; Robert Gates; James Steinberg; Alan Greenspan; Richard C. Holbrooke. About 90% of members are Rothschild Zionists.

Insider Accidentally tells All!

One of the most informative and penetrating revelations concerning the CFR power network came in **1966,** with the publication of *Tragedy and Hope: A History of the World in Our Time* by **Professor Carroll Quigley** of Georgetown University. This book is massive, like an old phone book and was supposed to be read by insiders only. Think of it as the "history of the New World Order" written by an insider, for the insiders. The celebrated historian was very sympathetic to the CFR's globalist agenda, and wrote:

Carroll Quigley
(1910 – 1977)

"I know of the operations of this network [the international Round Table groups, including the Council on Foreign Relations] because I have studied it for twenty years and was permitted for two years, in the early 1960's, to examine its papers and secret records. I have no aversion to it or to most of its aims and have, for much of my life, been close to it and too many of its instruments.... In general, my chief difference of opinion is that it wishes to remain unknown." (Quigley, 1966)

And what are the "aims" of this network? According to Dr. Quigley:

> Nothing less than to create a world system of financial control in private hands able to dominate the political system of each country and the economy of the world as a whole.

The network to which Quigley referred had provided the "brain trust" and the financial impetus behind the drive for the **League of Nations.** This was the "first try" at a New World Order. Leading that drive for the network was **Col. Edward Mandell House**, the key advisor and "alter ego" of **President Woodrow Wilson**, the man that sold America to the Banksters. When the *League of Nations* was thwarted, Col. House and his colleagues were determined to continue their struggle by other means.

House was part of a cabal called "**The Inquiry**," a group of 100 "forward-looking" social engineers who created the **Versailles Peace Treaty** at the close of World War I – and we all know how that worked out. Germany bankrupt, and the Rothschild Zionists get Palestine. By the way, the *Versailles Treaty* created the perfect storm for Hitler to take control of Germany and launch World War II.

This group formed the American nucleus of what was to become the **Council on Foreign Relations**. The Inquiry's British counterparts created a companion organisation - the **Royal Institute of International Affairs** (RIIA), who still tell the US what to do on a daily basis. Dr. Quigley explains:

> *"In this secret society Rhodes was to be leader; Stead, Brett (Lord Esher), and Milner were to form an executive committee; Arthur (Lord) Balfour, (Sir) Harry Johnston, Lord Rothschild, Albert (Lord) Grey, and others were listed as potential members of a 'Circle of Initiates'; while there was to be an outer circle known as the 'Association of Helpers' (later organized by Milner as the Round Table organization)...Thus the central part of the secret society was established by March 1891."*

The plan developed by Rhodes and his small circle of co-conspirators was one in which *"a world system of financial control in private hands"* would be used to bring about world government. This system," notes Quigley,

> *was to be controlled in a feudalist fashion by the central banks of the world acting in concert, by secret agreements arrived at in frequent private meetings and conferences.*

Again, this is happening right now with the secret **Trans Pacific Partnership** (TPP). Professor Quigley explained further:

> *The apex of the system was the Bank for International Settlements (BIS) in Basle, Switzerland, a private bank owned and controlled by the [Rothschild] worlds' central banks which were themselves private corporations. Each central bank, in the hands of men like Montagu Norman of the Bank of England, Benjamin Strong of the New York*

*Federal Reserve Bank, Charles Rist of the
Bank of France, and Hjalmar Schacht of the
Reichsbank, sought to dominate its government
by its ability to control Treasury loans, to
manipulate foreign exchanges, to influence the
level of economic activity in the country,
and to influence cooperative politicians by
subsequent economic rewards in the
business world.*

The **BIS** and all of the other banks mentioned above are Rothschild created, owned, and operated. This description by Quigley sounds a lot like the plans in *The Protocols of The Learned Elders of Zion*.

In January **1924**, **Reginald McKenna**, who was then chairman of the board of the Midland Bank (and had been Britain's Chancellor of the Exchequer in 1915-16 - equivalent to the role of Secretary of the Treasury or Minister of Finance in other nations), confirmed that the British system was completely dominated by the conspiratorial greedy aristocracy.

"I am afraid the ordinary citizen will not like to be told that the banks can, and do, create money," said McKenna. "And they who control the credit of the nation direct the policy of Governments and hold in the hollow of their hands the destiny of the people."

Reginald McKenna
(1863 – 1943)

On November 11, 1927, the Wall Street Journal called **Montagu Norman**, governor of the Bank of England, *"the currency dictator of Europe."*

Norman was a strange, secretive, weirdo, given to wearing disguises, using assumed names, and incessantly flitting about the world on "mysterious missions", confirmed the Journal's assertion before the **Macmillan Committee** on March 26, 1930.

Serving Higher Powers

But as Professor Quigley points out, Norman answered to powers who stood in the shadows.

> *It must not be felt that these heads of the world's chief central banks were themselves substantive powers in world finance,"* write Quigley. *"They were not. Rather, they were the technicians and agents of the dominant investment bankers of their own countries, who had raised them up and were perfectly capable of throwing them down.*

Those bankers to whom Quigley refers were members of the **Rhodes-Milner-Rothschild network**. Their immense power and influence were exercised through the **Royal Institute of International Affairs**, the **CFR**, and their many other levers of control in the government, the major political parties, academe, business, and the media. As Rhodes biographer **Sarah Millin** put it:

> *The government of the world was Rhodes' simple desire.*

The **Rhodes Scholarships**, like the Round Table groups, were integral to this global scheme. Part of Rhodes' plan was to bring bright, ambitious young men to Oxford University for indoctrination and recruitment into his grand conspiracy. Co-conspirator **William Stead** said that Rhodes' own words were that after 30 years there would be,

> *between two and three thousand men [mathematically selected] in the prime of life scattered all over the world, each one of whom will have had impressed upon his mind in the most susceptible period of his life the dream of the Founder [Rhodes].*

What were the qualities looked for in these specially selected "scholars"? According to Rhodes himself: *"smugness, brutality, unctuous rectitude, and tact."* Which perfectly described the ruthless Cecil Rhodes, and **corporate psychopaths**. And just as aptly, his most famous Rhodes Scholar and one-world acolyte is **Bill Clinton**. I should also mention that ex-Australian Prime Minster (1983 to 1991), **Robert James Lee "Bob" Hawke** AC, GCL (1929 -) was also a Rhodes Scholar.

Over the years, Round Table-style groups parallel to the CFR have been established in France, Germany, Italy, Belgium, Norway, Sweden, India, Canada, Japan and dozens of other countries. Rhodes' disciples have thus built a global network of unprecedented power, capable of influencing, manipulating, sabotaging, and controlling political and economic events on a scale previously unimaginable.

> ❝ *When the influene which the [Royal] Institute wields is combined with that controlled by the Milner Group in other fields — in education, in administration, in newspapers and periodicals — a really terrifying picture begins to emerge,* ❞

Quigley wrote that in **The Anglo-American Establishment**, which was published posthumously in 1981. He explained:

> ❝ *The picture is terrifying because such power, whatever the goals at which it may be directed, is too much to be entrusted safely to any group... No country that values its safety should allow what the Milner Group accomplished in Britain — that is, that a small number of men should be able to wield such power in administration and politics, should be given almost complete control over the publication of the documents relating to their actions, should be able to exercise such influence ove the avenues of information that create public opinion, and should be able to monopolize so completely the writing and the teaching of the history of their own period.* ❞

Admiral Chester Ward, who was himself a member of the CFR for 16 years, saw that "*terrifying picture*" up close. Admiral Ward, who resigned in disgust, was not exaggerating when he charged that the CFR agenda is to promote,

> ❝ *Disarmament and submergence of U.S. sovereignty and national independence into an all-powerful one-world government.* ❞

Below is a CFR news article by **Mathew Kroenig** (Rothschild Zionist) Jan/Feb 2012, trying to start World War III. These dangerous Rothschild Zionist want to bring the world another war, but this time, it will destroy us all.

"Military men are dumb, stupid animals to be used as pawns for foreign policy"

-- Henry Kissinger
Nobel Peace Prize recipient

Henry Kissinger, picks his nose

and eats it - in public...

ROYAL INSTITUTE OF INTERNATIONAL AFFAIRS (RIIA)

The **Royal Institute of International Affairs** is slightly older than the CFR and just as dangerous. Born from the ashes of war-ravaged Europe following World War I, the idea for the RIIA was forged at an informal session during the 1919 Paris peace conference. The Institute was formalised the next year, first as the *British Institute of International Affairs*, and then, after receiving its Royal Charter, as the Royal Institute of International Affairs. Note the Royal connection!

The group became synonymous with **Chatham House**, its headquarters in St. James' Square, London, and is widely recognised among foreign policy experts as the most influential think tank in the world. Indeed, it is at the centre of the British Establishment.

In the years since its inception, the RIIA has opened branches in countries across the British Commonwealth and around the world, including the Council on Foreign Relations, born largely from the same 1919 Paris meeting that birthed the Institute itself, the Australian Institute of International Affairs, the South African Institute of International Affairs, the Pakistan Institute of International Affairs, the Canadian International Council, and similar organisations.

Officially, the Royal Institute of International Affairs, like its various branch organizations, is a non-profit, non-governmental think tank that promotes analysis of international issues and world affairs in four main research areas: (1) Energy, Environment and Resources, (2) International Economics, (3) International Security, and (4) Area Studies and International Law. Also like its branch organisations, the majority of the group's publications and proceedings are open to the public and freely available via their website or their journal, International Affairs. But following their founder's ambition to create secret societies with circles within circles, you will never read about their secret agendas.

Funded by partners, patrons and corporate members that read like a Who's Who of the Fortune 500, including Chevron, AIG, Bloomberg, Toshiba, Morgan Stanley, Goldman Sachs, Lockheed Martin, Royal Dutch Shell, the European Commission, and dozens of other corporations, institutions and foreign governments, Chatham House consistently attracts some of the best known speakers on a wide range of topics, releasing reports that set the global policy agenda, not only for Britain, but for much of the rest of the developed world as well.

Although the majority of its activities are publicly accessible, it is, perhaps tellingly, for its policy on keeping certain meetings private that the organisation is best known. The policy is called **The Chatham House Rule** and states:

> When a meeting, or part thereof, is held under the Chatham House Rule, participants are free to use the information received, but neither the identity nor the affiliation o the speaker(s), nor that of any other participant, may be revealed.

In other words, what is said in the House – stays in the House.

The rule is ostensibly invoked to encourage debate on contentious issues, the theory being that prominent individuals would not be willing or able to discuss their full views on these subjects if their identity and affiliations were to be publicly known. Some of the most infamous and criticized secretive meetings in the world, including the Bilderberg conference, adhere to Chatham House Rules, inviting charges of secrecy and hidden influence.

When it comes to a group like the Royal Institute of International Affairs, it is hard to argue that such charges are misplaced. In a public lecture by researcher and author **G. Edward Griffin** (true hero of the people), he presented the history of the *Round Table* group founded by **Cecil Rhodes** and how it functioned as a structure of "circles within circles" where the members of the outer, public Round Table fronts had little understanding of what went on in the inner circles of the group's secretive core membership. It was precisely from this Rhodes-created secret society that the *Royal Institute of International Affairs* and its various branches, including the *Council on Foreign Relations*, emerged.

Milner was a journalist who was plucked from obscurity by **Stead**, who made him assistant editor at the **Pall Mall Gazette**. After a series of political appointments, Stead and Rhodes used their influence to have him appointed **High Commissioner for Southern Africa** in 1897, an important and influential position in the years leading up to the Boer War.

Milner mentored a group of young lawyers and administrators, mostly affiliated with **Oxford University**, w ho b ecame k nown a s "Milner's Kindergarten." These figures went on to become some of the most influential figures in the foreign affairs of the early 20th century British Empire, including Lord Lothian, Philip Henry Karr, Robert Henry Brand of Lazard Brothers, 1st Baron Tweedsmuir, and **Lionel Curtis**, the founder of the *Royal Institute of International Affairs*.

In a rare recorded interview, **Professor Quigley** described in detail how this Rhodes-founded Round Table Group exerted power in international affairs in the first half of the 20th century through organizations like Chatham House. According to Quigley, the group was responsible for the Boer War, the establishment of the Rhodes Trust, the control of *The Times*, the formation of the *League of Nations*, the formation of the *Royal Institute of International Affairs*, and the appeasement of Nazi Germany, amongst other events.

In recent years, *Chatham House*, its most visible mouthpiece, has been responsible for reports on why gold is not a viable alternative to the current international monetary system, an analysis of the 2009 Iranian election that informed reports around the globe about the "irregularities" of that election, an op-ed from the British Foreign Secretary urging for a thorough weaponization of cyberspace, amongst many other influential documents, publications, conferences and presentations.

In the end, what is perhaps most intriguing to those who are interested in examining how power functions in society is not necessarily the secretive origins of a group like the *Royal Institute of International Affairs*, or even the way that it has covertly manipulated, shaped and controlled British foreign policy for decades, or how it has managed to wield such considerable influence over world affairs through its various branch organisations. Instead, what is most fascinating about *Chatham House* is that it is so very much open.

Many of its meetings and proceedings are publicly available. Its partners and corporate members are published on its website. Its journal is accessible to all. Its history, once shrouded in mystery, has been laid bare for over half a century thanks to the work of scholars like Quigley. And yet still, for all that, the RIIA is rarely discussed as an important power centre in 21st century society.

In some ways, perhaps this is its greatest accomplishment: to hide its enormous influence and its ongoing role in steering global geopolitics, not by hiding under a blanket of secrecy like the Bilderberg Group, Skull and Bones, or other secret societies, but by putting itself so much in the public spotlight that it seems mundane. It should be noted, after all, that this is precisely the way that Rhodes envisioned such an organization to function, and the continued existence and influence of that idea, manifested most openly in *Chatham House*, the *CFR*, and their brethren think tanks around the world, might serve as the perfect example of how some of the world's biggest secrets are hidden in plain sight.

TRILATERAL COMMISSION (TC)

Zbigniew Brzezinski
(1928 -)

"*The technetronic era involves the gradual appearance of a more controlled society. Such a society would be dominated by an elite, unrestrained by traditional values. Soon it will be possible to assert almost continuous surveillance over every citizen and maintain up-to-date complete files containing even the most personal information about the citizen. These files will be subject to instantaneous retrieval by the authorities.*" - *Zbigniew Brezinski, Between Two Ages, America's Role in the Technotronic Era, 1970.*

The Trilateral Commission is a similar group to the CFR that brings together global power brokers. Founded by **David Rockefeller** and **Zbigniew Brzezinski** (Pronounced Zar-big-new Bra-zin-ski), both of whom are also leading **Bilderberger** and **CFR** members. In fact, Rockefeller was **Chairman Emeritus** of the CFR, and he continues to finance and support them. On page 405 of his Memoirs, David Rockefeller wrote:

David Rockefeller
(1915 -)

"*Some even believe we are part of a secret cabal working against the best interests of the United States, characterizing my family and me as 'internationalists' and conspiring with others around the world to build a more integrated global political and economic structure – one world, if you will. If that's the charge, I stand guilty, and I am proud of it.*"

The Trilateral Commission came into being in July 1973, and is headquartered in Washington D.C. It is composed of approximately

TC Logo

325 elites in business, banking, and politics. It is propagated as being an economic cooperation between America, Europe, and Japan, but in reality it is another secretive society/organisation - this one specialising in creating the trilateral economic interdependence necessary to bring in the New World Order system of world currency and world governance.

However, its main purpose over the years has been to launder money. As more Congressmen and private citizens became aware of the **CFR** and the **Federal Reserve Bank** during the 1950's and 60's, the Committee of 300 planners realised that they had to be more covert. Their American and European drug money would have to be sent to Japanese Industrialists and Arab oil magnates, who would use it to buy up Western businesses and real estate. With this system in place, economic woes in the West resulting from the globalists control, could then be blamed on the Japanese and Arabs.

Arab leaders, who could not agree on anything for centuries, then suddenly came together to create the **OPEC Oil Embargo** in 1973. High petrol (gas) prices, caused the American population to flock to cheap Japanese cars. This system of Western, Eastern and Middle-Eastern trade created global inter-dependence, which made LOTS of money.

Committee members meet several times annually to discuss and coordinate their work. The Executive Committee chooses members, and at any time, around 350 belong for a three-year renewable period.

Everyone is a consummate insider with expertise in business, finance, politics, the military, or the media, including past presidents, secretaries of state, international bankers, think tank and foundation executives, university presidents and selected academics, and former senators and congressmen, among others.

Although it's annual reports are available for purchase, its inner workings, current goals, and operations are secret – with good reason. Its objectives harm the public, they must not be revealed. Legendary researcher and author **Antony Sutton** wrote:

> *This group of private citizens is precisely organized in a manner that ensures its collective views have significant impac on public policy."* He added that *"Trilateralists have rejected the US Constitution and the democratic political process.*

An official Trilateral Commission report was fearful about,

> *the increased popular participation in and control over established social, political, and economic institutions and especially a reaction against the concentration of power of Congress and of state and local government.*

To address this, media control was essential to exert "restraint on what newspapers may publish (and TV and radio broadcast)." Then according to **Richard Gardner** in the July 1974 issue of **Foreign Affairs** (a CFR publication):

> *CFR's leadership must make an end run around national sovereignty, eroding it piece by piece, until the very notion disappears from public discourse. (Gardner, 1974)*

The Trilateral Commission is widely perceived as an off-shoot of the Council on Foreign Relations. According to **Christopher Lydon**, writing in the **July 1977 Atlantic**,

> *The Trilateral Commission was David Rockefeller's brainchild.*

At the time, David Rockefeller was Chairman of the Council on Foreign Relations, having been elected to that post in 1970. However, Rockefeller became the founding Chairman of the Trilateral Commission with one plan - his plan - to control the world, economically.

"WE ARE ON THE VERGE OF
A GLOBAL TRANSFORMATION.
ALL WE NEED IS THE RIGHT
MAJOR CRISIS AND THE
NATIONS WILL ACCEPT
THE NEW WORLD ORDER."

- David Rockefeller

TC Logo – The Illuminati Rule: Hiding in Plain Sight

The word "Trilateral" means "three-sided" - the three sides in this case being North America, Europe, and Japan. However, the actual meaning of the name and symbol, embodies 666. Each arrow, when separated from the logo, is a 6, making 666.

TRILATERAL COMMISSION

Trilateral Commission Logo Revealed

Their true plan...

Trilateralist Zbigniew Brzezinski wrote in his book, **Between Two Ages: America's Role in the Technotronic Era**

> 66 *People, governments and economies of all nations must serve the needs of multinational banks and corporations. (The Constitution is) inadequate....the old framework of international politics, with their sphere of influence....the fiction of sovereignty....i clearly no longer compatible with reality... TC today is now global with members from countries as diverse as Argentina, Ukraine, Israel, Jordan, Brazil, Turkey, China and Russia. (Brzezin´ski, 1970* 99

In his book, **Trilaterals over America**, Antony Sutton believes that TC's aim is to collaborate with Bilderbergers and CFR in,

> 66 *establishing public policy objectives to be implemented by governments worldwide. (Sutton, 1995)* 99

Current Heads of the Trilateral Commission

- **Chairmen North America** (2015): **Joseph S. Nye, Jr.**, University Distinguished Service Professor and former Dean, John F. Kennedy School of Government, Harvard University, Cambridge, MA; former Chair, National Intelligence Council and former U.S. Assistant Secretary of Defense for International Security Affairs.
- **Chairmen Europe** (2015): **Jean-Claude Trichet**, former President of the European Central Bank (ECB), Honorary Governor of the Banque de France, Chairman of the Group of Thirty. and Chairman of the BRUEGEL Institute. Jean-Claude Trichet is also a member of the Institut de France (Académie des Sciences morales et politiques). He was appointed Chairman of the Group of 30 in November 2011 and elected Chairman of the BRUEGEL Institute (Brussels) in March 2012 and European Chairman of The Trilateral Commission to serve through the 2013-2015 Triennium.
- **Chairmen Asia Pacific** (2015): **Yasuchika Hasegawa**, is president and chief executive officer of Takeda

Pharmaceutical Company Ltd. He joined Takeda Chemical Industries, Ltd., in 1970 and has served the company with a three-year posting in Germany and a ten-year posting in the United States as vice president and then president of TAP Pharmaceuticals, Inc., Chicago. He became president of Takeda in 2003 and concurrently chief executive officer in 2009. Mr. Hasegawa is chairman of the Keizai Doyukai (Japan Association of Chief Executives). He graduated from Waseda University.

Some notable members

Some notable members of the Trilateral Commission include George Bush, Dick and Lynne Cheney, Bill Clinton, Al Gore, Jimmy Carter, Walter Mondale, David Rockefeller, Zbigniew Brzezinski, Henry Kissinger, David Gergen, Richard Holbrooke, Madeleine Albright, Robert McNamara, Paul Volcker, Alan Greenspan and Paul Wolfowitz.

US Senators Diane Feinstein, Robert Taft Jr., Charles Robb, William Cohen, and John Glenn, Congressmen, Ambassadors, Secretaries of Treasury, State and many other political figures are Trilateralists.

There are also many banking institutions represented at Trilateral meetings including the European Central Bank, World Bank, IMF, the Federal Reserve, Chase-Morgan, Citibank, Bank of America, Bank One, Bank of Tokyo, Bank of Japan and more.

Also plenty of multi-national corporate interests are represented including Fuji Xerox, Goldman Sachs, AIG, Exxon-Mobil, Shell, Chevron, Texaco, Sony, Samsung, Comcast, Time Warner, Carlyle Group, Levi-Strauss, Daikin, Sara Lee, GE, GM, Ford, Chrysler, Toyota, Mitsubishi, Johnson and Johnson, IBM, Boeing, and Citigroup.

> **" "** *Many of the original members of the Trilateral Commission are now in positions of power where they are able to implement policy recommendations of the Commission; recommendations that they, themselves, prepared on behalf of the Commission. It is for this reason that the Commission has acquired a reputation for being the Shadow Government of the West ...The Trilateral Commission's tentacles have reached so far*

in the political and economic sphere that it has been described by some as a cabal of powerful men out to control the world by creating a supernational community dominated by the multinational corporations." – Researcher **Laurie K. Strand** *"Who's in charge—Six Possible Contenders" People's Almanac #3.*

THE CLUB OF ROME

Club of Rome logo

Founded in 1968 in Rome, **The Club of Rome** describes itself as *"a think tank and a centre of research and action, of innovation and initiative."* It is a group of scientists, economics, businesspeople, high-level public servants, Heads of State and former Heads of State from around the globe that was established as a new way of addressing the larger questions confronting global society because the existing ways were too narrow and governments too compartmentalised.

These inter-related questions and issues are referred to as the *"problematique"* by Club members.

The Club views itself as "a group of world citizens, sharing a common concern for the future of humanity and acting as a catalyst to stimulate public debate, to sponsor investigations and analyses of the problematique and to bring these to the attention of decision makers". To put that another way, The Club of Rome examines present global problems and possible future trends, to try to understand what is happening, and then to encourage action at different levels, from individuals to governments.

Club members share the belief that each human being can contribute to the improvement of societies (CLUB OF ROME, 2015).

Now the REAL story

This group was organised in 1968 by the **Morgenthau Group** with funding from the Rockefellers, for the purpose of accelerating the plans to have the **New World Order** in place by the year 2000. *The Club of Rome* developed a plan to divide the world into ten regions or kingdoms (Morgenthau Group, 2000) and how to control the population (Rockefeller's contribution).

In 1976, the United States Association of the Club of Rome (**USACOR**) was formed for the purpose of shutting down the U.S. economy gradually. If you have been following the US economy lately you will realise this plan has almost come to fruition in 2015. It is only a matter of time before the US economy completely collapses.

The Technetronic Era

The Club of Rome commissioned **Zbigniew Brzezinski**, US President Carter's National Security Advisor, (who also with David Rockefeller formed The Trilateral Commission in 1973), to write **Between Two Ages: America's Role in the Technetronic Era** (Brzezinski, 1982). This is a post-industrial, zero growth plan designed in part to cripple U.S. industry in order to prepare America for the New World Order. Another book, **The Chasm Ahead** was also commissioned and written by **Aurelio Peccei** (Comm 300, 33° Freemason).

Peccei had been the chairman at a previous conference held in May 1967. It was organised by the *Scientific and Technological Committee of the North Atlantic Assembly* and the *Foreign Policy Research Institute*. It was called **Conference on Transatlantic Imbalance and Collaboration** and it was held at Queen Elizabeth's palatial property in **Deauville**, France.

Aurelio Peccei (1908 - 1984)

The meeting was attended by *Club of Rome* and NATO officials. Notable attendees were Harland Cleveland, Joseph Slater, Claiborne K. Pell, Walter J. Levy, George McGhee, William Watts, Robert Strausz-Hupe (U.S. ambassador to NATO), and Donald Lesh.

The basic purpose and intent of the conference at Deauville was to end U.S. technological and industrial progress. Out of the conference came the two books mentioned. Peccei's book largely agreed with Brzezinski, but added that there would be chaos in a future world if it is **NOT RULED BY A ONE WORLD GOVERNMENT.**

> *"Why should I concern myself with how many die? Even the Christian Bible says what is man that God should be mindful of him? For me, men are nothing but a brain at one end and a shit factory at the other." - Aurellio Peccei*

Henry Kissinger was then, and still is, an important agent in the service of the *Royal Institute for International Affairs*, a member of the *Club of Rome*, the *Council on Foreign Relations* and a regular attendee at the *Bilderberg* conferences. Yes, he certainly gets around doesn't he? And imagine how much influence he has, yet he has never been elected by anyone – ever!

Kissinger's role in destabilizing the United States by means of three wars; the Middle East, Korea and Vietnam, is well known, as is his role in the Gulf War, in which the U.S. Army acted as mercenaries for the *Committee of 300* in bringing Kuwait back under its control and at the same time making an example out of Iraq, so that other small nations would not be tempted to work out their own destiny.

The Club of Rome, acting on Committee of 300 orders to eliminate **General ul Haq**, had no compunction in sacrificing the lives of a number of U.S. servicemen on board the flight, including a U.S. Army Defence Intelligence Agency group headed by **Brigadier General Herber Wassom**. General ul Haq had been warned by the Turkish Secret Service not to travel by plane, as he was targeted for a mid-air bombing. With this in mind, ul Haq took the United States team with him as "an insurance policy," as he commented to his inner circle advisors.

Club of Rome and its financiers under the title of the **German Marshall Fund** were two highly-organised conspiratorial bodies

North
Atlantic
Terrorist
Organization

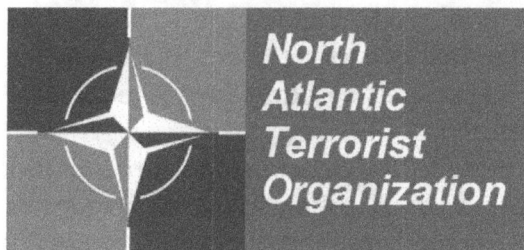

The true meaning of NATO

operating under cover of the **North Atlantic Treaty Organization (NATO)** and that the majority of *Club of Rome* executives were drawn from NATO. The *Club of Rome* formulated all of what NATO claimed as its policies and, through the activities of the *Committee of 300* member **Lord Carrington**, was able to split NATO into two factions, a political (left wing) power group, and its former military alliance.

The *Club of Rome* is still one of the most important foreign policy arms of the *Committee of 300*, and the other being the *Bilderbergers*. It was put together in 1968 from hard-core members of the original **Morgenthau Group** on the basis of a telephone call made by the late, Aurelio Peccei.

Peccei called for a new and urgent drive to speed up the plans of the One World Government now called the **New World Order**. Peccei's call was answered by the most subversive "future planners" drawn from the United States, France, Sweden, Britain, Switzerland, and Japan that could be mustered.

During the period 1968-1972, The *Club of Rome* became a cohesive entity of new-science scientists, Globalist, future planners and inter-nationalists of every stripe. As one delegate put it,

> *"We became Joseph's Coat of Many Colours."*

Peccei's book **Human Quality** (Peccei, 1977) formed the basis of the doctrine adopted by NATO's political wing. Peccei headed the **Atlantic Institute's Economic Council** for three decades while he was the Chief Executive Officer for **Giovanni Agnellis' Fiat Motor Company**. Agnelli, a member of an ancient Italian **Black Nobility** family of the same name, is an important member of the *Committee of 300*. He played a leading role in development projects in the Soviet Union.

The *Club of Rome* is a conspiratorial umbrella organisation, a marriage between Anglo-American financiers and the old Black

Nobility families of Europe, particularly the so-called "nobility" of London, Venice, and Genoa. The key to the successful control of the world is their ability to create and manage savage economic recessions and eventual depressions.

The Committee of 300 looks to social convulsions on a global scale, followed by depressions, as a softening-up technique for bigger things to come, as its principal method of creating masses of people all over the world who will become its "welfare" recipients of the future.

The committee appears to base much of its important decisions affecting mankind on the philosophy of Polish aristocrat, **Felix Dzerzhinsky**, who regarded mankind as being slightly above the level of cattle. As a close friend of British intelligence agent **Sydney Reilly** (Reilly was actually Dzerzhinsky's controller during the Bolshevik Revolution's formative years), he often confided in Reilly during his drinking bouts. Dzerzhinsky was of course, the beast who ran the **Red Terror** apparatus. He once told Reilly, while the two were on a drinking binge that,

"Man is of no importance. Look at what happens when you starve him. He begins to eat his dead companions to stay alive. Man is only interested in his own survival. That is all that counts.

Felix "Iron Felix" Dzerzhinsky. Founder of the Cheka Secret Police (KGB. 1978-1991)

With regard to the **Third World**, the *Club of Rome's* **Harland Cleveland** prepared a report which was the height of cynicism. At the time, Cleveland was the United States Ambassador to NATO. Essentially, the paper said it would be up to Third World nations to decide among themselves which populations should be eliminated.

As Peccei later wrote (based on the Cleveland Report):

> *Damaged by conflcting policies of three major countries and blocs, roughly patched up here and there, the existing international economic order is visibly coming apart at the seams....The prospect of the necessity of the recourse to triage deciding who must be saved is a very grim one indeed. But, if lamentably, events should come to such a pass, the right to make such decisions cannot be left to just a few nations because it would lend themselves to ominous power over life of the world's hungry.*

Limiting Growth and Population

The Club of Rome is best known for its 1972 report **The Limits to Growth**. The work of a group of **MIT** (Massachusetts Institute of Technology) scientists targeted to a non-specialist audience, the publication predicted dire consequences to unchecked economic and population growth. More than 12 million copies have since been sold in 27 languages. The book was discussed in hundreds of seminars, roundtables, newspaper articles, radio, and television programmes. This report was part of the human de-population movement set up by the **Eugenics cult**.

As a so-called non-profit, non-governmental organisation, the *Club of Rome* brings together scientists, economists, businessmen, international high level civil servants, heads of state and former heads of state from all over the world and seems to have no problems funding its multi-million dollar budget and agenda. They manipulate and distort global issues related to the environment, demography, development, ethical values and governance, society in the age of information technology and education.

Revolving Doors for the Membership

1999 **HRH Prince Hassan bin Talal** (member of the Jordanian Royal family) was appointed as President of the Club of Rome at a ceremony in Madrid under the patronage of Spain's **King Juan Carlos and Queen Sofi** . The King congratulated the members of the Club on their "*excellent choice.*" Yes, of course he was an excellent choice, because little Prince Hassan is the consummate Insider.

He just happens to be a member of the *Council on Foreign Relations, Trilateral Commission,* and *Club of Rome* 1999–2007. Prince Hassan replaced **Ricardo Diez-Hochleitner** (World Bank, Unesco and United Nations) Spain's media mogul who has been heading the Club since 1991.

Prince El Hassan bin Talal of Jordan - the little fella in the middle!

In 2015, The Club has two Co-Presidents - **Anders Wijkman** and **Ernst Ulrich von Weizsäcker**; two Vice-Presidents - **Ms. Susana Chacón** and **Roberto Peccei** and one Honorary President - **Dr. Ricardo Díez-Hochleitner** (again).

Club of Rome founders Alexander King (left) and Aurelio Peccei (right) were both unapologetic Malthusians who sought to establish the language of 'system analysis' to prove that mankind was condemned to destruction unless world government and population reduction were not made global policy.

THE UNITED NATIONS

"*The age of nations must end. The governments of nations have decided to order their separate sovereignties into one government to which they will surrender their arms.*" (*U.N. World Constitution*)

Paul-Henri Spaak (1899 - 1972)

The first president of the United Nations General Assembly, **Paul-Henri Spaak**, who was also a prime minister of Belgium and one of the early planners of the *European Common Market*, as well as a secretary-general of NATO, affirmed,

> "*We do not want another committee, we have too many already. What we want is a man of sufficient stature to hold the allegiance of all the people and to lift us up out of the economic morass into which we are sinking. Send us such a man, and whether he be God or devil, we will receive him.*"

The "idea" for creating the **United Nations** was born a few years before the First World War. The idea was named **League of Nations** and came from a book of fiction called **Phillip Dru: Administrator**. The author was Woodrow Wilson's (the man who sold America to the Banksters) socialist right hand man, **Colonel House**, the real power in the White House at this time. House later admitted the book was fact, presented as fiction. President Wilson's biographer, **George Sylvester Viereck** said:

> "*The Wilson Administration transferred the Colonel's ideas from the pages of fiction to the pages of history*".

In his novel, published anonymously two years before the First World War had even begun, he proposed "*...a League of Nations*". After the war, despite enormous influence and money backing, the idea came to nothing because the United States would not support it. That was because the White House was still dominated by Senators that held the United States in high esteem and did not want to sell it down the One World Government toilet. My how things changed...

But not to worry, the socialist backing for the League already had its sights on a successor, the **United Nations**. All that was needed to coerce the "sheep" into the fold was another BIG war. This was not to be a problem, because the seeds for this war were already planted at Versailles Treaty at the end of World War I as we have already discussed.

Following Germany's surrender, two committees were established to administer details of post-war policies. Woodrow Wilson (the man who sold America to the Banksters) appointed **Bernard Baruch** to represent the US on the economic committee and **Thomas W. Lamont** of **J.P. Morgan** spoke for US (US banks, that is) interests on the financial committee. Baruch's group decided that Germany would pay $12 billion (worth: over $190 billion in 2015 money) in reparations and, together with other limitations on the German economy, the new German republic (The Weimar Republic) was doomed to fail. In doing so, social conditions would ripen for the rise to power of Adolph Hitler.

Once the banksters were assured that Hitler was their man, rivers of money flowed out of the **Federal Reserve** to build Germany's infrastructure and Adolph's war machine. Remember, Adolf was a Rothschild, so no expense was spared. This all occurred during the **Great Depression** while the people of the United States were losing their farms, homes and jobs, and starving on their feet because there "wasn't enough money."

Again, remember after the *Federal Reserve Act 1913* enabled private banks to control the money. So sometimes they restricted the money (depression) because they channelled it elsewhere (in this case Germany) and other times they expand the amount of money in circulation – this creates inflation, which creates a boom, or "bubble" which always must burst, which means more unemployment and the cost of living increases. Both are designed to make the bankers richer, and the people poorer.

The people are then easier to control, and reliant on the banks "loaning" them money. People with an income are a threat to their agenda. They don't want the people to have money in case they use it to fight back.

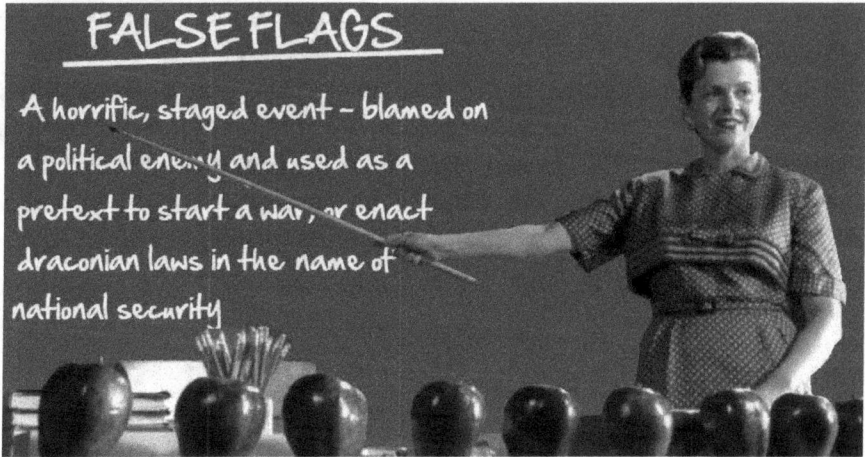

The bombing of Perl Harbour was a false flag

Similar actions were occurring in the Pacific to bring Japan towards war and eventually the Second World War became history with the loss of millions of lives. The banks made uncountable profits along with the industrial powers. For some, WWII was another successful venture, and for the usual people, it was a nightmare.

The same people who made profit from these wars now resurrected the *League of Nations* under a new banner, **The United Nations**. They were able to do this under one of their favourite play books – the **Hegelian Dialectic** or *Problem-Reaction-Solution*. This time it was the horrors of World War II. By the way, the US got into that war by a False Flag – the bombing of **Perl Harbour**.

In 1945, representatives of 50 countries met in San Francisco at the United Nations Conference on International Organization, to draw up the United Nations Charter. Those delegates deliberated on the basis of proposals worked out by the representatives of China, the Soviet Union, the United Kingdom and the United States at Dumbarton Oaks, United States in August-October 1944. The Charter was signed on 26 June 1945 by the representatives of the 50 countries. Poland, which was not represented at the Conference, signed it later and became one of the original 51 Member States.

The United Nations officially came into existence on 24 October 1945, when the Charter had been ratified by China, France, the Soviet

Union, the United Kingdom, and the United States and by a majority of other signatories.

But that was only the public culmination of years of behind-the scenes manoeuvring by the Council on Foreign Relations, which controlled the administration of **Franklin D. Roosevelt**. In his book, ***The Shadows of Power: The Council on Foreign Relations and the American Decline***, **James Perloff** uncovers the details of what really happened:

> **"** In January 1943, the Secretary of State, Cordell Hull, formed a steering committee composed of himself, Leo Pasvolsky, Isaiah Bowman, Sumner Welles, Norman Davis, and Morton Taylor. All these men - with the exception of Hull - were in the CFR. Later known as the Informal Agenda Group, they drafted the original proposal for the United Nations. It was Bowman - a founder of the CFR and member of Colonel House's old 'Inquiry' - who first put forward the concept. They called in three attorneys, all CFR men, who ruled that it was constitutional. Then they discussed it with Franklin Roosevelt on June 15th, 1944. The President approved the plan, and announced it to the public the same day. (Perloff, 1988) **"**

The US delegation at the founding meeting of the UN was like a roll call of the CFR. It included 74 CFR members who all served on Roosevelt's Advisory Committee during the war and on Post-War Foreign Policies. This was the vehicle through which the United Nations was manipulated into being. The US delegation included two interesting CFR members.

The Men that Created the United Nations

One was **John J. McCloy** (CFR chairman from 1953-70, a member of the *Committee of 300*, *Bilderberg Group*, the chairman of the *Ford Foundation* and the Rockefellers' *Chase Manhattan Bank*, and friend and advisor to nine presidents from Roosevelt to Reagan).

He was also best friends with **John Foster Dulles** (Hitler supporter, CFR founder, and soon to be Secretary of State); and **Nelson Rockefeller** (master manipulator, four times elected Governor of New York, and vice president).

McCloy was also the financial advisor to the Italian fascist government of **Benito Mussolini** and he played a significant role in Nazi Germany for the **Harriman/Bush** bank which was helping to financing Hitler (Prescott Bush, President George HW's father was later prosecuted for Trading with the Enemy). McCloy sat in Hitler's private box at the 1936 Olympics in Berlin at the invitation of **Rudolf Hess** and Hermann Göring. He was one of the ultimate "insiders." He didn't care who he mixed with, who he supported, or who he called friend. It is typical of these people. It is all about the power – never mind the money.

The other CFR delegation member was **Alger Hiss**. He was the Secretary General of the UN conference, and the State Department official. Hiss was also Executive Secretary of the 1944 **Dumbarton Oaks Conference**, where he worked with Stalin's man, **Vyacheslav Molotov**, on the details of the UN Charter. He was described as President Roosevelt's *'top international organisation specialist'* at the **Yalta Conference** in the Crimea in February 1945, which was also attended by Churchill and Stalin.

After guiding the UN into existence, Hiss was made president of the infamous *Carnegie Endowment for International Peace*, an appointment made by non-other than **John Foster Dulles**. Dulles ignored information about Hiss's espionage when he was told about it in 1946. Later in 1948, Hiss was exposed as a secret agent employed by the Soviet Union. He was sent to prison for 44 months. He was also charged with perjury in 1950, in connection with the 1948 case. But nothing happened to Dulles over his, or his "covering" for a friend.

There were other Soviet spies in the US delegation in San Francisco for the launch of the UN. Among them **Harry Dexter White**. White was the senior American official at the 1944 *Bretton Woods* conference, and reportedly dominated the conference and imposed his vision over the objections of **John Maynard Keynes**, the British representative. According to economic historian **Brad Delong**, Keynes was later proved correct by events, on almost every point where the Americans overruled him.

After the war, White was closely involved with setting up what were called the Bretton Woods institutions—the **International Monetary Fund** (IMF) and the **World Bank**. Both of these are Rothschild banks, and the Rothschilds funded and created the Soviet Union, so no wonder they had busy little bees working in every powerful group in the US. This may also explain why, when **J. Edgar Hoover** of the FBI charged that White was an active agent of Soviet espionage, and despite the fact he had sent five reports to the White House warning the President of White's activities, **President Truman** promoted him to a position at the United Nations!

This then, is the organisation (the CFR), and their men, which created the United Nations. The UN was given land in New York to build their headquarters, free of charge by the Rockefellers. All the while, the sneaky little bankers like JPMorgan, Warburg, Schiff, and Marburg were pulling the strings in the background, behind the politicians and advisors. As mentioned, these are the very bankers that funded the Bolshevik revolution that created the Soviet Union and worldwide Communism, and created the Federal Reserve Bank and the IRS. They are all Rothschild Zionists.

The Public View

The United Nations was sold to the public as a means to bring peace to the world, to solve differences by diplomacy, not war – but given who created it, and who funded it, do you really still buy that? Not to mention, there have been more wars in the world since the UN was created than there was before. So they fail big time on that Mission Statement. But let's face it, that is not really why the UN was created.

The UN was created to usher in a One World Government – the global fascist/communist tyranny known as the New World Order. It is the mask that hides world government, a one world army, and a one world religion. The public are being manipulated and softened up by conflicts and propaganda, to accept this policy as the only way to bring peace and stability to human affairs.

The United Nations has given birth to a stream of connected organisations which coordinate the New World Order plan in areas like Health (**World Health Organisation**), Population Control or - more accurately - eugenics, (**UN Population Fund - UNFPA**),

Economic development and environment (the **UN Environment Programme - UNEP**), Education, Science and Culture (**UNESCO**), and the list is getting longer all the time. These are organisations which are designed to globalise control of all areas of our lives. The two I feel are the most dangerous and frightening right now are **Agenda 21** (recently rebranded as the UN 2030 Agenda) and **Codex Alimentarius**.

AGENDA 21: SUSTAINABLE DEVELOPMENT

Are you concerned about your private property? Do you own a house, land, or apartment? If so, then this is extremely important information you need to know.

Agenda 21: Sustainable Development is the model for the 21st Century, as the UN, and every country that signs on to it see it. It is the action plan to inventory and control all land, all water, all plants, all minerals, all animals, all information, all means of production, and all human beings in the world.

Agenda 21 Trojan horse (art by David Dees)

The United Nations *Agenda 21: Sustainable Development* was signed onto by 179 nations, including the United States, United Kingdom, China, Australia, Canada, France, Germany, Netherlands, New Zealand, Ireland, Japan, Romania, Russia, Spain, Sweden, in 1992, during the UN Earth Summit held in Rio de Janeiro (see full list here: Ramirez, 2015).

In the United States, it was **George HW Bush**, the same man that publicly stated his eagerness to create a New World Order that signed America onto "sustainable development" plan, and has been re-endorsed by every President since. It is a global plan, implemented locally. By implementing it locally, it becomes a strength for the globalists, but for those opposing it, it may turn out to be their weakness.

It is possibly the biggest public relations scam in the history of the modern world. Make no mistake, the Agenda for the 21st Century is a recipe for destruction. It enables and justifies the monitoring, metering, and restricting of **our** energy and water usage, but not that of the corporations. It will implement a carbon tax that makes it ok for the corporations to pollute, but not the people. It will exhaust the economy, and coupled with endless wars in foreign lands, most countries, especially the US, will go bankrupt.

They intend to "diagnose" a large portion of the population with "mental illness" and prescribe mind numbing drugs. Basically any child they deem is disruptive will be forced onto psychotropic drugs. They also want to redesign the schooling system with sustainable development principles in every level from kindergarten to post grad students. In the United States you may be familiar with the new schooling disaster known as **Common Core**? Common Core says 2+2=5. Common Core is part of Agenda 21, and is designed to dumb our kids down and produce obedient workers rather than independent thinkers. The ultimate goal is to have the average population no more educated than Grade 6 level.

They want to declare public, "wild" lands off limits to humans (except for the billionaires) and change every land usage document in each nation to reflect this. So if you are used to walking your dog through a beautiful nature strip, forget it. It will be OUT OF BOUNDS.

Smart Growth Cities

They want to rezone all non-nature land to incorporate high density housing and city centres. They want to create what they call **Smart Growth Cities**. These cities are high density, crammed packed. The only roads in and out are monitored, and only lead to the next Smart Growth City. All travel will be highly restricted and monitored. Land outside the Smart Growth City is deemed OUT OF BOUNDS. Huge transport arterial highways will be constructed whose sole purpose is to ship merchandise. The NAFTA super highway is already being constructed, and reclaiming hundreds of generational farms along the route with Texas farmers being hit the worst.

Another aspect of Agenda 21 is it allows for warrantless searches and surveillance on domestic properties, and identifies Libertarians, Veterans, Preppers, and Christian groups that have compounds as potential "combatants" (their word not mine!). It also redefines torture as "enhanced interrogation." If your country was invaded by a foreign army, it couldn't do a better job than Agenda 21.

In effect, it is a Corporatocracy[10], a global totalitarian state, and it is happening now. It does not come with flashing lights and bells and whistles saying AGENDA 21. Indeed, that is how they have been quietly implementing all this over the last 20 years and people are only finding out about it now. But they won't openly call it Agenda 21 in your local Council meetings, but I can assure you it is there. It is part of your government, school system and your life.

The final push to openly implement Agenda 21 into your life whether you want it or not will come via a Hegelian Dialectic – Problem-Reaction-Solution. It will create a new normal that would never have been accepted before their manufactured "crisis." And think for a second, in the "sustainable" genre, what is the number one crisis right now? **Global warming!**

WARNING – WARNING - Sea levels are rising, the polar bears are drowning, and in 50 years we are all going to be under water because the poles melted!!!...The greedy, selfish humans destroyed the planet. What are we going to do!

---

[10] Corporatocracy is a term used as an economic and political system controlled by corporations and/or corporate interests.

Sound familiar?

Enter the UN to the rescue!! So the only way we can save the planet the UN tells us, is to implement a draconian system that creates a new class system – well, old really – the **feudal system**, with the mega rich, and the horrendously poor. Global warming is all bunk. I did some very deep research and wrote an article proving (scientifically) why global warming is a scam. You can read this in *ANNEX 3.9.1 The Carbon Tax Scam.*

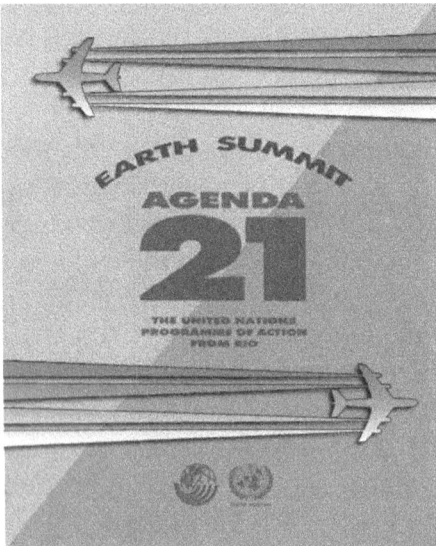

Agenda 21 Earth Summit with **Chemtrails Cover**

A man that features largely in that article is **Maurice Strong**, and just like all the other consummate insiders, I bet you have never heard of him. It was Strong that penned the Agenda 21 book which is the blueprint, or text book for implementing "sustainable development" worldwide.

It is 300 pages, with 40 Chapters and it covers every aspect of your life. Once again, we have a non-elected, "grey man" who has affected you more than

any government official could have. Let's take alook at Mr. Strong's view of the world.

What Does Maurice Strong Think About You?

Strong, a multi-millionaire, said at the time of delivering his diabolical plan (1992 UN Earth Summit, Rio de Janeiro), that the "*affluent middle-class*" is unsustainable. The so-called affluent middle-class in all developed countries usually includes families with 2-4 children. They have two cars, a four bedroom house in the suburbs, and they take an annual vacation somewhere within 2-4 hours' drive of where they live.

Further to this, they eat meat regularly, they have multiple appliances in the house, including air-conditioning and heat. They use water from dams and reservoirs. These people, Strong says, must go! They cannot continue to live this "affluent" lifestyle. But he doesn't stop there. For the farmers in developing countries he says "**tillage**" that is, disturbing the earth's surface in order to plant crops, releases greenhouse gases into the atmosphere, therefore they must stop doing that.

For most people, the way you are living right now, is unsustainable according to this character Maurice Strong. I might add that Mr. Strong, originally from Canada, lives in China (hiding there after a scandal) in a high rise, luxury penthouse, with six servants. He has to use an elevator all day every day just to get into his house. He has two luxury Bentley cars that have 6-litre, V12 engine. These are very heavy cars with huge engines that consume about the same amount of fuel as six, small economy cars. His penthouse has air-conditioning and air filtering (because the air in China is so polluted)

FACT: AGENDA 21 CALLS FOR THE ELIMINATION OF PRIVATE PROPERTY OWNERSHIP, SINGLE-FAMILY HOMES, PRIVATE CAR OWNERSHIP, INDIVIDUAL TRAVEL CHOICES, AND FAMILY FARMS. IT FULLY PROHIBITS PERSONAL FREEDOMS AND THE RIGHTS OF CITIZENS TO OWN PROPERTY, HOMES, CARS, AND FARMS.

that requires articulated water to run. This guy is a complete hypocrite and a joke.

To really sell this idea to the next generation, they have produced a children's propaganda piece called **Rescue Mission: Planet Earth: A Children's Edition of Agenda 21** in Association With the United Nations (Children of the World., 1994), allegedly authored by **Bourtros Boutros Ghali**, 6th Secretary-General of the United Nations. I think it is more likely it was written by the **Tavistock Institute**, which we will be looking at in detail in **Book III: Secrets of the Mind Control Programs**.

Rescue Mission: Planet Earth: A Children's Edition of Agenda 21

Speaking of books, most of this information on Agenda 21 comes from the brilliant book by **Rosa Koire**, *Behind the Green Mask - U.N. Agenda 21* (Koire, 2011).

If you want to learn how they managed to ram this through your local council, indoctrinate people into the system, and how they created bogus statue law to "legalise' their land theft, then I strongly recommend Rosa's book. She covers everything you need to know about Agenda 21 and more.

What do others think?

13th January 2012, the **Republican National Committee** asserted that,"*Agenda 21 is a comprehensive plan of extreme environmentalism, social engineering, and global political control.*"

Here is a great video on YouTube that is quick and easy: *Agenda 21 in 5 minutes* (Agenda 21, 2013).

"Megacities on the Move - Planned-Opolis" – Creepy AGENDA 21 Utopia Promotion

Several years ago, a creepy cartoon video showed up on the web called *Megacities on the Move - Planned-Opolis*. The video struck a nerve, and sent a chill down everyones spine who knew about Agenda 21. We all knew we were looking at what the global planners in the UN had install for us. So people starting asking questions like who produced this video? Who funded it etc.? The video was made by a group calling themselves **Forum for the Future** who are a PR group for the globalists. Just their list of clients is a who's who of Fortune 500 companies.

About Forum for the Future

Founded in 1996, Forum for the Future is an independent, non-profit organisation with a mission to promote sustainable development.

Keep in mind that this is a not-for-profit group. They boast 70 staff, and their clients include mega-companies like PepsiCo and Coca-Cola, Vodafone, Starbucks, MacDonald's, Unilever, Shell, Sky TV, Du Pont, Kellogg's, Johnsons, Heineken and The Crown Estate (that is a giveaway!) and hundreds of others (Members, 2015).

How does a not-for-profit group get so many mega-companies to sign up for them to do their marketing? Wouldn't PepsiCo rather use a high profile advertising company to lift their profile? Normally they would, but when they need to sell a lie convincingly, they turn to *Forum for the Future.*

Speaking of **PepsiCo**, perhaps they were trying to soften the fact that they used **aborted foetuses** to flavour their drink? Yes, hard to believe, but **Pepsi admitted** they did it, and promised (publicly) they would not use aborted HUMAN foetuses any longer to flavour their drinks (Pepsi, 2012). But it wasn't just Pepsi that got caught doing the most disgusting thing possible – they had their buddies in the fake food industry also doing it! Indeed, many other famous brands were also using **Aborted Human Foetal Cells for Stimulating Artificial Flavours.**

Campbell's Soup, Oreo, Ritz, Maxwell House, Kraft, Nestle and more (Human foetal cells, 2015).

HEK 293 is the code for aborted human kidney cells that are used to generate taste receptors, that can stimulate a type of protein known as G *protein,* familiar to human's taste. So if you can, check the packaging for this code in the ingredients section.

I think you get the point. What sort of respectable company would want to be involved with criminals like this? That is why the Illuminati have hundreds of "front" companies, which are almost always not-for-profit companies or Foundations set up all over the world to handle the inevitable slip ups. Forum for the Future is one such company, whose expertise is in propaganda.

This series of four short videos were shown to different groups of school children under 11 years old, to gauge their reactions and get input. The idea is that they want to include this type of environmental-sustainable future propaganda in regular school curriculum.

Life in planned-opolis

Vee is living in a future city called *Planned-Opolis* in the year 2040. She is a happy slave. She works as a virtual doctor, but even she doesn't earn enough to eat meat and fresh veggies regularly, own a car, or travel abroad. She loves her life despite having no real freedoms. Vee and others living in *Planned-Opolis* don't have the choice to decide what to eat and how much to eat. She can't even move around freely and use the transportation she likes. Food and travel are restricted by a "calorie card." She and her kids don't even decide their future work, they are allocated careers in their last year of school.

Even talking about freedom is considered bad. In fact, those people who show their discontent are forced to live in the *Cry Freedom Ghetto*, a kind of "lord of the flies" feral-land. People who live there have to do without high speed transportation system, no internet and they also miss out on jobs and essential services (and don't wash by the look of them). In fact, the dissenters in the *Cry Freedom Ghetto* look like medieval peasants fighting over a dead rat.

To conclude, Vee is just happy to be a slave. She is someone **Aldous Huxley** (author of Brave New World, 1932) would be proud of. Huxley wanted people to love their servitude. People living there indeed love their oppression and slavish existence.

I don't think that any sane person would like to live in that city planned by the global elite. Therefore, they need to drip feed our children that this is what they deserve, and get used to it. They do this via propaganda and mind control that I will be discussing in depth in **Book III: Secrets of the Mind Control.**

Key points to note from that video

- All movement and activities are limited, as one is rationed an amount of energy through a **Calorie Card**. In the future, it is more likely this will be done with a computer chip in your arm or elsewhere.
- Mega computers run everything, and are everywhere – always watching.
- Transportation is highly regulated and only the elite own cars.
- In schools, children are designated their future work/profession. They don't have the choice to decide their future career.
- Global Food Council controls all food supply and also decides what all people can eat, and how much they can eat. The food council in the real future will be the UN Codex Alimentarius.

- Those who oppose the system are forced to live in the *Cry Freedom Ghetto*. If you watch the movie/book *Brave New World*, this is the same - people who live "outside" the city are savages, feral and dirty.

The Illuminati are forever trying to force people into living situations that are not natural. It is because they see us a cattle, and therefore, need to keep us in a cattle yard. The rest of the farm is for the farmers.

You can watch it on YouTube: (Opolis, 2011)

To fully grasp what they are planning, watch the movie ***THX 1138*** (George Lucas' first movie from 1971). This movie is uncanny on how accurately it predicts the future living conditions under Agenda 21. And of course, it's all being rolled out under the fraudulent label of "progress" and "sustainable development."

Next, we will examine Agenda 21's strange bedfellow, and partner in crime - **Codex Alimentarius**.

CODEX ALIMENTARIUS

The Codex Alimentarius (Latin for "Book of Food") is a collection of internationally recognised standards, codes of practice, guidelines and other recommendations relating to foods, food production, and food safety. Its texts are developed and maintained by the **Codex Alimentarius Commission**, a body that was established in early November 1961 by the **Food and Agriculture Organization** of the **United Nations** (FAO). It was joined by the **World Health Organization** (WHO) in June 1962, and held its first session in Rome in October 1963.

They operate under the guise they are here to protect the health of consumers and ensure fair practices in the international food trade. The Codex Alimentarius is recognised by the **World Trade Organization** as an international reference point for the resolution of disputes concerning food safety and consumer protection. This means, if two countries are in the WTO, and country A complains to the WTO that country B is not using Monsanto GMO seeds, and it is costing country A more money to use GMO seeds, then the WTO orders country B to start using GMO or be heavily penalised. See how they keep everything even.

So what is so bad about this you say? In 1996, the German delegation put forward a proposal that no herb, vitamin or mineral should be sold for preventive or therapeutic reasons, and that supplements should be reclassified as drugs or toxins, which means you could only get them via prescription from a doctor. It also means herbalist, homeopaths, naturopaths, Chinese herbalists, or any other alternative health service cannot legally sell you remedies, or advise you to take any natural, non-patent cure.

And that is what this is all about. They want to destroy any competition to **Big Pharma** – that is the name we give to the huge, mega companies that dominate the drug market. Big Pharma cannot patent any plant or natural remedy. So without a patent, anyone can cure themselves. But with a patent, Big Pharma literally earn billions.

In 2002, the FAO (Food and Agriculture Organization of the United Nations) and WHO (World Health Organisation of the United Nations) had serious concerns about the direction of Codex and hired an external consultant to determine its performance since 1962 and to designate which direction to take the trade organisation.

The consultant concluded that Codex should be immediately scrapped and eliminated. It was at this time that big industry realized the full monetary potential of this organization and exerted its powerful influence. The updated outcome was a toned down report asking Codex to address 20 various concerns within the organisation.

Since 2002, the **Codex Alimentarius Commission** has covertly surrendered its role as an international public health and consumer protection organisation. Under the helm of big industry, the sole sneaky purpose of the new codex is to increase profits for the global corporate juggernauts while controlling the world through food. The implicit understanding of their philosophy is that if you control food, you control the world *(Laibow, 2011)*. I guess they were getting tips from **Henry Kissinger**, because he once said:

> *"Who controls the food supply controls the people; who controls the energy can control whole continents; who controls money can control the world."*

Codex is run by the Big 5

The most dominant country behind the agenda of Codex is the United States, whose sole purpose is to benefit multinational interests of the **Big 5**: **Big Pharma**, **Big Chema**, **Big Biotechna**, **Big Agra**, and **Big Medica**.

At the latest meeting in Geneva, the U.S. recently became the chair of Codex, which will facilitate an exacerbation of the distortion of health freedom and will continue the promulgation of misinformation and lies about **genetically modified organism** (GMOs) and nutrients while fulfilling the unspoken population control agenda.

The reason the U.S. continues to dominate Codex is because other countries falsely believe the U.S. possesses the latest and greatest safety technology when it comes to food and hence, whatever the U.S. asks for, its allies (E.U., Argentina, Brazil, Canada, Mexico, Australia, Malaysia, Indonesia, Japan, Singapore) follow suit nearly every time. Many of the countries who wish to participate and want to voice their opinions are not allowed to attend the Codex meetings as the U.S. denies most visas for these representatives whenever they feel like it.

Many of these countries (South Africa, Swaziland, Kenya, Ghana, Egypt, Cameroon, Sudan, and Nigeria) realise that Codex has been altered from a benevolent food organisation, to one that is fraudulent, lethal, and illegitimate. The fact that Codex meetings are held all over the world is also no accident and allows the U.S. to maintain its tight grip on the Codex agenda as the less economically viable countries are not able to attend (Laibow, 2011).

While the NWO agenda of the media is busy driving fear into the hearts of the world by focusing on terrorism, global warming, salmonella, and food shortages, the real threats are clandestinely becoming a reality. Soon every single thing you put into your mouth (with the exception of pharmaceuticals of course) will be highly regulated by *Codex Alimentarius*, including water.

The standards of Codex are a complete affront to the freedom of clean and healthy food, yet these regulations have no legal international standing. Why should we be worried? These soon-to-be mandatory standards will apply to every country who are members of the **WTO** (World Trade Organization).

If countries do not follow these standards, then enormous trade sanctions will result. Some Codex standards that took effect on December 31, 2009 and once they were initiated, are now completely irrevocable include:

- **All nutrients** (vitamins and minerals) are to be considered toxins/ poisons and are to be removed from all food because Codex prohibits the use of nutrients to *"prevent, treat, or cure any condition or disease"*

- **All food** (including organic) is to be irradiated, removing all toxic nutrients from food (unless eaten locally and raw).
- **Nutrients** allowed will be limited to a Positive List developed by Codex which will include such "beneficial" nutrients like Fluoride (3.8 mg daily) developed from environmental waste. All other nutrients will be prohibited nationally and internationally to all Codex-compliant countries.
- **All nutrients** (e.g., CoQ10, Vitamins A, B, C, D, Zinc and Magnesium) that have any positive health impact on the body, will be deemed illegal under Codex and are to be reduced to amounts negligible to humans' health. You will not even be able to obtain these anywhere in the world, even with a prescription.
- **All advice** on nutrition (including written online or journal articles or oral advice to a friend, family member or anyone) will be illegal. This includes any reports on vitamins and minerals and all nutritionist's consultations.
- **All dairy cows** are to be treated with Monsanto's recombinant bovine growth hormone.
- **All animals** used for food are to be treated with potent antibiotics and exogenous growth hormones.
- **The reintroduction** of deadly and carcinogenic organic pesticides that in 1991, 176 countries (including the U.S.) have banned worldwide, including 7 of the 12 worst at the Stockholm Convention on Persistent Organic Pesticides (e.g., Hexachlorobenzene, Toxaphene, and Aldrin) will be allowed back into food at elevated levels.
- **Dangerous and toxic levels** (0.5 ppb) of aflatoxin in milk produced from mouldy storage conditions of animal feed will be allowed. Aflatoxin is the second most potent (non-radiation) carcinogenic compound known to man.
- **Mandatory use** of growth hormones and antibiotics on all food herds, fish and flocks
- **Worldwide implementation** of unlabelled GMOs into crops, animals, fish, and trees.
- **Elevated levels** of residue from pesticides and insecticides that are toxic to humans and animals.

Some examples of potential permissible safe levels of nutrients under Codex include:

- **Niacin** - upper limits of 34 mcg daily (effective daily doses include 2000 to 3000 mcgs).
- **Vitamin C** - upper limits of 65 to 225 mcg daily (effective daily doses include 6000 to 10000 mcgs).
- **Vitamin D** - upper limits of 5 µg daily (effective daily doses include 6000 to 10000 µg).
- **Vitamin E** - upper limits of 15 IU of alpha tocopherol only per day, even though alpha tocopherol by itself has been implicated in cell damage and is toxic to the body (effective daily doses of mixed tocopherols include 10000 to 12000 IU).

The Door is Open for Codex

In 1995, the U.S. **Food and Drug Administration** (FDA) created an illegal policy stating that international standards (i.e., Codex) would supersede U.S. laws governing all food even if these standards were incomplete. Furthermore, in 2004 the U.S. passed the **Central American Free Trade Agreement** (illegal under U.S. law, but legal under international law) that required the U.S. to conform to Codex by December of 2009.

Once these standards were adopted there is no possible way to return to the standards of the old. Once Codex compliance begins in *any* area, as long as you remain a member of the WTO, it is totally irrevocable. These standards are then unable to be repealed, changed, or altered.

Population control for money is the easiest way to describe the new Codex which is run by the U.S. and controlled by Big Pharma and the like to reduce the population to a sustainable 500 million - a reduction of approximately 93 percent. The FAO and WHO have the audacity to estimate that by the introduction of just the vitamin and mineral guideline alone, a minimum of 3 billion deaths (1 billion from starvation and another 2 billion from preventable and degenerative diseases of under nutrition, e.g., cancer, cardiovascular disease, and diabetes) will result. Those are their numbers - not mine!

Degraded, demineralized, pesticide-filled, and irradiated foods are the fastest and most efficient way to cause a profitable surge in malnutrition, preventable and degenerative disease which the most appropriate course of action is always pharmaceuticals. Death for profit is the new name of the game. Big Pharma has been waiting for this opportunity for years.

Fighting Back

Dr. Rima Laibow, M.D., who is the medical director for **Natural Solutions Foundation**, has undertaken legal action against the U.S. government, and continues to attend every Codex meeting while fighting for your health freedom. The latest Codex meeting in Geneva heard some dissenting voices that were tired of the U.S. bullying every other country in the world with its population control agenda.

Brazil and China have stated that when smaller, underrepresented countries are unable to attend Codex meetings (due to the U.S. not allowing Visas or for lack of monetary means) then every decision made in their absence is invalid.

As a result, Codex may soon fall apart under the weight of its own corruption, but pressure needs to be unilaterally applied.

Dr. Rima has also been meeting with delegates from other countries and making them aware of something called *Private Standards*. Private standards allow countries to draft food standards which are safer and higher than those mandated by Codex. Obviously, this is not a very difficult task and many countries can seemingly circumvent the flawed and irrevocable guidelines Codex is attempting to implement.

What Can You Do?

The only way to avoid such cataclysmic events are to fight with the dissemination of knowledge to everyone you know. It does not matter whether they are still asleep or hypnotized by the enslavement of daily life, or too busy to pay attention -- the time to wake up is now.

The U.S. government and the collaborating media have been trying to distract America and the world, while all these egregious and mandatory standards are covertly passed. It is time to take action and you can do so by going to www.healthfreedomusa.org and following the latest updates on Codex. You can also sign a legal citizen's petition (US citizens only for now) here: (Petition, 2015).

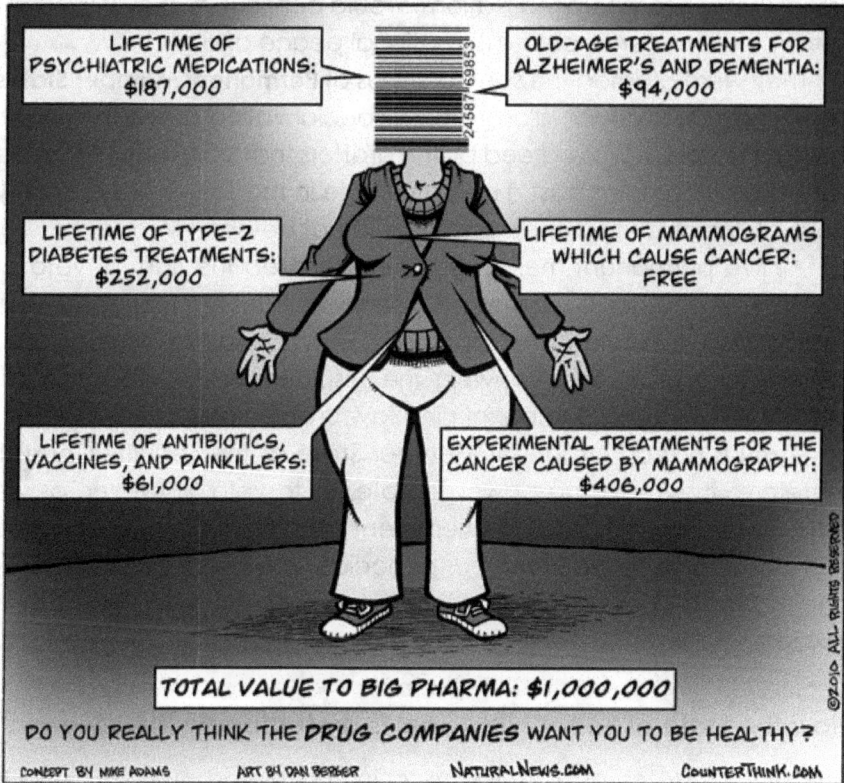

COUNTERTHINK - *"BIG PHARMA'S MILLION-DOLLAR WOMAN"*

LIFETIME OF PSYCHIATRIC MEDICATIONS: $187,000	OLD-AGE TREATMENTS FOR ALZHEIMER'S AND DEMENTIA: $94,000
LIFETIME OF TYPE-2 DIABETES TREATMENTS: $252,000	LIFETIME OF MAMMOGRAMS WHICH CAUSE CANCER: FREE
LIFETIME OF ANTIBIOTICS, VACCINES, AND PAINKILLERS: $61,000	EXPERIMENTAL TREATMENTS FOR THE CANCER CAUSED BY MAMMOGRAPHY: $406,000

TOTAL VALUE TO BIG PHARMA: $1,000,000

DO YOU REALLY THINK THE **DRUG COMPANIES** WANT YOU TO BE HEALTHY?

CONCEPT BY MIKE ADAMS   ART BY DAN BERGER   NATURALNEWS.COM   COUNTERTHINK.COM

©2010 ALL RIGHTS RESERVED

One person cured, is one less dollar for Big Pharma!

The Health Ranger

I would also strongly recommend visiting the website of **Mike Adams**, the "Health Ranger," an outspoken consumer health advocate, award-winning investigative journalist, internet activist, and science lab director. If you are interested in alternative health, healthy eating, and lifestyle, or just want a laugh, Mike's site is awesome (HealthRanger, 2015).

THE RIGHT TO VETO

The creators of the United Nations Charter conceived that five countries — China, France, the Union of Soviet Socialist Republics (USSR) [which was succeeded in 1990 by the Russian Federation], the

United Kingdom and the United States, because of their key roles in the establishment of the United Nations, would continue to play important roles in the maintenance of international peace and security.

They were granted the special status of **Permanent Member States** at the Security Council, along with a special voting power known as the **right to veto**. It was agreed by the drafters that if any one of the five permanent members cast a negative vote in the 15-member Security Council, the resolution or decision would not be approved.

All five permanent members have exercised the right of veto at one time or another. If a permanent member does not fully agree with a proposed resolution, but does not wish to cast a veto, it may choose to abstain, thus allowing the resolution to be adopted if it obtains the required number of nine favourable votes.

Israel is not a Permanent Member State at the Security Council, therefore, they have no power to vote, or to veto. However, as we have already learnt, the US government is run by Rothschild Zionist, so all you need to do, to hide your genocide from the world, is to bully and control a country that is on the permanent members. Here is how it works.

How the State of Rothschild/Israel is protected by the US

The United States cast its first veto in the United Nations Security Council in 1970, during the presidency of Richard Nixon, when **Henry Kissinger** was the national security adviser. The first U.S. veto in history was a gesture of support for Britain, which was under Security Council pressure to end the white minority government in southern Rhodesia (the land of **Cecil Rhodes**).

Two years later however, on Sept. 10, 1972, the United States employed its veto for the second time—to shield Israel.' That veto, as it turned out, signalled the start of a cynical policy to use the U.S. veto repeatedly to shield Israel from international criticism, censure, and sanctions.

Before this practice stopped 18 years later, Washington used its veto 29 times to shield Israel from critical draft resolutions. This constituted nearly half of the total of 69 U.S. vetoes cast since the founding of the U.N. The Soviet Union cast 115 vetoes during the same period.

The initial 1972 veto to protect Israel was cast by **George Bush** in his capacity as U.S. ambassador to the world body. Ironically, it was Bush as president who stopped the use of the veto to shield Israel 18 years later. The last such veto was cast on May 31, 1990, killing a resolution approved by all 14 other council members to send a U.N. mission to study Israeli abuses of Palestinians in the occupied territories.

The rationale for casting the first veto to protect Israel was explained by Bush at the time as a new policy to combat terrorists. The draft resolution had condemned Israel's heavy air attacks against Lebanon and Syria, starting Sept. That was the day after 11 Israeli athletes were killed at the 1972 Munich Olympic Games, in an abortive Palestinian attempt to seize them as hostages, to trade for Palestinians in Israeli prisons. Between 200 and 500 Lebanese, Syrians and Palestinians, mostly civilians, were killed in the Israeli raids.

Nonetheless, Bush complained that the resolution had failed to condemn terrorist attacks against Israel, adding:

> *"We are implementing a new policy that is much broader than that of the question of Israel and the Jews. What is involved is the problem of terrorism, a matter that goes right to the heart of our civilized life."*

Unfortunately, this "policy" proved to be only a rationale for protecting Israel from censure for violating a broad range of international laws. This became very clear when the next U.S. veto was cast a year later, on July 26, 1973. It had nothing to do with terrorism. The draft resolution affirmed the rights of the Palestinians and established provisions for Israeli withdrawal from occupied territories, as embodied in previous General Assembly resolutions. Nonetheless, Washington killed this international effort to end Israel's occupation of Palestinian lands.

Washington used the veto four more times in 1975-76 while **Henry Kissinger** was Secretary of State. One of these vetoes arguably may have involved terrorism, since the draft condemned Israeli attacks on Lebanese civilians in response to attacks on Israel. But the three other vetoes had nothing at all to do with terrorism.

One, in fact, struck down a draft resolution that reflected U.S. policy against Israel's alteration of the status of Jerusalem and establishment of Jewish settlements in occupied territory. Only two days earlier, U.S. Ambassador **William W. Scranton** had given a speech in the United Nations calling Israeli settlements illegal and rejecting Israel's claim to all of Jerusalem. Yet on March 25, 1976, the U.S. vetoed a resolution reflecting Scranton's positions which had been passed unanimously by the other 14 members of the council.

The two other vetoes during Kissinger's reign also were cast in 1976. One, on Jan. 26, killed a draft resolution calling for recognition of the right of self-determination for Palestinians. The other, on June 29, called for affirmation of the "inalienable rights" of the Palestinians.

The **Carter** administration cast only one veto. But it had nothing to do with terrorism. It came on April 30, 1980, killing a draft that endorsed self-determination for the Palestinian people.

The all-time abuser of the veto was the administration of **Ronald Reagan**, the most pro-Israel presidency in U.S. history, with the most pro-Israel secretary of state, **George Shultz**, since Kissinger. The Reagan team cynically invoked the **veto 18 times to protect Israel**. A record six of these vetoes were cast in 1982 alone. Nine of the Reagan vetoes resulted directly from Security Council attempts to condemn Israel's 1982 invasion of Lebanon, and Israel's refusal to surrender the territory in southern Lebanon which it still occupies today. The other nine vetoes shielded Israel from council criticism for such illicit acts as the Feb. 4, 1986, skyjacking of a Libyan plane.

Illicit Skyjacking or "Self-Defence"

Israeli warplanes forced a private, executive jet to land in Israel, allegedly in an effort to capture Palestinian terrorist **Abu Nidal**. He was not aboard and after interrogation, the passengers were allowed to leave. The U.S. delegate explained that this act of piracy was excusable,

> *"because we believe that the ability to take such action in carefully defined and limited circumstances is an aspect of the inherent right of self-defence recognised in the U.N. Charter."*

Other vetoes employed on Israel's exclusive behalf included the Jan. 20, 1982 killing of a demand that Israel withdraw from the **Golan Heights** it had occupied in 1967; the April 20, 1982 condemnation of an Israeli soldier who shot 11 Muslim worshippers at the Haram Al-Sharif in the Old City of Jerusalem's; the Feb. 1, 1988 call for Israel to stop violating Palestinian human rights in the occupied territories, abide by the Fourth Geneva Convention and formalise a leading role for the United Nations in future peace negotiations; the April 15, 1988 resolution requesting that Israel permit the return of expelled Palestinians, condemning Israel's shooting of civilians, calling on Israel to uphold the **Fourth Geneva Convention** and calling for a peace settlement under U.N. auspices.

The Bush administration used the veto four times to protect Israel: on Feb. 17, 1989, to kill a draft strongly deploring Israel's repression of the Palestinian uprising and calling on Israel to respect the human rights of the Palestinians; on June 9, 1989, deploring Israel's violation of the human rights of the Palestinians; on Nov. 7, 1989, demanding Israel return property confiscated from Palestinians during a tax protest and calling on Israel to allow a fact-finding mission to observe Israel's suppression tactics against the Palestinian uprising; and, finally, on May 31, 1990, calling for a fact-finding mission on abuses against Palestinians in Israeli-occupied lands.

The May 31, 1990 veto was quashing a commission to investigate murder of seven Palestinian workers, presumably, as the result of a secret understanding, if not an official agreement, with Russia and the three other Security Council members with veto power. By then it had become obvious that the council could not be effective in a post-Cold War world if Britain, China, France, Russia, and the United States recklessly invoked their vetoes.

And so it continues. Here is a summary by US President. It really shows who the hard core Rothschild Zionist is out of this group of criminals doesn't it.

Bill Clinton (3)

- May 17, 1995 (S/1995/394) Confirming Israeli Expropriation of Land in East Jerusalem as Invalid
- March 7, 1997 (S/1997/199) Calling Israeli Authorities to Refrain From All Settlement Activity
- March 21, 1997 S/1997/241) Demanding Israel Cease Construction of Settlements in East Jerusalem

George W Bush (9)

- March 27, 2001 (S/2001/270) Calling for UN Observers Force in West Bank & Gaza
- December 14, 2001 (S/2001/1199) Demanding Immediate Cessation of Israeli-Palestinian Violence

- December 20, 2002 (S/2002/1385) Condemning Israeli Killing UN employees of World Food Programme
- September 16, 2003 (S/2003/891) Demanding Israel Halt Threats to Expel Yasser Arafat
- October 14, 2003 (S/2003/980) Seeking to Bar Israel from Extending Security Fence
- March 25, 2004 (S/2004/240) Condemning Israel for Killing Hamas Leader Ahmed Yassin
- October 5, 2004 (S/2004/783) Calling Israel To Halt Gaza Operation
- July 13, 2006 (S/2006/508) Calling Israel To Halt Gaza Operation
- November 11, 2006 (S/2006/878) Calling Israel To Halt Gaza Operation

Barack Obama (1)
- February 18, 2011 S/2011/24) Condemning Israeli settlements Established Since 1967 as Illegal

(Vetoes, 2015); (UN Vetoed, 2015)

These resolutions brought the total passed by the council against Israel since its birth to 81. If the United States had not invoked its veto, the record against Israel would now total 110 resolutions condemning or otherwise criticizing its behaviour or suppressing the rights of Palestinians.

"The United Nations is the greatest fraud in history. Its purpose is to destroy the United States." (John E. Rankin, a U.S. Congressman)

John E. Rankin
(1921 - 1953)

UNITED NATIONS

ONE WORLD - ONE GOVERNMENT

The UN: Advocates global taxation
The UN: Entrenches and rewards racism
The UN: Appeases dictators
The UN: Has been caught trafficking children for prostitution
**The UN: Peacekeeper's missions destroy the sovereignty
of nations and they work to outlaw individual rights**

Secretary Generals follow the script

All seven of the UN secretary generals since 1945 have promoted such thinking. The last holder of the office, **Dr Boutros Boutros-Ghali** called for a permanent UN Army (world army) and for the UN to have the right to levy taxation (world government). His successor, **Kofi Annan**, wants the same.

The UN is a front for the Illuminati/New World Order hierarchy. In a speech in 1970, **Robert Welch**, the founder of the **John Birch Society** in America, predicted with remarkable accuracy what the United Nations would become:

> "The United Nations hopes and plans - or, more accurately, the insiders, the conspiratorial bosses above it, hope and plan for it- to use population controls, the secret government, 145 controls over scientific and technological developments, control over arms and military strength of individual nations, control over education, control over health, and all the controls it can gradually establish under all of the different excuses for international jurisdiction that it can devise. These variegated separate controls are to become components of the gradually materialising total control that it expects to achieve by pretence, deception, persuasion, beguilement, and falsehoods, while the enforcement of such controls by brutal force and terror is also getting under way."

Robert Henry Winborne Welch, Jr. (1899 - 1985)

The United Nations 2030 Agenda

In 2015 the United Nations rebranded their Agenda 21 to **2030 Agenda**, indicating they have now implemented a timeline of 2030 to get Agenda 21 in place and fully operational. From what I can tell, 2030 Agenda basically pushes the same things as Agenda 21.

It still reads like a blueprint for the global enslavement of humanity under the boot of corporate masters. This document describes nothing less than a global government takeover of every nation across the planet.

The "goals" of this document are nothing more than code words for a corporate-government fascist agenda that will imprison humanity in a devastating cycle of poverty, while enriching the world's most powerful globalist corporations like Monsanto and DuPont.

Total enslavement of the planet by 2030

As the UN document says,

> " We commit ourselves to working
> tirelessly for the full implementation
> of this Agenda by 2030. "

If you read the full document and can read beyond the "feel good" and public relations phrases, you'll quickly realise that this UN agenda is going to be forced upon all the citizens of the world through the invocation of government coercion. Nowhere does this document state that the rights of the individual will be protected. Even the so-called *"Universal Declaration of Human Rights"* utterly denies individuals the right to self-defence, the right to medical choice and the right to parental control over their own children.

The UN is planning nothing less than a global government tyranny that enslaves all of humanity while calling the scheme "sustainable development" and "equality."

That is what the United Nations was always intended to do; that is what it was created to do; that is what it is now doing.

Annexes:

ANNEX 3.7.1 - Committee of 300 Institutions
ANNEX 3.9.1 - The Carbon Tax Scam
ANNEX 3.9.2 - Bilderberg Conference 2015 Attendance List

References:

Adams, M. (2015). *The United Nations 2030 Agenda decoded: It's a blueprint for the global enslavement of humanity under the boot of corporate masters.* [online] NaturalNews. Available at: http://www.naturalnews.com/051058_2030_Agenda_United_Nations_global_enslavement.html# [Accessed 18 Nov. 2015].

Agenda 21, (2013). *Agenda 21, in under 5 minutes.* [online] YouTube. Available at: https://youtu.be/6l79Qa92DeU [Accessed 21 Oct. 2015].

Agenda 21, (2013). *Agenda 21, in under 5 minutes.* [online] YouTube. Available at: https://www.youtube.com/watch?v=6l79Qa92DeU [Accessed 16 Nov. 2015].

Alimentarius, C. (2015). *Codex Alimentarius.* [online] Wikipedia. Available at: https://en.wikipedia.org/wiki/Codex_Alimentarius [Accessed 20 Oct. 2015].

Allen, G. (1976). *The Rockefeller file.* Seal Beach, Calif.: '76 Press.

Babiak, P. and Hare, R. (2006). *Snakes in suits.* New York: Regan Books.

Babiak, P., Neumann, C. and Hare, R. (2010). Corporate psychopathy: Talking the walk. *Behavioral Sciences & the Law.*

Benko, R. (2013). *1.6 Billion Rounds Of Ammo For Homeland Security? It's Time For A National Conversation.* [online] Forbes.com. Available at: http://www.forbes.com/sites/ralphbenko/2013/03/11/1-6-billion-rounds-of-ammo-for-homeland-security-its-time-for-a-national-conversation/ [Accessed 18 Oct. 2015].

Borghese, L. and Grinberg, E. (2015). *Gay priest to be stripped of duties of Vatican - CNN. com.* [online] CNN. Available at: http://edition.cnn.com/2015/10/03/world/gay-vatican-priest-krzystof-charamsa-feat/ [Accessed 18 Oct. 2015].

Brzezinĺ ski, Z. (1970). *Between two ages.* New York: The Viking Press.

Casualties, V. (2015). *Vietnam War.* [online] Wikipedia. Available at: https://en.wikipedia.org/wiki/Vietnam_War [Accessed 18 Oct. 2015].

CEO, B. (2015). *Executive Management Team | Brisbane City Council.* [online] Brisbane. qld.gov.au. Available at: http://www.brisbane.qld.gov.au/about-council/governance-strategy/organisational-chart/executive-management-team [Accessed 24 Oct. 2015].

Children of the World., (1994). *Rescue Mission Planet Earth.* New York: Grisewood & Dempsey, Inc.

Client List, (2015). *Our members | Forum for the Future.* [online] Forumforthefuture.org. Available at: https://www.forumforthefuture.org/our-members [Accessed 16 Nov. 2015].

Clinton, H. (2010). *Hillary Clinton accidentally admits that the CFR runs this nation. Wow..* [online] YouTube. Available at: https://www.youtube.com/watch?v=Kfpgl6NqF0I [Accessed 17 May 2015].

Corbett, J. (2013). *Chatham House Rule: Inside the Royal Institute of International Affairs : The Corbett Report.* [online] Corbettreport.com. Available at: https://www.corbettreport.com/chatham-house-rule-inside-the-royal-institute-of-international-affairs/ [Accessed 15 Nov. 2015].

Daily Mail, (2011). *Bill Clinton and George Bush Snr reveal surprising friendship as former presidents are honoured at country music charity gala.* [online] Mail Online. Available at: http://www.dailymail.co.uk/news/article-1368842/Bill-Clinton-George-HW-Bush-reveal-firm-friendship-Points-Light-Institute-gala.html [Accessed 18 Oct. 2015].

Damato, D. (2008). *Codex Alimentarius: Population Control Under the Guise of Consumer Protection.* [online] NaturalNews. Available at: http://www.naturalnews.com/024128_CODEX_food_health.html [Accessed 21 Oct. 2015].

Domhoff, G. (1967). *Who rules America?.* Englewood Cliffs, N.J.: Prentice-Hall.

Estulin, D. (2009). *The true story of the Bilderberg Group.* Walterville, OR: TrineDay.

Harnden, T. (2014). *Bush: My Sweet Dad, a Wonderful Father to Bill Clinton and Me | RealClearPolitics.* [online] Realclearpolitics.com. Available at: http://www.

realclearpolitics.com/articles/2014/11/18/bush_my_sweet_daddy_a_wonderful_father_to_bill_clinton_and_me_124685.html [Accessed 18 Oct. 2015].

HealthRanger, M. (2015). *HealthRanger.com - Sharing empowering videos to help improve personal and planetary health*. [online] NaturalNews. Available at: http://www.healthranger.com/ [Accessed 18 Nov. 2015].

Herbers, J. (1969). *250,000 War Protesters Stage Peaceful Rally In Washington; Militants Stir Clashes Later*. [online] Nytimes.com. Available at: http://www.nytimes.com/learning/general/onthisday/big/1115.html [Accessed 18 Oct. 2015].

Hiss, A. (2015). *Alger Hiss*. [online] Wikipedia. Available at: https://en.wikipedia.org/wiki/Alger_Hiss [Accessed 20 Oct. 2015].

Home, C. (2015). *CODEX Alimentarius: Home*. [online] Codexalimentarius.net. Available at: http://www.codexalimentarius.net [Accessed 21 Oct. 2015].

Horizon: Season 48, Episode 5 - Are You Good or Evil?. (2011). [video] UK: Nikki Stockley.

Howe, F. (1968). *The Confessions of a Monopolist*. Upper Saddle River, N.J.: Gregg Press.

Human foetal cells, (2015). *Aborted Human fetal cells for stimulating artificial flavors*. [online] Seattleorganicrestaurants.com. Available at: http://www.seattleorganicrestaurants.com/vegan-whole-food/aborted-fetus-cells-artificial-flavors.php [Accessed 18 Nov. 2015].

Koire, R. (2011). *Behind the green mask*. Santa Rosa, CA: Post Sustainability Institute Press.

Laibow, D. (2012). *Dr Rima Laibow Codex Alimentarius*. [online] YouTube. Available at: https://youtu.be/wFIpvi5KfLQ [Accessed 21 Oct. 2015].

Laibow, R. (2011). *Nutricide-Criminalizing Natural Health, Vitamins, and Herbs - NaturalNews.tv*. [online] Tv.naturalnews.com. Available at: http://tv.naturalnews.com/v.asp?v=098B99C326DFEAF10F257768813CEF52 [Accessed 15 Nov. 2015].

Members, (2015). *Our members | Forum for the Future*. [online] Forumforthefuture.org. Available at: https://www.forumforthefuture.org/our-members [Accessed 18 Nov. 2015].

One-heaven.org, (2015). *One-Heaven: Canons - Canonum De Ius Rex - Canons of Sovereign Law - Article 81 - Lucifer*. [online] Available at: http://one-heaven.org/canons/sovereign_law/article/81.html [Accessed 19 Apr. 2015].

Opolis, (2011). *YouTube - four visions of city life in 2040 - planned-opolis.flv*. [online] YouTube. Available at: https://youtu.be/IRFsoRQYpFM [Accessed 16 Nov. 2015].

Pepsi, T. (2012). *Pro-lifers drop boycott after Pepsi disavows use of aborted fetal-cells*. [online] The Washingtion Times. Available at: http://www.washingtontimes.com/news/2012/apr/30/pro-lifers-drop-pepsi-boycott/ [Accessed 18 Nov. 2015].

Perloff, J. (1988). *The shadows of power*. Boston: Western Islands.

Petition, (2015). *Sign Citizenâ€™s Petition*. [online] Healthfreedomusa.org. Available at: http://www.healthfreedomusa.org/?page_id=184 [Accessed 18 Nov. 2015].

Ramirez, A. (2015). *Which Nations Signed Agenda 21?*. [online] The Post Sustainability Institute. Available at: http://www.postsustainabilityinstitute.org/which-nations-signed-agenda-21.html [Accessed 21 Oct. 2015].

SEC, (2015). *U.S. Securities and Exchange Commission | Homepage*. [online] Sec.gov. Available at: https://www.sec.gov/ [Accessed 24 Oct. 2015].

Self Driving Car, G. (2015). *CNN test-drives Googles "self-driving car"*. [online] YouTube. Available at: https://youtu.be/VCpPPVvGqTY [Accessed 6 Jun. 2015].

Sutton, A. (1995). *Trilaterals Over America*. Boring, OR: CPA Book Publishers.

UN Vetoed, (2015). *List of Vetoed United Nation Security Council Resolutions*. [online] Wikipedia. Available at: https://en.wikipedia.org/wiki/List_of_Vetoed_United_Nation_Security_Council_Resolutions [Accessed 15 Nov. 2015].

Vetoes, (2015). *U.S. Vetoes of UN Security Council Resolutions Critical to Israel | Jewish Virtual Library*. [online] Jewishvirtuallibrary.org. Available at: https://www.jewishvirtuallibrary.org/jsource/UN/usvetoes.html [Accessed 15 Nov. 2015].

White, H. (2015). *Harry Dexter White*. [online] Wikipedia. Available at: https://en.wikipedia.org/wiki/Harry_Dexter_White [Accessed 20 Oct. 2015].

Why NAFTA is Bad, (2015). *Why NAFTA is Bad for the U.S. | Economy In Crisis*. [online] Economyincrisis.org. Available at: http://economyincrisis.org/content/why-nafta-is-bad-for-the-u-s [Accessed 6 Jun. 2015].

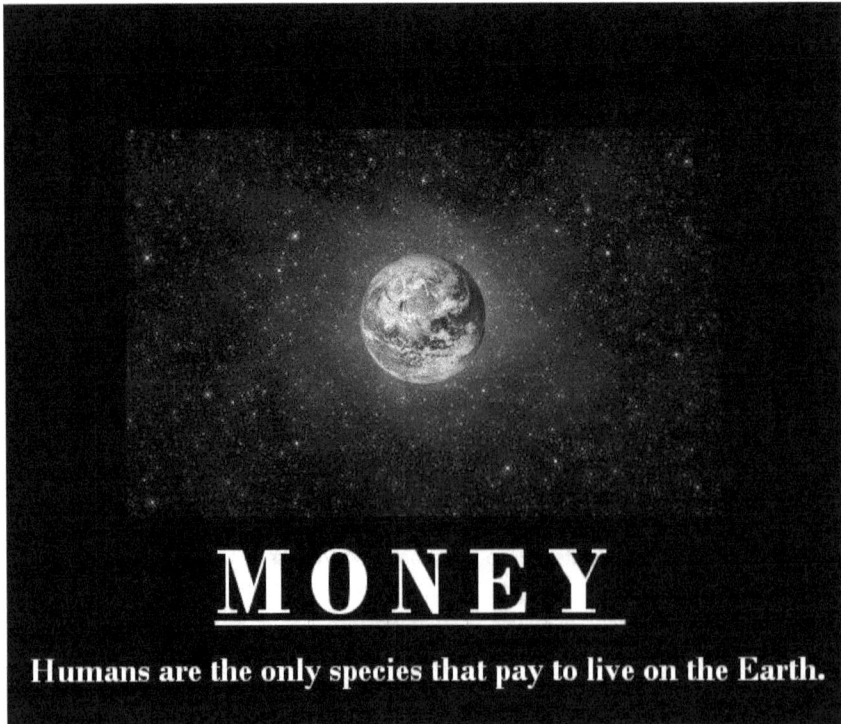

10

10 CONSPIRACY THEORIES THAT TURNED OUT TO BE TRUE!

"Society is one vast conspiracy for carving one into the kind of statue it likes, and then placing it in the most convenient niche it has"

—RANDOLPH BOURNE

*H*ere are some of the top 10 Conspiracies of all time. There have been hundreds of books and documentaries on these topics, however the majority of the population is not aware of them. Therefore, it is not my intention to give an in-depth analysis, or to provide a mountain of evidence to support the claims. As stated, this has already been done by other hard working and diligent researchers. I present them here now to highlight them, and in some cases, inspire the reader to investigate them further. Even though I numbered them, there is no real best to worst or anything. The numbering is arbitrary, but I did want to start with the most recent:

1. GENETICALLY MODIFIED ORGANISMS (GMO)

GMO's cause cancer, 2012

Few things exemplify more absolutely the fact that we are living in a world of deception, manipulation, and fraudulent science than GMOs. Over the past few years, a number of studies (both independent and peer-reviewed) have emerged, which clearly outline why GMOs should not be approved as completely safe for human consumption. Despite this fact, their status has not changed. The truth of their danger was also demonstrated by the **March against Monsanto**, a worldwide protest where millions of people around the world gather every year to peacefully protest the biotech giant. There is a reason why so many countries around the world have now completely banned GMOs and the pesticides that go with them.

In November 2012, the Journal of Food and Chemical Toxicology published a paper titled, *Long Term Toxicity of Roundup Herbicide and a Roundup-Tolerant Genetically Modified Maize*, by Gilles-Eric Seralini and his team of researchers at France's Caen University (Séralini, 2012).

It was a very significant study that made a lot of noise worldwide, the first of its kind under controlled conditions that examined the possible effects of a GMO maize diet treated with Monsanto's **Roundup Herbicide** (Walia, 2014).

In March **2015**, **The World Health Organization's** (WHO) cancer arm, the International Agency for Research on Cancer (IARC), said **glyphosate**, the active ingredient in Monsanto's herbicide **Roundup**, was "*classified as carcinogenic to humans.*" It also said that *glyphosate* was carcinogenic in humans for non-Hodgkin lymphoma (Polansek, 2015).

Case closed! Monsanto GMO's will kill you!

2. GLOBAL WARMING IS A FRAUD

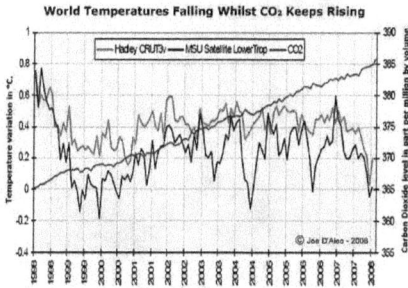

World Temperatures Falling Whilst CO₂ Keeps Rising

Climategate *began in Nov 2009*

The suggestion of a conspiracy to promote the theory of global warming was put forward in a 1990 documentary **The Greenhouse Conspiracy,** broadcast by Channel Four in the United Kingdom on 12 August 1990.

It was part of the Equinox series, which asserted that scientists critical of global warming theory were denied funding.

William Gray, PhD (a pioneer in the science of hurricane forecasting) has made a list of 15 reasons for the global warming hysteria. The list includes the need to come up with an enemy after the end of the Cold War, and the desire among scientists, government leaders and environmentalists to find a political cause that would enable them to 'organise, propagandise, force conformity and exercise political influence.

A **One World Government** could best lead (and control) us to a better world!' In this article, Gray also cites the ascendancy of **Al Gore** to the vice presidency as the start of his problems with federal funding. According to him, the **National Oceanic and Atmospheric Administration** stopped giving him research grants, and so did **NASA**.

Global warming has all but been debunked, especially when the **Climategate** scandal broke in 2009, which showed climate scientist were fudging their data to support the global warming hoax.

Three themes emerged from the leaked emails: (1) prominent scientists central to the global warming debate were taking measures to conceal, rather than disseminate, underlying data and discussions; (2) these scientists view global warming as a political "cause" rather than a balanced scientific inquiry and (3) many of these scientists frankly admit to each other that much of the science is weak and dependent on deliberate manipulation of facts and data (Taylor, 2011).

In reality, all the data from NASA shows a global cooling, and it has nothing to do with manmade activities (NASA, 2015). Furthermore, all of the carbon taxes would be paid directly into **Rothschild owned banks**.

Case closed! Manmade warming is a scam!

3. 9/11 WAS PLANNED BY THE US GOVERNMENT

Building 7 - not hit by a plane, but collapses into its own footprint hours after the attack, 2001

Many conspiracy theories have been presented concerning the September 11, 2001 attacks. Many of them claiming that **President George W. Bush** and/or individuals in his administration knew about the attacks beforehand and purposefully allowed them to occur because the attacks would generate public support for militarisation, expansion of the police state, and other intrusive foreign and domestic policies by which they would benefit.

Proponents point to the **Project for the New American Century**, a conservative think tank that argues for increased American global leadership, whose former members include ex-Secretary of Defence **Donald Rumsfeld**, Vice President **Dick Cheney** and several other key Bush administration figures. A 1990 report from the group stated that:

> **❝** *Some catastrophic and catalysing event — like a new Pearl Harbor,* **❞**

would be needed to budge public opinion in their favour. Whilst there are hundreds of items of evidence that proves without doubt that 9/11 was an inside job, one only needs to watch one, **30 second video clip**. It shows the implosion of **Building 7**.

For those that do not know, Building 7 was a large building near the World Trade Centre. It was not hit by a plane, or anything else. It did not catch on fire. It was however the main control centre for the **CIA**. This was the command centre for the CIA to manoeuvre the remote controlled planes into the World Trade Centre, as well as the place where they controlled and detonated the explosions, to bring down the Twin Towers in a controlled demolition – implosion.

The BBC had a live cross to their reporter who was announcing that Building 7 had collapsed. The only problem was Building 7 could still be seen behind her, standing, and it was 20 minutes before the building actually collapsed (BBC video, 2001). Oops!

The "job" was planned by the **Israelis**, and was funded by the **Saudis**. There is overwhelming evidence to support this information.

Building 7 was conveniently "imploded" hours after the towers fell. This was to hide all evidence of the remote controlled planes that were controlled from this building (Building 7, 2001).

If you want the full story about what really happened on 9/11, then I would recommend the documentary *9/11: In Plane Site* (vonKleist, 2004), or *Loose Change: Final Cut* (Avery, 2007).

The evidence shown in these two documentaries is breathtaking, and demonstrates the absolute, systemic level of corruption within the United States government. I can assure you that after watching these documentaries, you will have no problem agreeing.

Case closed! 9/11 was an inside job!

DID YOU KNOW

One week before September 11, 2001, the Zim Shipping Company broke its lease it had held for 30 years and moved out of the World Trade Center.

Zim is half-owned by the Rothschilds.

4. PRINCESS DIANA WAS MURDERED BY THE ROYAL FAMILY

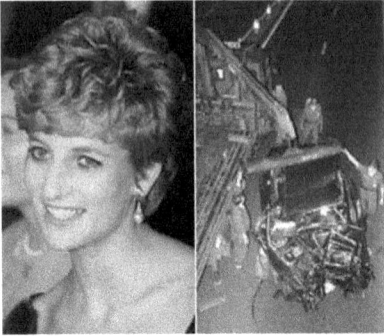

Princess Diana was assassinated, 1997

In 1997, Princess Diana (Princess of Wales) and Dodi Fayed (son of Mohamed Fayed, owner of the Ritz Hotel and Harrods), were killed in a car accident while trying to get away from press photographers in Paris. The scandal surrounding their relationship (Dodi was Muslim whilst Diana was the mother of the future head of the Church of England) has led many people to speculate that they were actually killed in order to prevent further scandal to the throne of England.

Polls suggest that around a quarter of the UK public, and a majority of people in some Arab countries, believe that there was a plot to murder Diana, Princess of Wales.

Motivations which have been advanced for such a conspiracy include suggestions that Diana intended to marry Dodi Fayed that she intended to convert to Islam, that she was pregnant, and that she was to visit the holy land and expose the Jewish genocide of Palestinians.

Organisations which are responsible for her death have included French Intelligence, the British Royal Family, certain members of the press, the British Intelligence services MI5 or MI6 (Diana, 1997).

In 2011, **Keith Allen**, father of the singer Lilly Allen, wrote and directed the best documentary about the death of Diana. Called ***Unlawful Killing***, it proves beyond any doubt that Diana and Dodi were murdered.

The "hit" was called for by **Prince Phillip**, himself a Nazi sympathiser and hard-core racist. Although the Queen did not have anything to do with the murder, she knew all about it in advance, and said nothing. Allen also tracks down the driver of the "White Fiat" that caused the accident – something the Police failed to do, or did not want to know about. Unsurprisingly, the driver of the Fiat, a British national, "committed suicide" (no doubt with a little help), before he could be brought to trial (Allen, 2011). He was found in a burning car with two bullet holes in the back of his head.

Case closed! Diana was murdered by MI6, under orders from Prince Phillip.

5. APOLLO MOON LANDINGS WERE A HOAX

Apollo pictures faked, 1969

The Apollo Moon Landing hoax accusations are claims that some or all elements of the Apollo Moon landings were faked by NASA and possibly members of other involved organisations like the CIA. Some groups and individuals have advanced alternate historical narratives which tend to varying degrees, to state that the Apollo Astronauts did not land on the moon, and that NASA created and continues to perpetuate this hoax.

The majority of Moon hoax evidence comes from NASA's own photos. They point to various issues with photographs and films taken on the Moon and aboard their craft. Indeed, in one film, NASA forgot to edit out the on-board filming, where the astronauts were blocking half of the window to make the Earth look further away. In reality, they were in **Low Earth Orbit**. And there you have it.

All images and film while "on" the moon surface where taken in a movie studio. If you have ever seen the James Bond movie **Moonraker** (Moore, 1979), then you have some idea what I am talking about. That movie was an insiders attempt to get the truth out. All rocket takes offs were real, however the space craft and astronauts only went into Low Earth Orbit – about 600 - 800 km (372.8 - 497.1 mi) up (LEO, 2015).

They were originally going to try and go to the moon, however, before the schedule launch, **James Van Allen** came forward with evidence of a radiation belt of energetically charged particles, approximately 1,000 to 60,000 kilometres above the surface of the Earth (Van Allen, 1958). They became known as the **Van Allen Radiation Belt**. Going through them would be akin to sitting inside a microwave oven. No living thing can survive the Van Alan belt. You could not even use the Apollo astronaut suit in Chernobyl, yet alone the Van Allen belt! And no pictures could have been taken on the moon as the extreme temperature of hot and cold and the extreme radiation would make all the pictures completely useless.

Unfortunately, it was too late to redesign the Apollo Lunar Module, and besides, it would need to be completely enveloped in lead, which would prove to be way too heavy to get into space. Thus, with no alternative, they decided to stage the moon landing as there was too much riding on it.

America could not face another embarrassing failure in the space program. Russia had beat them at everything, and were also preparing their own, non-manned moon landing. Interesting that the Russians, who had hundreds of hours more Space time and experience than the Americans, deemed sending men to the moon to be too dangerous. Yet the Americans decided to go?

Originally the Americans were only going to hoax the first mission, however, a fix was never found, and filming on a sound stage was lot cheaper! Famed Hollywood director **Stanley Kubrick** was brought in to make the movie of his life. In fact, it was his work on his movie *2001: A Space Odyssey* (1968) that really impressed the powers that be and that is why he was selected. Kubrick admitted this in 1999, three days before his death, during a filmed interview (Adl-Tabatabai, 2015).

Researchers asked NASA for a copy of the Apollo Lunar Module blueprints. They literally wanted to build a scale replica and launch it into space, to prove once and for all that its 4 mm thin walls could not protect a human from the Van Allen radiation belt. NASA informed them that the blue prints had been destroyed years ago and they no longer had any copies.

So let's get that straight – potentially the greatest engineering feat in human history, and they did not think it was necessary to keep the blueprints? Imagine what those blueprints would be worth today, just for their historical value. But no, NASA thought nothing to throw them out with the garbage. How odd? Unless you were trying to hide something.

Not everyone at NASA was in on the scam. Indeed, all of the technicians, engineers etc., were being fed a "simulation" transmission, and had no idea it was fake. Only the astronauts, a handful of top ranking politicians, and the movie makers were in on the whole story. All the film makers except Kubrick were bumped off by the CIA, as were any other potential leaks.

Neil Armstrong refused to give interviews about his time on the moon, he rarely attended reunions and lived a hermit existence up till his death in 2012. However, in 1994, during the Apollo 11 25th Anniversary celebrations at the Whitehouse, Armstrong gave a very enigmatic speech that has convinced many people that he did not go to the moon. Here is an excerpt:

".. Today we have with us a group of students, among America's best. To you we say - we've only completed the beginning. We leave you much that is undone (he becomes emotional and cries). There are great ideas undiscovered. Breakthroughs available to those, who can remove one-up truth's protective layers. There are places to go beyond belief. Those challenges are yours..." (Armstrong, 1994)

Neil Armstrong
(1930 - 2012)

There are several brilliant film documentaries on the Moon Landing Hoax. The best researched and presented in my opinion are: **A Funny Thing Happened On The Way To The Moon** (Sibrel, 2001) and **What Happened on the Moon: Hoax Lies & Videotape** (The Moon Hoax, 2010). Another brilliant film is **Dark Side of the Moon** (Kubrick, 2002). They try and claim it is a "mockumentary," but it is a typical CIA script – they spread real information with a touch of disinformation, then have a few "authority" figures laugh. Is it real? Is it a joke? Nope, no joke here. NASA have never sent humans to the Moon.

A 'Moon rock' given to Holland, by Apollo 11 astronauts, Neil Armstrong and Buzz Aldrin in 1969, has turned out to be a fake. Curators at Amsterdam's **Rijksmuseum**, where the rock has attracted tens of thousands of visitors each year, discovered that the "lunar rock," valued at £308,000, was in fact petrified wood. NASA gave moon rocks to more than 100 countries following lunar missions in 1969 and the 1970s. No doubt, these also will be fakes, but who would want to admit it, especially when they are such crowd pullers. Well done to **Xandra van Gelder**, who oversaw the investigation. She said the museum would continue to keep the stone as a curiosity (Telegraph, 2009).

Case closed! The Apollo Moon Landings were hoaxed!

6. JOHN F. KENNEDY'S ASSASSINATION

John F. Kennedy assassinated, 1963

The assassination of John F. Kennedy, the thirty-fifth President of the United States, took place on Friday, November 22, 1963, in Dallas, Texas, USA at 12:30 p.m. CST (18:30 UTC).

Kennedy was fatally wounded by gunshots while riding with his wife Jacqueline in a presidential motorcade through Dealey Plaza.

The official investigation by the **Warren Commission** was conducted over a ten-month period, and its report was published in September 1964. The Commission concluded that the assassination was carried out solely by **Lee Harvey Oswald**, an employee of the Texas School Book Depository in Dealey Plaza.

A number of conspiracy theories exist with regard to the assassination of U.S. President John F. Kennedy. Such theories began to be generated soon after his death, and continue to be proposed today. Many of these theories propose a criminal conspiracy involving parties such as the Federal Reserve, the Central Intelligence Agency (CIA), the Mafia, Federal Bureau of Investigation (FBI) director J. Edgar Hoover, Vice President Lyndon B. Johnson, Richard Nixon, Fidel Castro, George H. W. Bush, Cuban exile groups opposed to the Castro government and the military and/or government interests of the United States (Kennedy, 1963).

However, all doubt was put to rest when in **1988**, the best researched and documented TV Mini-Series ever on this subject was produced.

In *The Men Who Killed Kennedy*, it is proven beyond doubt that **Lyndon B. Johnson** was involved, that **George H. W. Bush** was involved, and that there were multiple shooters. They even name the shooters who were non US nationals. Time to set history straight on this one (JFK, 1988).

Case closed! JFK was assassinated by the CIA,
with full support from Lyndon B. Johnston!

7. ADOLF HITLER SURVIVED WORLD WAR II

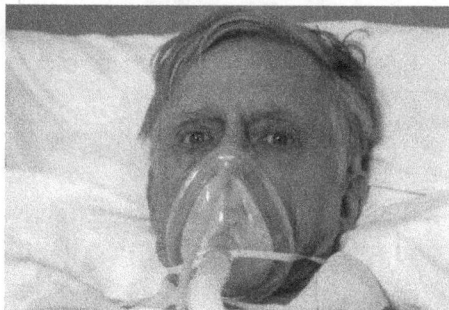

Adolf Hitler died on February 13, 1962 at 3:00pm

The world was told that **Adolf Hitler** committed suicide inside his bunker in 1945, just a day before the Red Army entered the bunker. The true story, known to Stalin, and the FBI was very different.

Adolf Hitler died on **February 13, 1962**, aged 73 in Argentina after living there for 17 years.

One of his two daughters, **Ursula** "Uschi" Hitler still lives in Buenos Aires and has children of her own. **Eva Braun** (Hitler's wife) lived to well into her 90's, also in Buenos Aires.

There are FBI documents that state Hitler survived the war, and boarded a submarine from Spain to Argentina. The escape from Berlin and relocation to Nazi friendly Argentina was organised by **Martin Bormann** (Hitler's 2IC), who started making plans as early as 1943.

The route they took is now well documented. They flew out of Berlin on 28 April 1945 with Eva, Uschi and Hitler's dog Blondie. Leaving from Hohenzollerndamm (near Berlin), they detoured to Magdeburg to avoid an Allied bomber group. They then continued to the abandoned Zeppelin base at Tønder, Denmark. The party now transferred to a new plane with a longer range to get to the Luftwaffe base at Travemunde, Germany (Uschi was dropped off here to be looked after by a Nazi loving family until it was safer for her to travel by air.) From here, they continued to **Reus** (near Barcelona), Spain.

This was made possible by Hitler's long term friend, Spanish dictator, **General Francisco Franco**. On arrival in Spain, the Spanish air force took over and flew the fleeing Nazis' to **Fuerteventura** in the Canary Islands, first having a short refuelling stop over in Morón Air force Base (near Seville).

They transferred to the Nazi base at **Villa Winter** to rendezvous with the U-boats (submarines) of **Operation Seawolf**.

After 53 days at sea, **U-518**, carrying Adolf Hitler, Eva, and Blondie, the submarine arrives at **Necochea** on the Argentine coast. A dedicated team of hard-core Nazis are there to meet them. The next day, the party flies to the **Estancia San Ramon** on the outskirts of San Carlos de Bariloche to begin their exile in five-star luxury.

Their first daughter (Uschi) joined them once they were safely embedded about one year later. She was about 4 or 5 years old. A second daughter was conceived during these early years in Argentina.

Eventually, Hitler's health began to fail, and Eva can't handle his erratic behaviour and leaves him, with the children, to live a relatively normal life in Buenos Aires. By 1953, Hitler realises that his closest ally, Martin Borman has betrayed him, and the dream of revitalising the 3rd Reich is gone.

Hitler now descends into a form of dementia, plagued by neural pain and horrific nightmares. He is tended to by an ex-Nazi physician, and an ex-Nazi sailor. These are the only two people he sees in his final years.

On his death bed, Eva and his children return to say their final goodbyes, but by this stage, Hitler did not even recognise them.

Adolf Hitler died at 3:00pm on February 13, 1962, aged 73 years old. His ashes were spread in the forest, on the mountain, near where he lived out his final years in Patagonia.

Martin Bormann was able to pull off the greatest theft of gold, jewels, and priceless artworks in the history of planet earth. He too died of old age, and died a very wealthy man.

All this and more is available to read in great detail in **Gerrard Williams** and **Simon Dunstan's** book: *Grey Wolf: The Escape of Adolf Hitler* (Dunstan and Williams, 2013). The book was also turned into a dramatized TV documentary of the same name. Gerrard Williams, is the former Duty Editor at Reuters Television and Foreign Duty Editor at The BBC, Sky News, and APTN.

Case closed! Adolf Hitler did not commit suicide in 1945. He escaped to Argentina and died from old age!

8. UFO RECOVERED AT ROSWELL

Roswell UFO crash, 1947

The Roswell UFO Incident involved the recovery of materials near Roswell, New Mexico, USA, in July 1947, which have since become the subject of intense speculation, rumour, questioning, and research.

There are widely divergent views on what actually happened, and passionate debate about what evidence can be believed. The United States military maintains that what was recovered was a top-secret research balloon that had crashed.

By the early 1990s, UFO researchers such as **Stanton Friedman, William Moore, Karl Pfloc** , and the team of **Kevin Randle** and **Don Schmitt** had interviewed several hundred people who had, or claimed to have had, a connection with the events at Roswell in 1947.

Additionally, hundreds of documents were obtained via **Freedom of Information Act** requests, as were some leaked by insiders, such as the **Majestic 12** documents.

Their conclusions were that at least one alien craft had crashed in the Roswell vicinity, that five aliens, one still alive, were recovered, and that a massive cover-up of any knowledge of the incident was put in place. Then in 1997, a man of impeccable credentials came forward and blew the whistle well and truly on Roswell (Roswell UFO, 1947).

Colonel Phillip J. Corso, a member of **President Eisenhower's** National Security Council and former head of the Foreign Technology Desk at the U.S. Army's Research and Development Department. Corso

Opposite angle, Roswell UFO crash, 1947

was the steward of Roswell alien artefacts and personally oversaw the Army's reverse-engineering project that gave the world micro-chips; fibre optics; laser; and Velcro to name but a few!

All is detailed in his book **The Day After Roswell** (Corso and Birnes, 1997). The Roswell incidence was turned into a movie in 1994 staring Kyle MacLachlan, Martin Sheen and Dwight Yoakam called **Roswell**. This movie was based on the facts around Roswell and is a very good starting point.

Case closed! Aliens really did crash at Roswell!

9. THE PHILADELPHIA EXPERIMENT

The Philadelphia Experiment, 1943

The Philadelphia Experiment was a naval military experiment at the **Philadelphia Naval Shipyard** in Philadelphia, Pennsylvania on October 28, 1943.

During the experiment, the U.S. destroyer escort **USS Eldridge** was to be rendered invisible for a brief period of time. It is also referred to as **Project Rainbow**. The U.S. Navy has stated that the experiment never occurred, and furthermore, details of the story contradict stated facts about the Eldridge.

It has nonetheless caused a significant ripple effect in many conspiracy theory circles, and elements of the Philadelphia Experiment are featured in many other government conspiracy theories (Philadelphia, 1943).

The experiment was conducted by a **Dr. Franklin Reno** as a military application of a **Unified Field Theory** (based on Tesla technology). The theory, briefly, proposes there is an interrelated nature of the forces that comprise electromagnetic radiation and gravity. Through a special application of the theory, it was thought possible, with specialised equipment and sufficient energy, to bend light around an object in such a way as to render it, invisible. The Navy considered this application of the theory to be of obvious military value (especially as the United States was engaged in World War II at the time) thus both approved and sponsored the experiment. The USS Eldridge was fitted with the required equipment at the naval yards in Philadelphia before setting sail.

Two young technicians **Edward** and **Duncan Cameron** manned the main switch room. When they tripped the switch, the ship went radar and optically invisible. Twenty minutes later, when the ship reappeared, the test had managed to render the entire ship 'out of phase' with the surrounding universe, which is why it was able to travel from **Philadelphia** to **Norfolk** (a distance of 444 Km / 276 mi) instantly.

Indeed, the Eldridge had not only vanished from the view of observers in Philadelphia, it had vanished from Philadelphia all together! The ship had been instantly transported several hundred miles - from Philadelphia to Norfolk, Virginia. After a few minutes, the ship once again vanished, to return to Philadelphia. Hundreds of eyewitnesses saw the Eldridge appear, then disappear in Norfolk, Virginia.

Unfortunately, the phasing effect had drastic effects on the crew members. During the experiment, crew members found they could walk through solid objects, and when the field was shut off, men were found embedded in the bulkheads, decks, and railings of the ship. The results were gruesome enough that some men went mad. A few disappeared into thin air.

In fact, a year or so later, one crewman of the Eldridge was eating dinner with his family and when he rose, he walked through a wall and was never seen again. Some men entered into what was called the '**Freeze**'. This is where a man faded from view; unable to move, speak or otherwise affect his surroundings. Initially, the *Freeze* effect lasted only a few minutes to a few hours. Interestingly enough, invisible crewmen were still visible to other sailors who had survived the original experiment.

As time went on, the Freeze effect lasted for days or months, and became known as the '**Deep Freeze**' (other terms include '*Caught in the Flow*', '*Caught in the Push*', '*Get Stuck*', '*Go Blank*', '*Hell Incorporated*' or '*Stuck in Molasses*').

The Deep Freeze could drive a man insane in very short order, and was only able to be counteracted if other crewmen performed a *'Laying on of Hands'* technique. Unfortunately, two men burst into flames while laying on of Hands, burning for 18 days, despite all attempts to quench the fire.

Finally, a crew man called **Alfred Bielbek**, who later became an outspoken advocate of the Philadelphia Experiment, went from 1943, to 1983 instantly! (Bielek, 1983)

Bielbek and the USS Eldridge story was made into a movie in 1984, called **The Philadelphia Experiment**. It was remade under the same name in 2012 as a TV movie. (Ziller, 2012).

A man called **Preston B. Nichols** tried to tie himself to the Philadelphia Experiment via the **Montauk Project**. The Montauk Project is a figment of Nichols' imagination and never happened. The Philadelphia Experiment really did happen – the movie tells all, well worth a look!

Case closed! The Philadelphia Experiment really did happen!

10. PEARL HARBOR WAS ALLOWED TO HAPPEN

Pearl Harbor attack, 1941

It is now fact that **President Franklin D.Roosevelt** (FDR) was warned three days before the attack on Pearl Harbor, that the Japanese empire was coming. He knew about it in advance and covered up his failure to warn the Hawaiian commanders, costing the lives of **2,400** US troops.

The information, contained in a declassified memorandum from the **Offi e of Naval Intelligence**, adds to proof that Washington dismissed red flags signalling that mass bloodshed was looming and war with Japan was imminent (Goddard, 2011). Roosevelt deliberately ignored intelligence of an imminent attack in Hawaii, suggesting that he allowed it to happen so that he would then have a legitimate reason for declaring war on Japan and joining the war in Europe.

Up to that point, public and political opinion had been against America's entry into what was seen largely as a European war, despite Roosevelt's private support for the Allies' fight against the so-called Axis - Germany, Italy, and Japan.

FDR needed the attack to sucker Hitler into declaring war, since the public and Congress were overwhelmingly against entering the war in Europe. It was his backdoor to war (Pearl Harbor, 2015).

It is now fact that the US was warned by at least the governments of Britain, Netherlands, Australia, Peru, Korea and the Soviet Union that a surprise attack on Pearl Harbor was coming. All of the important Japanese codes had already been broken.

FDR, Marshall and others knew the attack was coming, and allowed it and covered up their knowledge. By entering World War II, America was able to break out of a sluggish economy and become the greatest manufacturing nation of all time. Washington became a global power base. This is the usual thinking of the world elites – war is money, and you get to cut down on some of your excess population, eliminating almost everyone from your welfare system.

Franklin D. Roosevelt was just another puppet carrying out orders from his bankster masters (The Rothschilds). And just like the Rothschilds, Roosevelt married his first cousin.

Case closed! FDR Killed 2,400 Troops at Pearl Harbor and forced America into WWII!

There are so many conspiracy theories that turned out to be true that if I included them all in this book, there would be no room left for anything else! Who knows, maybe I will write a book just on conspiracy theories that turned out to be true in the future!

HISTORY IS A LIE.
RELIGION IS A CONTROL SYSTEM.
MONEY IS A HOAX.
DEBT IS A FICTION.
MEDIA IS MANIPULATION.
GOVERNMENT IS A CORPORATION.

THE SYSTEM IS AN ILLUSION.

#WAKEUP

Annexes:

ANNEX 3.10.1 - The Climate Change Scam

References:

Adl-Tabatabai, S. (2015). *Stanley Kubrick Confesses To Faking The Moon Landings – Your News Wire.* [online] Your News Wire. Available at: http://yournewswire.com/stanley-kubrick-confesses-to-faking-the-moon-landings/ [Accessed 12 Dec. 2015].

Allen, K. (2011). *Unlawful Killing (2011).* [online] IMDb. Available at: http://www.imdb.com/title/tt1979385/ [Accessed 25 Jun. 2015].

Armstrong, N. (1994). *Moon landing FAKE ...Neil Armstrong talks.* [online] YouTube. Available at: https://youtu.be/SFPiwnVL9ic [Accessed 29 Jul. 2015].

Avery, D. (2007). *Loose Change Final Cut (FULL VERSION).* [online] YouTube. Available at: https://youtu.be/ynROamW80O0 [Accessed 30 Jul. 2015].

BBC video, (2001). *BBC video about WTC7 is a hoax.* [online] YouTube. Available at: https://youtu.be/s0qdLoobkUI [Accessed 17 Aug. 2015].

Bielek, A. (1983). *The Philadelphia Experiment and Montauk Survivor Accounts.* [online] Bielek.com. Available at: http://www.bielek.com/ [Accessed 29 Jul. 2015].

Building 7, (2001). *30-Second Reel of Building 7 Collapse Footage.* [online] YouTube. Available at: https://www.youtube.com/watch?v=Mamvq7LWqRU [Accessed 25 Jun. 2015].

Corso, P. and Birnes, W. (1997). *The day after Roswell.* New York: Pocket Books.

Diana, (1997). *Diana, Princess of Wales*. [online] Wikipedia. Available at: https://en.wikipedia.org/wiki/Diana%2C_Princess_of_Wales [Accessed 25 Jun. 2015].

Dunstan, S. and Williams, G. (2013). *Grey wolf*. New York: Sterling.

Goddard, J. (2011). *Pearl Harbour memo shows US warned of Japanese attack*. [online] Telegraph.co.uk. Available at: http://www.telegraph.co.uk/news/worldnews/northamerica/usa/8932197/Pearl-Harbour-memo-shows-US-warned-of-Japanese-attack.html [Accessed 17 Jul. 2015].

JFK, (1988). *The Men Who Killed Kennedy (TV Mini-Series 1988)*. [online] IMDb. Available at: http://www.imdb.com/title/tt0254033/ [Accessed 25 Jun. 2015].

Kennedy, (1963). *Assassination of John F. Kennedy*. [online] Wikipedia. Available at: https://en.wikipedia.org/wiki/Assassination_of_John_F._Kennedy [Accessed 25 Jun. 2015].

Kubrick, S. (2002). *Dark Side of the Moon (TV Movie 2002)*. [online] IMDb. Available at: http://www.imdb.com/title/tt0344160/ [Accessed 29 Jul. 2015].

LEO, (2015). *Low Earth orbit*. [online] Low Earth orbit. Available at: https://en.wikipedia.org/wiki/Low_Earth_orbit [Accessed 29 Jul. 2015].

Moore, R. (1979). *Moonraker (1979)*. [online] IMDb. Available at: http://www.imdb.com/title/tt0079574/ [Accessed 29 Jul. 2015].

NASA, (2015). *Earth's Temperature Tracker : Earth is Cooling...No It's Warming*. [online] Earthobservatory.nasa.gov. Available at: http://earthobservatory.nasa.gov/Features/GISSTemperature/giss_temperature2.php [Accessed 25 Jun. 2015].

Pearl Harbor, (2015). *Attack on Pearl Harbor*. [online] Wikipedia. Available at: https://en.wikipedia.org/wiki/Attack_on_Pearl_Harbor [Accessed 17 Jul. 2015].

Philadelphia, (1943). *Philadelphia Experiment*. [online] Wikipedia. Available at: https://en.wikipedia.org/wiki/Philadelphia_Experiment [Accessed 25 Jun. 2015].

Polansek, T. (2015). *Monsanto weed killer can 'probably' cause cancer: World Health Organization*. [online] Reuters. Available at: http://www.reuters.com/article/2015/03/20/us-monsanto-roundup-cancer-idUSKBN0MG2NY20150320 [Accessed 17 Jul. 2015].

Raffill, S. (1984). *The Philadelphia Experiment (1984)*. [online] IMDb. Available at: http://www.imdb.com/title/tt0087910/ [Accessed 29 Jul. 2015].

Roswell UFO, (1947). *Roswell UFO incident*. [online] Wikipedia. Available at: https://en.wikipedia.org/wiki/Roswell_UFO_incident [Accessed 25 Jun. 2015].

Séralini, G. (2012). Long term toxicity of a Roundup herbicide and a Roundup-tolerant genetically modified maize. *Food and Chemical Toxicology*, 50(11), pp.4221-4231.

Sibrel, B. (2001). *A Funny Thing Happened on the Way to the Moon*. [online] YouTube. Available at: https://youtu.be/xciCJfbTvE4 [Accessed 29 Jul. 2015].

Taylor, J. (2011). *Climategate 2.0: New E-Mails Rock The Global Warming Debate*. [online] Forbes. Available at: http://www.forbes.com/sites/jamestaylor/2011/11/23/climategate-2-0-new-e-mails-rock-the-global-warming-debate/ [Accessed 25 Jun. 2015].

Telegraph, (2009). *'Moon rock' given to Holland by Neil Armstrong and Buzz Aldrin is fake*. [online] Telegraph.co.uk. Available at: http://www.telegraph.co.uk/news/science/space/6105902/Moon-rock-given-to-Holland-by-Neil-Armstrong-and-Buzz-Aldrin-is-fake.html [Accessed 22 Dec. 2015].

The Moon Hoax, (2010). *Amazon.com: What Happened on the Moon: Hoax Lies & Videotape: What Happened on the Moon-Hoax Lies & Videotape: Movies & TV*. [online] Amazon.com. Available at: http://www.amazon.com/What-Happened-Moon-Hoax-Videotape/dp/B0040BJH54 [Accessed 29 Jul. 2015].

Van Allen, (1958). *Van Allen radiation belt*. [online] Van Allen radiation belt. Available at: https://en.wikipedia.org/wiki/Van_Allen_radiation_belt [Accessed 29 Jul. 2015].

vonKleist, D. (2004). *9/11 In Plane Site - Directors Cut*. [online] YouTube. Available at: https://youtu.be/igX7Z8VstN4 [Accessed 30 Jul. 2015].

Walia, A. (2014). *New Study Links GMOs To Cancer, Liver/Kidney Damage & Severe Hormonal Disruption*. [online] Collective-Evolution. Available at: http://www.collective-evolution.com/2014/07/15/new-study-links-gmos-to-cancer-liverkidney-damage-severe-hormonal-disruption/ [Accessed 17 Jul. 2015].

Warner, B. (2013). *The Girls From Argentina: Daughters of Nazi Boss Adolf Hitler Who Escaped From Berlin On April 27th 1945 Thanks to Franco in Spain.*. [online] Better Call Bill Warner Investigations Cheaters-Child Custody Cases Sarasota to Panama City Fl 941-926-1926. Available at: http://billwarnermyblog.wordpress.com/2013/08/21/the-girls-from-argentina-daughters-of-nazi-boss-adolf-hitler-who-escaped-from-berlin-on-april-27th-1945-thanks-to-franco-in-spain/ [Accessed 17 Jul. 2015].

Ziller, P. (2012). *The Philadelphia Experiment (TV Movie 2012)*. [online] IMDb. Available at: http://www.imdb.com/title/tt2039399/ [Accessed 29 Jul. 2015].

11

EXPOSED: THE HOUSE OF ROTHSCHILD

---

*"Though they control scores of industrial,
commercial, mining and tourist corporations,
not one bears the name Rothschild. Being private
partnerships, the family houses never need to, and
never do, publish a single public balance sheet, or
any other report of their financial condition."*

—FREDERIC MORTON, 1962

---

*T*his is the richest man in the world, and if you have any cash in your wallet or purse, then you have an IOU made out to him. He owns your mortgage, your car loan, your credit cards, your savings, and even your land. In fact, you could even say he owns you. Your Birth Certificate makes you a commodity on the Stock Exchange, he controls that as well.

His official name and title is **Nathaniel Charles Jacob Rothschild**, 4th Baron Rothschild Bt, OM, GBE, FBA (born 29 April 1936). He is listed as a British investment banker and a member of the prominent Rothschild

Nathaniel Charles Jacob Rothschild, 4th Baron Rothschild

banking family. He is also Honorary President of the Institute for Jewish Policy Research.

He is more commonly regarded as simply **Jacob Rothschild**. Even though he looks like a caring, gentle old man, make no mistakes, Jacob Rothschild and his ancestors have handpicked Presidents and Prime Ministers, crashed stock markets, bankrupted nations, orchestrated wars, and sponsored the mass murder and impoverishment of millions. The wealth of this one family alone could feed, shelter and educate every human being on earth today for the next 100 years or more.

However, you won't see his family's wealth listed in the Forbes list of the world's richest, nor will you hear much about him in the news. The reason is simple. Not only does he own **Forbes**, but also the **Associated Press** (AP), **Reuters**, and just about every other media outlet in the modern world. Over the centuries, his family have hoarded the world's gold supplies to the tune of trillions, and store it in mass subterranean vaults. He also owns the world's central banks. This includes the **Federal Reserve Bank** in the United States. The Federal Reserve controls every bank in the United States and the **International Monetary Fund** (IMF). The bankers control the governments, the Rothschilds control the bankers, and on it goes. In fact, there are Rothschild-owned/controlled central banks in all but 3 countries in the world.

Before 9/11, there were only 8 countries in the world without a Rothschild owned Central Bank: Afghanistan, Iraq, Libya, **Syria**, Cuba,

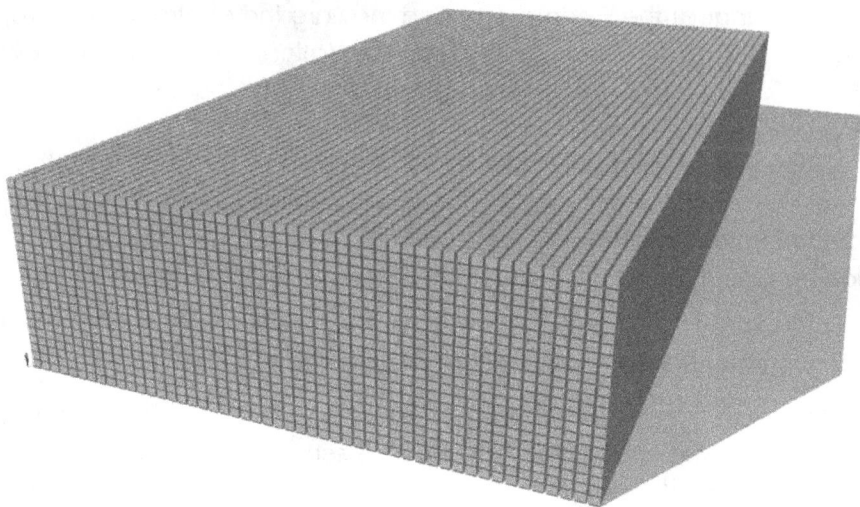

This is $9 trillion. Even if we called it $10 trillion, Rothschild has another 51.5 stacks like this one. You can just see the man on the far left.

North Korea, and **Iran**. Now, there are only 3 left to invade (Cuba is now a spent force and no longer on the hit list), conquer, and acquire. Notice which countries the Rothschild corporate media demonise all the time?

How much rich is filthy rich

His wealth is an estimated **$515 TRILLION**. A trillion, is a MILLION x MILLION. To put it in perspective, if his wealth was $100 bills, then it would stack all the way to the sun and back - 15 times! Or, if you were to spend $1 million per day, it would take about 2,738 years to spend all of the Rothschild wealth.

What does this kind of money buy you?

Every war, every peacetime, every food shortage; are all controlled by the Rothschilds. Every financial boom, and every bust – controlled by them. Every revolution, social upheaval, and terrorist attack – controlled by the Rothschilds. They rig the price of gold and other precious metals, as well as manipulate and rig the Stock Exchange. They have amassed the world's largest store of gold bullion and they have the ability to manipulate markets in order to increase their wealth and decrease others'. They created the Illuminati, they took over (and changed) the Freemasons, and they are the control and power behind Zionism, Nazism, Communism, The Vatican, Feminism, the New Age Movement, TV, Hollywood, Pop/Rap/Rock/Country Music and the New World Order.

They could feed and cure the Third World overnight. In fact, they could give every single person on Earth (7 billion) about $73,500 each, and they would still have some change left over. Obviously it is no longer about money, it is about power.

Fiefs in the Middle Ages

In the Middle Ages (5th to the 15th century), a parcel of land was known as a *fief*. When a Knight gave his services to a King, usually in the way of battle defence of the kingdom, the King would give fief to him. In other words, the King would lease a parcel of land in his kingdom to the Knight. The fief usually came with servants and farming peasants to tend the land. As well as his military services, the Knight was also required to hand over a portion of the produce produced on the land to the king (taxation). This system was known as medieval feudalism or the **feudal system**.

Additionally, the fief came with rent, dignities, and offices. The person who was given the fief was called a **Vassal**. The Vassal was a free man. His duty was to protect the King. He was of a rank of a Lord of the Manor also known as a **Baron**, who was lesser than a Noble or the King (Newman, 2015).

Barons

A Baron was responsible first to his king and second to the people who lived on his manor. The king might require the Baron to serve in the military or engage in various other activities. By complying with the King's requirements, it was possible for the Baron to earn a higher title, more land, or prosperous marriages for his children and other family members. If he did not comply, the Baron could lose his manor, his luxurious lifestyle, or maybe even his life. As a percentage of each manor's crops was sent to the King, a baron also had to make sure that all of the serfs on his estate were protected in order to ensure that a plentiful crop was produced. A Baron also served as judge in a court of crime or passed out sentences in court (Newman, 2008).

In **1822**, the Emperor of Austria was up to the eyeballs in debt to the Rothschilds family. They said, forget the debt, but give us titles instead. So the Emperor granted the five Rothschild brothers the official title of Baron. If a Baron is a Vassal, and a Vassal controls a fief, what fief were the Rothschilds given?

Quite simply - the land of **Palestine!** After the theft of the land that was once Palestine, the Rothschilds became the Lords of their own fiftem, which they called the **State of Israel**. But the State of Israel is not a country like many people believe it is. And many countries around the world do not even recognise Israel as a "legal" State.

Indeed, they had to bribe President **Harry S. Truman** with a very large sum of money so the USA would recognise Israel as an official, legal State. But if you live in a Rothschild controlled country, you will never hear about this stuff.

To find out how the Rothschild family amassed over half the world's wealth, stole a nation, and control governments all over the world, we need to go back to the beginning of their dynasty.

Oh, and earlier in this book, I said they based the Simpsons character Mr. Burns on Jacob Rothschild, the man we just met. What do you think? Is there a likeness?

Jacob Rothschild   Charles Montgomery "Monty" Burns
from The Simpsons

A DYNASTY IS BORN

Mayer Amschel Bauer (1743 – 1812)

1743: Mayer Amschel Bauer, an Ashkenazi Jew is born in Frankfurt, Germany, the son of Moses Amschel Bauer, a money lender and the proprietor of a counting house. Moses Bauer hangs a red hexagram sign above the entrance door to his counting house. Two hundred years later, this same symbol will become the flag of Israel. At a very early age, Mayer showed that he possessed immense intellectual ability, and his father spent much of his time teaching him everything he could about the money lending business and in the basic dynamics of finance.

1760: During this decade, Mayer Bauer works for a bank owned by the Oppenheimers' in Hanover, Germany. He is highly successful and becomes a junior partner. Whilst working at the bank he becomes acquainted with **General von Estorff**.

Red Sign

The Seal of Solomon is the Rothschild Logo

After his father's death, Mayer Bauer returns to Frankfurt to take over the family business. Mayer recognises the significance of the red hexagram. It was the Seal of Solomon – remember, on his ring. That represents Occult Power, so Mayer dedicates his soul to Satan right there and changes the family from Bauer to **Rothschild**, after the red hexagram sign hanging over the entrance door. "Rot," is German for, "Red," and "Schild" is German for "Sign." Thus, Rot-Schild = Rothschild = Red Sign. As we have already learnt, this is not the Star of David as many

Jews and non-Jews believe it to be. Historians and archaeologist (including Jews) have never found any text or reference to the Star of David. That, is a Rothschild/Vatican myth to confuse.

Hessian Soldiers

Prince William IX of Hesse-Hanau (1743 - 1821)

Now as **Mayer Rothschild**, he catches up with his acquaintance, General von Estorff, who is attached to the court of **Prince William IX of Hesse-Hanau**, one of the richest royal houses in Europe. Prince William IX was the grandson of George II of England, a cousin to George III, a nephew of the King of Denmark, and a brother- in-law to the King of Sweden. This royal family earnt its money by hiring out mercenary soldiers (Hessian soldiers) to foreign countries for vast profits - a practice that continues today in the form of exporting, "peacekeeping" troops throughout the world.

Through the General, Rothschild arranged a meeting with the Prince under the pretext of selling him some valuable coins and trinkets at discounted prices. All goes as planned, and Prince William is more than pleased with discounted prices he charges for his rare coins and trinkets. It is also then that Rothschild offers the Prince a bonus for any other business he can direct his way (a "spotters" fee). Rothschild subsequently becomes close associates with Prince William, and ends up doing business with him and members of the court. He soon discovers that loaning money to governments and royalty is far more profitable than loaning to individuals, as the loans are bigger and are secured by the nation's taxes.

1769: Mayer Rothschild is given permission by Prince William to hang a sign on the front of his business premises declaring that he is, "*M. A. Rothschild, by appointment court factor to his serene highness, Prince William of Hanau.*"

1773: During this period, Mayer Rothschild along with Jacob Frank, draw up plans for the creation of the Illuminati. They hire and entrust

Adam Weishaupt, a Crypto-Jew who was outwardly Roman Catholic – a Jesuit Priest no less, with its organisation and development. It was these three men that formulated the document that was to be known as *The Protocols of the Learned Elders of Zion*.

Amschel Mayer Rothschild (1744 -1855)

1744: Mayer Rothschild marries Gütle Schnapper (1753 - 1849), and their first son, **Amschel Mayer Rothschild** is born. Amschel, like all his brothers who follow him, will enter the family business at the age of 12. On the death of his father in 1812, he succeeded as head of the bank at Frankfurt-am-Main (Germany), and died "childless" in 1855. He did however father an illegitimate son named Alois, who in turn was the father of Adolf Hitler.

Salomon Mayer Rothschild (1744 - 1855)

1774: Their second son, **Salomon Mayer Rothschild** is born. He was sent to Vienna (Austria) in 1820 to formalise the family's existing involvements in financing Austrian government projects. His bank, the S M von Rothschild, financed various government undertakings where large amounts of capital had to be raised. He made connections amongst the country's aristocracy and its political elite, and in recognition of his services he was made part of the Austrian nobility when awarded the hereditary title *Freiherr* (Baron) in 1822. In 1824 he married his own niece, the daughter of his brother Jacob.

In **1843**, he became the first Jew to ever be given honorary Austrian citizenship. Under his control, the Viennese bank was highly successful. But the concentration of wealth in the hands of a few members of the elite resulted in growing civil unrest in the countryside. A national anti-Rothschild sentiment, and ultimately Rothschild involvement in Austrian banking and financing lead to the revolutions of 1848; after which Salomon left the business in the hands of his son, **Anselm Salomon**, and retired to Paris where he died in 1855.

1775-1783: During the American Revolution, the House of Rothschild brokered a deal between the Throne of England and Landgrave Frederick II of Hesse-Kassel (a small independent country in northern Hesse, Germany) and other German princes. Prince William was to provide 16,800 Hessian soldiers to help England stop the Revolution in America. Rothschild was also made responsible for the transfer of funds that were to pay the German soldiers. The transfer was never made. The soldiers were never paid, which may account for their poor showing. The Americans prevailed. At this point, Meyer Rothschild set his sights on America.

1776: May 1st (May Day), they hired Adam Weishaupt (code named Spartacus) to establish a secret society called the **Order of the Illuminati**. Their objective? To create a world government ruled by men of superior intellect - namely themselves and their bloodlines.

1777: Adam Weishaupt officially completes his organisation of the Illuminati. The purpose of the Illuminati is to divide the Goyim (what they call all non-Jews) through political, economic, social, and religious means. The opposing sides were to be armed and incidents were to be provided in order for them to: fight amongst themselves; destroy national governments; destroy religious institutions; and eventually destroy each other. This agenda is documented in *The Protocols of the Learned Elders of Zion*.

Johann Adam Weishaupt
(1748 - 1830)

Freemasons Under Attack

Weishaupt soon infiltrates the Continental Order of Freemasons with this Illuminati doctrine and establishes lodges of the *Grand Orient* to be their secret headquarters. This was all under the orders and finance of big daddy, Mayer Rothschild and the concept was spread and is followed within Masonic Lodges worldwide to the present day.

John Robison publishes a book entitled, *"Proofs of a Conspiracy Against All the Religions and Governments of Europe Carried on in the Secret Meetings of Freemasons, Illuminati and Reading Societies."* (1798) In this book, Professor Robison of the University of Edinburgh, one of the leading intellects of his time, who in 1783 was elected general secretary of the Royal Society of Edinburgh, gave details of the whole Rothschild Illuminati plot. He advised how he had been a high degree Mason in the Scottish Rite of Freemasonry, and had been invited by Adam Weishaupt to Europe, where he had been given a revised copy of Weishaupt's conspiracy. However, although he pretended to go along with it, Professor Robison did not agree with it and therefore published his informational book which included details of the Bavarian government's investigations into the Illuminati and the French Revolution.

Subvert Governments, Education, Ethics, Policies, Measures, Religions, Banks and the Press.

Weishaupt also recruits 2,000 paid followers, including the most intelligent men in the field of arts and letters, education, science, finance and industry. They were instructed to follow the methods below in order to control people:

1) *Use monetary and sex bribery to obtain control of men already in high places, in the various levels of all governments and other fields of endeavour. Once influential persons had fallen for the lies, deceits, and temptations of the Illuminati, they were to be held in bondage by application of political and other forms of blackmail, threats of financial ruin, public exposure, fiscal harm, and even death to themselves and loved members of their families.*

2) *The faculties of colleges and universities were to cultivate students possessing exceptional mental ability belonging to well-bred families with international leanings, and recommend them for special training in internationalism, or rather the notion that only a one-world government can put an end to recurring wars and strife. Such training was to be provided by granting scholarships to those selected by the Illuminati. The Rhodes scholarship is one such organisation.*

3) *All influential people trapped into coming under the control of the Illuminati, plus the students who had been specially*

educated and trained, were to be used as agents, and placed behind the scenes of all governments as experts and specialists. This was so they would advise the top executives to adopt policies which would in the long-run serve the secret plans of the Illuminati one-world government and bring about the destruction of the governments and religions they were elected or appointed to serve.

4) *To obtain absolute-control of the media, at that time the only mass-communications media which distributed information to the public, so that all news and information could be slanted in order to make the masses believe that a one-world government is the only solution to our many and varied problems*

Nathan Rothschild (1777 - 1836)

1777: The third son, **Nathan Mayer Rothschild** is born. Nathan exhibited a superior affinity for the banking business. When he moved to London at age 21, he became a merchant banker and began to cement ties between the House of Rothschild and the Bank of England. These ties are still going strong today in 2015. Nathan proves to be the most ruthless and soulless of the Rothschilds. Many of the changes he instigated in banking are still used today.

1784: Adam Weishaupt issues his order for the French Revolution to be started by **Maximillian Robespierre** in book form. This book was written by one of Weishaupt's associates, **Xavier Zwack**, and sent by courier from Frankfurt to Paris. However en route to Paris, the courier is struck by lightning, and the book detailing this plan is discovered by the police, and handed over to the Bavarian authorities.

As a consequence, the Bavarian government orders the police to raid Weishaupt's masonic lodges of the *Grand Orient*, and the homes of his most influential associates. Clearly, the Bavarian authorities were convinced that the book that was discovered was a very real threat by a private group of influential people, to use wars and revolutions to achieve their political ends.

1785: The Bavarian government outlaw the Illuminati and close all the Bavarian lodges of the Grand Orient. Of course, the Illuminati just went underground and have survived to this day, far more corrupted and disfigured than even Weishaupt had envisioned.

Weishaupt fled to **Gotha**, Germany. That is the same Gotha that gave Queen Elizabeth II her original surname - **Saxe-Coburg-Gotha**. Yes, the Queen of England's ancestors took in Weishaupt and fed him, and bed him, until his death many, many years later. What nice people they were. I suppose that is why Queen Elizabeth II is head of the Illuminati today.

Meyer Rothschild moves his entire family to a five story luxurious dwelling he shared with the Schiff family. In **1865**, the Schiffs' not-yet-born grandson Jacob would move to New York in 1917 and become the mastermind behind the funding of the Bolshevik Revolution in Russia. This action would successfully instate Communism as a major world movement, which was, (and still is), a basic tenet of the Illuminati and their collectivist agenda. From this point on the Rothschilds and the Schiffs would play a central role in the financial history of Europe, and subsequently that of the United States and the world.

1786: The Bavarian government publishes the details of the Illuminati plot in a document entitled, *"The Original Writings of The Order and Sect of The Illuminati."* They then send this document to all the heads of church and state throughout Europe, but sadly their warning is ignored.

*Carl Mayer von Rothschild
(1788 - 1855)*

1788: The fourth son, **Kalmann (Carl) Mayer Rothschild** is born. The 1821 occupation of Naples by the Austrian army provided the opportunity for Carl to set up his business in the Kingdom. As such, Carl was sent to Naples where he established *C M de Rothschild & Figli* to operate as a satellite office to the Rothschild banking family in Germany. He established a good working relationship with **Luigi de' Medici**, the *Direttore della Segreteria di Azienda del Regno di Napoli* (Finance Minister), and his operation became the dominant banking house in Naples.

In **1829**, Carl was appointed *Consul-General of Sicily*, and in January **1832**, the Jewish banker was given a Ribbon and Star of the **Sacred Military Constantinian Order of Saint George,** at a ceremony with the new Roman Catholic **Pope, Gregory XVI.** This was the Pope's way of getting rid of his vast gambling debts he owed to Carl Rothschild. Why else would a Catholic Pope award a Catholic accolade to a Jew? Mind you, Carl was really chuffed, and wore it with pride.

1789: Due to the European ignorance of the Bavarian government's warning, the Illuminati's plan for a **French Revolution** succeeded from this year to 1793. This revolution was a bankers' dream, it established a new constitution and passed laws that forbade the Roman Church from levying tithes (taxes) and also removed its exemption from taxation.

1790: Mayer Rothschild, the patriarch of the Rothschild dynasty states,

> *"Let me issue and control a nation's money and I care not who writes the laws."*

From this moment onwards, the Rothschilds, like the Monarchies of the world, are above the law, and nothing they do will ever see them having to face a court of justice ever again.

1791: Benjamin Franklin, having become very familiar with the Bank of England and fractional reserve banking, understood the dangers of a privately owned Central Bank controlling the issue of the Nation's currency and resisted the charter of a central bank until his death in 1791. That was the same year that **Alexander Hamilton** (the Rothschilds agent in George Washington's cabinet) pushed through legislation that would provide for the charter of The First Bank of the United States. This is established with a 20 year charter. Ironically, the bank was chartered by the **Bank of England** to finance the war debt of the Revolutionary War. Nathan Rothschild (from England) invested heavily in that first bank. He immediately set about to control all financial activity between banks in America.

There were a couple of problems though. The U.S. Constitution put control of the nation's currency in the hands of Congress, and made no provisions for Congress to delegate that authority. It even established the basic currency unit, the dollar. The dollar was constitutionally mandated to be a silver coin based on the Spanish pillar dollar and to contain 375 grains of silver. This single provision was designed to keep the American money supply out of the hands of the banking industry. The Bank of England made several attempts to usurp control of the U.S. money supply but failed. Still, through their Illuminati agents, they continued to enlist supporters through bribery, blackmail, and kickbacks.

ANY PROPONENT OF A FRACTIONAL RESERVE BANKING SYSTEM IS AN ECONOMIC PREDATOR.

During the next twenty years, the country would fall prey to contrived financial havoc as a result of the banker's policies of creating cycles of inflation and deflation (tight) money. During times of inflation, the economy would boom, there would be high employment, and people would borrow money to buy houses and farms. At that point, the bankers would raise interest rates and incite a depression, which would obviously cause unemployment. People who could not pay their mortgages would have their homes and farms repossessed by the bank for a fraction of their true value. This is the essence of the Illuminati ploy, and it would recur, time and time again. In fact, it's still happening today.

1792: The fifth son, **Jacob (James) Mayer Rothschild** is born. Jacob was sent to Paris where he had great success. However, it's worth mentioning that the Rothschilds were, and are, supporters and the engineers of the State of Israel. Indeed, James' grandson, **Edmond** Benjamin James de Rothschild, was a huge supporter of Zionism, and his generous donations lent significant support to the movement during its early years which helped lead to the establishment of the State of Israel.

James Mayer de Rothschild (1792 - 1868)

He was also a patron of the first Zionist settlement in Palestine at **Rishon-LeZion**, and bought from Ottoman landlords many parts of the land which now makes up present-day Israel.

In **1917 Walter Rothschild** was the addressee of the Balfour Declaration, which committed the British government to the establishment in Palestine of a national home for the Jewish people. James A. de Rothschild financed the **Knesset building** as a gift to the State of Israel. The Supreme Court of Israel building was donated to Israel by Dorothy de Rothschild (remember, she has her name permanently chiselled to the outside of the Supreme Court building); Outside the President's Chamber is displayed the letter Mrs Rothschild wrote to Prime Minister **Shimon Peres** expressing her intention to donate a new building for the Supreme Court. Of course, not many people realise that the flag of Israel – the so-called Star of David is in fact the Rothschild Family Flag. If you remember back to the Rothschild patriarch – Mayer, he used this symbol as a sign above his door. Even Orthodox Jews dismiss the Star of David as a symbol to represent Jews.

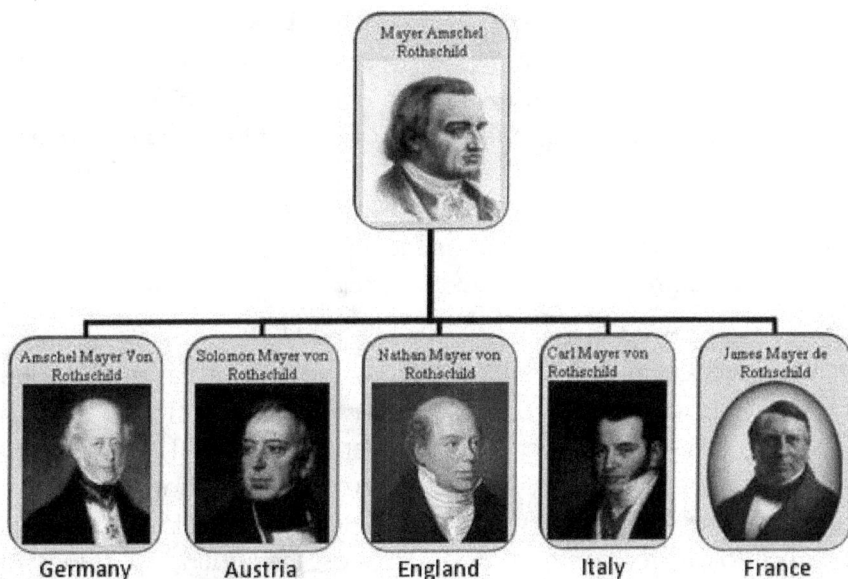

(Cibella and Baron, 1998)

THE FIRST GENERATION OF THE DYNASTY IS COMPLETE

1812: Mayer Amschel Rothschild dies. In his Will, he lays out specific laws that the House of Rothschild were to follow:

> 1) All key positions in the family business were only
>   to be held by family members;

2) *Only male members of the family were allowed to participate in the family business, this included a reported sixth secret bastard son. It is important to note that Mayer Rothschild also had five daughters, so today the spread of the Rothschild Zionist dynasty without the Rothschild name is far and wide, and Jews believe the mixed offspring of a Jewish mother is solely Jewish;*

3) *The family was to intermarry with its first and second cousins to preserve the family fortune. Of the 18 marriages by Mayer Rothschild's grandchildren, 16 were between first cousins - a practice known today as inbreeding, which is still carried out;*

4) *No public inventory of his estate was to be published;*

5) *No legal action was to be taken with regard to the value of the inheritance;*

6) *The eldest son of the eldest son was to become the head of the family (this condition could only be overturned when the majority of the family agreed otherwise). This happened immediately when Nathan was elected head of the family following his father's death. Nathan was considered by far the best, and most clever banker among them.*

After amassing huge fortunes, the name Rothschild became synonymous with extravagance and great wealth. By the end of the century, the family owned, or had built, at the lowest estimates over 41 palaces, of a scale and luxury perhaps unparalleled even by the richest Royal families. The British Prime Minister **Lloyd George** claimed in 1909, that Lord Nathan Rothschild was the most powerful man in Britain. The business magazine referred to Mayer Amschel Rothschild as the *"founding father of international finance,"* and Forbes magazine as the *"20th most influential businessmen of all times"*. Ironically, the British Royal Family always (and still do) refer to their Rothschild banker as "Haus Jude" or "House Jew." It is a reminder that they are not born of the Nephilim hybrids, therefore, they will always serve the Black Nobility, even though the Rothschild's wealth dwarfs theirs. Even among the elite, it is all about your bloodline.

From the mid-19th century, many people had their eyes on the Rothschilds and their activities. Suspicion and an anti-Rothschild sentiment spread throughout Europe. Thus, for the Rothschild's, it was time to keep a low public profile and to put in place a network of front men to take care of their businesses. By the later 19th century, almost all Rothschilds had started to marry outside the family, usually into the aristocracy or other financial dynasties, like Warburg, Oppenheim, House of Bonaparte, Wellington, Guinness, House of Borghese, Walpole, Wodehouse, and others.

Funding Both Sides of War

1815: The five Rothschild brothers work to supply gold to both Wellington's army (through Nathan in England) and Napoleon's army (through Jacob in France), and begin their policy of funding both sides in every war for profit. The Rothschilds love wars because they are massive generators of risk free debt. Thus, over the next 200 years they make it their business to ignite as many wars and conflicts as they can. Indeed, their mother, Gütle Rothschild, famously states:

> *"If my sons did not want wars, there would be none."*

Whilst the Rothschilds are funding both sides in this war, they use the banks they have spread out across Europe to give them the opportunity to set up an unrivalled postal service network of secret routes, fast couriers and their secret weapon – carrier pidgins (never used before this time). This also doubled as a spy network, and gave the Rothschilds advanced information, keeping them one step ahead of their rivals.

Conveniently, these Rothschild couriers were the only merchants allowed to pass through the English and French blockades during the Napoleonic Wars (1803–1815). It was these couriers who also kept Nathan Rothschild up to date with how the war was going, so he could use that intelligence to buy and sell from his position on the stock exchange in accordance with that intelligence. Today we call that "insider trading" and it is illegal – for good reason.

One of Rothschild's couriers was a man named **Rothworth**. When the outcome of the **Battle of Waterloo** was won by the British, Rothworth took off for the Channel and was able to deliver this news to Nathan Rothschild a full 48 hours before Wellington's own courier.

On this news, Nathan instructed all his workers on the floor of the English Stock Exchange to start selling all his British stocks. This made all the other traders believe that the British had lost the war, so they started selling frantically as well. Thus, British stock prices plummeted in value which was when Nathan Rothschild discreetly instructed his workers to purchase all the British stock they could lay their hands on. They were now able to buy back the British stocks for pennies on the pound.

When news came through that the British had actually won the war, the stock went up to a level even higher than before the war ended, leaving Nathan Rothschild with a return of approximately 20 to 1 on his investment.

This gave the Rothschild family complete control of the British economy, which was by now the financial centre of the world. Following Napoleon's defeat, Rothschild was able to force England to set up a new Bank of England (Central Bank), which Nathan Rothschild controlled.

Still in 1815, this is the year Nathan Rothschild makes his famous and arrogant statement,

"I care not what puppet is placed upon the throne of England to rule the Empire on which the sun never sets. The man who controls Britain's money supply controls the British Empire, and I control the British money supply."

Nathan Rothschild
(1777 - 1836)

He would go onto brag that in the 17 years he had been in England, he had increased the £20,000 stake given to him by his father, 2500 times to £50 million (about $5.4 billion in 2015)

The Rothschilds also use their control of the Bank of England to replace the method of shipping gold from country to country and instead, used their five banks spread across Europe to set up a system of paper debits and credits, which is still used by the banking system of today.

By the end of this century, a period of time that was known as the, *"Age of the Rothschilds,"* it is estimated that the Rothschild family had already controlled half the wealth of the world at this time.

Congress of Vienna

Something that did not go as planned for the Rothschilds this year was the Congress of Vienna. The Congress started in September, 1814 and concluded in June 1815. The Rothschilds, now more confident, and arrogant than ever before, formulated a plan to create a world government with them leading it. This would give them complete political control over much of the civilised world.

Tsar Alexander I (1777 – 1825)

After the French Revolutionary Wars and the Napoleonic Wars, many of the European governments and monarchies were in huge debt to the Rothschilds. Nathan and his brothers figured they could use that debt owed to them as a bargaining tool and essentially blackmail the governments into handing over control to them. However, Tsar Alexander I of Russia, who had not succumbed to a Rothschild central bank, would not go along with the plan. In fact, he convinced the other rulers not to fold, so the Rothschild world government plan failed.

Enraged by this, Nathan Rothschild swore that someday he or his descendants would destroy Tsar Alexander's entire family and his descendants. Unfortunately he was true to his word and 102 years later, the Rothschilds funded the (Jewish) Bolsheviks would act upon that promise during the Russian Revolution.

1816: The American Congress passes a bill permitting yet another Rothschild dominated central bank, which gives the Rothschilds control of the American money supply again. This is called the **Second Bank of the United States** and is given a twenty year charter to help cover the cost of the American War of Independence. This was yet another war which the Rothschilds funded both sides. Now they were able to use that war to get the Central Bank back up and running again.

1818: Following the French securing massive loans in 1817 in order to help rebuild after their disastrous defeat at Waterloo, Rothschild agents bought vast amounts of French government bonds causing their value to increase. On November 5th they dumped the lot on the open market causing their value to plummet and France to go into a financial panic. The Rothschilds then stepped in to take control of the French money supply. This was the same year the Rothschilds were able to loan £5,000,000 (around $500,000,000 today) to the Prussian government – an immense amount of money during that time and the greatest amount of wealth ever seen to that date.

1821: Carl Rothschild was sent to Naples, Italy. He would end up doing a lot of business with the Vatican and Pope Gregory XVI, who subsequently conferred upon him the Order of St. George in exchange for clearing some of his debts to the Rothschild bank. An odd title to bestow upon a Jew, given the title was a Catholic title. But it is a title that holds much prestige and honour none the less. Also, whenever the Pope received Carl, he would give him his hand, rather than the customary toe to kiss, which showed the extent of Carl's power over the Vatican.

The Jewish Encyclopaedia (Vol. 2, p.497) states:

> " It is a somewhat curious sequel to the attempt to set up a Catholic competitor to the Rothschilds that at the present time the latter are the guardians of the papal treasure. "

1822: Again, to clear enormous debts owed to the Rothschilds, Francis I the Emperor of Austria, made the five Rothschild brothers **Barons**. Nathan Rothschild chose not to take up the title. This was really a big deal to the Rothschilds. They had always been on the outer of European aristocracy. Even though they had more money, they were Jews, and they had no "official" titles of nobility. Finally, their dream came true. They could finally rub elbows with the aristocracy. Even though they manage to buy their Titles, the Black Nobility is not impressed.

1823: The Rothschilds take over the financial operations of the Catholic Church worldwide, including the Vatican. Leading up to the year 1814, Carl had been using his influence over Pope Pius VII to reinstate the powerful **Society of Jesus** (The Jesuits).

They had been outlawed around 100 years earlier for raising forces against the Pope and the Vatican. Carl, like everybody else, knew that the Jesuits had the best, and most sophisticated network of spies, hit men, and political heavies in the world. If you wanted to carry out a false flag, an assassination, a coup de tête or rig an election, then the Jesuits were the go-to organisation. Whoever controlled the Jesuits, could control the entire planet at that time.

Therefore, Carl made it his business to get the Jesuits (who had still been operating underground) reinstated officially by the Pope.

Carl also knew it was only a matter of time before he owned the Vatican through financial control – thus, he could control and use the Jesuits to his family's own ends. Carl had bought off Jesuit leader **Tadeusz Brzozowski** years early with funding and the promise of having his Order reinstated.

The Jesuits

The Jesuits have a Jewish Boss!

The Rothschilds now controlled the equivalent of the CIA, MI6 and Mossad all rolled up into one, coherent and well-oiled machine. They were well on the way to world domination. The Jesuits have been credited with all manner of conspiratorial actions. Indeed, this has led to many people believing that the Jesuits / Vatican run the world. But as we have learnt by now, if you want to get to the truth – follow the money. And we know for a fact, Rothschild controls the Vatican Bank, the Vatican runs the Jesuits – and the Rothschilds run the Vatican. So who is behind the Jesuits? Irony at its best. The largest Catholic organisation in the world is run by Khazarian, Ashkenazi Jews!

Thus, the Society of Jesus was restored to the world by the Papal letter *Solicitudine Omnium Ecclesiarum* on August 14, 1814.

1827: Sir Walter Scott publishes his nine volume set, *The Life of Napoleon*. In volume two, he states that the French Revolution was planned by the Illuminati (Adam Weishaupt) and was financed by the money changers of Europe - the Rothschilds (Scott, 2008).

THE UNITED STATES UNDER ATTACK FROM ROTHSCHILD BANKS

1832: President Andrew Jackson (the 7th President of the United States from 1829 to 1837), runs the campaign for his second term in office under the slogan, "Jackson And No Bank!" This is in reference to his plan to take the control of the American money system to benefit the American people, not for the profiteering of the Rothschilds.

1833: President Andrew Jackson starts removing the government's deposits from the Rothschild controlled Second Bank of the United States and instead, deposits them into banks directed by democratic bankers. This causes the Rothschilds to panic and so they do what they do best - restrict the money supply causing a depression. President Jackson knows what they are up to and later states:

What President Jackson said back then, is exactly what happened in 2008. The bankers made bad bets with your money, and when they lost, they got the tax payers to bail them out to the tune of $2 trillion in the United States alone. Below are $100 bills in those stacks, and this is $1 trillion. So double the amount below, and that is what the TAX PAYERS gave to the banks, which 40% of them were foreign banks. Meanwhile, tens of thousands of innocent people lost their houses to the same banks they gave all this money to. Are you starting to see the scam yet?

A stack of $100 notes that make $1 trillion

"Gentlemen! I too have been a close observer of the doings of the Bank of the United States. I have had men watching you for a long time, and am convinced that you have used the funds of the bank to speculate in the breadstuffs of the country. When you won, you divided the profits amongst you, and when you lost, you charged it to the bank. You tell me that if I take the deposits from the bank and annul its charter I shall ruin ten thousand families. That may be true, gentlemen, but that is your sin! Should I let you go on, you will ruin fifty thousand families, and that would be my sin! You are a den of vipers and thieves. I have determined to rout you out, and by the Eternal, (bringing his fist down on the table) I will rout you out!"

President Andrew Jackson
(1767 – 1845)

(Taken from the original minutes of the Philadelphia committee of citizens sent to meet with President Jackson (February 1834), according to Andrew Jackson and the Bank of the United States (1928) by Stan V. Henkels - online PDF)

1835: On January 30, there was a failed assignation attempt on President Jackson's life. By a miracle, both the assassins' pistols jammed and would not fire. Jackson later stated publicly that it was the Rothschilds behind the plot. The assassin, **Richard Lawrence**, who was found not guilty by reason of insanity, later bragged that powerful people in Europe had hired him and promised to protect him if he were caught. No charges were laid.

The Rothschilds acquire the rights in the Almadén quicksilver mines in Spain. This was at the time the biggest concession in the world and as quicksilver was a vital component in the refining of gold or silver, this gave the Rothschilds a virtual world monopoly.

1836: Following his years of fighting against the Rothschilds and their central bank in America, President Andrew Jackson finally succeeds in throwing the Rothschilds Central Bank out of America when the bank's charter is not renewed. It would not be until **1913** that the Rothschilds would be able to set up their third central bank in America, the **Federal Reserve**, and to ensure no mistakes are made, this time they will put one of their own bloodline, **Jacob Schiff** in charge of the project who left nothing to chance.

Nathan Mayer Rothschild dies and the control of his bank, N. M. Rothschild & Sons is passed on to his younger brother, James Rothschild.

1837: The Rothschilds send one of their own, August Belmont, a Rothschild Zionist, to America to salvage their banking interests defeated by President Andrew Jackson.

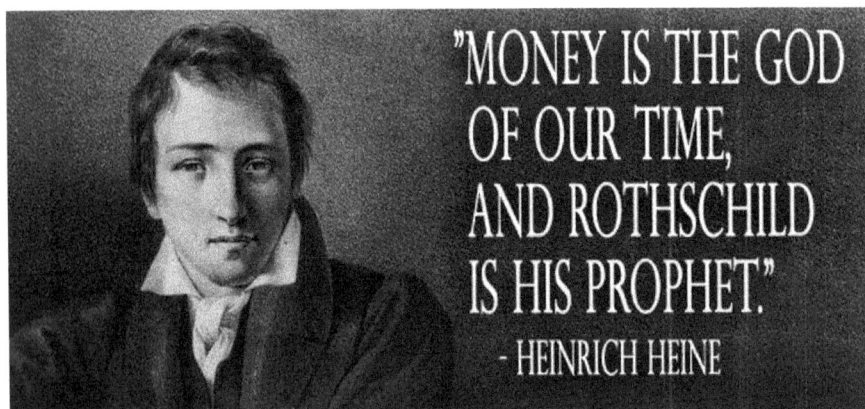

"MONEY IS THE GOD OF OUR TIME, AND ROTHSCHILD IS HIS PROPHET."
- HEINRICH HEINE

ROTHSCHILDS RIG THE PRICE OF GOLD AND SILVER

1840: The Rothschilds become the Bank of England's bullion brokers. They set up agencies in California and Australia. They still control the price of gold and silver to this day (in 2015). Each day they meet in the London Bullion Market Association (LBMA) head office and decide what the gold and silver price will be. The price is then set twice daily in US $ at 10:30 am and 3:00 pm each business day. This small group of men decide each day what "they think" the price around the world should be. No room for conflict of interest there right? (Gold and Silver Prices, 2011).

1841: President John Tyler (the 10th President of the United States From 1841 to 1845) vetoed the act to renew the charter for the Bank of the United States. He goes on to receive hundreds of letters threatening him with assassination.

1844: Salomon Rothschild purchases the United Coal Mines of Vítkovice and Austro-Hungarian Blast Furnace Company that would go on to be one of the top ten global industrial concerns.

Benjamin Disraeli, a Rothschild Zionist (who would go on to become British Prime Minister twice - the only admitted Rothschild Zionist to do so) publishes **Coningsby**, in which he characterises Nathan Rothschild as,

"...the Lord and Master of the money markets of the world, and of course virtually Lord and Master of everything else. He literally held the revenues of Southern Italy in pawn, and Monarchs and Ministers of all countries courted his advice and were guided by his suggestions."

Benjamin Disraeli
(1804 - 1881)

He may as well have stuck his tongue straight down the back of Nathan's trousers. No wonder he got to be PM twice! But no guess where he was getting his orders from to run England.

CHOO-CHOO, THE NEW MONEY MAKING MACHINES

1845: James Rothschild (who by now had married his niece Betty, Salomon Rothschild's daughter), is now known as **Baron James de Rothschild**. He wins the contract to build the first major railway line in Europe through bribery, cohesion, and blackmail. This was called the **Chemin De Fer Du Nord** and ran initially from Paris to Valenciennes and then joined with the Austrian rail network, built by his brother's wife's father, Salomon Rothschild - all sounds a bit sordid doesn't it. With a small loss of control during WWII, the Rothschilds have owned and operated **Du Nord Railways** in Europe at a huge profit.

Edmond Benjamin James de Rothschild is born to James and Betty in Boulogne-Billancourt, France. Edmond, a product of in-breeding, is a very strong supporter of Zionism, and his generous donations lent significant support to the movement during its early years which helped lead to the establishment of the State of Israel, otherwise known as the Fiefdom of Rothschild.

1847: Lionel De Rothschild now married to the daughter of his uncle, Kalmann (Carl) Rothschild, is elected to the parliamentary seat for the City of London. More inbreeds to come!

1848: Karl Marx, an Ashkenazi Jew, publishes The **Communist Manifesto**. Interestingly at the same time as he is working on this, Karl Ritter of Frankfurt University was writing the antithesis, which would form the basis for Freidrich Nietzsche's, **Nietzscheanism**. This Nietzecheanism was later developed into Fascism and then into Nazism and was used to propel the first and second world wars.

Marx, Ritter, and Nietzsche were all funded and under the instruction of the Rothschilds. The idea was that those who direct the overall conspiracy, could use the differences in those two so-called ideologies, to enable them to divide larger and larger factions of the human race into opposing camps, so that they could be armed and then brainwashed into fighting and destroying each other, and particularly, to destroy all political and religious institutions. The same plan put forward by Weishaupt 72 years earlier in 1776.

1849: *Gütle Schnaper, Mayer Rothschild's wife dies.*

1850: Construction begins this decade on the manor houses of **Mentmore** in England and **Château de Ferrières** in France. More Rothschild's manors will follow throughout the world, all of them filled with works of art, and more luxurious than any royal palace.

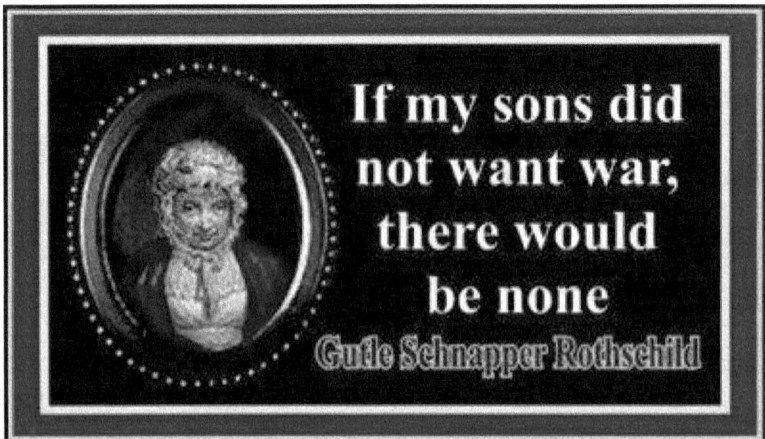

If my sons did not want war, there would be none

Gutle Schnapper Rothschild

A Rothschild House - Château de Ferrières in France

A Rothschild House - Mentmore Towers, Buckinghamshire, England

James Rothschild in France is said to be worth **600 million francs**, which at the time was 150 million francs more than all the other bankers in France put together!

1852: N.M. Rothschild & Sons begins refining gold and silver for the Royal Mint and the Bank of England and other international customers including the Perth Mint in Australia.

1853: Nathaniel de Rothschild, the son in law of James Rothschild, purchases Château Brane Mouton, the Bordeaux vineyard of Mouton, and renames it **Château Mouton Rothschild**.

1855: The eldest brother, Amschel Mayer Rothschild dies. The 2nd son, Salomon Mayer Rothschild dies and the 4th son, Kalmann (Carl) Mayer Rothschild dies. Not a very good year for the Rothschild brothers that is for sure!

1858: Lionel De Rothschild takes his seat in parliament and becomes the first Jewish member of the British parliament, and possibly the first that married his cousin.

1861: President Abraham Lincoln (16th President of the United States from 1860 till his assassination in 1865) approaches the big banks in New York to try to obtain loans to support the ongoing American Civil War. As these large banks were heavily under the influence of the Rothschilds, they offer him a deal they know he cannot accept, 24% to 36% interest on all monies loaned. The bankers do not want to free slaves, so they do not want to support Lincoln. Lincoln is very angry about this high level of interest and so he prints his own debt free money called **Greenbacks**. He informs the public that this is now legal tender for both public and private debts.

1862: By April $449,338,902 worth of Lincoln's debt free money (the Greenback) has been printed and distributed. He states of this,

> *"We gave the people of this republic the greatest blessing they ever had, their own paper money to pay their own debts."*

That same year The **Times of London** publishes a story containing the following statement,

> If that mischievous fiancial policy, which had its origin in the North American Republic, should become indurated down to a fixture, then that government will furnish its

own money without cost. It will pay off debts and be without a debt. It will have all the money necessary to carry on its commerce. It will become prosperous beyond precedent in the history of civilized governments of the world. The brains and the wealth of all countries will go to North America. That government must be destroyed or it will destroy every monarchy on the globe.

1863: President Abraham Lincoln discovers the Tsar of Russia, Alexander II (1855 – 1881), was having problems with the Rothschilds as well, as he was refusing their continual attempts to set up a central bank in Russia. The Tsar then gives President Lincoln some unexpected help.

The Tsar issued orders that if either England or France actively intervened in the American Civil War, and help the South, Russia would consider such action a declaration of war, and take the side of President Lincoln. To show that he wasn't messing about, he sent part of his Pacific Fleet to port in San Francisco and another part to New York.

The Rothschild banking house in Naples, Italy, C. M. de Rothschild e figli, closes following the unification of Italy.

The Rothschilds use one of their own in America, **John D. Rockefeller**, to form an oil business called **Standard Oil** which eventually takes over all of its competition.

1864: Rothschild, August Belmont, who by now is the Democratic Party's National Chairman, supports General George McClellan as the Democratic nominee to run against President Abraham Lincoln in this year's election. Much to the anger of Belmont, President Lincoln wins the election.

1865: In a statement to Congress, President Abraham Lincoln states,

"I have two great enemies, the Southern Army in front of me, and the financial institutions in the rear. Of the two, the one in my rear is my greatest foe."

Abraham Lincoln
(1809 – 1865)

Later that year, on April 14, President Lincoln is assassinated, less than two months before the end of the American Civil War. Lincoln was assassinated by the Rothschilds (who funded **John Wilkes Booth** to pull the trigger) because Lincoln refused Rothschilds money and their central bank. Lincoln broke the cardinal rule of banking – he created competition with his debt free Greenbacks currency. The next President to make this fatal mistake was **John F. Kennedy** – and we all know what happened to him.

Following a brief training period in the Rothschilds London Bank, Jacob Schiff, a Rothschild, Rothschild Zionist, born in their house in Frankfurt, arrives in America at the age of 18, with instructions and the finance necessary to buy into a banking house there.

The purpose of this was to carry out the following tasks:

Jacob Schiff (1847 – 1920)

1. Gain control of America's money system through the establishment of a central bank.
2. Find desirable men, who for a price, would be willing to serve as stooges for the Illuminati and promote them into high places in the federal government, the Congress, Supreme Court, and all the federal agencies.
3. Create minority group strife throughout the nations, particularly targeting the whites and blacks.
4. Create a movement to destroy religion in the United States, with Christianity as the main target.

1865: Nathaniel de Rothschild becomes Member of Parliament for Aylesbury in Buckinghamshire, UK.

1868: The youngest of the original brothers, Jacob (James) Mayer Rothschild dies, shortly after purchasing Château Lafite, one of the four great premier grand cru estates of France. He is the last of Mayer Amschel Rothschild's sons to die.

1870: Nathaniel de Rothschild dies.

1873: The failing **Rio Tinto** copper mines in Spain are purchased by a group of foreign financiers including the Rothschilds. These mines represented Europe's largest source of copper. Today, Rio Tinto Group is a British-Australian multinational metals and Mining Corporation with headquarters in London, United Kingdom, and a management office in Melbourne, Australia. Its 2014 profit was $US9.3 billion (Rio Tinto, 2015).

1875: On January 1 of this year, Jacob Schiff, now Solomon Loeb's son-in-law after marrying his daughter Teresa, takes control of the banking house **Kuhn, Loeb & Co**. He goes on to finance **John D. Rockefeller's** Standard Oil Company, **Edward R. Harriman's** Railroad Empire, and **Andrew Carnegie's** Steel Empire. This is all with Rothschild money, thus each is controlled by the Rothschilds.

Schiff then identifies the other largest bankers in America at that time. They are, **J.P. Morgan** who controls Wall Street, the **Drexels** and the **Biddles** of Philadelphia. All the other financiers, big and little, danced to the music of those three houses. Schiff then gets the European Rothschilds to set up European branches of these three large banks on the understanding that Schiff, and therefore the Rothschilds, is to be the boss of banking in New York and therefore America.

This is also the year **Lionel De Rothschild** loans **Prime Minister Benjamin Disraeli** the finances for the British government to purchase shares in the **Suez Canal**, from **Khedive Said** of Egypt. This was done as the Rothschilds needed this access route to be held by a government they controlled, so they could use that government's military to protect their huge business interests in the Middle East, and their future theft of Palestine.

Otto Eduard Leopold, Prince of Bismarck, Duke of Lauenburg, known as Otto von Bismarck (1815 – 1898)

"The division of the United States into two federations of equal force was decided long before the civil war by the high financial power of Europe. These bankers were afraid that the United States, if they remained in one block and as one nation, would attain economical and financial independence, which would upset their financial domination over the world. The voice of the Rothschilds predominated. They foresaw the tremendous booty if they could substitute two feeble democracies, indebted to the financiers, to the vigorous Republic, confident and self-providing. Therefore they started their emissaries in order to exploit the question of slavery and thus dig an abyss between the two parts of the Republic."
—OTTO VON BISMARCK, 1876

1879: Lionel de Rothschild dies.

1880: Rothschild agents begin fomenting a series of massacres, predominantly in Russia, but also in Poland, Bulgaria, and Romania. These massacres resulted in the slaughter of thousands of innocent Jews, causing approximately 2 million to flee mainly to New York, but also to Chicago, Philadelphia, Boston, and Los Angeles. The reason these pogroms were initiated was to create a large Jewish base in America, who when they arrived, would be educated to register as **Democrat** voters. Some twenty years later, this would result in in a massive Democratic power base in the United States and be used to elect Rothschild front men such as **Woodrow Wilson** (the man who sold America to the Banksters) to the Presidency, and to carry out the bidding of the Rothschilds.

1881: President James A. Garfield (The 20th President of the United States who lasted only 100 Days) states two weeks before he is assassinated:

*President James A.
Garfield
(1831 a– 1881)*

"Whoever controls the volume of money in our country is absolute master of all industry and commerce…and when you realize that the entire system is very easily controlled, one way, or another, by a few powerful men at the top, you will not have to be told how periods of inflation and depression originate."

Edmond James de Rothschild has a son Maurice de Rothschild.

1885: Nathaniel Rothschild, son of Lionel De Rothschild, becomes the first Jewish peer and takes the title of **Lord Rothschild**. In the past, the title of Lord was reserved for Noble or Royal bloodlines. However, when the nobles and royals are in hock to you, you can buy whatever you want – including silly titles!

1886: Alphonse Rothschild of the Rothschild banking family of France obtains substantial amounts of Russia's oil fields and forms the **Caspian and Black Sea Petroleum Company** (Bnito), which quickly becomes the world's second largest oil producer. In 1911, the company was acquired by **Royal Dutch Shell** (Black Nobility Family).

1887: Opium trafficker in China, **Edward Albert Sassoon**, marries **Aline Caroline de Rothschild**, the grand-daughter of Jacob (James) Rothschild. Aline Caroline's father, **Gustave**, together with his brother, **Alphonse**, took over the Rothschild's French arm following their father Jacob's death.

The Rothschilds finance the amalgamation of the **Kimberley Diamond Mines** in **South Africa**. They subsequently become the biggest shareholders of the new company **De Beers**, and mine precious stones in Africa and India without the locals receiving any subsidy for this. They used their vast media network to promote diamonds as a "girl's best friend" and as a tradition for engagement rings. Prior to this, diamonds were not considered rare or expensive at all, and engagement rings were not heard of.

During this period, the Rothschilds set up and finance their new buddy **Cecil Rhodes**, who invents a new job description – "Blood Diamonds." Without Rhodes and the Rothschilds, the tragedy of blood diamonds would have never happened. There is a movie called **Blood Diamond** (2006) starring Leonardo DiCaprio and Djimon Hounsou that tells the modern story.

1891: The **British Labour Leader** makes the following statement on the subject of the Rothschilds,

> *"This blood-sucking crew has been the cause of untold mischief and misery in Europe during the present century, and has piled up its prodigious wealth chiefly through fomenting wars between States which ought never to have quarrelled. Whenever there is trouble in Europe, wherever rumours of war circulate and men's minds are distraught with fear of change and calamity you may be sure that a hook-nosed Rothschild is at his games somewhere near the region of the disturbance."*

Comments like this worry the Rothschilds and towards the end of the 1800's, they purchase the **Reuters** news agency. That way, they can have some control of the media and make sure comments like this never make it to print.

1895: Edmond James de Rothschild, the youngest son of Jacob (James) Mayer Rothschild visits **Palestine** and subsequently supplies the funds to found the first Jewish colonies there. This is to further their long term objective of creating the Fiefdom of Rothschild/State of Israel.

Theodor Herzl on the Israeli $100 bill

1897: The Rothschilds found the **Zionist Congress** to promote Zionism (a political movement with the sole aim of moving all Jews into a singularly Jewish nation state) and arrange its first meeting in Munich, Germany. However due to extreme opposition from local Jews who are quite happy where they are, this meeting has to be moved to Basle, Switzerland and takes place on 29 August.

The meeting is chaired by Rothschild Zionist, **Theodor Herzl**, who would state in his diaries:

> *It is essential that the sufferings of Jews become worse...this will assist in realization of our plans...I have an excellent idea...I shall induce anti-Semites to liquidate Jewish wealth...The anti-Semites will assist us thereby in that they will strengthen the persecution and oppression of Jews. The anti-Semites shall be our best friends.*

Now you should realise why they funded Hitler during WWII – re-read Herzl's ideas if you are not sure.

Herzl is subsequently elected President of the Zionist Organisation which adopts the Rothschild Red Hexagram/Sign as the Zionist flag, which 51 years later will end up as the flag of Israel, much to the disgust of many other (non-Zionist) Jews. The Zionist created the Nazi Party to carry out Herzl's plan.

♀ ♀ ♀ ✡ ✡ ✡ ✡

Edward Henry Harriman becomes a director of the **Union Pacific Railroad** and goes on to take control of the **Southern Pacific Railroad.** This is all financed by the Rothschilds.

1901: The Jews from the colonies set up in Palestine by Edmond James de Rothschild send a delegation to him which tell him,

Edmond James de
Rothschild
(1845 – 1934)

"If you wish to save the Yishuv (The Jewish settlement) first take your hands from it, and...for once, permit the colonists to have the possibility of correcting for themselves what needs correcting." Edmond is very angry about this and replies, "I created the Yishuv, I alone. Therefore no men, neither colonists nor organisations have the right to interfere in my plans!"

Control freak much? The Rothschild banking house in Frankfurt Germany, M. A. von Rothschild und Söhne, closes as there is no male Rothschild heir to take it on.

1902: Baron Philippe de Rothschild (1902 – 1988) is born in France. He became a Grand Prix race-car driver, a screenwriter and playwright, a theatrical producer, a film producer, a poet, and one of the most successful wine growers in the world – but only because he could afford to buy the best people and information to do it for him.

1905: A group of Rothschild backed Zionist Jews led by **Georgi Apollonovich Gapon** attempt to overthrow the Tsar in Russia in a

Communist Coup. They fail and are forced to flee Russia only to be given refuge in Germany.

1903: The Swedish Nobel and the French Rothschild's *Far East Trading*, financed by **King Wilhelm III**, combined with Samuel and Oppenheimer's **Shell Oil** to form the *Asiatic Petroleum Company*.

1906: The Rothschilds claim that due to growing instability in the region and increasing competition from Rockefeller (the Rockefeller family are Rothschild descendants through a female bloodline) who owned Standard Oil, this is why they sell their Caspian and Black Sea Petroleum Company to Royal Dutch and Shell. This is another example of the Rothschilds trying to hide their true wealth.

By **1927 Royal Dutch Petroleum** discovered oil at Seria off the coast of Brunei, who's Sultan would become one of the world's richest men as a result of his loyalty to Royal Dutch. The Dutch and British monarchs who control Royal Dutch merged their company with the Oppenheimer and Samuel's Shell Oil and Nobel and Rothschild's *Far East Trading* and **Royal Dutch Shell** was born (Henderson, 2011). **Queen Beatrix** of the Dutch **House of Orange** (Black Nobility) and **Lord Victor Rothschild** (Bloodline) are its two largest shareholders. Queen Beatrix is a regular at **Bilderberg** meetings. Her **SS Nazi** father, Prince Bernhard of Lippe-Biesterfeld, co-founded the Bilderberg Group.

1907: Rothschild front man, **Jacob Schiff**, the head of **Kuhn, Loeb and Co.**, in a speech to the New York Chamber of Commerce, warns that:

> *"Unless we have a Central Bank with adequate control of credit resources, this country is going to undergo the most severe and far reaching money panic in its history."*

Suddenly America finds itself in the middle of another typical run of the mill Rothschild engineered financial crisis (false flag), which as usual, ruins the lives of millions of innocent people throughout America and makes billions for the Rothschilds. We will see this repeated in 1930 and as recently as 2008.

1909: Jacob Schiff founds the National Advancement for the Association of the Coloured People (**NAACP**). This was done to incite black people into rioting, looting, and other forms of disorder, in order to cause a rift between the black and white communities. Jewish historian Howard Sachar, states the following in his book, *A History of the Jews in America*,

> "*In 1914, Professor Emeritus Joel Spingarn of Columbia University became chairman of the NAACP and recruited for its board such Jewish leaders as Jacob Schiff, Jacob Billikopf, and Rabbi Stephen Wise.*" (Sachar, 1992)

Other Rothschild Zionist co-founders included Julius Rosenthal, Lillian Wald and Rabbi Emil G. Hirsch. It was not until 1920 that the NAACP appointed its first black president, **James Weldon Johnson.**

1911:   Werner Sombart, in his book, *The Jews and Modern Capitalism*," stated that from 1820 on, it was the, "*Age of the Rothschild*," and concluded that there was, "*Only one power in Europe, and that is Rothschild.*"

1912: In the December issue of *Truth Magazine*, **George R. Conroy** states of banker Jacob Schiff,

---

"*Mr Schiff is head of the great private banking house of Kuhn, Loeb, and Co., which represents the Rothschilds interests on this side of the Atlantic. He has been described as a financial strategist and has been for years the financial minister of the great impersonal power known as Standard Oil. He was hand in glove with the Harrimans, the Goulds, and the Rockefellers in all their railroad enterprises and has become the dominant power in the railroad and financial power of America.*"

THE MAN WHO SOLD AMERICA TO THE BANKSTERS

Woodrow Wilson (the man who sold America to the Banksters)

1913: On March 4, **Woodrow Wilson** (the man who sold America to the Banksters) is elected the 28th President of the United States thanks to Rothschild money. Shortly after he is inaugurated, he is visited in the White House by Rothschild agent **Samuel Untermyer** of the law firm **Guggenheim, Untermyer, and Marshall.**

Untermyer tries to blackmail Wilson for the sum of $40,000 in relation to an affair Wilson had whilst he was a professor at Princeton University with a fellow professor's wife. This is a common tactic of the Rothschilds – to go out of their way to either find some blackmail worthy events, or set the person up to blackmail them (Bill Clinton knows all about that!).

Wilson does not have the money (in 1904 that is over $100,000), so Untermyer volunteers to pay the $40,000 out of his own pocket. However, there is a catch. Wilson must promise to appoint to the first vacancy on the **United States Supreme Court**, a nominee to be recommended to Wilson by Untermyer (Rothschilds). Wilson agrees to this.

Woodrow Wilson is the man that sold America to the bankers. He did more to hurt America than any other President since. Contrary to many conspiracy websites and books, Wilson never regretted helping to make the Federal Reserve, and the "regret speech" people use to prove he did regret his move was made in 1911 – 2 years before the Federal Reserve Act was put into Law.

Via e-mail, **John M. Cooper**, a professor of history at the **University of Wisconsin**, and the author of several books on Woodrow Wilson, stated:

> *"I can tell you categorically that this is not a statement of regret for having created the Federal Reserve. Wilson never had any regrets for having done that. It was an accomplishment in which he took great pride."*

So there you have it. Wilson was a 100% New World Order stooge and sell out. He was a traitor to the American people, and should be remembered as such. Indeed, if not for Woodrow Wilson, the United States would be the wealthiest, most prosperous, and highest living civilization in the world by far. Instead, it is on the verge of economic collapse, there are more people on food stamps then in the history of the US, and manufacturing, production, and jobs have all gone off shore.

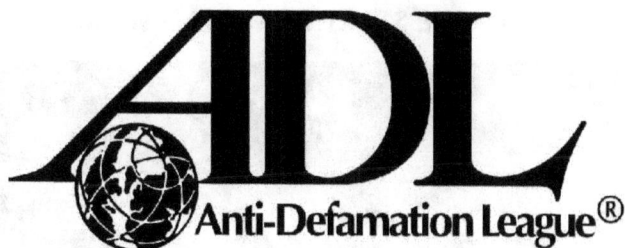

The **Anti-defamation League** was created in 1913 to protect the Jewish Banksters that had just hijacked America that same year with the **Federal Reserve** and their Criminal Collection Agency, the **IRS.**

It was set up by Rothschild man, Jacob Schiff. This organisation is formed to slander anyone who questions or challenges the Rothschild global conspiracy as, "anti-Semitic." If they can't find a legitimate excuse to publicly destroy you, they will make one up. I will not be at all surprised if they come after me after this book is published! Also, I should add at this time that I have no intention of shooting two bullets into the back of my head, while my arms are tied behind my back. No, I am not being funny (much), they have done this several times and try and say it is "suicide." So for the record, I have no intention of committing suicide – ever. But that doesn't rule out a bizarre accident I suppose.

1913 proves to be the most successful year ever for the Rothschilds, for it is in this year they pull off the greatest theft in the history of planet earth. They finally get their PRIVATE Central Bank in the United States. President Woodrow Wilson (the man who sold America to the Banksters) signed the **Federal Reserve Act** into law on December 23, 1913. More on that in Chapter 14.

If the United States ever wants to become strong and wealthy again, they must first shut down the Federal Reserve, and start printing their own, interest free money. Within 10 years, the only Americans that are poor, are those that choose to be. There could be free healthcare, free higher education, and the lowest unemployment rate in the world. This is not socialism. It would be a very wealthy country looking after its citizens, just like **Brunei** does. In Brunei, the money is tax free, no GST, no petrol (gas) tax and no income tax. Everything is cheaper. Brunei is a peaceful, quiet country which highly values family and family life. It's safe to walk around at night in the city, nobody hassles you, and no drunken youths vomiting and fighting. Kind of like the USA, back in the 1950's.

1914: THE START OF WORLD WAR I

No-man's land: This U.S. soldier, who lies dead, entangled in barbed wire. Thanks to the greedy Rothschild murderers.

In this war, the German Rothschilds loan money to the Germans, the British Rothschilds loan money to the British, and the French Rothschilds loan money to the French. Furthermore, the Rothschilds have control of the three European news agencies, **Wolff** (est. 1849) in Germany, **Reuters** (est. 1851) in England, and **Havas** (est. 1835) in France.

The Rothschilds use Wolff to manipulate the German people into a fervour for war. From around this time, the Rothschilds are rarely reported in the media, because they own the media. It is also important that in the early years of the war, American news was pro-German. But when the British did a deal to get America into the war, the newspapers turned horrific on the Germans.

1916: On June 4, Rothschild Zionist, **Louis Dembitz Brandeis** is appointed to the Supreme Court of the United States by President Wilson as per his agreed blackmail payment to Samuel Untermyer some three years earlier. Justice Brandeis is also the elected leader of the Executive Committee for Zionist Affairs, a position he has held since 1914.

If you remember back, the Rothschilds had a pathological hatred for the Tsar in Russia. During World War I, this was the reason why the German's were winning. Germany was being financed by the Rothschilds to a greater extent than France, Italy, and England, because Rothschilds did not want to support the Tsar in Russia, and of course, Russia was on the same side as France, Italy, and England.

Then a significant event occurred. Although Germany was winning the war and not one foreign soldier had set foot on their soil, they went ahead and offered armistice to Britain with no requirement of reparations. The Rothschilds were anxious to make sure this armistice didn't happen, as they were expecting to make far more money off this war. Therefore, they played yet another card they had up their sleeve.

The Start of the Strife in the Middle East

Whilst the British were considering Germany's offer, Rothschild agent Louis Brandeis sends a Zionist delegation from America to Britain to promise to bring America into the war on the side of the British, provided the British agree to give the land of Palestine to the Rothschilds.

The Rothschilds had huge business interests in the Middle East and desired their own state in that area, along with their own military force which they could use as an aggressor to any state that threatened those interests. (Somehow they missed their homeland by about 800 miles in Georgia, Russia – the old lands of Khazaria!)

The British subsequently agree to the deal for Palestine, even though it was not their land to give. At no point were the Palestinians informed of this deal. In fact, the Arabs were under the impression that they would be receiving an Arab homeland, ruled independently by Arabs. This is what they were told they would get if they helped the British fight the Ottomans (Turks) in Turkey and North Africa.

I am sure you have heard of **Lawrence of Arabia**? He was the man in charge of training and leading the Arabs against the Ottomans. Lawrence was also led to believe that the deal he made with the Arabs was for real. However, at the end of the war, he learnt that it was a cruel lie just to get the Arab's support, otherwise the British could never have won.

Captain Lawrence had become very close with his Arab fighters. When he was forced to tell them they had been betrayed, he could not bear it. After many years of PTSD, heavy drinking and living as a recluse back in England, the famous war hero, Lawrence of Arabia, shot himself in the head while sitting on his front porch.

The "official story" says he died in a motorbike accident – after all, we couldn't have a celebrated war hero commit suicide - not good for the country's morale you know (Lawrence, 2015).

Captain Thomas Edward Lawrence CB DSO was a great man, but a tortured man. Betrayed by his country, and disowned by the people he loved. For me, Lawrence was the first of many fatalities that have stained the sand red over the years, because of the State of Israel.

Meanwhile, after England "promised" the land that wasn't theirs to the Zionists, the Zionists in London contacted their counterparts in America to inform them of this fact. America at this point had a very large German immigrant

TE Lawrence (1888 - 1935)

population, and as such, most American media had been pro-German.

However, once the Zionist were promised Palestine, literally overnight, the same previously pro-German media turned on them, running propaganda pieces such as: German soldiers were killing Red Cross Nurses; German soldiers were cutting off babies hands, etc., in order to manipulate the American public against the Germans.

ABSOLUTELY NONE OF THESE CLAIMS WERE TRUE!

This trick has been used again and again. In fact, the most emotionally moving testimony on October 10, 1990 came from a 15-year-old Kuwaiti girl, known only by her first name of **Nayirah**. According to the Caucus, Nayirah's full name was being kept confidential to prevent Iraqi reprisals against her family in occupied Kuwait. Sobbing, she described what she had seen with her own eyes in a hospital in Kuwait City. Her written testimony was passed out in a media kit prepared by Citizens for a Free Kuwait.

> *"I volunteered at the al-Addan hospital,"* Nayirah said. *"While I was there, I saw the Iraqi soldiers come into the hospital with guns, and go into the room where … babies were in incubators. They took the babies out of the incubators, took the incubators, and left the babies on the cold floor to die." (Nayirah, 2010)*

Three months passed between Nayirah's testimony and the start of the first Gulf War. During those months, the story of babies torn from their incubators was repeated over and over again.

President Bush retold the story, over and over

It was recited as fact in Congressional testimony, on TV and radio talk shows, and at the UN Security Council.

> *"Of all the accusations made against the dictator,"* MacArthur observed, *"none had more impact on American public opinion than the one about Iraqi soldiers removing 312 babies from their incubators and leaving them to die on the cold hospital floors of Kuwait City."* (MacArthur, 2004)

At the Human Rights Caucus, however, Hill & Knowlton and Congressman Lantos had failed to reveal that Nayirah was a member of the Kuwaiti Royal Family. Her father, in fact, was **Saud Nasir al-Sabah**, Kuwait's Ambassador to the US, who sat listening in the hearing room during her testimony. The Caucus also failed to reveal that H&K vice-president **Lauri Fitz-Pegado** had coached Nayirah in what even the Kuwaitis' own investigators later confirmed was false testimony. That is right, the removing of babies from their incubators was a lie – propaganda – false. But it helped to convince a nation (the US) to launch an illegal war. (MacArthur, 2004)

This same year the American media turned on Germans, President Woodrow Wilson (the man who sold America to the Banksters), ran a re-election campaign under the slogan,

"Re-Elect the Man Who Will Keep Your Sons out Of the War."

On December 12, **1916**, Germany and her allies offer peace terms to end the war. If accepted, the soldiers could have returned home for Christmas, and millions of soldiers and civilians would have been saved. Instead, the Rothschild's deal delays the war for two more years.

1917: As a result of Germany's offer of peace, the Rothschild war machine goes into overdrive in America, spreading propaganda which leads to President Wilson, under the instructions of American Zionist leader and Supreme Court Justice, Louis Dembitz Brandeis, reneging on his promise to the electorate.

On April 2, **1917**, President Woodrow Wilson (the man who sold America to the Banksters), Mr. "Re-Elect the Man Who Will Keep Your Sons out Of the War", went before a joint session of Congress to seek a Declaration of War against Germany in order that the world "be made safe for democracy." How this man can sleep at night I will never know.

Four days later, Congress voted to declare war. By the time the war ended a year and a half later, an entire generation was decimated— France alone lost half its men between the ages of twenty and thirty-two. The maimed bodies of millions of European men who survived bore mute testimony to the war's savagery. Over 90% of the returned veterans suffered what we call today Post Traumatic Stress Disorder (PTSD) which caused almost 1/3 to take their own lives rather than live with the bloody and terrifying nightmares. Many turned to drink to dull the memories generating domestic violence, mass divorce, and broken families.

I say again, Woodrow Wilson (the man who sold America to the Banksters) did more harm to America than any other President since.

The **Nobel Peace Prize 1919** was awarded to Woodrow Wilson (the man who sold America to the Banksters). This just shows what a joke the Nobel Peace Prize is. In fact, they gave it to **Barack Obama** for "services rendered" in 2009. Again, contrary to what people "think" about Obama, he has started and supported more wars than George W Bush during his time. He has also personally signed off over 1,500 drone strikes that have killed hundreds of children.

He also failed to close the concentration camp and government sanctioned torture facility at **Guantanamo Bay** - even though he made that an election promise whilst campaigning in 2007.

Just a heads up, ANYONE they give a Nobel Peace Prize to, is a hard–core Insider "puppet," and will have more blood on their hands

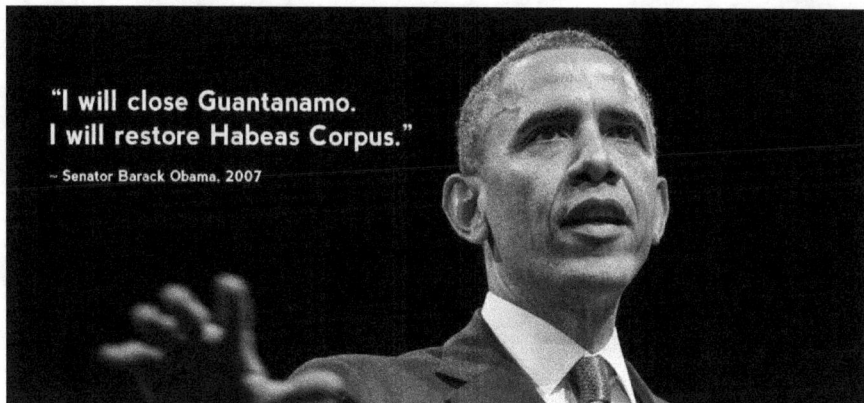

"I will close Guantanamo.
I will restore Habeas Corpus."
~ Senator Barack Obama, 2007

*Barack Obama, Habeas Corpus and close Guantanamo election pledge 2007.
He lied about both.*

than any serial killer. In fact, if I were offered this prize, I would use it as toilet paper to clean my backside!

THE BALFOUR DECLARATION

1917: As per the Rothschild Zionist promise to the British to take America into the war, they decide they want something in writing from the British to prove that they will uphold their side of the bargain.

The British Foreign Secretary, Arthur James Balfour therefore drafts a letter which is commonly known as the "Balfour Declaration," reproduced in its entirety below:

*British Foreign Secretary, Arthur James Balfour and the typed letter called
the Balfour Declaration*

THE PALESTINE POST

STATE OF ISRAEL IS BORN

THE BALFOUR DECLARATION LETTER

Foreign Office
November 2nd, 1917

Dear Lord Rothschild,

I have much pleasure in conveying to you, on behalf of His Majesty's Government, the following declaration of sympathy with Jewish Zionist aspirations which has been submitted to, and approved by, the Cabinet.

His Majesty's Government view with favour the establishment in Palestine of a national home for the Jewish people, and will use their best endeavours to facilitate the achievement of this object, it being clearly understood that nothing shall be done which may prejudice the civil and religious rights of existing non-Jewish communities in Palestine, or the rights and political status enjoyed by Jews in any other country.

I should be grateful if you would bring this declaration to the knowledge of the Zionist Federation.

Yours sincerely,
Arthur James Balfour

Prior to the Balfour Declaration, the Middle East was relatively peaceful. Arabs, Jews, and Christians lived side by side for hundreds of years in peace. They tolerated and respected each other's observance to their religions, and ways of life. That is until the Rothschilds took over ownership.

This single letter is responsible for all of the strife, murders, massacres, wars, genocide, and terrorism in the Middle East since 1918 to now, and in the future. Shame on you Mr. Balfour.

(Pryor, 1998)

A Note on Zionism

Zionism is a movement for (originally) the re-establishment and (now) the development and protection of a Jewish nation in what is now Israel. It was established as a political organisation in 1897 under Theodor Herzl, and was later led by Chaim Weizmann.

The Jewish faith and Zionism are two very different philosophies. They are as opposite as day and night. In their years of divinely decreed exile no Jew ever sought to end this exile and establish independent political sovereignty anywhere.

The people's sole purpose was the study and fulfilment of the Divine commandments of the Torah. The Zionist movement created the Israeli state. The latter is a fiction less than one hundred years old. Its essential goal was and is to change the nature of the Jewish people from that of a religious entity to a political movement. From Zionism's inception the spiritual leaders of the Jewish people stood in staunch opposition to it. To this day Torah Jewry remains forever loyal to its faith. Zionists want the world to believe that they are the representatives of the entire Jewish people. This is false! The Jewish people never chose them as their leaders.

Today, there are Christians, Jews, and anyone that wants to get ahead that calls themselves "Zionist." Till now I was identifying these false Jews as Ashkenazi Jews who were hiding behind the title of Jew. But from now, I will refer to anyone that works for or sucks up to the Rothschilds, or anyone who really believes in a Jewish home state (so they can rebuild the Temple and bring about Armageddon), as Rothschild Zionist, because that is what they are.

Rothschilds get their revenge

Czar Nicholas II and family -- murdered by the Rothschilds

1918: The Rothschilds, who finance and control the Jewish Bolsheviks in Russia, now order them to murder Tsar *Nicholas II and his entire family,* *even though the Tsar had already abdicated months earlier and left the capital.*

This is both to get control of the country, as well as an act of revenge for Tsar Alexander I blocking their world government plan in 1815 at the Congress of Vienna, and Tsar Alexander II siding with President Abraham Lincoln in 1864.

It is extremely important for them to slaughter the entire family, including women and children in order to make good on the promise made by Nathan Mayer Rothschild in 1815. It is designed to show the world what happens if you ever attempt to cross the Rothschilds.

The Rothschilds can take 100% responsibility for the Russian Civil War (1917-22), which means they are also responsible for the 9,000,000 deaths that resulted from it (White, 2011).

Many more than the less than 1,000,000 Jews they condemned to death in WWII.

It is reported that the Rothschilds were angry with the Russians because they were not prepared to allow them to form a central bank within their nation. They therefore gathered groups of Jewish spies and sent them into Russia to drum up a revolution for the benefit of the common man, which was actually a takeover of Russia by a Rothschild controlled elite.

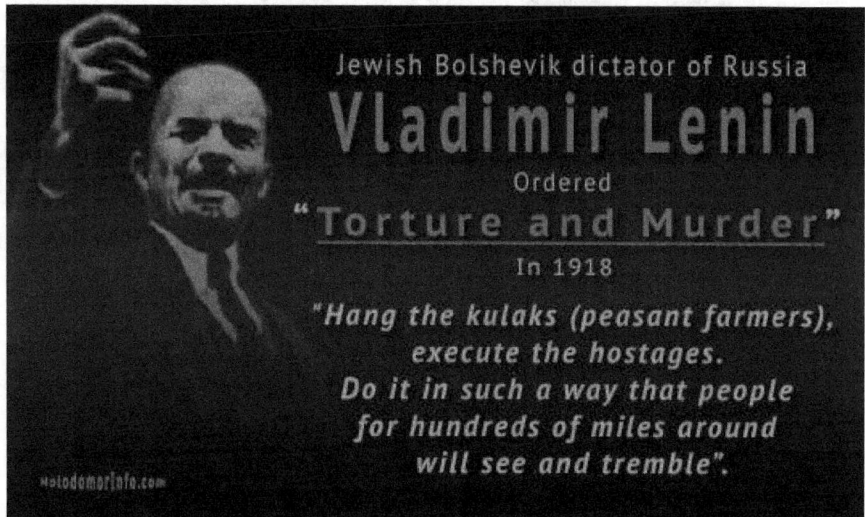

Jewish Bolshevik dictator of Russia
Vladimir Lenin
Ordered
"Torture and Murder"
In 1918
"Hang the kulaks (peasant farmers), execute the hostages. Do it in such a way that people for hundreds of miles around will see and tremble".

Holodomorinfo.com

Vladimir Ilyich Ulyanov (Lenin) was an Ashkenazi Jew that slaughtered millions. His Khazarian ancestors would be proud.

These Jewish spies were, in age old deceptive Ashkenazi tradition, given Russian names. For example, **Trotsky** was a member of the first group and his original name was **Bronstein**. These groups were sent to areas throughout Russia to incite riots and rebellion.

The Jewish Post International Edition, week ending January 24th 1991, confirms **Vladimir Lenin** was Jewish (Khazarian). Lenin is also on record as having stated,

> *"The establishment of a central bank is 90% of communizing a nation."*

These Jewish, Rothschild funded Bolsheviks would go on in the course of history to slaughter 30 million Christians and Non-Jews in Soviet controlled territory. Indeed, the author **Aleksandr Solzhenitsyn** in his work, **Gulag Archipelago, Vol 2**, affirms that Zionist Jews created and administered the organised Soviet concentration camp system in which tens of millions of Christians and Non-Jews died. On page 79 of this book he even names the administrators of this the greatest killing machine in the history of the world. They are Aron Solts, Yakov Rappoport, Lazar Kogan, Matvei Berman, Genrikh Yagoda, and Naftaly Frenkel. All six are Rothschild Zionist (Solzhenitsyn, 1974).

In 1970 Solzhenitsyn would be awarded the Nobel Peace Prize for literature. No one has set up a multi-million dollar Holocaust Memorial Museum for these 30 million yet. But they weren't Jews, so I guess they don't count.

1919: U.S. Congressman **Oscar Callaway** informs Congress that **J. P. Morgan** is a Rothschild front and has taken control of the American media industry. He states,

"In March, 1915, the J.P. Morgan interests, the steel, shipbuilding, and powder interest, and their subsidiary organizations, got together 12 men high up in the newspaper world and employed them to select the most influential newspapers in the United States and sufficient number of them to

*Oscar Callaway
(1872 – 1947)*

control generally the policy of the daily press...They found it was only necessary to purchase the control of 25 of the greatest papers...An agreement was reached. The policy of the papers was bought, to be paid for by the month, an editor was furnished for each paper to properly supervise and edit information regarding the questions of preparedness, militarism, financial policies, and other things of national and international nature considered vital to the interests of the purchasers."

In January, Rothschild Zionist, **Karl Liebknecht** and **Rosa Luxemburg** are killed as they attempt to lead another Rothschild funded Communist coup, this time in Berlin, Germany. Communism is favoured by the Rothschilds because it centralises power and control. A democracy costs them too much money (to buy Presidencies) and to push their agendas through can take far too long. That is why Red China is their model for the rest of the world. No voting, no answering to the public, no individual thought, and very little social unrest.

The Versailles peace conference is held to decide reparations that the Germans need to pay to the victors following the end of the First World War. A delegation of 117 Zionists headed up by Rothschild Zionist, **Bernard Baruch** bring up the subject of the promise of Palestine for them.

At this point the Germans realised why America had turned on them and under whose influence - the Rothschilds. The Germans naturally felt they had been betrayed by the Zionists. This is because at the time the Rothschilds made their deal with Britain for Palestine, in exchange for bringing America into the war, Germany was the friendliest country in the world towards the Jews.

Indeed, the **German Emancipation Edict** of 1822 guaranteed Jews in Germany all civil rights enjoyed by Germans. Also, Germany was the only country in Europe which did not place restrictions on Jews, even giving them refuge when they had to flee from Russia after their first attempted Communist coup failed there in 1905.

Nevertheless, the Rothschilds had held up their side of the bargain to spill the blood of millions of innocent American boys, and as a result, Palestine is confirmed as a Jewish homeland, and whilst its handover to the Rothschilds takes place, it is to remain under the control of Britain.

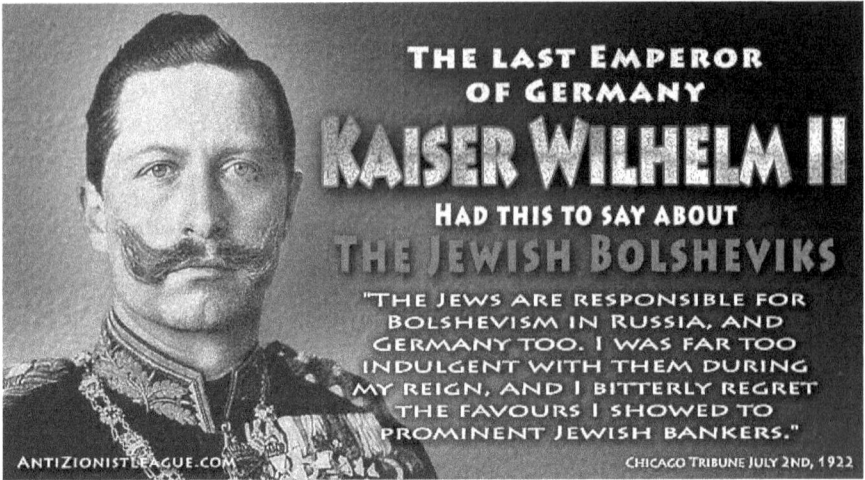

THE LAST EMPEROR
OF GERMANY
KAISER WILHELM II
HAD THIS TO SAY ABOUT
THE JEWISH BOLSHEVIKS
"THE JEWS ARE RESPONSIBLE FOR BOLSHEVISM IN RUSSIA, AND GERMANY TOO. I WAS FAR TOO INDULGENT WITH THEM DURING MY REIGN, AND I BITTERLY REGRET THE FAVOURS I SHOWED TO PROMINENT JEWISH BANKERS."
ANTIZIONISTLEAGUE.COM   CHICAGO TRIBUNE JULY 2ND, 1922

That is because the Rothschild have not yet amassed their own army, so since they control Britain, they use the British army to enforce their takeover of Palestine.

At that time, less than one percent of the population of Palestine was Jewish. Interestingly, the host of the Versailles peace conference is **Baron Edmond de Rothschild**. Remember Edmond? Edmond de Rothschild was the founding father of Zionism and the Yishuv – the Jews settling in Palestine. No conflict of interest there right! Honestly, you can't make this stuff up...

On March 29th, **The Times** of London reports on the Bolsheviks in Russia,

> One of the curious features of the Bolshevist movement is the high percentage of non-Russian elements among its leaders. Of the twenty or thirty commissaries, or leaders, who provide the central machinery of the Bolshevist movement, not less than 75% were Jews.

1920: Winston Churchill (whose mother Jenny (Jacobson) Jerome, was Jewish – meaning he is Jewish under Ashkenazi law, as he was born of a Jewish mother). Churchill was a *Committee of 300* member and 33rd degree Mason. He spoke from personal knowledge regarding the global conspiracy when he writes in an article in the *Illustrated Sunday Herald*, dated February 8, 1920:

"From the days of Illuminati leader Weishaupt, to those of Karl Marx, to those of Trotsky, this worldwide conspiracy has been steadily growing. And now at last this band of extraordinary personalities from the underworld of the great cities of Europe and America, have gripped the Russian people by the hair of their heads and become the undisputed masters of that enormous empire."

Winston Churchill
(1874-1965)

Churchill's mother, now known as **Lady Randolph** of New York in the United States, had numerous lovers before and during her marriage, including the Prince of Wales (the future King Edward VII), Karl Kinsky, and Herbert von Bismarck. It was her dalliance with the Prince of Wales (later became **King Edward VII**) that got her pregnant with Winston. There was no way the Prince could marry her, so he paid off one of his sycophants, **Lord Randolph Churchill** to marry her, so as to avoid a scandal. Winston was born less than eight months after the wedding, and no, he wasn't premmie. King Edward VII did do the right thing on one account and helped finance Winston's upbringing. He made sure he got into good schools and financed his education. He also secured him his first big job as **First Lord of the Admiralty**. This position had previously always gone to senior statesman, usually with a title ("Sir"/"Lord"/"Baron" etc.) who had outstanding military experience and leadership skills.

However, the relatively young (at 37) Winston was given the position in a true example of nepotism, even though he was not qualified for such a position.

His incompetency and lack of qualifications were demonstrated during the fatal **Gallipoli** campaign in the Dardanelles (Turkey). Tens of Thousands of Australian, New Zealand, English, Indian and French soldiers were slaughter by the waiting Turkish (Ottoman) forces. It was one of the greatest military defeats of World War I and World War II combined. For his failure as a war planner, he later got the job of British Prime Minister less than 20 years after the fatal Gallipoli campaign and got a second crack at sending men to their deaths in World War II. In fact, he delayed the first ever WWII victory in Africa to send half those troops to an already doomed Greece, for no strategic reason. All of his Generals protested but he would not listen. Greece fell (as expected), thousands of British soldiers died, and the Germans still occupied North Africa and were threatening the Suez Canal. Only by a miracle by one of his homosexual Generals – **Montgomery,** did the Empire forces, with help from America, did they win their first victory, and save North Africa.

Winston Churchill is always portrayed as a great war leader and icon of British politics. That fact is he only got the job because of who his real father was, and he really did suck at everything he did. That may be why he drank so heavily and suffered from Bi-Polar disorder, or maybe that was caused by all the blood on his hands due to false pride and arrogance. Churchill should have been tried as a war criminal, not celebrated as a hero. But this is such a typical trick by the elites through history.

1921: Under the orders of Jacob Schiff, the **Council on Foreign Relations** (CFR) is founded by Rothschild Zionist, **Bernard Baruch**, and Colonel **Edward Mandell House**. Schiff gave his orders prior to his death in 1920, as he knew an organisation in America needed to be set up to select politicians to carry on the Rothschild conspiracy, and the formation of the CFR was actually agreed in a meeting on May 30, 1919 at the Hotel Majestic in Paris, France.

The CFR membership at the start was approximately 1,000 people in the United States. The membership included the heads of virtually every industrial empire in America, all the American based international bankers, and the heads of all their tax free foundations. In essence, all those people who would provide the capital required for anyone who wished to run for Congress, the Senate, or the Presidency.

Controlling the Press

The first job of the CFR was to gain control of the press. This task was given to **John D. Rockefeller** who set up a number of national news magazines such as **Life**, and **Time**. He financed **Samuel Newhouse** to buy up and establish a chain of newspapers all across the country, **Eugene Meyer** also would go on to buy up many publications such as the **Washington Post**, **Newsweek**, and **The Weekly Magazine**.

The CFR also needed to get control of radio, television and the motion picture industry. This task was split amongst the international bankers from, Kuhn Loeb, Goldman Sachs, the Warburgs, and the Lehmanns.

1925: The Jewish Encyclopaedia, 1925 edition, Vol. 5, page 41, states, "*Edom is in modern Jewry.*"

With the startling admission that the so called enemy of the Jews, Esau (also known as Edom, see Genesis 36:1), now actually represents the Jewish race, when on page 41 of Volume V it is stated, "*Edom is in modern Jewry.*" So what they are basically saying is that these Ashkenazi Jews and Rothschild Zionists, who represent 95% of the so-called Jewish population, are actually gentiles or goyim themselves! As we have already seen, DNA science has now confirmed this fact. But it is interesting that they knew as far back as 1925!

1926: N. M. Rothschild & Sons refinance the Underground Electric Railways Company of London Ltd which has a controlling interest in the entire London Underground transport system.

Maurice de Rothschild has a son, Edmond de Rothschild.

1929: The Rothschilds crash the United States economy by contracting the money supply. They wanted to consolidate the American banks. Some 4,000 banks and other lenders ultimately

Rothschild puppet J.P Morgan Jr. (1867 - 1943) and Uncle Pennybags

failed, which gave the Rothschilds more control of those banks that were left. It was the Rothschild puppet J.P Morgan Jr. that started the crash by spreading rumours that caused a run on the banks. **Rich Uncle Pennybags**, the mascot of the game **Monopoly** was based on J.P Morgan.

1930: The first Rothschild World Bank, the **Bank for International Settlements** (BIS) is established in Basle, Switzerland. The same place as where 33 years earlier the first ever World Zionist Congress was held. By the way, **Switzerland** is a country that was created by the bankers and oligarchs. That is why they have the secret Swiss Banks Accounts – so the elites and criminals can hide their money somewhere. It is also why Switzerland is always neutral in war. They do not want to risk blowing up their rich stuff! It is also home to The **Large Hadron Collider** (LHC) tunnel, where they are trying to create a portal to other dimensions and invoke demons/spirits/aliens. Also the home of **CERN** which is the world's largest laboratory and also the birthplace of the World Wide Web. And finally, the place the Nazis laundered billions of Reichsmarks, exchanging them for British Pounds Sterling. No Swiss banker ever appeared at the World War II war tribunal over this.

1933: On January 30, Adolf Hitler becomes Chancellor of Germany (similar to President). He drives Jews, many of which were Communist, out of Governmental positions within Germany. He is a Rothschild agent and a relative.

As a result of this, in July the Jews hold a World Conference in Amsterdam during which they demand that Hitler re-instate every Jew back to his former position. Hitler refuses and as a result of this, Samuel Untermyer (the Rothschild Zionist who blackmailed President Wilson) who is now the head of the American delegation and the president of the whole conference, returns to the United States and makes a speech on radio which was transcribed in the *New York Times*, Monday, August 7, 1933. In the speech he made the following statements on the next page.

This is the same dirt bag that blackmailed Woodrow Wilson, and later was on the Steal Palestine Committee.

As two thirds of Germany's food supply had to be imported, and could only be imported with the proceeds of what they exported, if Germany could not export, two thirds of Germany's population would

Samuel Untermyer
(1858-1940)

"...the Jews are the aristocrats of the world...Our campaign is...the economic boycott against all German goods, shipping and services...What we are proposing...is to prosecute a purely defensive economic boycott that will undermine the Hitler regime and bring the German people to their senses by destroying their export trade on which their very existence depends...Each of you, Jew and Gentile alike...must refuse to deal with any merchant or shopkeeper who sells any German-made goods or who patronizes German ships or shipping."

starve, as there would be not enough food for more than one third of the population.

As a result of this boycott, Jews throughout America would protest outside and damage any stores in which they found any products with, "Made in Germany," printed on them, causing stores to have to dump these products or risk bankruptcy.

Once the effects of this boycott began to be felt in Germany, the Germans, who had demonstrated no violence towards the Jews up to this point, simply began boycotting Jewish stores in the same way the Jews had done to stores selling German products in America. Perhaps this vandalising by Jews in America is what inspired the German **Kristallnacht** ("Crystal Night") also referred to as the *Night of Broken Glass* where Nazis went berserk smashing the glass at Jewish shops, then rounding up the owners and beating them, and in some cases killing them.

Rothschilds financed **IBM**, who supply machines to the Nazis which produce punch cards to help organise and manage the initial identification and social expulsion of Jews, the confiscation of their property and their extermination.

IBM, like many other Rothschild funded front companies were never prosecuted after the war under the Trading with the Enemy Act.

Satanic symbol on the US $1 Bill from 1933

Other TRAITORS included Ford Motor Cars, Dunlop Tyres, and General Electric. For a full account of US companies that helped the Nazis, and got away with it, I highly recommend the video series **Corporatocracy**: by Antony C. Sutton (1980).

On November 16, **1933** President Roosevelt recognises the Zionist regime of Stalin in Russia without consultation with Congress, even as 8,000 Ukrainians march in protest in New York. In **1935**, President Roosevelt, born of a Jewish mother, therefore satisfying Ashkenazi rules of being Jewish, orders the Illuminati all-seeing eye to be placed upon the new US $1 bill, along with the motto, **Novus Ordo Seclorum**. This is Latin for, A New Order of the Ages or **New World Order**.

Nicholas Roerich (1874 – 1947)

It was actually his Vice President and 33° Freemason, **Henry A Wallace** that insisted on including the all-seeing eye and pyramid. Wallace was a hard-core occultist with a fascination with symbolism. The man he publicly referred to as his "guru" in all things Occult was the enigmatic Russian mystic, **Nicholas Roerich**, and it was he who first pointed out the significance of the all-seeing eye and pyramid.

Roerich, was a Russian mystic and occultist. He was also a painter, writer, archaeologist, theosophist, perceived by some in Russia as an enlightener, philosopher, and public figure, who in his youth was influenced by a movement in Russian society around the occult. He was interested in hypnosis and other spiritual practices and his paintings are said to have hypnotic expression. It is said he had a tremendous influence of his pupil Wallace.

This later became a public embarrassment to Wallace, but the damage was done. Many people wrongly believe a New World Order is coming, however, by placing their symbol on the $1 note in 1935, they were announcing to the world that they were already here, and now running the show in the United States at least.

This is the date when the United States had officially been usurped by foreign bankers. What were the American people thinking when they allowed this satanic symbol to be put on their money I will never understand.

The Weirdo Roosevelt Love Life

Roosevelt, in true "elite" style married his cousin and allowed the bombing of Pearl Harbour to take place, sacrificing thousands of young American sailors. He then used this false flag event to commit millions of boy Soldiers, Sailors, Air force, and Marines to World War II. Roosevelt was a joint player – i.e. part of the New World Order, as well as a practising Illuminist (Illuminati).

Eleanor Roosevelt

Lorena Hickok

Eleanor Roosevelt and her lesbian lover Lorena Hickok

His kissing cousin wife Eleanor Roosevelt was high up in the Illuminati – a **Mother of Darkness preistess** to be exact, and had a long term lesbian affair with **Lorena Hickok**.

They began their decades-long relationship in 1933, right before FDR's inauguration. Lorena, or Hick (as Eleanor called her) was a highly successful reporter, and Eleanor was about to become First Lady. They shared an emotional, sexual, and romantic relationship that peaked in passion and later developed into a friendship that endured until death.

The relationship these two women shared has been--not surprisingly--heavily censored over the years. While they lived, photographs of family dinners were cropped to remove Hick's image. If she was included in a photograph, she was not identified. And she was certainly not talked about, even to biographers. After Eleanor's death, Hick herself edited and retyped much of their X rated correspondence.

She burned some of Eleanor's letters and many of her own. After Hick's death, her sister Ruby read the original versions of their first year of correspondence and was horrified by the depravity and explicitly. She threw them in the fireplace, saying, "*This is nobody's business.*"

Even Doris Faber, author of **The Life of Lorena Hickok: ER's Friend** (Faber, 1980) was horrified by the correspondence. She tried to get the letters sealed from the public until after the year 2000, and when she couldn't do that, she decided to ignore content and reflect on the relationship.

The collection **Empty Without You: The Intimate Letters of Eleanor Roosevelt and Lorena Hickok**, published in 1998, gave the public a new glimpse into the life of one of America's most beloved and twisted First Ladies (Roosevelt, Hickok and Streitmatter, 2000). We do know that Eleanor was partial to Hick giving her a "hand," (or two) with closed fingers...let's leave it at that.

1934: Swiss banking secrecy laws are reformed and it becomes an offence resulting in imprisonment for any bank employee to violate bank secrecy. This is all in preparation for the Rothschild engineered Second World War in which, as usual, they will fund both sides.

Edmond de Rothschild dies aged 89 in Boulogne-Billancourt (France). His body was then laid to rest in Ramat HaNadiv (Israel).

1936: With regard to the increase in anti-Semitism in Germany, Samuel Landman (at the time, secretary to the World Zionist Organisation), in his 1936 book, Great Britain, The Jews, and Palestine states the following of the United States entry into World War 1:

> 	The fact that it was Jewish help that brought USA into the War on the side of the Allies has rankled ever since in Germany – especially Nazi minds, and has contributed in no small measure to the prominence which anti-Semitism occupies in the Nazi programme." (Landman, 1936)

1938: On 7th November, an Ashkenazi Jew, **Herschel Grynszpan**, assassinated **Ernst vom Rath**, a minor official at the German Embassy in Paris. As a result of this, German hostility towards Jews in Germany started to turn violent. This was yet again a False Flag event instigated by the Rothschilds, designed to anger the Germans.

The Rothschilds Austrian banking house in Vienna, S. M. von Rothschild und Söhne, closes following the Nazi occupation of Austria. This is part of the bluff.

1939: I.G. Farben, the leading producer of chemicals in the world and largest German producer of steel dramatically increases its production. This increased production is almost exclusively used to arm Germany for the Second World War. This company was controlled by the Rothschilds and would go on to use Jews and other disaffected peoples as slave labour in the concentration camps.

On 1 September, 1939, the Second World War starts when Germany invades Poland. World War I never really finished. It stopped only because of an armistice (cease fire). The Treaty of Versailles left Germany with a crippling debt, mathematically impossible to pay back, and was the perfect recipe to re-ignite hostilities. Germany was allowed enough time to re-arm, right under the noses of the Allies. In reality, all this was allowed to happen because the powers that be not only wanted to continue the war, but they felt the needed to. The new unified Germany was potentially too economically powerful and had to be taken down until the Rothschild could control it fully. Furthermore, they still had to fill up Israel will more Jews – not such an easy task at the moment.

1940: Hansjurgen Koehler in his book, **Inside The Gestapo**, states the following of Maria Anna Schicklgruber, Adolf Hitler's grandmother,

> *"A little servant girl...came to Vienna and became a domestic servant...at the Rothschild mansion ...and Hitler's unknown grandfather must be probably looked for in this magnificent house."* *(Koehler, 1940)*

Baron Amschel von Rothschild   Alois (Rothschild) Hitler   Adolf (Rothschild) Hitler

This is backed up by Walter Langer in his book, **The Mind of Hitler**, in which he states,

> *Adolf's father, Alois Hitler, was the illegitimate son of Maria Anna Schicklgruber... Maria Anna Schicklgruber was living in Vienna at the time she conceived. At that time she was employed as a servant in the home of Baron [Amschel Mayer von] Rothschild. As soon as the family discovered her pregnancy she was sent back home...where Alois was born.*

1941: President Roosevelt takes America into the Second World War by refusing to sell Japan any more steel scrap or oil. Japan was in the midst of a war against China and without that scrap steel and oil, Japan would be unable to continue that war. Japan was totally dependent upon the United States for both steel scrap and oil. Roosevelt knew this action would provoke the Japanese to attack America, which they subsequently did at Pearl Harbor. Roosevelt was informed days before the Pearl Harbour attack, that the Japanese were coming but did nothing, allowing the strike to take place.

1942: Prescott Bush, father of future American Presidents' George Herbert Walker and George W, has his company seized under the *Trading With The Enemy Act*. He was funding Hitler from America, whilst American soldiers were being killed by German soldiers. Jews are also being slaughtered by these same soldiers. Interestingly, the ADL (Anti-Defamation League) never criticises any of the Bush family for this.

1943: February 18th, Rothschild Zionist, **Izaak Greenbaum**, head of the Jewish Agency Rescue Committee, in a speech to the Zionist Executive Council states,

> *"If I am asked, could you give from the UJA (United Jewish Appeal) monies to rescue Jews, I say, no and I say again no!" He would go onto state, "One cow in Palestine is worth more than all the Jews in Poland!"*

This is not a surprise, the whole idea of Zionist support for the slaughter of innocent Jews was to scare the survivors into believing that their only place of safety was Israel. How else do you think the Zionists could ensure Jews would leave the beautiful European cities in which they live, in order to settle in a dusty old desert!

1944: On 6 November **Lord Moyne**, British Minister Resident in the Middle East was assassinated in Cairo by two members of the Jewish

IMF and World Bank Group Meetings

terrorist group, the **Stern Gang**, led by future Prime Minister of Israel, **Yitzhak Shamir**. He is also responsible for an assassination attempt against **Harold MacMichael**, the High Commissioner of the British Mandate of Palestine, this same year. Interestingly, he also masterminds another successful assassination this year against the United Nations representative in the Middle East, **Count Folke Bernadotte** who, although he had secured the release of 21,000 prisoners from German camps during World War II, was seen by Yitzak Shamir and his terrorist collaborators as an anti-Zionist.

In **Bretton Woods**, New Hampshire (USA), two further Rothschild world banks are created. The **International Monetary Fund** (IMF), and the **World Bank**.

The World Bank gives ridiculous loans to Third World countries or poorer countries, knowing full well they will not be able to make the repayments. When the country defaults on its World Bank loan, they make the country an offer: Give us your national assets - companies and resources, e.g. State run Electricity Company, Water Company, Telephone Company, mines, water etc. or we will come in by force and take over the country.

They are forced to privatise these government departments, further restricting them from earning money to pay back the bank, and all their assets go into private, Rothschild hands. This is still going on today in Greece, Spain, Portugal, and Ireland to name but a few.

In any country in the world where you see a push to sell State owned assets, you know it is the Rothschilds behind it.

1945: The end of the Second World War. It is reported that I.G. Farben plants were specifically not targeted in the bombing raids on Germany. Amazingly at the end of the war, they were found to have only sustained 15% damage. The tribunals held at the end of the Second World War to investigate Nazi War Crimes, censored any materials recording Western assistance to Hitler.

The Rothschilds take a giant step towards their goal of world domination when the second, League of Nations, called the **United Nations**, was approved this year. The United Nations headquarters in New York City sits on 6.5 Ha / 16 acres of land purchased with an $8 million donation made in 1946 by **John D. Rockefeller Jr**, a bloodline stooge of the Rothschilds.

1946: On July 22, the future Prime Minister of Israel, Rothschild Zionist **David Ben-Gurion**, orders another future Prime Minister of Israel, Rothschild Zionist, **Menachem Begin**, to carry out a terrorist attack on the King David Hotel in Palestine, to try and drive out the British. As a result of this, 91 people were killed, most of them civilians: 28 British, 41 Arabs, 17 Jews, and 5 others. Around 45 people are injured.

Menachem Begin went on to proudly proclaim himself as, "*the father of modern terrorism.*" Just to put the gravity of the attack on the King David Hotel into perspective, it was at the time the biggest death toll as a result of single terrorist action ever and was only surpassed over 40 years later by the Bombing of Pan Am flight 103 over Lockerbie.

1947: The British, who prior to World War II declared that there would be no more immigration of Jews to Palestine in order to protect the Palestinians from their acts of terror against both them and British soldiers, transfer control of Palestine to the United Nations. The United Nations resolve to have Palestine partitioned into two states, one Zionist and one Arab, with Jerusalem to remain as an international zone to be enjoyed by all religious faiths.

This transfer was scheduled to take place on May 15, 1948. The United Nations had no right, or no mandate to give Arab property to anyone. At the time the Jews owned 6% of Palestine, however **Resolution 181** granted the Rothschild Zionist 57% of the land, leaving the Arabs who at that time had 94% with only 43%.

1948: In the Spring of this year, the Rothschilds bribe President Harry S. Truman (33rd President of the United States 1945 – 1953) to

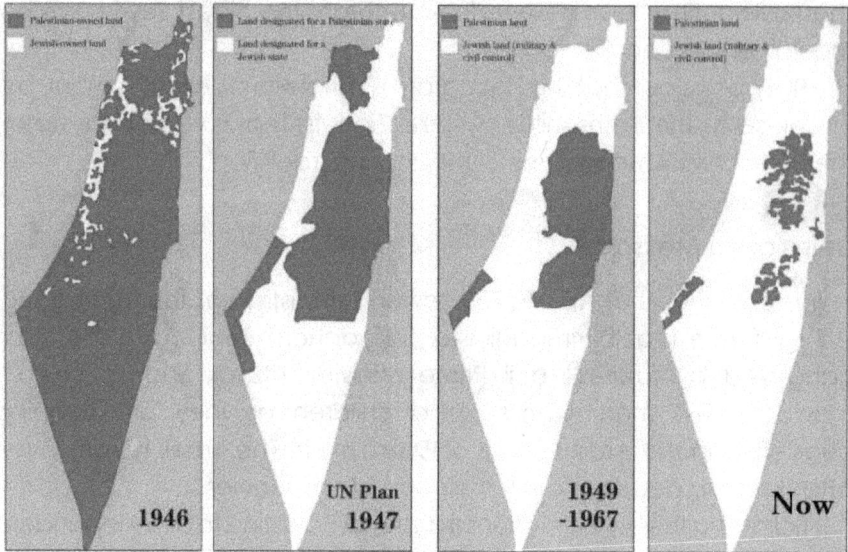

Israeli land theft from 1946 to 2015 (Palestinian owned land is dark / Jewish land theft is white)

recognise Israel (Fiefdom of Rothschild) as a sovereign state with a $2,000,000 bribe (worth $20,000,000 in today's money). Truman the gutless, greedy snake accepts the bribe. The Zionist then declare Israel to be a sovereign Jewish state in Palestine and within half an hour of receiving the money, President Truman declared the United States to be the first foreign nation to recognise it.

The Flag of Israel is unveiled. Despite tremendous opposition from non-Zionist Jews, the emblem on the flag is a blue coloured version of the Rothschild, "Red Hexagram Sign." This angers many Jews who realise this Hexagram was used in the ancient mystery religions as the symbol of **Moloch**, (described as a demon that demands child sacrifice and is also the name of the stone owl the elite worship at Bohemian Grove).

Flag of Israel - Flag of Rothschild - Flag of Zionist – The Satanic Seal of Solomon

The Hexagram was also used to represent Saturn, which has been identified as the esoteric name for Satan. This indicates that anyone killed in the name of Israel is actually a sacrifice to Satan.

These dissenting Jews believe the **Menorah**, the oldest Jewish symbol should be used on the flag.

They point out that the Hexagram is not even a Jewish symbol, but of course as the Rothschilds own the Zionists, that is what ends up on the Rothschild, I mean Zionist, I mean, the Israeli flag.

Deir Yassin Massacre

In the early hours of April 9, 132 Jewish terrorists from the **Irgun gang**, led by future Israeli Prime Minister Menachem Begin, and the Stern gang, led by future Israeli Prime Minister Yitzhak Shamir, brutally massacre 260 men, women and children as they are sleeping peacefully in the Arab village of **Deir Yassin**. The Israeli hordes even attacked the dead to satisfy their bestial tendencies.

Following the United Nations transfer of Palestine to an independent Jewish State and an independent Arab state on May 15, the Israelis launched a military assault on the Arabs with blaring loudspeakers on their trucks informing the Arabs that if they did not flee immediately, they would be slaughtered.

800,000 Arabs with the recent memory of the Deir Yassin massacre at the forefront of their minds, fled in panic. They asked for help from neighbouring Arab states, but those states did not get involved as they were no match for the Israelis, whose up to date military hardware had been supplied by the Jewish Stalinist regime in Russia. Following this assault, the Jews now controlled 78% of the former Palestine as oppose to the 57% that had been given to them illegally by the United Nations. They stole an extra 21% of the land, and the number keeps going up. The Zionist Jews will not stop until they occupy 100% of Palestine, and eliminate or enslave all the true Semites. But their ultimate goal is to own, and control **The Levant**, an old Biblical term which includes Cyprus, Israel, Jordan, Lebanon, Palestine, Syria, Turkey, and the Hatay Province. Notice which country the US has taken out, or is trying to take out?

The Palestinians, many of them Christians, were never paid compensation for their homes, property, and businesses stolen from them during this illegal Jewish assault, and these people ended up in slum refugee cities of tents. Furthermore, at least half of the Palestinians in their hurry to flee left their birth certificates behind. The State of Israel / Fiefdom of Rothschild then passed a law that only those who could

Palestinian refugees

prove citizenship were allowed to return to Israel, meaning these 400,000 Palestinians could not return and lost all their property they had left there.

Are you beginning to understand why the Palestinians throw stones and fire bottle rockets at Israel? Do you see why young Palestinians who have lost everything, and have nothing to live for, strap bombs to their bodies and blow up an Israeli bus, along with themselves? Palestine is now nothing more than an open air concentration camp. Meanwhile, the United Nations paper tiger does nothing.

What these pretend Jews are doing in Palestine is genocide, in the very literal sense of that word –

"Genocide: the deliberate killing of a large group of people, especially those of a particular nation or ethnic group."

And the world does nothing. No one can go to the United Nations because the Ashkenazi Jews run the US, and the US have veto power to quash any criticism of Israel. The Ashkenazi Jewish run media only tell lies to make themselves out to be the victims. When Palestinian teenagers fire bottle rockets, Israel responds with tanks and air strikes.

Do you really think this is fair? If this was any other country in the world there would be an outcry. But instead, Palestinian children go hungry, sleep in holes in the ground, watch their parents and siblings get blown up, or shot to pieces.

Israel have bombed their schools, hospitals, and homes. Every week, Israel bulldoze Palestinian homes so they can build Jewish homes on top of the rubble. And why? Because of some idiotic, childish, ancient vendetta.

Rothschild Zionist, David Ben-Gurion, one of the founding fathers of Israel and its first Prime Minister, candidly describes Zionist aims in his diary (21 May 1948) as follows,

> *The Achilles heel of the Arab coalition is the Lebanon. Muslim supremacy in this country is artificial and can easily be overthrown. A Christian State ought to be set up there, with its southern frontier on the river Litani. We would sign a treaty of alliance with this State. Thus when we have broken the strength of the Arab Legion and bombed Amman, we could wipe out Trans-Jordan, after that Syria would fall. And if Egypt still dared to make war on us, we would bomb Port Said, Alexandria, and Cairo. We should thus end the war and would have but paid to Egypt, Assyria, and Chaldea on behalf of our ancestors.*

The world really needs to rally to the Palestinian cause. At the very least, all land from the United Nations treaty of 1947 should be returned to them immediately. The Palestinians should be financially compensated, just like the Jews that were kicked out of Germany in World War II.

Germany and Switzerland have paid out over **$14 billion** in compensation to European Jews that were injured or displaced during WWII. How about Israel afford the Palestinians the same courtesy? Finally, given Israel's long and brutal history of terrorism, they should be immediately disarmed of nuclear weapons. I would certainly feel a lot safer knowing these psychopaths can't "press the button."

Melbourne, Australia Gaza Protest, 2015

Mao Zedong
(1893-1976)

1949: On October 1, **Mao Tse-tung** (Zedong) declares the founding of the People's Republic of China in Tiananmen Square, Beijing. He is funded by Rothschild created Communism in Russia and also the following Rothschild agents: **Solomon Adler**, a former United States Treasury official who was a Soviet Spy; **Israel Epstein**, the son of a Jewish Bolshevik imprisoned by the Tsar in Russia for trying to foment a revolution there; and **Frank Coe**, a leading official of the Rothschild owned IMF.

1950: Israel passes their law of return, guaranteeing every Jew worldwide the right to dwell in the state of Israel, however the Palestinians, even though they had lived there for 1300 years, were denied that right.

John Davitt, former chief of the Justice Department's internal security section, notes that the Israeli intelligence service is the second most active in the United States, after the Soviets, and of course, both Israel and the Soviet Union are run by Rothschild Zionist leadership.

1951: On 1 April, the Israeli Secret Intelligence Agency the **Mossad**, which will go on to terrorize the world, is formed. The motto of the Mossad is probably the most disgusting secret service motto in the world being: "*By Way Of Deception, Thou Shalt Do War.*"

1953: N. M. Rothschild & Sons found the British Newfoundland Corporation Limited to develop 60,000 square miles of land in Newfoundland, Canada, which comprised a power station to harness the power of the Hamilton (later renamed Churchill) Falls. At the time this was the largest construction project ever to be undertaken by a private company.

1954: The **Lavon Affair**: Israeli agents recruit Egyptian citizens of Jewish descent, to bomb Western targets in Egypt, and plant evidence to frame Arabs, in an apparent attempt to upset American/Egyptian relations (False Flag). Israeli Defence Minister, Rothschild Zionist, **Pinhas Lavon** is eventually removed from office, though many know that terrorist leader and now Prime Minister David Ben-Gurion is responsible.

A hidden microphone planted by the Israelis is discovered in the Office of the US Ambassador in Tel Aviv.

1955: Edmond de Rothschild founds Compagnie Financiere, Paris.

1956: Telephone taps are found connected to two telephones in the residence of the US military attaché in Tel Aviv.

1957: James de Rothschild dies and it is reported (by the Rothschild owned media) that he bequeaths a large sum of money to the state of Israel to pay for the construction of their parliament building, the **Knesset**. He states that the Knesset should be,

> *a symbol, in the eyes of all men, of the permanence of the State of Israel.*

On page 219 of his book, ***Tales of the British Aristocracy***, **L.G. Pine**, the Editor of **Burke's Peerage**, states that the Jews,

> *Have made themselves so closely connected with the British peerage that the two classes are unlikely to suffer loss which is not mutual. So closely linked are the Jews and the lords that a blow against the Jews in this country would not be possible without injuring the aristocracy also. (Pine, 1956)*

Maurice de Rothschild dies in Paris.

1962: de Rothschild Frères establishes Imétal, as an umbrella company for all their mineral mining interests.

Frederic Morton publishes his book, *The Rothschilds*, in which he states,

> *Though they control scores of industrial, commercial, mining and tourist corporations, not one bears the name Rothschild. Being private partnerships, the family houses never need to, and never do, publish a single public balance sheet, or any other report of their financial condition. (Morton, 1962)*

This attitude reveals the true aim of the Rothschilds, to eliminate all competition and create their own worldwide monopoly,

President John F. Kennedy (1917-1963)

secretly behind the curtain. Remember the MOSSAD logo *By Way Of Deception, Thou Shalt Do War.*

1963: On June 4th, President John F. Kennedy (the 35th President of the United States 1961 – 1963) signs **Executive Order 11110** which returned to the U.S. government the power to issue currency, without going through the Rothschild's owned Federal Reserve. Less than 6 months later on November 22nd , president Kennedy is assassinated by the Rothschilds for the same reason as they assassinated President Abraham Lincoln in 1865 - he wanted to print American money for the American people with no interest or tax, as oppose to, for the benefit of a money grabbing, warmongering, foreign elite.

This Executive Order 11110, is rescinded by **President Lyndon Baines Johnson** (the 36th President of the United States 1963 to 1969) on Air Force One from Dallas to Washington, **the same day** as President Kennedy was assassinated.

Johnston had full knowledge that Kennedy was to be assassinated, and even held an early "victory" party the night before. Many of those who attended spoke out about how he bragged he would be the next President, sooner than everybody thought he would. Another, and probably the primary reason for Kennedy's assassination is however, the fact that he made it quite clear to Israeli Prime Minister, David Ben-Gurion, that under no circumstances would he agree to Israel becoming a nuclear state. If you are interested in who, how, and why Kennedy was assassinated, I strongly recommend the excellent documentary *The Men Who Killed Kennedy* (1988).

*"In the case of John F.
Kennedy, the assassination
was carried out with great
attendant publicity and
with the utmost brutality to
serve as a warning to world
leaders not to get out of
line. Pope John Paul I was
quietly murdered because*
he was getting close to the Committee of 300 through Freemasons in
the Vatican hierarchy. His successor, Pope John Paul II, was publicly
humiliated as a warning to cease and desist – which he has done..."*
   – DR JOHN COLEMAN, CONSPIRATORS' HIERARCHY:
   THE COMMITTEE OF 300

The Israeli newspaper **Ha'aretz** on February 5, 1999, in a review of,
Avner Cohen's book, *Israel and the Bomb*, states the following,

> The murder of American President John
> F. Kennedy brought to an abrupt end to the
> massive pressure being applied by the U.S.
> administration on the government of Israel
> to discontinue the nuclear program...The book
> implied that, had Kennedy remained alive, it
> is doubtful whether Israel would today
> have a nuclear option.

Edmond de Rothschild establishes *La Compagnie Financière Edmond
de Rothschild* (LCF), in Switzerland as a venture capital house. This later
develops into an investment bank and asset management company
with many affiliates. He also marries his wife Nadine and they have a
son, **Benjamin de Rothschild.**

   1965: Israel illegally obtains enriched uranium from NUMEC (Nuclear
Materials and Equipment Corporation).

   1967: The treatment of the Palestinians by the Zionist Jews, finally ignites
enough anger in the Arab world for Egypt, Jordan, and Syria to mobilize on
Israel's borders. All of these three countries are suddenly attacked by Israel
and as a result, the Sinai, which included Gaza, was stolen from Egypt,
and the West Bank and the Jordan River stolen from Jordan.

USS Liberty attached by Israeli fighter jets

USS Liberty Attacked by Israel

As a result of this, on June 8, the Israelis launch an attack on the **USS Liberty** with Israeli aircraft and motor torpedo boats in an effort to blame it on Egypt, and to bring America into the war on their side (false flag). Of course to do this, they must follow to the letter their Mossad motto, **By Way Of Deception, Thou Shalt Do War.** As a result of their attack, 34 American servicemen were killed and 174 wounded. Israel lies as usual, claiming it mistook this warship that was flying a large United States flag, for an ancient, out-of-service Egyptian horse carrier, *El Quseir,* that was 180 feet shorter. They also claim the ship was in the war zone, when it was actually in international waters, far from any fighting.

The Israeli's attack on this warship lasts for 75 minutes during which time they shoot up one of the United States flags, resulting in the sailors desperately raising another one.

In the aftermath of this attack, the American sailors who survived are warned by the United States military not to discuss the matter with anyone due to, "national security."

This story gets no prominence in the Rothschild controlled mainstream media and as usual, Israel is in no way even rebuked for their crimes by their subservient country America. Imagine if North Korea suddenly, and without provocation, attacked a United States Navy ship? What do you think the US would do?

The following day, June 9th, Israel illegally occupies the **Golan Heights** which it seizes from **Syria**. This area goes on to provide Israel with one third of its fresh water. Israeli General **Matityahu Peled**, is quoted in Ha'aretz (19 March 1972) with the following statement,

> **"** *The thesis that the danger of genocide was hanging over us in June 1967 and that Israel was fighting for its physical existence is only bluff, which was born and developed after the war.* **"**

Another sickening and deceptive statement, but again at least he's consistent with the Mossad motto, *By Way Of Deception, Thou Shalt Do War*.

de Rothschild Frères is renamed **Banque Rothschild**.

1968: Noémie Halphen, wife of Maurice de Rothschild dies. But this author, **Danny Searle** is born, and makes it his life's purpose to wake up humanity and usher them into a **Golden Age of Spiritual Enlightenment**.

USS Liberty survivors trying to get the truth out

THE CAREER OF A ROTHSCHILD FRONT MAN
RICHARD PERLE

*Richard Perle is the type of guy that makes your skin crawl. He is a pathological liar, cheat, thief, traitor, and con man, yet he has been granted a life of material wealth and comfort. How is this possible? It is very simple. Perle, like many of his colleges in the New World Order, are prepared to sell their souls, betray their people, their country, and their families, all for power and money. I know I should not single out Richard, for he is only doing what he has been trained to do, and been allowed to get away with. However, this vile man's career, is a text book example of the typical Rothschild's, New World Order front men, and what they do. Not to mention, he was a great friend of **George W Bush**, who kept him close, and listen to Perle's "advice." That advice led to the second invasion of Iraq and the loss of thousands of innocent lives. You can easily judge the character of a man by the company he keeps - hey Georgie boy!*

RICHARD PERLE

*1970: While working for Senator Henry "Scoop" Jackson, Ashkenazi Jew and Rothschild front man **Richard Perle** is caught by the **FBI** giving classified information to Israel. Nothing is done. No charges are laid.*

*1978: While working with the **Senate Armed Services Committee**, Perle was caught in a security breach by **CIA** director **Stansfield Turner**. Although Turner urged **Senator Jackson** to fire him, Perle received a warning and was kept on staff. No charges are laid.*

*1981 to 1987, Perle was **Assistant Secretary of Defence** for international security policy in the **Reagan** administration. In a **New York Times** article, Perle was criticised for recommending that the Army purchase an armaments system from an **Israeli** company that a year earlier had paid him $50,000 in consulting fees. No charges are laid.*

*1996: During the **Clinton** administration, Perle lead a study group with **Douglas Feith** and **David Wurmser** who produced a report on balancing power in the Middle East, specifically in Israel's favour. Perle argued that the removal of **Saddam Hussein** from power in Iraq should be a key objective for the Israeli state.*

*2001: George W. Bush appointed Perle chairman of the **Defence Policy Board Advisory Committee**, which advises the **Department of Defence**. Perle stood to profit financially by influencing government policy, which would allow him to profit from a war in Iraq. He was under pressure for conflict of interests charges but managed to deflect them for several years.*

THE CAREER OF A ROTHSCHILD FRONT MAN RICHARD PERLE

Former US Vice President **Dick Cheney** *was in charge of the September 11, 2001 "False flag" operation (9/11) in the United States along with help from Donald Rumsfeld, Paul Wolfowitz, Richard Perle, General Richard Myers, Rudy Giuliani, Larry Silverstein, and other members of the Zionist community, especially in New York (Fetzer, 2015).*

2003: While chairman of the **Defence Policy Board**, *Perle was caught red handed accepting bribes and doing under the table deals with China. Perle was forced to resign as chairman, though he remained on the board. No legal action is taken against him.*

2004: As Director of **Hollinger International**, *Perle received over $3 million in bonuses on top of his salary, bringing the total to $5.4 million. A U.S. Securities and Exchange Commission (SEC) report singled out Perl as having breached his fiduciary responsibilities as a company director. The investigating committee called for him to return the money. To date, he has not returned any money. No charges are laid.*

2006: As a member of the Cambridge, Massachusetts-based consulting firm **Monitor Group**, *Perle was an advisor to Libyan dictator* **Muammar al-Gaddafi**. *Perle travelled to Libya with several other advisers to hold lectures and workshops, and promote the image of Libya and its ruler. It was really to gain Intel (spy) to find out how the US (Dick Cheney) could take Gaddafi down. Gaddafi was murdered in 2011 under orders from Dick Cheney.*

2008: Perle invested heavily in oil interests in Iraq, in collaboration with Iraqi Kurdish leaders in northern Iraq. He used his "contacts" from the Gulf War to source the most lucrative oil wells (Perle, 2015).

Richard Perle is a classic white collar criminal. He is a habitual liar, cheat, thief, thug, war monger, and all round bad person. Yet, he is part of a system that encourages this type of behaviour. Perle is in no way unique, however his example is used to highlight how things work on **Capitol Hill** *and the* **White House**. *In a different situation, he could easily be a bigwig for the Mafia or organised crime. But because he works for the Rothschilds, he gets away with all manner of crime. One final note, Perle has expressed support for a theoretical first strike, using* **thermonuclear weapons** *on* **North Korean** *and* **Iranian** *nuclear facilities. Remember back to the beginning of this chapter which countries do not have a Rothschilds Central Bank in them. This man is not a Jew, he is not an American, and he is not an Israeli. This man is a Zionist Rothschild Front Man, loyal to that cause only, and that is what makes him so frightening. He would start WWIII for $1.*

None Dare Call It Conspiracy

1970: British Prime Minister **Edward Heath**, who by the way is now a known paedophile of the highest order, makes **Lord Victor Rothschild** the head of his policy unit. Whilst he is in that role, Britain enters the European Community.

1972: In his book, which I highly recommend, *None Dare Call It Conspiracy*, Gary Allen, a true hero of the people states,

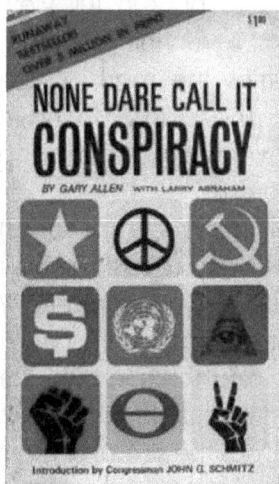

"One major reason for the historical blackout on the role of the international bankers in political history is the Rothschilds were Jewish...The Jewish members of the conspiracy have used an organisation called The Anti-Defamation League (ADL) as an instrument to try and convince everyone that any mention of the Rothschilds and their allies is an attack on all Jews. In this way they have stifled almost all honest scholarship on international bankers and made the subject taboo within universities. Any individual or book exploring this subject is immediately attacked by hundreds of ADL communities all over the country. The ADL has never let the truth or logic interfere with its highly professional smear jobs. Actually, nobody has a right to be more angry at the Rothschild clique than their fellow Jews...The Rothschild Empire helped finance Adolf Hitler." (Allen, 1972)

Universal Product Code

1973: George J. Laurer, an employee of the Rothschilds controlled IBM Company, invents the **UPC** (Universal Product Code) barcode which will eventually be placed upon every item traded worldwide and bear the number, **666**.

The Book of Revelation, Chapter 13, Verse 17 through 18, states the following in relation to this number,

And that no man might buy or sell, save he that had the mark, or the name of the beast, or the number of his name. Here is wisdom. Let him that hath understanding count the number of the beast: for it is the number of a man; and his number is Six hundred threescore and six.

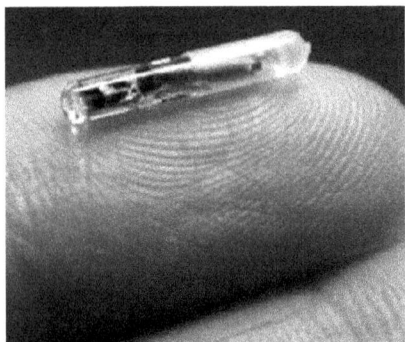

The whole satanic aims of the Rothschilds are now in full view of the world, everything bought or sold carries the mark of the beast, 666. The plan is to have this UPC eventually embedded into a micro-chip.

They will persuade (or force) all humans (regardless of their social status) to be implanted/ marked with a microchip (into their right arm/hand or into their heads); so that no one can buy or sell without using the microchip or the microchip's code for shopping.

This technology is already available, and about the size of a grain of rice, but will eventually be even smaller.

A Swedish company is forcing its employees to have the implant just so they can use special security doors and operate the photocopier. It also talks with the cell phones and can transfer data and contact information. It is being sold as "convenient" and "safe" and pushed as "cool".(Reuters, 2015)

It will store all of your financial records, health records, school records, driver's licence, gun registration, job applications, current work status, and what type of work you are recommended for (ABC News, 2015).

If you protest the government/system in any way, they can turn the chip off. This means you cannot buy or sell, get medical help, travel, or get a job. They intend to have a cashless society, so people will have no option but to have a chip.

Aaron Russo (February 14, 1943 - August 24, 2007), a true hero of the people, is best known for producing the movies *Trading Places*, *Wise Guys*, and *The Rose*. Later in life he created the documentaries **Mad as Hell**, which calls into question the current state of governmental affairs and *America: Freedom to Fascism*, which investigates the breadth of the Sixteenth Amendment to the United States Constitution, the IRS, and the Federal Reserve System. After a six year battle with bladder cancer, Russo died on August 24, 2007.

About 11 months before 9/11, Aaron Russo spent time with **Nicholas Rockefeller** who admitted that the elite's goal is to microchip the world's entire population in order to control and enslave everyone. He also revealed that the events on 9/11 and the so called 'War on Terror' was a complete fraud in order to achieve their goals (Russo, 2001).

1974: N. M. Rothschild & Sons British Newfoundland Corporation, Churchill Falls project in Newfoundland, Canada, is completed. N. M. Rothschild & Sons also create a new asset management part of the company which traded worldwide. This eventually became, **Rothschild Private Management Limited.**

Edmond de Rothschild, a great-grandson of Jacob (James) Mayer Rothschild, bought the *Cru Bourgeois estate of Château Clarke* in Bordeaux.

Château Clarke in Bordeaux, France owned by Edmond de Rothschild

THE HAROLD WALLACE ROSENTHAL INTERVIEW

1976: *In a highly confidential, 17 page interview conducted by Charles A. Weisman, is basically a confession by an insider to the globalist - Zionist elite. This classic interview is one of the "must have" pieces for the library of the NWO investigator. It gives insights into the thinking of the* **Committee of 300**, *and the* **Black Nobility** *generally.*

Ashkenazi Jew, **Harold Rosenthal**, *aide to Rothschild Zionist,* **Senator Jacob Javits**, *who admittedly had a few whiskies under his belt before he just let loose states,*

"Most Jews do not like to admit it, but our god is Lucifer."

As a Jewish administrative assistant to one of America's high ranking senators, Rosenthal continues:

"It is a marvel that the American people do not rise up and drive every Jew out of this country."

Mr. Harold Wallace Rosenthal made this statement after admitting Jewish dominance in all significant national programs. He said,

"We Jews continue to be amazed with the ease by which Christian Americans have fallen into our hands. While the naive Americans wait for Khrushchev to bury them, we have taught them to submit to our every demand."

Asked how a nation could be captured without their knowing it, Mr. Rosenthal attributed this victory to absolute control of the media. He boasted of Jewish control of **all news**. *Any newspaper which refused to acquiesce to controlled news was brought to its knees by withdrawing advertising. Failing in this, the Jews stop the supply of news print and ink. "It's a very simple matter," he stated. Asked about men in high political office, Mr Rosenthal said that no one in the last three decades has achieved any political power without Jewish approval.*

"Americans have not had a presidential choice since 1932. Roosevelt was our man; every president since Roosevelt has been our man."

If you remember back, this is the year they announce their **New World Order** *on the US $1 note. While I do not believe it to be a "Jewish" conspiracy, it is without doubt a Rothschild Zionist conspiracy.*

THE HAROLD WALLACE ROSENTHAL INTERVIEW

Mr. Harold Wallace Rosenthal, age 29, was assassinated by Rothschild agents (Mossad) during a fake PLO sky-jacking attempt on an Israeli airliner in Istanbul, Turkey, August 12, 1976, after this interview went public (Rosenthal, 1976).

*He had to be shut up. This type of "truth" could ruin everything, and all their plans from **The Protocols of the Elders of Zion**.*

Although Harold Wallace Rosenthal is pretending to be a Jew, he is actually a Rothschild Zionist, so one should use the word Zionists wherever Harold Rosenthal says Jews.

The original Mossad motto is: "By way of deception, thou shalt do war." Is certainly apt in both his assignation and his interview. Deception = lies. Satan is the father of all lies. Sort of ties in when you think about it...The full 17 page document is available at: (Weisman, 1976).

THE HIDDEN TYRANNY

THE ISSUE THAT DWARFS ALL OTHER ISSUES

This is the Most Sensational Manuscript of Its Kind. *Also known as:*

"The Rosenthal Document"

1978: Rothschild Zionist, **Stephen Bryen**, then a **Senate Foreign Relations Committee** staffer, is overheard in a Washington D.C. hotel offering confidential documents to top **Israeli** military officials. Bryen obtains a lawyer, **Nathan Lewin**, and the case heads for the grand jury, but is mysteriously dropped. Bryen later goes to work for **Richard Perle**. No charges were laid.

1979: The Egyptian-Israeli peace treaty in 1979 was underwritten by United States aid which pledged **$3 billion annually to Israel** from the United States taxpayer. In 2015, Israel is still receiving this $3 billion in taxpayer funded money. Meanwhile, US veterans can't get health-care.

Shin Bet (the Israeli internal security agency) tries to penetrate the **US Consulate General** in Jerusalem through a "Honey Trap," using a clerical employee who was having an affair with a Jerusalem girl.

Baron and Baroness Phillipi de Rothschild in a joint venture with **Robert Mondavi**, begin the construction of a pyramid in Napa Valley, California, where the leader/founder of the **Church Of Satan**, Rothschild Zionist, **Anton LaVey**, was based. This is known as **Opus 1** (which means, the first work), and the front for this temple is masked as a winery. Inside (underground) is one of the main Illuminati sacrificial temples where regular human sacrifices, *Eye Wide Shut* type parties and satanic worship are performed regularly.

1980: The global phenomenon of privatisation starts. The Rothschilds are behind this from the very beginning in order to seize control of all publicly owned assets worldwide.

1981: Banque Rothschild is nationalised by the French government. The new bank is called, **Compagnie Européenne de Banque**. The Rothschilds subsequently set up a successor to this French bank, **Rothschild & Cie Banque** (RCB), which goes on to become a leading French investment house.

Opus 1 – one of the main Illuminati sacrificial temples

1982: From September 16 to 18, future Prime Minister of Israel and then Defence Minister, Rothschild Zionist, **Ariel Sharon**, orchestrates Israel's invasion of **Lebanon**, which provided aerial lighting in order to facilitate the killing of **3,500 civilians**, mostly Palestinians and Lebanese Shiites, men, women and children. It became known as the *Sabra and Shatila massacre.*

1985: Eustace Mullins, a true hero of the people, publishes, *Who Owns the TV Networks*, in which he reveals the Rothschilds have control of all three major U.S. Networks, which are: NBC; CBS; and ABC. Since then **Fox**, owned by Rothschild Zionist, Rupert Murdoch, has hit the lead of US TV networks.

The **New York Times** reports the **FBI** is aware of at least a dozen incidents in which American officials transferred classified information to the **Israelis**, quoting (former Assistant Director of the F.B.I.) **Raymond Wannal**. The Justice Department does not prosecute. No charges were laid.

Richard Smyth, the owner of **MILCO**, is indicted on charges of smuggling nuclear timing devices to **Israel**.

N. M. Rothschild & Sons advise the British government on the privatisation of **British Gas**. They subsequently advise the British government on virtually all of their other privatisations of state owned assets including: British Steel; British Coal; all the British regional electricity boards; and all the British regional water boards.

A British MP heavily involved in these privatisations is future **Chancellor of the Exchequer** (equivalent to the President of the Federal Reserve), **Norman Lamont**, a former Rothschild banker.

Mordechai Vanunu
(1954 -) – A True Hero

1986: Mordechai Vanunu, a true hero, and technician at **Dimona**, Israel's nuclear installation, from 1976 to 1985, discovers that the plant was secretly producing nuclear weapons. His conscience made him speak out and in 1986, he provided the **London Sunday Times** with the facts and photos they used to tell the world about Israel's nuclear weapons programme. His evidence showed that Israel had stockpiled up to **200 nuclear warheads**, with no debate or authorisation from its own citizens.

On 30th September 1986, Vanunu was lured from London to Rome. There he was kidnapped, drugged, and shipped to Israel. After a secret trial, he was sentenced to 18 years for, "treason," and, "espionage," (something Israel is very familiar with) though he had received no payment and had communicated with no foreign power. He goes on to be held in complete isolation for 11 years, only allowed occasional visits from his family, lawyer and a priest, conducted through a metal screen. Although he completes his sentence, the Israeli government continues to hold him against his will. Once again, shame on Israel, shame.

1987: Edmond de Rothschild creates the **World Conservation Bank** which is designed to transfer debts from Third World countries to this bank and in return, those countries would give land and natural resources to this bank. This is designed so the Rothschilds can gain control of the Third World which represents 30% of the land surface of the Earth. And that is the thing. The Rothschilds, and the Black Nobility, are land owners. They have all the gold and money, but what they really want is land. Lots, and lots of land.

On April 24 the **Wall Street Journal** reveals the, "*Role of Israel in Iran-Contra Scandal Won't be explored in Detail by Panels*" (Britton, 1955).

1988: The ADL initiate a nationwide competition for law students to draft anti-hate legislation for minority groups. That competition is won by a man named **Joseph Ribakoff**, whose thesis proposes that not only must hate motivated violence be banned, but also any words which stimulate: suspicion; friction; hate; and possible violence, these must also be criminalised. This ADL prize-winning paper suggests that not only should state-agencies monitor and restrict free speech in general, but they should also censor all films that criticise identifiable groups. Furthermore, even if the person making the statement can justify it, for example Christians criticising Satan worshippers because the bible expressly forbids it, Ribakoff asserts that the truth is to be no defence in court.

The only proof a court will need in order to secure a conviction of hate speech, is that something has been said, and a minority group or member of such group has felt emotionally damaged as a result of such criticism. Therefore, under these proposals which the ADL will have forced into law all over the world less than 15 years later, Jesus would have been arrested as a hate criminal. This law is designed to protect the Rothschild conspiracy from being revealed in that if you criticise the Rothschilds criminal cabal, you will be targeted as anti-Semitic, and thus risk imprisonment. I wonder if the Jews in Gaza who regularly call Arabs "dogs" and "pigs" will be charged?

Philippe de Rothschild, the man who built **Opus 1** dies.

1989: Many of the satellite states in Eastern Europe, through the influence of **Glasnost**, become more open in their demands of freedom from Communist governance in their Republics. Many revolutions happen in 1989, most of them involving the overthrow of their respective Communist governments and the replacement of them with Republics. Thus, the hold the Communists had over Eastern Europe (the Iron Curtain) becomes very weak. Eventually, as a result of **Perestroika** and Glasnost, Communism collapses, not only in the Soviet Union but also in Eastern Europe.

In Russia, **Boris Yeltsin** (whose wife is the daughter of Joseph Stalin's marriage to Rosa Kaganovich) and the Republican government, takes steps to end the power of the Communist party by suspending and banning the party and seizing all their property. This symbolised the fall of Communism in Russia, and resulted in the start of a mass exodus of 700,000 Jews from the former Soviet Union to Israel. That is because Communism was a Rothschild Zionist creation which they controlled for years.

In the Israeli Journal, **Hotam** (24 November 1989), there is a report of a speech that then Israeli Deputy Foreign Minister, Rothschild Zionist, **Binyamin Netanyahu**, gave to students at Bar Ilan University in which he states,

> *"Israel should have exploited the repression of the demonstrations in China, when world attention focused on that country, to carry out mass expulsions among the Arabs of the territories."*

The London and Paris Rothschilds announce the launch of a new subsidiary, **Rothschild GmbH**, in Frankfurt, Germany.

Highway of Death - victim burnt to death while fleeing

Gulf War I – Massacre in the Desert

1991: Following the Iraqi invasion of Kuwait on August 2, 1990, on January 16 of this year the United States and Britain began an aerial bombing campaign of targets within Iraq. On 24 February, the ground campaign commenced which was to last 100 hours until on February 28 when a horrendous war crime occurred.

This crime was the slaughter of **150,000 Iraqi troops** with Napalm[11] bombs. These Iraqis were fleeing on a crowded highway from Kuwait to Basra. President **George Herbert Walker Bush** ordered United States military aircraft and ground units to kill these surrendering troops. They were then bulldozed into mass, unmarked graves in the desert, some still alive. More than 2,000 vehicles and tens of thousands of charred and dismembered bodies littered the 100 Km/60 miles of highway.

---

[11] Napalm is flammable liquid used in warfare. It is a mixture of a gelling agent and petroleum or a similar fuel. It was initially used as an incendiary device against buildings and later primarily as an anti-personnel weapon, as it sticks to skin and causes severe burns when on fire.

The infamous "Highway of Death," Iraq 1991

President Bush then ordered an end of hostilities. What was the significance of this slaughter and President Bush declaring the war over on this day? Well, it was the **Day of Purim** which fell on this day. *The Day of Purim* is the day Jews celebrate their victory over Ancient Babylon (Enlil's army vs, Marduk's army), now based within the borders of Iraq, and a day when the Jews are encouraged to get bloody revenge against their perceived enemies. Of course, no one was charged with war crimes. President George Herbert Walker Bush, and his son's, are all Christian Zionist. The word "holocaust" means "burnt offering." I think this counts as that:

1992: In March, former **Federal Reserve Board Chairman** Rothschild Zionist, **Paul A. Volker** becomes Chairman of the European banking firm, **J. Rothschild, Wolfensohn and Co.**

Stephen Bryen, caught offering confidential documents to Israel in 1978, is serving on the board of the pro-Israeli Jewish **Institute for National Security Affairs** while continuing as a paid consultant, with security clearance, on exports of sensitive US technology.

The Samson Option, by Seymour M. Hersh reports,

> "Illicitly obtained intelligence was flying so voluminously from
> LAKAM (a secret Israeli intelligence unit, a Hebrew acronym for
> Scientific Liaison Bureau) into Israeli intelligence that a special code
> name, JUMBO, was added to the security markings already on the
> documents. There were strict orders, Ari Ben-Menashe recalled,
> "Anything marked JUMBO was not supposed to be discussed with
> your American counterparts."

The Wall Street Journal reports that Israeli agents apparently tried to steal **Recon Optical Inc's** top-secret airborne spy-camera system.

Controlled recession designed for Britain

On September 16th, Britain's pound collapses when currency speculators led by Rothschild agent, Rothschild Zionist, **George Soros** borrows pounds and sells them for German Deutsche Marks in the expectation of being able to repay the loan in devalued currency and to pocket the difference. This results in the British Chancellor of the Exchequer, **Norman Lamont** announcing a rise in interest rates of 5% in one day and as a result, drives Britain into a recession which lasts many years as large numbers of businesses fail and the housing market crashes.

This is right on cue for the Rothschilds, after they had privatised Britain's state owned assets during the 1980's, driven the share price up, and then collapsed the markets so they could buy them up for pennies on the pound, a carbon copy of what Nathan Rothschild did to the British economy 180 years before in 1815. It cannot be overstated that the *Chancellor of the Exchequer* at that time, Norman Lamont, prior to becoming an MP, was a Merchant Banker with N. M. Rothschild and Sons, who he joined after reading Economics at Cambridge.

The Revolving Doors in Politics

1993: **Norman Lamont** leaves the British government to return to **N. M. Rothschild and Sons** as a director, after his mission to collapse the British economy, to profit the Rothschilds is accomplished. This is a very common phenomena, particularly in America known as the *Revolving Door*.

In politics, the "revolving door" is a movement of personnel between roles as legislators and regulators and the industries affected by the legislation and regulation. In some cases, the roles are performed in sequence, but in certain circumstances may be performed at the same time.

The movement of high-level employees from public sector jobs to private sector jobs and vice versa has been going on for years. The idea is that there is a revolving door between the two sectors as many legislators and regulators become consultants for the industries they once regulated and some private industry heads receive government appointments that relate to their former private posts. It would be simple to stop this obvious corrupt system, but who would want to stop it right? The problem is of course, is that the people who make the laws, are the same people who exploited this little loophole. So much for "democracy."

Probably one of the best, and most blatant examples of this was **Dick Cheney**, the war criminal, and the boss behind the 9/11 crime.

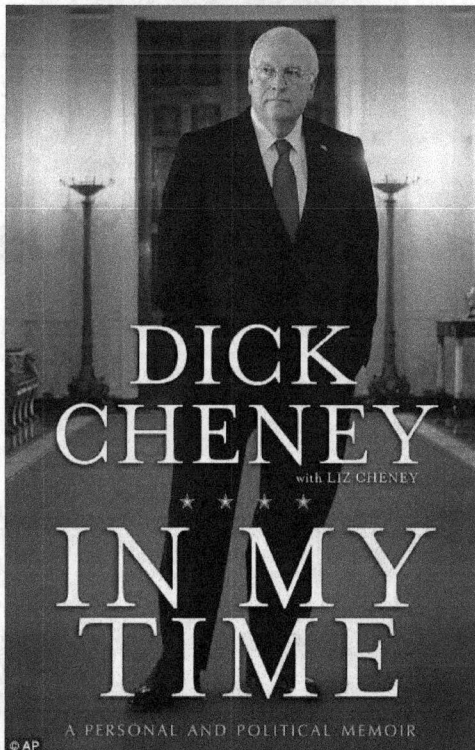

Dick Cheney - War criminal

THE REVOLVING DOORS OF DICK CHENEY

Richard Bruce "Dick" Cheney (1941 -), has been described as the 'real' President of the Unites States (making George W Bush a puppet), and possibly the most evil person on earth during his term as the 46th Vice President of the United States from 2001 –2009.

Between 1987 and 1989, during his last term in Congress, Cheney was a director of the Council on Foreign Relations (CFR). He also served a second term as a Council on Foreign Relations director from 1993 to 1995.

He was also a member of the board of advisors of the Jewish Institute for National Security Affairs (JINSA) before becoming vice president.

From 1995 until 2000, he served as Chairman of the Board and Chief Executive Officer of Halliburton, a warmongering Fortune 500 Company which is part of the Military Industrial Complex.

1991: Following the end of Operation Desert Storm, the Pentagon, led by then Defence Secretary Dick Cheney, paid Halliburton subsidiary Brown & Root Services over $8.5 million to study the use of private military forces (mercenaries) with American soldiers in combat zones.

In the early 1990s, Halliburton was found to be in violation of federal trade barriers in Iraq and Libya. After having pleaded guilty, the company was fined $1.2 million, with another $2.61 million in penalties. For a company that has profits in the tens of billions, this is less than a smack on the wrist!

1995: Cheney resigns as Defence Secretary and replaces Thomas H. Cruikshank, as chairman and CEO of Halliburton.

1998: Halliburton merged with Dresser Industries, which included Kellogg. Prescott Bush (the Nazi supporter in WWII) was a director of Dresser Industries, which is now part of Halliburton; his son, former President George H. W. Bush, worked for Dresser Industries in several positions from 1948 to 1951, before he founded Zapata Corporation.

2000: George W Bush surprised some pundits by asking Cheney to join the Republican ticket. Halliburton reached an agreement on July 20 to allow Cheney to retire, with a severance package worth $36 million. Cheney now goes back to politics.

Cheney resigned as CEO of Halliburton on July 25, 2000. As vice president, he argued that this step removed any conflict of interest. Cheney's net worth, estimated to be about $86 million, which was largely derived from his post at Halliburton.

2001: Michael Ruppert published a stunning book, entitled Crossing the Rubicon, that laid out the evidence — many proofs — that Dick Cheney was in charge of the events of 9/11.

THE REVOLVING DOORS OF DICK CHENEY

Following 9/11, Cheney was instrumental in providing a primary justification for a renewed war against Iraq. Cheney helped shape Bush's approach to the "War on Terror," making numerous public statements alleging Iraq possessed weapons of mass destruction (which they did not).

Cheney continued to allege links between Saddam Hussein and al-Qaeda, even though a classified President's Daily Brief on September 21, 2001 indicating the U.S. intelligence community had no evidence linking Saddam Hussein to the September 11 attacks and that "there was scant credible evidence that Iraq had any significant collaborative ties with Al Qaeda".

In the run-up to the Iraq war, Halliburton was awarded a $7 billion contract for which 'unusually' only Halliburton was allowed to bid. Yes, no other company was even allowed to bid for this contract!

Following the US invasion of Iraq, Cheney remained steadfast in his support of the war, stating that it would be an "enormous success story". It was not a success for the US Military, but it was a huge win fall for Halliburton, who made billions from the war in Iraq.

2004: Cheney has received a further $398,548.00 in deferred compensation from Halliburton while still USA Vice President.

2006: Dick Cheney shot Harry Whittington, a 78-year-old Texas attorney, while participating in a quail hunt at Armstrong ranch in Kenedy County, Texas. No charges were laid, and Whittington later "apologised" to Cheney.

2010: Cheney is named in a corruption complaint filed by the Nigerian government against Halliburton, which the company settled for $250 million – a drop in the Halliburton Ocean.

Due to Cheney's involvement as an architect of the so-called "enhanced interrogation techniques" program (torture), multiple prominent figures and groups have called for his prosecution under various anti-torture and war crimes statutes. To date, neither Cheney nor his cronies have been brought to justice, and probably never will be.

SOME INTERESTING FACTS ABOUT HALLIBURTON

Halliburton is a *Committee of 300* company, as are all of the **Military Industrial Complex**. War is good for money making, but making the bombs and bullets is even more lucrative even in so-called peace time. He are some key points on Halliburton the company, and how it conducts itself in the world.

Bribery:

2010: Halliburton officials were accused of coordinating a scheme to bribe Nigerian government officials over a period of years in association with the **Bonny Island** liquid natural gas (LNG) project. Bribing foreign governments is a criminal offense under the U.S. Foreign Corrupt Practices Act. The settled out of court for $250 million.

Tax issues:

On March 4, **2004**, Senators Levin (D-MI) and Dorgan (D-ND) released a GAO report on tax avoidance by federal contractors. At the time, Halliburton had 17 subsidiaries in tax haven countries, including 13 in the Cayman Islands which does not impose a corporate tax.

In **2002**, Citizen Works Citizen Works found that Halliburton ranked 8th Among the Fortune 500 companies with the most offshore tax haven subsidiaries.

During Dick Cheney's tenure as Halliburton's CEO, the number of company subsidiaries located in offshore tax havens increased from 9 (in 1995) to 44 (in 1999).

One of these subsidiaries (Halliburton Products and Services Ltd.), was incorporated in the Caiman Islands, and was used to get around sanctions on doing business in Iran. (Erwin Seba, Reuters, March 20, 2003)

Labour:

Much of Halliburton/KBR's government business in Iraq and Kuwait, already worth tens of billions, is being carried out by the world's poorest people. Many of these people are underpaid, working for wages that are one-tenth of what U.S. workers receive, thereby creating more profits on the margins for Halliburton and its subcontractors. For example, NPR reported in October 2007 a Pakistani dishwasher at a forward operating base in Diyala was being paid $1.25 an hour for two years work for the Saudi-based food-services firm, Tamimi, a KBR subcontractor.

Political influence:

Vice President Dick Cheney told NBC's **Meet the Press**

> *"I have absolutely no influence of, involvement of, knowledge of in any way, shape or form of contracts"* that Halliburton received in Iraq.

But an internal **Pentagon** email later obtained by **Time** magazine indicated that months before the war "action" on the Iraqi oil contract was "coordinated" with Cheney's office.

Two months before the U.S.-led invasion of Iraq, the **Wall Street Journal** reported,

> 66 The Bush administration is eager to secure Iraq's oil fields and rehabilitate them, industry officials say. They say Mr. Cheney's staff hosted an informational meeting with industry executives in October, with Exxon Mobil Corp., Chevron Texaco Corp., ConocoPhillips and Halliburton among the companies represented. Both the Bush administration and the companies say such a meeting never took place." (Thaddeus Herrick, "U.S. Oil Wants to Work in Iraq," Wall Street Journal, Jan. 17, 2003.) 99

In addition, Cheney has resisted public requests for disclosure of documents relating to his secret Energy Task Force that proved he was investigating Iraq's oil fields prior to the war. Some of the documents were released only after a judge ordered Cheney to make them public. (Halliburton, 2015)

Sources: (Cheney, 2015); (Halliburton, 2015); (Ruppert, 2004); (Shooting, 2006)

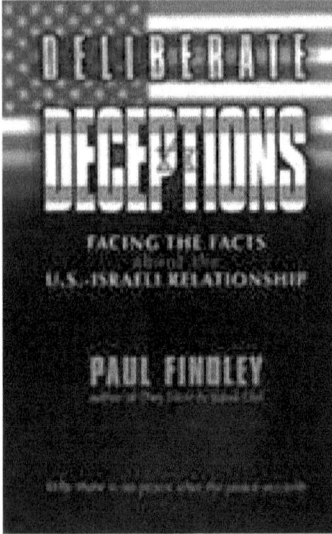

Former Congressman, **Paul Findley** publishes his seminal book, **Deliberate Deceptions: Facing the Facts about the U.S. Israeli Relationship** (Findley, 1993). In this book he lists the 65 United Nations Member Resolutions against Israel from the period 1955 to 1992, and the 30 United States vetoes on Israel's behalf, which if not made, would have seen Israel have 95 resolutions against them at this point. No matter, even with Israel's puppet the United States helping them terrorise others, the 65 Resolutions passed against Israel are more than all the Resolutions passed against all other countries combined. This alone condemns Israel's occupation of Palestine.

Not that Israel cares too much about the views of the United Nations when you consider that less than two weeks after Israel's attack on the USS Liberty (an attack designed to sink the Liberty and blame it on Egypt, prompting the USA into a war with Egypt on behalf of Israeli Lies, remember the Mossad motto, **"By Way Of Deception, Thou Shalt Do War"**), the Israeli Foreign Minister, Aba Eban, stated of the United Nations,

> *"If the [UN] General Assembly were to vote by 121 votes to 1 in favour of Israel returning to the armistice lines (pre June 1967 borders), Israel, would refuse to comply with the decision."*

New York Times – 19 June 1967, says:

> The UN is simply another Rothschild front of International Jewry.

It goes on to report that the ADL (Anti-defamation League) is caught operating a massive spying operation on critics of Israel, which included such diverse groups and organisations such as the Arab-Americans, the San Francisco Labour Council, ILWU Local 10 TV Network, Oakland Educational Association, NAACP, Irish Northern Aid, International

Indian Treaty Council, the Asian Law Caucus, and the San Francisco Police.

Data collected was sent to Israel and in some cases to South Africa. Pressure from Jewish organisations forces the city to drop the criminal case, but the ADL settles a civil lawsuit for an undisclosed sum of cash. No charges were laid.

1995: Former atomic energy scientist and whistle blower, **Dr. Kitty Little**, reveals to the world that the Rothschilds now control 80% of the world's uranium supplies giving them a monopoly over nuclear power.

> *Israel aggressively collects (US) military and industrial technology.*

The report stated that Israel obtains information using, *"ethnic targeting, financial aggrandizement, and identification and exploitation of individual frailties,"* of US citizens.

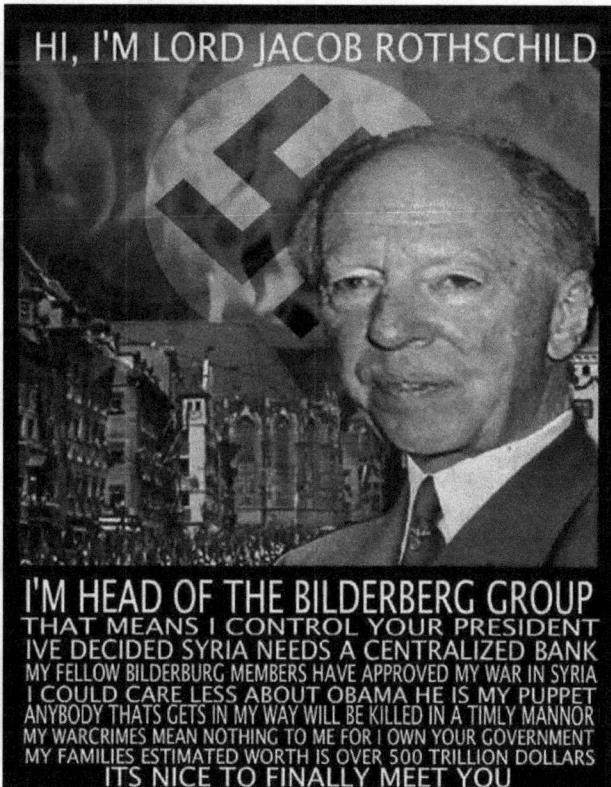

THE HOUSE: HI, I'M LORD JACOB ROTHSCHILD

I'M HEAD OF THE BILDERBERG GROUP
THAT MEANS I CONTROL YOUR PRESIDENT
IVE DECIDED SYRIA NEEDS A CENTRALIZED BANK
MY FELLOW BILDERBURG MEMBERS HAVE APPROVED MY WAR IN SYRIA
I COULD CARE LESS ABOUT OBAMA HE IS MY PUPPET
ANYBODY THATS GETS IN MY WAY WILL BE KILLED IN A TIMLY MANNOR
MY WARCRIMES MEAN NOTHING TO ME FOR I OWN YOUR GOVERNMENT
MY FAMILIES ESTIMATED WORTH IS OVER 500 TRILLION DOLLARS
ITS NICE TO FINALLY MEET YOU

ISRAEL CLAIMS TO BE AMERICA'S BEST FRIEND AND ALLY – YET CHEATS, LIES, AND STEALS FROM THE USA, OVER, AND OVER, AND OVER...

1996: A General Accounting Office report, «Defense Industrial Security: Weaknesses in US Security Arrangements With Foreign-Owned Defense Contractors,» found that according to intelligence sources, «Country A,» (identified by intelligence sources as Israel), «conducts the most aggressive espionage operation against the United States of any US ally."

The report described, "An espionage operation run by the intelligence organization responsible for collecting scientific, and technologic information [for Israel] paid a US government employee to obtain US classified military intelligence documents." (Washington Times, 22 February 1996)

The Jerusalem Post (30 August 1996) quoted the report, "Classified military information and sensitive military technologies are high-priority targets for the intelligence agencies of this country."

The Washington Report on Middle East Affairs (Shawn L. Twing, April 1996) noted that this was, "a reference to the 1985 arrest of **Jonathan Pollard**, a civilian US naval intelligence analyst who provided Israel's LAKAM espionage agency an estimated 800,000 pages of classified US intelligence information."

The GAO report also noted that, "Several citizens [of Israel] were caught in the United States stealing sensitive technology used in manufacturing artillery gun tubes."

An Office of Naval Intelligence document, "Worldwide Challenges to Naval Strike Warfare" reported that, "US technology has been acquired [by China] through Israel in the form of the Lavi fighter and possibly SAM (surface-to-air) missile technology."

Jane's Defense Weekly (28 February 1996) noted that, "until now, the intelligence community has not openly confirmed the transfer of US technology [via Israel] to China." The report noted that this, "represents a dramatic step forward for Chinese military aviation." (Flight International, 13 March 1996).

Mossad logo: **"By Way Of Deception, Thou Shalt Do War"**

THE ROTHSCHILD'S KILL ONE OF THEIR OWN

Amschel Mayor James Rothschild, (1955-1996), pictured here in 1977 at age 22

1996: Amschel Mayor James Rothschild, aged 41, is strangled with the heavy cord of his own towel robe in his hotel room in Paris. The French Prime Minister orders the French Police to close their investigation, and **Rupert Murdoch**, born of a Jewish mother and so a Jew by Ashkenazi standards, instructs his editors and news managers around the world to report it as a heart attack.

According to British broadcast reporter **Ian Gooding**,

> *"Murdoch sent a hotline fax to his 600-odd editors and news managers around the world, ordering them to report Amschel's death as a heart attack, if at all. No one around here has ever seen such pressure to kill a front-page story. But in the end, the cover-up was complete."*

People used the word "gentle" to describe Amschel. He was the only son of **Victor Rothschild's** second marriage to **Theresa Mayor**, and heir to the Rothschild dynasty after his older half-brother Jacob (yes, the same guy at the beginning of this chapter).

The Rothschilds have a secret pact. Each member of the dynasty will die if he refuses to advance the plan for the subversion and enslavement of the human race outlined in *The Protocols of Zion*.

Obviously Amschel Rothschild did not have "the killer instinct", which shows that even at the top level of the Rothschild dynasty, you are not immune from a lethal attack. It demonstrates what soulless predators these people are.

Amschel's story is a great tragedy. A sensitive, intelligent, and good man is born into a megalomaniac family of generational Satanists. He discovers he must be a ruthless predator, but it's not in his character. He has a soul. He resists and is murdered. Amschel's soul came into this family to teach them compassion and tolerance, but because they could not understand these concepts, they lashed out in fear and murdered their own flesh and blood. If anything, we should pity this family.

This yet again demonstrates that the Nephilim hybrid bloodline lacks the "empathy" gene written about by **Richard Dawkins** in his classic book, *The Selfish Gene* (Dawkins, 1989).

It's OK to murder 500,000 children – as long as they are Arabs!

On 12 May, 1996, United Nations Ambassador and Rothschild Zionist, **Madeleine Albright**, appeared on *60 Minutes*. She was asked the following question by correspondent Lesley Stahl, in reference to the years of United States led economic sanctions against Iraq,

Madeleine Albright (1937 -)

> *"We have heard that half a million children have died. I mean, that is more children than died in Hiroshima. And, you know, is the price worth it?"*

To which Ambassador Albright replied without blinking,

> *"I think that is a very hard choice, but the price, we think, the price is worth it."*

Her comments cause no public outcry. In fact, the holocaust of half a million Iraqi children is positively admired by the United States government when you consider that less than 8 months later, President Clinton appointed Albright as Secretary of State.

Whilst appearing before the Senate Committee who were considering her appointment, Albright is literally chomping at the bit for the blood of more Iraqi children and she states,

> *"We will insist on maintaining tough UN sanctions against Iraq unless and until that regime complies with relevant Security Council resolutions."*

1997: An Army mechanical engineer and Rothschild Zionist, **David A. Tenenbaum**, "inadvertently," gives classified military information on missile systems and armoured vehicles to Israeli officials (New York Times, 20 February 1997).

The Washington Post reports US intelligence has intercepted a conversation in which two Israeli officials had discussed the possibility of getting a confidential letter that then-Secretary of State **Warren Christopher** had written to Palestinian leader **Yasser Arafat**.

One of the Israelis, identified only as **Dov**, had commented that they may get the letter from **MEGA**, the code name for Israel's top agent inside the United States. US ambassador to Israel, **Martin Indyk**, complains privately to the Israeli government about heavy-handed surveillance by Israeli intelligence agents.

Israeli agents place a tap on Rothschild Zionist and daughter of a Rabbi, **Monica Lewinsky's** phone at the Watergate and record phone sex sessions between her and President Bill Clinton. The **Ken Starr** report confirms that Clinton warned Lewinsky their conversations were being taped and ended the affair. Interestingly, at the same time, the FBI's hunt for MEGA is called off.

On 29 October **Edmond de Rothschild** dies in Geneva. Interestingly, on the exact same day **Anton Szandor LaVey**, the founder of the Church of Satan also dies, who in his book Satan Speaks, he states in relation to *The Protocols of the Elders of Zion*,

> **❝** *The first time I read the Protocols of the Elders of Zion, my instinctive reaction was, so what's wrong with THAT? Isn't that the way any master plan should work? Doesn't the public deserve - nay, demand - such despotism?* **❞**

Kofi Annan becomes Secretary General to the United Nations. He is married to **Nane Lagergren**, a Rothschild, who he wed in 1984.

1998: The European Central Bank is set up in Frankfurt, the city from which the Rothschilds originate.

2000: George W. Bush is elected (so they tell me) President of the United States. Bush and his family claim to be descendants of the **House of Plantagenet** (British Royalty) which is descended from the **Royal House of Judah** (the original REAL Jews).

2001: On September 11th the attack on the World Trade Center is orchestrated by Israel with the complicity of Saudi Arabia, Britain and America, under the orders of the Rothschilds as a pretext for removing the liberty of people worldwide, in exchange for security, just as happened with the Reichstag fire in Germany, where the

citizens were lied to in order to give up liberty for security. They also will use the attacks to gain control of the few nations in the world who don't allow Rothschild central banks and so, less than one month after these attacks, US forces attack Afghanistan, one of only seven nations in the world who don't have a Rothschild controlled central bank. Less than a week before the 9-11 attack on 5 September, the so-called lead hijacker **Mohamed Atta** and several other hijackers made a still-unexplained visit on-board one of Pro Israeli lobbyist Rothschild Zionist, **Jack Abramoff's** casino boats. No investigation is undertook as to what they were doing there.

The September 11, 2001 attacks, also known as the 9/11 attacks, were a series of strikes in the US which killed nearly 3,000 people and caused about $10 billion worth of property and infrastructure damage. US officials assert that the attacks were carried out by **al-Qaeda** terrorists, but many experts have raised questions about the official account.

They believe that rogue elements within the US government (Dick Cheney, Donald Rumsfeld, Paul Wolfowitz, Richard Perle, General Richard Myers, Rudy Giuliani, Larry Silverstein and others) orchestrated or at least encouraged the 9/11 attacks in order to accelerate the US war machine and advance the Zionist agenda.

On 9/11, **5 Israelis** are arrested for dancing and cheering while the World Trade Towers collapse. Supposedly employed by *Urban Moving Systems*, the Israelis are caught with multiple passports and a lot of cash and explosives. Two of them are later revealed to be Mossad. As witness reports track the activity of the Israelis, it emerges that they were seen at *Liberty Park* at the time of the first impact, suggesting a foreknowledge of what was to come. The Israelis are interrogated, and then eventually sent back to Israel. The owner of the moving company used as a cover by the Mossad agents, abandons his business and flees to Israel. The United States Government then classifies all of the evidence related to the Israeli agents and their connections to 9/11. No charges were laid.

All of this is reported to the public via a four part story on Fox News by **Carl Cameron**. Pressure from Jewish groups, primarily **AIPAC**, forces Fox News to remove the story from their website. Two hours prior to the 9/11 attacks, **Odigo**, an Israeli company with offices just a few blocks from the World Trade Towers, receives an advance warning via the internet. The manager of the New York Office provides the FBI with the IP address of the sender of the message, but the FBI does not follow this up.

The FBI is investigating 5 Israeli moving companies as possible fronts for Israeli intelligence. It is revealed that prior to the attack, millions of dollars of put options[12] on both American Airlines and United Airlines, were traded. The FBI have promised to follow the purchasers up, but have never revealed their findings. That is because this would lead directly to Israel, the state behind the 9/11 attacks.

More Spying on their "Best" Friends

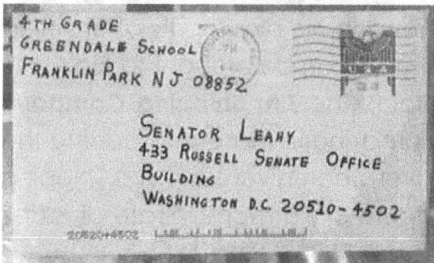

A letter containing Anthrax that was cooked up in a US Dept. of Defence lab was sent to Sen. Leary.

It is discovered that US drug agents' communications have been penetrated. Suspicion falls on two companies, **AMDOCS** and **Comverse Infosys**, both owned by Israelis. AMDOCS generates billing data for most US phone companies and is able to provide detailed logs of who is talking to whom. **Comverse Infosys** builds the tapping equipment used by law enforcement to eavesdrop on all American telephone calls, but suspicion forms that *Comverse Infosys*, which gets half of its research and development budget from the Israeli government, has built a back door into the system that is being exploited by Israeli intelligence and that the information gleaned on US drug interdiction efforts is finding its way to drug smugglers.

The investigation by the FBI leads to the exposure of the largest foreign spy ring ever uncovered inside the United States, operated

---

[12] Put Option: an option to sell assets at an agreed price on or before a particular date.

by Israel. Half of the suspected spies have been arrested when 9/11 happens. No charges were laid.

Following the World Trade Center attack, anonymous letters containing anthrax are sent to various politicians and media executives. Like the 9/11 attack, this is immediately blamed on Al-Qaeda, until it is discovered that the anthrax contained within those letters is a specific type of weaponized anthrax made by a United States military laboratory. The FBI then discover that the main suspect for these anthrax letters is a Rothschild Zionist **Dr. Philip Zack**, who had been reprimanded several times by his employers, due to offensive remarks he made about Arabs. Dr. Philip Zack was caught on camera entering the storage area where he worked at **Fort Detrick** which is where the anthrax was kept. At this point, both the FBI and the mainstream media stopped making any public comments on the case. No charges were laid.

Jewish Defence League Chairman since 1985, Rothschild Zionist, **Irv Rubin,** is jailed for allegedly plotting to bomb a mosque and the offices of an Arab-American congressman. He dies shortly after slitting his throat in a suicide attempt, before he can be brought to trial.

One week prior to the 9/11 attack, the **Zim Shipping Company** moves out of its offices in the WTC, breaking its lease and costing the company $50,000. No reason has ever been given, but Zim Shipping Company is half owned by the Fiefdom of Rothschild/State of Israel. No charges were laid.

On October 3, Israeli Prime Minister **Ariel Sharon**, makes the following statement to Rothschild Zionist **Shimon Peres**, as reported on **Kol Yisrael radio:**

"Every time we do something you tell me America will do this and will do that...I want to tell you something very clear, don't worry about American pressure on Israel. We, the Jewish people, control America, and the Americans know it."

Ariel Sharon
(1928 - 2014)

2002: *Webster's Third New International Dictionary* (Unabridged), reprinted in 2002 provides a new definition of Anti-Semitism which has not been updated since 1956. It reads,

> *Anti-Semitism: (1) hostility toward Jews as a religious or racial minority group, often accompanied by social, political or economic discrimination (2) opposition to Zionism (3) sympathy for the opponents of Israel.*

It was definition (2) and (3) that were added in the 2002 edition, just before the USA decide to invade Iraq under orders from the State of Rothschild, I mean Israel.

Also this year, the Prime Minister of Israel and war criminal Ariel Sharon, orders the massacre in the Jenin refugee camp in the West Bank. The definition was updated to protect these criminals. No charges were laid.

The **DEA** issues a report that Israeli spies, posing as art students, have been trying to penetrate US Government offices. Police near the **Whidbey Island Naval Air Station** in southern Washington State stop a suspicious truck and detain two Israelis, one of whom is illegally in the United States. The two men were driving at high speed in a Ryder rental truck, which they claimed had been used to, "deliver furniture."

The next day, police discovered traces of TNT and RDX military-grade plastic explosives inside the passenger cabin and on the steering wheel of the vehicle. The FBI then announces that the tests that showed explosives were, "false positive," by cigarette smoke, a claim test experts say is ridiculous and impossible. Based on an alibi provided by a woman, the case is closed and the Israelis are handed over to **INS** to be sent back to Israel. One week later, the woman who provided the alibi vanishes. No charges were laid.

2003: The United States invade Iraq for the second time, on 19 March, which this year is the holy **Day of Purim** in the Jewish calendar. This "Day of Purim," is a day the Jews celebrate their victory over Ancient **Babylon**, now based within the borders of Iraq. What is also significant is that the previous U.S. led invasion of Iraq ended on the Day of Purim ten years earlier with the slaughter of 150,000 fleeing Iraqis under President George Herbert Walker Bush.

Ancient Babylon, I mean Iraq, is now one of six nations left in the world who don't have a Rothschild controlled central bank. Make no mistake about it, this is the so called "Benchmark" which the puppet GW Bush references in his "War on Arab" speeches. This war is mainly about genocide of the entire Muslim world and is being fought with the blood of the American military, which the Fiefdom of Rothschild/ State of Israel control. It is the most immoral depraved act of horror being perpetrated to bring on World War III.

Israel has always struggled for water, it had to steal the Golan Heights from Syria which provided Israel with one third of its fresh water 36 years before, yet still in Israel water extraction has surpassed replacement by 2.5 billion litres in the last 25 years. This means the water is far more precious to them than the oil reserves which are the second largest reserves of oil on the planet.

Malaysian Prime Minister Mahathir Mohamed states in a speech,

> *"Jews rule the world by proxy. They get others to fight and die for them."*

The Police Chief of Cloudcroft stops a truck speeding through a school zone. The drivers turn out to be Israelis with expired passports. Claiming to be movers, the truck contains junk furniture and several boxes. The Israelis are handed over to immigration. The contents of the boxers are not revealed to the public. No charges were laid.

Israel deploys assassination squads into other countries, using forged passports, including the United States and Australia. The US Government does not protest, nor does the Australian Government. No charges were laid.

The American Israel Public Affairs Committee (AIPAC)

AIPCA logo

2004: Two years into an investigation of **AIPAC**, the largest political lobbying group in the USA with over 65,000 members, AIPAC has been called *Israel's Fifth Column in Washington*, whose only purpose is to use the USA for the purposes of Israel. It is also a spy front for Israel, after Rothschild Zionist **Larry Franklin**, a mid-level Pentagon Analyst is observed by the FBI giving classified information to two officials of AIPAC, suspected of being Israeli spies.

AIPAC hires lawyer **Nathan Lewin** to handle their legal defence, the same lawyer who defended suspected Israeli spy **Stephen Bryen** in 1978.

Larry Franklin worked in the **Pentagon Office of Special Plans**, run by **Richard Perle**. Perle was caught giving classified information to Israel back in 1970. But now he was insisting that Iraq was crawling with **weapons of mass destruction (WMD)**, requiring the United States to invade and conquer Iraq. There were no WMDs of course, and Perle has dumped the blame for the, "bad intelligence," on **George Tenet**. No charges were laid.

But what is known is that the *Pentagon Office of Special Plans* was coordinating with a similar group in Israel, in Ariel Sharon's office. With two suspected Israeli spies (at least) inside the office from which the lies that launched the war in Iraq originated, it appears that the people of the United States are the victims of a deadly hoax, a hoax that started a war using the blood and money of American citizens for the purposes of Israeli oppression. The leaking of the investigation of AIPAC to the media on August 28th, 2004 gave advance warning to other spies working with Franklin.

The damage to the FBI's investigation was completed when **United States Attorney General John Ashcroft** ordered the FBI to stop all arrests in the case. Like the Stephen Bryen case and the hunt for "MEGA," this latest spy scandal was destined by officials, who have their own secret allegiances to protect, to be buried, barring a massive public outcry. And you guessed it - No charges were laid.

New Zealand Stands Up to Israel

Helen Clark Prime Minister New Zealand (1999 - 2008)

The Prime Minister of New Zealand, **Helen Clark** angrily denounced Israel and imposed diplomatic sanctions on it after two Mossad agents were jailed for six months, for trying on false grounds to obtain a New Zealand passport.

The plot, which involved obtaining a passport in the name of a tetraplegic man who had not spoken in years. Ms Clark said Israel had ignored requests made three months earlier for an explanation and an apology.

Ms. Clarke stated,

> "This type of behaviour is unacceptable internationally by any country. It is a sorry indictment of Israel that it has **again** taken such actions against a country with which it has friendly relations."

Not the First Time

She said **again**, referring to a 1997 incident in which Mossad agents used fake Canadian passports in an attempt to assassinate the Hamas leader, **Sheikh Khaled Mashal**, which caused the Israeli ambassador to be ordered out of Canada until Tel Aviv promised to cease the practice.

The good news is that the Clarke government had the guts to jail these two spies for six months, and imposed diplomatic sanctions, something that US law enforcement is incapable or unwilling to do. In typical fashion, **Silvan Shalom**, the Israeli foreign minister, said Israel was disappointed with New Zealand's reaction. Really Mr. Shalmon, and what would you do if you found an Iranian spy in your country? Yes, Israel SHOOTS spies! You hypocrite.

More Israeli Spies are let go

Police near the **Nuclear Fuel Services** plant in **Tennessee** stop a truck after a 5 Km / 3 mile chase, during which the driver throws a bottle containing a strange liquid from the cab. The drivers turn out to be Israelis using fake identifications. The FBI refuses to investigate and the Israelis are released. In a separate event, two Israelis try to enter **Kings Bay Naval Submarine Base**, home to eight **Trident submarines**. The truck tests positive for explosives. No charges were laid.

The National Director of the **ADL, Abraham H. Foxman**, publishes a book entitled, **Never Again? The Threat Of The New Anti-Semitism**, in which he states that the **New Testament's** "lie," that the ancient Pharisees were responsible for the death of Jesus, has been responsible for anti-Semitism throughout the millennia and thus the **New Testament of the bible** is, "**hate speech**," and should be censored or banned.

Do you remember what we found in the Torah earlier? **TALMUD, Kethuboth 11b** states: "*When a grown up man has intercourse with a* *little girl it is nothing, for when the girl is less than this (3 years), it is as if one puts the finger into the eye."* The footnote to this passage says: *"As tears come to the eye again, and again, so does virginity come back to the little girl under three years."* The same section confirms that sexual activity with small boys is in the same category. *"The intercourse with a small boy is not regarded as a sexual act."*

Mr. Foxman needs to explain why religious sanctioned paedophilia is less harmful than the New Testament.

2005: On January 20, **President Bush** makes the following statement as part of his second inaugural address, *"When our Founders declared a new order of the ages."* This is not true. The founders did not declare a, "new order of the ages," **President Roosevelt** did when in 1933, he put its Latin translation, *Novus Ordo Seclorum*, on the US 1 dollar bill.

On 7 July the **London Underground Network is bombed.** Israel's Finance Minister, **Binyamin Netanyahu** is in London on the morning of the attacks in order to attend an economic conference in a hotel over the underground station where one of the blasts occurred. However, he stayed in his hotel room instead after he had been informed by **Israeli intelligence** officials attacks were expected. All evidence points to the Undergrounding bombing being a false flag event, planned and executed by Mossad - *By way of deception, thou shalt do war.*

There are now only **5 nations** in the world left without a Rothschild controlled central bank: Libya, Iran; Syria, North Korea, and Cuba.

Physics Professor, **Stephen E. Jones** of **Brigham Young University** publishes a paper in which he proves the **World Trade Center** buildings were brought down by internal explosives, in a controlled implosion demolition. He receives no coverage in the mainstream media for his scientific and provable claims (Jones, 2013).

2006: The **Edmond De Rothschild Banque**, a subsidiary of Europe's Edmond De Rothschild family bank group in France, becomes the first foreign family bank that has obtained approval of the **China Banking Regulatory Commission** to enter China's financial market. Interesting, because in August 2015, China's stock market is collapsing. I wonder who orchestrated that.

The **ADL** *(Anti-Defamation League)* ruthlessly leans on governments throughout the world to pass hate crimes legislation, as they are scared that the criminal cabal that is **Israel** and the **Rothschilds** is being exposed more and more on a daily basis, predominantly on the internet. Their job is to protect this criminal network and what better way to do it than by passing laws in which anyone who exposes a Jewish criminal becomes a criminal.

David Irving is sentenced to three years in jail in Austria for **denying the holocaust**. It is important to note that the only historical event you can be arrested for questioning, is the holocaust. This is because this has been the Rothschilds greatest weapon in brainwashing you, **THE STUPID GOYIM**! They continually perpetuate the lie that the Jews are so poor and persecuted, when in actual fact they control the vast majority of international finance and international corporations throughout the world.

2007: Secret British cabinet paper from the 1950's emerge and read: *"When the French Prime Minister, Monsieur Mollet, was recently in London, he raised with the prime minister the possibility of a union between the United Kingdom and France."* Britain and France talked about a "union" in the 1950s, even discussing the possibility of the Queen becoming the French head of state. This is part of the bigger Rothschild plan to merge all of Europe into a Super State with One World Government.

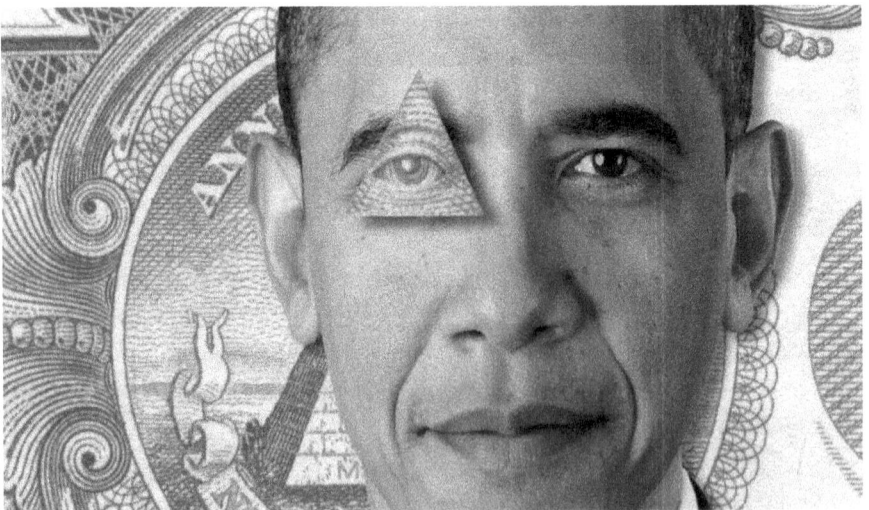

THE OBAMA / ROTHSCHILD PRESIDENCY

2008: Barack Hussein Obama is selected and paid for by the Rothschild Wall Street Bankers to play the role of **CEO / US President**. But not just the bankers, he first had to be selected by the **Bilderberg Group**.

Many people really thought Obama would be different, but as soon as we saw who he gave jobs to, it was known he was working for Wall Street Banksters.

Even though Ashkenazi Jews only make up about 2% of the United States population, they regularly make up to 80% of all White House appointments. That is a huge disparity that no one ever questions. If the White House was made up of almost entirely Asians, or Blacks, or Latinos or Italians, or Irish, then I am sure there would be a huge outcry.

Not for racist reasons, but for reasons that such a small minority get to represent the whole nation of over 350,000,000 people.

But since Obama was "selected," as opposed to "elected," he had to follow the company policy and employ his owner's people.

Of course, the owners are the Rothschild, and their people are the Wall Street banksters and Zionists. Whilst most of Obama's people are Jewish Zionists, some are Christian fundamentalist and also Zionists.

Zionism in its public expression, is a political ideology based on a homeland for Jewish people in Palestine and a belief that the Jews are God's "chosen race," with a God-given right to the "promised land" of Israel. Historically, this is nonsense, as I demonstrated in Chapter 3. They also believe that the real borders of Israel must encompass what is now Israel, including Gaza and the West Bank still officially owned by the Palestinians, plus Lebanon, Iraq, Syria, Egypt and Jordan, an area known as the Levant, or, as Genesis puts it: '... *from the brook of Egypt to the Euphrates'*.

That is why now in 2015, NATO and the US are trying every trick in the book to start a war with Russia so they can bomb Syria, then invade Iran. Once they get Syria and neutralise Russia, they will attack Iran. This is the Israel plan that will use the US army to fight a proxy war on their behalf.

The problem is that they have underestimated Russia. If the US/Israel gang attack Russia, Syria, or Iran, not only will it spark World War III, it will also be the END of the United States of America, and the State of Israel. No ifs, buts, or maybes.

But that is the public expression of Zionism, however at its inner core it is a secret society created and controlled by the **House of Rothschild**.

They have sought to sell the 'Zionism-means-all-Jewish-people' lie so that they can condemn as 'anti-Semites' and 'racists' anyone who exposes the truth about Rothschild Zionism and its agents in government, banking, business, media, military etc.

Racism is the ultimate ignorance. Racists are ridiculous, juvenile, and silly, but no way is the threat of being branded as one (they have already tried and failed) going to stop me exposing what must be exposed if the **Control System** is to fall.

The world's most extreme racists are, after all, the Rothschild Zionists. Israel is an apartheid state every bit as much as was the apartheid South Africa and apartheid America. And by that I don't only mean the evil that is inflicted upon the Palestinian people minute-by-minute, day-by-day, but also the extraordinarily racist divisions within Jewish society with the black Jews from Ethiopia.

For example, Ethiopian Jews are treated as little more than vermin by the Jews in Israel. So let us get past the calculated smokescreen that challenging Rothschild Zionism and the horrors of Israel means you are anti-Jewish and instead, look at the simple facts that they don't want you to know and acknowledge.

John C. Hagee

Firstly, as stated, you don't have to be Jewish to be a Rothschild Zionist, as US Vice-President, **Joe Biden** publicly said while bum kissing his masters in Tel Aviv (ultimately his masters at *Chateau Rothschild*).

Indeed, some of the most vehement Rothschild Zionists are the Christian Zionists in the United States and elsewhere, led most vocally by their 'spiritual' leader, **John C. Hagee**. Think of the worst kind of extreme Bible-bashing hypocrite and you've got him to a tee. Hagee has built a multi-million dollar empire with his fake Christian clap trap.

Hagee is the founder and National Chairman of the Christian-Zionist organization, **Christians United for Israel**, and he is a regular visitor to Israel and has met every prime minister since **Menachem Begin**. His **John Hagee Ministries** have given more than **$8.5 million** to relocate Jews from the former Soviet Union to Israel and he is the founder and Executive Director of an event called **A Night to Honor Israel**, which pledges solidarity between Christians and the State of Israel.

The Rothschilds have a network of organisations, including **B'nai B'rith** and its offshoot, the **Anti-Defamation League** (ADL) that work with other Rothschild controlled groups to target anyone who gets close to seeing the elephant in the room and exposing it for all to see.

They attack and undermine them in every way they can to stop the simple and devastating truth coming to light – that the Rothschild Zionists control the mainstream media; Hollywood and the movie industry; governments, not least in the United States; and crucially in the light of current events, they control global finance and commerce.

Therefore, I am going to take you through the personnel of the Obama administration that 'he' appointed after his election in late 2008, to give you an idea of how the very few, dictate to the very many, via the Rothschild networks.

Remember as we go through the names, that only 2% of the population of the United States is Jewish and significant numbers of those will not be Rothschild Zionists.

Obama and the true life psychopath Rahm Emanuel BFF's

Thus, Obama appointed **Rahm Emanuel** (Rothschild Zionist) to be his White House Chief of Staff (handler). Emanuel, who served in the Israeli army, is the son of a former operative with the **Irgun** terrorist group that helped to bomb Israel into existence in 1948 and caused some 800,000 Palestinians to flee their homeland in terror.

Obama's White House Senior Advisor (handler) is **David Axelrod** (Rothschild Zionist), a close associate of Emanuel and the man who ran Obama's 'change you can believe in' election campaigns against Hillary Clinton and John McCain. Axelrod now oversees the words on the teleprompter screens to which Obama is fused to, for even the most minor announcement. Axelrod, like Emanuel, is the product of the Rothschild Zionist 'political' Mafia that controls Chicago where Rahm Emanuel is now mayor.

One of Obama's chief funders and controllers is the Rothschild Zionist agent, **George Soros**, the multi-billionaire financial speculator and manipulator of countries, not least in the former Soviet Union.

Obama appointed a stream of Rothschild Zionist 'advisors' and 'czars' in various subject areas, including infamous Rothschild Zionist agent, **Henry Kissinger**, and the obnoxious **Cass Sunstein**.

As 'Administrator of the White House Office of Information and Regulatory Affairs', Sunstein has called for 'conspiracy theories' to either be banned or taxed. This is another Rothschild goal – to ban any view or research that exposes the Rothschild agenda.

Sunstein (Rothschild Zionist) says the opinion that 'global warming' is a manipulated hoax is a good example of what should be banned or taxed. So it is no wonder that Obama appointed **Carol Browner** (Rothschild Zionist) and **Todd Stern** (Rothschild Zionist) to take charge of his 'global warming'/'climate change' policies.

The key economic post in the United States is the chairman of the **Federal Reserve**, the privately-owned and Rothschild-controlled cartel of banks. The US Federal Reserve, which, as the saying goes, is no more Federal than the Rothschild-controlled **Federal Express**. The 'Fed' prints money for literally cents on the dollar and then 'lends' it to the government at interest and for profit. What a great scam if you can get away with it, and because the Rothschild networks control the government and media as well as the Federal Reserve banks – they have... (Thank you Woodrow Wilson!).

We can pick up the 'Fed' story with the appointment of **Paul Adolph Volcker** to head the Fed during the presidencies of **Jimmy Carter** and **Ronald Reagan** (in truth George Bush senior).

Volcker was a former vice president and director of planning with the Rockefeller (Rothschild)-controlled **Chase Manhattan Bank** (who own ANZ bank in Australia and New Zealand) and left the Fed in 1987 to become chairman of the New York investment banking firm, **J. Rothschild, Wolfensohn & Co.**, run by **James D. Wolfensohn** (Rothschild Zionist), who later became president of the **World Bank**.

Next in line at the Federal Reserve was 'Mr Big', **Alan Greenspan** (Rothschild Zionist), a practising Satanist according to some who say they have attended rituals with him. Greenspan was 'appointed' by President Reagan (presidents don't 'appoint' Fed chiefs, they are told who it is going to be) and he remained head of the Fed and thus American economic policy through all the Clinton years and most of **George W. Bush** before stepping down in early 2006.

In that time he oversaw the systematic dismantling of financial regulation such as getting rid of the **Glass-Steagall Act 1933**, that allowed greed and corruption to run riot and in the same period that vicious and despicable duo, **Tony Blair** and his Chancellor and later successor, **Gordon Brown**, were doing the same in Britain.

Greenspan received unquestioning support for this policy from **Bill Clinton's** Treasury Secretaries, **Robert E. Rubin** (Rothschild Zionist), former co-chairman of the Rothschild-controlled **Goldman Sachs**, and **Larry Summers** (Rothschild Zionist), former Chief Economist at the Rothschild owned World Bank.

Bill Clinton's Special Assistant to the President for Economic Policy in this same period and Senior Economist and Senior Adviser on the Council of Economic Advisers during the Clinton administration was **Peter Orszag** (Rothschild Zionist).

Timothy Geithner - Yes Man

Another Greenspan supporter of deregulation was **Timothy Geithner** (Rothschild Zionist), the President of the Federal Reserve Bank of New York, the most powerful in the Federal Reserve cartel. Without the collective demolition of financial checks and balances by this cabal of Rothschild Zionists there would not have been the crash of September 2008 with its catastrophic consequences for billions worldwide.

But when Barack Obama became US President a few months later, everyone thought there would be a fresh start. So there was much shock and horror when Obama chose an 'economic team' that he 'appointed' to 'sort out the mess' that turned out to be the very same people who created it! It was all done from a White House controlled by Rahm Emanuel (Rothschild Zionist) and David Axelrod (Rothschild Zionist).

Obama made **Timothy Geithner** (Rothschild Zionist) his Treasury Secretary – Obama's mother worked for Geithner's father, **Peter F.**

Geithner (Rothschild Zionist), the director of the Asia programme at the Ford Foundation in New York.

Larry Summers (Rothschild Zionist) was appointed director of the White House National Economic Council, and **Paul Adolph Volcker**, business partner of the Rothschilds, was made Chairman of the Economic Recovery Advisory Board.

The gang that trashed the town was now back in town to trash it even more and you'll never guess ... they decided that the only way to save an economy brought to its knees by their collective actions and the banking system they represent was to hand trillions of taxpayer-borrowed dollars to the Rothschild-controlled banks and insurance companies like **CitiGroup** (advised to disaster, by Rothschild Zionist **Robert E. Rubin**), **J. P. Morgan**, **AIG**, **Deutsche Bank** and a long list of others.

Overseeing this and all other American government spending was Obama's Budget Director, the already-mentioned, **Peter Orszag** (Rothschild Zionist), who worked closely with Rahm Emanuel (Rothschild Zionist) to impose the **North American Free Trade Agreement** (NAFTA) which has devastated American industry in line with Rothschild policy.

Peter Orszag was the founder and president of the economic consultancy firm which advised the **Central Bank of Iceland** in the period before it went bankrupt and he advised the **Russian Ministry of Finance** when the country's resource assets were being given to Rothschild Zionist oligarchs like **Chelsea football club** owner, **Roman Abramovich**, who became instant billionaires.

Peter Orszag

Orszag resigned as Budget Director in July 2010 with his job done, but, no matter, Obama announced that **Jacob Lew** (Rothschild Zionist), an under-secretary of state to Hillary Clinton, would take over and resume the same post he held under Bill Clinton.

By the time the economy was in full decline in September 2008, **Alan Greenspan** (Rothschild Zionist) had stepped down from the Fed before the crash he knew was coming. But, once again, no matter, he was replaced by **Bernard Bernanke** (Rothschild Zionist) the smirking, smug, you know what, who printed even more money (at interest to the taxpayer) to hand to his Rothschild Zionist pals in Wall Street.

Since 2008, the Federal Reserve has printed and given to their Rothschild banks almost **$5 trillion** (that is a 5 with 12 zeros after it!). That is $5 trillion plus interest the United States tax payers are expected to pay back. It is a debt your great, great, great grandchildren will still be paying off.

Meanwhile, Treasury Secretary **Timothy Geithner** (Rothschild Zionist), who has been centrally involved in handing trillions of dollars of public money to his banking associates, with no strings attached, asked the opinion of a private international Rothschild Zionist 'law firm' called **Squire, Sanders & Dempsey** to see if American states could, as some requested, legally use bail-out money or **TARP** – the *Troubled Asset Relief Program* – to support the legal bills of people trying to protect their homes from foreclosure by the bailed out banking system. The privately-owned Rothschild Zionist **Squire, Sanders & Dempsey** said 'no' and so Timothy Geithner said the money could not be used to protect the public who had bailed out the banks from foreclosure by those same banks. Thus, hundreds of thousands of people in the United States lost their homes to the banks they helped bail out. Are you beginning to smell a rat?

David Millstone is a very active Rothschild Zionist, partner at *Squire, Sanders & Dempsey* and regional chairman of the **Anti-Defamation League's** international affairs committee. His firm says that public money can go to the Rothschild Zionist banks, but not to the innocent victims of the banks. And while all this has been going on, these have been the heads of the major international financial institutions with the power to impose global economic policies.

The President of the World Bank was **Robert Zoellick** (Rothschild Zionist), a big-time George W Bush administration insider who was a fervent advocate of invading Iraq long before 9/11. Zoellick took over at the World Bank from the disgraced **Paul Wolfowitz** (Rothschild Zionist), another orchestrator of the Iraq invasion as Deputy Defence Secretary.

Sexual Predator walks free!

The Managing Director of the **International Monetary Fund** (IMF) was **Dominique Strauss-Kahn** (Rothschild Zionist), the French politician. In 2011, Strauss-Kahn raped **Nafissatou Diallo**, a 32-year-old maid at the **Sofitel New York Hotel**. After charges were filed against Strauss-

Dominique Strauss-Kahn, sexual predator and pervert

Kahn, the Rothschild heavies paid a visit to Nafissatou Diallo. After that, she changed her story repeatedly, until the charges were finally dropped. The charges were dropped even though investigators matched semen samples taken from Nafissatou's clothing, and a DNA sample obtained from Strauss-Kahn. Strauss-Kahn paid Nafissatou Diallo an undisclosed amount over the civil suit. Why would he do that if he was innocent?

Strauss-Kahn was later implicated in the attempted rape of journalist **Tristane Banon**, however French public prosecutors dropped the investigation. No charges were laid.

2012, Strauss-Kahn organised a prostitution ring, hiring prostitutes for sex parties at hotels in **Lille, Paris** and **Washington; 2012**, a French prosecutor announced that they will not continue the investigation of Strauss-Kahn's connection to a gang rape in Washington, D.C. Strauss-Kahn was acquitted of all charges on 12 June 2015. If it were you or me, we would be doing 15 to life, but these Rothschild goons are above the law.

Still in 2012, the head of the **European Central Bank** (ECB) is **Jean-Claude Trichet** (Rothschild Zionist), another Frenchman who took over in 2003, following his acquittal in a trial over 'financial irregularities' at **Crédit Lyonnais**, one of France's biggest banks.

At the heart of the Irish 'bail out' (the bail out of Irish banks and the elite investors, like the Rothschilds, by the people of Ireland) were Jean-Claude Trichet (Rothschild Zionist) at the European Central Bank and sexual predator Dominique Strauss-Kahn (Rothschild Zionist) at the IMF.

And the banks that caused the crash to which the Rothschild Zionists in power are 'responding' for their benefit are also invariably controlled, directly or ultimately, by Rothschild Zionists.

These include **Goldman Sachs** headed by **Lloyd Blankfein** (Rothschild Zionist) and created by Rothschild Zionists **Marcus Goldman** and **Samuel Sachs** who came like so many of these people, from families that settled in America from the country where the name Rothschild originated – Germany. Even more specifically, the German region of **Bavaria** comes up again and again – the home of the infamous Bavarian Illuminati of **Adam Weishaupt. Pope Benedict XVI** and **Henry Kissinger** are just two more examples of 'born in Bavaria', Rothschild sociopaths.

Goldman Sachs was fundamentally responsible for the crash of 2008, but by that time, its former Chairman and Chief Executive Officer, **Henry 'Hank' Paulson** had been installed as **US Treasury Secretary** to begin the bank bailout policy, with enormous benefit to Goldman Sachs, in the closing weeks of the Bush administration.

Goldman Sachs was also instrumental in the collapse of the economy in Greece that started the 'euro panic' that later engulfed Ireland, Spain, and Portugal.

They have the whole thing stitched up because the Rothschild Zionist secret society network have their agents in governments, the banking system, including the international institutions like the IMF, and control the reporting of their activities through ownership of the mainstream media.

As a result, if it is happening economically and politically, it's because the Rothschilds want it that way – be it in banking, stock markets, commodity markets, currency valuation, and the price of gold -- the lot.

Peter Mandelson, on the right, with his owner, Jacob Rothschild. Notice how he must walk behind the master.

The world of finance is dictated by 'investor confidence' and who controls that? Those who have the power to control the media, government and central bank financial statements and have the financial resources to move trillions around the financial markets every day. In other words, the Rothschilds and their lackeys.

Rothschild Zionism is an elite secret society at its rotten core and the people I am naming here and so many more are not agents of Jewish people as a whole, but agents of the secret society that has mercilessly manipulated the Jewish population for centuries to advance its goals.

It is impossible to become President of the United States without support from the **American Israel Public Affairs Committee** (AIPAC), a massive Rothschild Zionist lobby group currently headed by Obama friend and funder, Ashkenazi Jew **Lee Rosenberg**. It is also very difficult to hold high office of any kind if AIPAC doesn't approve and a real struggle to even become a member of Congress or the Senate if AIPAC is against you.

As former BBC and Independent Television News correspondent, **Alan Hart**, wrote in *Zionism: The Real Enemy of the Jews*:

> *'Jewish people make up less than two per cent of the American population, but account for 50 per cent of the political campaign contributions.'*

And that 50 percent is overwhelmingly made up of a few Rothschild Zionists and is not in the least representative of half the Jewish population.

In Britain and so many other countries around the world they have the same tail wagging the dog. The British version of the American Israel Public Affairs Committee (AIPAC) is the **Friends of Israel** network in every major party.

One investigation discovered that 80% of Members of Parliament in the now ruling **Conservative Party** are members of the *Friends of Israel* – which has the stated goal of supporting anything that is good for Israel.

The British Prime Minister, **David Cameron**, is a Rothschild Zionist and so is the leader of the Labour 'opposition', **Ed Milliband**, who got the job after a campaign in which his brother, **David Miliband** (Rothschild Zionist), was the other major candidate. This in a country where the Jewish population (with many not Rothschild Zionists) is around 280,000 in a national population of 62 million.

The key manipulating force in the previous UK governments of **Tony Blair** and **Gordon Brown** was **Peter Mandelson** (Rothschild Zionist), who flaunts his close connections to the Rothschilds with holidays at their mansion on the Greek island of **Corfu**.

The Rothschilds controlled Blair as they controlled Bill Clinton and George W. Bush and this was the connection that led to Blair going into wars in support of both presidents who were being urged on by Israel (the Rothschilds).

It was the Rothschild network that orchestrated the invasions of Afghanistan and Iraq, the War of Terror and its justification, September 11th.

9/11: THE ROTHSCHILD ZIONIST CONNECTION

The lease of the twin towers at the World Trade Center was bought just weeks before September 11th by businessmen, **Larry Silverstein** (Rothschild Zionist) and **Frank Lowy** (Rothschild Zionist), who both have very close links to Israeli leaders, including current Prime Minister **Benjamin Netanyahu**, who said that what happened on 9/11 was *'good for Israel'.*

Larry Silverstein and his partner Frank Lowy acquired a 99-year lease on the entire World Trade Center complex just weeks before the 9/11/01 attack.

The World Trade Center deal was struck with **Lewis Eisenberg** (Rothschild Zionist), the former chairman of the *Port Authority of New York and New Jersey.* Eisenberg was recently appointed chairman of the Republican National Committee. Eisenberg had resigned from Goldman Sachs in the 1980s after his secretary accused him of sexually harassing her. When New Jersey Gov. **Christine Todd Whitman** appointed Eisenberg chairman of the Port Authority, in February of 1996, **Forbes Magazine** wrote that it was "*a strange political appointment, considering the part he played in the sex scandal that rocked Goldman and the financial community in the late 1980s.*"

Eisenberg was also the vice president of the American Israel Public Affairs Committee (AIPAC) and is also close to the Israel leadership. The man who lobbied heavily for the *New York Port Authority* to sell the lease into private hands was **Ronald S. Lauder** (Rothschild Zionist) from the **Estée Lauder** cosmetics family.

He is involved with a stream of Rothschild Zionist organisations, including the **Jewish National Fund, World Jewish Congress, American Jewish Joint Distribution Committee,** and our old favourite, the **Anti-Defamation League.** It seems if you are going to get up to no good, then you better be a member of the ADL.

Buying the World Trade Center lease was a terrible business deal for Silverstein and Lowy because the towers were known as the 'white elephants', given the state they were in and the massive amount of asbestos that needed to be dealt with. Asked why he had bought the lease Silverstein said,

'*I felt a compelling urge to own them*'. Especially because he knew what was coming,

When the deal was done Silverstein and co massively increased the insurance for a '**terrorist attack**' and were awarded **$4.55 billion** after the towers were hit. The lease had cost $3.2 billion and Silverstein reportedly only invested **$14 million** of his own money. That is over a $1 billion profit for Lucky Larry and Franky. Not a bad days deal right? The judge who oversaw the litigation between Silverstein and the insurance companies was **Michael B. Mukasey** (Rothschild Zionist) who later became US Attorney General. I am sure Larry and Frank looked after him as well.

'Lucky Larry' Silverstein and Frank Lowy had originally been outbid by $50 million for the World Trade Center lease by a company called **Vornado**, whose chief shareholder was the Jewish businessman, **Bernard Mendik**. He was Silverstein's former brother-in-law and they had fallen out big time after his divorce from Silverstein's sister. Then Vornado, despite having the best bid, 'suddenly changed their minds' and 'suddenly pulled out' leaving the field free for Silverstein and Lowy. No wonder they call him 'Lucky Larry'.

Weeks after Silverstein and Lowy presented their final bid for the WTC, Vornado's Bernard Mendik died after becoming 'suddenly ill'. So many 'suddenlys'.

Silverstein had breakfast every morning with his children in the **Windows on the World Restaurant**, more than 100 floors up in the North Tower, but none of them showed on 9/11. Silverstein said he had a last minute 'dermatologist appointment' when in truth, as one his bodyguards has said privately, he had a phone call in his car telling him to stay away from the World Trade Center that morning. He then got on his car phone to tell his children.

Where's Larry today? It was Silverstein who said in a television interview (which he now deeply regrets) that when another of his buildings in the World Trade Center complex, **Building Seven** or the **Salomon Brothers Building**, was on fire the decision was made to '*pull it*' – the classic term for a controlled demolition. Soon after this decision, the building, which had not been hit by a plane, did indeed come down in a controlled implosion demolition.

The problem with Silverstein's story is that it can take weeks to place the charges in a building like the 47-storey Building Seven to make it collapse in on itself as it did. How could the decision be made to 'pull it' and then down it comes? Building Seven collapsed perfectly onto the land on which it stood – and that could only happen with a controlled demolition. The charges were planted long before the official decision was made to '**pull it**' and the whole 9/11 scenario unfolded from a pre-planned script. The BBC announced on live television that Building Seven had collapsed half-an-hour before it actually did, because the authorities released the 'news' too early.

Security at the World Trade Center was the responsibility of the Rothschild Zionist- owned **Kroll Associates** which has close links to the CIA and Mossad. Security at all three airports involved on 9/11 was run by **ICTS International / Huntsleigh USA**, companies owned by Rothschild Zionists, **Ezra Harel** and **Menachem Atzmon**, and dominated by 'former' agents of **Shin Bet**, Israel's internal security service and counter-intelligence agency that handles security for the Israeli airline, **EL AL**.

The Missing Security Tapes for the World Trade Center

Late on the night of **August 23, 2001**, at about 3 a.m., security cameras in the parking garage of the World Trade Center captured the arrival of two or three truck vans.

Visual examination determined the vans were separate and unique from trucks used by janitorial services, including different colours and devoid of markings. More curious, all the janitorial trucks had pulled out of the Towers by about 2:30 a.m.—about half an hour before the second set of vans arrived. According to high-level State Department source with a top security clearance, who disclosed the unusual nightly activity, no vans matching that description had entered the World Trade Center at such an hour in any of the weeks or months prior to that date. It was a unique event.

Security cameras caught the vans leaving the Towers at approximately 5 a.m.—before the first wave of AAA personality types on Wall Street, driving Mercedes and BMWs, arrived to track the markets.

For the next 10 to 12 nights, the same mysterious truck vans arrived at the World Trade Center at the same mysterious hour— after the janitorial crews had left the building and before the most fanatic robber barons on Wall Street showed up for work. The vans appeared at the World Trade Center from approximately August 23, 2001 until

September 4, 2001. After that last night, they never appeared at the Towers again. In fact, the vans were never heard of again, either. The 9/11 Commission was never informed of their surprising presence in the Towers three weeks before the 9/11 attack.

Video from the security cameras could be the most significant missing part of the 9/11 puzzle. This State Department source was convinced the mysterious trucks were used to transport explosives into the building, and that an unidentified orphan team wired the World Trade Center for a controlled demolition in those late night hours.

The Shoe and Undies Bombers

Rothschild Zionist-owned ICTS was also responsible for security at the Paris airport as well where the alleged 'shoe bomber', **Richard Reid**, boarded his plane in 2001 to the United States and ICTS was providing the 'security' at Amsterdam airport in 2009 when the underpants bomber, **Umar Farouk Abdulmutallab** boarded his flight after paying cash for a high-priced last-minute ticket, boarded without checked baggage and, reportedly, even a passport. As a result, travellers are now being radiated in full-body scanners.

The CIA at the time of 9/11 was headed by **George Tenet** (Rothschild Zionist) and the 'investigation' into the attacks was overseen by Assistant Attorney General, **Michael Chertoff** (Rothschild Zionist), the son of an agent with the Israeli (Rothschild) enforcement agency, **Mossad**. Chertoff co-authored the notorious **Patriot Act** which deleted basic rights and freedoms on the justification of 9/11 and then became the second head of **Homeland Security**, an organisation also created on the back of 9/11. Chertoff now runs his own company, the **Chertoff Group**, a 'risk management and security consulting firm', which employs several senior colleagues from Homeland Security and also **Michael Hayden**, a former Director of the **National Security Agency** (NSA) and the **CIA**. Chertoff was all over the TV networks after the engineered 'underpants bomber' incident urging the government to introduce full body radiation scanners, which they then did. They are produced by one of the Chertoff Group clients, **Rapiscan Systems**.

The underpants bomber was allowed onto the plane despite a string of red flags, and apparently no passport, through a 'security' system operated by the Rothschild Zionist, ICTS.

The Pentagon at the time of 9/11 was controlled by people like **Paul Wolfowitz** (Rothschild Zionist), the Deputy Defence Secretary who went on to head the World Bank; and **Dov Zakheim** (Rothschild Zionist), a dual Israeli/American citizen and the Pentagon Controller who managed to 'lose' $2 trillion from the Pentagon budget – a fact that was announced on September 10th, 2001. Anyone wonder why this announcement was not widely reported? Did something happen the next day then? It had to be a coincidence, surely, they couldn't have known what was coming, could they??

Dov Zakheim also wrongly classified squads of **US F16** and **F15 fighters** as military surplus so they could be sold to Israel at a knock-down price (and bought with American 'aid' money, anyway). This and other military sales (often gifts) means that Israel, with a population of just seven and a half million, has one of the biggest air forces on the planet - With love from **Dov**. Remember back to earlier:

*"One of the Israelis, identified only as **Dov**, had commented that they may get the letter from **MEGA**, the code name for Israel's top agent inside the United States."*

Did we just identify the mysterious Israeli that was talking with MEGA? But if I could work it out – why can't the FBI? Unless they don't really want to know...

When Neocons are in Charge

The Bush administration was famously controlled at the time of the September 11th attacks by the so-called *neocons* or *neo-conservatives*. These were led by a cabal of Rothschild Zionists war mongers like Richard Perle, Paul Wolfowitz, Dov Zakheim, Robert Kagan, Douglas Feith, Lewis 'Scooter' Libby, the disbarred American attorney and convicted felon who was former 'advisor' to Dick Cheney, and William Kristol, editor of the Rothschild Zionist neocon propaganda sheet, the **Weekly Standard**, owned at the time by Rupert Murdoch (Rothschild Zionist). Oh yes, and this gang also included Robert Zoellick, now head of the World Bank, who took over in that post from his neocon and Rothschild Zionist colleague, disgraced **Paul Wolfowitz**. Every one of them a Rothschild Zionist.

I repeat – Jewish people make up only 2% of the American population and many of those are not Rothschild Zionists. The ratio to positions of power is simply fantastic and I am only highlighting here what you might call a 'headline list'. It goes much, much deeper.

The neocon leadership wrote to **Bill Clinton** urging him to attack Iraq before 9/11 and they then went into overdrive to advocate the invasions of Iraq and Afghanistan after the World Trade Center attacks under Bush. Interestingly, these same Rothschild Zionists, along with puppet Defence Secretary **Donald Rumsfeld** and Vice-President **Dick Cheney**, both vehement supporters of Israel, launched a 'think tank' before Bush came to office called the **Project for the New American Century** (PNAC).

In September **2000**, this organisation published a document called *Rebuilding America's Defenses: Strategies, Forces, and Resources for a New Century* in which they called for American forces to 'fight and decisively win multiple, simultaneous major theatre wars' with emphasis on places like Iraq, Iran, and North Korea (countries that did not yet have a Rothschild Central Bank).

But the document said that this,

> ❝ *... process of transformation ... is likely to be a long one, absent some catastrophic and catalysing event – **like a new Pearl Harbor**' to justify it to the people.* ❞

One year to the month after that document was published and nine months after most of these Rothschild Zionists came to power in the Bush administration, America did indeed have 'a new Pearl Harbor' which was then used to justify the agenda laid out in the document.

The Bush **State of the Union** address in 2002 which called Iraq, Iran and North Korea the 'axis of evil' was written by the neocon, **David Frum** (Rothschild Zionist), and was straight from the pages of the *Project for the New American Century* document.

The official 9/11 Commission 'investigation' into what happened that day was only forced upon Bush and Cheney kicking and screaming and the man they first appointed to head the Commission was **Henry Kissinger** (Rothschild Zionist). This was so ludicrous and incredible that even he agreed to resign, citing 'conflicts of interest', which had never stopped him before.

The fact is, they would not pay him the exorbitant fee he demanded (for lying under oath for the biggest inquiry in America's history.) If he was going to have his name on this document scam for the rest of history, he wanted to be paid well for it. But the 'investigation' and the final report was overseen by **Phillip Zelikow** (Rothschild Zionist) and it decided that the official story was basically true after failing to interview or quote key witnesses that gave another version of events.

If there is one person that should have the whole 9/11 debacle pinned squarely on them it is **Phillip Zelikow**. No, he did not order the hit, he did not set the charges, and he did not call off the air defence. He did not have any part in the actual attack. But what he did do, was to allow the true criminals to get away with it. He created the lie that has become the "official story" – the lie that will forever be in history unless the truth comes out.

His accomplices were **Alvin K. Hellerstein** (Rothschild Zionist) who has major family ties to Israel. He was the

Phillip Zelikow

federal judge assigned to deal with all wrongful death and personal injury cases filed by the families of those who died on September 11th.

Attorney **Kenneth Feinberg** (Rothschild Zionist) oversaw the 9/11 victim's compensation fund and 97% of the families were persuaded to take the money in exchange for not pressing for an independent investigation of the September 11th atrocities. Those that did demand an investigation or rejected the limitations of the compensation fund were dealt with through a 'special mediator', **Sheila Birnbaum** (Rothschild Zionist). Feinberg went on to become the 'Special Master' for **TARP** Executive Compensation related to the bank bail outs, and is currently the government-appointed administrator of the compensation fund for victims of the BP oil disaster in the Gulf of Mexico.

The Dancing Israelites

Then there is the story of the five 'dancing Israelis' that I already mentioned, who were arrested after police received several calls from New Jersey residents outraged that 'middle-eastern' men were high-fiveing, whooping and cheering as they videotaped the burning Twin Towers.

> *"They were like happy, you know … They didn't look shocked to me," one witness said.*

Police and FBI officers reportedly discovered maps of New York in the Israelis' white van with locations highlighted, and also $4,700 in cash, hidden in a sock, foreign passports, and box cutters of the type alleged to have been used by the 'Arab hijackers'.

It was further reported that sniffer dogs found traces of explosives in the van, which belonged to a Mossad front company called **Urban Moving Systems** owned by Israeli **Dominick Suter** (Rothschild Zionist), who dropped everything (literally judging by the haste the office was evacuated) and fled back to Israel immediately after the attacks.

The Forward, a Jewish newspaper, said the FBI found that at least two of the five arrested Israelis were Mossad agents and that *Urban Moving Systems* was a Mossad front operation. The five were held for 71 days, but then **released without charge** and allowed to return to Israel where three of them appeared on television to say that *'our purpose was to document the event'* (Dancing Israelis, 2012).

Yes, an event they knew was going to happen. They knew when, how, and where. What does that tell you? Yet in the final "Official" 9/11 Report by Zelikow, they were not even mentioned once.

Dr. Alan Sabrosky, former director of studies at the **US Army War College** has said publicly that US military leaders now know that Israel *'and those traitors within our nation'* were responsible for the 9/11 attacks (Sabrosky, 2012).

Is Israel Controlling Phony Terror News?

Following September 11th, we had been subjected to a series of '**Bin Laden**' videos and other 'information' promoting fear of Arab terrorism from two organisations called **IntelCenter** and **S.I.T.E.**, or the *Search for International Terrorist Entities Institute*.

IntelCenter is headed by **Ben Venzke** (Rothschild Zionist) and S.I.T.E was co-founded by **Rita Katz** (Rothschild Zionist). In an article headed,

Is Israel Controlling Phony Terror News? Writers **Gordon Duff** and **Brian Jobert** ask some key questions:

- Who says Al Qaeda takes credit for a bombing? Rita Katz.
- Who gets us bin Laden tapes? Rita Katz.
- Who gets us pretty much all information telling us Muslims are bad? Rita Katz

Rita Katz is the Director of *Site Intelligence*, primary source for intelligence used by news services, Homeland Security, the FBI, and CIA. What are her qualifications? She served in the Israeli Defence Force. She has a college degree and most investigative journalists believe the Mossad "helps" her with her information. We find no evidence of any qualification whatsoever of any kind. A bartender has more intelligence gathering experience.

Nobody verifies her claims. SITE says Al Qaeda did it, it hits the papers. SITE says Israel didn't do it and that hits the papers too. What does SITE really do? They check the internet for "information," almost invariably information that Israel wants reported and it is sold as news, seen on American TV, reported in our papers and passed around the internet almost as though it were actually true. Amazing.

Rita Katz admitted to receiving more than **$130,000** for her work as an FBI consultant on the case for the hunt for **Osama Bin Laden**.

Adam Gadahn AKA Adam Pearlman a Jew dressed as an Arab

But not quite so amazing if you have read this far and seen the extent to which the Rothschild Zionist secret society networks control and manipulate world events.

Rothschild Zionists Katz and Venzke provide 'intelligence' and Bin Laden videos for 'security' agencies and the media, and **Adam Gadahn** is an alleged spokesman for 'Al Qaeda' who releases videos of himself supporting terrorism. His name is on the FBI 'most wanted' terrorist list.

How strange then that 'Adam Gadahn' turns out to be a Jewish man called **Adam Pearlman**, grandson of **Carl Pearlman**, who served on the Board of the rabid, Rothschild Zionist, **Anti-Defamation League** (ADL).

By way of deception, thou shalt do war!

Controlling the Media

The Chairman of the US Homeland Security and Governmental Affairs Committee is Senator **Joseph Lieberman** (Rothschild Zionist) who, like the Rothschild cesspit in general, is desperate to use the 'threat of terrorism' to censor the Internet, to block the truth from coming out.

Rothschild Zionists have kept exposure from the door, up to now, through ownership of the mainstream media.

Shahar Ilan, a daily features editor with the leading Israeli newspaper, *Ha'aretz*, wrote:

> The Jews do control the American media. This is very clear, and claiming otherwise is an insult to common knowledge.

Not only in America, either, and not only the 'news' media of Rothschild Zionist moguls like Rupert Murdoch. The **Los Angeles Times** columnist, **Joel Stein** (Rothschild Zionist), wrote an article proclaiming that Americans who don't think Jews (Rothschild Zionists) control Hollywood are just plain 'dumb':

> I had to scour the trades to come up with six Gentiles in high positions at entertainment companies. But lo and behold, even one of that six, AMC President Charles Collier, turned out to be a Jew! As a proud Jew, I want America to know of our accomplishment. Yes, we control Hollywood.

The mass of Jewish people have been mercilessly used and abused by the Rothschild networks that don't give a damn about them. They are not pursuing what is best for Jewish people as a whole, but what suits the Rothschild conspiracy for global domination on behalf of their hidden masters.

The Rothschilds and their Zionist secret society web control American government policy on Israel and everything else – and it's the same in Britain and country after country, including France,

Germany (of course), Italy, Belgium and the European Union, which was a Rothschild creation from the start.

Obama's first major speech on the Middle East in 2008 was, according to the *Wall Street Journal*, written for him by **James Steinberg** (Rothschild Zionist), **Daniel Kurtzer** (Rothschild Zionist) and **Dennis Ross** (Rothschild Zionist). It was delivered to the Rothschild Zionist lobby group, the *American Israel Public Affairs Committee* (AIPAC). Any chance of it being biased against the Palestinians, do you think?

The man appointed to oversee the war in Afghanistan and the targeting of Pakistan was **Richard Holbrooke** (Rothschild Zionist), Obama's 'Special Representative' for Afghanistan and Pakistan who died in December 2010.

Holbrooke served the Rothschild Zionist cabal in positions of 'diplomacy' from the **Vietnam war** to the conflict in **Afghanistan**, taking in posts as a special envoy to the Balkans before and during the war in the former Yugoslavia; as

Richard Holbrooke (1941 - 2010)

United Nations Ambassador; as the man given responsibility for selling the Aids agenda, and so much more.

It is the Rothschilds' duel control of America and Israel that has led to astonishing amounts of American tax dollars being transferred to Israel in military and financial 'aid'. One arm of the Rothschilds is simply giving it to another.

John J. Mearsheimer and **Stephen M. Walt** write in their book, *The Israel Lobby and U.S. Foreign Policy*:

> *Israel receives about $3 billion in direct foreign assistance each year, which is roughly one-fifth of America's entire foreign aid budget. In per capita terms, the United States gives each Israeli a direct subsidy worth about $500 per year. This largesse is especially striking when one realizes that Israel is now a wealthy industrial state with a per capita income roughly equal to South Korea or Spain. (Mearsheimer and Walt, n.d.)*

The US House of Representatives recently approved another $205 million in military aid for Israel for an 'anti-missile' system.

> 'When it comes to defence, military, and intelligence cooperation, the relationship between the US and Israel has never been stronger',

said Democrat Representative **Steve Rothman** (Rothschild Zionist), a member of the House Appropriations Defense Subcommittee.

As he spoke, the Israeli authorities were using their American-supplied military might to continue the blockade of the Gaza Strip which has been stopping supplies of food, fuel, medicine, and basic needs for 1.5 million Palestinians since 2007. Hundreds of Palestinian children are dying per week due to starvation and lack of basic medical supplies – all thanks to the Obama government. But remember what Rothschild Zionist Madelaine Albright said, that ½ million dead Arab children in Iraq was worth it.

2010: A former Mossad officer has alleged the Israeli spy agency has its own "passport factory" to create or doctor passports for use in intelligence operations. Three Australian passports were used by Israeli suspects in the killing of top Hamas leader **Mahmoud Al Mabhouh** in Dubai. Dubai police say they are 99 per cent sure Mossad was behind the operation to smother Mabhouh with a pillow in his hotel room. No charges were laid.

The new face of Rothschild

Nat Rothschild (1971 -) - the new face of greed and corruption

2013: Nathaniel (Nat) Philip Rothschild - the 44-year-old son of **Jacob Rothschild** (the guy at the beginning of the chapter), is described by the **New York Times** as having an extraordinary metamorphosis from playboy to hedge fund prince, and tipped him as,

> *...a kingmaker in his own right, and an investor who some say may become the richest Rothschild of them all.*
> *(Rothschild, 2013)*

Nat Rothschild was well known for ordering up high priced prostitutes by the dozen, to come to the family palace/home, and fulfilling his worst, filthiest, sexual fantasies, all on big daddy's credit card! All this while he was in High School. Apparently he has a liking for black working girls.

Now however, he says he has turned over a new leaf, and wants to knuckle down, work hard, and make billions, like his good old Dad did.

As we have seen, many of these so-called elites have perverted sexual tastes, probably due to their inbreeding. At any rate, I will wage a bet that Nat will have a "sex scandal" before he reaches 45 years old, but no doubt, the public will never hear about it.

And as for working hard? I think my version of working hard is a little different to Nat's version of working hard. I guess it is all relative. But good luck to the young man. Let's hope he takes after his murdered uncle Amschel Mayor James Rothschild. If ever there was a generation of Rothschilds that could make significant changes to the way the family conducts itself, it is this one. But I know they are also under pressure from minders to keep the status quo. It would take a very strong personality with a thick skin to bring change to this family.

2014: A US technology company which had 20 senior staff on board **Malaysia Airlines Flight MH370** had just launched a new electronic warfare gadget for military radar systems in the days before the Boeing 777 went missing. With the disappearance of MH-370, **Jacob Rothschild** became the sole owner of the **Freescale Semiconductors Patent**. This invention is said to revolutionise modern warfare.

2015: Their latest money grab is the **Carbon Tax scam** – see **ANNEX 3.9.1 The Carbon Tax Scam**. Any country that pays a carbon tax – pays it into a Jacob Rothschild's controlled bank. Think of the Rothschild family as the family of puppet masters, always hiding behind the curtain, but always in control of the illusion.

The Lowdown

The Rothschild family is the richest in the world, with an estimated net worth of $400 trillion in personal assets, and $115 trillion in financial assets. They have been at the heart of global finance since the 1760's, when Mayer Amschel Bauer /Rothschild sent his five sons out into the world's five financial centres. The brothers made their millions with their combined global reach in the 19th Century by funding monarchies, governments, both sides of every war, crashing stock markets and murdering or intimidating rivals. A newspaper at the time described the family as the:

> *Brokers and counsellors of the kings of Europe, and the republican chiefs of America.*

Today in 2015, the Rothschild family controls the **US Federal Reserve bank**, and every other Central Bank in the world, as well as the **World Bank**, the **IMF**, and the **Bank of International Settlements** (BIS). They decide what the price of gold and silver will be on a daily basis and profit from its ups and downs. With their agent **Paul Warburg**, they were able to create the powerful, secret, or shadow government of the United States back in **1913**.

The Rothschilds set up and funded organisation like **Bilderberg**, the **United Nations**, the **CFR**, the **Trilateral Commission** etc. by proxy, using the other mega rich families they help to set up, who are thus, beholden to them, like the **Rockefeller** (Chase Manhattan Bank, Exxon Mobile, Chevron and BP); **J.P Morgan** (GE; AT&T, US Steel, US Gold Market); **Du Pont** (Explosives and plutonium for atom bombs for the War Machines of the world, they prohibited farming and use of hemp/marijuana, Nylon, GMO seeds, "Doomsday Seed Vault"); **Bush** (Skull and Bones, Nazis, George HW and George W were both *selected* – not "elected" to be President of the US, and both start wars in Iraq, Oil, banking and real estate).

SOUL DEED

I hereby "unconditionally" surrender my soul

..and my U.S. Constitutional Rights to;

THE ROTHSCHILD FAMILY

In exchange for food stamps, "Obamacare" and a life of servitude

Date	Signature

Rothschilds in the Natural World

There are no fewer than 153 species or sub-species of insect that bear the Rothschild name, as well as 58 birds, 18 mammals, 14 plants, 3 fish, 3 spiders, and 2 reptiles (eg. *Ornithoptera rothschildi* - **Rothschild's birdwing Butterfl** ; Giraffa Camelopardalis *rothschildi* - **Rothschild's giraffe** and *Paphiopedilum rothschildianum* - **Gold of Kinabalu orchid**).

Ornithoptera rothschildi - Rothschild's birdwing Butterfly

In the world of culinary delights, they have also been honoured by having a soufflé (**Rothschild Soufflé**) and a savoury (**Shrimp toast to Rothschild**) named after them. There are towns and numerous streets named after members of the family in their **Fief of Israel**. Rothschilds own several vineyards whose wines are drunk the world over. There is even a Rothschild Island in the Antarctic!

They energetically pursued and acquired decorations, titles and other honours in an attempt to be seen as equal with the European aristocracy. They had the money, but they didn't have the pedigree or class – until, they secured the ultimate prize – an **English Peerage**[13] in 1885. The 3rd generation also threw themselves into hunting and horse racing, those quintessentially, aristocratic pastimes.

They have funded and supported a very long list of politicians in the UK, America, Australia and Canada and no doubt elsewhere. Many of these politicians become Presidents and Prime Ministers, all who owe the Rothschilds a great deal, thus, the Rothschilds get things done their way.

They have also been funding, loaning, and controlling the British Royals since the early 1800's, starting with **King George IV** (when he was still a prince), right up till now with **Queen Elizabeth II**. In 1824, Nathan Rothschild loaned £10,000 (£98,500 in 2015) to the **Duke of York**. This started a stampede of British Royals lining up for "special" loans (mostly for gambling debts). In fact, these two extended German families – Saxe-Coburg-Gotha (British Royals) and the Rothschilds, rose from obscurity to glory in the course of the 19th century. Indeed, theirs

---

[13] The ranks of the English peerage are, in descending order, Duke, Marquess, Earl, Viscount, and Baron.

was to be an almost **symbiotic** relationship. Therefore, in the next chapter, let's blow the lid of secrecy off the **British Royal Family**!

In Conclusion

I have set out here to reveal the true face of Zionism – the House of Rothschild and its networks – and how its agents in Big Government, Big Banking, Big Business, Big Pharma, Big Biotech, Big Media and so on, are working as one unit to impose a global, Orwellian dictatorship on the human population – including the mass of Jewish people.

Zionism is a subject that all but a few are either too ignorant or too frightened to tackle and expose, but it must be made public and the web dismantled if global tyranny is to be avoided in the very near future.

In fact, it's not even about the 'future'; the tyranny is already here and it is just a case of how deeply we are going to allow ourselves to be enslaved by it.

The Rothschilds have spent a century hiding the true and ever-gathering extent of their global control and that veil must be lifted for the mass of the people to see. I should also stress that when I say 'Rothschild', I don't only mean those called 'Rothschild', nor even all of the people who are known by that name. There are many in the Rothschild family and its offshoots who have no idea what the hierarchy is doing and there are many 'Rothschilds' who don't carry the name itself. When I say 'Rothschild', I am referring to the Rothschild bloodline because, they have had a long breeding programme that produce offspring that are brought up under other names.

So when these people come to power, they carry the Rothschild genetics and answer to their control system, but they are not officially called 'Rothschild', and in this way the scale of the Rothschild infiltration of government, finance and so on, remains hidden behind an army of offspring known by different names. Adolf Hitler was a good example of this. It is time to put the Rothschilds on public display because that's the last place they want to be. They have operated from the shadows for long enough and we must urgently ensure that those days are over.

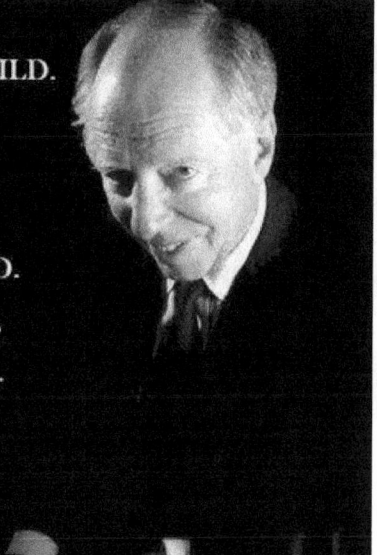

HELLO THERE,

MY NAME IS JACOB ROTHSCHILD.

MY FAMILY IS WORTH
500 TRILLION DOLLARS.

WE OWN NEARLY EVERY
CENTRAL BANK IN THE WORLD.

WE FINANCED BOTH SIDES OF
EVERY WAR SINCE NAPOLEON.

WE OWN YOUR NEWS,
THE MEDIA, YOUR OIL,
AND YOUR GOVERNMENT.

I bet you remember me now thanks to the damn Danny Searle!

References:

ABC News, (2015). *Breaking News: RFID Microchip Implant Available NOW 2015 (Abc news)*. [online] YouTube. Available at: https://youtu.be/afVbbn8PHEU [Accessed 24 Aug. 2015].

Allen, G. (1972). *None dare call it conspiracy*. Rossmoor, Calif.: Concord Press.

Britton, F. (1955). *Behind communism*. Los Angeles, Calif.: F.L. Britton.

Cheney, D. (2015). *Dick Cheney*. [online] Wikipedia. Available at: https://en.wikipedia.org/wiki/Dick_Cheney [Accessed 25 Aug. 2015].

Cibella, R. and Baron, D. (1998). *Jewish Families of Frankfurt - ROTHSCHILD FAMILY*. [online] Goldschmidt.tripod.com. Available at: http://goldschmidt.tripod.com/roths.htm [Accessed 22 Aug. 2015].

Dancing Israelis, (2012). *Dancing Israelis Our purpose was to document the event*. [online] YouTube. Available at: https://youtu.be/wIeP84WEZLU [Accessed 16 Oct. 2015].

Dawkins, R. (1989). *The selfish gene*. Oxford: Oxford University Press.

Duff, G. and Jobert, B. (2009). *IS ISRAEL CONTROLLING PHONY TERROR NEWS?*. [online] Whale.to. Available at: http://www.whale.to/c/who_is.html [Accessed 16 Oct. 2015].

Faber, D. (1980). *The life of Lorena Hickok*. New York: W. Morrow.

Fetzer, J. (2015). *PressTV-'Cheney was in charge of 9/11 false flag'*. [online] Presstv.ir. Available at: http://www.presstv.ir/Detail/2015/07/25/421797/Cheney-911-false-flag- [Accessed 24 Aug. 2015].

Fickling, D. (2004). *'Mossad spies' jailed over New Zealand passport fraud*. [online] The Guardian. Available at: http://www.theguardian.com/world/2004/jul/16/israel [Accessed 16 Oct. 2015].

Findley, P. (1993). *Deliberate deceptions*. Chicago, Ill.: Lawrence Hill Books.

Gold and Silver Prices, (2011). *How the Gold and Silver Prices Are Determined ?*. [online] Goldbroker. com. Available at: https://www.goldbroker.com/how-gold-silver-prices-are-determined [Accessed 22 Aug. 2015].

Griffin, G. (2002). *The creature from Jekyll Island*. Westlake Village, Calif.: American Media.

Halliburton, (2015). *CorpWatch : Halliburton*. [online] Corpwatch.org. Available at: http://www. corpwatch.org/section.php?id=15 [Accessed 16 Oct. 2015].

Halliburton, (2015). *Halliburton*. [online] Wikipedia. Available at: https://en.wikipedia.org/wiki/ Halliburton#1990s [Accessed 25 Aug. 2015].

Henderson, D. (2011). *The Four Horsemen Behind America's Oil Wars*. [online] Global Research. Available at: http://www.globalresearch.ca/the-four-horsemen-behind-america-s-oil-wars/24507 [Accessed 22 Aug. 2015].

Hitchcock, A. (2012). *Synagogue of Satan - updated, expanded, and uncensored*. [S.l.]: Lulu Com.

Jones, S. (2013). *Professor Steven Jones on the Controlled Demolition Of WTC Demolition*. [online] YouTube. Available at: https://youtu.be/wkaX5n3pfZE [Accessed 26 Aug. 2015].

Koehler, H. (1940). *Inside the Gestapo*. London: Pallas Pub. Co.

Landman, S. (1936). *Great Britain, the Jews and Palestine*. [London]: [New Zionist Press].

Lawrence, T. (2015). *T. E. Lawrence*. [online] Wikipedia. Available at: https://en.wikipedia.org/wiki/ T._E._Lawrence [Accessed 14 Oct. 2015].

MacArthur, J. (2004). *Second front*. Berkeley: University of California Press.

Mearsheimer, J. and Walt, S. (n.d.). *The Israel lobby and U.S. foreign policy*.

Michel Ph.D., N. and Moore, S. (2014). *Quantitative Easing, The Fed's Balance Sheet, and Central Bank Insolvency*. [online] The Heritage Foundation. Available at: http://www.heritage.org/research/ reports/2014/08/quantitative-easing-the-feds-balance-sheet-and-central-bank-insolvency [Accessed 16 Oct. 2015].

Morton, F. (1962). *The Rothschilds*. New York: Atheneum.

Nayirah, (2010). *Faked Kuwaiti girl testimony*. [online] YouTube. Available at: https://youtu.be/ LmfVs3WaE9Y [Accessed 14 Oct. 2015].

Newman, S. (2008). *Social Classes in the Middle Ages | Middle Ages*. [online] Thefinertimes.com. Available at: http://www.thefinertimes.com/Middle-Ages/social-classes-in-the-middle-ages. html#sthash.zqTbZpKA.dpuf [Accessed 10 Aug. 2015].

Newman, S. (2015). *Fief in the Middle Ages | Middle Ages*. [online] Thefinertimes.com. Available at: http://www.thefinertimes.com/Middle-Ages/fief-in-the-middle-ages.html [Accessed 10 Aug. 2015].

Passports, (2010). *Mossad 'factory' churned out fake Australian passports*. [online] Abc.net.au. Available at: http://www.abc.net.au/news/2010-02-26/mossad-factory-churned-out-fake-australian/343612 [Accessed 16 Oct. 2015].

Perle, R. (2015). *Richard Perle*. [online] Wikipedia. Available at: https://en.wikipedia.org/wiki/Richard_ Perle [Accessed 24 Aug. 2015].

Pine, L. (1956). *Tales of the British aristocracy*. [London]: Burke.

Pryor, G. (1998). *1944-Which begat the Balfour declaration*. [pen, ink and wash on bainbridge board] Canberra: Part of Pryor collection of cartoons and drawings - National Library of Australia.

Reuters, (2015). *Microchips implanted under the skin of office workers*. [online] YouTube. Available at: https://youtu.be/NBTK8cFajYE [Accessed 24 Aug. 2015].

Rio Tinto, (2015). *Rio Tinto delivers underlying earnings of $9.3 billion and announces a 12 per cent increase in full year dividend and a $2.0 billion share buy-back - Rio Tinto*. [online] Riotinto.com. Available at: http://www.riotinto.com/media/media-releases-237_14294.aspx [Accessed 22 Aug. 2015].

Roosevelt, E., Hickok, L. and Streitmatter, R. (2000). *Empty without you*. [Cambridge, Mass.]: Da Capo Press.

Rosenthal, H. (1976). *Harold Wallace Rosenthal interview*. [online] Iamthewitness.com. Available at: http://iamthewitness.com/DarylBradfordSmith_Rosenthal.html [Accessed 6 Aug. 2015].

Rothschild, A. (1996). *The Rothschild They Murdered*. [online] HenryMakow.com. Available at: http://www.henrymakow.com/remembering_the_rothschild_who.html [Accessed 25 Aug. 2015].

Rothschild, N. (2013). *The richest Rothschild of them all*. [online] Mail Online. Available at: http://www.dailymail.co.uk/femail/article-446056/The-richest-Rothschild-all.html [Accessed 7 Aug. 2015].

Ruppert, M. (2004). *Crossing the Rubicon*. Gabriola, BC: New Society Publishers.

Rush, J. (2014). *Underpants bomber failed 'because he wore underwear for two weeks'*. [online] Mail Online. Available at: http://www.dailymail.co.uk/news/article-2705644/Underpants-bomber-failed-mission-blow-airliner-wore-pair-underwear-two-weeks.html [Accessed 16 Oct. 2015].

Russo, A. (2001). *Nicholas Rockefeller admitted the elite's goal is a 100% microchipped and enslaved World population*. [online] YouTube. Available at: https://youtu.be/oygBg6ETYIM [Accessed 6 Aug. 2015].

Sabrosky, D. (2012). *Israel DID 9/11 (Israeli Mossad) Dr. Alan Sabrosky*. [online] YouTube. Available at: https://youtu.be/TT1AzrKuEtM [Accessed 16 Oct. 2015].

Sachar, H. (1992). *A history of the Jews in America*. New York: Knopf.

Shooting, (2006). *Dick Cheney hunting incident*. [online] Wikipedia. Available at: https://en.wikipedia.org/wiki/Dick_Cheney_hunting_incident [Accessed 25 Aug. 2015].

Silverstein, L. (2001). *9/11-WTC7 Larry Silverstein says 'PULL IT' (INSIDE JOB)*. [online] YouTube. Available at: https://youtu.be/p34XrI2Fm6I [Accessed 16 Oct. 2015].

Solzhenitsyn, A. (1974). *The Gulag Archipelago, 1918-1956*. New York: Harper & Row.

Standley, J. (2001). *BBC Reports Collapse of WTC Building 7 Early-- TWICE*. [online] YouTube. Available at: https://youtu.be/6mxFRigYD3s [Accessed 16 Oct. 2015].

Stockbauer, B. (2011). *PNAC "REBUILDING AMERICA'S DEFENSES" – A Summary*. [online] Informationclearinghouse.info. Available at: http://www.informationclearinghouse.info/article3249.htm [Accessed 16 Oct. 2015].

Stockham, R. (2015). *UK now has third highest number of super-rich in the world*. [online] Left Foot Forward. Available at: https://leftfootforward.org/2015/10/uk-now-has-third-highest-number-of-super-rich-in-the-world/ [Accessed 16 Oct. 2015].

Strauss-Kahn, D. (2015). *Dominique Strauss-Kahn*. [online] Wikipedia. Available at: https://en.wikipedia.org/wiki/Dominique_Strauss-Kahn#Personal_life [Accessed 16 Oct. 2015].

The Money Masters, (2015). *Famous Quotations on Banking*. [online] Available at: http://www.themoneymasters.com/the-money-masters/famous-quotations-on-banking/ [Accessed 29 May 2015].

Thomson, M. (2007). *BBC NEWS | UK | When Britain and France nearly married.* [online] News.bbc. co.uk. Available at: http://news.bbc.co.uk/2/hi/uk/6261885.stm [Accessed 16 Oct. 2015].

Weisman, C. (1976). *The Hidden Tyranny - 'Our God is Lucifer' : Free Download & Streaming : Internet Archive.* [online] Internet Archive. Available at: http://www.archive.org/details/ TheHiddenTyranny-ourGodIsLucifer [Accessed 21 Nov. 2015].

White, M. (2011). *Twentieth Century Atlas - Death Tolls.* [online] Necrometrics.com. Available at: http://necrometrics.com/20c5m.htm [Accessed 22 Aug. 2015].

.

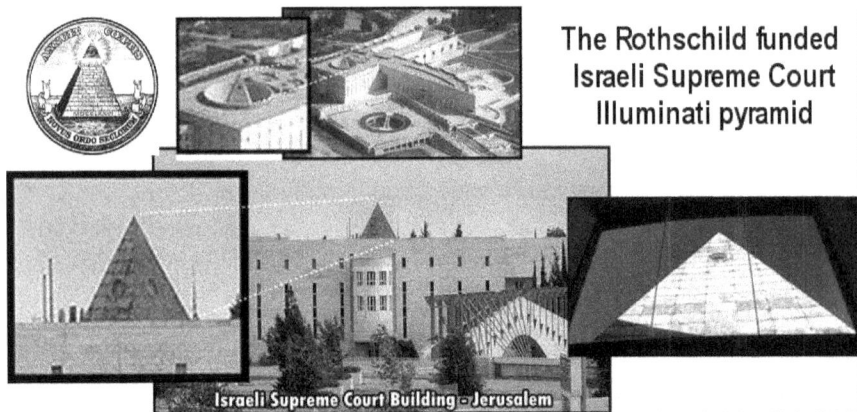

The Rothschild funded Israeli Supreme Court Illuminati pyramid

Israeli Supreme Court Building - Jerusalem

12

EXPOSED: THE HOUSE OF WINDSOR

"It has always been the aim of royalty and aristocracy to lower the individual liberty and independence of the common people. A baron and a minute-man could not breathe the same air."

—JOHN BOYLE O'REILLY

*T*here are people who believe that they have a God given right to rule over others. They believe, that their outward appearance is superior to all others. They harbour selfish ambitions to be rich and to have power over what they describe, as common people. They lie, cheat, steal, strangle, stab and slash their way to power. They believe that their actual Will power, what the British occultist, **Aleister Crowley** described as the *Will of Thelema* is The Royal Will, and must be obeyed. Literally millions of people have been slaughtered at the behest of the Royal lust for war. And thousands of people have been assassinated so that demonic Dukes, and Killer Queens can reign supreme.

This cabal of crowned killers use the global network of Secret Societies, described as the Illuminati, to do their bidding and their killing. The conspiratorial view of history, is the correct view of history. Conspiracy to grant property, conspiracy to make illegal profits, and conspiracy to assassinate has been the driving force behind the Royal political elite for thousands of years.

For the crowned killers of England, torture, disembowelling, impaling, hanging, burning, strangling, poisoning, and killing in the most satanic manner, is the order of the day. This, is the *modus operandi* (MO) of Royal Families. For centuries, the Royal elite devised terrible punishments for anyone accused of treason. The monarchy reserved the most disgusting forms of torture and death for those who questioned the Royal Will. A so-called traitor would often have each arm and leg tied to four horses, which were whipped to gallop in opposite directions, thus ripping the victim into four parts, while still alive. Regularly, the Royal elite would divide the victim's heart into sections, and send these for public display to different parts of the country as a macabre warning. The head would be put on a spike and displayed in a prominent location for the same reasons.

The British throne has been bathed in blood for centuries. At one time, Britain contained several small kingdoms. These small kingdoms were ruled over by inter-marriage and wars. The self-elected elite were gradually amalgamated into the single monarchy which rules over Wales, Scotland, Northern Ireland, England, Canada, Australia, New Zealand, as well as 53 other smaller nations, and secretly controls the United States of America.

Things Are Never As They Seem

In July, 2015, *The Sun* newspaper published an article "*Secret 1933 ilm shows Edward VIII teaching this Nazi salute to the Queen.*" The 1933 film showed the then, Princess Elizabeth (later Queen Elizabeth II), being taught the Nazi salute by her uncle Edward VIII, Prince of Wales who would later be known as King Edward VIII, and Emperor of India (Salute, 2015). He would be quietly removed from the throne less than 12 months later, but more on that later.

The point is, the so-called British Royal Family known as the Windsors, are actually German. But how far back have these German parasites sat on the English throne? The lineage is long, but begins with the ***Act of Settlement*** of **1701**.

The Parliament of England granted the English throne to protestant heir, **Sophia of Hanover,** a German lineage of **King George's** soon followed, as did the **American War for Independence**.

American Resistance

The United States was founded on July 4th, 1776 in resistance to the hegemonic, despotic, tyrannical rule of King George III and his abuse against the colonies. Most of the British parliament was against going to war with their fellow Englishmen because the King was also very unpopular there as well. It was well know that he was a German King, and his father was brought over to rule England. These people could barely speak English.

What is not common knowledge is that the United States did not technically win the ***War of Independence***. King George III had a cunning plan. He offered to stop the war, grant them "independence", as long as they paid the British Crown a tribute every year, they were not allowed to grant noble titles (in case they tried to rise up again), and they must allow free trade between the two nations. To achieve this, they set up the United States as a corporation.

Washington and his soldiers had put up a good fight, but by now they were a spent force. He agreed to the terms, and the rest is history. Again, the Royals create the illusion that the people are free, all the while they rule from behind the curtains.

They did a similar stunt in Australia, Canada, and New Zealand, but avoided a war. Instead, they called these countries "Dominion" countries, which meant they could have their own government, money, laws (within reason) and for all intents and purpose seem like a free, independent country. Much better for productivity.

Interestingly, India, while under British occupation, lobbied tirelessly to be granted Dominion status, however it was always refused, no doubt because the Indians had dark skin. So what happened? Revolution, and Mahatma Gandhi. India got full independence from Britain in **1947**.

To this day, the United States still pays a tribute to the British Royal family, and they still take their daily orders from the **CFR** (who get their orders from the RIIA in the UK).

In the Modern Era

It is a fine drama which spans well over 300 years, with tales of lust and betrayal, of heroism and cruelty, of mysteries, murders, tragedies, and trials.

In **1840,** the German bloodline was given another injection when **Victoria** married her German cousin **Albert**. You may ask what did lust have to do with the matronly Queen Victoria?

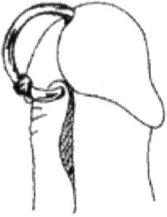

Well, she was young once and her husband **Prince Albert** gave his name to more than just a bridge, a concert hall, and a memorial. Indeed, no other British Royal has a body piercing named after him. It obviously kept Victoria happy, she had nine children to Albert.

Another interesting fact is that the present Queen's grandfather **George V**, actually took over the running of the country, with a secret, personal rule for a few days in 1931. He believed it was the only way to save the country from revolution. Most of the papers relating to this are still hidden. How much do we really know about what goes on?

Prince Albert Piercing

The Power behind the Throne

In 1867, **Walter Badger** wrote a book on the British Constitution which said that it had two parts. The **efficient part**, and the **dignified part**. The dignified part was headed by the Queen (Victoria). It was a piece of theatre, whose only purpose was to make people feel loyalty. The actual power was entirely held by the efficient part, which he said was a secret committee called **The Cabinet**. Everyone accepted Badger's book. In fact, the government encouraged people to believe in it. So did the Royal family then and now. Well, they would wouldn't they. The truth however, is very different.

Obviously, when the 18-year-old Victoria came to the throne in **1837**, she was not in much of a position to try and run the country. She had a rather odd upbringing. Her father had been a brother of **George IV** and **William IV**, but he died when she was a baby. Her mother was a straight-laced, **German Princess** who was determined that her daughter should not be part of the disreputable life of the court. Furthermore, she was convinced the young Victoria would be murdered by one of her terrible uncles, who wanted the thrown for himself. Thus, she was brought up in isolation in **Kensington Palace**, which in those days was fairly cut off from London. Her main interest on becoming Queen, was to finally cut free from her mother and supervisor, and move out of her mother's bedroom. When she was 19, she fell hopelessly, utterly, in love with her first cousin, the 20-year-old, younger son, of the Duke of **Saxe-Coburg-Gotha.**

> *He is excessively handsome. Such beautiful eyes. My heart is quite going..."*
> *Victoria's diary*

He certainly tried hard to look good. That notorious ring was attached to a chain, to assist in moving the line in his britches. They married in 1840, but Victoria wasn't hugely popular at the time. She was headstrong, and wilful. She actually blocked a change of government because it would have upset her domestic arrangements.

The Prime Minister at the time, **Lord Melbourne,** had given Victoria the wives and daughters of his own supporters, as the ladies of the bedchamber. When his weak government fell, and **Robert Peel** came to power, Peel insisted that the Queen should replace at least some of the members, so that the court wasn't a complete one-party state. Victoria refused. Peel felt forced to resign and Melbourne came briefly back to power.

The people did not like what she was doing, and they didn't like her. Contrary to what the royal spin doctors have written in the school history books, Queen Victoria was not popular. She was often hissed at in public and there were no less than seven attempts to assassinate her. Keeping the populace ignorant with no public schooling, using adults and children alike as virtual slaves in workhouses, providing no adequate protection against hypothermia, working every man, woman and child to exhaustion, and imposing a crippling poll tax was the *modus operandi* of Queen Victoria and all her relatives sitting on the thrones across Europe. No wonder they were despised by the general public. So-called Victorian values allowed children to be used as slave labour. Inhumane slums and widespread poverty were common across the whole the Europe, right up until the 1970s.

Child labour in coal mines was very common during Victoria's reign

If Victoria was hated, Albert was positively despised and viewed as a stiff German Prince that did not care about England.

Peel came back to power and refused to grant Albert much more than half the allowance Victoria demanded, saying the people were very hard up - which they were. The position of the throne seemed pretty shaky. It didn't seem likely that this would become the most secure and richest monarchy in the world. How did that happen?

The Rise to Power

When Victoria came to the throne, all she had as her own, was the revenue of the **Duchy of Lancaster**, £27,000 per year (£2,500,200.00 / US$3,778,177.00 in 2015). The **Sunday Times Rich List** for 1990, showed Queen Elizabeth II as being worth £6.7 billion. That is nearly £15 billion in today's money (2015). She is the richest person in Britain by a huge margin, and second only to the Rothschilds on the world stage, even though they answer and bow to her.

It is true that the latest Rich List shows her being worth a mere £250 million. Has she lost 97% of her money on the horses? Did she give it all away to charity? No. The latest figure is a guess, based on

Queen Victoria and Prince Albert photo-graphed at Buckingham Palace in 1860

an instruction to *The Sunday Times* not to count anything she holds in trust for the nation. Obviously she can't sell the crown jewels and pocket the proceeds. However, most rich people actually hold much of their wealth in trust, yet it still treated as theirs, because they have the use of it.

The Royal move into profit began when Albert took charge of the Royal finances. He wasn't allowed to be King, there was deep suspicion of him. But Victoria let him manager her affairs and he did an astonishing job of it. The Royal household was an incredible gothic antique. To clean a window in Buckingham Palace, it was a job for the **Lord Chamberlain's** staff, unless it was a kitchen or scullery window, then they had to call on the **Lord Stuart**, and neither could touch the outside of the glass, because that was looked after by the **Office of Woods and Forests**. Laying a fire was the Lord Stuart's job, but lighting of it was done by the Lord Chamberlain's staff. So whenever they were not on good terms, the palace froze. Other Palace staff were paid for jobs whose very purpose and even existence had been forgotten.

Enter Albert with boiling water and a hatchet, and he soon sorted that lot out, and cut Victoria's costs dramatically. He had a huge capacity for work and organisation, so when he came up with the idea for a great exhibition of the world's arts and industry, no one should have doubted that he could make it happen. But they did. They had no confidence in the exhibition hall, the **Crystal Palace** - a giant greenhouse – the brainchild of **Joseph Paxton**, and when they realised that thousands would congregate there, they thought that it would be a rallying point for revolutionaries.

The opening of **The Great Exhibition** was on May 1st, **1851**, and was a thrilling day for the nation and for Queen Victoria. The Royal couple began to be viewed with some enthusiasm and it was quite

The Great Exhibition 1851, in the Crystal Palace, Hyde Park London

understandable that the next year, an eccentric miser should leave the Queen half million pounds in his will.

Albert's influence in the government rose visibly, which of course soon put an end to his popularity. By **1854**, it was generally believed that Albert the foreigner, was a traitor, in league with Russia forcing loyal ministers out of office. Crowds gathered around the **Tower of London** under the impression that Albert and Victoria had been arrested for treason. That frenzy died down, but at the back of it were two things that were going to be permanent problems.

One, was that the Queen and her consort must have some role in running the country. But that could not be squared with any kind of representative government. The other issue was that people were realising that the monarch was making a profit, and they didn't like it. The solution was to conceal what was really happening under a cloak of secrecy, and that cloak is still in place to this very day.

Indeed, many researchers over the years have been denied documents that should not have been denied, but were, because they contained information about the Royal family. Some of these documents go back past Victoria, and still they are deemed "*a matter of national security*," a catch all phrase to block us plebs from seeing their secret business.

Albert's own role was very secret. He was in reality acting as King of England, but that was behind the scenes. The title he was eventually given in **1857** was just **Prince Consort**. He took it very seriously and worked himself to death. His last act as the hidden King of England was at the end of **1861**, to stop the Prime Minister from sending an angry dispatch to the American government. If it had been sent, England would probably have been pushed into the **American Civil War**, on the side of the South.

Albert Dies, Victoria drops her bundle

When Albert died, Victoria let go a terrible shriek. She never recovered. She retired to Scotland and went into what seemed to be an everlasting mourning.

Victoria with her uncouth, arrogant, and heavy-drinking Highland gillie, John Brown

She and Albert had built a number of retreats for themselves. **Osborne** on the Isle of Wight, **Sandringham** in Norfolk and her favourite, **Balmoral**, in Scotland. It was here that she hid for months at a time with the faithful Highland *Gille*[14], **John Brown**. He was allowed enough familiarity for the Queen to be widely referred to as **Mrs. Brown**. Brown was a hard-drinking man. Initially, when he was a young *gillie* with a lot of physical duties, his drinking does not seem to have adversely affected him, but as

---

[14] Gillie is a Scots term that refers to a man or a boy who acts as an attendant on a fishing, or hunting expeditions, primarily in the Highlands. In origin it referred especially to someone who attended on his employer or guests.

he grew older and his duties became more indoors and sedentary, his alcoholism began to catch up with him, to the disgust of the court. Victoria occasionally had to excuse him from attending her at dinners because he was "bashful," a Victorian euphemism for completely drunk. It was also rumoured that they had a secret child together, a daughter (Lamont-Brown, 2000).

The Public ask – Why are we Paying for Her?

Victoria herself could see no reason to take part in public ceremonies like the *Opening of Parliament*. She thought that her hidden role as the head of government was enough. But that of course led many people to wonder why they had to pay for her up keep at all. She received, as she had done so from the start of a reign, £385,000.00 (£41,965,000.00 in 2015) a year from the government. It was way more than she needed. Indeed, her court was nowhere near as expensive as for instance, George IV's expenses, and without her being visible, many people could see no point in her having this money.

By the **1870**'s, there was a strong Republican movement expressing itself in newspapers, large public meetings, and in parliament. The nature of the country was changing dramatically. New industrial cities were darkening the landscape with smoke and soot. A new kind of society was emerging. A society of low-paid factory workers, artisans, builders, miners and metalworkers. These were people outside the political world, with no natural attachments to traditional political structures, and there were a lot of them.

The anti-Royalist got angry and loud every time Parliament was asked for extra grants to Victoria's children, when they came of age or were married. But in fact, it was very probably these children who saved her thrown.

No British Statesman wanted to see the Royal family given its marching orders when their marriages offered such a useful back door into the Royal families of Europe. Victoria's eldest daughter was married to the heir to the **Kaiser** of the new German Empire and was a strong and useful influence on her husband, and a thorn in Bismarck's flesh. The heir to the British throne was **Albert Edward**, who married **Alexandra**, daughter of the **King of Denmark** and sister to the **King of Greece**.

The Greek Crown had actually been offered to another of Victoria's sons, **Alfred**. The Greeks had sacked their own King and held a national vote on who should get the throne. 95% of them voted for Alfred, who was at the time an 18-year-old midshipmen in the Royal Navy. The government made him turn it down, because they had promised to keep their hands off Greece. Never mind, it went as a sort of hand-me-down to the son of England's good friend, the King of Denmark.

In **1874**, Alfred married the daughter of **Czar Alexander II**, which was very useful given the Anglo/Russian competition on the edges of India.

These were marriages that would produce many, many, well distributed children. By the time Victoria died in **1901**, she had over 90 living descendants. It was a full-time job just getting them birthday presents. The rulers of **Germany, Greece, Romania, Norway, Russia, Yugoslavia, Spain,** and **Sweden** would all trace their descent from this one lady.

There was a downside to all this Royal intermarriage and inbreeding though. Victoria was a carrier of **haemophilia**, the condition that prevents blood from clotting and the Spanish, Prussian, and Russian Royal families were consequently affected by it. But even if the British government had known about that, they wouldn't have shed many tears over it. As a system for exercising influence abroad, the monarchy was well worth the money. It also ought to have the advantage at home, with inducing people to be loyal to their country, even if they detested its government, which is obviously very useful if you ran that government. But to sell monarchy to the British and Commonwealth public, monarchy had to be rebranded.

Victoria the Brand Name / Logo

In 1867, a new Tory Prime Minister, and Rothschild Zionist, **Benjamin Disraeli**, was just the man to do it. He flattered, flirted, and lured Victoria out of mourning and back to public life. He re-created her as *Empress of India*, turning her into the **Queen Empress** (not that the Indians had any say in it). The classic, posed picture (on the next page) becomes the new logo for Victoria (Rebrand, 2015).

Britain was now a world power with an international trade that dwarfed all others thanks to the Council of 300's **East India Company**. Britain's Navy also dominated the oceans and its empire expanded on the simple principle that *trade follows the flag*, and if the Union

January 1, 1877, Queen Victoria was proclaimed Empress of India

Jack is flying in each remote corner of the globe, then other flags aren't. The problem was however, for a small country with a very small army, to rule ever more of the Earth's surface. That rule couldn't be maintained by force, it required the consent of the governed. It was the grand theatrics of Disraeli's Victorian Imperialism that invited people throughout the Empire to take pride in being subjects. But not by a bunch of industrialists and politicians, but of a Prim and Matronly Great Sovereignty. The Queen lavished foreign leaders with medals, and titles, and held fancy dinners when they visited. This left the idiotic foreign leaders eating out of her hand. She had them right where she needed them – at her feet, and they were happy to keep their own people down and obedient to her.

Victoria became the logo of the British Empire. Her portrait spread all over the world thanks especially to the introduction of postage stamps. A statue would appear in virtually every town and city of the British Empire, and where there was no statue, there would certainly be a Victoria Street, Victoria Park, Victoria Hotel, or Victoria something. The whole process came to a glorious climax in her **Golden Jubilee** of **1887**.

The great processions in London, with representatives of "her" dominions, were followed by an eruption of ugly public halls, clock towers, fountains and statues, disfiguring public spaces over about a quarter of the planet. By the time Victoria died, hardly anyone even remembered that her thrown had once seemed endangered. In fact, she reigned so long, 64 years, that hardly anyone could even remember any other sovereign.

Her death in **1901** at age 81, was just 22 days into the new century, and seemed portentous. She'd become synonymous with Britain and its Empire. Now, Britain's would leave the 19th century without the security of the Great Mother Hen.

Victoria would cast a long shadow. Elizabeth II, coming to the throne 51 years later, would be the first of her successors, who had no personal memory of her. Victoria's eldest son, **Albert Edward** became the new **King Edward VII**, was already 59 years old. The funeral of the Queen Empress and Edward's coronation involved a huge invention of traditions and ceremonies. In this atmosphere, it's not surprising that Edward was granted an annual allowance even greater than Victoria's. A few voices said that it was unnecessary for the King to have as big an income as **Andrew Carnegie**, the Bill Gates of his day, but no one took much notice.

King Edward VII

Edward VII (1841-1910)

Edward had been given a miserable and oppressive childhood. Victoria had measured him by the impossible yardstick of her hero worship of the perfect man, his father. Naturally, young Bertie rebelled. Of course, his first visit to a prostitute shocked his parents deeply. It happened to be followed by his father Albert's fatal illness, which Victoria had inevitably blamed on "her wicked son."

She had arranged his marriage shortly afterwards in the hope that domestic discipline would rein him in. **Princess Alex of Denmark** was beautiful, but she was also deaf, and dull company. With nothing much else to do, Bertie had become the living epitome of the life of a playboy. A life of champagne drinking, cigar-smoking, horse racing, gambling, and entertaining show girls, and pretty married ladies. He was naturally drawn to the company of outsiders. Not just shady characters, but the "Jews and Catholics", "bankers and foreigners," and he was outspokenly outraged by the casual racism of the Empire,

> Because a man has a black face and a different religion than our own, there is no good reason why he should be treated as a Brute"
> - Albert Edward

He sat on a commission on working-class housing and even invited a member of the working class to stay at Sandringham. Admittedly, the man in question was an MP and a fellow member of the Commission, and he had to eat in his bedroom because he didn't have the right clothes to come down to dinner...but still...

By the time Bertie came to the throne, he was a big, fat old man, with a social conscience and a comforting mistress, **Alice Campbell**, who understood him perfectly. Edward saw himself as something like a nursery rhyme monarch, magnificent and jolly, caring and helpful.

In **1903**, completely ignoring his government, he went to France and started negotiations for a treaty that would become the **Entente Cordiale**, which saw a significant improvement in Anglo-French relations. However, this isolated Germany. He detested his nephew, the Kaiser. He persuaded the press, and then the government, to back the treaty which guaranteed that if Germany attacked France, Britain would go to war in their defence. And that is exactly what happened in 1914.

He determinedly resisted any increase in democracy in Britain, and was a firm opponent of the vote for women. The crunch over his reactionary views came when **Lloyd George** planned to introduce old-age pensions in **1909.**

To raise the cash, there would have to be new taxes on income. The Tory (conservatives) majority in the **House of Lords** voted down what was called the "*people's budget*" and when the Liberal government drew up legislation to take that power away from the Lords, they voted that down to – obviously. So the Prime Minister told the King he needed to create about 250 new peers to swing the vote. Edward was not enthusiastic, but would he actually defy the government?

In May **1910**, in the middle of the battle, Edward died. Edward's 44 year-old son **George** inherited the throne.

Hey there, Georgy boy

George V was the second son of Edward VII. His mother was **Alexandra of Denmark**, sister of **Empress Marie of Russia**. He joined the Royal Navy aged 12 and served until 1892, when he became heir to the throne on the death of his elder brother Albert, Duke of Clarence, who died of pneumonia. In order to step into his brother shoes, he left his job and married the woman who been betrothed to Clarence. She was related of course, and her name was Princess **Mary of Teck**. Teck was

King George V (1865-1936)

in the Kingdom of Württemberg, Germany. "May," as she was known, now inherited a fortune worth around £250/$380 million in today's prices, and a political crisis.

They became Duke and Duchess of York and lived on the Sandringham Estate, in Norfolk. They had six children Edward, Albert, Mary, Henry, George, and John (George V, 2015). The youngest, Prince John, suffered from epilepsy and was locked up in a farm house. He allegedly died at aged 13, most likely from "assisted" suffocation.

As part of the deal with the government to pass the budget and cut the power to the House of Lords, it was agreed that the Crown could **stop paying any income tax.** In return, the King would pay for his own trips abroad (which they never did – they just get the host country they are visiting to pay the costs). The new constitutional deal drew the teeth of the House of Lords. Whatever the elected government in the Commons decided to do, it now could do. The only possible break on its power now was the King, and the question was of course, was whether he would ever exercise it, and what would happen if he tried.

At first, the Crown was too weak to try. But when war began with Germany in **1914**, George V was seen naturally enough, as German, which he was. He kept a bit quiet about his official titles of *Field Marshall General of the Prussian Army* and *Admiral of the Imperial German Navy*.

What's in a name?

The Windsor name now used by Queen Elizabeth II and other British royal's only dates back to 1917. Before that, the British Royal family bore the German name Saxe-Coburg-Gotha (Sachsen-Coburg und Gotha in German), popularly known as Brunswick or Hanover. Why the drastic name change?

The answer to that question is simple: **World War I**. Since August **1914**, Britain had been at war with Germany. Anything German had a bad connotation, including the German name Saxe-Coburg-Gotha. Not only that, Germany's **Kaiser Wilhelm** was a cousin of the British King. So on July 17, 1917, to hide his German ancestry, Queen Victoria's grandson, **King George V,** officially declared that *"all descendants in the male line of Queen Victoria, who are subjects of these realms, other than female descendants who marry or who have married, shall bear the name* **Windsor***."*

Thus the king himself, who was a member of the House of Saxe-Coburg-Gotha, changed his own name and that of his wife, Queen Mary, and their children to **Windsor***.* The new English name Windsor was taken from one of the King's favourite castles.

His granddaughter Queen **Elizabeth II** confirmed the Royal Windsor name in a declaration following her accession in **1952.** But in 1960, Queen Elizabeth II and her husband **Prince Philip** announced yet another name change. Prince Philip of Greece and Denmark, whose mother had been **Alice of Battenberg**, had already Anglicized his name to **Philip Mountbatten** when he married Elizabeth in 1947. (Interestingly, all four of Philip's sisters, all now deceased, married Germans.) In her 1960 declaration to the **Privy Council**, the Queen expressed her wish that her children by Philip (other than those in line for the throne) would henceforth bear the hyphenated name **Mountbatten-Windsor.** For whatever reason, the request was rejected and the British royal family's name has remained Windsor.

Queen Victoria and the Saxe-Coburg-Gotha Line

The British House of Saxe-Coburg-Gotha began with Queen Victoria's marriage to the German Prince Albert of Sachsen-Coburg und

QUEEN CHRISTMAS BROADCAST EXCLUSIVE

'MY HUSBAND AND I ARE RELATED TO THE GERMAN ARISTOCRACY BEHIND THE WORLD WARS AND OUR FAMILY NAME WAS CHANGED TO WINDSOR TO HIDE THIS. WE ALSO SENT THE RUSSIAN SPY AND PAEDOPHILE ANTHONY BLUNT TO GERMANY TO HIDE COLLABORATION WITH OUR NAZI FAMILY DURING WW2.

WE FURTHER INVITED THE PAEDOPHILE AND PROCURER OF CHILDREN JIMMY SAVILE INTO OUR INNER CIRCLE KNOWING WHAT HE WAS DOING. WE WISH YOU ALL A HAPPY CHRISTMAS.'

DAVIDICKE.COM

Gotha in 1840. Prince Albert (1819-1861) was also responsible for the introduction of German Christmas customs (including the Christmas tree) in England. The British Royal family still celebrates Christmas on December 24th, when Germans celebrate, rather than on Christmas Day as is normal in English custom.

Just as Victoria and Albert shared one grandfather (Duke Francis of Saxe-Coburg-Saalfeld) and one grandmother (Countess Augusta Reuss) in common, two pairs of their grandchildren married each other. In 1888, **Princess Irene** of Hesse and by Rhine, whose mother was Queen Victoria's daughter Alice, married **Prince Henry** of Prussia, a son of Victoria's daughter Victoria. Another of Alice's children, Grand Duke **Ernest Louis** of Hesse, married **Princess Victoria Melita**, a daughter of Alice's brother Alfred, Duke of Saxe-Coburg and Gotha, in 1894, but divorced in 1901 (Victoria and Albert, 2015).

It was also one of the inbred grandsons of Victoria and Albert, also called **Prince Albert** who was a strong suspect in the **Jack the Ripper** murders of 1888.

Queen Victoria's eldest daughter, the **Princess Royal Victoria**, also married a German prince in 1858. Most people know right away the **Wedding March** song right? "*Here comes the bride... da, da, da, da....*" But not many people realise that the most familiar wedding march, the one most English-speaking people associate with weddings, comes from a well-known German composer of operas. The "***Bridal Chorus, G Major***" is borrowed from the **Richard Wagner** (1813-1883) opera *Lohengrin*.

Prince Philip, the Nazi supporter, is a **direct descendent of Queen Victoria**, through her daughter **Princess Alice**, who married another German, **Ludwig IV** Duke of Hesse and by Rhine. So the Queen of England and her husband are German "**kissing cousins**" as well. In-breeding is very common among the House of Winsor and indeed all of the Black Nobility. This is a custom carried through since the time of the **Egyptian Pharaohs** who married sisters as well as cousins and mothers.

Victoria's son, **King Edward VII** (Albert Edward, "Bertie"), was also a British monarch who was a member of the House of Saxe-Coburg-Gotha. He ascended to the throne at the age of 59 when Victoria died in 1901. "Bertie" reigned for nine years until his death, brought on from excessive alcohol, drug, and food abuse in 1910. His son **George Frederick Ernest Albert** (1865-1936) became **King George V**, the man who renamed his line to Windsor. His other illegitimate son was **Winston Churchill**.

However even today, we never really hear them called by their last name. We hear "Prince William" and "Prince Charles." They are never referred to as "Prince Charles Windsor." Most of the slave public in England who support these people don't even know their last names, because they do not want you to know their last name.

Royals are Cold Hearted

Revolution was a real danger, as cousin Nikki in Russia, the Czar of Russia had recently found out. Russia was deposed of its Royal family in February **1917**.

Czar Nicholas II of Russia – cousin to King George V of England

The new Russian government asked Britain to give Czar Nicholas II of Russia and his family (the Romanovs) asylum, and Lloyd George agree to it. However, his own cousin, **King George V**, supposedly was terrified of being associated with the Romanovs, who were now labelled as tyrants by revolutionaries. So he forced the government to withdraw the offer. The Bolsheviks took over Russia in October and Nicholas and his family were slaughtered. To protect the King's reputation, it was put about that Lloyd George was the one who had refused to rescue them.

In November **1918**, a German Revolution forced the **Kaiser**, cousin Willie, to abdicate, and Germany gave up the war.

Consolidate the Empires

The whole political landscape had been transformed. There had been six (Sax-Coburg-Gotha) Empires when George V was crowned. Britain, France, Italy, Austria, Germany, and Russia. But by 1925, George was the only one left, but his world was not exactly safe just yet. Most of the southern Irish were committed republicans. Attempts to hold back that country by force was disastrous and in 1922, the Irish Free State had come into being.

King George had lost a considerable chunk of his kingdom (which they had originally stolen anyway), but the wealth of the Royal family continued to grow. This could be attributed to Queen Mary's enthusiasm for collecting valuable trinkets at "special" prices. The Romanovs hadn't been allowed to join the British Royals, but a substantial chunk of their jewellery did. In fact, people began hiding their treasures if the Queen was coming to call, as she would hint strongly that she expected to be given them. Sometimes, she would just take them anyway, and the embarrassed aides had to quietly return the items back later. She was a true, Royal kleptomaniac.

The Bankers Really Rule England

In 1924, **Ramsay MacDonald** became Britain's first Labour Prime Minister. The good old political establishment had been given a real kicking. No one knew where this might lead. Then came the Wall Street Crash of 1929 (false flag by Rothschilds) and financial disaster. The UK government needed huge loans which were conditional (by the Rothschild bankers), on cuts in unemployment benefits, and the pay of public servants and the armed forces.

The Labour cabinet would not do it, and McDonald went to the King to resign. George was pretty sure that this was a decisive moment. If these harsh and draconian policies were forced through by the Conservatives (Tories), a class war would probably break out and everything, including himself, might very well be swept away.

So he refused to accept the resignation and persuaded MacDonald that it was his patriotic duty to stay on as the leader of a new "coalition" government to force through the cuts. That way, they were more likely to be accepted. This was an extraordinary exercise of Royal power (by proxy for the Rothschilds) and it wasn't over yet.

When the cuts were announced in September **1931,** the entire **British Atlantic Fleet** went on strike. This was the most powerful military force in the world and it was gathered in **Invergordon**. There was total panic in the Admiralty. Mutiny! The intelligence services warned that it was a communist plot and that the sailors were going to march to London rallying all the disaffected, including the police on the way.

The financial markets went into a tailspin and the **Bank of England** (Rothschild) was forced to stop exchanging pounds for gold, going off the gold standard. The Admiralty drew up plans to bomb the mutinous fleet from the land and sink its own ships. The King decided he had to save the Navy and the country. He knew sailors, and they were not revolutionaries. They just needed to be spoken to in the right way. Therefore, in complete secrecy, he took control, appointing a retired admiral to deal with the situation. **Admiral John Kelly** was not appointed by the government, or by the Admiralty, and was instructed not to report to any of them, but directly to King George.

He offered the sailors a deal - if they sailed back to their home ports, the King would see to it that their grievances were taken seriously and they would **not** be punished. It was a sensible approach and it worked, but all evidence of the King's role and Kelly's appointment were hidden. We're not supposed to know what power Royalty can wield, because the bit about mutineers not being punished was a lie. Once the danger was passed, the leaders were identified, rounded up, and quietly removed. The following year Admiral Kelly was awarded the **Grand Cross of the Royal Victorian Order** (awarded for distinguished personal service to the monarch of the Commonwealth realms) in the same year. What a coincidence!

In **1932**, King George V gave the first Christmas radio message. He was now a presence in homes throughout his empire. The Empire had changed its form of course and in 1931 the dominions, the "white principalities" of the Empire - Canada, Australia, and New Zealand and so on, had become legally independent of Westminster. They were the **Commonwealth** and the Sovereign was its institutional core.

As part of his program to make the monarchy seem more British and so he hoped, more secure, King George decreed that his children need not marry partners of royal descent. This would indeed transform the position of the monarchy, but not in the way he expected.

In **1936,** when George was 70 years old and dying, his doctor, Lord Dawson, decided to ensure that the death would not be reported first in the *"vulgar evening papers"*. **Bertrand Edward Dawson**, 1st Viscount Dawson of Penn, had a poem made about him by the people of England:

> *You've heard of Lord Dawson of Penn,*
> *He's killed any number of men,*
> *And that's why we sing,*
> *Oh God save the King,*
> *From Bertrand Lord Dawson of Penn*

Lord Dawson met **The Times's** deadline by giving the King a fatal injection, called a **whiz-bang**. George was told he would soon be convalescing in Bognor. His last words were *"bugger Bognor,"* however The Times reported his last words as being, *"How is the Empire?"*

Edward VIII and Wallis Simpson – Nazi Collaberators

His successor was his son **Edward VIII**, Duke of Windsor, who was 38 at the time. He was a poorly educated child of rather dysfunctional parents. The Queen had been completely distant and King George V famously said

Edward VIII, Duke of Windsor (1894-1972)

"My father was frightened of his father, I was frightened of my father, and I'm damn well going to see to it, that my children are frightened me"

Edward had escaped by travelling widely, and as the world's most eligible bachelor, enjoyed a series of affairs with married women, culminating in the love of his life, the twice married American, **Wallis Simpson**.

At the time of Edward's succession, the affair was in full swing and her husband had resigned himself to a divorce. The British press completely censored the whole subject. However, the rest of the world was fascinated by it.

Edward insisted that he was going to marry Wallis and make her Queen. The Prime Minister and the Archbishop of Canterbury said the country wouldn't stand for it. Edward was actually very popular, and he wanted to go on the radio and appeal to the nation. He wasn't allowed to do that, and was told it would be unconstitutional.

Without a written document, the Constitution is what the government can get away with. They have their reasons and these went beyond the court gossip that Wallace was said to be lesbian/bi-sexual, or a man in drag, engaged in a sadomasochistic relationship with Edward and so on.

The crucial issue wasn't even that the head of the **Church of England** shouldn't marry a divorcee, or that secret investigators had reported that Wallis Simpson had two other lovers - a car salesman and an Irish MP. The real reason only came to light in 2002 when secret documents released under Freedom of Information, showed that the FBI told the British government that Wallace had another lover, the German Ambassador **Joachim von Ribbentrop**.

Edward VIII and Wallis Simpson meet with Adolf Hitler, 1936

In fact, the FBI said she was a Nazi agent, and that was why the government insisted that Edward must give her up to keep the throne. Edward was also a big fan of Hitler. He abdicated and took Wallis Simpson to live in France.

The couple remained pro-Nazi, even after the war accelerated. His scandalous marriage to a doubly divorced American woman would be his downfall as the history books would have you believe, however the once and future King was pigeon-holed at the Bahamas as its Governor, because his Nazi sympathies became widely known during World War II (Edward VIII, 2015).

Two years before his death, Edward told an interviewer that he never thought Hitler was such a bad chap. An MI5 report featuring a British

Edward, Duke of Windsor chats to Hitler's propaganda chief Joseph Goebbels at a party in Berlin in 1937

Wallis Simpson and Prince Edward did not marry for love - they were both Nazi collaborators – or she really was a man?

Admiral who had attended Hitler's 1937 Nuremberg rally said that Hitler would soon invade, but there was no reason to worry about it because he would bring the **Duke of Windsor,** formerly King Edward, over as King. Indeed, the Duke was angered at being forced to abdicate the throne in 1936 and was willing to work with Adolf Hitler to regain it (Morton, 2015).

Prince Edward gives a Heil Hitler salute, surrounded by his Nazi buddies!

King George VI with Lady Elizabeth Bowes-Lyon on the day of their engagement.

Albert - George VI

After the abdication of his Nazi brother, **Albert** was crowned as **King George VI** in 1936. He was 18 months younger than Edward, and completely lacked his brother's social grace. He had a chronic stutter when he spoke, and he was extremely shy, but at least he was safely married to **Elizabeth Bowes Lyon**, the daughter a minor Scottish aristocrat. Albert was the first royal to legally marry a "commoner" since **Henry VIII**.

George didn't have much in the way of winning ways, but his

Windsor Castle was much safer from bombing

wife, enraged at what Edward had done, was determined to help him through. She arranged speech therapy to cure his stutter (see movie *The King's Speech*). But when war with Germany began in 1939, they were not seen as a rallying point for patriotic fervour, especially as they publicly supported Neville Chamberlain's appeasement of Hitler.

When the Royal couple visited the first bomb sites in London, they were booed and hissed at. George VI and Queen Elizabeth (that's the woman we remember as Elizabeth the Queen Mother) as full members of the Fabian Society, refused to allow themselves any doubt as to the outcome of the Second World War. When Buckingham Palace was bombed, the Queen said she was glad, because it meant she could look the East Enders in the face (and because she didn't have to pay for the repairs no doubt). At least it meant the Royal couple wouldn't be booed anymore when they visited other people's bombed-out homes.

Actually, while they spent their days in London, they retreated for the night to Windsor Castle, which was considerably safer. As the war went on, the Royal couple became more and more identified with Churchill as the spirit of Britain.

When the victory celebrations came in 1945, it seemed natural that they should revolve around Buckingham Palace. By the time of his premature death from smoking in 1952, this shy, country gentleman and his queen had gone a very long way to restoring the monarchy to its central place in British life. It had vanished virtually everywhere else. There had been 16 monarchies on the continent of Europe when Victoria died, now there was only one - Sweden.

Monarchs were restored to Belgium, Holland, Norway, and Denmark, but as a pale shadow of the old European Royalty.

The Dragon Queen - Elizabeth II

The new Queen, the 25-year-old Elizabeth II, seem to be a fairy tale remnant of a lost world of glamour. Her coronation was a celebration of pageantry itself, in a country that was a vast bomb site. Four houses out of 10 have been damaged or destroyed. But the show must go on, so the Coronation was even shown on the new medium of television, though the Archbishop of Canterbury feared that the peasants, I mean people, would be watching it in pubs, without removing their hats. By her side in the coronation

25-year-old Elizabeth II (1926-)

coach, rode her husband Philip. Like Albert, he would never be crowned King.

Philip, Duke of Edinburgh, was from the Royal House of **Schleswig-Holstein-Sonderburg-Glücksburg**, and was born into the Greek and Danish Royal Families. He was born in Greece, but his family was exiled from the country when he was still an infant. After being educated in France, Germany, and the United Kingdom, he joined the British Royal Navy in 1939, at the age of 18.

From July 1939, he began corresponding with the 13-year-old Princess Elizabeth (his third cousin through Queen Victoria and second cousin once removed through Christian IX of Denmark) whom he had first met in 1934. During World War II he served with the Mediterranean and Pacific fleets.

There was no question of the Queen becoming a modest suburban sovereign like the restored European royals. George's widow was sure her daughter should be regal and grand. Royalty required flunkies and castles and palaces and gold and coaches. She herself made do with six cars, three chauffeur's, five chefs, two pages, three-foot men, two dressers, and 30 secretaries, maids, treasurers, and housekeepers, and she was absolutely against Royalty paying tax.

For a long time, this life of extravagance was met with an extraordinary degree of complicity from the governments of the day. However, in 1947, when Labour came to power amid all the nationalisations, of the class war declaration of *"We are the Masters now!"*, somehow came to the agreement that the government would take over the cost of running Buckingham Palace, including paying for all the staff. This meant that the Queen, and all her family, could live rent free, food and drink free, utility bill free, staff to do everything for you free, cars, horses, animals all free etc. etc. No wonder they have so much money.

Now the conservatives said the government would take over the cost to the Royal train and royal visits abroad and freed the Queen from paying tax on property, apart from rates on Sandringham and Balmoral. In **Edward Heath's** (known head of paedophile ring) time as Prime Minister, it was officially stated for the first time that the Queen pays no tax.

In 1973, she was exempted from the new **Companies Bill** that could force shareholders to identify themselves, even if they hid behind the names of nominees. Her shares are hidden in a company called the

Bank of England Nominees, and the **Crown Corporation**, which can only be used by heads of state, and is uniquely exempt from disclosure laws.

Indeed, in 1965, when the Labour government introduced capital gains tax, they declared that the Queen was exempt. Under these arrangements, immense and unknowable riches were built up. She has for example, **600** works by Leonardo da Vinci, paid for from the public purse – your taxes! The public is told that these riches are not really hers, because she's not free to sell them, but most of these "Royal Collections" are never publicly displayed, and not even academics have access to them. Why? Whose interest is being served?

Before She Was Crowned Queen

Before the young Elizabeth could be crowned Queen, she first had to undergo a Druid (Pagan) ritual. Without being accepted and anointed by the High Druid Council, she could not rule. Therefore, the ritual was held in Balmoral on the monarchy's private estate. Lucky for us, a picture of the event was taken. This once again supports the fact that the Queen of England is the top leader of the Illuminati, and all of their Luciferian groups.

Queen Elizabeth II is initiated into a Druid Coven. Note who stands higher.

The Cost of Monarchy

Just as in medieval times, the Royal family live a life of unfettered privilege and luxury, with Commonwealth Nation's tax paying "subjects" funding their lavish existence. The idea of a hereditary ruler is as absurd as having a hereditary mathematician, but for some reason people let them get away with it.

Officially, the Royal Family costs British taxpayers £40,000,000 per year. They get a similar tithing from Australia, Canada, and New Zealand. But that is just the tip of a very large iceberg. The Royal Palaces are maintained by the tax payers, even their private houses like Balmoral. Windsor Castle is their private residence as well, except when it burnt down and the cost of rebuilding it fell on the public purse. The Queen owns more than half the land of England, Canada, Australia, and New Zealand, as well as over 50% of all the smaller Commonwealth nations – 53 in total. As a matter of fact, she also owns almost 50% of the real estate on Manhattan Island, New York.

That is also the reason why the Queen's head appears on more coins, bank notes, and stamps than any other head of state in world history. She actually receives a "royalty" for every time her likeness appears on anything. That is why Australia for example is forced to pay the "crown" millions and millions of dollars every year, even though she lives on the other side of the world, and does not perform any service for Australia.

Queen Elizabeth II is the wealthiest person in the world, only being slightly outdone by the Rothschilds on a "family" wealth basis. It obviously means that the monarchy can put on a heck of a show that goes far beyond their demand on the public purse, and they don't need to run the risk of asking us to fund the whole thing from taxes. Each person in England must contribute 61 pence a year. However, that money, just over £40/$56 million is not enough to put on the grand, regal show each week which the British monarchy seems to be about. Therefore, the **Commonwealth Nations** must pick up the shortfall.

The Commonwealth Nations Scam

Firstly, as someone that lives in a Commonwealth Nation, I can assure you that no one here enjoys the "common wealth." In fact, the Crown Corporation and its front companies rip billions of dollars' worth of minerals from the Australian soil and give nothing back to the locals. All of the wealth goes directly to overseas bankers and private family Trusts. Anyway, back to the Royal's scam. Originally, it worked like this:

The Queen had her likeness put on every coin and note – all currency, including gold and silver bullion coins. For the "honour" of having the Queen's picture on all money, the nations had to pay a "royalty" for using her trademarked face picture. However, after a while, it became too difficult to know how much money was in circulation. Therefore, it was decided that they should all pay a set percentage per GDP. This is the kind of issues and decisions that are made at the **Commonwealth Heads of Government Meeting** (CHOGM), held every two years.

The solution they came up with is similar to the extortion racket **King George III** set up with the United States to end the War of Independence. The US still pays the House of Windsor 5% of its GDP annually, forever! (see Chapter 6).

In the Commonwealth it varies slightly. Commonwealth Dominion nations pay 5%, however the smaller and poorer countries pay between 2.5% and 3.75%. The British Commonwealth still has 53 members with a total population of about **2.328 billion**. In 2014, the total GDP estimate for the Commonwealth was **$14.623 trillion** (Commonwealth, 2015).

I am not sure what the exact figures work out to be, but if we do the math on just the dominions, Canada ($1.628 trillion), Australia ($1.241 trillion), New Zealand ($170.59 billion) and also include South Africa ($725.004 billion), the combined GDP is $3,764,594,000,000 (three trillion seven hundred sixty-four billion five hundred ninety-four million). 5% of that is $188,229,700,000 (one hundred eighty-eight billion two hundred twenty-nine million seven hundred thousand). There are still another 49 countries that contribute as well per year, so it is probably safe to say she earns about £2 billion a year from her Empire.

This is a staggering amount of money in anyone's language. Queen Elizabeth II gets this money every year for allowing her face to appear on money, and in every town hall or club that hangs a picture of her. It also covers statues and monuments that use her likeness. This is also why every other royal clamours to have their images placed on merchandise every time they get married or have a baby. Only the Queen can use the face on money scam, but the others get a "royalty" every time their face appears on a coffee cup or a tea towel and so on.

Queen Elizabeth's likeness on Australian $5 note, Canadian $20 note, New Zealand $20 note, Australian $1 coin. All coins and notes in every Commonwealth Dominion Nation has the Queen's face. Over 2 billion people look at her every day.

They have the audacity to earn billions, and not pay tax, or pay for the upkeep of their own homes, or for their holidays abroad. But for me, what really stung me the most, was their profits from wars. As an example, I will just look at World War I, because this is when it all started for the Royals to make a profit from war, a trick they learnt from the Rothschilds.

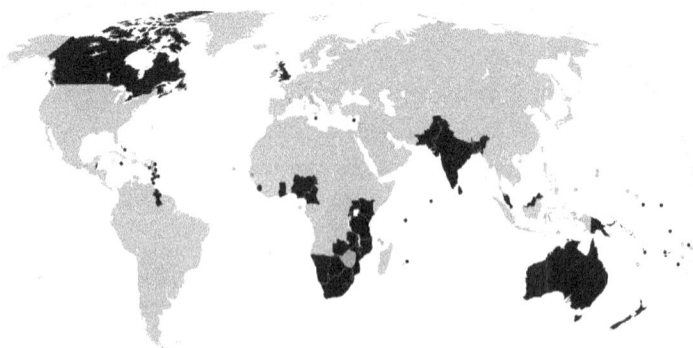

53 members of the Commonwealth Nations (old British Empire)

How Rich is Filthy Rich?

The Queen is the wealthiest person on earth. Her gold carriage alone is made of four tonnes of solid gold, worth over $370 billion at today's gold prices. Until 1992, all of the Queen's income was tax free. In 1977, the Bank of England Nominees Limited (Rothschild bank) was established to hide the Queen's income and investments. Secrecy about her wealth protected her from a public lynching.

Government and banking officials inform the Queen on where to invest her wealth. That is called "insider trading" and it is illegal, yet the Queen gets away with it scot free. Why? Because she is the Queen, and immune from prosecution – literally. She could go out in the street, shoot someone dead in front of 1000 people and TV cameras, and the British legal system is not allowed to lay charges or arrest her.

The Queen owns more than 300 residences, including castles and palaces, over 50% of **Manhattan Island** (New York) real estate and more. She owns the Crown Jewels, 27,000 painting masterpieces, prize race horses, and a fleet of Bentleys and Rolls Royce cars. Her colossal wealth also includes **Crown Land** and investments that she inherited from her **Black Nobility** ancestors. The Queen's Crown Estate includes over 50% of the UK's coastline, as well as Regent Street, and Windsor Great Park. Her trillions in wealth pass down to her descendants, untaxed.

But the Royals are Good for the Tourist Economy Aren't they?

Would British tourism collapse if the Monarchy was abolished? No. Statistically, Buckingham Palace does not even make the top 20 list for best tourist attractions in the UK. When the Queen's parasitical income from British tax payers was reduced, she pretended to share the suffering of commoners from austerity programs. That drop in tax payer income was a tiny drop in the Royal bucket. In fact, the interest she earns on the other money she makes is more than the money she allegedly lost.

It was Prince Phillip that famously called us, the people, "*Useless eaters,*" but the reality is, these people could not even put a nail in a piece of wood. They are the useless eaters, not us. Conservatively, the Queen is said to be worth **$55 trillion**. She could single handily solve world poverty overnight. Instead, she just sits in her ivory tower and laughs at us.

Of the billions of families on planet earth, how did this one family mange to collect and hoard most of the world's wealth over the centuries? Before the "Face on Money" scam, before the insider trading and even before the tax-free income, the Royals made their money from:

- The Slave Trade and
- The Drug trade

The Royal Slave Traders

Author **Nick Hazlewood**, in his book, *The Queen's Slave Trader*, traces the slave trade back to **Queen Elizabeth I**, who sent **Captain John Hawkin**s to collect human slaves, using any means necessary (Hazlewood, 2004). Queen Elizabeth I started the British slave trade in 1564. As head of the Church of England, her slave trading of African blacks upset the moral foundations of the Church.

Queen Elizabeth II is now head of the Church of England. 200 years after the slave trade was abolished, the Church was pressured into confessing its horrific crimes, and apologise for profiteering from the African slave trade. At first, the Queen and the Church only admitted to owning slaves and plantations. But the public soon discovered that the Church had given their blessing to something far worse.

The **Church of England** had approved the beating, mutilation, rape, kidnapping, and murder of tens of millions of Africans, by declaring that Africans **had no soul**. This gave the Church divine license to profit from their diabolical crimes.

Queen Elizabeth I was Britain's first slave trader, and the head of the Church of England. Today, the public is demanding Queen Elizabeth II remove Queen Elizabeth I from the crypt in Westminster Abby.

The Royal Drug Trade

Even more lucrative than Queen Elizabeth I slave trade, was Queen Victoria's drug trade. Opium was grown and manufactured in the British owned opium factories in British India. China banned the importation of opium, but once the British monarch secured a drug trade monopoly, over 17,000 illegal chests of opium worth millions, were forced onto the Chinese population. When the Chinese government resisted, the British waged three drug wars on them and forced them to pay for the illegally imported opium. China's Emperor didn't stand a chance against the British East India gun boats and Royal Navy. The British destroyed, plundered, looted, and raped their way along the coast of China until there was nothing left to loot or plunder.

On August 29, **1842**, the **Treaty of Nanking** forced the Chinese government to pay £15,000,000 ($676,894,423 in 2015) to the British merchants to open up its ports to opium trade and to cede **Hong Kong** to the British (Nanking, 1842). This was the ugly origin of Hong Kong's 155 years as a stolen, British Crown colony.

The Cost of their Wars

In World War I, Australia, and all Commonwealth Nations, were asked to send their young men to Europe to help England defeat the Germans. After World War I, England was literally bankrupt.

Therefore, the government of the day went to the monarchy (King George V) and asked for financial assistance, just to get the country back on its feet. They were told that it was not up to the monarchy to bail them out, and that they should get the money from the Commonwealth Nations.

For Australia, as for many nations, the First World War remains the most costly conflict in terms of deaths and casualties. From a population of fewer than five million at the time, 416,809 men enlisted, of which over 60,000 were killed and 156,000 wounded, gassed, or taken prisoner. For this sacrifice, the Australian government was sent a bill for their participation (for food, bombs, bullets etc. that they used during operations). They got the bill in 1919, and finally paid it off in 1984 (65 years). But that is not the worst of it. The English government repaid the outstanding £1.9 billion of their debt from a 3.5% War Loan on 9 March 2015 (UKDebt, 2015). All of this money went to the House of Rothschild and their Bank of England shareholders – the House of Windsor.

The Royal Racists

In return for a free, lavish lifestyle, the British Royal family refuse to obey many British laws, such as the **1968 Race Relations Act**. You will be very hard pressed to find any non-whites on the Royal staff, even in the kitchens. The Royal family are notorious for their racism. The **Queen Mother** (deceased) was always referring to dark skinned people as **Nig-nogs** and **blackamoors**, much to the embarrassment of her handlers. **Prince Philip**, in public said to an Olympic (black British) decathlon athlete *"still throwing spears I see…"* and referring to Asians as *"…slitty-eyed"*.

Princess Anne (Queen's sister) is on record saying, *"He's everything I despise. He's black and he's married to a Jew"* (really showing the Nazi traits there). All these phrases have been said by the Royals in public, so one can only guess what they say in private.

How do they get away with it?

Certainly for a very long time it was simply not permitted to suggest that the monarchy should be anything less than grand. In 1957, **Lord Altrincham** wrote an article arguing for a modernised monarchy. He called the court *"complacent and out of touch"*. He even said that the Queen sounded like a *'priggish schoolgirl'* and said that the monarchy should not be as it was, *"intimately associated with the upper classes"* (Altrincham, 2015).

Wow! The Duke of Argyll said that he should be *"hanged, drawn, and quartered"* for talking about the Queen and her monarchy like that. The BBC immediately dropped him from any questions. In fact, Altrincham got it wrong. Lavish splendour was just what most of the

Sex Pistols, 1977 God Save the Queen album cover

public wanted from their monarchy. They would have despised the Queen on a bicycle. They wanted to be deferential. They probably still do. There were 20 more years of this kind of thing to come.

In 1977, the year of the Queen's Jubilee, the Sex Pistols song **God Save the Queen** and her fascist regime was banned from being broadcast, even when it outsold all other records. The puzzle becomes even more intriguing when you look at the apparent shrinking roll the Crown plays in public affairs. The imperial title had already disappeared in the days of George VI, when India and Pakistan became independent.

The Empire became the Commonwealth and if the 58 past and present members are part of that organisation, 16 realms, including Australia and Canada, still have Elizabeth as their Head of State.

Why does it matter so much to protect and sustain Royalty? Partly perhaps, it's more to do with the Queen herself than the institution of monarchy.

Elizabeth I, Victoria, Elizabeth II - the rule of elderly matriarchs seems to be particularly proper to the English. It may even provide an important social glue as the population of Britain became more heterogeneous, with substantial immigration from Commonwealth countries, by people who feel excluded from political life and often from the legitimate economy. Perhaps there was a hope that the Queen would be a focus of patriotic attachment? After all, she's the linchpin of the Commonwealth, its graciously enthusiastic figurehead promoting the image of glamorous and golden royalty, above and outside politics that is synonymous with Britain. It may be a very useful way of creating legitimacy for a State that might otherwise look rather shabby.

The Next Generation

Possibly the last great thing Camilla Parker-Bowles ever did. She goes for the big dig at a Gala Ball

Camilla Parker-Bowles, great-granddaughter of Alice Keppel, and famous for picking her nose in public on a regular basis.

Diana said that on her honeymoon with Charles, he was more interested in reading eight books by **Laurens van der Post**, than in her. He also wore Charles-Camilla cufflinks for the entire time, and when Diana became distressed, she felt strongly that the Royal family turned against her.

Annus Horribilis

In 1992, it all blew apart in what the Queen called her *Annus horribilis*, a Latin phrase, meaning "horrible year." Her second son **Andrew** (a known paedophile) separated from his wife **Sarah Ferguson**, who was pictured topless, while having her toes sucked by **John Bryan**, an American financial manager (Toes, 2009). Her daughter, **Princess Anne**, divorced **Captain Mark Phillips. Charles and Diana** split up with spectacular accusations being made in the press and on television, and lastly, Windsor Castle caught fire.

That is when the ground really began to shift. At least when it was explained that the £40 million repair bill would be paid for by the public. There was a huge collective breath of "*Oh no it won't!*"

So the Queen decided it would be much wiser to offer to pay 70% of the cost. She opened up some of her homes to the public to raise the cash. There was still astonishingly, little direct criticism of the Queen over this. In an age when television and the press have the power to destroy anyone, the Queen and her mother were treated with respect, even devotion. But the rest of the Royal family had become fair game and was subjected to a ferocious assault of public humiliation. I am sure the others are sacrificed as a distraction to keep people away from what the Queen really gets up to.

People started to ask the legitimate questions - why do we support the Royal family and all their wealth? Why are we giving them all this money? The press pack was baying at their heels. That's when the Queen agreed that she should voluntarily start paying income tax and refund the parliamentary allowances received by other members of the royal family. Perhaps people started to realise that this was just a front – they wouldn't really start paying anything. Whatever the reason, things didn't get any better and the Queen herself began to be criticised in **1997**, when Princess Diana was murdered in a car crash in Paris.

We all remember the shock and horror and the debate about the lack of public reaction by the senior members of the Royal family. There was a widespread feeling that at that moment, they were not in fact part of the nation.

Was the program started by **George V** of integrating the monarchy into the life of the nation becoming unravelled?

Instead of the monarch playing the role of warning and advising the Prime Minister, which is supposed to be their constitutional role, the Prime Minister warned and advised the Queen, to take public action. She had to be seen to grieve, or the monarchy itself might be in danger.

Now we wait to see what happens next. The heir to the throne (Charles) and his ex- mistress, now wife, the vulgar Camilla Parker-Bowles, are forever tainted with the image of the Princess that was publicly destroyed.

The Queen is an old lady now at 89. Can anyone be certain that the country would accept Charles as King? There's always been a bargain at the heart of monarchy in England. The monarch has always been dependent on the people, and that bargain has been the key to their survival. It began when **William the Conqueror** realised that he and his friends couldn't actually run a country where they didn't speak the language, or know the laws, traditions, or even the geography. It was restated in a series of crises, in which monarchs who tried to rule without consent, were simply dumped. Indeed, Matilda, Jane Grey, Richard Cromwell, and James II did not get the consent required by the people to feel that the Sovereign is entitled to be there. They must respect laws, even though no court can enforce them. Laws which today, probably include having to pay tax. The throne will no doubt go to her grandson, **Prince William.**

In **2015**, Elizabeth, who is also the nation's oldest ever monarch, officially surpassed the 63 years, 7 months, 2 days, 16 hours and 23 minutes that her great-great-grandmother Queen Victoria spent on the throne.

Why do people bow down to these disgusting parasites?

Queen Elizabeth II enjoying the elites most favourite pastime.

Queen Elizabeth II enjoys a good old dig.

Queen Elizabeth II doesn't even mind getting her gloves dirty

In this enthusiastic pick, she is up to the first knuckle!

In this technically difficult method, she manages to get a thumb up there! Well done ma'am.

William and Kate

Before their fairy tale wedding, not everything was perfect for Kate and William. The couple split up at least half a dozen times over eight years.

Both Kate Middleton and Diana Spencer (Princess Diana) come from old, and fabulously wealthy, aristocratic families with Titles. Their families have been mixing with Royals for centuries. In fact, the Spencers actually financially bailed out several Monarchs over the years, and also aided George Washington's ancestors.

Yet with both these women, the public is told they are "commoners'. This is such a lie and obfuscation of the facts. The reason these families are kept so close to the Royals is because the female offspring are used at different times as "broodmares" for the Royals. They need to bring in some fresh blood every so often to avoid more deformities, brain damage, and impediments that have plagued them for years due to their inbreeding.

Diana only became aware of this after it was too late. Kate on the other hand had the advantage of seeing Diana's fate, and did not want to follow suit. That is why William and Kate were on again, off again. Every time William and his minders put pressure on Kate to marry, she bolted. Eventually though, she was convinced. I am not sure what she was promised or threatened with, but whatever it was, she seems to have accepted her fate happily.

Thus, the couple set their wedding day for **April 29th 2011**. Coincidentally, it was the exact same day as Hitler's wedding day, and it marked the 66th anniversary of Hitler's marriage to **Eva Braun**.

William finally slid a ring on to Kate's finger. It was the used ring that belonged to his deceased mother. The same ring she wore during her doomed and loveless marriage to Williams two-timing father, Prince Charles.

William on the other hand, refused to wear a wedding band, and stayed as ringless as a bachelor. Even if the eight year on-again / off-again relationship wasn't absolutely perfect, at least their fairy-tale wedding would be perfect because it was a well-rehearsed, choreographed event that left nothing to chance.

The Royals of the modern era are given celebrity status as this over the top event proved. Even in America, where they are taught from an early age to be wary of Kings and Queens, the public and the news people where beside themselves with excitement and anticipation. They could not get enough of the Royals of England getting married. The same happened when they produced a new born child. How is it that within 50 years, Victoria, and the Queen's mother were often hissed at and booed?

The Origins of Propaganda

This goes back to **Edward Bernays**, who wrote the book *Propaganda* in 1928. This one book became the greatest "bible" for the CIA, for advertising companies, for Hollywood, and for the British Royals. I will cover this book and Bernays in **Book III: Secrets of the Mind Control**, but for now, just be aware that it helped lift the Royals from being barely tolerated, to being "rock star" popular. Basically, they applied Bernays' theories and started to include the Royals at A list events. They photographed them with real, "A list" celebrities like Hollywood stars, famous musicians and other celebrities. Before long, people would see the Royals with other celebrities at parties and assume they were popular as well, so they must be "cool." This got ramped up during the reign of George V (Reign 1910 – 1936).

The Royals greatest fear is that the people will wake up one day, and start a revolution. There is even a secret, private, super-fast train and station under Buckingham Palace. If the Queen is ever in trouble, the underground train will rush her at Mach 2 to Heathrow Airport where her private Jumbo Jet is waiting. They really do fear an uprise, because they know what they are getting away with is so criminal.

But if the people think you are "cool" and popular, they will never want to lynch you. So a lot of money is spent every year showing the Royals at the right events at the right time, in the best light. I know this to be true, because once you begin to read what they really get up to, you will be shocked. It is not the kind of things you read about in glossy magazines.

On TV screens around the globe, billions watched as the ringless William twisted, squeezed and fumbled a gold wedding ring on to Kate's finger, but denied her the same honour. Every flag-waving commoner wanted a royal souvenir that they could take home and cherish forever and ever. They were even selling "Royal condoms" souvenirs. Remember, they make a buck from every item they sell with their heads on it. These "royalties" will help set up William and Kate to become the next multi-billionaires. **Wills'n'Kate**: the comic book was particularly a good seller, and a good "propaganda" for brainwashing the kids (Good, 2011).

© REUTERS/Dylan Martinez

The sour, flower girl (left)

Yes, everything was going great until the balcony kiss that Royal Wedding watchers waited for breathlessly. That magical moment was stolen by a three year old flower girl, whose sour expression cast a giant shadow over the Royal kiss. The flower girl is the daughter of **Lady Rose Astor** and she is also Prince William's goddaughter. Kate finally bent down and whispered something like *"put on a happy face and get used to it. You're ruining everything."*

Why is the pouting flower girl important enough to be named Prince William's goddaughter? Because she's an **Astor**!

Fritz Springmeier identifies the Astor's as one of the **13 bloodlines** who made billions from opium slave trading and loansharking. His book gives referenced documentation of their criminal history. Many within these unsavoury power circles were on the wedding guest list like **James Rothschild**, of the Rothschild bankster dynasty.

James Rothschild brought along his pass-around girlfriend **Astrid Harbord**, who according to the tabloids had previously been bedfellows with **Prince Harry**. Her father, **Charles Harbord**, shot himself in the head in 2012 (Gould and Constable, 2012).

Also on the guest list was **Gary Goldsmith**, Kate's uncle. The tabloids report that Uncle Gary is a filthy rich, cocaine snorting, pill popping, porn peddling, and horny, hedonistic playboy.

Kate's Uncle Gary was photographed at the wedding, popping pills with his female escort (part time prostitute for the rich and porn star by day). Uncle Gary Goldsmith is the younger brother of Kate's mother, **Carole Goldsmith**. Kate's uncle Gary was filmed covertly by undercover reporters for the UK's **News of the World** at his sprawling $10 million villa, on the Spanish party island of **Ibiza**.

He named his villa **La Maison de Bang Bang**, which is French slang for **House of Sex**. Guarded by **MI6 agents**, Prince William, and his bride to be, holidayed, partied, and sailed at Uncle Gary Goldsmith's house of bang-bang in 2006. The undercover reporters, reported that Kate's Uncle Gary entertains his guests with hard-core porn on a massive 152" screen. He supplies marijuana, cocaine, ecstasy, hookers, and a door-to-door delivery service. Does anyone really believe that William and Kate just held hands and sipped tea on their bang-bang holiday?

And speaking of Uncles, which Uncle is slimier? Kate's Uncle Gary, or William's **Uncle Andrew**?

Prince Andrew is the brother of William's father, Charles and the son of Queen Elizabeth II. He is the fourth in line to the British throne.

Andrew, who was also a featured guest at William's wedding, has been exposed in the news as a client and close friend of **Jeffrey Epstein**. Epstein is a convicted **paedophile** who served up underage girls to Prince Andrew like lollipops. Epstein also gave Andrew $30,000 to help pay for his ex-wife Fergie's massive debts, that she was blackmailing him for. Andrew was finally forced to step down as Britain's trade ambassador because of:

1) His criminal behaviour with underage girls.
2) A $6,000,000 tax evasion charge, and
3) Conflicts of interest from friendships with a convicted paedophile and with then Libyan leader Gadhafi's son **Saif**, whose country was being bombed by the British military at the time. He was also a close friend with convicted Libyan gun smuggler **Tarek Kaituni**.

Despite their criminal activities, neither of William and Kate's sleazy uncles have ever been arrested or prosecuted for their crimes. That is because they are royals, and therefore, **ABOVE THE LAW**.

Ok, so two rotten apples in the newlyweds family doesn't make them all rotten does it? William's brother **Harry** isn't such a bad bloke is he? It can't be easy being the ginger top, younger brother, and second fiddle to the perfect, handsome William, who is destined to be King. It can't be easy wondering why you look so much like **James Hewitt**, the man your mother publicly admitted that she cheated with while Charles was cheating with Camilla. Diana confessed her affair with James Hewitt in an interview with the program *Panorama*.

> *"Your relationship goes beyond a close friendship?"*
> *Diana, "Yes, it did."*
> *"Were you unfaithful?"*
> *Diana, "Yes I adored him...I was in love with him".*

It can't be easy hearing your real father admit that the Royal family threatened to kill him.

> *"Where they threatening?"*
> *JH, "Yes they were, in as much as they said that it was not conducive to my health to continue the relationship."*

**Who's the Daddy? Hewitt (left), Harry (centre) Charles (right)
Harry sure looks like Hewitt!**

James Hewitt said he also receive warnings from Diana's personal police protection and members of the Royal Household. He says that he even had a conversation with a senior member the Royal Family (Prince Phillip).

It can't be easy hearing news reports that your mother slept around with lots of men including **Barry Mannakee**; **David Waterhouse**; **James Gilbey**; **James Hewitt**; **Oliver Hoare**; **William Carling**; **Doctor Hasnar Khan**; **Bryan Adams** (the singer) and finally **Dodi Fayed**.

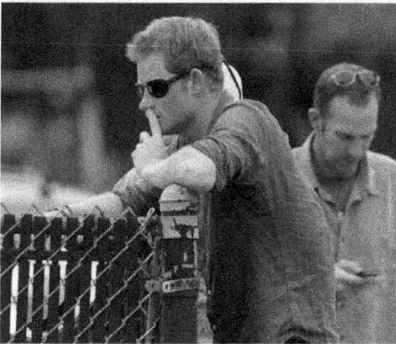

Harry seems to have inherited the Royal addiction to nose picking

Worst of all was the fact that your mother got pregnant by Muslim playboy **Dodi El-Fayed**, and that your family murdered her because she was an embarrassment to the Crown.

Harry has a lot to be angry about. It's understandable that he acted out his anger and got caught by the Paparazzi drinking, drugging, brawling, groping breasts, and making racist comments about dark-skinned people.

The Nazi Link Won't Go Away

What was not so understandable to the world was why Harry wore a Nazi uniform and a swastika armband to an upscale fancy-dress party

Prince Harry at fancy dress party

in 2006. The news was a reminder of the Royal family's links to Hitler's Nazi Party.

Indeed, Prince Philip is William and Harry's grandfather and the Queen's husband. Both of Philip's sisters married high-ranking German officers in the Nazi Party. His sister **Sophie** married Nazi SS Colonel (Prince) **Christoph von Hesse**, who was a director in the Third Reich's Ministry of Air Forces, Commander of the Air Reserves. He also headed up **Hermann Göring's** Secret Intelligence Service. Prince Philip's German uncle, **Lord Louis Mountbatten**, was a central figure in secret communications between the British Royal Family and their pro Hitler cousins in Germany.

The authors of *War of the Windsors*, state that Lord Louis Mountbatten had been nicknamed **Dickey** and for good reason. Philip's Uncle Dickey was the last Viceroy in India, where he was a known paedophile who sexually exploited young working-class Indian peasant boys (Picknett, 2002).

Finally, their great Uncle **Edward** was best friends and fan boy of **Adolf Hitler**. That is why he abdicated, and still supported Hitler even after England joined the war. The story that he abdicated to marry the woman he loved (Wallis Simpson) is complete nonsense and a lie. But that is what was sold to the public – Britain couldn't have a King who worshipped Adolf Hitler.

The Royals admiration for the Nazis was finally confirmed in 2015 when the Royal family's private archives of them practising their Heil Hitler salute. The black-and-white footage is believed to have been filmed by the Queen's father, the future **King George VI**, on the family's Balmoral estate in Scotland in 1933 or 1934. It shows the future Queen – then aged six or seven – raising her right arm in the air as the Queen Mother does the same. The group were apparently being encouraged by the Adolf Hitler loving, future King Edward VIII (Tominey, 2015).

It is really no surprise that Prince Harry turns up at a party with a Nazi armband on. The Royal spin doctors have been trying for years to bury this history, but with the advent of the Internet, they are fighting a losing battle.

Prince Philip (circled) at the Nazi funeral in 1937

The British Royal Family are German Jews?

The so called British Royal Family is basically German. They were once seated on almost every thrown in Europe. They are from the German Saxe-Coburg and Gotha bloodline which often intermarries with the Hesse-Kassel German nobility bloodline. It is from this union they claim Jewish descent, from the **Royal House of David** in ancient Israel, who of course answered to, and worshipped Enlil, the Anunnaki Earth Base Commander. But as we know, Enlil left the planet, and Marduk remained. That is why they are all members of the **Brotherhood of the Dragon**.

They raise their children without love or compassion. Breeding each successive generation to be at the head of a military establishment, who keep an angered peace, by using fear, surveillance, and war. Prince Charles is obsessed with his family tree connecting him to **Vlad the Impaler** of Romania. Vlad was the real life character of **Bram Stocker's Count Dracula**. Charles has bought up almost an entire village in Romania since learning of his link.

More Royal Paedophiles!

Another book, The **Kincora Scandal**, connects Lord Dickey Mountbatten to a child prostitution ring operating in Belfast, Ireland. Authorities failed to intervene at the Kincora care home for boys, until 1981, despite reports over the years of child sexual abuse. The operators of the Kincora child prostitution ring were eventually convicted in 1981 of the ritual, sexual abuse of defenceless young boys, who were sold like prostitutes. No charges were ever brought against the VIP customers which included Royals, politicians, lawyers, and judges (Moore, 1996). Belfast citizens finally had reason to celebrate when Prince Philip's paedophile Uncle Dickey Mountbatten was killed by an IRA bomb planted in his boat.

Lord Mountbatten, now 79 years old when on August 27 1979, a day he set sale for a "*pleasure group*," in the **Shadow 5**, his 27-foot runabout. Only about 10 minutes after they set off, there was a tremendous explosion, and the boat seemed to lift off the surface of the water before it splintered into a million whirling pieces. Bodies, oil, and blood rained down to float upon the water. Lord Mountbatten's grandson **Nicholas**, and the boat boy were both dead and face down in the water. Lord Mountbatten himself had both his legs nearly torn off by the blast. He was still alive but died very shortly thereafter on the boat that rescued them. Of course, in true Royal Family fashion, Lord Dickey Mountbatten was given a lavish funeral at **Westminster Abby**. His body laid in state for three days before it was interred. One of the British newspapers of the day said simply on the banner headline "**These Evil Bastards**." I wonder who they were referring to (Rodrigues, 1979).

What kind of childhood did Prince Phillip have?

The answer can be found in a biographical book called **Elizabeth: Behind The Palace Doors** (Davies, 2000). Phillip's mother was Princess **Alice Mountbatten Burg** – granddaughter of Queen Victoria. She was diagnosed as a paranoid schizophrenic and committed to a mental institution in Switzerland. Phillip's German father ran off with a wealthy mistress, which left the boy parentless.

Phillip's Uncle, **George Mountbatten** became his surrogate father and legal guardian. Unfortunately, Uncle George had the same perverse reputation as Uncle Dickey. George Mountbatten kept a scandalous collection of child pornography that he bound into volumes and emblazoned with the family crest. Most disturbing, were pictures of family orgies and bestiality in which children and animals were sexual participants. The question is, was George's adopted son Phillip a participant?

George Mountbatten's porn collection now resides at the British Museum, where it is kept in a secret repository of artefacts deemed pornographic and unfit for public viewing. It is a well-known fact that child victims of sexual predators commonly identify with their abusers, and grow up to become sexual predators themselves.

Like her husband Prince Phillip, Queen Elizabeth also came from a family of name changers, and for precisely the same reasons – to cover up their German identity. Before **1917**, the British Royals bore the name **Saxe-Coburg Gotha**, which was changed to the more British sounding name of Windsor. The Queen and Phillip are both the great, great grand-children of Queen Victoria, who married her German first-cousin. That makes Elizabeth and Phillip, inbred kissing cousins.

According to genetic researchers, the marrying of relatives is not a very good idea. Indeed, when it comes to inbreeding horror stories, the **Appalachian Mountain** families are no match for the British Royals.

The Queen's first cousins **Katherine** and **Nerissa Bowes-Lyon** were severely mentally handicapped. They were institutionalised in a state run asylum in **1941**. Cousin Nerissa died in 1986, and the Queen's look-alike cousin Katherine died at age 87 in **2014**.

She was mentally retarded, neglected, and NEVER visited or mentioned. The Queen also has three second cousins who were also sent to the same mental hospital on the same day as Katherine and Nerissa.

Burke's Peerage is a prestigious directory that records the "who's-who" lineage of the British aristocracy. It falsely recorded that the Queen's first cousins Katherine and Nerissa Bowes-Lyon, died in 1940 and 1961.

"I'm not an Anglophobe ladies and gentlemen. I love the British, and a lot of their culture. It's amazing, and led by the Magna Carta, and then the real renaissance worldwide. So much has come out of the British Isles, but not the globalist and the Transylvanian Royal family, perched like giant, stinking vultures on the carcass of the UK"

Alex Jones (1974 -)
Infowars.com

THE QUEEN'S HIDDEN COUSINS

(CHANEL 4 TV DOCUMENTARY)

Every family has secrets they would rather the world not know. Even the most famous of them all. But every family occasion over the past 70 years, two of the Queen's cousins have been absent from the feast. Declared dead by family and society. Staff at the hospital were sworn to secrecy, and it was something they did not talk about among themselves. For decades, the cousins remained hidden in an institution for so-called mental defectives. One of the carers stated,

> *"It just seemed like such a waste of life. I couldn't put my children in there."*

Many thousands of others condemned as "idiots" and "imbeciles" shared their fate and were hidden out of sight, and out of mind. But the Royal secret, was exposed. A private investigator and whistle-blower's camera revealed the truth. Katherine Bowes-Lyon, niece to the Queen Mother, and cousin to the Queen was alive until February

Queen Elizabeth's mentally handicapped cousin Katherine

23, 2014. Sheila Rule had cared for Nerissa and Katherine for over a decade, and was one of the few to attend Nerissa's funeral. According to Sheila, at Nerissa's funeral there was no family present – only staff from the hospital. When you consider the lavish funeral they put on for Lord Dickey Mountbatten the paedophile, it makes you wonder where these royals are coming from. For Nerissa's funeral, there were no flowers, no fancy wake, and no fancy coffin. It was a State welfare affair, attended only by staff. To me, that is sad for anybody, but for a cousin of the Queen?

Indeed, the Queen, with all her vast wealth, did not spend a penny on her look-alike cousin Katherine or her sister Nerissa during their entire lives. Their care was paid for by the tax payer. No birthday gift, no Christmas card, and not a single visit from the Queen or Royal Family in over 60 years (Channel 4, 2015).

Nerissa and Katherine are not the only mentally defective relatives of the Queen. The Queen's great Uncle – **Prince Albert Victor**, was mildly retarded and deaf in one ear. He was also a suspect in the murderous rape and mutilation of slum prostitutes using a carving knife. The killer became known as **Jack the Ripper** (BBC Video – The Lost Prince). The Queen's Grandfather, **King George V**, had an epileptic son. When the boy suffered an epileptic seizure at age four, the King hid the child in an isolated farm house. The boy never saw his Royal parents again, and reportedly died in his sleep (most likely suffocated). **King George III** was Queen Elizabeth's third great grandfather. Because of his episodes of prolonged psychosis, he was put in a straitjacket and kept behind bars at Windsor Castle were he became increasingly insane and blind. **Queen Anne** and **George IV** inherited the same genetic madness. (Bennett, 1995)

The Queen's mother-in-law, **Alice Battenberg**, had regular visions that she was Christ's bride. She was diagnosed as a paranoid schizophrenic and committed to an asylum in 1930. Alice is Prince William's great grandmother.

Hollywood, and the Royal Spin-doctors invest millions in propaganda movies that rewrite history. They do this to help the world forget the crimes, cruelty, madness, and the heartless past of the British Royal Family. The Oscar winning movie **The Queen**, was all about resuscitating the Queen's dying popularity after Diana's murder. Another propaganda Oscar winner, **The King's Speech**, focused on the Queen's father, **King George VI** and his speech impediment. The movie failed to mention Royal inbreeding as a potential cause of his disability. Monarchy movies sell the belief that the Royals are sensitive, caring, human, and deserving of worship and tax payers support, but the fact is, they are not.

Missing Children

In mid-October of 1964, kissing cousins Elizabeth and Philip paid a Royal visit to a Catholic residential school for Aboriginal children, in **Kamloops**, British Columbia Canada. **William Combes** was 12 years old at the time of the Royal visit.

> *"I was an inmate at the Kamloops school and we were visited by the Queen of England and Prince Phillip. I remember it was strange because they came by themselves, no big fanfare, or nothing. But I recognised them and the school principal told us it was the Queen and we all got given new clothes and good food for the first time in months the day before she arrived.*
>
> *The day the Queen got to the school, I was part of a group of kids that went on a picnic with her and her husband and some of the priests, down to a meadow near Dead Man's Creek. I remember it was weird because we all had to bend down and kiss her foot, a white laced boot.*
>
> *After a while, I saw the Queen leave the picnic with ten children from the school, and those kids never returned. We never heard anything more about them and never met them again even when we were older. They were all from around there but they all vanished.*
>
> *The group that disappeared was seven boys and three girls, in age from six to fourteen years old. They were all from the smart group in class. Two of the boys were brothers and they were Metis from Quesnel. Their last name was Arnuse or Arnold. I don't remember the others, just an occasional first name like Cecilia and there was an Edward.*
>
> *What happened was also witnessed by my friend George Adolph, who was 11 years old at the time and a student there too. But he's dead now."*

William Combes was the sole survivor of a group of three aboriginal boys who claim to have witnessed the abduction of ten children during a royal visit to the Kamloops residential school in mid-October, 1964, when both the Queen and Prince Philip were in Canada.

William, aged 59 and in good health, was scheduled to be a primary witness at the opening session of the **International Tribunal into Crimes of Church and State** (ITCCS) on September 12, **2011** in London, England. But William Combes never made it to the tribunal. He died suddenly, just days before his testimony, from a still-undisclosed cause. The Vancouver Coroner's Office refuses to comment on William's death. Remember the "suddenlys' from the Rothschild story? Well, they are happening again...

But his murderers did not win. William's videotaped statements, including his witness of the 1964 abductions, were registered in the archives of the ITCCS, and were made public at the opening session on September 12, 2011(ITCCS, 2015), (Combes, 2011).

WORLD WILDLIFE FUND – PRIVATE HUNTING CLUB

The Queen and Phillip's trip to Canada was not the only shopping trip they took together in the 1960's. In 1961, the couple went on another

The caged hunt of a rare Tiger 1961 - Prince Philip (left) and the Queen (centre)

shopping spree, but not for children this time, but for endangered tigers and elephants.

Only a few short months before, Phillip launched the **World Wildlife Fund**. After arriving Jaipur, India with the Royal pair slipped into matching safari jackets and journeyed into India's *Ranthambhore Jungle* with their hunting guide, the **Maharajah of Jaipur**. Despite protests from British and Indian politicians, the hunt party continued deep into the Indian jungle.

An endangered **Bengal tiger** was lured into the cross hairs of Philip's hunting rifle by tying a group of goats together as prey. Philip then shot and killed the defenceless animal in what can only be described as a "caged hunt." There was a British TV crew that accompanied the hunt. They recounted a tale of how Philip had earlier shot and killed a mother elephant while her orphaned calf ran off into the jungle in terror.

Later that day, the party came across an extremely rare and endangered **Indian Rhino**. At the time, there were only about **250** left in the entire world. Other members of the party were horrified because they knew there would be no stopping the now blood crazed Philip from bagging a Rhino. Locals literally stood in the way of the Rhino to stop the Duke from shooting it. However, Philip would have none of it. He took aim and **BANG!** One less rare Indian Rhino to worry about. He went on to shoot and kill a **crocodile** and six **Urials** (a type of mountain sheep) on that trip (Batchelor, 2015).

As the Royals continued their holiday on the Sub-Continent, they travelled north to Kathmandu in Nepal. Another caged tiger hunt was organised, and another 8.5 ft. tiger was shot. They also bagged another rare rhino (TigerKill, 1961).

Philip co-founded the WWF in 1961

Philip co-founded the *World Wildlife Fund* (WWF) in 1961, with former Nazi SS Officer **Prince Bernhard** of the Netherlands. Prince Bernhard also helped found the **Bilderberg group** of royals, politicians, bankers, and business men who meet annually for secret talks.

When the WWF was founded, there were about **3 million** African elephants left in the wild. Since then, numbers have plummeted to about **200,000**.

The **African Rhino** once had a population of around **100,000**. Today they are virtually extinct in the wild, and are only kept on private reserves and in captive breeding programs (Kasnoff, 2015). The last herd of wild African Rhinos numbered about **700** and were destroyed by the WWF. They were all rounded up "for conservation." Some were sent to "*pay-for-kill*" game farms (ala Cecil the Lion) to raise money to save the species we are told? The rest were sent to game farms in the United States, Australia, Asia, England, and elsewhere as tourist attractions. Many did not survive the drugging and shipping to all parts the world (Douglas, 1994).

At the start of the 20th century, India was home to **100,000** tigers, but numbers crashed in the years following independence in 1947, even though the WWF controlled most of the breeding grounds in India. Over the past 30 years, Prince Philip has hunted and killed many kinds of animals. Indeed, figures compiled from press reports by the anti-blood sports lobby suggest that in Britain alone he has shot at least **30,000** pheasants.

The real WWF

He has also killed deer, rabbit, hare, wild duck, snipe, woodcock, teal, pigeon, and partridge in the UK. In his native land of Germany, Prince Philip brags how he and his son, Prince Charles, once shot and killed 50 wild boar in one day. These were not feral hogs that plague Australia and America. These were a particular pure strain of animal that has lived in Europe since the end of the last Ice Age.

The Duke frequently invites rich sporting friends to the Royal Family's 20,000-acre Norfolk estate at Sandringham.

The scam is simple. Set up the World Wild Life Fund, then grab huge areas of land all over the world and deem them "off limits" to local farmers and indigenous hunters, all in the name of "conservation." Then, a few times a year, Prince Phillip and his blood lust band of crazies get to go on a killing spree claiming they are "culling" the animals for conservation. The World Wildlife Fund is basically a private hunting club for rich elites of the world. And just like medieval times, anyone "poaching" on the "King's land" will be arrested and imprisoned, even if they were only trying to feed their families.

Prince Philip's total "bag" over the past 30 years stretches over continents, species and runs into mind-boggling numbers.

In **1993**, while out shooting for up to four days a week during his seven-week stay at Sandringham, he hit his target of **10,000** pheasants. His shooting parties are estimated to have killed about **150,000** pheasants over the last two decades.

When it comes to blood sports, it is a family affair. Like father, like son, like grandson. On a trip to **Kenya** in Africa, **Prince William** took lessons in spearing African wildlife from a Masai tribal member. According to news reports, Prince William drove a 2 metre/7 foot spear into a small antelope and killed it (Antelope, 2003). In fact, the Dik-dik antelops only grow 30 – 40 cm / 15" high at the shoulder. Doesn't take a man to kill one of them does it.

Prince William speared a Dik-dik Antelope just like this one!

Prince William recently purchased **250** birds including pheasants, ducks, and partridges. But not as pets, but for shooting targets. As

Patrons of the "Duke and Duchess of Cambridge" Conservation Fund (Cambridge, 2015) – another fund scam.

the birds were set free, William shot them out of the sky like skeet, at the Queen's Sandringham Estate. Prince William and daddy Charles set packs of bloodhounds after foxes. It's jolly great fun chasing after terrorised foxes on horseback, then watch the bloodhounds tear them to shreds.

The World Wildlife Fund was not created to save endangered wild life species. On the contrary, it has made a fortune from the illegal ivory trade which is was supposed to prevent. Phillip and Bernhard's World Wildlife Fund raised massive funds from corporations and public donations. They use the funds to confiscate huge tracts of land all over the world. The Fund is being used as a land and power grab. The Royal Families "green" policies have pushed native people off their ancient land, shut down their farming, and caused food shortages and starvation. Saving animals and the environment is a phoney excuse they use to pass international laws that advance their world government agenda.

Prince Phillip's son Charles, is now the new President of the World Wildlife Fund, which has been renamed **World Wide Fund for Nature**. It is one of the largest contributors to human and animal de-population. The so-called conservation parks in Africa and elsewhere, are covertly used to train terrorist groups and mercenaries.

These **kill for profit** soldiers cross borders, create social unrest, start civil wars, and commit genocide in places like Rwanda, Kenya, Liberia and Sierra Leone (Douglas, 1994).

Sadly, the trusting public have donated millions under the false illusion that they are supporting wildlife.

Prince Harry also has a conservation Fund (Harry, 2015).

Not to be outdone, William's half brother, Prince Harry, has also got into the scam. He set up a conservation fund he promotes on his website and makes millions from it. But he still likes to go to foreign countries and shoot the native animals. He even came to Australia to shoot kangaroos – just for fun!

He who controls the food, controls the world

There are only 10 – 12 corporations that run the world's food supply, which are all grouped around Britain's Royal House of Windsor. The Windsor led cartel includes Cargill, Continental, Monsanto, and Archer Daniels Midland (ADM) which dominate world food supplies including dairy, meat, grains, edible oils and fats, fruits, vegetables, sugar and spices. This cartel is hoarding food, minerals and raw materials and it has the power to shut down food production and export supplies worldwide.

Prince Philip was once famously quoted as saying,

> *"If I were reincarnated I would wish to be returned to earth as a killer virus to lower human population levels."*

Prince Phillip Mountbatten, alias Battenberg, and the power elite view themselves as the inheritors of the earth. Culling the population through eugenics is their answer to freeing up planet earth's resources that are being consumed by what they consider as racially inferior commoners and *useless eaters*.

Groom of the Stool

This is a tyrannical group pushing eugenics, population control, and carbon taxes. Prince Philip, the Queen's husband, another German Prince, is tied to eugenics and Nazism. The point is that these people are the most filthy, degenerate people you can imagine.

So any time you see some mind numbing zombie telling you how exciting the Royal wedding is, or the next Royal visit (paid for by the tax payers) and how they watched it, remind yourself that they are watching a bunch of inbred, human hating, idiots that cannot even dress themselves. Yes, they still employ Valets (Valet de chamber) to dress them.

Something they try and keep quiet is that the Queen still has a **Groom of the Stool**, a person who literally wipes her bottom for her. Google *Groom of the Stool* and see what I am talking about. Even though they say she doesn't have one anymore, leaked insiders have said she does. At a Royal visit to Canada a couple of years ago, people took photos of the Queen's portable toilet being unloaded from her plane. She actually takes her own toilet with her wherever she goes.

Why do Americans Worship the Royals?

It is sad that Americans carry on like giggling school girls when the British Royals visit. If only they knew their history, they would know that the 4th July was all about **resisting** this usurping, German family. Most people in the UK now days don't even like the Royal family. In fact, the UK has a secret police system that threatens people who speak out about getting rid of the monarchy.

There are servile people that have been raised to worship this family all over the world. Little old ladies who think it's cute. Do you know, Princess Diana on record, told her butler and close friends that her husband was going to try and kill her in an automobile accident?

American's get really excited when they get to meet Royalty, but the Royal protocol should be offensive to any free thinking humanist.

"When you meet the Queen, bow slightly at the waist, and never look her in the eyes. Do not offer your hand unless she offers hers first, and never ever touch her."

Self-claimed Satanist, Lady Gaga bows to the Great Dark Mother of the Dragon Brotherhood.

The Queen has real power, and uses it

The media has misled the people into believing that the British monarch is a symbolic, ceremonial figure head, with little or no real power. That she is a harmless old relic who passes her time sipping tea at the palace. Nothing could be further from the truth.

The Queen embodies the Crown and supreme world power. Presidents of the United States are forbidden any titles of nobility and are subservient to the monarch. Prime Ministers in Commonwealth Nations like Canada, Australia, and New Zealand are her "Prime" Ministers, and she, is their Head of State.

Just like the Masonic symbols hidden in the American 1$ bill, the one percent that rule the one percent, that rule the 99 percent, are also hiding in plain sight.

They are hiding by **reigning**, instead of **ruling**. The British monarch *reigns*, but she has chosen instead to delegate her power to Presidents and Prime Ministers to *rule* on her behalf. This protects her from becoming a target of political hostilities. Meanwhile the general public is kept in the dark about her true powers.

So what exactly are the supreme powers the monarch possesses?

She has the power to grant titles like Sir and Dame, but also:

- The Power to dismiss Prime Ministers and government
- The Power to dissolve parliament and call new elections
- The Power to refuse legislation passed by Parliament
- The Power to enact laws in her Majesty's name
- The Power to declare a state of emergency and issue proclamations
- The Power to command the armed forces and raise a personal militia
- The Power to declare war without the agreement of the Parliament
- The Power to read confidential government documents and intelligence reports
- The Power to pardon convicted criminals

Three times in three years the Parliament of Canada didn't do what the Queen of England wanted, so she suspended their Parliament.

She did the same thing in the early 1970's in Australia – she fired the Prime Minister **Gough Whitlam**, because he stood up to the American Military Industrial Complex (and CIA).

In the late 1960's the British-controlled Indian Ocean island of **Diego Garcia** was handed over to the US Military who wanted to build a massive Airforce and Naval base there so they had a staging platform to invade Iraq some years later (Yes, the Iraq invasion had been in the planning for a full decade before they went in). The only problem was there were people living on the island, and had been for generations. The locals were brutally expelled by British Governments in the late 1960s and early 1970s to make way for an American military base. The actions of the British were described as a **crime against humanity.** The good old **United Nations** did nothing to stop them.

In November **2000**, the **High Court of Britain** agreed that the islanders should be allowed to return to their homes and that their expulsion was illegal. After a 30 year battle, the islanders had finally won – they were going home, or so they believed.

When the **Pentagon** found out, they made a call. Next thing, **Tony Blair**, Prime Minster of Britain gets a call from the **Queen**. She tells him to overturn the High Court decision, and do not allow those islanders to return. The Queen got her way.

Now that is power, when a royal decree can over turn a humanitarian High Court ruling!

John Pilger - *Stealing a Nation* (2004) is a 1 hour documentary that tells the whole story and one worth watching (Pilger, 2004).

Consolidation of Power

Without counting the rulers of the kingdoms and duchies that went to make up the German empire, there were 20 reigning monarchs before World War One, most of which were related to the British monarchy in some way or another - with a crowned sovereign in every country except France and Switzerland. By the end of World War One, the three great monarchies of Central Europe - Germany, Russia, and Austria-Hungary - had fallen. In the main, it was those sovereigns without outwardly personal power who kept their thrones. So this was one of the greatest strategic ploys the British monarchy ever did to guarantee longevity – to create the illusion that they have no power.

THE PRINCESS DIARIES

Diana, Princess of Wales (1961-1997)

There is no doubt what so ever that Princess Diana was murdered. Most people do not know that Diana survived the crash. **Dodi Fayed** and the driver **Henri Paul** were killed instantly, and the body guard **Trevor Rees-Jones** was seriously injured. Diana on the other hand was injured, but conscience and alert, and had she received prompt treatment, she would have survived (Barton, 2007).

The on-board ambulance doctor, **Jean-Marc Martino** (he should go to jail), treated Diana at the scene for almost 40 minutes before the ambulance set off. He then ordered the ambulance to take Diana to the **Pitie-Salpetriere** hospital where she died, instead of the **Hotel-Dieu**, which the ambulance passed on the way. The doctor also ordered the ambulance to drive extremely slowly, even though there was little traffic. (Batty, 2007). It took an amazing **1hr and 43 minutes** before Diana arrived at the hospital for treatment. She was still alive. Somehow though, they managed to let her pass away in the following hours, alone, in the hospital, and all her blood samples disappeared (Reid, 2007). The creepy Royal body snatchers grabbed Diana's body and partially embalmed her, even though she was no longer a Royal and in a French hospital, and without French Police or hospital permission. This destroyed any evidence that she had been murdered in the hospital.

The Patsies

Before they even checked his blood, the press had already blamed her driver **Henri Paul,** who they said was "*drunk as a pig*," even though the video footage of him leaving the venue showed him as sober as a judge. Later, the restaurant receipt confirmed Henri had consumed just two *Pernod Ricards*, an unsweetened aniseed flavoured liqueur that is often enjoyed after dinner as a digestive. Yet, all blame was put on Henri Paul.

Even though all of the CCTV cameras in the tunnel were conveniently turned off for the first time in their history on the night of the crash, dozens of eye witnesses saw a **white Fiat Uno** flash a bright light, then collide with Diana's car. White paint from the Uno was found on Diana's car. This car was solely responsible for the crash – so who was driving it?

James Andanson was a photographer who freelanced for MI-5, MI-6 and the CIA. He had been stalking Diana and Dodi earlier in the month while they were on holiday in the Mediterranean. He told French Police he was not in Paris on the night of the crash, but told two different versions of events. His wife and son also gave him contradictory alibies. Privately, he admitted to friends he had been there in the tunnel on the night of the crash. Less than six hours after the fatal crash in Paris, and for reasons that have never been revealed, Andanson boarded a flight at Paris's Orly airport, bound for Corsica. And surprise, surprise, surprise...Andanson owned a white Fiat Uno.

The question of who was driving the white Fiat Uno was never raised in the Inquest. This was possibly the most important part of the trial, and it was not brought up. Why?

In May **2000**, Andanson's body was found in a blazing vehicle in the French countryside. He had two bullet holes in the back of his head. The official verdict was suicide (Evans, 2007).

The Insiders Version of Events – the Inquest

The Inquest into her death was like the JFK inquest and the 9/11 inquests – a farce. It was conducted in the Royal family's own court house, by one of their own, handpicked insiders, **Lord Justice Scott Baker** (he should go to jail). He made sure none of the Royal family were called as witnesses. What is amazing, is that they had a hand written note from Diana, saying that her husband had threatened to kill her in a staged car accident. If Mary Jones had written that note, and she died from a car accident, I am pretty sure Mr. Jones (the husband of Mary) would be a star suspect for the prosecution. He would have at least been interviewed by the police. Not in this case. Prince Charles (he should go to jail) was never questioned, nor did he even go to the Inquest into his wife's death.

Lord Snot, I mean Lord Scott Baker, made sure crucial evidence was ignored, or covered up and he pushed the inquest into a pre-scripted direction to completely protect the Royal family, and blame everything on Henri Paul.

During the Inquest, the Metropolitan Police Commissioner (1993-2000) **Lord Condon** admitted he had suppressed crucial evidence implicating **Prince Phillip** in the assassination of Diana. He sat on this evidence for three years. He later lied under oath, and perjured himself (he should go to jail).

During the Inquest, the next Metropolitan Police Commissioner (2000-2005) **Lord Stevens** lied under oath, and perjured himself (he should go to jail).

Sir Robert Fellows, the Queen's Private Secretary, hated Diana's guts, lied under oath, and perjured himself (he should go to jail). As a reward for lying and protecting the royals, he was made a Lord two years later.

MI-6 Planed the whole thing

Former MI-6 Officer **Richard Tomlinson** blew the whistle by producing a secret document from MI-6 that showed a detailed plan to assassinate a Serbian leader in a car crash, in a tunnel, by flashing a very bright light into the driver's eyes. This is exactly what happened to Diana's car. The man that drove the white fiat that blinded Diana's driver was James Andanson who was later suicided.

The Verdict

If you ask any person in the street what the verdict was for the death of Diana, they will tell you it was "accidental." And who caused the accident? They will say *"the Paparazzi was to blame."*

This is **NOT** what the verdict was, but it **IS** what the British media spun. The Jury concluded that it was not an accident, and that the Paparazzi had nothing to do with it. The actual verdict was that it was an *Unlawful Killing*.

Unlawful Killing is defined as murder or manslaughter, and the Jury blamed the driver of the **white Fiat Uno**. But because they were never told who the driver was, no charges were ever laid on anyone. Nice and tidy.

There is no doubt that the Inquest was manipulated by powerful, unelected forces to the advantage of the British Royal family. This could only happen because in essence, Britain is a monarchy, not a democracy.

Pay Day

Figures released on the coroner's website show that the inquest that took six months cost £2,885,618.66 - paid for by the **Ministry of Justice**. A three-year inquiry by the Metropolitan Police cost just under £3.7m. Someone made a lot of money...

The Unelected Power of Britain

Much of Britain still operates under a system of unelected power, and at its centre are the Windsors (Saxe-Coburg-Gotha), the old aristocracy, and their vast wealth. So why does Britain (and all the Commonwealth nations) still tolerate this racist, parasitic family? Despite presenting itself as a charming and picturesque relic of the past, the royal family retains a ruthless grip on power in 21st century Britain. It presides over a corrupt and corrosive **Honour System** (giving people medals and titles) that keeps thousands of public officials in permanent obedience to the monarchy, all hoping for a Knighthood or an OBE, in return for a lifetime of loyal service. These are the people who operate Britain's system of government, judges, coroners, civil servants, police chiefs, private secretaries, members of the secret services and Privy Councillors (lawyers). They demand absolute secrecy from their subjects and stifle descent.

What Happened After the Inquest?

Since the crash and the Inquest, Charles has married Camilla, as he had always wanted to; MI-6 now publicly admits that they have been involved with assassinations in the past; Diana has been air-brushed out of official Royal history. No action has been taken against the Police Chiefs that suppressed Diana's sworn statement predicting that the Royal family would kill her in a car accident. Instead, they both got promoted and now sit in the House of Lords.

    Mohamed Al-Fayed (father of Dodi who died in the crash) was ordered by Prince Phillip to take down the Royal Warrants that hung for decades outside Harrods of London. The royal crests of The Queen, the Duke of Edinburgh, the Queen Mother, and the Prince of Wales

Mohamed Al-Fayed private investigators found:

The coroner outlined ten claims which Mohamed Al Fayed, pictured below yesterday, says back up his theory of a conspiracy to kill Diana and Dodi.

1 THE DRIVER WORKED FOR MI6: Henri Paul was a paid informant of the British and French security services and persuaded Dodi to let him drive the car as part of the murder plot.

2 HE WAS NOT DRUNK: The security services have deliberately disseminated the false idea that the driver was drunk.

3 THE ENGAGEMENT: Diana was under surveillance by both MI6 and the CIA who were aware she was about to announce her engagement to Dodi.

4 ASSASSINS IN THE SECURITY SERVICE: MI6 was known to be involved in assasination plots, including a plan to kill former Serbian leader Slobodan Milosevic.

5 THE MI6 PLOT: Senior MI6 agents were stationed at the British Embassy before and after the crash.

They engineered a plan to kill Diana and Dodi using junior officers.

6 THE PREGNANCY: Diana's body was illegally embalmed to conceal the fact that she was expecting Dodi's child.

7 THE BLOOD TEST: Henri Paul's blood tests were fixed by the security services to give the impression he was drunk and speeding.

8 THE CCTV CAMERAS: CCTV cameras along the car's last route were deliberately disabled by the security services.

9 THE WHITE FIAT UNO: The car was ambushed using a combination of a blinding flash of light, a stun gun and a white Fiat Uno driven by paparazzi James Andanson, who was employed by MI6.

10 THE CHANGED ROUTE: There is no explanation why Henri Paul took the route via the Alma Underpass through Paris instead of a quicker route to Dodi's apartment via a slip road.

Mohamed Al-Fayed spent millions on uncovering the truth

were removed in 2000. Mohamed later burnt the crests in a symbolic gesture.

What got Diana killed?

There are several valid theories why Diana was assassinated. It was well known that **Prince Philip** hated her with passion. When it was learnt that she was pregnant to Dodi el Fayed, a Muslim *"Nig-nog"* and that the two were planning to marry, that was like a red flag to a bull for a racist imperialist. The British Royal Family could never have a "darky" in the fold, especially a Muslim – it would ruin Christmas!

But another fact that came out, admitted by Diana herself, was that she really upset the **Military Industrial Complex** with her anti-mine program she got behind. She was called and abused, threatened and intimidated by the **Lords of War** who she had panicking.

No doubt, it was a combination, and the Duke - Prince Philip was more than happy to give the order to take her out. He relayed this to MI-6 who carried out the operation without question, using one of their disposable operatives (James Andanson). They even used an older plan they dreamt up for a different assassination. Although the Queen was not directly involved, she was certainly aware of the plot. Her cold and distant behaviour in the weeks after Diana's death was only changed when Tony Blair, the then Prime Minister, went and told her that the public were turning against her and she better "pretend" to be upset about Diana's death. The trick worked, and the sycophants were appeased.

Of course, the Queen did go and strip Diana of all of her Royal titles after she was buried. I wonder why the known tramp, and gold digger, the **Duchess of York – Fergie,** is still allowed to keep her titles and attend Royal banquets and parties? Maybe she is blackmailing her ex-husband Price Andrew the paedophile?

The Royal Family then relied on the old boys club known as the **"*Establishment*,"** with their unerring instinct for mutual, self-preservation, to rally around and cover it up, and cover for each other, and suppress uncomfortable facts. The British monarchy got away with murder yet again, because they have been getting away with murder for centuries, and they are very good at it now.

Ultimately, I think I know deep down what got Diana killed, and here it is in her own words, quoted directly:

"I do things differently. I don't go by a rule book. I rule from the heart, not from the head. And although that has got me into trouble in my work, I understand that. But someone has got to go out there and love people and show it."

Unlawful Killing, the Documentary

To get the whole story in a brilliant and gripping documentary, I cannot recommend highly enough *Unlawful Killing (2011)* directed and written by **Keith Allen**, father of the pop singer Lily Allen and *Game of Thrones* star Alfie Allen (Theon Greyjoy). It was banned in Britain when it first came out. After you watch it, you will know why (Allen, 2011). If you live in Britain, you should run public showings of this documentary and share it on Facebook.

Diana's handwritten note saying her husband was planning to have her killed in a car accident. It was withheld for three years by then Police Commissioner, Lord Condon. He admitted he did it to protect Prince Charles. This letter never mentioned at the Inquest.

WHO IS THE REAL ROYAL FAMILY?

The well-known British TV host **Tony Robinson** (Black Adder, Time Team etc.), made a documentary called **Britain's Real Monarch** (2004), about a remarkable discovery regarding the current Royal family. According to research, there was an illegitimate son born in the **Middle Ages**. If that is the case, then every King or Queen since should not have sat on the thrown. But if not them, then who?

500 years ago, **Edward IV** was King, but his claim to the throne was fatally flawed. Evidence suggests that he was not fathered by the previous King, but by a humble archer (surnamed **Blaybourne**).

It was the summer of **1441**, and England was at war with France. Edward's mother had gone along with her husband the King. While the King was off fighting, it was widely rumoured that she had a fling with an English archer. Nine months later, Edward was born. Within 20 years, Edward became Edward IV. But gossip about his parentage persisted during his lifetime and even after his death.

In fact, **Shakespeare** mentions it in his play *Richard III* (Shakespeare, 1993), when he penned,

> ❝ *Tell them, when that my mother went with child*
> *Of that unsatiate Edward, noble York*
> *My princely father then had wars in France*
> *And, by just computation of the time,*
> *Found that the issue was not his begot;* ❞

The gossip was plenty, but still just gossip. Historians put the rumours down to political mud-slinging. That was until British Historian **Dr. Michael Jones** came across some hard evidence in the archives of the French, **Rouen Cathedral**. He discovered a document that substantiated the rumours that Edward was indeed a bastard. The document Dr. Jones found clearly states that the King, **Richard Duke of York**, was away on campaign from July to August, the very time his wife conceived. During this period, they were separated by about 160 Km (100 mi).

Edward was born 28 April 1442, so if we count back 40 weeks to the time of conception, it is smack bang in the middle of the period the King was away. Conception dates are not an exact science, however five weeks is a fairly big gap, and a reasonable window of error. Premature babies in the Royal families were always recorded, as they posed a threat of infant mortality. No record was recorded that Edward was premmie. Furthermore, this bombshell evidence helps to cement previous circumstantial evidence that was glossed over.

The Rouen Cathedral records show that Edward's christening was a hushed up affair in a side chapel. I know when the modern Royals have a Christening, it is a media circus, and so it was back then. But not for this Christening. Indeed, in contrast, his younger brother had the whole Cathedral opened up and hundreds of people attended.

The strong jawed, wide jowls Edward looked absolutely nothing like the thin faced King.

(Left) Richard Plantagenet, 3rd Duke of York (Right) Edward IV

Neutral sources declare that Edward's own mother, **Cecily of York** confided that Edward was a bastard, even making a legal deposition. She knew the truth of his lineage was vital in protecting the Royal line.

You may be asking why it matters if Edward IV was legitimate or not. Basically, after the **War of the Roses**, most of the legitimate kings were dead. With no more sons of kings left, this left the throne open to claims from outside the direct line. Enter one **Henry VII**. His claim was dodgy at best, and was actually barred from ever taking the Crown. Therefore, the only way to legitimise himself, was to marry a "royal."

Enter **Elizabeth of York**. Elizabeth's claim is based on the fact that she is the daughter of Edward IV (the bastard). But if Edward IV is illegitimate, that invalidates the claim of both Elizabeth, and of Henry.

What that means is very significant. It means that every King or Queen that follows, is illegitimate.

That includes: Henry VIII > Elizabeth I > The Georges > Victoria > Edward VII > George V> Edward VIII> George V > VI> **Elizabeth II** – ALL of these people should never have reigned as Kings or Queens of England – including the current **Queen Elizabeth II** (Barrow, 2013).

The story of Edward IV's illegitimacy did come out during his life. In fact, his own spin doctors came out in force to try and cover it up. They produced many eulogies that continually emphasised what should be obvious – that he was *"conceived in wedlock," "positive Royal blood"* which is odd, because he is already on the throne. Methinks thou doth protest too much! They even tried to move his conception date to a time before Richard and Cecily left for the battle in France. That would have been a full 11 month pregnancy. They tried so hard to cover it up, they shot themselves in the foot, – we know that an eight week, overdue baby is impossible.

So Who Should Be King or Queen?

The obvious question now is of course, who is the legitimate Royal family. Forget the history you know. Prepare to meet Queen Margaret I, King Henry X, and Queen Barbara I. There is a very strict way genealogist follow royal procession, and that is what Tony did next.

Edward IV had two other brothers, Richard III and George Duke of Clarence, the middle brother, had children of his own – the last of the Plantagenet line. His children would have actually taken precedence over Edward IV's. George's eldest was mentally handicapped (another one!), and so was locked up in a tower till his death – unmarried. His daughter was Margaret, Countess of Salisbury who lived and had children of her own. Thus, she should have been **Queen Margaret I**. As last of the Plantagenets, she was a threat to Henry VIII's legitimacy, so he had her, and her sons arrested on false charges of treason and locked up in the Tower of London and finally executed. From here, an alternative family had to be found.

Queen Margaret I's granddaughter married into the **Hastings** family. From this family, the true king should have been King **Henry** (Hastings) VIII – Not Henry (Tudor) VIII. **Henry Hastings** was no less vicious than Tudor, and was known as the **Puritan Arm**. Jumping ahead to Queen Victoria, this should have been the reign **King George** (Hastings) now called **Loudoun**, who at this time was living in Scotland. Soon, the Hastings / Loudoun fortune was squandered by **Henry Hastings**. He spent the last of the family fortune of £5.5 million on a horse race – the whole amount on the win. The horse came in second. The Hastings now had to work for a living. In the 20th century, the family had tragic deaths in both World Wars, but would have left us with **Queen Barbara I** as of 2004. Barbara had a son, now living in Australia.

In 1960, a young man of 17 set sail from England in search of a new life abroad. He didn't know it at the time, but he was leaving his kingdom behind. The true King of Great Britain now lives in a small outback town of **Jerilderie** in New South Wales. His name is **Michael Hastings**. Technically, Michael is not Mr. Hastings, he is a Peer of the realm. His official title is **Michael Abney-Hastings, 14th Earl**

Michael is an impressive, tall man with an heir of dignity and grace. But he is also your typical Aussie working class bloke. He is so down to earth - it is humbling. Whilst he is well aware of his Title, he chooses to stay in Jerilderie and just be Mr. Michael Hastings. When Tony asked him why he stayed in Australia, and not return to England and live among the aristocracy as is his birthright, Michael shrugs his shoulders and says,

Michael Hastings – The Real King of England dies in Australia 2012

> *"Because I love it here. I arrived when I was 17, I married here, I had five children here, and I have five grandchildren now, and I have a wonderful life here.*

Michael lives in a typical, modest home. He raised his children there, you can see the love that has permeated the household for many years. Ironically, as King of Britain, he would also be King of Australia. But he admits, like most Australians, that Australia should be a republic.

What strikes me is Michael is just not interested in living a Royal life. He genuinely loves the life he made for himself. Yet, I think of those sad, lonely Rothschilds, which had to buy their titles, and mix and hob-nob with the aristocracy, just to feel worthy in life. Here is a man that has titles, could be filthy rich, but he chose love. Michael Hastings is a beautiful soul.

Queen Elizabeth's day is planned minute by minute. A Royal Piper blows the bagpipes at 9:30 am after the Royal breakfast every day. She spends her time going through Royal rituals, and Satanic rituals, pressing the flesh with plastic people and scroungers.

Michael's day begins at 7:30am when he sets out on a 30 minute drive to work. He works at the Australian Rice Research Instituted, trying to develop a rice crop that can grow in arid conditions. Michael died on 30 June **2012**. He is succeeded by his son **Simon Abney-Hastings, 15th Earl of Loudoun.**

Compared with the parasitic, dysfunctional, no love, Windsors, the true Monarch lives right at the heart of a close-knit family and community. They are at such extremes. But if not for accidents, and lucky breaks, and coming first instead of second in a horse race, history could have been very different.

This proves beyond a doubt, that there is no such thing as the **Divine Right of Kings.**

References:

Allen, K. (2011). *Unlawful Killing (2011)*. [online] IMDb. Available at: http://www.imdb.com/title/tt1979385/ [Accessed 28 Oct. 2015].

Altrincham, L. (2015). *Elizabeth II Facts, information, pictures | Encyclopedia.com articles about Elizabeth II*. [online] Encyclopedia.com. Available at: http://www.encyclopedia.com/topic/Elizabeth_II.aspx [Accessed 7 Dec. 2015].

Antelope, (2003). *BBC NEWS | UK | William 'kills antelope'*. [online] News.bbc.co.uk. Available at: http://news.bbc.co.uk/2/hi/uk_news/3139181.stm [Accessed 9 Dec. 2015].

Barrow, M. (2013). *Timeline of the Kings and Queens of England*. [online] Resources.woodlands-junior.kent.sch.uk. Available at: http://resources.woodlands-junior.kent.sch.uk/customs/questions/kings.htm [Accessed 5 Nov. 2015].

Barton, F. (2007). *I thought Diana would live, says first doctor at the crash scene*. [online] Mail Online. Available at: http://www.dailymail.co.uk/news/article-493383/I-thought-Diana-live-says-doctor-crash-scene.html [Accessed 28 Oct. 2015].

Batchelor, T. (2015). *PICTURED: Queen and Prince Philip pose with dead tiger 50 years before Cecil the lion*. [online] Express.co.uk. Available at: http://www.express.co.uk/news/royal/595424/Queen-Prince-Philip-pose-dead-tiger-50-years-before-Cecil-lion-controversy [Accessed 9 Dec. 2015].

Batty, D. (2007). *Ambulance driver defends slow Diana journey*. [online] the Guardian. Available at: http://www.theguardian.com/uk/2007/nov/14/monarchy.davidbatty [Accessed 28 Oct. 2015].

BBC, (1961). *Royal Tour Of India - Reel 1 (1961)*. [online] YouTube. Available at: https://youtu.be/IRyEJ0IltOY [Accessed 9 Dec. 2015].

Bennett, A. (1995). *The madness of King George*. New York: Random House.

Cambridge, (2015). *Conservation*. [online] Dukeandduchessofcambridge.org. Available at: http://www.dukeandduchessofcambridge.org/features-0/conservation [Accessed 9 Dec. 2015].

Channel 4, (2015). *The Queen's Hidden Cousins*. [online] Channel 4. Available at: http://www.channel4.com/programmes/the-queens-hidden-cousins [Accessed 8 Dec. 2015].

Combes, W. (2011). *Star Eyewitness who named Queen of England in Abduction of Aboriginal Children dies suddenly in Vancouver Hospital | Welcome to ITCCS.ORG and The International Tribunal into Crimes of Church and State*. [online] Itccs.org. Available at: http://itccs.org/2011/02/28/star-eyewitness-who-named-queen-of-england-in-abduction-of-aboriginal-children-dies-suddenly-in-vancouver-hospital/ [Accessed 8 Dec. 2015].

Commonwealth, (2015). *Commonwealth of Nations*. [online] Wikipedia. Available at: https://en.wikipedia.org/wiki/Commonwealth_of_Nations [Accessed 7 Dec. 2015].

Davies, N. (2000). *Elizabeth*. Edinburgh: Mainstream Pub. Projects.

Douglas, A. (1994). *The oligarchs' real game is killing animals and killing people*. 1st ed. [ebook] Washington D.C.: Executive Intelligence Review, pp.41-47. Available at: http://www.larouchepub.com/eiw/public/1994/eirv21n43-19941028/eirv21n43-19941028_041-the_oligarchs_real_game_is_killi.pdf [Accessed 9 Dec. 2015].

Edward VIII, (2015). *Edward VIII*. [online] Wikipedia. Available at: https://en.wikipedia.org/wiki/Edward_VIII [Accessed 8 Dec. 2015].

Entente Cordiale, (1904). *Entente Cordiale*. [online] Wikipedia. Available at: https://en.wikipedia.org/wiki/Entente_Cordiale [Accessed 7 Dec. 2015].

Evans, M. (2007). *Diana: Fiat driver 'shot in the head'*. [online] Express.co.uk. Available at: http://www.express.co.uk/news/uk/12839/Diana-Fiat-driver-shot-in-the-head [Accessed 28 Oct. 2015].

George V, (2015). *King George V*. [online] Britroyals.com. Available at: http://www.britroyals.com/kings.asp?id=george5 [Accessed 26 Dec. 2015].

Good, O. (2011). *Wills'n'Kate: the comic book*. [online] the Guardian. Available at: http://www.theguardian. com/books/2011/jan/16/kate-william-public-love-story [Accessed 8 Dec. 2015].

Gould, L. and Constable, N. (2012). *Prince Harry in shock as father of close friend shoots himself in suicide tragedy after becoming 'plagued by depression and financial problems'*. [online] Mail Online. Available at: http://www.dailymail.co.uk/news/article-2150459/Charles-Harbord-suicide-Prince-Harry-shock-close-friend-Astrids-father-dies.html [Accessed 8 Dec. 2015].

Harry, (2015). *Prince Harry Africa Conservation*. [online] Princehenryofwales.org. Available at: http://www. princehenryofwales.org/ [Accessed 9 Dec. 2015].

Hazlewood, N. (2004). *The Queen's Slave Trader*. New York: William Morrow.

ITCCS, (2015). *Welcome to ITCCS.ORG and The International Tribunal into Crimes of Church and State | Our Mandate: (1) To lawfully prosecute those people and institutions responsible for the exploitation, trafficking, torture and murder of children, past and present, and (2) To stop these and other criminal actions by church and state, including by disestablishing those same institutions.*. [online] Itccs.org. Available at: http://itccs.org/ [Accessed 8 Dec. 2015].

Kasnoff, C. (2015). *Black Rhinoceros: an Endangered Species*. [online] Bagheera.com. Available at: http://www. bagheera.com/inthewild/van_anim_rhino.htm [Accessed 9 Dec. 2015].

Lamont-Brown, R. (2000). *John Brown*. Stroud: Sutton.

Longest, (2015). *Queen Elizabeth 'never aspired' to be Britain's longest-reigning monarch*. [online] ABC News. Available at: http://www.abc.net.au/news/2015-09-09/crowds-cheer-queen-elizabeth-as-uk-longest-reigning-monarch/6763522 [Accessed 7 Dec. 2015].

Moore, C. (1996). *The Kincora scandal*. Dublin: Marino Press.

Morton, A. (2015). *Unmasked: Edward, the Nazi King of England*. [online] Mail Online. Available at: http:// www.dailymail.co.uk/news/article-2973681/Edward-Nazi-King-England-Princess-Dianas-biographer-reveals-Duke-Windsor-s-collusion-Hitler.html [Accessed 8 Dec. 2015].

Moyes, J. (1996). *Royals' shooting passion draws bad blood*. [online] The Independent. Available at: http://www. independent.co.uk/news/royals-shooting-passion-draws-bad-blood-1315283.html [Accessed 9 Dec. 2015].

Nanking, (1842). *Treaty of Nanjing | China-United Kingdom [1842]*. [online] Encyclopedia Britannica. Available at: http://www.britannica.com/event/Treaty-of-Nanjing [Accessed 23 Oct. 2015].

Philip, (2015). *Prince Philip, Duke of Edinburgh*. [online] Wikipedia. Available at: https://en.wikipedia.org/wiki/ Prince_Philip,_Duke_of_Edinburgh [Accessed 7 Dec. 2015].

Picknett, L. (2002). *War of the Windsors*. Edinburgh: Mainstream.

Pilger, J. (2004). *John Pilger - Stealing A Nation [2004]*. [online] YouTube. Available at: https://youtu. be/0zhGvId4fcc [Accessed 28 Oct. 2015].

Rayner, A. (2009). *Queen Mother on King George VI's death*. [online] Telegraph.co.uk. Available at: http:// www.telegraph.co.uk/news/uknews/theroyalfamily/6200485/Queen-Mother-biography-on-George-VIs-death.html [Accessed 8 Dec. 2015].

Rebrand, (2015). *The 1st of January 1877 AD, Victoria Proclaimed Empress of India*. [online] Information-britain. co.uk. Available at: http://www.information-britain.co.uk/famdates.php?id=1223 [Accessed 8 Dec. 2015].

Reid, S. (2007). *Diana: The unseen evidence which has been mysteriously ignored until now*. [online] Mail Online. Available at: http://www.dailymail.co.uk/femail/article-483701/Diana-The-unseen-evidence-mysteriously-ignored-now.html [Accessed 28 Oct. 2015].

Rodrigues, J. (1979). *IRA bomb kills Lord Mountbatten: Guardian reporting from 1979*. [online] the Guardian. Available at: http://www.theguardian.com/news/from-the-archive-blog/2015/may/19/ mountbatten-lord-prince-charles-ira-1979 [Accessed 8 Dec. 2015].

Salute, (2015). *Their Royal Heilnesses*. [online] Available at: http://www.thesun.co.uk/sol/homepage/news/ royals/6548665/Their-Royal-Heilnesses.html [Accessed 8 Dec. 2015].

Shakespeare, (1993). *Richard III: Entire Play*. [online] Shakespeare.mit.edu. Available at: http://shakespeare. mit.edu/richardiii/full.html [Accessed 5 Nov. 2015].

TigerKill, (1961). *Queen on Tiger Shoot in Katmandu (1961)*. [online] YouTube. Available at: https://youtu.be/ q4CmB9c852s [Accessed 9 Dec. 2015].

Toes, (2009). *The Duchess of York's Toe Scandal*. [online] Iconic Photos. Available at: https://iconicphotos. wordpress.com/2009/06/03/the-duchess-of-yorks-toe-scandal/ [Accessed 13 Dec. 2015].

Tominey, M. (2015). *Truth about Royal 'Nazi salute': Queen was just waving*. [online] Express.co.uk. Available at: http://www.express.co.uk/news/uk/592170/Truth-picture-Queen-Nazi-salute [Accessed 9 Dec. 2015].

UKDebt, (2015). *Government to pay off WW1 debt - BBC News*. [online] BBC News. Available at: http://www. bbc.com/news/business-30306579 [Accessed 7 Dec. 2015].

Windsor, (2015). *House of Windsor*. [online] Wikipedia. Available at: https://en.wikipedia.org/wiki/House_of_ Windsor [Accessed 8 Dec. 2015].

WWF, (2015). *History | WWF*. [online] World Wildlife Fund. Available at: http://www.worldwildlife.org/about/ history [Accessed 9 Dec. 2015].

13

YOU AND YOUR GOVERNMENT ARE CORPORATIONS

"Money and corruption are ruining the land, crooked politicians betray the working man, pocketing the profits and treating us like sheep, and we're tired of hearing promises that we know they'll never keep."
—RAY DAVIES (FROM THE SONG "MONEY & CORRUPTION / I AM YOUR MAN")

I bet you did not know that every Federal, State, and County / local government in the Rothschild run countries are listed on the **US Securities and Exchange Commission** as corporations, with a business number, and each has a non-elected CEO as the head. According to their website,

> The mission of the U.S. SEC is to protect investors, maintain fair, orderly, and efficient markets, and facilitate capital formation.

Search Results

SEC Home » Search the Next-Generation EDGAR System » Company Search » *Current Page*

COMMONWEALTH OF AUSTRALIA CIK#: 0000805157 (see all company filings)
SIC: 8880 - UNKNOWN SIC - 8880
State location: DC | Fiscal Year End: 0630
(Assistant Director Office No 99)

SEC website shows Australia as a corporation

I did a search for my Federal government just to see for myself. My Federal government is Australia. Here is what I found:

The official name of the corporation is **COMMONWEALTH OF AUSTRALIA** with a business number **0000805157**. The business address for the Commonwealth of Australia is 1601 Massachusetts Ave, NW, C/o Australian Embassy, Washington DC 20036 (SEC, 2015).

Home | Latest Filings | Previc

U.S. Securities and Exchange Comm

Search the
Next-Generation EC
System

ϴ

ings)   Business Address   Mailing Address
1601 MASSACHUSETTS AVE NW
C/O AUSTRALIAN EMBASSY
WASHINGTON DC 20036

Australia Corporation address

You can see all the documents they lodge like Profit/Loss etc. The typical forms corporations have to lodge each year. If you want to do your own search, go to https://www.sec.gov/.

Commonwealth of Australia is the company, and **Australia** is the country/nation. It is the same for America, as in the company is called the US and the country is the USA. Every country in the Rothschild controlled world has two names.

Brisbane City Council Inc.

I checked to see if my Local Council (Brisbane City Council) was on SEC, and sure enough it was. So then I went to the BCC website to see who their CEO was.

It lists a man called **Collin James**. Colin James has never appeared on a ballot paper ever for the BCC. Nor has he ever run for office within the BCC. So Collin has been hired (or appointed) by the BCC. According to the job description,

> *Colin oversees the delivery of Council's key initiatives in the pursuit of achieving the Brisbane Vision…Colin is a director of several boards including CitySmart and the City of Brisbane Investment Corporation (CEO, 2015).*

Brisbane City Council
Dedicated to a better Brisbane

Site help | Contact Us

About Council | Planning & building | Traffic & transport | Environment & waste | Facilities & recreation | Laws & permits | What's on & events | Community

GO

HOME › ABOUT COUNCIL › GOVERNANCE & STRATEGY › ORGANISATIONAL CHART › EXECUTIVE MANAGEMENT TEAM

Executive Management Team

The Chief Executive Officer (CEO) and divisional managers form Brisbane City Council's Executive Management Team. The CEO reports to the Lord Mayor.

Chief Executive Officer

Colin Jensen, Chief Executive Officer

Colin Jensen is the Chief Executive of Brisbane City Council, the largest local government in Australia. Council has an annual budget of $3.1 billion, an asset base of $22.5 billion and serves a population of 1.1 million people.

Colin oversees the delivery of Council's key initiatives in the pursuit of its Living in Brisbane 2026 vision. Prior to joining Council in August 2010, Colin had a successful career in the Queensland Government, most recently as the Coordinator-General and Director-General of the Department of Infrastructure and Planning.

In these roles, Colin was responsible for

- overseeing the delivery of the largest infrastructure program in Queensland's history
- modernising the state's planning and development system

- **ABOUT COUNCIL**
- **Governance & strategy**
- Organisational chart
- **Executive Management Team**

Brisbane City Council website explains the roles of Executive Team

I am sure Colin is a nice man, but I did not vote for him to head my city. There is another man, the **Lord Mayor** who is voted in to do the running of the council. So what does a CEO do? Well, basically he is there to make sure the company runs smoothly, but most importantly, he is there to make sure the company makes a profit for the company's shareholders.

So how does a Council make a profit for shareholders?

And who are the shareholders? Maybe I am? After all, it is my Council where I live.

Guess again…the shareholder profits come from your property taxes, fines, levies, parking meters etc. The shareholders are private, foreign investors. So in a nutshell, all the money you pay to your government on any level – Council, State, Federal, is going to private investors, that most probably do not even live in your country. I know, sticks in the throat a little bit right.

Unfortunately this is all true, and you can find out for yourself. It is part of a much bigger conspiracy where you as a person is listed as an "asset," as in a property asset, like a chair or a computer that a company owns. Are you beginning to see now why your government is listed on the **US Stock Exchange**?

Every person in your country that has a registered **Birth Certificat** is registered as an "asset" on the Stock Exchange.

How they own you – by consent

Because most people can do labour or work of some kind, that labour or work transfers into paying back bank debts (loans)? It is the same as collateral. It keeps your owners, the Illuminati – New World Order very happy, and very rich.

Using your Birth Certificate, the "company" – the State, can create a fictional company called "your name" – except the company name is always spelt in capital letter. For example, the real "you" may be called *Jason Bourne*, but the fictional, company name is always referred to as JASON BOURNE. Every time you get a letter from the government, it is always in capital letters. Whether it is for a fine, tax notice, or drivers licence renewal. That is because they are writing to the fiction. By opening the letter and responding to it, you have agreed to be the caretaker of that company – like the CEO/CFO.

Common Law vs. Statute Law

Now, try and follow me on this. As a real, flesh and blood person, you live under **Common Law**. As soon as you are born, you have rights under Common Law. Common Law is the body of law based on judicial decisions and customs that everyone in your area agrees to. For example, everyone agrees that murder or rape are crimes. These fall under Common Law, because it is widely accepted. Common Law, in its most basic form says – **do no harm**. If you harm anyone, any property, or yourself, it is a crime.

The other kind of laws we have in our societies are called **Statute Law**. Statute law are laws made by governments, however, Statute laws are more like "rules", like when a government cannot fix a problem. For example, *"Do not go fishing in this creek during the month of May on every second Tuesday."* This is just made up nonsense, and that is what Statute Law is. Sometimes statute laws make sense, like fire bans on very hot, windy days. But as I said, they are normally when Councils or governments cannot solve a problem, they make a Law. And that is called Statute Law. And many come with fines, levies, and fees. That is the other difference. Natural Law - Common Law, should never cost anything – they are your birth right.

The other entities that use Statue Law are corporations. For example, McDonalds may have a law or rule that says all employees must wear a McDonald's hat during working hours. That is fair enough, and if you are an employee you agree to do this.

But what would you think if you went into McDonalds and they said they cannot serve you if you don't wear their hat. Besides being confused, I am sure you agree that it is ridiculous, because you do not even work for them, so why should you have to wear the hat if you are not an employee?

That is a reasonable response. So what if I told you that you have agreed to the rules of a company that you are not even aware of, but you actually work for.

That is exactly what you, and every person in a Rothschild controlled state has done.

The Scam and how it Works

When you were born, your parents did what they thought was right and they had you registered with the State. They receive a birth certificate, and feeling proud as punch, they take you home. For them, that is where the paperwork ends. But for the corrupt Illuminati, the paperwork is just starting.

Using your birth certificate, they register a new company. They call this company your name in capital letters (e.g.: MARY JONES). This then generates a business number. That business number is then registered on the Stock Exchange, just like any other business.

As I explained earlier, you have a certain value placed on your company.

At birth, they take a heel prick of your baby. This blood test is for an in-depth genetic test. From this, they have the technology that can determine how you will grow, what your average weight will be, and your height, even your eye colour and your overall physical make up. They can also scan for potential diseases like cancer, diabetes, heart condition etc. After this screening, your company is allocated a score. The better your genes, the higher your score.

This score is then associated with your company. During your life, every new blood test you have, medical procedure or change in health is recorded and your company is updated. You are probably wondering why they go to all this trouble right?

It is all about the money

Have you ever heard on the news that your government has X dollars in deficit? The US is up to about $18 trillion at the time of writing. That means your government borrowed money from somewhere to build a bridge or a road or something. Just like when you go to the bank and ask for a loan, the bank asks you for **collateral**. You may have a house or a second car or something you can put up.

For a country under the Rothschild central bank scam, you and everyone else in the country is the collateral, along with natural resources (mining), agriculture, and GDP etc. Every bit helps. Thus, the more "companies" that are fit and healthy that they have on the stock exchange, the more money they can borrow. So right now, assuming you are fit, your company may be worth $150,000.

As you grow, finish a degree, or have more children, your company's worth goes up. By the age of 40 years, it may be worth $350,000.00. If you did not finish high school, or you got sick very early, your company may only be worth $50,000.00 – but it is still something.

But you will never see that money, simple because you are not even aware that the company exists. However, it does, and the company number is usually on the birth certificate somewhere. I know in America at least, people have been able to look up their number and find it on the US Securities and Exchange Commission. They will see their name there in all capital letters, listed as a company.

I have simplified this topic a little bit because it is quite involved and confusing when you first come across it. The fact is, your company is still subordinate to the **Crown Corporation**. The long story short, your company is an employee of the Crown Corporation. That is why all their rules/laws are Statute Laws. They are made up, and they are not real. Some really are for our own good, but most are not. That is why the Queen of England, and all the other Royals and Elites never get into trouble for their crimes. They are above their own Statute law, because they are the CEO's.

When you go to Court

Let's say you did the wrong thing and got a speeding ticket. They send you a letter in the mail, addressed to you in all capital letters. You assume it is addressed to you, so you pay the fine. But what if you end up in court for something.

The first thing they do is to ask you to state your name for the record. They then say, "are you JASON BOURNE?" If you say yes, then you just agree to be judged in **Admiralty Law** or **Maritime Law**, which is **THEIR** law. I spoke briefly about Admiralty Law in Chapter 6.

Admiralty law is the law of the Bench – the Temples – the Inns, and of course, Corporations.

The Law for you the person is the law you were born with - **Common Law**. Common Law does not recognise Statue Law and vice versa.

The Judge can only rule under the Law he is sworn in for

At the beginning of each day, a judge in any court must "swear in" under the Law he will be ruling with. Therefore, a judge cannot, and will not judge you under Common Law if he was not sworn in that morning for Common Law. The same is true if he swore in for a Common Law hearing and you asked him to judge you under Admiralty Law.

I can tell you now that judges everywhere sign in under Admiralty law, because that is what they trained for. During their six years in University training, they may spend less than one day studying Common Law. They are corporate lawyers, so they learn international corporate laws. They call this legal system **Admiralty law.**

So like the McDonalds story – would you agree to wear their hat just to get served?

When you agree that the name they read out is you, in their weird Law language and rules that means you just took responsibility for the Company, and you are its representative.

That is because you agreed to be judged under their Statue Admiralty law. Once you agree, all goes as normal. You either pay a fine or do time. Whatever the outcome, it was all decided under Admiralty law.

If you remember back to Chapter 6, I showed the US flag with gold fringe – note, not USA flag. The US is a corporation. The USA is a country.

The flag tells you what court you are i

If you enter a Court, and they have a flag with a gold fringe (in any country), it means you are being judged under the International Admiralty law. If before you agree that is your name, and ask, "*Is this a Common Law court?*" the Judge will have to answer "*No.*" If you then say, "*I wish to be heard under Common Law,*" the Judge would have to leave the room, remove the gold fringe flags, re-sign in under Common Law, then hear the case. A big muck around for them, but not many people know enough about it to make it happen.

You broke *THEIR* law

However, the thing is, you broke a law that is their corporation's rules. The judge works for the corporation.

Imagine you work for IBM, and you broke an IBM rule. You are brought into the boardroom where the CEO and executive team are waiting, and maybe your immediate Manger is there to announce the rules you broke (you were late for work for the last 21 days).

The charges are read, you agree or disagree, the CEO passes sentence. Case closed.

But what if you went into that meeting and said, I want to be ruled under Apple Inc. laws. Everyone would look at you as if you were crazy. It is EXACTLY the same when you go into court. It is their "boardroom." The judge is the CEO, your Manager is the prosecutor, and the executive team are the jury. And you work for IBM, so they will only be looking at IBM rules you broke.

They cannot, and will not judge you under Common Law, simply because you did not break a Common Law rule (unless you harm someone/something), then they have their own laws to cover that.

Under Common Law, a speeding fine is no longer valid unless you injured someone, or damaged property. But because you drove on their roads, and you paid for a licence to drive on their roads, they assume you are an employee of the company, and that you will be judged under company rules/laws.

That is why they hide this from you. That is why it is the biggest scam (next to Banking) in the history of the world.

Admiralty Law

According to the definition,

> ❝ Admiralty law or maritime law is a distinct body of law that governs maritime questions and offenses. It is a body of both domestic law governing maritime activities, and private international law governing the relationships between private entities that operate vessels on the oceans. ❞

Note how it says it governs "international law, both domestic and private law." In other words, it covers everything.

Jordan Maxwell, a true hero of the people, is a pioneer of the truth movement, and he was the first person to really get his head around this topic and teach others about it. Jordan is a true hero of humanity and I cannot speak highly enough about him. It was Jordan that told us why certain words are the way they are.

For example you are birthed, like a ship is berthed. You come from your Mother's waters, like a ship is in the water. But I will let him explain it – so much better:

LAWS OF THE LAND VS LAWS OF THE SEA

From back in the Roman Empire, there are two things on earth, land, and water. Rome once ruled the world. Caesar once ruled from "the hill." Washington DC, the new Rome, as Washington DC, is the new Rome, or Empire.

Subsequently, we have law of the land, and the law of the water. Law of the land is the law of the people in the land in which they live. However laws of the sea/water are international. They are the banking laws. When you get a credit card in the USA, it works in Europe or in India.

All ships are female, and she delivers a product. Females produce products. Labour, delivery room, birth, ship, "she" delivers products. When products are delivered, they need a certificate of manifest. What is on the ship is on its manifest.

Humans are maritime admiralty products; they also have certificate of manifest. "Birth certificate." On the bottom of birth certificate, shows our "informant" are our parents. We are then property of the department of commerce.

All humans are "stock." As soon as people are born, they are property of the government in which they live. See US vs USA. United States is different than the United States of America. Constitution of USA formed in 1776 and the constitution for the US 1871. US Inc. United states is a corporation. Formed in Delaware in 1871. All citizens are governed under corporate law. All corporations must have a President, Vice President, Secretary, and Treasurer. Hence, the USA Inc. formed in act of 1871. A US citizen is an employee of the US Inc. (Maxwell, 2015).

Legalese Language

The language used by lawyers that is difficult for most people to understand is called **legalese**. I do not mean simply the technical language of lawyers (i.e. terms like tort, bona fide, plaintiff etc...), although legalese may start from that. Every niche has its own technical language after all, and that's fine.

But Legalese is different. Legalese doesn't just use technical terms but also long and complex sentences, ridiculous archaic words, cascades of subordinate sentences, whatever is useful to make things less understandable. It is a language which is with no apparent reason, extremely difficult to grasp. When it is not totally unintelligible to laymen (and to lawyers themselves). It is a language which doesn't communicate. That makes them "indispensable".

So, for instance, this is a horrible sentence in legalese (source Plain Language Association International)

> *Due to the fact that the plaintiff-appellant had up to this point in time supplied an insufficient number of widgets, defendant-appellee specified that, in the event that an insufficient number was supplied in the future, the contract would be held to be terminated, and deemed to be null and void and of no further effect. (55 words)*

And this is the translation:

Because Smith Co. had not supplied enough widgets, Jones Co. said that, if this happened again, Jones would terminate the contract. (21 words)

So why do lawyers use legalese?

1) They want to make things less understandable for the clients/the laymen in general. And why?
   a. They want to show off (like a pianist who plays a baroque sonata)
   b. They want the client not to understand anything of what they wrote, for avoiding remarks/critiques
   c. They want to dominate - as understanding something that other people do not understand is a huge form of domination. They share the information but they do it

in such a mysterious way that the reader still needs an interpreter to make sense of it. And they are both the creator of the information and the interpreter.

2) I also found out that legalese is a distinctive sign for lawyers. I have a friend who is a lawyer. He told me that once, his law professor commented that a judicial decision was poorly drafted because the judge had used very simple constructions and linear sentences. Of course, it was not legalese. It was not complicated enough. So I realised that to a certain extent, writing legalese is a way for lawyers to show to other lawyers how good they are. It is the signature of the virtuoso.

3) The same friend also told me that sometimes he had the feeling that the client expected some legalese in his work, and he felt compelled to use it. The more shadowy the sentence, the better the job. I have the feeling that clients want to see the magician who spells out some mysterious words and makes the magic - so the whole thing gets quite trivial if you understand all of it. Not to mention clients who expected long papers instead of short, quick pieces of information. And yes, one way to achieve long papers is being verbose and using legalese (Long subordinate sentences).

4) Of course, it is nothing new to say lawyers use legalese as a form of power. (see Benson, *The End of Legalese*) (Kimble, 1996). But why do some people expect it? Why do they want to see the wizard in action?

5) Finally, they want to keep themselves in a job. Just try defending yourself in their Courts. Most people can't. You need a well trained Lawyer to act on your behalf, because they made the system so only they could understand it. That is why they charge so much. They rigged the system and we have no choice.

How to not participate

In order to not play this game any longer, it is not that simple, but it is doable. I have personal experience, but I am NOT an expert. I watched a lot of videos on YouTube by a Canadian man I believe is the expert in what is known as the **Freeman** movement. His name is **Dean Clifford**.

They call themselves a *Freeman* or a *Freeman on the Land*. Basically these people have opted out of the Company, and now live completely under Common Law. That means they no longer pay for a driver's licence, they don't pay property tax, and they never go to Admiralty Law Court.

Some have got off, many have not. The problem is most Judges are not even aware of the scam, so they do not know what to make of it. Others know about it and "abandoned" the court. That means they leave the room, and as they do they announce the Court is abandoned. They then go to the back room and hide until everyone leaves. This means the charges are no longer valid.

The main problem though is many people go off half-cocked, and don't do enough study before they try and take on the system. So they look like a complete goose, and the Judge throws the book at them. There are hundreds of videos of actual court cases using the Freeman system.

My own experience

Again, I say, I am not an expert, and will positively not answer any questions or give advice outside of this book. So please don't ask me how – there are hundreds of websites, videos, and tutorials. And that is what I used. Just Google "Freeman on the land [your country]"

As I live in Australia, we are still beholden to Queen Elizabeth II in the UK. Therefore, my experience will be different for someone living in the USA.

I first downloaded some MS Word templates that had all the words and format required. I just had to type my name and address, then print them out. I had to make copies which were signed and stamped as original copies. I had to send the documents by registered mail, thus, someone had to sign for them – and then you know they got it.

I also included a **Notice of Fee Schedule** documented which basically listed my fees to interact with them. For example, to open a letter, I charge a minimum of 15 minutes at a rate of $1,500 per minute. To send a reply will cost them $100,000. Etc. It is playing them at their own game. Again, everything must be signed as originals and copies (which you must keep safe) by a Justice of the Peace or similar. I had to send letters to the Queen, her Privy Council (they are the British Lawyers that made up this Admiralty Law), then to my own country's Attorney General (equivalent to the US Attorney General) in my State and Federal level.

The letters basically say I am not DANIEL I am Daniel, and I do not speak for that name, nor do I have anything to do with it. I acknowledged it was a fiction. I then stated I am not an employee or member of the Crown Corporation or any other Company that I am not aware of.

Furthermore, as I am not an employee, I am not answerable to that company's laws. Finally, I stated that if I do not receive a reply from them within four weeks, acknowledging that either they agree that I am out, or that they do not know what I am talking about, then I can assume I am right, and that I am no longer answerable to their company laws. I also mentioned that from time to time I may use their roads and promise to drive within the limits that they required etc.

I signed it off with a witness (JP), and had to include my real mailing address, and physical address. I must admit I was waiting for the police or some other "security" people to break down my door at 3am on any given night for two weeks after I sent the letters. But nothing happened.

The Incident

About three months later, I was driving on one of their roads. I was going around a corner on a green arrow, however, as I went around the corner some school kids were running across. So I had to stop until they were safely on the footpath. By the time that happened, the light had changed to red. Because I was already over the "white line," the automatic camera took my picture, and sent me a letter in the mail with a fine for $300.00.

I did open this letter because I was curious. It was addressed to the ALL CAPITALS name, which is not me. I called them up and told I had mitigating circumstances, but the lady on the other end was rude and not interested and said bad luck – just pay the $300 fine.

Ok, so that is how they want to play – just raise revenue. No problem, I can do that as well.

So with a red permanent marker, I drew diagonal lines across the page and wrote the word VOID in between them. I sent that back, with a copy of my original letter to the Attorney General, and my Fee Schedule.

Again, I said if I do not hear back from them within a certain time frame, I will consider the matter closed.

About one week before the deadline for them to reply came, I was driving home from somewhere. Next thing, I had a police car right behind me with his lights flashing, wanting me to pull over. I pulled over and got my phone out, and hit "record." I informed the Policeman that I had a recording device and I was recording our conversation.

He was angry, rude, and obnoxious. I remained calm. I asked him why he pulled me over. He said that an **unpaid fin** had come up when his system **automatically** scanned my number plate on the back of my car. He admitted that he did not know what the unpaid fine was for. I informed him that I was waiting for a reply and they had 4 days left. He said he doesn't know anything about that and just pay the fine if I "*know what is good for me*." He was really angry when he said that. I thanked him and we went our own way.

That was over five years ago now, and I have never received another letter, phone call, or random Police stop. I am not holding my breath, maybe if my house is on fire they will let it burn rather than save me hahaha!

The problem is not with the Police. Indeed, most of them do not know what is going on, so be polite and courteous to them. My complaint is with the Crown Corporation, whose CEO is Queen Elizabeth II.

My True Intentions

I went through a lot of work for this to have a so-far positive outcome. I never did all this just to get out of paying fines, or to be a smartarse. If I ever brake a law that I thought I deserved to be fined for, I would pay the fine. But when they are just raising revenue, and no one is in danger, then I will not play that game.

Don't think for a minute that you can break the law tomorrow, then you can get off the fine or jail time by saying you are a Freeman. Like I said, I spent months in advance educating myself, sending the letters and making my Fee Schedule. I honestly hoped I would never have to fall back on this, but I did.

Promissory Notes

A promissory note is an IOU. Some of you may be used to writing your friends or family IOUs for say $10 or $20 or some other amount. But governments and banks deal in much bigger amounts with slightly more complex arrangements.

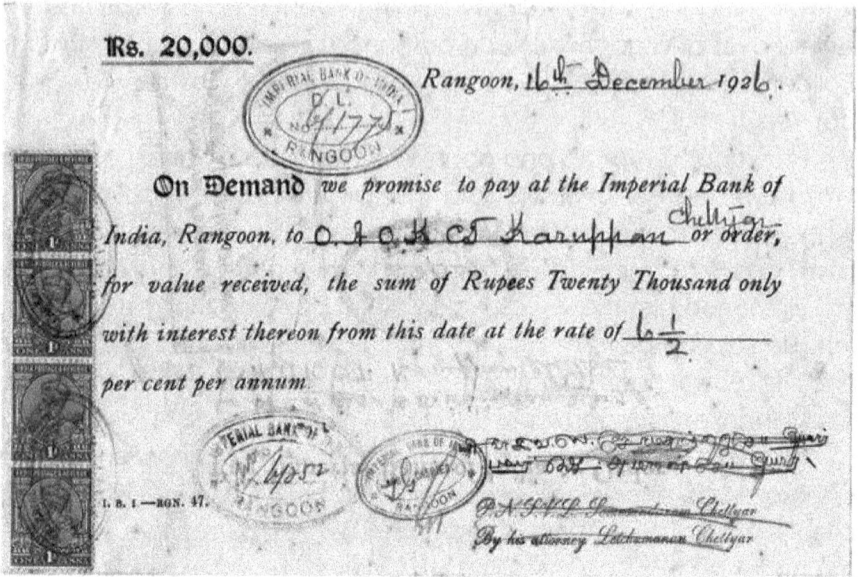

Promissory note

However the fundamentals are similar. Usually promissory notes will carry conditions such as agreeing to pay back a specific sum at a fixed date in the future with interest and crucially, distinguishing them from actual IOUs, they contain a specific promise to pay the money.

Above is an old promissory note made out to the Imperial Bank of India in 1926.

A promissory note, quite simply, is a promise to pay back a loan. In terms of buying a house or other property, a promissory note is the key document that dictates the loan payment process. It specifies the amount being borrowed, the term of the loan, the interest rate, the monthly payment, and what happens if payments are not made on time.

The actual mortgage contains this information. However, it also describes the property, and makes an additional provision. In the case that you do not pay the loan as specified in the promissory note, the lender has the power to foreclose (sell the property). The mortgage document serves as a legal lien that is filed in city or county records. Voluntary liens are imposed by a contract between the creditor and the debtor, such as when a lender holds a mortgage on a property, it has a lien against the home. Involuntary liens are imposed by law, such as when a lien is placed on property for outstanding taxes and other unpaid debts.

The mortgage and the promissory note are inherently interlocked, and give meaning to the other. The promissory note, then, is an extremely important document that you should understand thoroughly.

Michael Tellinger's Experience

Author and a true hero of humanity Michael Tellinger, tells his story, and how to make your own promissory note. Basically, the bank were trying to take Michaels house. They wanted him to pay $55,920.00 USD or they would take his house and sell it. After going through many legal battles, and losing badly, one of the banker's insiders secretly told him about promissory notes. It is what the Illuminati themselves use to borrow money.

So Michael set about learning everything he could and put this new knowledge to good use. He made several promissory notes to pay off the bank, and so far, it looks like it worked.

Michael said in the promissory note that he would pay back a certain amount every month, but that they (the bank) must come to his house to receive it. If they did not come to his house to receive the payment, he can assume they have sold the debt to a 3rd party, and thus, he is no longer required to pay it back – the debt is finalised. If you want to know more, I strongly advise you to watch Michael's video (Tellinger, 2014).

Michael's website has MS Word templates you can download to make a promissory note, as well as tips and useful information about the terminology they use (Ubuntu, 2015). NOTE: you cannot use promissory notes to pay other people or businesses - they are meant for Banks and Government departments only.

Educate Yourself

If you really want to learn more, then it is a fascinating journey. The most valuable information I found for my situation came from:

- **Southern Freemen:** This is where I got the letter templates from (Freemen, 2015).
- **Dean Clifford**: (Clifford, 2013). Dean was arrested on trumped up charges in 2013 (Dean Arrested, 2013).

- The same thing happened to friend of mine in Australia, **Santos Bonacci** in 2014. Santos has also done some fantastic lectures on Law and Language (Bonacci, 2013).
- Larry Hannigan's Australia (Hannigan, 2015)

It is all about Debt

This whole, convoluted system is all designed for one thing - to create more debt. They have managed to reduce everything, including you, me, and every other human into a commodity with a value. But for every value, there is a debt.

Once you understand that money is debt, you will understand how the whole system works, and how we can eventually bring it down. Therefore, in the next chapter, you will learn some of the greatest secrets about money that the Illuminati do not want you to know about, and for good reason.

References:

Bonacci, S. (2013). *Law and Language - Santos Bonacci Part One*. [online] YouTube. Available at: https://youtu.be/dnxO1eU2PX8 [Accessed 16 Nov. 2015].

Clifford, D. (2013). *Making it Simple - Dean Clifford - Part 1/2*. [online] YouTube. Available at: https://youtu.be/9xpisHFB0jw [Accessed 16 Nov. 2015].

Dean Arrested, (2013). *Dean Clifford, Freemen guru, arrested on Canada-wide warrant*. [online] Cbc.ca. Available at: http://www.cbc.ca/news/canada/hamilton/news/dean-clifford-freemen-guru-arrested-on-canada-wide-warrant-1.2439237 [Accessed 16 Nov. 2015].

Freemen, S. (2015). *Southern Freemen*. [online] Southernfreemen.com. Available at: http://www.southernfreemen.com/ [Accessed 16 Nov. 2015].

Hannigan, L. (2015). *Larry Hannigan's Australia*. [online] Larryhannigan.com. Available at: http://larryhannigan.com/ [Accessed 16 Nov. 2015].

Kimble, J. (1996). *Writing for Dollars, Writing to Please*. 1st ed. [ebook] Plain Language Network. Available at: http://www.plainlanguagenetwork.org/kimble/Writing1.pdf [Accessed 3 Dec. 2015].

Maxwell, J. (2015). *The Jordan Maxwell Show*. [online] The Jordan Maxwell Show. Available at: http://jordanmaxwellshow.com/blog/ [Accessed 16 Nov. 2015].

Tellinger, M. (2014). *How to create your own Promissory Notes - Michael Tellinger*. [online] YouTube. Available at: https://youtu.be/dbku5XULgIA [Accessed 3 Dec. 2015].

Ubuntu, (2015). *ubuntu: Michael Tellinger*. [online] Ubuntuparty.org.za. Available at: http://www.ubuntuparty.org.za/ [Accessed 3 Dec. 2015].

14

SECRETS OF MONEY: THE BIGGEST SCAM IN HISTORY

"It is well enough that people of the nation do not understand our banking and monetary system, for if they did, I believe there would be a revolution before tomorrow morning."

—HENRY FORD (1863 - 1947)

*I*magine for a minute that you could click your fingers, and any amount of money you had in mind would suddenly appear in your bank account. Sounds like a crazy fantasy right? Well for you and me it is, but for the bankers of the world, it is exactly how they conduct business every day.

Here is how the scam works, just so we're clear. Banks don't lend deposits when they make a loan. In fact, it's the complete opposite. They create a deposit when they make a loan. They create money, from nothing! Then they charge us interest for the privilege.

The interest bills alone all over the world are staggering. The profits are enormous. The bankers will never, ever surrender this privilege. So how did it get to this? How was this was made possible?

THE SECRETS OF THE FEDERAL RESERVE ACT

It was the night of November 22, 1910, and a group of the richest and most powerful men in America were boarding a private rail car at an unassuming railroad station in Hoboken, New Jersey. The car, waiting with shades drawn to keep onlookers from seeing inside, belongs to **Senator Nelson Aldrich**, the father-in-law of billionaire heir to the Rockefeller dynasty, **John D. Rockefeller, Jr**. A central figure on the influential **Senate Finance Committee** where he oversaw the nation's monetary policy. Aldrich was referred to in the press as the "General Manager of the Nation." Joining him that evening was his private secretary, **Shelton**, and a who's who of the nation's banking and financial elite: **A. Piatt Andrew**, the Assistant Treasury Secretary; **Frank Vanderlip**, President of the National City Bank of New York; **Henry P. Davison**, a senior partner of **J.P. Morgan** Company; **Benjamin Strong, Jr.**, an associate of J.P. Morgan and President of Bankers Trust Co., and **Paul Warburg**, heir of the Warburg banking family and son-in-law of **Solomon Loeb** of the famed New York investment firm, **Kuhn, Loeb & Company**.

The men had been told to arrive one by one after sunset to attract as little attention as possible. Indeed, secrecy was so important to their mission that the group did not use anything but their first names throughout the journey and the meeting so as to keep their true identities secret, even from their own servants and wait staff. The movements of any one of them would have been reason enough to attract the attention of New York's voracious press, especially in an era where banking and monetary reform, especially in an era where banking and monetary reform was seen as a key issue for the future of the nation; a meeting of all of them, now that would surely have been the story of the century.

THE SECRETS OF THE FEDERAL RESERVE ACT

And it was.

Their destination? The secluded Jekyll Island off the coast of Georgia, home to the prestigious Jekyll Island Club whose members included the Morgans, Rockefellers, Warburgs and their boss, the Rothschilds. Their purpose? Davison told intrepid local newspaper reporters who had caught wind of the meeting that they were going duck hunting. But in reality, they were going to draft a reform of the nation's banking industry in complete secrecy. Yes, private, unelected bankers writing government legislation that will impact on the entire nation.

Frank Vanderlip wrote later in the Saturday Evening Post,

> *...it would have been fatal to Senator Aldrich's plan to have it known that he was calling on anybody from Wall Street to help him in preparing his bill...I do not feel it is any exaggeration to speak of our secret expedition to Jekyll Island as the occasion of the actual conception of what eventually became the Federal Reserve System.*

At Jekyll Island, the true draftsman for the Federal Reserve was Paul Warburg.

Paul Warburg, a friend and associate of the Rothschilds and an expert on European central banking arrived in the United States from Germany in 1902. He was brought in as a supposed partner in Kuhn, Loeb and Company. He married the daughter of Solomon Loeb, one of the founders of the firm, however, as already stated, the head of Kuhn and Loeb was Jacob Schiff at this time (a Rothschild). The truth is, Warburg was brought over to America to help take control of that country's money.

The plan was simple. The new central bank could not be called a central bank, because America did not want one. If you take you mind

THE SECRETS OF THE FEDERAL RESERVE ACT

back, the banksters had already tried twice to get a permanent Central Bank and failed.

That was mainly due to men like Andrew Jackson and Abraham Lincoln who blocked the previous attempts. But now they had the President and Senator Aldrich in their pocket, so the time was right. But to make sure, they would not call it a Central Bank – they had to give it a deceptive name that would fool the people. Thus, they chose The Federal Reserve Bank of America. But it would remain a private bank no matter what the name implied.

Superficially, the bank was to be controlled by Congress, but a majority of its members were to be selected by the private banks that would own all of its stock. Yes, the Federal Reserve banks are owned solely by private bankers. No Central Bank anywhere in the world is owned by a government. To keep the public from thinking that the Federal Reserve would be controlled from New York (Wall Street), a system of twelve regional banks was designed.

Given the concentration of money and credit in New York, the Federal Reserve Bank of New York controlled the system, making the regional concept initially nothing but a ruse.

According to **G. Edward Griffin**, the author of the bestselling **The Creature from Jekyll Island** and a long-time Federal Reserve researcher, explains:

> **“** *This banking cartel wrote their own rules and regulations, and called it "The Federal Reserve Act," Using their puppet Woodrow Wilson, they had their "law" passed on the 23rd December at 11 pm, when most of Congress was away for the holidays. (Griffin, 2002* **”**

The new law was very much to their liking because they wrote it. And in essence, what they had created was a set of rules that made it possible for themselves to regulate their own industry, but they went even beyond

THE SECRETS OF THE FEDERAL RESERVE ACT

that. The board and chairman were to be selected by the President, but in the words of **Colonel Edward House**, the board would serve such a term as to *"put them out of the power of the President."*

The power over the creation of money was to be taken from the people and placed in the hands of private bankers who could expand or contract credit as they felt best suited their needs. They do the same with the price of gold, silver and other precious metals.

This Act literally allowed Congress to give away the sovereign right to issue the nation's money to the private banks. But what really stings, is that it was this Act that created the **Federal Tax Act**. You see, the banksters required someone or something to cover their bad bets, so as surety, they forced the American people to pay income tax to cover their debts. Yes, that is right, Americans NEVER paid Income Tax before 1913. However, the late film maker **Arron Russo** questioned the legality of the Income Tax laws and his findings may surprise you. He made a short documentary *about this (Russo, 2012).*

Congressman **Charles Lindbergh** stated following at the passing of the Federal Reserve Act on December 23, 1913:

> *"The Act establishes the most gigantic trust on earth. When the President signs this Bill, the invisible government of the monetary power will be legalized ... The greatest crime of the ages is perpetrated by this banking and currency bill."*

It is important to note that the Federal Reserve is a private company, it is neither Federal, nor does it have any Reserve. It is conservatively estimated that profits exceed $190 billion per year and the Federal Reserve has never once in its history published accounts. In other words, it has never been audited.

In the 2008 after the so-called **Global Financial Crisis**, the then President of the Reserve Bank, Ashkenazi Jew and Rothschild man **Ben Bernanke** was asked by Congress to explain where $2 trillion dollars (of tax payers money) had disappeared to.

THE SECRETS OF THE FEDERAL RESERVE ACT

He smugly replied – "I don't know" and shrugged the question off. The President of the Federal Reserve Bank did not know where $2 trillion dollars went. He is either a liar, or he is incredibly incompetent. Either way, Obama re-appointed Bernanke as head of the Federal Revere when he took office. (That is because Wall Street paid $500 million dollars to get Obama elected – so Obama has done the bidding of Wall Street during his entire Presidency.)

What was the purpose of the Fed?

The Federal Reserve Act was implemented for two reason.
1. To make as much money as possible for the Illuminati Banksters.
2. To enslave the average person in a world of perpetuating debt.

Ben Bernanke (rear) and Alan Greenspan. Both past Presidents of the Fed (art by David Dees)

"You are a den of vipers! I intend to rout you out, and by the Eternal God I will rout you out. If the people only understood the rank injustice of our money and banking system, there would be a revolution before morning."

—U.S. PRESIDENT ANDREW JACKSON

Andrew Jackson
(1829-1837)

You are about to learn one of the biggest secrets in the history of the world. It's a secret that has huge effects for everyone who lives on this planet. Most people can feel deep down that something isn't quite right with the world economy, but few know what it is. Gone are the days where a family can survive on just one pay cheque. Every day it seems like things cost more and more, and it is going out of control.

Yet only one in one million understand why.

You are about to discover the system that is ultimately responsible for most of the inequality in the world today. The powers that be do not want you to know about this, as this system is what has kept them at the top of the financial food chain for last 300 years.

Learning this will change your life, because it will change the choices that you make. If enough people learn about it, it will change the world, because it will change the system. Never in human history, have so many been plundered by so few, and it's all accomplished through this, the biggest scam in the history of mankind.

Where does money come from?

They say that money doesn't grow on trees, but the truth is, the modern banking system creates currency far faster than trees can grow. Most people don't have a clue how currency is created and economists and bankers make it sound so complex that people think they can't understand it. Furthermore, no school in the world includes this subject on their curriculum – and for very good reason as we will see.

I'm going to try and strip the monetary system down into its essence, so that you can see the scam behind the curtain, and just how it affects you.

Government Creates Glorified I.O.U'

Every modern society creates currency in pretty much the same way. But since the US dollar is the majority of the world's currency, I'm going to use the United States as our example. If your country has a Central Bank, then it is part of the same Rothschild owned and operated scam. So what is going on in the US Federal Reserve, is exactly what is going on in your country's Central Bank.

It all starts when some politicians says "vote for me and I'll make sure the government provides more free stuff than my opponent does." But there is no such thing as a free lunch, so to provide that supposedly "free stuff," the politicians vote for the country to spend more than its income.

This is called **deficit spending**. To pay for that deficit spending, the **Treasury borrows currency** by issuing a **bond**.

Treasury Bonds

So what is a bond? If you think about it, a bond is really nothing more than a glorified "I owe you." It is a pretty piece of paper with numbers

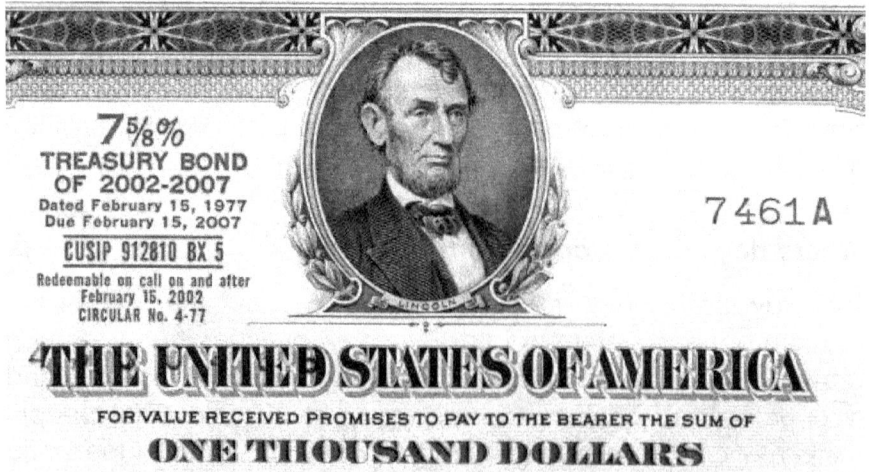

Bond US Treasury (2002)

printed on it that says *"loan me a trillion dollars today and I promise over a 10-year period, I'm going to pay you back that trillion dollars plus interest"*

What you need to understand is that Treasury Bonds are your national debt. These glorified IOU's are to be paid back by you, me, and our descendants through future taxation. Therefore, when the government issues a bond, it steals prosperity out of the future, so that it can spend it today.

The Treasury then hold a bond auction and the world's largest banks show up and compete to buy part of your national debt, and make a profit by earning interest on it.

Indeed, the largest portion of U.S. debt, 68 cents for every dollar or about $10 trillion, is owned by individual investors, corporations, state, and local governments and, yes, even foreign governments such as China that hold US Treasury bills, notes and bonds.

Foreign governments hold about 46 percent of all U.S. debt held by the public, more than $4.5 trillion. The largest foreign holder of U.S. debt is China, which owns more than $1.2 trillion in bills, notes and bonds, according to the Treasury (Murse, 2015).

You'll notice that as we move through this process, the big banks are there taking a cut every step along the way. This isn't by chance as you'll see shortly.

So after the Treasury sells its bonds, through a kind of shell game (swaps) called **open market operations**, banks get to sell some of those bonds to the **Federal Reserve** at a **profi** .

To pay for the bonds, the Federal Reserve opens up its big old cheque book and writes a bad, bogus counterfeit cheque that should bounce, because the cheque is drawn from an account that always has a zero balance. Indeed, there isn't one penny in there.

To quote from the Boston Federal Reserve,

> *When you or I write a check, there must be sufficient funds in our account to cover that check, but when the Federal Reserve writes a check, there is no bank deposit on which that check is drawn. When the Federal Reserve writes a check, it is creating money"*
> – from **Putting it Simply,** Boston Federal Reserve.

The Fed then hands those cheques to the banks and at this point, currency (money) springs into existence! It was literally created out of thin air! Now days, currency is just numbers on a screen. The Fed types in these numbers, and that becomes currency.

The banks then take that currency and buy more bonds at the next Treasury auction.

What is a cheque?

A cheque (US spelling is "check") is also an IOU. When you write a cheque, you are making a note that says *"here's my I.O.U. for cash, all you have to do is go to the bank and pick it up."*

Now it is very, very important that you understand this process, because I am going to come back later and show you the devastating effect this has on you.

1) The Treasury issues IOU's – (bonds).
2) The banks then buy those IOU's with currency.
3) The Fed Reserve then writes IOU's – (cheques), and hands them to the banks, in exchange for the Treasury's IOU's (the bonds) and currency is created.

So what is really happening is the Federal Reserve and the Treasury are just swapping IOU's, using the banks as middlemen and abracadabra, hey presto! Currency (money) magically springs into existence. This process repeats and repeats, over and over again, enriching the banks and indebting the public by raising the national debt.

Money vs. Currency

The end result, is that there is a build-up of bonds at the Federal Reserve and a build-up of currency at the Treasury. This process is also where all paper currency comes from. The Federal Reserve and the government mistakenly call this **base money**. That is because they do not know the difference between money and currency. But I will correctly referred to it as **base currency** because it is not money - it is currency, and there is a big difference.

Money has a stored value and maintains its purchasing power over long periods of time. For example, a piece of gold or silver. Earlier in US history, the paper currency was just a claim cheque. It was a representation for real money of intrinsic value (gold and silver) that was held in deposit at the Treasury. This saved people from having to travel around town with a heavy bag of gold over your shoulder. Instead, you had a piece of paper to represent your gold.

In fact, you could walk into any bank and slap your currency, like a twenty dollar bill on the counter, and redeem it for real money - a twenty dollar gold piece.

But now, this base currency that's piling up in the Treasury is really nothing but a receipt, or a claim cheque on IOU - the bonds. It is not tied to anything of intrinsic value. It is really nothing but a supply of numbers on a screen. The Treasury does not hold any supplies of gold or silver – just IOU Bonds.

The Government gets the loan

The Treasury then deposits the newly created currency into the various branches of the government and the politicians say *"hey, thanks for that!"* The government then uses the currency to do some deficit spending on public works, social programs, and war.

The government employees, contractors and soldiers then deposit their pay into the banks.

Now this may come as a shock to you, but when you deposit your currency with the bank, you're not actually depositing it into an account to be safely held in trust for you. Instead, you're actually loaning the bank your currency, and within certain legal limits, they can do with it, pretty much anything they please. This includes gambling in the stock market and loaning it out at a profit, of course!

Now this is where the currency creation machine really gets cranking, because this is where something called **fractional reserve lending** comes into play.

Fractional reserve lending

Fractional reserve lending is exactly what it says. The banks are allowed to reserve only a fraction of your deposit and loan the rest out. Although reserve ratios may vary, I'm going to use a 10 percent reserve ratios as our example.

If you deposit $100.00 in your account, the bank can legally take $90.00 of it and loan it out without telling you.

The bank must hold $10 of your deposit in reserve, just in case you want some of it.

These reserves are called **vault cash**. But why does your bank account still say you have $100.00 in if the bank has stolen $90.00 of it? Because the bank left an IOU it created at the time of your deposit that is called **Bank Credits** in its place. Now I know this sounds crazy, but here it is in black and white from the Fed itself,

> *Commercial banks create checkbook money whenever they grant a lone, simply by adding new deposit dollars in accounts on their books in exchange for a borrower's I.O.U." – Federal Reserve Bank of New York, "I Bet You Thought, p.19*

These are nothing but numbers that the bank's type into their computers. Even though these bank credits are just IOU's (numbers), they are no different from base currency numbers. They are all just numbers that exist in computers, but to the Fed, they are all currency. Therefore, there is now **$190.00** in existence.

The reason people take out loans from the banks is to buy something they want. They are going to buy a house or, a car or, a vacation or something like that.

Greed gone wild

Bob wants to buy a new TV that cost $90.00. So Bob (the borrower) goes to the bank and takes out a loan for $90.00. The bank loans Bob the $90.00 from your account deposit. Bob takes the money home, and buys his new TV.

The seller now deposits that $90.00 into his account, and his bank loans out ninety percent of that, and leaves bank credit numbers in its place. So now there is **$271.00** in existence.

This process repeats and repeats until it can no longer retain a 10% reserve ratio.

An initial deposit of just **$100.00** can create up to **$1,000.00** of bank credit, all backed by $100.00 of vault cash - just 10%. The result is that the expansion of the currency supply by the bank is far greater than even this example would lead you to believe.

Indeed, as I said, reserve ratios vary wildly. On some deposits it is 10%, on others it is 3%, and on some forms of requirements it is 0%.

In the real world, many deposits and loans are for millions of dollars, even billions of dollars. Each deposit is loaned out hundreds and thousands of times. The bank earns interest on each loan it makes.

So once again, when currency is deposited in a banks vault, the banks get to lend it out, and then it gets redeposited and lent out, and redeposited and lent out again, and redeposited, and lent out again, over and over again, creating bank credits each step along the way.

This is where the vast majority of our currency supply comes from. In fact 92-96% of all currency in existence, is created not by the government, but in the banking system. And only about 2% of US currency is in paper (notes) circulation. The majority is just numbers on a screen.

Too much money is bad

People may think that massive amounts of currency pouring into society may at first sound like a fun idea. That is until you remember one of the most important hidden secrets of money created from thin air is - that the prices of everyday goods and services act as a sponge on an expanding currency supply. The more currency we have, the more prices rise. This is where **inflatio** comes from.

Indeed, just ask your parents or grandparents how much things cost when they were children. I know myself things cost a lot less when I was a child. But during your life, the government keeps adding more and more money to the economy, which means it loses its value.

For example, if you lived in a village and you were the only person who grew, and sold bananas. You could get a very good price for your bananas, because people cannot get them from anywhere else. But what if each year, a new banana grower came to town. After only 10 years, you would have to compete with 10 other growers, and now there are so many bananas for sale, the price has crashed.

The true definition of inflation is an expansion of the currency supply. Rising prices are merely the symptom. Thus, our entire currency supply is nothing but a couple of papers, swept up in this hocus-pocus scam, where the Treasury and the Federal Reserve swap glorified IOU's and a bunch of numbers the banks just typed into their computers.

That is it. That is our entire currency supply. It is nothing but a supply of numbers. Some of them printed, most of them typed, and there is nothing else. But if you thought that was crazy, get ready for the twilight zone of modern day economics.

You are a debt slave

We work for some of that currency supply. True wealth is your time. But we trade away moments in our lives, hour by hour, day by day, year by year, for numbers that somebody printed on pieces of paper, or just typed into a computer. Now those numbers represent our time, sweat, tears, labour, ideas, and talent.

We, are what gives the currency its value. But here comes the really cruel joke. We work hard so that we can save some of that currency, so that we can pay the **tax collector**. In the United States it is known as the IRS, and in Australia, the ATO, but they perform the same operation. They take your currency, and turn it over to the Treasury so that the Treasury can pay the principal, plus interest on that Bond that the Fed Reserve bought with a cheque, drawn on an account that has nothing in it!

Now let's do a recap on this section because this is where the system begins to rob you and me on a massive scale.

The Creation of Money and Debt 101

Most of our taxes are not used for schools, hospitals, roads, and public services etc. Our taxes are used to pay interest on the Bonds that the Federal Reserve bought with a cheque, drawn on an account that has nothing in it.

The Federal Reserve is committing fraud, but here is one of the biggest secrets of them all. Before the establishment of the Federal Reserve, there was no need for personal income tax. The Federal Reserve was created in 1913, and that very same year, the Constitution was amended to allow income tax. Do you really think this was just a coincidence?

Ask yourself, how much income tax have you paid over your lifetime? Did you know the average employee that works full time, works for almost three months a year for free! Yes, the money you pay in tax is usually equivalent to 1-3 months' pay. Remember that the next time you want to go home early for something important and you are feeling guilty.

Indeed, most of your salary/pay has been silently siphoned away, into the hands of those who **own the system**.

Yes, this system has owners. Who they are is an even bigger secret that we will get to shortly. But first we need to understand the mumbo jumbo of the so-called **debt ceiling**.

Money is Debt

It's all based on a huge paradox. There was interest due on that Bond and there was interest due on every one of those loans that the banks made. That mean there is interest due one every dollar in existence.

Think about this for a minute. If you borrow the very first dollar into existence and that is the only dollar that exists on the planet, but you promised to pay it back, plus another dollar worth of interest, where do you get the second dollar to pay the interest?

The answer is, that you have to borrow that dollar into existence as well, and promised to pay that dollar back with interest as well, so now there are two dollars in existence, but you owe four, and so on and so on. The result is, there is never enough currency to pay the debt. There is always more debt in the system then there is currency in existence to pay the debt.

Therefore the whole system is impossible. It is finite - it will come to an end, one day. Let's just hope we are not around when it happens.

What would happen if the government stopped borrowing to do deficit spending? Are the payments on those Treasury Bonds going to stop? What would happen if the public stop borrowing and going deeper into debt? Are your house and car payments going to stop? No, there is a payment due every month, on the principal, plus the interest, on every dollar in existence, and those payments do not stop.

If we stop borrowing, then no new currency is created to replace the currency that we used to make those payments.

Whether you're making a payment on a loan, or paying tax to make a payment on a Bond, the portion of the payment goes to pay off the principal which extinguishes that portion of the debt. But the debt also extinguishes the currency.

Currency and debt are like matter and anti-matter. When they meet, they annihilate each other. If we just pay off the principal only on all the loans and Bonds that exist, the entire currency supply just vanishes.

Try it for yourself

Try this little experiment. Make two stacks of coins of the same size. The one on the left is Debt, and the one on the right is Currency. Because we create twice as much debt for every dollar we borrow, the stack on the left must be twice as high as the stack on the right.

Start removing the currency, one at a time, and remove two currency coins, you must remove one debt coin. Eventually all of your currency coins will disappear, and a big stack of debt coins are still there. Because this stack is not held up by currency, it gets too big and heavy and collapses.

In other words, if we don't go deeper into debt every year, what happens is the whole thing goes into a **deflationary collapse** under the weight of those payments.

Why you can never balance the budget

Politicians and pundits alike talk about balancing the budget, paying down the debt, and living within our means. They don't understand that this is deflationary. It is impossible to do under our current monetary system without collapsing the whole economy.

This is why any talk of a debt ceiling is not only ridiculous, it is delusional.

The system is designed to require ever-increasing levels of debt just to continue. That is why politicians will always kick the can down the road and raise this so-called debt ceiling, over and over again, until the whole system finally collapses under its own weight.

Simply put, they don't want it to collapse on their watch. The Founding Fathers in the United States knew the dangers of Central Banking and fought to free themselves from this very thing.

The **Revolutionary War** started out as a tax revolt, but now US citizens must pay tax, just to have a monetary system.

Having just suffered through the hyperinflation of the Continental dollar which was printed into oblivion to finance the Revolutionary War, they understood the dangers of a **fiat currency**[17] and debt based monetary systems. So to protect future generations from institutional

---

[17] Currency that a government has declared to be legal tender, but is not backed by a physical commodity.

when you work for a wage
that leaves you broke or in debt
after purchasing the necessities
like food, rent and hydro;
you are working for FREE...

THAT, my friends, is SLAVERY

theft and out-of-control government, they wrote into the Constitution that only gold and silver can be money, for the simple fact that you can't print them.

The US's current system is not only unconstitutional, but it robs people of the liberty and prosperity their forefathers fought and died for.

We are all feeling the effects of ignoring the Constitution right now. By forcing more currency into the circulation, our purchasing power is diluted.

Inflation is a slow and in insidious, stealth tax. It is simply the result of this debt based monetary system.

Who benefits

This system empowers and benefits those who create the currency and receive it first, as they get to spend it into circulation before it has an effect on the economy. They are stealing purchasing power from you, and transferring it to the banks and the government every hour, of every day, because of this false monetary system.

It is not like the people at the top don't know this. To quote the Federal Reserve:

> 66 *The decrease in purchasing power,*
> *incurred by holders of money, due to*
> *inflation imparts gains to the issuers* 99
> *of money.*

This is a fraud. It is a **Pyramid scheme**. It is a **Ponzi scheme**. It is a scam and it is a **LIE**.

The entire monetary system is nothing but a form of legalised theft. But here is the biggest con job of them all.

The Federal Reserve is not federal. It has stockholders. There is no federal agency that has stockholders.

What is a stockholder?

A share of stock represents a percentage of ownership in a corporation. So the stockholders are the owners of that corporation.

Therefore, the Federal Reserve is a private corporation with owners. You can see it for yourself if you go to the Federal Reserve's website and it will say this stockholders receive an annual dividend of 6% (Fed Shareholders, 2015).

Wow, 6% of billions of dollars every year, for doing nothing, and spending nothing. For just $1 billion, they get $3,600,000.

Who are the Federal Reserve Shareholders?

J. W. McCallister, an oil industry insider with **House of Saud** connections, wrote in *The Grim Reaper* that information he acquired from Saudi bankers, cited 80% ownership of the New York Federal Reserve Bank, by far the most powerful Fed branch, by just eight families, four of which reside in the US. They are the Goldman Sachs, Rockefellers, Lehmans and Kuhn Loebs of New York; the Rothschilds of Paris and London; the Warburgs of Hamburg; the Lazards of Paris; and the Israel Moses Seifs of Rome.

CPA **Thomas D. Schauf** corroborates McCallister's claims, adding that ten banks control all twelve Federal Reserve Bank branches. He names N.M. Rothschild of London, Rothschild Bank of Berlin, Warburg Bank of Hamburg, Warburg Bank of Amsterdam, Lehman Brothers of New York, Lazard Brothers of Paris, Kuhn Loeb Bank of New York, Israel Moses Seif Bank of Italy, Goldman Sachs of New York and JP Morgan

Chase Bank of New York. Schauf lists William Rockefeller, Paul Warburg, Jacob Schiff and James Stillman as individuals who own large shares of the Fed. The Schiffs are insiders at Kuhn Loeb. The Stillmans are Citigroup insiders, who married into the Rockefeller clan at the turn of the century.

Goldman Sachs is the most powerful financial group in the world. It is a fully Zionist organisation that selects all US Treasury positions for the last 30 years. In fact, in that last 30 years, every Fed Reserve President and 2IC have been Rothschild Zionist, Ashkenazi Jews.

Eustace Mullins, true hero of the people, came to the same conclusions in his book **The Secrets of the Federal Reserve**, in which he displays charts connecting the Federal Reserve Bank and its member banks to the families of Rothschild, Warburg, Rockefeller, and the others. The control that these banking families exert over the global economy cannot be overstated and is quite intentionally shrouded in secrecy. Their corporate media arm is quick to discredit any information exposing this private central banking cartel as "conspiracy theory." Yet the facts remain.

The True FAT CATS

The owners of the primary banks are the same people that wrote this legislation in 1913, and who now line up to buy the Treasury Bonds at the Treasury Auction.

There are five families in particular that have grown very fat from the theft of American prosperity. They are: **Rothschild**, **Schiff**, **Warburg**, **Rockefellers**, and **Morgan**.

These are the main shareholders, or rather, their families are. Yes, part of the Federal Reserve Act they wrote, included a clause that stated that those individuals would be the shareholders (all Ashkenazi Jews, all Comm 300, all Bloodlines), and that after their deaths, the shares would pass to their immediate families, forever, and ever, and ever...Your hard work, your toil, your sweat, your talent, your time is going to support an already fabulously wealthy handful of families, who do absolutely nothing to earn it. They keep us in debt to keep themselves wealthy. If you have money in the bank or in your wallet/purse, then they are your owners, and you are their slave. The note in your wallet is an IOU to one of these families.

On top of their shares, these greedy banksters get to make a profit by selling part of your national debt - those Bonds to the Federal Reserve, who buys them with a cheque from nothing. Then you pay tax, to pay the principal and the interest on those Bonds (to the banks), so that the Federal Reserve can pay the shareholders a 6% dividend.

Don't be alarmed if you don't quite comprehend the deception of this system at first glance. Very few people do. It is purposely complex. The economist **John Maynard Keynes** once wrote,

> 66 *By this means government may secretly and unobserved, confiscated the wealth of people, and not one man in a million will detect the theft. – John Maynard Keynes* 99

I believe, that presented correctly, anyone can understand the system, regardless of how complex it is. So let's do a recap and break it down even more.

Step 1: The government creates glorified IOU's.

These Bonds increase our national debt, and put the public on the hook to pay it back.

Step 2: IOU's are swapped to create currency.

The Treasury sells the bonds to the banks. The banks then turn around and sell our national debt, at a profit, to the Federal Reserve, which they own. The Federal Reserve then opens its chequebook that doesn't have a penny in it, and buys those IOU's with IOU's that it writes - cheques on a chequeing account that has a 0 balance. Then they give those cheques to the banks, and currency just springs into existence. Then the whole process repeats. This results in a build-up of bonds at the Federal Reserve and Currency at the Treasury, which is really just a supply of numbers. The Treasury then deposits the numbers in the various branches of the government.

Step 3: The government spends the numbers on promises, Public Works, Social Programs, and War.

Then the government employees, contractors, and soldiers, deposit their pay into the banks.

Step 4: The banks multiply the numbers

By magically inventing more IOU's through fractional reserve lending, where they steal a portion of everyone's deposit and lend it out. That currency gets redeposited and then a portion is stolen again, and the process repeats over and over, magnifying the currency supply exponentially. Then we work for some of those numbers.

Step 5: Our numbers are taxed

We pay taxes to the IRS, who then turns our numbers over to the Treasury, so the Treasury can pay the principal, plus the interest on bonds that were purchased by the Federal Reserve, with a cheque from nothing.

Step 6: The debt ceiling delusion

The system is designed to require ever-increasing levels of debt that will eventually collapse under its own weight, because politicians always kick the can down the road. They don't want it to collapse on their watch so they always increase the debt ceiling.

Step 7: The secret owners take their cut

The world's largest banks own the Federal Reserve. Those banks make a profit selling the national debt each day. They make a profit when the Fed pays them interest on the reserves held at the Fed and the Fed pays them a 6% dividend on their ownership.

Can a bank foreclose on your house if they have provided nothing of real value in the mortgage?

A little remembered footnote in banking history occurred in December 1968. A bank was moving to foreclose on a house, and the homeowner decided to fight the foreclosure in court, arguing that contract law requires two contracting parties to agree to swap two items of value, legally called the "consideration."

In the case of First National Bank of Montgomery vs. Jerome Daly, Daly argued that since the bank simply wrote a number in a ledger to create the loaned money out of thin air, there was no real value and therefore no legally binding consideration. The lawyers for the bank admitted that this is how the bank works. They create money out of thin air as a ledger or computer entry, which you must repay with your labour. And there was no law in 1968 that specifically gave banks the legal right to do that. Daly argued that because there was no equal consideration, the mortgage was null and void and the attempt to foreclose invalid. The jury agreed! So did Judge Mahoney, who resisted demands to over-rule the jury in favour of the bank, and wrote a simple straight forward decision that stated that there was no question that the mortgage contract was void, because the claim that the bank simply made up the money out of thin air, was not disputed by the bank itself.

Judge Mahoney was murdered with poison less than six months later, and Jerome Daly, who was an attorney, was debarred. The decision in favour of Daly was then nullified on procedural grounds and the entire matter has been kept out of the media! (Jones, 2014).

Perhaps if Daly had of created a Promissory Note (see Chapter 13), he would have had more luck.

This system is fundamentally evil. It funnels wealth from the working population, to the government and to the banking sector.

It is the cause of the artificial booms and busts of modern economies and it creates a great disparity of wealth between the rich and the working class. It is only possible because we no longer use real money (gold or silver) but instead we use fiat currency.

But worst of all, it is a form of enslavement. **Bond** is the root word of **bondage**. Whenever a government issues a bond, it is a promise to make us pay tax in the future.

Nobody asked you if you wanted to pay tax today for the prosperity we all enjoyed in the last century. Nobody is asking our children if they want to work hard in the future to pay for the prosperity we're enjoying now.

George Washington once wrote to James Madison,

> *No generation has the right to contract debts greater than can be paid off during the course of its own existence.*

By stealing the prosperity from tomorrow, so we can spend it today, we enslave ourselves and future generations.

Federal Reserve in Washington DC

Now this all sounds pretty bad but there is great hope, for YOU are the greatest threat to this false monetary system. This system relies on the public being ignorant of its workings. Please share this knowledge with everyone you know, because an informed public, that fully understands this system, can build a better future for generations to come.

Above is the Federal Reserve in Washington DC. It is located on **Constitution Street** and that is just as much of a joke as the New York Federal Reserve being located on **Liberty Street**.

Both of them are unconstitutional, both of them limit our Liberty, and they transfer wealth away from us every second, of every day to the Federal Reserve, to the government, and to the banking sector. You are now among the one in a million who can detect the theft of your prosperity. The big question is, what can you do about it?

1) Read this section again, and again, until you can describe and teach it to others. Those who understand the system can make preparations for its unavoidable collapse and protect themselves. History shows those who don't will probably be wiped out.

Federal Reserve in New York

2) Share this chapter, or even the whole book with people you care about. All it takes is a few mouse clicks to share this book on Facebook, or tweet it, or email the Amazon link to loved ones. Please share it wherever you can.

3) Get Involved. There is a great group called **Campaign for Liberty** that are actively protesting to get the Fed audited. Yes, since the Federal Reserve came into being over 100 years ago, it has never been audited, even though it administers the public money. That is why Senator **Rand Paul** (son of Ron Paul) is pushing the Audit the Fed in Congress. Check them out and join in!

http://www.campaignforliberty.org/

Josiah Stamp, 1st Baron Stamp (1880 – 1941)

"The modern banking system manufacturers money out of nothing. The process is perhaps the most astounding piece of sleight of hand that was ever invented. Banking was conceived in inequity and born in sin. Bankers own the earth. Take it away from them, but leave them the power to create money and control credit, and with the flick of a pen, they will create enough money to buy it back again…But if you want to continue as the slaves of bankers and pay the cost of your own slavery, let them continue to create money and to control credit"

– SIR JOSIAH STAMP, DIRECTOR OF THE BANK OF ENGLAND.

References:

Fed Shareholders, (2015). *FRB: Federal Reserve Act: Section 7*. [online] Federalreserve.gov. Available at: http://www.federalreserve.gov/aboutthefed/section7.htm [Accessed 25 Nov. 2015].

FEDACT, (1913). *FRB: Federal Reserve Act*. [online] Federalreserve.gov. Available at: http://www.federalreserve.gov/aboutthefed/fract.htm [Accessed 25 Nov. 2015].

Griffin, G. (2002). *The creature from Jekyll Island*. Westlake Village, Calif.: American Media.

Jones, S. (2014). *Montgomery vs. Daly*. [online] The Banking Swindle. Available at: https://criminalbankingmonopoly.wordpress.com/montgomery-vs-daly/ [Accessed 29 Nov. 2015].

LaRouche, L. (2015). *Debt Fraud: Greece Actually Owes Nothing!*. [online] Larouchepac.com. Available at: https://larouchepac.com/20150219/debt-fraud-greece-actually-owes-nothing [Accessed 13 Oct. 2015].

Liberty, (2015). *Campaign for Liberty - Reclaim the Republic. Restore the Constitution.*. [online] Campaign for Liberty. Available at: http://www.campaignforliberty.org/ [Accessed 25 Nov. 2015].

Money, (2015). *Facts About U.S. Money*. [online] Factmonster.com. Available at: http://www.factmonster.com/ipka/A0774850.html [Accessed 25 Nov. 2015].

Murse, T. (2015). *How Much U.S. Debt Does China Own?*. [online] About.com News & Issues. Available at: http://usgovinfo.about.com/od/moneymatters/ss/How-Much-US-Debt-Does-China-Own.htm [Accessed 25 Nov. 2015].

Press, A. (2015). *IMF says Iceland repays its remaining $332 million in debt ahead of schedule*. [online] US News & World Report. Available at: http://www.usnews.com/news/business/articles/2015/10/09/imf-says-iceland-has-repaid-its-remaining-debt [Accessed 13 Oct. 2015].

Russo, A. (2001). *Nicholas Rockefeller admitted the elite's goal is a 100% microchipped and enslaved World population*. [online] YouTube. Available at: https://youtu.be/oygBg6ETYIM [Accessed 6 Aug. 2015].

15

ALL WARS ARE BANKERS' WARS

"Banks do not have an obligation to promote the public good."
— ALEXANDER DIELIUS, CEO, GERMANY, AUSTRIAN,
EASTERN EUROPE GOLDMAN SACHS, 2010, SOURCE:
WALL STREET JOURNAL, MAY 2010

It is a matter of historical truth, that the bankers financed both sides of World War I and II. If anyone had the cream of the profits, it was the bankers. War is also good for banks because a lot of material, equipment, buildings, and infrastructure get destroyed in war. So countries go into massive debt to finance war, and then borrow a ton more to rebuild.

As stated, it is easily demonstrated that the Rothschilds, and their banker minions have financed both sides of very war, and unrest since Napoleon. This also includes the American Revolutionary War and War of Independence. But aside from bullets and bombs, infrastructure and

rebuilding, the main reason banks like wars, is because they can infest the newly vanquished nation with their Central Bank scam. As history shows, every war in modern times that the US and/or NATO have been involved with, have been against sovereign nations that did not have a Rothschild controlled Central Bank.

The Petro Dollar

In the final days of World War II, 44 leaders from all of the Allied nations met in **Bretton Woods**, New Hampshire in an effort to create a new global economic order. With much of the global economy decimated by the war, the United States emerged as the world's new economic leader.

In addition to introducing a number of global financial agencies (World Bank, IMF etc.), the historic NWO meeting also created an international gold-backed monetary standard which relied heavily upon the U.S. Dollar. Initially, this dollar system worked well. However, by the 1960's, the weight of the system upon the United States became unbearable.

On August 15, **1971**, President **Richard M. Nixon** (33° Freemason, Comm 300) shocked the global economy when he officially ended the international convertibility from U.S. dollars into gold, thereby bringing an official end to the Bretton Woods arrangement (Bretton Woods, 2015).

Two years later, in an effort to maintain global demand for U.S. dollars, another system was created called the **petrodollar** system.

In **1973**, a deal was struck between **Saudi Arabia** and the **United States** in which every barrel of oil purchased from the Saudis would be denominated in U.S. dollars. Under this new arrangement, any country that sought to purchase oil from Saudi Arabia would be required to first exchange their own national currency for U.S. dollars. In exchange for Saudi Arabia's willingness to denominate their oil sales exclusively in U.S. dollars, the United States offered weapons and protection of their oil fields from neighbouring nations, including Israel.

By **1975**, all of the **OPEC** nations had agreed to price their own oil supplies exclusively in U.S. dollars in exchange for weapons and military protection.

This petrodollar system, or more simply known as an *"oil for dollars"* system, created an immediate artificial demand for U.S. dollars around the globe. And of course, as global oil demand increased, so did the demand for U.S. dollars. But this artificially boosted the American dollar, so if you remove the oil-pegged-to the US dollar, then the US dollar would collapse overnight, and America would be bankrupt.

As the U.S. dollar continued to lose purchasing power, several oil-producing countries began to question the wisdom of accepting increasingly worthless paper currency for their oil supplies.

Today, several countries have attempted to move away, or already have moved away, from the petrodollar system. Examples include Iran, Syria, Venezuela, and North Korea... or the "axis of evil," if you prefer. What is happening in our world today makes a whole lot of sense if you simply read between the lines and ignore the "official" reasons that are given in the mainstream media. Additionally, other nations are choosing to use their own currencies for oil like China, Russia, and India, among others.

So what happens when a nation decides to sell oil on its own terms, and not use the petrodollar system?

Saddam Hussein and the lie of Iraq's nuclear weapons

Iraq, already hostile to the United States following **Desert Storm**, which was a double cross by the US, demanded the right to sell their oil for

Euros in 2000 and in 2002. The United Nations agreed to allow it under the "Oil for food" program instituted following *Desert Storm*. One year later, the United States re-invaded Iraq under the lie of Saddam's nuclear weapons, lynched Saddam Hussein, and placed Iraq's oil back on the world market only for US dollars.

The clear US policy shift following 9-11, away from being an impartial broker of peace in the Mideast to one of unquestioned support for Israel's aggressions only further eroded confidence in the Petrodollar deal and even more oil producing nations started openly talking of oil trade for other global currencies.

Gaddafi and the Gold Dina

Over in Libya, **Muammar Gaddafi** had instituted a state-owned central bank and a value based trade currency, the **Gold Dinar**.

Libyan Gold Dinar

Gaddafi announced that Libya's oil was for sale, but only for the Gold Dinar. Other African nations, seeing the rise of the Gold Dinar and the Euro, even as the US dollar continued its inflation-driven decline, flocked to the new Libyan currency for trade. This move had the potential to seriously undermine the global hegemony of the dollar. French President **Nicolas Sarkozy** reportedly went so far as to call Libya a "threat" to the financial security of the world. So, the United States invaded Libya, brutally murdered Qaddafi (the object lesson of Saddam's lynching not being enough of a message, apparently), imposed a private central bank, and returned Libya's oil output to dollars only. The gold that was to have been made into the Gold Dinars, 144 tons of it, is as of last report, unaccounted for.

General Wesley Clark blows the whistle on US plans to conquer the oil-rich Middle East

According to **General Wesley Clark**, the master plan for the "dollarification" of the world's oil nations included seven targets, Iraq,

Syria, Lebanon, Libya, Somalia, Sudan, and Iran (Venezuela, which dared to sell their oil to China for the Yuan, is a late addition).

Full transcript of interview:

> *About ten days after 9/11, I went through the Pentagon and I saw Secretary Rumsfeld and Deputy Secretary Wolfowitz. I went downstairs just to say hello to some of the people on the Joint Staff who used to work for me, and one of the generals called me in. He said, "Sir, you've got to come in and talk to me a second." I said, "Well, you're too busy." He said, "No, no." He says, "We've made the decision we're going to war with Iraq." This was on or about the 20th of September. I said, "We're going to war with Iraq? Why?" He said, "I don't know." He said, "I guess they don't know what else to do." So I said, "Well, did they find some information connecting Saddam to al-Qaeda?" He said, "No, no." He says, "There's nothing new that way. They just made the decision to go to war with Iraq."*
>
> *He said, "I guess it's like we don't know what to do about terrorists, but we've got a good military and we can take down governments." And he said, "I guess if the only tool you have is a hammer, every problem has to look like a nail. So I came back to see him a few weeks later, and by that time we were bombing in Afghanistan. I said, "Are we still going to war with Iraq?" And he said, "Oh, it's worse than that." He reached over on his desk. He picked up a piece of paper. And he said, "I just got this down from upstairs" -- meaning the Secretary of Defense's office -- "today." And he said, "This is a memo that describes how we're going to take out seven countries in five years, starting with Iraq, and then Syria, Lebanon, Libya, Somalia, Sudan and, finishing off, Iran." I said, "Is it classified?" He said, "Yes, sir." I said, "Well, don't show it to me." And I saw him a year or so ago, and I said, "You remember that?" He said, "Sir, I didn't show you that memo! I didn't show it to you!"*
> *- General Wesley Clark*

What is notable about the original seven nations originally targeted by the US is that none of them are members of the **Bank for International Settlements** (BIIS), the private central banker's private central bank, located in **Switzerland** (a country created by the Bankers). This meant that these nations were deciding for themselves how to run their nations' economies, rather than submit to the international private banks.

America has been at war 222 out of 239 years since 1776. Let that sink in for a moment.

Now the bankers' gun sights are on Iran, which dares to have a government central bank and sell their oil for whatever currency they choose. The war agenda is, as always, is to force Iran's oil to be sold only for US dollars and to force them to accept a privately owned central bank. Malaysia, one of the few remaining nations without a Rothschild central bank, is now being invaded by a force claimed to be "Al Qaeda" and has suffered numerous suspicious losses of its commercial passenger jets.

With the death of President **Hugo Chavez**, plans to impose a US and banker friendly regime on **Venezuela** are clearly being implemented.

Germany's gold bullion. Where is it?

The German government recently asked for the return of some of their gold bullion from the **Bank of France** and the **New York Federal Reserve**. France has said it will take **5 years** to return Germany's gold. The United States has said they will need **8 years** to return Germany's gold. This suggests strongly that the Bank of France and the NY Federal Reserve have used the deposited gold for other purposes, most likely to cover gold futures contracts used to artificially suppress the price of gold to keep investors in the equities markets. Now the Central Banks are scrambling to find new gold to cover the shortfall and prevent a gold run.

So it is inevitable that suddenly France invades **Mali** (Africa), ostensibly to combat **Al Qaeda**, with the US joining in. Mali just happens to be one of the world's largest gold producers with gold accounting for 80% of Mali exports. War for the bankers does not get more obvious than that!

Mexico has demanded a physical audit of their gold bullion stored at the **Bank of England**, and along with Venezuela's vast oil reserves (larger than Saudi Arabia), Venezuela's gold mines are a prize lusted after by all the Central Banks that played fast and loose with other peoples' gold bullion. So we can expect regime change if not outright invasion of Venezuela soon.

The Plan is in Plain Sight

In the diagram on the other page, the dark coloured countries are members of the **WTO** (World Trade Organisation). The WTO is a Rothschild Central Bank organisation. I have placed explosion signs in the countries that are not WTO compliant countries that also just happen to be the same countries that NATO and the US have invaded or bombed in the last couple of years. Other countries that are not WTO or have Central Banks in them are Russia and Ukraine, which NATO and the US just happen to be belligerent toward in the last couple of years.

Note how many of these countries that are being bombed are on General Wesley Clark's list. The only country that has not been invaded or bombed yet from General Wesley Clark's list is Iran. But that is about to change.

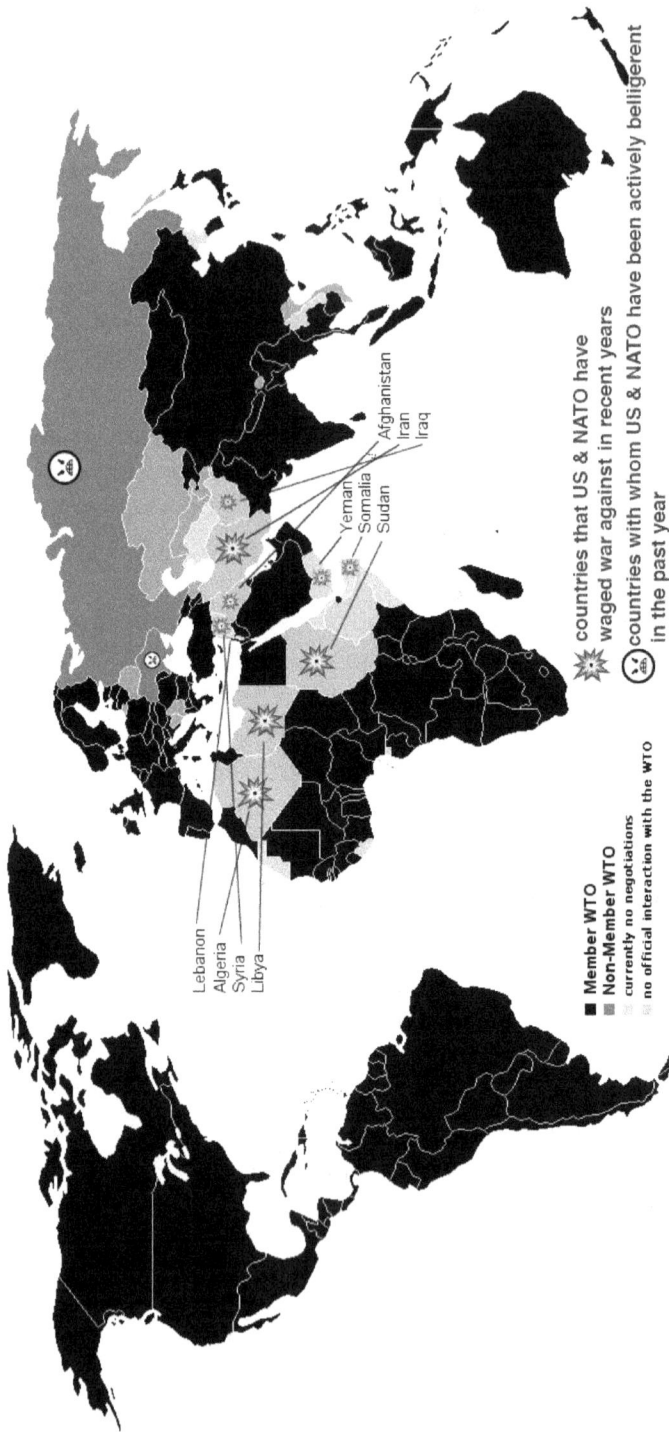

Member WTO
Non-Member WTO
currently no negotiations
no official interaction with the WTO

Lebanon
Algeria
Syria
Libya

Yemen
Somalia
Sudan

Afghanistan
Iran
Iraq

countries that US & NATO have
waged war against in recent years

countries with whom US & NATO have been actively belligerent
in the past year

*I appreciate the image above will be hard to see, however a full sized version
is available on my website.*

HOW DID WE GET TO THIS POINT?

Zbigniew Brzezinski (Left)

Throughout 1998 and leading up to 2000, the People with the money and their influential think tanks forecast the mobilisation of an aggressive American foreign policy.

In his book **'The Grand Chessboard'**,Zbigniew Brzezinski, advocates the policies of the Predatory Ruling Classes (Brzezinski, 1997).

Throughout the years **2001-2003** In the wake of the 'Pearl Harbor' type attacks of 9-11, General Wesley Clark learns that the pro-Israeli neo-conservatives within the Bush-Cheney administration plan to overthrow the governments of Iraq, Libya, Syria, Iran and several other states. General Clark alleged that the traumatic destruction of 9/11 enabled an aggressive foreign policy to be implemented; even though none of the targeted nations had anything to do with 9/11. He did not go public with this until 2007. Though plans did not exactly unfold according to the Pentagon's five year time-table, they have followed the plan and are still on track.

2006 and the formulation of the Chinese/Russian trade-block:

BRICS: Brazil, Russia, India, China

BRICS is the acronym given to the trade association between the five major emerging economies of Brazil, Russia, India, China, and South Africa. BRICS members are all developing countries with large, fast-growing economies. With Russia and China comprising its foundation, BRICS has since grown so much in both economic and political influence, that its members can no longer be controlled by the outside forces of global affairs.

> *"The West is scared of BRICS as it has no control over it."* - **Coneel Sebal** India's ex- Foreign Secretary

Putin Gives US Inc. the Finger

And what the Western (Rothschild) financial Cartels cannot control, they will seek to destroy.

By **2014**, BRICS have established its own international financing mechanism to circumvent the International Monetary Fund (IMF).

Russian President **Vladimir Putin** visited Israel in the June of 2013 to speak to Prime Minister, **Benjamin Netanyahu**. In strong yet diplomatic terms, the pro-Syrian President Putin expressed his opposition to any strike against Syria or Iran. Russia and China have consistently urged for peace in the region. In response, an angry **Hillary Clinton** declared: *"Russia and China will pay a price for standing up for the Assad regime."*

With the advent of the **Arab Spring** of 2013, U.S and Saudi supplied **Terrorists-for-hire** are losing the fight to overthrow the Syrian leader Assad. The U.S and Israel, under the pretext of helping these suppressed "rebels" overthrow a "corrupt government" begin bombing Syrian Government positions.

How convenient is the sudden rise of **ISIS**, the events in **Ukraine**, and the anti-China manoeuvres in Africa and the Pacific, and its beneficial consequences for the Globalist agenda of the New World Order.

In the Summer of **2013** an alleged 'gas attack' occurs in Syria and is blamed on Assad-just a few weeks after Obama's warning. It is claimed in the Western Press that children were among the victims of Assad's 'gas'. Images of the "poison gas" attack had a staged quality smacking of a False Flag Operation by the Western Powers.

The Attack if it had occurred, would have been more beneficial for the 'rebel's' to blame Assad and draw the US directly into the conflict. President Assad strongly denies the accusation and invites an international investigation into the alleged occurrence. Assad compares the accusation to the false claims of "**Weapons of Mass Destruction**" which were levelled against Iraq in 2002 & 2003.

Pulitzer Prize winning investigative journalist **Seymour Hersh** is convinced that Assad was framed for the gas attacks. It wasn't the first time that the US government and the **New York Times** tried to lie America into a war. The Obama administration ignores Assad's denials and begins preparations for war. But no surprise, actual video footage comes out showing it was the US/Saudi backed "rebels" (Al Nusrah Front) that released the deadly nerve gas and tried to blame it on the Syrian army (Gayle, 2013). But not one apology from the Western media or governments (Waterman, 2013).

Meanwhile, Netanyahu continues his attempts to provoke a Syrian attack against Israel by bombing the outskirts of Damascus. Assad remains resolute and does not attack, but he does threaten retaliation in the event of a full scale attack upon Syria.

Russia & China announce they will defend Syria and Russia, China, Syria and Iran stage war games in the Mediterranean. The strong hand played by Putin and his alliance affords Obama the out that he needs and he backs off. China and Russia conduct massive military drills in response to American aggression drawing Russia and China closer together. Russia offers a deal in which Syria agrees to surrender its chemical weapons in exchange for peace and Russia's continued protection.

Later the same year pro-EU/US mobs, CIA backed 'rent-a-mobs', and activists begin forming in Kiev, **Ukraine**. Their ultimate aim is to overthrow the Russia-friendly (elected) government in Ukraine and replace it with US-EU stand-ins from the Ukrainian Nazi Party (yes, they really are Nazis). **Senator McCain** arrives in Kiev to incite the restless mob with shouts of "America stands with you!" Also stirring trouble is US Under-Secretary of State **Victoria Nuland**. Nuland is the wife of arch 'neo-conservative' luminary **Robert Kagan**; one of the principal architects of the **War on Terror**. Nuland has helped to dole out billions of dollars in 'pro-democracy investment' in Ukraine, most of which came from **George Soros** and US taxpayers. Among the violent thugs in Kiev were a group of former Israeli commandos. What would be Israel's motivation to establish a new anti-Russian Ukrainian government on Putin's front door-step?

In the Far East, the US friendly states of Japan, Vietnam and Philippines continue to agitate China. Japan announces that it will amend its pacifist Constitution and build up its military.

Although Obama's Globalist faction and the anti-Obama neo-cons share a common interest in weakening the Russia-China alliance, the motives are different. Obama still would prefer to avoid a Middle Eastern war, and focus on inciting wars against Russia and China instead. That is mainly due to the fact that Obama is a Muslim, and it would literally mean he cannot fight his brother Muslims (Obama Admits, 2009).

What will the response from Russia, Iran, and China be? That may be the decisive question in which the Baltic States and China Sea Stakes are played against the Russia-China alliance. More importantly, the question remains where will the war between the First World Powers vying for control of the last of the World's natural resources be launched? In the Middle East on behalf of Israel and the Neo-cons, or in Eastern Europe?

Just Follow the bombs

There is a piece of land that is home to about 22 million people. It is slightly bigger than the State of North Dakota in the US.

American is bombing it, France is bombing it, Turkey is bombing it, Israel is bombing it, Kurds are attacking it, US- backed, and armed and trained rebels are bombing and attacking it. ISIS is bombing and attacking it, then there is Iran with a military presence there, and now we have Russia starting to bomb that land as well (on invitation). Finally, in the UK, David Cameron is chomping at the bit for his chance to join in the bombing game. I am talking about **Syria**.

The Moral High Ground

If anyone ever needed confirmation that we live in a lunatic asylum, then the events in Syria in 2015 are the confirmation. Does anyone really think that all this is going on, all this bombing, death, and destruction and refugee creation, is happening because the West morally feels that **President Assad** is a tyrant? Do they really think he is depressing his people, and therefore, the West is in opposition to him, and the country must be supported? Does anyone really believe that? The idea that the United States and Britain have any interest whatsoever in the oppression of the people of Syria, when the British and American Empires have spent centuries oppressing people all over the world for their own economic benefit and accumulation of Power.

They could not give a damn about what is happening in Syria in terms of oppression of the people or whatever else they claim.

In fact, we have a situation where one of the greatest oppressors of humanity on the planet is **Saudi Arabia**. It executes someone on average about every two days at the moment, usually via beheading.

They routinely cut the hands off of thieves, the feet off of other criminals, and they have stoned to death women for adultery. All this is carried out under **Sharia Law**. Saudi Arabia is part of the coalition to stop oppression in Syria? Give me a break...

The Muslim Rift

Muslims are split into two main branches, the **Sunnis** and **Shias**. The split originates in a dispute soon after the death of the Prophet Muhammad over who should lead the Muslim community. The great majority of Muslims are Sunnis - estimates suggest the figure is somewhere between 85% and 90%.

Shia Islam hold that the Islamic prophet Muhammad's proper successor as Caliph was his son-in-law and cousin **Ali ibn Abi Talib**. On the other hand, Sunnis believe that Muhammad's father-in-law **Abu Bakr**, and not Ali ibn Abi Talib, was his proper successor. Hundreds of thousands of innocent Muslims have died over this dispute (Shia–Sunni, 2015).

The Muslim Terrorists

It is now a fact that over 80% of Muslim extremists (terrorists) are radicalised in **Wahhabi Mosques**. Wahhabism is a branch of fundamentalist **Sunni Islam**, named after an eighteenth-century preacher and scholar, **Muhammad ibn Abd al-Wahhab** (1703–1792) (Wahhabi, 2015). It is by far the most dangerous form of Islam.

The Muslim Brotherhood was originally founded to unify Muslims against world Imperialism. However, a de facto of current Muslim Brotherhood and Morsi in Egypt is a Wahhabi group. The Saudis spent a lot of oil dollars and hijacked Morsi and the Muslim Brotherhood, which they currently have about 80% converted to Wahhabi. In fact, the current Muslim Brotherhood betrayed its founders by being sold to the Saudis and becoming a Wahhabi group.

The Muslim Brotherhood (which Obama openly protects) is a Sunni, Wahhabi Islam network, that literally funds, trains and arms radical Islam extremists, mainly via Wahhabi Mosques, to fight against non-Muslims and their Shia Islamic brothers (Brighton, 2014). Most of the Wahhabi Mosques for doing this are in Western countries, like America, Britain, Europe, Canada, and Australia.

Obama, Noble Peace Prize Winner, bringing Democracy to Yemen

As the militant group the Islamic State in Iraq and Syria, or ISIS, has seized vast territories in western and northern Iraq, there have been frequent accounts of fighters' capturing groups of people and releasing the Sunnis while the Shias are singled out for execution (Rubin, 2014). Indeed, we have **ISIS**, rightly vilified and condemned for the horrors of beheading as a tool of trauma, control, and terror and yet, we have Saudi Arabia beheading on a more regular basis, without a murmur from the same, moral West. Obama and his gang are bombing civilians mercilessly in Yemen without a murmur from the West.

In fact, Obama, who was named the **2009 Nobel Peace Prize laureate**, has personally signed off a total of **98 US drone attacks** against **Yemen** since 2009; 41 in 2012, 26 in 2013 and 14 in 2014. Thousands of mostly civilian children have been murdered in these drone strikes, and the US Congress have never signed off on declaring war against Yemen (Yemen, 2015). This is something Obama just went and did without Congressional approval. This is Obama assuming dictatorial powers, which will only get worse.

So it comes as no surprise that Obama and his Western Allies, on record, arm the Syrian rebels and ISIS, and allows them to do what they do. It is clear that the cover story of *"we must help the people of Syria"* is nonsense.

The True Price of Democracy

Shaker Aamer with two of his children before his abduction by the US

The moral hypocrisy of Obama, Cameron, Blair, and Bush is breathtaking. They are all war criminals and psychopaths, who talked about how they must stand for freedom and justice, while bombing the crap out of a country, then leaving mayhem and violence behind. We have a moral United States that has held a British citizen, **Shaker Aamer,** in **Guantanamo Bay** for 14 years without charge or trial, and who was beaten and tortured by his American guards (Davies et al., 2015). An innocent man taken from his family and his children. A man denied seeing his children grow up. He has a child he has not even seen, because he was born after he was taken into captivity by these psychopaths. We have children who've been denied a father in their childhood, by a government, representing a nation and even more so, a hidden hand behind governments. We have an American administration that can do that to a human being and still claim the moral high ground.

The Truth About al-Qaeda

> *"The truth is, there is no Islamic army or terrorist group called Al Qaida. And any informed intelligence officer knows this. But there is a propaganda campaign to make the public believe in the presence of an identified entity representing the 'devil' only in order to drive the TV watcher to accept a unified international leadership for a war against terrorism. The country behind this propaganda is the US . . ." - Pierre-Henri Bunel*

Al Qaeda was an intelligence construct used by Washington to destabilise and destroy sovereign countries, while sustaining the illusion of an outside enemy, which threatens the security of the Western World.

Osama Bin Ladin (Tim Osman) at the White-house with Condoleezza Rice, Secretary of State under George W. Bush

It began in the early 1980's when the USSR was invading/occupying Afghanistan. The US still saw the USSR as an enemy, so it recruited, armed, and trained local Afghans who became known as the **Mujahidin** (freedom fighters). Incidentally, **Osama Bin Ladin** was a leader of the Mujahidin, and was trained by the CIA.

To keep track of the Islamic mercenaries fighting for the Mujahidin, the CIA created a database with all of their contact details, including those of their families. This database became known within the CIA as "Al Qaeda," meaning "the base" or "the database."

After the USSR pulled out of Afghanistan, the CIA thought it would come in handy to keep this database, and contacts with the Islamic mercenaries in case they ever need them in the future.

So in the early 1990's, when the US required a new "boogie man" to justify their out of control military budget, they decided to call up the guys in the Al Qaeda database. Most were still in the Mujahidin, so they rearmed, retained, and rebranded them **Al Qaeda** (al-Qaida, 2010).

The New World Order owned and controlled media went into overload and starting their fear mongering news about the new threat to the world – the spooky, Islamic terrorist group called Al Qaeda. But to really make it seem real, they needed an arch enemy – a leader for this evil group. Enter CIA operative Tim Osman (Osama Bin Laden).

Shortly before his untimely death, former British Foreign Secretary **Robin Cook** told the **House of Commons** that "Al Qaeda" is not really a terrorist group but a database of international Mujahidin and arms smugglers used by the CIA and Saudis to funnel guerrillas, arms, and money into Soviet-occupied Afghanistan (Bunel, 2015).

By 2012, the US had used up all of its "Al Qaeda is scary" points, so that had to go back to the drawing board. They decided to recruit new freedom fighters from all over the Middle East. In doing so, they took any psychotic cutthroat they could find, and created a new brand called **ISIS**.

One problem with recruiting any old alpha-male psycho that will kill for money, is many of them want to be in charge. That is why soon after the release of the new world boogie man – ISIS, they changed their name to ISIL, to IS, and then the derogatory word used by Muslim enemies – **Daesh**. Daesh, an adapted acronym of their Arabic name - **Dawlat** al-Islamiyah f'al-Iraq w Belaad al-Sham - is similar to another Arabic word - **das** - which means 'to trample down' or 'crush', which could therefore be the source of their dislike (Doré, 2015).

Because of too many Chiefs and not enough Indians, the CIA and Saudi handlers have lost control (after arming them) in certain areas. There is no honour among criminals. So the US/Saudi "leaders" are scrambling to gain control.

Clear as mud

ARE you confused by what is going on in the Middle East? Let me explain.

We support the Iraqi government in the fight against Islamic State. We don't like IS, but IS is supported by Saudi Arabia, whom we do like.

We don't like President Assad in Syria. We support the fight against him, but not IS, which is also fighting against him.

We don't like Iran, but Iran supports the Iraqi government against IS. So, some of our friends support our enemies and some of our enemies are our friends, and some of our enemies are fighting against our other enemies, whom we want to lose, but we don't want our enemies who are fighting our enemies to win.

If the people we want to defeat are defeated, they might be replaced by people we like even less. And all this was started by us invading a country to drive out terrorists who weren't actually there until we went in to drive them out. Do you understand now?

AUBREY BAILEY, Fleet, Hants.

They try and confuse you on purpose. That way people lose interest, and they can get away with murder.

Enter Russia. Putin knows what is going on, and has very expensive military and naval bases in Syria that he does not want to lose or get trashed by these out of control mad men.

Drugs are still good for business

Afghanistan is, by far, the largest grower and exporter of opium in the world today, cultivating a **92 percent** market share of the global opium trade. But what may shock many is the fact that the US military has been specifically tasked with guarding Afghan poppy fields, from which opium is derived, in order to protect this multibillion dollar industry that enriches Wall Street, the CIA, MI6, and various other groups that profit big time from this illicit drug trade scheme.

Prior to the tragic events of September 11, 2001, Afghanistan was hardly even a world player in growing poppy, which is used to produce both illegal heroin and pharmaceutical-grade morphine. In fact, the Taliban had been actively destroying poppy fields as part of an effort to rid the country of this harmful plant, as was reported by the Pittsburgh Post-Gazette on February 16, 2001, in a piece entitled *Nation's opium production virtually wiped out* (Gannon, 2001).

But after 9/11, the US military-industrial complex quickly invaded Afghanistan and began facilitating the reinstatement of the country's poppy industry. According to the United Nations Drug Control Program (UNDCP), opium cultivation increased by **657 percent** in 2002 after the US military invaded the country under the direction of then-President **George W. Bush** (Nimmo, 2010). More recently, The New York Times (NYT) reported that the brother of current Afghan President **Hamid Karzai** had actually been on the payroll of the CIA for at least eight years prior to this information going public in 2009. Ahmed Wali Karzai was a crucial player in reinstating the country's opium drug trade, known as **Golden Crescent**, and the CIA had been financing the endeavour behind the scenes (Watson, 2009)

"The Golden Crescent drug trade, launched by the CIA in the early 1980s, continues to be protected by US intelligence, in liaison with NATO occupation forces and the British military," Prof. Michel Chossudovsky in a 2007 report

Professor Chossudovsky wrote this before it was revealed that Ahmed Wali Karzai was on the CIA payroll.

> *"The proceeds of this lucrative multibillion dollar contraband are deposited in Western banks. Almost the totality of revenues accrue to corporate interests and criminal syndicates outside Afghanistan"*
> *(Chossudovsky, 2007)*

But the mainstream media has been peddling a different story to the American public. **FOX News**, for instance, aired a propaganda piece back in 2010 claiming that military personnel are having to protect the Afghan poppy fields, rather than destroy them, in order to keep the locals happy and to avoid a potential "security risk" -- and FOX News reporter **Geraldo Rivera** can be heard blatantly lying about poppy farmers being financially supported by the Taliban, rather than the CIA and other foreign interests. You can watch that clip here (Rivera, 2011).

So while tens of thousands of Americans continue to be harmed or killed every year by overdoses from drugs originating from this illicit opium trade, and while cultivation of innocuous crops like marijuana and hemp remains illegal in the US, the American military is actively guarding the very poppy fields in Afghanistan that fuel the global drug trade. Something is terribly wrong with this picture.

U.S. Marines with Fox Company, 2nd Battalion, 5th Marine Regiment, Regimental Combat Team 6, patrol through a poppy field during Operation Lariat in the Lui Tal district, Helmand province, Afghanistan, April 16, 2012.

But as I have already stated in earlier chapters, the **Black Nobility** made their first millions in the illegal Opium Wars against China (1839 – 1860). Then from late 1969, during the Vietnam War, Hong Kong chemists associated with the **Chiu Chua syndicate** and the CIA began refining opium into No.4 heroin — up to 99% pure — in the **Golden Triangle**, an area encompassing the hills of eastern Burma, the mountain crests of Thailand, and the high plateaus of northern Laos. It soon found its way to US troops. Within 18 months, it was estimated that between 10% and 15% of them were using it. Later estimates went as high as 34% (Rainford, 2013).

These troops took the habit back home with them, and some of them became involved in the trade. At this point, the US addict population had risen to 500,000 and Australia was seeing the start of its own heroin problem.

By the time the war was over, Vietnam was in ruins and Golden Triangle heroin was being exported around the world.

Now the US Marines are protecting and growing poppies for heroin production, so I guess nothing has really changed. Bankers' wars are really good for profits in many areas.

The Reality of ISIS

More people are finally beginning to wake up and understand what is truly going on in Syria and what the real objective has been all along for the US government and the Military Industrial Complex.

I will let you in on a little secret, the Obama administration have never been interested in removing ISIS at all. In fact, it is the total opposite. ISIS is a Frankenstein creation, by the merging of Ajnad al Sham, Ahrar ash-Sham and the **Al-Qaeda** branch **Al Nusrah Front**, plus Western mercenaries/special forces to lead them. This "beast" was created by Western intelligence to destabilise Syria, in an effort to remove **President Bashir al-Assad** from power. That is because the global banking cartels, can't wait to get their greedy little paws on Syria's natural resources, specifically natural gas, and its transit through the Middle East. They also want to control another very vitally important piece on the Grand Chessboard and in the process, the US Government has armed, funded, and trained, ISIS terrorist to do Washington's and Israel's dirty work.

> *Pro war propagandist Sean Hannity asks senator John McCain "I am concerned about this report about Syrian rebels in the cease-fire with ISIS Senator"*
>
> *Senator John McCain, "It is not true, it is not true. I don't care about the report and I know all these people intimately. We talk to them all the time" [the ex- al-Qaeda now calling themselves Free Syrian Army] (Hannity, 2015)*

There is no doubt that the US Government is responsible for the creation of ISIS, and the Obama White House say that they are only arming the so-called "moderate" rebels in Syria. These were the same "moderate" rebels that used US supplied weapons to shoot down a Russian bomber, then shoot the pilots in the air after they ejected from their plane, then fired a missile at a Russian rescue helicopter killing everyone aboard (Weaver, Tran and Quinn, 2015).

In fact, there has been a whole trail of evidence throughout the entire country, like US weapons airdrops, that somehow magically, mysteriously, and accidentally keep ending up in the hands of ISIS. Then there were the hundreds of Toyota pickup trucks, which clearly demonstrate US involvement and support.

Of course, we also have declassified secret US Government documents that were obtained by the law firm **Judicial Watch,** that

ISIS supplied with hundreds of Toyota pickup trucks that were made in Texas, USA.

show that the US deliberately allied with **al-Qaida**, and other Islamist extremist groups to take out Bashar al-Assad.

So the evidence is there, and Russia isn't stupid. **Vladimir Putin** knows what's going on, and I can assure you, he is on the side of Right!

In fact, Putin has publicly declared that Obama has indeed armed ISIS. Putin gave a speech before the Russian air strikes in Syria, where he states that the USA armed ISIS, and the Syrians that are fighting against Bashar al-Assad,

Vladimir Putin fighting the NWO

"Another threat that President Obama mentioned was ISIS. Well, who on earth armed them? Who helped to arm the Syrians that are fighting against Assad? Who created the necessary political climate that facilitated the situation for the delivery of arms? Who pushed the arms into the area? Really, you really do not understand who is fighting in Syria?" (Putin, 2015).

Make no mistake about it. The fact that the Russians are now involved is a game changer. Obviously, the Obama administration and the global banking cartels are not very happy with the idea of Russian air strikes in Syria. This is where it starts to get very dangerous, because this is how WWIII starts to escalate.

British defence officials have instructed fighter jet pilots to shoot down Russian jets over Syria. Furthermore, US Senator and huge warmonger **John McCain** says he would like to arm the Syrian rebels with weapons to shoot down the Russian Air Force.

> *John McCain: "We need to have a no fly zone. We need to have a buffer zone for refugees. We need to provide the very guys who we want to see topple Assad... I might do what we did in Afghanistan many years ago to give those guys the ability to shoot down those planes. That equipment is available.*
>
> *Neil Cavuto Fox news, "Who would be shooting them down?"*
>
> *John McCain: "The Free Syrian army" (NOTE – the "moderate rebels") (FoxNews, 2015)*

24 November 2015, A Russian Sukhoi Su-24M bomber aircraft was shot down by a Turkish Air Force F-16 fighter jet near the Syria–Turkey border

Meanwhile **Al Nusrah** forces, who are infamously known for being the real culprits behind the chemical attacks on Syrian civilians a few years ago, launched rocket strikes on the Russian embassy in Damascus. Rockets that were more than likely supplied by US-led forces. This is a build up to a global conflict.

Zero Hedge reported that the commander of Iran's **Quds force**, **Qasem Soleimani**, violated a UN travel ban to visit Russia, and held meetings with the Kremlin.

The Pentagon says those meetings were very important and helped accelerate the timetable for Russia's involvement in Syria. This looks like the biggest standoff between Russia and the United States since the Cold War, and don't expect Saudi Arabia and Israel to just stand there on the sidelines either, especially now that it looks like Iran wants to join the fight.

Thousands of Iranian forces have arrived in Syria in October 2015. They will soon join the fight in a major ground offensive backed by Russian airstrikes. That's according to Reuters (Rothschilds).

So there is an emerging military alliance between Russia, the Syrian Army, and its allies, Iran and China.

They are focused on recapturing the territories that were taken over by US-sponsored ISIS, and now that the Russians appear to be succeeding in taking out radical militants inside Syria, the President of Iraq is considering asking the Russians to conduct a similar operation inside his own country soon.

So the Russians may very well end up launching air strikes in Iraq as well. Call it what you like, but to me, it looks like a preview of World War III, but this time, Russia is on the side of Righteous, and the US/Israel/NATO lead coalition are the "Axis of Evil".

John McCain

A quick note on John McCain. He comes across as a tough guy, take no prisoners, kind of war monger. His claim to fame, which he plays on, was that he was a Vietnam Fighter Pilot (hero) that was shot down, and he spent time as a POW. However, all of the other prisoners that were held with him tell a very different story. During his capture, John McCain cried and begged for his life. He gave the North Vietnamese Army (NVA) the information that allowed them to shoot down more US planes and kill/capture more US pilots. Documents and transcripts of his interviews by NVA have surfaced in 2008 that confirm this. According to Colonel Ted Guy, John McCain was a traitor who "Sang like a canary."

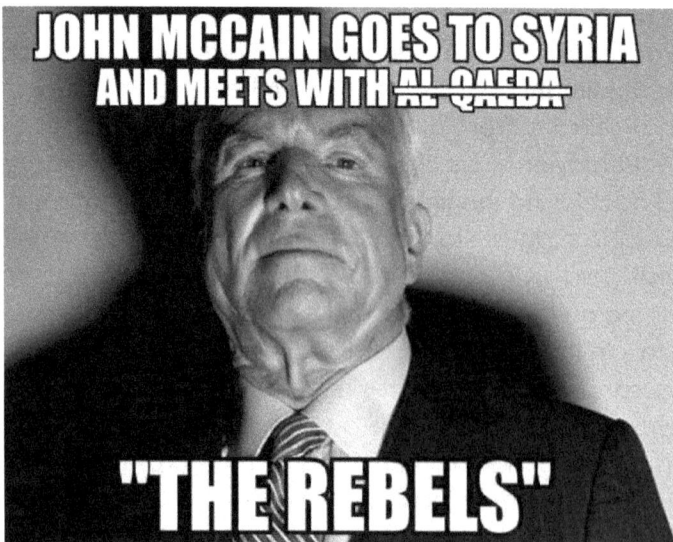

ALBERT PIKE AND THREE WORLD WARS

Albert Pike (1809 - 1891) Head Freemason, founder of KKK, Highest ranked Illuminist in US.

Very few outsiders know about the intimate plans of **Albert Pike** and the architects of the **New World Order**. In the 19th Century, Albert Pike established a framework for bringing about the One World Order. Based on a vision revealed to him, Albert Pike wrote a blueprint of events that would play themselves out in the 20th century, with even more of these events yet to come. It is this blueprint which I believe unseen leaders are following today, to engineer the planned Third and Final World War. What Pike wrote seems like a very accurate "prediction," however, we must remember that Pike wrote this letter in 1871 - over 40 years before WWI. This shows that the world elites have been planning wars to Pike's plan all along. And it looks like the next one is following Pike's script.

> **The First World War** must be brought about in order to permit the Illuminati to overthrow the power of the Czars in Russia and of making that country a fortress of atheistic Communism. The divergences caused by the "agentur" (agents) of the Illuminati between the British and Germanic Empires will be used to foment this war. At the end of the war, Communism will be built and used in order to destroy the other governments and in order to weaken the religions.

Students of history will recognise that the political alliances of England on one side and Germany on the other, forged between 1871 and 1898 by Otto von Bismarck, co-conspirator of Albert Pike, were instrumental in bringing about the First World War. The Jewish Bolshevist also assassinated the Czar of Russia and brought in Communism, with the funding of Wall Street (Jewish) Bankers.

> **The Second World War** must be fomented
> by taking advantage of the differences between
> the Fascists and the political Zionists. This
> war must be brought about so that Nazism is
> destroyed and that the political Zionism be
> strong enough to institute a sovereign state
> of Israel in Palestine. During the Second
> World War, International Communism must become
> strong enough in order to balance Christendom,
> which would be then restrained and held in
> check until the time when we would need
> it for the final social cataclysm.

After this Second World War, Communism was made strong enough to begin taking over weaker governments. In 1945, at the Potsdam Conference between Truman, Churchill, and Stalin, a large portion of Europe was simply handed over to Russia, and on the other side of the world, the aftermath of the war with Japan helped to sweep the tide of Communism into China.

Readers who argue that the terms Nazism and Zionism were not known in 1871 should remember that the Illuminati *invented* both these movements. In addition, Communism as an ideology, and as a coined phrase, originates in France during the Revolution. In 1785, Restif coined the phrase four years before revolution broke out. Restif and Babeuf, in turn, were influenced by Rousseau - as was the most famous conspirator of them all, Adam Weishaupt.

> **The Third World War** must be formented
> by taking advantage of the differences caused
> by the "agentur" of the "Illuminati" between
> the political Zionists and the leaders of
> Islamic World. The war must be conducted
> in such a way that Islam (the Moslem Arabic
> World) and political Zionism (the State of
> Israel) mutually destroy each other. Meanwhile
> the other nations, once more divided on this
> issue will be constrained to fight to the

*point of complete physical, moral, spiritual
and economical exhaustion...We shall unleash
the Nihilists and the atheists, and we shall
provoke a formidable social cataclysm which
in all its horror will show clearly to the
nations the effect of absolute atheism, origin
of savagery and of the most bloody turmoil.
Then everywhere, the citizens, obliged to
defend themselves against the world minority
of revolutionaries, will exterminate those
destroyers of civilization, and the multitude,
disillusioned with Christianity, whose deistic
spirits will from that moment be without
compass or direction, anxious for an ideal,
but without knowing where to render its
adoration, will receive the true light through
the universal manifestation of the pure
doctrine of Lucifer, brought finally out in the
public view. This manifestation will result
from the general reactionary movement which
will follow the destruction of Christianity
and atheism, both conquered and
exterminated at the same time.*

Since the terrorist attacks of Sept 11, 2001, world events, and in particular in the Middle East, show a growing unrest and instability between Modern Zionism and the Arabic World. This is completely in line with the call for a Third World War to be fought between the two, and their allies on both sides. This Third World War is still to come, and recent events show us that it is not far off.

"And as we continue our tour of dead worlds, we come to this one, which the former inhabitants called "Earth", which is kinda weird because when it was still alive, the surface was mostly water. Go figure.
Anyway, near as we can tell, they burned their own world to a crisp because of a religious war over some god named 'Dol-Arh'. But happily, there was no intelligent life on that planet, so no real loss. Know what I mean?"

You have been brainwashed!

You have been raised by a public school system and media that constantly assures you that the reasons for all these wars and assassinations are many and varied, but necessary. The US claims to bring democracy to the conquered lands but they haven't; the usual result of a US overthrow is the imposition of a dictatorship, such as the **1953** CIA overthrow of Iran's democratically elected government of **Mohammad Mosaddegh** and the imposition of the **Shah**, or the **1973** CIA overthrow of Chile's democratically elected government of **President Salvador Allende**, and the imposition of **Augusto Pinochet**, or to save a people from a cruel oppressor, revenge for 9-11, or that tired, worn-out, catch all excuse for invasion, *weapons of mass destruction*. Assassinations are always passed off as "crazed lone nuts" to obscure the real agenda.

The real agenda is simple. It is enslavement of the people by creation of a false sense of obligation. That obligation is false because the Private Central Banking system, by design, always creates more debt than money with which to pay that debt.

Private Central Banking is not science, it is a religion; a set of arbitrary rules created to benefit the priesthood, meaning the owners of the Private Central Bank. The fraud persists, with often lethal results, because the people are tricked into believing that this is the way life is supposed to be and no alternative exists or should be dreamt of.

The same was true of two earlier systems of enslavement, *Rule by Divine Right* and *Slavery*. Both systems built to trick people into obedience, and both now recognised by modern civilisation as illegitimate. Now we are entering a time in human history where we will recognise that rule by debt, or rule by Private Central Bankers issuing the public currency as a loan at interest, is equally illegitimate. It only works as long as people allow themselves to believe that this is the way life is supposed to be.

But understand this above all; Private Central Banks do not exist to serve the people, the community, or the nation. Private Central Banks exist to serve their owners, to make them rich beyond the dreams of Midas and all for the cost of ink, paper, and the right bribe to the right official.

Behind all these wars, all these assassinations, the hundred million horrible deaths from all the wars lies a single policy of dictatorship.

The private central bankers allow rulers to rule only on the condition that the people of a nation be enslaved to the private central banks. Failing that, said ruler will be killed, and their nation invaded by those other nations enslaved to private central banks.

The so-called "*clash of civilisations*" we read about on the corporate media is really a war between banking systems, with the private central bankers forcing themselves onto the rest of the world, no matter how many millions must die for it.

Indeed the constant hatemongering against Muslims lies in a simple fact. Like the ancient Christians (prior to the Knights Templars private banking system), Muslims forbid usury, or the lending of money at interest. And that is the reason our government and media insist they must be killed or converted. They refuse to submit to currencies issued at interest. They refuse to be debt slaves.

So off to war your children must go, to spill their blood for the money-junkies' gold. We barely survived the last two world wars. In the nuclear/bioweapon age, are the private central bankers willing to risk incinerating the whole planet just to feed their greed? Apparently so.

Drums of War are Banging

This brings us to the current situation in the Ukraine, Russia, China, and Syria.

The European Union had been courting the government of the Ukraine to merge with the EU, and more to the point, entangle their economy with the private-owned European Central Bank. The government of the Ukraine was considering the move, but had made no commitments. Part of their concern lay with the conditions in other EU nations enslaved to the ECB, notably Cyprus, Greece, Spain, and Italy. So they were properly cautious.

Then Russia stepped in with a better deal and the Ukraine, exercising the basic choice all consumers have, to choose the best product at the best price, dropped the EU and announced they were going to go with Russia's offer. It should be noted that Russia have always rejected the Illuminati and the New World Order. There have been Russian leaders over the years that were Freemasons, but for whatever reason, they were never allowed to bring in the Rothschild Central Banks. Putin is by far the strongest anti-NWO leader to date.

That is why when Ukraine rejected the NWO offer of a debt creating Central Bank, it was at that point that agent's provocateurs flooded into the Ukraine, covertly funded by intelligence agency fronts like CANVAS and USAID (Soros funded), stirring up trouble, while the western media proclaimed this was a popular revolution. Snipers shot at people and this violence was blamed on then-**President Yanukovich**. However, a leaked recording of a phone call between the EU's **Catherine Ashton** and Estonia's Foreign Minister **Urmas Paet** confirmed the snipers were working for the overthrow plotters, not the Ukrainian government. Urmas Paet has confirmed the authenticity of that phone call.

This is a classic pattern of covert overthrow we have seen many times before. Since the end of WWII, the US has covertly tried to overthrow the governments of 56 nations, succeeding 25 times.

Examples include 1953: Iran; 1954: Guatemala; 1960: Congo; 1961: Dominican Republic; 1963: South Vietnam; 1964: Brazil; 1973: Chile, and of course, the current overthrow of Ukraine's elected government of Yanukovich and the imposition of the current unelected government, which is already gutting the Ukraine's wealth to hand to the western bankers. (Stuster, 2013)

Brazil, Russia, India, China, and South Africa have formed a parallel financial system called **BRICS**, scheduled to officially launch on January 1, 2015. As of this writing, some 80 nations are ready to trade

The Ruble and Yuan, enemies of the New World Order

with BRICS in transactions that do not involve the US dollar. Despite US economic warfare against both Russia and China, the Rouble and Yuan are seen as more attractive for international trade and banking than the US dollar. Hence, the US attempts to fan the Ukraine crisis into war with Russia, and attempts to provoke North Korea as a back door to war with China.

There is a war going on within the US Whitehouse right now between the **State Department**, most of the **Navy** brass, and a rouge faction of the **CIA** on one side (Red), and factions of the **CIA**, **Defence Intelligences**, and high ranking members of the **US Army** and **Airforce** on the other side (Blue). Red wants a war with Russia, so they created ISIS and continue to fund them. Blue are refusing to take part in theses illegal wars. At the moment it is a standoff. But it is about to heat up and if Red wins, this is what you can expect:

How it will play out

The Red side is the New World Order, and they do not want to strike first. Instead, they want push, poke, and agitate Russia and/or China to strike first with a tactical nuclear weapon. They are even willing to let the US military and NATO look like the bad guys if it means they can get Russia/China to attack first.

In the event Russia/China attack first (or even North Korea) there will be an **EMP** (Electro-magnetic Pulse) that will take out the electrical grid. Everything will go down for good – Internet, ATM's, phone system, and even cars that have computers running them. During this period there will be mass panic and confusion. Then about 1-15 minutes later, the nukes will start flying in. They want them to take out US Military targets in one stroke. In fact, they want to decimate the US Military so badly, that they are no longer a viable fighting force. Only then can they use this as a pretence to ask the rest of the world to form a **One World Army** to fight Russia/China.

Once the One World Army is formed, they will do a back door deal with China to take out Russia. They (Rothschilds) still hate Russia, and want it destroyed. They also know that China wants to run the New World Order, so they will trick China into playing ball with them. By this time, China would have occupied all of the Asia Pacific region, including all of Japan, Philippines, Australia, and New Zealand. Part of the deal will be to let China hang on to those regions.

Once China takes out Russia, an armistice will be called (cease fire). They will use the armistice to create a new **Cold War** with China. That way they can justify spending trillions of dollars on building a brand new, global army, that will be permanently installed. If all goes to plan, the new "army" will be made up of robot soldiers and drones.

There will only be two armies left in the world, China, and the New World Order, One World Army. The Cold War hostilities will not be real, but used to trick the people into spending so much money.

Currently, the "hot war" and nuclear exchange could be within the next 2-4 years (from 2015). Everything leading up to this is to agitate Russia/China into striking first. If they do not take the bait, then North Korea will be armed by the West, and used to nuke the US as a pre-emptive attack.

Many US cities will be wiped-out, but many areas in the mountains, countryside, and inner-country will be left alone. It is in these areas that people will come together and live in small communities. However, the Constitution, and the sovereignty of the US government will be no more. The US will be abolished, and a new dictatorial government will be put into power. A power that is friendly to the corporations, and uncaring about the population.

Only small pockets of patriots will still live under the old Constitution system. In these communities, the only energy power they will have is what they create. The national electrical grid will never be active again (outside the UN, Smart-Growth Cities) in the foreseeable future.

All Wars Are Bankers' Wars

Flag waving and propaganda aside, all modern wars are wars by and for the private bankers, fought and bled for by third parties, unaware of the true reason they are expected to gracefully be killed and crippled for. The process is quite simple. As soon as the Private Central Bank issues its currency as a loan at interest, the public is forced deeper and deeper into debt. When the people are reluctant to borrow any more that is when the **Keynesian economists** demand the government borrow more, to keep the pyramid scheme working.

When both the people and government refuse to borrow any more that is when wars are started, to plunge everyone even deeper into debt to pay for the war. Then after the war, to borrow more to rebuild. When the war is over, the people have about the same as they did before the war, except the graveyards are far larger and everyone is in debt to the private bankers for the next century. This is why **Brown Brothers Harriman** in New York was funding the rise of **Adolf Hitler**.

If you take your mind back to Chapter 11, you will remember that the Rothschilds tried and tried to take out Russia in **1917**. They funded the Bolshevik Revolution to do this. They funded Hitler to take out Russia in the 1940's. It is only in recent years, through Putin, that Russia has been able to break the shackles of Rothschild intervention and control, and that is why we are seeing this new **World War III** begin to play out. The Rothschild will not tolerate Russia being an independent world power.

As long as Private Central Banks are allowed to exist, inevitably as the night follows day, there will be poverty, hopelessness, and millions of deaths in endless World Wars, until the Earth itself is sacrificed into the flames of **Mammon**[18].

Mammon in the New Testament of the Bible, is greed or material wealth, and in the Middle Ages was often personified as a deity, and sometimes included in the seven princes of Hell.

The path to true peace on Earth lies in the abolishment of all private central banking everywhere, and a return to the state-issued, value-based currencies that allow nations and people to become prosperous.

References:

al-Qaida, (2010). *Al-Qaida timeline: Plots and attacks*. [online] msnbc.com. Available at: http://www.nbcnews.com/id/4677978/ns/world_news-hunt_for_al_qaida/t/al-qaida-timeline-plots-attacks/ [Accessed 30 Nov. 2015].

Bretton Woods, (2015). *Archives - Bretton Woods Monetary Conference, July 1-22, 1944*. [online] Web.worldbank.org. Available at: http://web.worldbank.org/WBSITE/EXTERNAL/EXTABOUTUS/EXTARCHIVES/0,,contentMDK:21826676~pagePK:36726~piPK:437378~theSitePK:29506,00.html [Accessed 1 Dec. 2015].

Brighton, J. (2014). *Sharia-ism is here*. [Place of publication not identified]: Sharia-ism Education Center.

Brzezinski, Z. (1997). *The grand chessboard*. New York, NY: BasicBooks.

Bunel, P. (2015). *Al Qaeda: The Database*. [online] Global Research. Available at: http://www.globalresearch.ca/al-qaeda-the-database-2/24738 [Accessed 30 Nov. 2015].

Chossudovsky, M. (2007). *Heroin is "Good for Your Health": Occupation Forces support Afghan Narcotics Trade Multibillion dollar earnings for organized crime and Western financial Institutions by Prof. Michel Chossudovsky*. [online] Thirdworldtraveler.com. Available at: http://www.thirdworldtraveler.com/Afghanistan/US_Forces_Narcotics_Trade.html [Accessed 22 Dec. 2015].

Clark, (2011). *General Wesley Clark: Wars Were Planned - Seven Countries In Five Years*. [online] YouTube. Available at: https://youtu.be/9RC1Mepk_Sw [Accessed 28 Nov. 2015].

Davies, C., Elgot, J., Norton-Taylor, R. and Pilkington, E. (2015). *Shaker Aamer lands back in UK after 14 years in Guantánamo Bay*. [online] the Guardian. Available at: http://www.theguardian.com/world/2015/oct/30/shaker-aamer-lands-back-in-uk-14-years-in-guantanamo-bay [Accessed 30 Nov. 2015].

Doré, L. (2015). [online] I100.independent.co.uk. Available at: http://i100.independent.co.uk/article/why-isis-will-hate-it-if-we-start-calling-them-daesh--bkC822p_zl [Accessed 30 Nov. 2015].

FoxNews, (2015). *John McCain: Arm Syrian Rebels to Shoot Down Russian Planes*. [online] YouTube. Available at: https://youtu.be/dx6s4jO9xNY [Accessed 30 Nov. 2015].

Gannon, K. (2001). *Pittsburgh Post-Gazette: Nation's opium production virtually wiped out*. [online] News.google.com - Google News Archive Search. Available at: https://news.google.com/newspapers?nid=gL9scSG3K_gC&dat=20010216&printsec=frontpage&hl=en [Accessed 22 Dec. 2015].

Gayle, D. (2013). *UN accuses Syrian rebels of carrying out sarin gas attacks which had been blamed on Assad's troops*. [online] Mail Online. Available at: http://www.dailymail.co.uk/news/article-2320223/UN-accuses-Syrian-rebels-carrying-sarin-gas-attacks-blamed-Assads-troops.html [Accessed 28 Nov. 2015].

Guy, C. (2008). *McCain Sang Like a Canary*. [online] Newtotalitarians.com. Available at: http://www.newtotalitarians.com/index_files/McCainSangLikeACanary.htm [Accessed 21 Dec. 2015].

Hannity, S. (2015). *Senator McCain Informs Foxnews That He Is Intimate With #ISIS*. [online] YouTube. Available at: https://youtu.be/AZqHUjOwUSU [Accessed 30 Nov. 2015].

Nimmo, K. (2010). *Fox News Makes Excuse for CIA's Afghan Opium Cultivation*. [online] Infowars.com. Available at: http://www.infowars.com/fox-news-makes-excuse-for-cias-afghan-opium-cultivation/ [Accessed 22 Dec. 2015].

Obama Admits, (2009). *Obama Admits He Is A Muslim*. [online] YouTube. Available at: https://youtu.be/tCAffMSWSzY [Accessed 28 Nov. 2015].

Pike, A. (1871). *Morals and Dogma*. [online] Sacred-texts.com. Available at: http://www.sacred-texts.com/mas/md/ [Accessed 10 Nov. 2015].

Putin, V. (2015). *Putin Openly Declares Obama Armed ISIS.* [online] YouTube. Available at: https://youtu.
be/9Z7vWEoogWs [Accessed 30 Nov. 2015].

Rainford, J. (2013). *How the Vietnam war boosted the drug trade | Green Left Weekly.* [online]
Greenleft.org.au. Available at: https://www.greenleft.org.au/node/55506 [Accessed 22 Dec.
2015].

Rivera, G. (2011). *U S Soldiers Grow Opium / Heroin Poppy in Afganistan Fox News.* [online] YouTube.
Available at: https://youtu.be/1kqbZy3EAmc [Accessed 22 Dec. 2015].

Rubin, A. (2014). *4 questions ISIS rebels use to tell Sunni from Shia - Times of India.* [online] The Times
of India. Available at: http://timesofindia.indiatimes.com/world/middle-east/4-questions-ISIS-
rebels-use-to-tell-Sunni-from-Shia/articleshow/37257563.cms [Accessed 21 Dec. 2015].

Shia-Sunni, (2015). *Shia-Sunni relations.* [online] Wikipedia. Available at: https://en.wikipedia.org/wiki/
Shia%E2%80%93Sunni_relations [Accessed 21 Dec. 2015].

Stuster, J. (2013). *Mapped: The 7 Governments the U.S. Has Overthrown.* [online] Foreign Policy.
Available at: http://foreignpolicy.com/2013/08/20/mapped-the-7-governments-the-u-s-has-
overthrown/ [Accessed 30 Nov. 2015].

Wahhabi, (2015). *Wahhabism.* [online] Wikipedia. Available at: https://en.wikipedia.org/wiki/
Wahhabism [Accessed 21 Dec. 2015].

WashingtonsBlog, (2013). *U.S. Occupation Leads to All-Time High Afghan Opium Production
Washington's Blog.* [online] Washingtonsblog.com. Available at: http://www.washingtonsblog.
com/2013/11/us-drug-afgahnistan-opium.html [Accessed 22 Dec. 2015].

Waterman, S. (2013). *Syrian rebels used Sarin nerve gas, not Assad's regime: U.N. official.* [online] The
Washington Times. Available at: http://www.washingtontimes.com/news/2013/may/6/syrian-
rebels-used-sarin-nerve-gas-not-assads-regi/ [Accessed 28 Nov. 2015].

Watson, P. (2009). *NY Times: Afghan Opium Kingpin On CIA Payroll.* [online] Infowars.com. Available
at: http://www.infowars.com/ny-times-afghan-opium-kingpin-on-cia-payroll/ [Accessed 22 Dec.
2015].

Weaver, M., Tran, M. and Quinn, B. (2015). *Nato meets as Russia confirms one of two pilots dead after
jet shot down - as it happened.* [online] the Guardian. Available at: http://www.theguardian.
com/world/live/2015/nov/24/russian-jet-downed-by-turkish-planes-near-syrian-border-live-
updates [Accessed 30 Nov. 2015].

Yemen, (2015). *Drone strikes in Yemen.* [online] Wikipedia. Available at: https://en.wikipedia.org/wiki/
Drone_strikes_in_Yemen#2015 [Accessed 30 Nov. 2015].

16

THE END GAME: ILLUMINATI PLANS REVEALED

---

*"The world is a dangerous place to live;
not because of the people who are evil, but
because of the people who don't do anything
about it."*

— ALBERT EINSTEIN

Let's begin this last chapter with a recap of the Illuminati bankers' history of the last hundred years in Russia. It has been about 98 years since the Ashkenazi led Bolshevik Revolution that was funded by the Wall Street bankers to bring down Russia, and then set up special client deals with the Soviet Union.

They had captured the Russian engine, which they used to project collectivism and tyranny all over the world. Then out of the dialectic, the West would counter that by its own militaristic expansions that would actually cover up the Imperial nature of what they were doing. Of course the irony is you have the old Soviet Union calling the West,

Imperialist, when they were acting like Imperialist, gobbling up all the satellite states of the Soviet Union. Then at the same time, the West were calling them Communists, when they're really Imperialist. That is all it is - Imperialism by another name. Conquest by another name.

A long story short, is about **Aleksandr Solzhenitsyn**, one of the people credited with bringing down the Soviet Union. It was not Ronald Reagan and the FBI, or the weapons and all the rest of it. It was ideological ideas that brought down the Soviet Union. Indeed, it was because young people and intellectuals read the book **The Gulag Archipelago** to a great extent. In fact, it was this same book that converted **Vladimir Putin**. He read it when he was in the KGB.

Solzhenitsyn became a national hero, and before his death he was praised on national television. Not long after, the Russians repudiated Communism and everything collapsed, almost overnight.

Since Putin came into power, Russia has gone from pushing an anti-family agenda, to promoting families, promoting male role models, paying people to have kids. This is the opposite of what happens in the United States. So for all of Russia's problems (and there are many) Russia has come out and said man-made global warming and carbon taxes are a global fraud, to establish planetary government, under a military assault on industry, all done in selective nations to shut down competition. Well, that is exactly what it is. It is not their opinion, it is exactly what it is. Next, Russia comes out and says the United States and others are funding and arming ISIS and al-Qaida. Again, that is exactly what it is. This has forced the mainstream media to say *"ok, it's actually true..."* and it just goes on and on.

You have to understand that people are hungry for opposition to globalism. They are hungry for strong leaders to stand up against it, like Vladimir Putin. The people of the United States are hungry for a George Washington type leader to come forward.

The truth is, Russia tried to go along with the West for the last 15, plus years since Putin got voted in, in 1999. But all we have seen is the West try to launch overthrows of the Government of Russia, overthrow satellites of Russia, overthrow border regions with Russia, start wars to take over their only two military bases outside Russia, and pushing the world towards conflict with Russia.

You have to understand that the globalist don't want us to have a culture. They want us to be an MTV/CNN plastic culture they can change day-to-day, week-to-week, month-to-month, every year.

They want emasculated men, they want dumb downed populations, and they've done it. The globalist have put the United States through the exact same program they tried to put Russia through. Russia, after 80 plus years of being under Bolshevik, nightmare rule, was able to struggle out of it to a certain extent. Indeed, they arrested scores of billionaire oligarchs (all Rothschild Zionists) who had been controlling the Soviet Union when it collapsed. In almost every case, (read the British newspapers) the Rothschilds sued over this and lost.

Every time the newspapers reported another oligarch's arrest, it turns out to be another Rothschild front. It also turned out, that all of these agents inside Russia had been controlling the country with **Boris Yeltsin**. Furthermore, inside operatives had been there since the beginning of the Bolshevik Revolution, when their families came out of England or out of the United States, came in, and took those areas over.

I am not trying to sound like a Jewish conspiracy, but the facts are all there. I am only reporting the facts. All these families, all call themselves Jews. It is a fact, that the Rothschilds didn't just fund the creation of Israel. The Rothschilds funded the Bolshevik Revolution and what happened to the Czar and his family. In fact, a large contingent of the fighters that were sent into Russia, were financed by the bank that became **Goldman Sachs** in the 1920's.

This is literally world conquest that we are dealing with. Russia, after having large portions of their population, and that of their neighbours terminated (20+ million), would get the blame for the extermination when it was the Bolsheviks that did it. They then turn around and blame Russia yet again. Yet, it was the globalist that put the criminals in control of Russia and then turn Russia into a giant engine of evil worldwide, all the while sucking the blood of the Russian people to fund this world government. To create the fake, bipolar world, so they could have the counter to it, that is the **Anglo-American** World Government.

The globalists actually call it the **Anglo-American System**. It has come to mean part of Europe, the UK, the United States, Canada, and Australia. That is the dominant world powers structure right now, and it is gobbling up what's left. It is putting sanctions on Russia, it's attacking on its borders, and it is putting Jihadist in to take out Russia's allies like Syria.

But what is most important to understand, is that the people attacking America, the people trying to take the basic liberties of the Republic, are at war with any culture - period.

I study the makeup of the New World Order. It is eugenics which is proto-pre Nazi. It is bizarre World Government dreams of the Rothschilds. It is mixed in with all sorts of bizarre occultism and it is very anti human. It is building a planetary government which the elite believe will give them life extension technologies that they don't want the general public to have access to. So they have to get a world government in now, to dictate energy, to dictate resources, and to dictate science, so that they can control the growth of what they call disruptive technologies. **Disruptive technologies** (covered in **Book IV: Secrets of the UFO's**) are simply technologies that unseat the monopoly power groups.

The central planners, who don't actually do the fighting and dying, are right now trying to start World War III. The only reason why it has not started already, is because there is a big struggle inside the US Government to stop the funding of Isis and al-Qaida and evil things America is doing. But here's the bottom line. There is an attack on countries happening worldwide and America and Russia are under attack by the very same world government forces. Russia knows this, and that is why it has not retaliated to NATO's hostilities. So what are the goals the New World Order hope to achieve after their next war?

NWO Objectives

1) Divide the world into two classes – the **Elite** and the **Serf**. No Middle class. It is a form of **neo-feudalism**.
2) To implement a one-world currency, only accessed by a chip scanned under the skin. There will be no currency in circulation, and precious metals like gold and silver will be outlawed for the Serf class.
3) Firearms and any other means to protect yourself will be outlawed for the Serf class.
4) To abolish all traditional religions, including Christian, Islam, Judaism, Buddhism, Hinduism, in order to replace them by a one-world religion based on **Luciferianism** and the "cult of man."
5) To abolish all borders, national identity, and national pride (patriotism) in order to establish a world identity and world pride, mainly to facilitate free-trade agreements.
6) The world will be divided into 'zones'. 1. The Euro Zone (includes

Africa), 2. The Asia-Pacific Zone (includes Australia and New Zealand), and 3. The Americas Zone (includes the United States, Canada, and South America).

7) To abolish the family unit as known today in order to replace it by individuals, all working for the glory of one-world government. Individuals are weak – families are strong. No families = no resistance.

8) No private property for Serf Class

9) To force all Serfs into "smart-growth" cities, and leaving the "wild" areas and rural areas for the pleasure of the Elites only.

10) To destroy all individual artistic and scientific creating works, to implement a world government's one mind sight. Only art and scientific investigation that they approve will be financed.

11) To implement a universal and obligatory membership to the United Nations. To assist the UN in achieving this, they will have a United Nations world army, air force, navy, marines, and a world police force. The United Nations will be the only body allowed to declare war and maintain a standing army except for China who will be the "enemy."

12) A worldwide Justice Department through the United Nations with an International Criminal Court;

13) A worldwide new Trade Agreement for all nations (e.g.: TPP).

14) In summary, they want One World government – One World Religion – One World Currency.

In the words of the late, great man, **George Carlin**, it is a big club (for billionaires) – and you ain't in it!

How the New World Will Look

The Council of 13 Ruling Families have carved the planet up into 13 regions (one each) that vary in size and populations. It is their plan to consolidate these regions into three main **Super States**. Their first objective was the **European Union**. The **Bilderberg Group** was given that task, and after they successfully implemented it, they are now focused on creating the other states.

Under the guise of **Free Trade Agreements** they will create a:

1) **North American Union** (Canada/USA/Mexico). Later on it will include the **South American Union** (all South American

countries will merge into one super state with North American Union).

2) **Asia Union** (China/India/Middle East). Later, the smaller vassal states of **Asia Pacific** (Asia/Australia/New Zealand/Pacific Islands) will be included.

3) **African Union** (all African countries will merge into one super state) will come into play. Eventually they will become part of the **European Union**.

The three interlocking super states form the core of the global government. **European Union - American Union - Asia Union**.

Main Governance and administration

American Union: will produce GMO crops for the Serf slaves and livestock, as well as cheap goods and clothing for the Serf slaves – similar to what Asia does now. The main production there however will be **Arms manufacturing**. America will supply the world police/military and arm them. The whole populace, except for the owners will be disarmed.

   European Union: will do most of the science and medical work. The **City of London** will still be the centre of the global economy. Small niche food production will still take place in certain, heavily controlled areas throughout Europe. There will still be a lot of work for servants and house staff. Imagine what it was like during the medieval times and that is a close approximation. You can only be born into nobility. Only nobility can own land, livestock, or merchandise. Areas like Switzerland, the south of France, Bavaria, Germany, and Brussels will remain strongholds of the globalist who will run these areas under the old feudal system. Places like Russia, Ukraine, Romania, Hungry will be the food production zones for Europe. Most of the population will be immigrants from Africa and Asia.

   All the populations that are not required for work details or the running of specialty equipment will either be transferred to **Asia** or **Africa** to live and work in the food production fields, or be exterminated. The sick, disabled, the elderly, or the very young (under 5) will go in the first wave of exterminations. If you remember the **Georgia Guide Stones**, they want to keep the world population under **500,000,000**, so about 95% of the people alive in 2015 will have to go.

   Asian Union: will produce most of the technological gadgets. Everything from computers and smart phones etc. right up to space satellites. They will work closely with the science groups in Europe, however, travel between the two will be strictly controlled.

Vassal Regions Include:

Australia: Most of Australia will be reduced to a moonscape as they strip mine the entire continent for minerals and resources. Some of the beautiful coast line and island resorts will remain for the Elites to unwind. Australians that are fit and can work in the mines will remain in Australia, however, everyone else will either be shipped to Asia or Africa for slave labour camps and food production duties, or be executed. A small amount of "service" personal and sex workers will remain to staff the resorts and restaurants used by the Elites. This will include children because we all know how the elites like having sex with children.

New Zealand: already has hundreds of global elites (billionaires) buying up huge tracts of land there and building mansions, complete with underground bunkers. So it looks like New Zealand will become the home base or redoubt for many of our owners. And no, unless you are a billionaire, you don't get to live there.

Pacific Islands: All islands will be completely de-populated and left empty for the enjoyment of our owners. There will be a small resident population of servants, cleaners, chefs etc. None will be permitted to breed or leave their island. When they become too old or sick to work, they will be euthanized, and replaced.

Africa: will merge into one super state, no more borders. Africa will become a major food production area. Everything from cereal crops, fruit trees, dairy, livestock etc. The people will be forced to live in tightly controlled super cities, and be taken out to the fields each day to work. Any riots or insurrections will be crushed, and ALL participants (not just the ring leaders) will be publicly executed. The days of African war lords and civil wars are coming to an end, but only to be replaced by a rigid, brutal, and uncompromising totalitarian police state. Similar to Australia, certain area s will be stripped mined, and others left as nature resorts for the Elites.

South East Asia: will be exactly the same as Africa, the only difference being is what food is produced. All workers, no matter what their ethnic background is, will be forced to survive on just over a bowl of rice a day. Diet will be supplemented by a "shake" type

Australia in the NWO future

drink that supposedly contains all of the daily energy requirements. This supplement will be "paid" for whether you want it or not.

South America: is another area that the billionaires have been buying up. The Bush family bought 42,000 hectares (over 100,000 acres) of land in Paraguay's northern "Chaco" region back in 2012. The area sits atop a huge natural gas reserve that none of the locals will ever benefit from. It is not clear at this point what their plans are, but considering how many of their Nazi friends live there, I would guess that it will be another living space or redoubt for our owners. They will exploit the gas and other natural resource in South America to increase their wealth and power.

Living in the New World

Even though I use the term "slaves" and "slave labour," it will not be total slavery like in the old days. They worked out a long time ago that if people are paid a wage, even if it is just enough to get by on, they will work harder than if you forced them to work for nothing.

How **Apple** treat its staff is a good indication of what to expect. The conditions and pay for the people that make iPhones is so bad, they (Apple) had to erect "suicide" nets around the building to stop depressed workers throwing themselves off the roof.

So even though you will be paid, the conditions will be akin to slave labour, like in current sweatshops that most top designer clothes manufacturers use. The poor Asian people have been living under these conditions for years in test runs. They will no doubt make the transition to world government a lot better than the spoilt and lazy 1st World people. The best analogy I have seen that best describes what they have in mind is in the 2012 version of the *Total Recall* movie.

In that future time, the world is controlled by private corporations. Workers live in filthy and squalled conditions, and must travel each day through the planet's core to get to the work area on the other side of the planet. Large sections of the planet are deem "no-go "areas. The corporations run everything, including the police force, which is really a private, corporate security force. The average "police" work is done by **robot cops**. We see this re-occurring theme in *Elysium* and *THX 1138*. That means it is already in the pipeline.

Indeed, Google spent a fortune acquiring **Boston Dynamics**, a "robot" manufacturer. They have come up with a series of robot

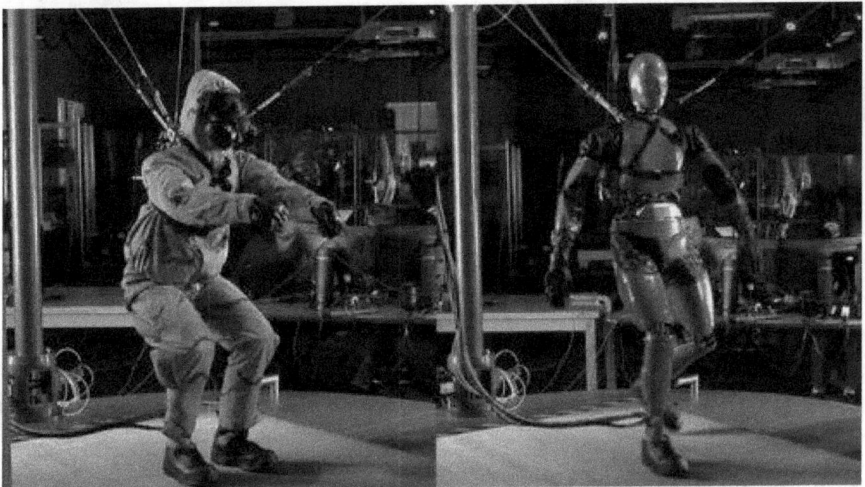

PETman 2014 (real prototype)

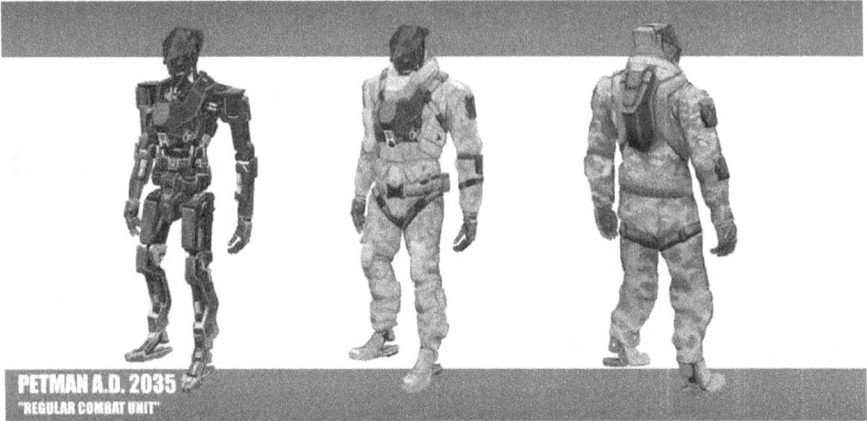

PETman 2035 (combat unit)

animal type creations for speed, and carrying large loads. But their crown piece is **PETman**.

PETman is a human size, human looking semi-autonomous robot. It can walk, run, jump, and climb stairs. The only, and ONLY thing stopping **PETman** going into full, "robot cop" production is they have not perfected an AI intelligence for it yet. But that is only a matter of time.

The City London in this future is still a shiny, modern place where everyone wears a tailored suit and sit in driverless cars. Again, Google is behind the push to roll out driverless cars.

Children will be bred based on genetics. Marriage will be outlawed, and selected people will be put together for the express purpose of breeding. Those not in the breeding program will be sterilised. People will be genetically tested and paired with an appropriate mate, or artificially inseminated (See **Brave New World** and **THX 1138**). The slaves will always breed slaves, and the elites will always breed elites. If a slave proves to be too smart, they will most likely be exterminated (can't chance them becoming a leader of an uprising).

Under **Agenda 21**, where areas the owners do not live, will be zoned as "wild" regions for them to enjoy. Just like in medieval times, if a serf was caught hunting in one of the King's forests (wild zones) so he could feed his family, then that serf would be publicly hanged. As proven through history, the elites always come up with most disgusting and bizarre ways to kill uncooperative serfs.

The new North American Union Ameros coin already in production

During a transition period for a cashless society, they will temporarily introduce a new currency for **North America**. It is called the **Amero**, which has already been released in small test batches. This will be like the Euro in Europe where every country uses it. In North America, it will be for the United States, Canada, and Mexico.

Watch their Plans in Hollywood Movies

Following the **Law of Return**, that they must inform the victim population of what they are planning in order to balance their Karma – a falsehood to be sure, but an idea they embrace nonetheless. They have produced several brilliant movies that explore the different scenarios they wish to employ. Even though the story lines change, the underlying theme does not – a totalitarian regime ruling over a subordinate "worker" class.

- Autómata (2014)
- Brave New World (1980) based on the book from 1932
- Elysium (2013)
- Ex Machina (2015)
- Nineteen Eighty-Four (1984) based on the book from 1949
- Soylent Green (1973)
- THX 1138 (1971)
- Total Recall (2012)

Total Recall (2012) or *Nineteen Eighty-Four* (1984) are the most likely outcomes (one or the other) after **World War III**. If the world continues without a major global war or catastrophe, then *THX 1138* (1971) leading to *Brave New World* (1980) will be the most likely outcome. Without doubt, *Nineteen Eighty-Four* is the darkest and most frightening to consider, but consider it we must.

But this is after years of trial and error in the *Total Recall/ Elysium / Soylent Green / Autómata/ Ex Machina* phase which will see the world ruled by a techno-elite. Societies will be openly run by technocratic companies (Apple, Microsoft, Intel, Dell, Boston Dynamics, and Google etc.)

Super Computers will run the world

Elections will be a thing of the past. Elections are always rigged, and we always get incompetent governments right? Notice how government all over the world is becoming more incompetent, more narcissistic, and more lies and scandals are breaking. This is by design – it is on purpose. They want a population that is so sick of useless politicians that they will embrace the "technological" marvel on offer. No more elections and corrupt candidates – we have a central computer that can run congress automatically, 24/7, at a fraction of the cost (of employing political staff). All decision will be based on the "peoples" needs. Sounds like an ideal system – until you realise who is running it, and who can rig the computer algorithms (the Elites!).

Indeed, they will sell all these ideas of *"let technology run your life"* as safer, more productive, cleaner and trendy. It starts with driverless cars, then a chip in the arm, then "smart" houses that feed all your information back to a central database for analysis. The dumbed-down and medicated masses will lap this up. In fact, the predominately Young Soul groups will want to be seen as "normal," so they will be lining up for it.

Enter the Age of Robotics

As robots replace more and more human jobs, the population of unemployed grows larger, and ever more dependent on welfare to survive. This is exactly what the planners want. By having a population on welfare, they are much easier to control. For example, they announce they are introducing a new, "convenient," "safer" and "trendy" micro-chip that will handle all of your financial and health transactions, and store the records for you. To buy or sell anything, just use the chip! To get your monthly pay check – use the chip!

Got to remember to pay your rent, mortgage, fine, licence renewal – the chip will automatically do these things for you! To keep this safe, so no one can rob you of your money, the "chip" will be inserted under your skin. If you are opposed to having this chip injected into your body, and you are on welfare – guess what – no chip, no welfare. The same goes for medical treatment, no chip – no health care. So how many people on welfare will reject the chip? Now do you understand why they want everyone on welfare? Oh, and one more thing about the chip – if you do something that they don't like, e.g. expose them, protest them, try and run away – they will just switch off your chip. And you guessed it, no chip – no travel.

By the way, the chip will also contain a tiny amount of nerve gas, about the size (in liquid form) of a pin head. One normal drop of this nerve gas on the skin will kill a fully grown man in about four seconds. This tiny amount in the bloodstream will kill you in about 6 minutes, but it is only released if you try and run away.

Drones will be in use everywhere. There will be flying drones whose sole purpose is to track down unauthorised travel. If they spot you walking down an abandoned country road, it will hover and scan you. If it does not detect a chip, it will assume you are a "hostile insurgent" and open fire killing you. If you have a chip, but are unauthorised to travel on that road, it will detain you with a Taser (if you try and run), and alert robot cops to come and pick you up.

The problem with robot cops is, they cannot reason with you. So they do not understand or care if you tell them you were walking to visit your sick and dying mother. Robots are emotionless. They don't get upset if their buddy is killed. They don't commit crimes of rage and revenge, but that is because robots are emotionless. They see an 80-year-old grandmother in a wheelchair the same way they see a T-80 tank: they're both just a series of ones and zeroes. Was this citizen authorised to be travelling on this road, on this day, at this time – Yes/No. No mitigating circumstances will be considered.

The Future Real-estate Bubble

Owning your own home will be impossible due to rising property prices in the future. Only the very wealthy can afford to buy property, drive cars, or travel abroad. Therefore, cheap, clean, and "smart" rental "cubicles" will be on offer! Designed by computer, fabricated by computer, all the same colour, all the same design. These "fantastic," "modern" cubicles will have all the mod cons, all squeezed into an area the size of your current single car garage. They won't have windows, but they will have flat screens that change automatically through the day to mimic the day and night – like you are looking out a window. Temperature will be controlled by a computer. Too cold or too hot? Bad luck, the computer will tell you what temperature to have. TV will be mind-numbing, with thousands of advertisements that try and sell you stuff you do not need, then C grade soap operas during the day, and reality TV shows about people degrading themselves for 15 minutes of fame at night...oh, so no real change to the TV we have right now.

Your food will consist of soups, porridges, and hard biscuit type things that are your vegetables (dehydrated and pressed). Things like fresh fruit and vegetables are only for the elite. The Serf's will never see these things unless they are black market contraband. But be careful what you sneak into your little mouse house. Every room is bugged and has cameras that can see in full colour and thermal. You are constantly "monitored" by the super computer – it can tell when you have a change in your hormone levels – when you sweat, or when you haven't eaten. As soon as it notices an irregularity, in come the Robot cops and drag you out for interrogation. All of these rental properties are located in a Smart-Growth mega city. No backyard, no leafy streets. Imagine a shoe box, divided into little squares. That is what the buildings in the living quarters of the future will look like.

Since 99% of the population will be forced to live in these cubicles, they will become hot property. Your chances of securing your new abode, will depend on your work, pro-activity, health and age records. They only want to look after the best and brightest. But just like now, I am sure there is someone, somewhere you can bribe. These types of tiny box accommodation has already been field tested in Japan. In fact, the Japanese love them so much they are starting to pop up everywhere in "Capsule Hotels" (Chong, 2010).

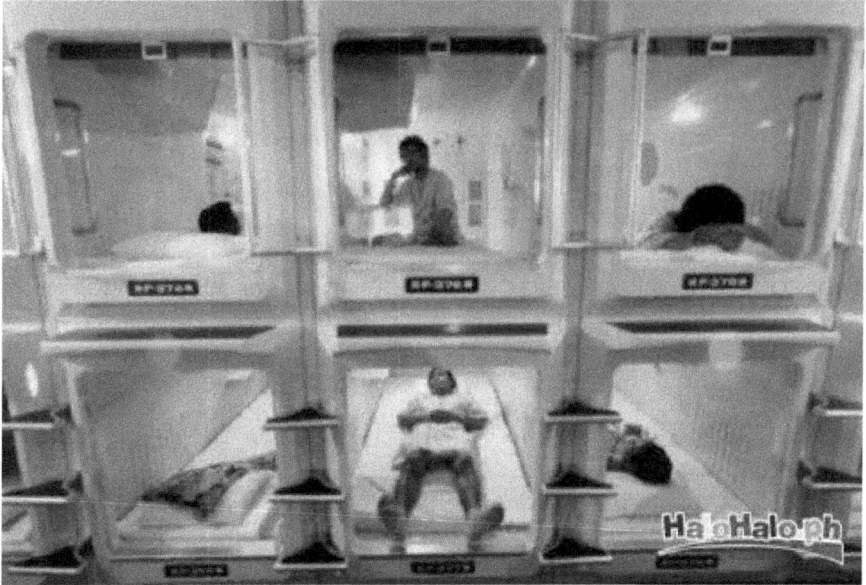

Popular Japanese Capsule Accommodation already spreading

Children in the Brave New World

As mentioned earlier, children will be bred – not born. In your housing cubicle, you will be placed with a compatible male or female. Looks, intelligence, hair colour, eye colour etc., no longer factor in matings. Your **genetics** are all that matter. When the Super Computer identifies a perfect genetic match, that will create the outcome they want, those two people will be matched up. One advantage is pregnant women will receive a slightly bigger food ration. Once the couple have passed their prime breeding age they will be separated. Women are usually euthanized, men are normally worked to death. You will never see or hear children running around playing and laughing.

By now, about 250 years in the future, they will have perfected their **Brave New World** civilisation. Great if you are an **Alpha** – not so hot if you are an **Epsilon**. Here is a short excerpt from *Brave New World*. It is a short conversation between two Beta children. Each child in each caste is brainwashed from birth to love their own caste only. Each caste believe they have the best jobs of all:

> *They hurried out of the room and returned in a minute or two, each pushing a kind of tall dumb-waiter laden, on all its four wire-netted shelves, with eight-month-old babies, all exactly alike (a Bokanovsky Group, it was evident) and all (since their caste was Delta) dressed in khaki. (Brave New World 2.8)*

That castes are distinguished by their clothing further dehumanises them. To any member of a higher caste, All Deltas will look exactly the same.

> *… all wear green," said a soft but very distinct voice, beginning in the middle of a sentence, "and Delta Children wear khaki. Oh no, I don't want to play with Delta children. And Epsilons are still worse. They're too stupid to be able to read or write. Besides they wear black, which is such a beastly colour. I'm so glad I'm a Beta.*

> *Alpha children wear grey. They work much harder than we do, because they're so frightfully clever. I'm really awfully glad I'm a Beta, because I don't work so hard. And then we are much better than the Gammas and Deltas. Gammas are stupid. They all wear green, and Delta children wear khaki. Oh no, I don't want to play with Delta children. And Epsilons are still worse. They're too stupid to be able…" (Brave New World 2.75-7)*

It's likely that the castes are kept separate for the sake of stability; this way there is no envy and no complications from intermingling. Each individual can view members of a different caste as a faceless, nameless "other". 1980 Tele-movie: (Movie, 1980), Book: (Huxley, 1998)

Travelling Around

Travel will be severely restricted, and all travel plans must be logged and recorded – because just like housing, no one can afford to own or

Brave New World caste system has five divisions: Alphas, Betas, Gammas, Deltas and Epsilons each having a specific set of careers and uniforms.

run a car, yet alone pay for fuel (unless you are a billionaire). But that doesn't mean you can't move around by car – no, they don't want an uprising! All cars will be driverless cars, controlled by computer and GPS. They are "community" cars, no personal ownership. You will go to a bus stop type of area where cars are waiting or retuning. You get in, verbally tell it where you want to go, scan your chip (which will deduct the fair, and check you have authorisation) and away you go. You will have to share it with complete strangers who may be going to the same location or dropped off on the way. Your designation, how long you stayed there, your time of return and all of your conversations are logged with the Super Computer. You are also video recorded.

Google and others have already perfected this technology (Urmson, 2015). The only reason why they have not rolled out the driverless cars is because they are still trying to work out the "insurance." True story, it is so typical of these globalists – always want to cover their butts "just" in case someone might sue them.

War and Cops

A common theme in the movies is to have a "none-corruptible," 24/7 cop, at a fraction of the cost of a human Police Force. This is something we will see sooner rather than later. Companies like the Google owned **Boston Dynamics** are very close to perfecting **PETMAN** – their man like warrior robot. They will have different models for different tasks – i.e.; military, police, search and rescue, firefighting, Hazchem etc. Military robots and the future of war is all the go now, and tech giants are scrambling to get their products to market (Singer, 2015).

Imagine how many jobs will go once PETMAN and other robots take over. Just like the political system, the movie **Robo Cop**, the machine can be programmed to ignore the illegal actions of the CEO of the company that created it, or any other "boss" they nominate.

Indeed, just like now, anyone who is in the elite gang gets a "get out of jail free card."

Wars are still big business and big profits for the New World Order and Illuminati, so don't expect them to go away too soon. However, people are getting tired and weary of endless war (just like in 1984). So the eggheads had to come up with something more palatable for the Serfs to swallow.

Even now, wars are fought very differently to how they were 50 years ago. We don't have a draft anymore. We don't have declarations of war anymore. We don't buy war bonds anymore. And now we have the fact that they are converting more and more soldiers that would normally be in harm's way into machines - drones, so we may take those already lowering bars to war and drop them to the ground. People will gladly allow autonomous robot soldiers and drones to do their dirty work for them. But as Pentagon robot engineer said,

> *"There's no real social, ethical, moral issues when it comes to robots. That is," he added, "unless the machine kills the wrong people repeatedly. Then it's just a product recall issue."*

The only outward appearance from a War robot and a Cop robot will be the outfit it wears. The Cop robot will still have all the strategic parameters and "kill" criteria as the War robot, but it will be wrapped around civil law instead of war's Rules of Engagement. Both are cold, emotionless, and efficient. They don't get scared, they don't get tired, and they don't get PTSD. When the time comes, people will be demanding them on our streets and in our wars.

Up, up, and Away!

After a couple of hundred years of this world, the elites themselves will splinter off into two groups. The **Super Nerd Class**, the **Technocrats**, will merge their bodies with machines in order to live forever. The movie *Surrogates* (2009) was a precursor to this phase. That was like the intermediate dream, next comes full mind, body, computer merging. Something along the lines of Johnny Depp's *Transcendence (I)* (2014) is their ultimate goal – to be a god! Or what they consider to be gods…

   Lucy (I) (2014) was another take on the same subject. This really is what they are striving toward. They are already experimenting with downloading a person's full brain content onto a computer. Then they hope to upload it to a new brain in a new body, or ultimately upload it to the cloud. Ironically, in both movies they make out they want to be beneficial gods helping humanity overcome all of its woes. Make no mistake. Benevolence is not even in their dictionary. Everything they do – everything - is for financial or personal gain. Globalist of any ilk NEVER perform altruistic acts.

   When I hear these Technocrats like **Ray Kurzweil** (Ashkenazi Jew) talk about merging with machines and becoming gods, I am always reminded of the conversation between Darth Vader and the Galactic Empire (globalists) stooges on board the Death Star. One Technocrat starts bragging about the awesome technology they have created, and how powerful they have become. However, Vader is quick to remind the Technocrats:

"Don't be too proud of this technological terror you've constructed. The ability to destroy a planet is insignificant next to the power of the Force." (Darth Vader, Star Wars: Episode IV

— A NEW HOPE (1977))

Head/Brain Transplants are coming!

On the other side is your hard core **Corporatocracy,** the old school Industrialist / Globalist. They want life extension technology as well, but they invest their money in "hands on" technology like cryogenics and brain transplants. Yes, both of these have been perfected. It started way back in the 1950's and 60's, then perfected in the 1970's. Russian doctors started with head transplants on dogs, then the United States went onto monkeys. The Chinese even did head transplants on mice!

New Scientist reported Feb. 25, **2015,** that **Dr Sergio Canavero** will announce at a conference in June a project to make the first human head transplant possible by **2017** (Mims, 2015). The procedure Canavero outlines is very much like that used by **Robert White,** who successfully transplanted the head of a rhesus monkey onto the body of a second rhesus in 1970. Canavero estimates that the total cost of a head transplant would be at least €10 million ($13 million.)

NWO "MAD" scientist Dr Sergio Canavero to perform first ever human head transplant

While this seems like fantastic technology on the surface, we need to scrape away the gloss and see it for what it is.

The downside of the head transplant is that the patient would be put into a three or four-week coma to let the body heal itself. The patient won't be able to get up and walk around after the surgery as the damage to the spinal cord would take about 12 months to heal fully. The patient would however, keep their old voice (Morrow, 2015). On the up side however, you get a brand new, young, fit body that will last another 50-60 years. Not bad for an 80 year old billionaire.

However, that is a long time for a narcissistic, psychopathic, megalomaniac to be out of action and away from his empire. But at the moment, it is the best chance of "living" forever. They think they can just get a new body every 60-70 and repeat the procedure. So Canavero's real purpose is to try new techniques to speed it up. They could easily do this in secret, but the best way to do expensive R&D is to get someone else to pay for it. This is a common ruse done by the Globalists.

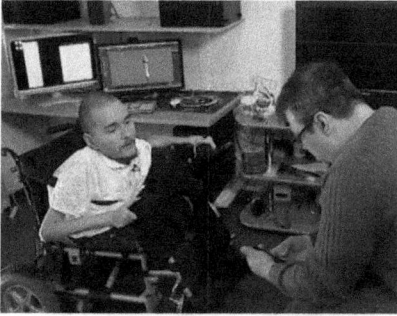

Valery Spiridonov will get the first human head transplant in 2017

Canavero will be working on a terminally man from Russia, who is battling the rare genetic **Werdnig-Hoffman** muscle wasting disease.

Step 1. Find someone that can solicit sympathy. People will happily donate, and so will governments. This will raise the money required for the NWO people to do research and development.

Step 2. Try new procedures. If they work, **patent them** and hide them away. Even if this man survives, you will never hear about the technology again. If it does not work, no harm, they lost a serf, not an elite.

I realise how hard and cold this sounds, but that is exactly how these people think. This is all about proving the technology, streamlining it, then once perfected, start taking orders from the filthy rich. Perhaps when enough elites sign up and pay, they will have a "coupon" day, and allow a Serf to benefit – once in a blue moon, just for PR.

Even though this is quite amazing, their ultimate goal is to transfer just the brain. Transplanting the head at the moment is possible, but complicated. Transferring a brain, intact, is a whole different challenge, but that is where they are headed (no pun intended). By just transplanting the brain, you don't have to worry about the 12 month healing process for walking. You also get a young head and body that match. Again, what they want is what was in the movie, Surrogates. But rather than have a "virtual" interface – that is more Ray Kurzweil, Technocrat tech, they want to have their brain, in a brand new, young, fit body. Because of this, they have been experimenting with cloning for decades.

For the Technocrats, they literally want to blast off and live on other planets or in space once they have perfected their brain transplant, or uploading their brain/mind to a machine.

The **Industrial Class** who remain will have been consolidated down to just a handful of families by this future time. Through internal wars and mergers, the 13 ruling families we have today will be gone. So too will the Committee of 300 be whittled down to about 30. Perhaps only three "super" families will remain. That is because the global resources will be scarce and dwindling. While the Families cooperate with each other for better prophets, they have no problem knocking each other off if they can get away with it. So like their uber-nerd buddies, they will send "others" out into space to locate new resources to plunder. Think of the movie *Avatar*. Even though the elite will enjoy a technologically, marvellous life, the life of the remaining worker class will not have changed much for hundreds of years. That is because humans do not cope well with change, so the less change, the less chance of an uprising or revolt. And by heavily restricting their daily news and information, because what they don't know, won't hurt them.

Back to the immediate future

Things to be aware of soon are False Flags that will include, "home grown" terrorism, global pandemics, and possibly a nuclear bombing of a US city. A **dirty bomb** or radiological dispersal device (RDD) is a weapon that combines radioactive material with conventional explosives. A dirty bomb is also a possibility for a false flag on an American city.

They will continue to rig elections, continue their never ending wars, and they will continue to collapse the US dollar and implode the economy. There is a hard-core group of Insiders within the US/ Israel Government (they are one and the same) that are hell bent on starting World War III with Russia/China. These same psychopaths will use foreign troops within the US to put down any opposition to their New World Order. They want a civil war. But they want gun control first, to disarm the nation before they announce their take over.

I will not be surprised if Obama suspends elections in 2016. I am not saying it will definitely happen, but it would not surprise me. It would be done as a result of a terrorist attack (nuclear bomb), and the sheeple will go along with it. One faction of the Illuminati want Hilary Clinton to be the next President, however Obama and his Chicago gang hate the Clintons and are trying to stop that from happening. Obama may leak some of Hilary's many crimes to take her out, or he may suspend elections under the guise of a benevolent dictator selling neo-Communism.

But how do we know so much about their plans?

Well, besides the hundreds of books and documents they put out there for anyone who is interested to read, they have set up a number of monuments that tell the tale of their proposed future. Therefore, just to prove this is not all "conspiracy theory" and nonsense, let's go on a road trip around the United States and see what the Illuminati have in mind for us in the near future. You can go to any of these locations and check them out for yourself.

Come on the Illuminati Road Trip!

Proof of the Illuminati takeover of the world is right under our noses. They love to brag, and show us what they are planning. These sites are also to their "brethren" know what the big plans are. Therefore, buckle up, and get ready for the Illuminati road trip across the United States, starting with Denver Colorado.

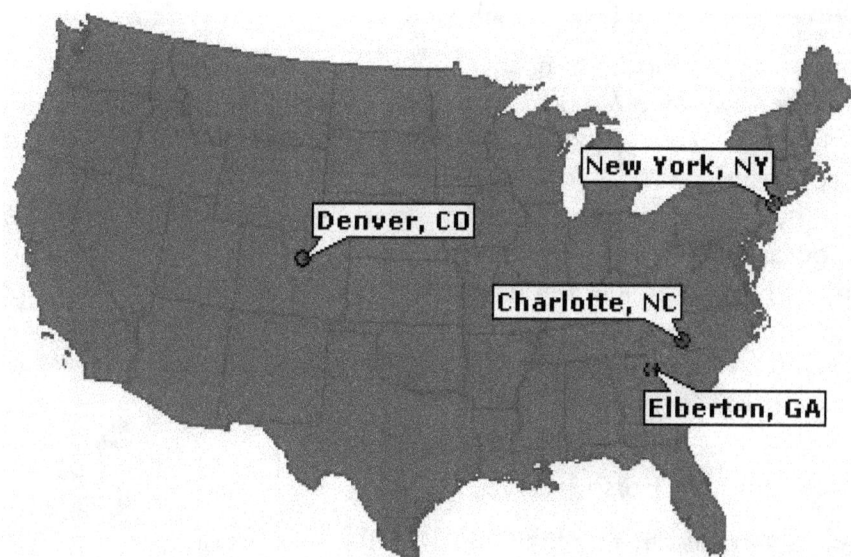

Illuminati Road Trip around the USA

Freemasonic dedication capstone in the atrium

Denver Colorado (Denver Airport)

Denver Colorado is home to America's largest airport called the **Denver New World Airport**. The airport was built by **Freemasons** in 1994 and features a Freemasonic dedication capstone in the atrium. A time capsule is buried underneath the stone to be opened in the year **2094**.

The Airport features a swastika shape runway, and there is a deep underground military base/city beneath the airport. It has miles and miles of secret subterranean tunnels connected to a large network of underground cities. Supersonic trains connect the underground cities. They can cross the US within 2 hours from coast to coast. If you drive 60 mph/100 Km per hour for 8 hours a day, it would take about 6 days.

Behold a Pale Horse

As passengers drive up to the main airport terminal, they are greeted by a sinister looking 10m / 32 ft. high, fibre glass blue stallion. It has veins popping out of its body and demonic eyes that glow bright

Blucifer outside as you arrive

Gargoyles inside greet you as you enter.

red. Not exactly a calming influence for travellers who are already spooked about getting on a plane. The sculpture is believed to symbolise the **Pale Horse** of the apocalypse mentioned in the Bible, whose name is **Death**. The sculptor, **Luis Jiménez**, died after a section of the 4,000 Kg / 9,000 pd sculpture fell on him and severed an artery in his leg. His official name is **Blue Mustang**, but locals call him **Blucifer** *(Morton, 2015)*.

Inside the airport travellers hurry past grotesque gargoyles sitting in suitcases that look down at them. Then there are the morbid, apocalyptic, murals that line the airport walls at the main gate.

Four panels of giant size wall murals in the baggage collection area tell a terrifying and prophetic story in pictures, of how humanity's future is going to unfold.

The Apocalyptic Murals

The first mural reveals a horrific, **Darth Vader** like figure wearing a Nazi General's uniform and a gas mask. The gas mask indicates that the next war will use depopulating, biological, or chemical agents. The white dove that he is killing symbolises peace. On the right are destroyed buildings reminiscent of the Twin Towers. The Nazi General's scimitar sword (a Muslim sword) has been swished through the air leaving behind a **rainbow chemtrail** that poisons the air, and the ethnic population below it. On the left, is an endless line of weeping women refugees, holding dead babies.

Mural Panel 1

Mural Panel 2

Barack Obama poses in front of Mural 2.

There is no trace whatsoever of violence to the dead children, who appeared to have died from the deadly gas of the toxic rainbow.

Why are there no men present? Presumably they have all been killed or are off fighting elsewhere. The Nazi General Scimitar sword that destroys piece, is a symbol used by the Shriners who are Freemasons. Freemasonry is a fraternity, within a fraternity. Outwardly, it is a friendly charitable organisation that conceals an inner Brotherhood of the 33rd degree elect.

The next airport mural shows a forest and a city in flames. The world's endangered animals and plants are all extinct. Buffalos, Wales, leopards, elephants, and sea turtles. The sickly haze and leaping flames suggest a nuclear or biochemical devastation. Children are the only survivors and they are weeping over three open caskets.

An African girl on the left, a native girl in the centre, and a white Judaeo-Christian girl on the right. They represent the death for the black, red and white root races, to make way for the New World Race. The dead white girl in the coffin holds the Bible and a yellow Judean star, which was used by the Nazis to identify Jews. It symbolises the death the Judaeo-Christian beliefs/God.

Another child holds a Mayan tablet depicting the end of the Mayan calendar and the end of the world as we know it. That is because the reign of Marduk is coming to an end. The **Quetzal** bird is alive, and protected by the container – but it is ready to break free. Quetzal was Ningishzidda's name in South America when he ruled there. Thus, the Quetzal bird represents **Ningishzidda**. He is in orbit, above the Earth, therefore protected. He is waiting to come back and help.

In the third mural, the apocalyptic war has ended. Children of all nations are joyfully giving up their nation's sovereignty to the blond-haired, blue-eyed German boy at the centre. They're all turning over their weapons, wrapped in their country's national flag to the German

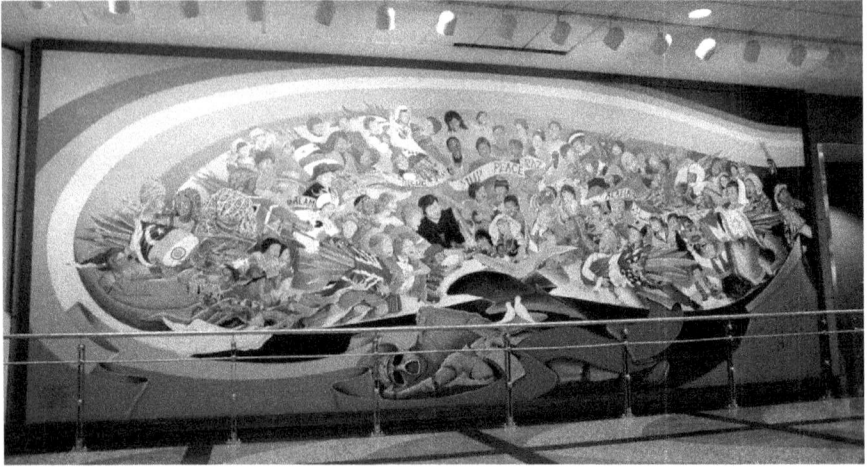

Mural Panel 3

Children of all nations hand over their weapons, wrapped in their flags.

Boy. The Bavarian jacket leaves no doubt whatsoever that the blond-haired, blue-eyed boy is German. He symbolises the **Bavarian illuminati** of Adam Weishaupt and the Rothschilds.

With an iron fist, the German boy destroys the weapons of war, symbolised by the Nazi General's sword. The German boy uses a hammer, which symbolises the hammer and sickle of **Communism** (a Rothschild invention).

In the foreground, the Nazi General is dead, with doves of peace perched on his corpse. The German boy symbolises a world leader and Saviour who brings peace through Communism to a devastated world.

Who is this boy that the world gives up their sovereignty and weapons to? We know he is German, with blonde hair and blue eyes, just like **Prince William**, who posed just like this boy for a **Papua New Guinea** stamp. Prince William's father, is the son of Prince Philip and Queen Elizabeth, who surnames were changed to cover up their German identities. Prince William's mother Diana, was the daughter of

Mural Panel 4

James Goldsmith, a German Jew. The German (Ashkenazi) Jews are the Rothschilds, who will use William to bring in their New World Order. In the fourth mural, the earth is restored, including the endangered species, along with the land and water. This was done by Ningishzidda, the new ruler of Earth. He did the same thing after the Biblical flood, when he also saved DNA to help repopulate the Earth.

This future world is populated not by adults, but by parentless children. What happened to the adults? They all died no doubt, and it was Ningishzidda that perfected the creation of humans along with his father, Enki and Aunty, Ninhursag/Ninmah originally. We can assume he is starting all over gain from scratch, because all of the humans died. Using saved DNA, he is able to create humans much quicker this time round.

The children are in a dance line that is led by the Scottish boy, who symbolises **Scottish Rite Freemasonry**. The Bavarian boy (Illuminati) is near the Scottish boy. On the right of the centre native child, is a child in a white hat. On the hat are the letters RC. These stand for the Freemason's bedfellow, **Rosicrucianism**. These Illuminati members believe they will inherit the world after Ningishzidda takes over. They are trying to suck up to him, and because they believe they are related to him by bloodline, that he will happily hand over the planet to them.

Also on the far left is an African woman carrying a snake banner. The snake has a black head, which symbolises **Marduk**.

It means that Marduk will relinquish his rule, and move out of Africa to allow Ningishzidda his turn to rule Earth. Indeed, with each New Age, a change in the astrological Houses of the Zodiac, the Anunnaki hand over ruling Earth among themselves. Enlil rule Earth during the Age of the Ram, Marduk rules during the Age of Pisces, and Ningishzidda will rule during the **Age of Aquarius**. I will cover this in depth in **Book IV: Secrets of the UFO's**.

The parentless children of the world are celebrating a new world religion. As they gather around and touch the light of Ningishzidda, who appears as a genetically engineered plant. The plant is a floral version of the colourful bird known as the **Quetzal**. It is symbolically inseparable from Ningishzidda, whose time it is to rule.

The main thing that the *Denver New World Airport* murals is an apocalypse with massive depopulation, extinction of species, the death a Judaeo-Christian beliefs. In fact, I think it will be the death of all religions. Once Ningishzidda returns and shows himself to the world, people will drop there phoney religions. They will realise that it was the Anunnaki that created humans, and they were their so-called gods. I seriously doubt Ningishzidda will ask humans to bow and worship him. He was not like that 5,000 years ago, and he will not be like that this time.

In fact, Ningishzidda was all about helping humanity, teaching them enlightening and spiritual ways. I think he will be viewed more as a Spiritual Teacher, and benevolent ruler. Like it or not, humans are incapable of ruling themselves just yet. They are too easily corrupted, and religions divide. It would be a Golden Age, but according to the Illuminati, none of us will be around to enjoy it.

Charlotte, North Carolina (Bank of America)

The next stop on our Illuminati Road Trip is **Charlotte, North Carolina** where the headquarters America's largest bank is located, the **Bank of America.** Here we find more eerie, bone-chilling paintings, describing the apocalyptic story of humanity's future in pictures. Three prophetic frescoes are prominently displayed in the Bank of America's main

Planning/Knowledge

lobby. Like the Denver murals, they tell a symbolic story which is understood by those in the know.

In the first mural, the central figure is a blue eyed, blonde haired German boy, wearing a Nazi overcoat, clicking his heels together and standing at attention on the checkerboard floor that is a classic symbol a Freemasonry. Who is he? He is the same boy found in the Denver Airport mural, but he is older in this continuation mural.

Notice the phallic, hand gesture in the comparison photo of the young, blond-haired, blue-eyed, Prince William. Similarly, the boy in the mural has a subliminal, erect phallus on his Nazi overcoat, symbolising power. By erasing the boy's right arm, it becomes clear that the flames and the burning bush are shaped like a hand, and the bush itself is shaped like an arm that is positioned at the boy's shoulder. It now becomes obvious that the German boy is making a straight arm, Nazi salute.

Prince William's **Knight of the Garter** crest is a Gold Lion. The image above Gold Lion is subliminally embedded into the blonde hair of the German boy in the mural. Notice the Egyptian pyramid (Freemasonry) and Black Sun (SS Nazis) behind him.

The second fresco in the Bank of America's

Chaos/Creativity

lobby, is an apocalyptic concentration camp where resistors are incarcerated. In the background, on the left, industrial chimneys and burning suggests a crematorium. The back, inside wall, are strung with barbed wire. Marines carrying rifles are seen in the crowd with their Nazi gold eagle flags. Notice the person wearing the white Bio-hazard protection gear. The hazard protection gear symbolises a pandemic, biochemical, or nuclear warfare. This is the same apocalyptic theme found in the Denver Airport mural, in which the Nazi General is wearing a gas mask.

Overhead, the elite are hovering and celebrating like gods, circling free and naked in their wealth and power. They are energised by the chaos below, where the world population is trapped in their net. All races and creeds are caught in the net are rioters and protesters, including a Catholic monk, a nun and a handcuffed black man. The protest signs are blank, implying they have no voice and are irrelevant. The street signs are also blank, implying that there is nowhere to go.

The last fresco has a mission accomplished theme. It illustrates the post-apocalyptic rebuilding era that creates order out of chaos. The Red Dragon (Marduk) in human form is edged into the hillside at the top of the fresco. He sleeps peacefully now in stasis. You can see a sign that says **EQ**. He sleeps above the EQ. EQ = equator, therefore, Marduk's resting place will be in the Northern Hemisphere. Meanwhile, all work is deep down in the Southern hemisphere. This is where the new world will be built. It shows new irrigated desert lands, and new lands/islands in the Southern Ocean. No humans will live in the Northern hemisphere at all.

The prophetic murals that are featured on America's largest airport and America's largest bank, express a New World Order agenda that is hidden in plain sight. The giant images on display for all to see, are designed to be understood only by a few. The commissioned murals share common themes. An apocalypse, a new world order, and a central figure who was a blond-haired, blue-eyed German boy. Many people think the blond-haired, blue-eyed German boy is **Prince William** of England. Those same people believe he is the Anti-Christ spoken of in the Bible.

Making/Building

Elberton, Georgia (Guide Stones)

The next stop on out Illuminati Road Trip is Elberton, Georgia. Elberton is

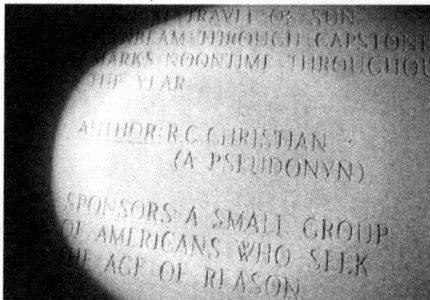

R.C. Christian was a pseudonym

the granite capital of the world, and is famous for its production at tombstones. In fact it exports some 250,000 tombstones every year. Oddly enough, the town that makes a living through death, is also the home of what some consider the most threatening monument in America.

It is the monument that some believe is a symbol for the coming holocaust, promoting a depopulation effort, on a massive scale.

It all started back in **1979** when a stranger came to Elberton, Georgia. Elberton is on the eastern part to Georgia, very close to the South Carolina border. This stranger said that he was part of a secret group, and they wanted to build a great, granite monument. The man, who called himself, **R. C. Christian**, was very well dressed in a tailored suit. He paid for the commission in cash, which was substantial. It was later realised that R.C. Christian was a pseudonym, as it said so on the monument. Nobody knows his real name, and nobody knows who put the money up. Furthermore, the "secret" group he claimed to be a part of is also unknown.

He gave very specific directions as to how this monument was to be built. He even specified how the granite was to be mined and cut up. It was built so as the monument would always be aligned with the **North Star**, so you it would be aligned with the moon, and various phases of the sun. In fact, it was very similar to **Stonehenge** in England. Indeed, this was to be the American Stonehenge, or as it is known, the **Georgia Guidestones**.

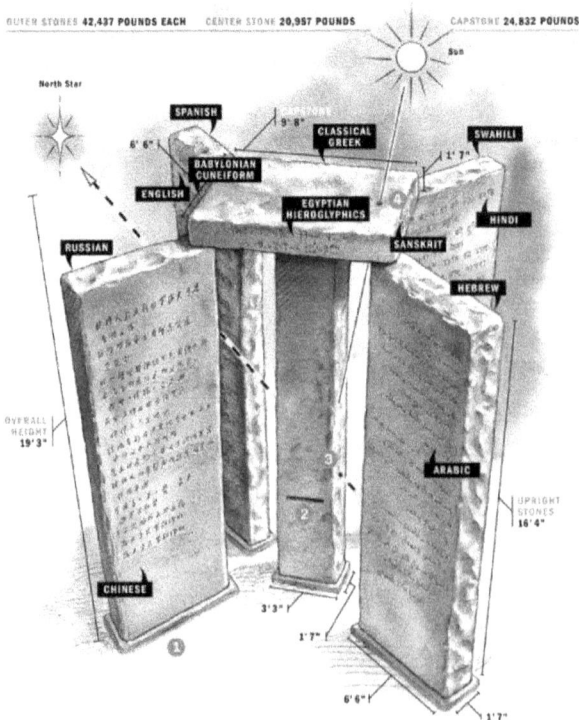

Georgia Guidestones

A man standing in front of the Georgia Guidestones

On each one of the guide stones is the same message, written in a different language. In fact, there are eight different languages the message has been translated into; English, Spanish, Swahili, Hindi, Hebrew, Arabic, Chinese and Russian — each relaying 10 "new" Commandments for "an Age of Reason." The message has come to be called, the **Ten Commandments of the Dark Side**. Coincidently, *The Age of Reason* was a book written by **Thomas Paine** and its intent was to destroy the Judeo-Christian beliefs (Guidestones, 2015).

The Message of the Georgia Guidestones

1) Maintain humanity under **500,000,000** in perpetual balance with nature.
2) Guide reproduction wisely - improving fitness and diversity.
3) Unite humanity with a living new language.
4) Rule passion - faith - tradition - and all things with tempered reason.

5) Protect people and nations with fair laws and just courts.
6) Let all nations rule internally resolving external disputes in a world court.
7) Avoid petty laws and useless officials.
8) Balance personal rights with social duties.
9) Prize truth - beauty - love - seeking harmony with the infinite.
10) Be not a cancer on the earth - Leave room for nature - Leave room for nature (Message, 2015).

Georgia Guidestones

The Real Message

Limiting the population of the earth to 500 million will require the extermination of nine-tenths of the world's people. That equates to about 6, 500,000,000 (six billion five hundred million) people must die / be killed. A true holocaust by any standard.

The Guidestones reference to establishing a world court foreshadows the current move to create an International Criminal Court and a World Government. The Guidestones' emphasis on preserving nature anticipates the environmental movement of the 1990s.

The reference to *"seeking harmony with the infinite"* reflects the current effort to replace Judeo-Christian beliefs with a new spirituality.

The message of the American Stonehenge also foreshadowed the current drive for Sustainable Development. Any time you hear the phrase *"Sustainable Development,"* you know it is talking about Agenda 21. Agenda 21 was compiled under the direction of **Mikhail Gorbachev** and **Maurice Strong**. In that document you will find an emphasis on the same basic issues: control of reproduction, world governance, the importance of nature and the environment, and a new spirituality. The similarity between the ideas engraved on the Georgia Guidestones and those espoused in the Agenda 21 Earth Charter reflect the common origins of both.

What is the true significance of the American Stonehenge, and why is its covert message important? Because it confirms the fact that there was a covert group intent on.

1) Dramatically reducing the population of the world
2) Promoting Agenda 21
3) Establishing a world government
4) Establishing a world court / legal system
5) Promoting a new spirituality (Luciferian) – Remember the letter by Albert Pike.

Just like the Masonic dedication stone at Denver Airport, which has a time capsule buried beneath it, the Georgia Guidestones also feature a capstone with a time capsule buried beneath it.

The fact that most Americans have never heard of the Georgia Guidestones or their message to humanity reflects the degree of control that exists today over what the American people think. All I can say is, ignore that message at your peril.

Certainly the group that commissioned the Georgia Guidestones is one of many similar groups working together toward a New World Order, a new world economic system, and a new world spirituality. But behind those groups, however, are dark spiritual forces. Without understanding the nature of those dark forces, it is impossible to understand the unfolding of world events, and that is what I will be getting into in **Book III: Secrets of the Mind Control**.

New York City (Saint John the Divine Cathedral)

Now it's off to New York City for the next stop on our Illuminati Road Trip. First stop is to one of the world's largest cathedrals. It is a New York City landmark called **Saint John the Divine Cathedral**, located at 1047 Amsterdam Ave. It was built with funding from the Grandmaster of the Masons of the State of New York.

Using the art style of the grotesque, this sculpture next to the cathedral features Sun worship, bizarre mythical creatures, and the upside down head of Satan. There is a John Lennon quote that says "*one day the world will live as one*"

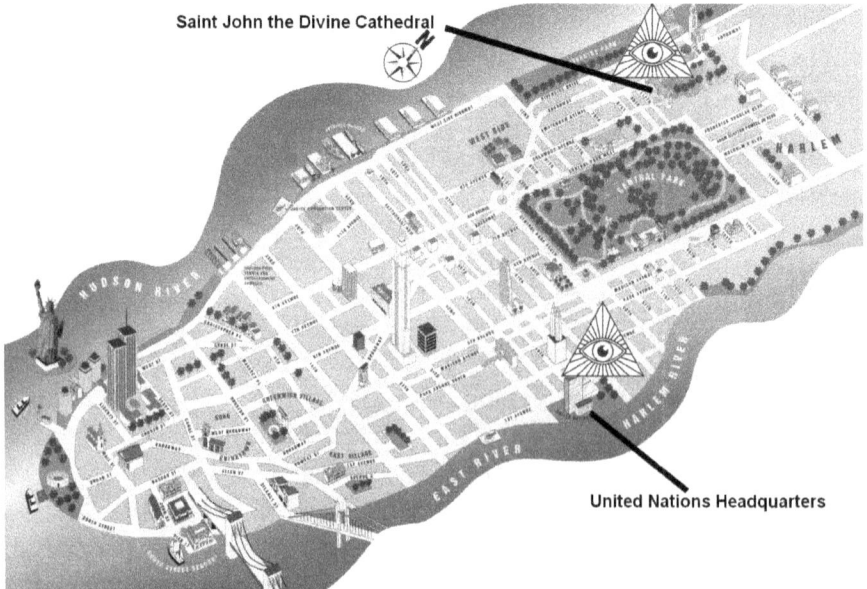

Map of Manhattan Island NY with Illuminati locations

This sculpture next to the Cathedral features a an upside down head of smiling Satan

Twin Towers destruction

On the western facade of the Cathedral, stonemasons have sculpted a chilling depiction the collapse of the Twin Towers and the destruction of New York City and its landmarks. This scene was created in 1997, four years before the destruction of the twin towers on 9/11. Other recognisable skyscrapers are the Chrysler Building and the Citigroup Center. The Cathedral's pillar on the left, shows the Brooklyn Bridge crumbling, cars and buses falling into the churning waters, and the Statue of Liberty sinking. Beneath this horrifying prophecy is the New York Stock Exchange, with street

Destruction of NY by a Wave   *Birth of Anti-Christ*   *Illuminati One Eye Pose of Priest*

people selling all around it. The pillar on the right depicts the Four Horsemen of the Apocalypse riding white, red, black, and pale horses that symbolise conquest, war, famine, and death. Another pillar depicts the birth of the anti-Christ, who is surrounded by mummies. Below the birth is a lamb with its legs tied. The book of Revelation refers to the anti-Christ as the beast, coming up, out of the earth, having two horns, like a lamb. Right below the tied lamb, is a spiral vortex, symbolising a change in consciousness.

Below it are people worshipping the energy vortex and the anti-Christ figure. The cathedral pillar on the left, is the Jewish Kabbalah's Tree of Life. The Kabbalah is linked to the occult practices and symbolism of Freemasonry. Standing above the Kabbalistic Tree of Life is a robed man pictured on the right. Only one eye is exposed, which symbolises the satanic all-seeing eye.

New York City, (United Nations HQ)

L U C I S   T R U S T

Lucis Trust logo is the rising or morning star, Lucifer

Our final stop in New York City is the United Nations headquarters, which was built in 1945 and financed largely by **John D Rockefeller** (Comm 300). Inside the UN headquarters is in ominous meditation room. The custodian to the meditation room is **Lucis Trust Company**, previous

UN Meditation / Ritual Room

known as **Lucifer Publishing Company**. At one time, the Lucis Trust Company was located at 666 United Nations Plaza.

The Rockefeller funded UN meditation room is 33 feet long and 18 feet wide. 18 feet is six, plus six, plus six. The small, dimly lit, windowless room was built in the shape of a pyramid that is laying on its side. At the centre of the room is a four foot high, black stone alter, which weighs 6.5 tonnes and

is extremely magnetic. This alter rests on a concrete pillar, and the pillar extends beneath the floor into the bedrock and taps into the earth's hyper dimensional energies to induce a state altered consciousness. It is also used to summon demons and make sacrifices in satanic rituals.

Not far from the meditation room is the United Nations

United Nations Security Council Chamber

UN Security Council Chamber mural

Security Council Chamber. This is the emergency room at the UN, where the world leaders meet when there is a threat to peace. They decide the fate of nations.

Even though Israel has over 200 uninspected nuclear weapons and has violated dozens of resolutions, no sanctions are ever imposed because of the United States veto powers.

Notice the giant mural that towers over the Security Council room. The central focus at the UN mural is the phoenix bird that has risen. In Greek mythology, a phoenix or phenix, is a long-lived bird that is cyclically regenerated or reborn. Associated with the sun, a phoenix obtains new life by arising from the ashes of its predecessor. A potential origin of the phoenix story is from Ancient Egypt where they venerated the **Bennu**, a solar bird. According to Egyptian mythology, the Bennu was a self-created being said to have played a role in the creation of the world. It was said to be the *ba* of Ra. The ancient Egyptians believed that a human soul was made up of five parts: the *Ren*, the *Ba*, the *Ka*, the *Sheut*, and the

The Phoenix and the newlyweds

Ib. In addition to these components of the soul, there was the human body called the *Ha*. The 'Ba' was everything that makes an individual unique, similar to the notion of 'personality'.

Ra was the name Marduk took while ruling over Egypt. Thus, the Phoenix rising in this mural symbolises Marduk, who rose to "heaven" (Nibiru) in the form of a Morningstar like Lucifer, after his death and rebirth (more on that in **Book IV: Secrets of the UFO's, Aliens and Ancient Astronauts**). Notice that the phoenix bird is not standing above his own ashes, he is standing above an old skin. That is because the old bird, Marduk, will no longer regenerate himself. Instead, a brand new bird – Ningishzidda will rise and rule.

At the top left, there is a church steeple without across. The missing cross symbolises the death of Christianity and the Judeo-Christian beliefs. Below that, a woman receives the rays of the Sun God, while the man in front of her plays Pan's flute. To their right are two pyramid symbols and people joined together by a long, blue, serpent like cloth.

Below the Risen Phoenix is sword, driven through a dragon beast. This represents the old Marduk (Brotherhood of the Dragon). The new world religion worships Ningishzidda as beautiful. Behind the Phoenix are the ghostly figures of the walking dead stepping into a void. They symbolise depopulation.

On the right panel, the pale horse from the book of Revelation is the bringer of death to humanity through weapons, hunger, and disease. The man is releasing him, and the chained black man represents slavery. There is a boy holding the slave's chain (the master). It is the blond-haired German boy again. We saw this same theme at the Bank of America and in Denver. The top panel shows the technologically advanced white race. They control industry, art, and science.

Pale horse and slave. Elites at the top

In this post-apocalyptic mural, the military man standing on the tail of the Beast, represents worldwide military power. He tips his helmet to the elite, who are climbing out from underground cities where they safely hidden from the apocalypse.

Elites climb out of their bunkers

Reptilian dances with a woman?

In the main oval panel, above the phoenix, a woman is holding flowers. She is the bride in a wedding ceremony. Who are these newlyweds that are kneeling submissively beneath the demon in the overhead tree? Could these newlyweds symbolise William and Kate? The general message of the UN's phoenix rising mural is that humanity is stepping into a new, Luciferian reality. After an apocalypse, the elites think they will rule, along with their Anunnaki overlord, and the rest of us will be slaves. It is the same common story with all of these murals. However, there is one really interesting part of this mural. On the right side of the top panel, a green, reptilian creature with scaly skin is dancing with a naked woman while musicians entertain him. Unfortunately it is too small to show you here. I recommend you get a hi-res picture of this mural to see it properly. Trust me, it is there, and I would love to know why.

Beneath this disturbingly prophetic mural, world leaders make global decisions that affect the lives of seven billion people. What is hard for most people to grasp, is that our elected government leaders are involved in an apocalyptic scheme to enslave the masses under a world government dictatorship.

Back to the Grove to absolve your sins!

How do these leaders sleep at night? How do they live with themselves, knowing they want to wipe out 95% of humanity? The answer can be found at the **Bohemian Grove Club** in Monte Rio, California. We already covered the Bohemian Grove in Chapter 8, but to recap, this is the summer camp for the elite, high-ranking politicians, billionaire banksters, businessman, and Hollywood executives. Members have included George Bush junior and senior, Newt Gingrich, Henry

Kissinger, Dick Cheney, Alan Greenspan, Dow Chemical Chairman Frank Popoff, as well as actor Danny Glover, and the list goes on. One thing is certain, these men don't believe in heaven and an afterlife for good behaviour.

They dress in long robes and gather before a 40 foot stone owl statue of the god **Molech**, where they conduct a mock, child sacrifice ritual. It is called the **Cremation of Care** Ritual to purge members of their guilt. The ritual symbolically burns up their cares and clears their conscience of the diabolical crimes they have committed against humanity.

That ends our road trip. Hopefully now you will be able to accept that our so-called leaders do not have our best interest at heart.

The Grand Plan – Bilderberg/CFR/ Trilateral Commission

The New World Order success depends on finding a way to get us to surrender our liberties in the name of some common threat or crisis. These "common threats or crisis" are known as **False Flags**.

They use a False Flag event like 9/11, Sandy Hook shoot-up; the Boston Bombing, Oklahoma bombing etc., that were carried out by rogue elements of the US government, with the express result of an erosion of individual liberty.

No doubt it will be a false flag that will breathe life into the ready to go **FEMA camps**. You may end up in one of these if you refuse the chip. In their own military documents they refer to these FEMA camps as "*re-education*" camps. A term borrowed directly from Communism.

Bilderbergers, Trilateralists, CFR, and UN members want "*an all-encompassing monopoly*" – over government, money, industry, and property that is "self-perpetuating and eternal." In **Confessions of a Monopolist** (1906), **Frederick C. Howe** explained its workings in practice:

> 66 *The rules of big business: Get a monopoly; let Society work for you. So long as we see all international revolutionaries and all international capitalists as implacable enemies of one another, then we miss a crucial point….a partnership between international monopoly capitalism and international revolutionary socialism is for their mutual benefit. (Howe, 1968* 99

In the **Rockefeller File**, Gary Allen wrote:

> 66 *By the late nineteenth century, the inner sanctums of Wall Street understood that the most efficient way to gain a monopoly was to say it was for the 'public good' and 'public interest. (Allen, 1976)* 99

David Rockefeller learned the same thing from his father, John D., Jr. who learned it from his father, John D. Sr. They hated competition and relentlessly strove to eliminate it – for David, on a global scale through a New World Order.

In the 1970s and 1980s, Trilateralists and CFR members collaborated on the latter's **1980 Project**, the largest ever CFR initiative to steer world events "*toward a particular desirable future outcome involving the utter disintegration of the economy.*"

Why do they want to destroy the economy?

Because by the 1950s and 1960s, worldwide industrial growth meant more competition. It was also a model to be followed, and "had to be strangled in the cradle" or at least, greatly contained. By the 1980s in America, they had set a course of no return. Great cities like Detroit Michigan, that was famous all over the world for being the car manufacturing heart, is now akin to a ghost town, or 3rd World city.

The result has been a transfer of wealth from the middle-class to the rich, and plan for its eventual demise. Remember, they want to take us back **neo-feudalism**.

The economic destruction of Detroit, and hundreds of other manufacturing cities around the world has been done by design. Simply put, they want to consolidate all manufacturing into a small group of mega companies that they own. These will all be placed in 3rd World countries where labour is at its cheapest. They do not have to pay pensions, sick days, or holiday pay. If a worker does not perform, then they are replaced, because there are another hundred starving people ready and willing to take their place. The other advantage they see in this arrangement is to get as many people in the 1st World countries onto welfare.

When people are on welfare, they are beholden to the State. If the person does not play along with the New World Order rules, they have the welfare cut off. Of course, it goes without saying that the more people they force onto welfare, the lower the payments will get. They will use the excuse that too many people are on welfare, and they can't afford to pay too much – even though they created the problem.

Controlling the masses

Eventually, this will lead to one of the Bilderberg Objectives to be fulfilled - One international identity for every citizen, observing one set of universal values. This will be in the form of a "chip" in your hand/arm or other part of the body. On the chip will be all of your financial records and means, health records, crime records and "citizen" number. They will make it look "cool" and convenient – just wave your wrist over the scanner to pay for your goods at the store. But what you will not be told until it is too late, is that if you buck the system, they will switch the chip off. That means you cannot buy or sell, get medical aid, or travel, because all major roads, trains, planes, and buses will require you to "scan" before you get on board – otherwise, you may be a terrorist!

Google, whose boss **Eric Schmidt** always attends Bilderberg meetings, is working aggressively to perfect the "driverless" car (Self Driving Car, 2015). In fact, they have already built it, but now they are debating about laws and liabilities. Typical of the NWO types, they bicker about who will have to pay if the car is in an accident – the manufacturer, or the person riding in it? So that is the only delay in full production at the moment. Regardless, I can assure you that by 2020 there will be driverless cars all over our roads. And just like other modes of transport, they will eventually require your ID (chip) scan before you can use them. It will all be sold as safety, convenience, and security.

Unfortunately, people will be lining up for one of these chips, even pushing and shoving to be first. This will all be done by a slick marketing campaign from **Tavistock** (more on them in **Book III: Secrets of the Mind Control**). They may even throw in a "medical" emergency like an airborne-Ebola virus – so, it would go like this. Come and get a vaccination, and while you are here, we will implant this chip. This tells us that you have been vaccinated, so you are free to travel. Otherwise, without the chip, we will have to quarantine you (indefinitely).

After you get the chip, they will offer free "upgrades" to include finances etc. Again, people will fight to get one of these chips.

The Political Parties work for the same boss - EVERYWHERE

The demise of America started with Republican, George Bush Sr. announcing the New World Order. Democrat Bill Clinton signed the US onto it. Independent Ross Perot warned everyone about it, but he was ignored. Republican George Bush Jr. let it happen. Democrat Obama is finishing the job. So you see, it does not matter which political party you vote for – they both have the same bosses – the 13 Ruling Families and Committee of 300.

Take your mind back to Chapter 1, where I asked the question, "Do [unelected] billionaires run the world?"

You bet they do!

Fear is their true master

Believe it or not, these so-called elites live in much more fear than you or me. They fear losing their wealth, their power, their status. They fear an uprising of the plebs (that is us). Thus, almost every decision they make, or action they take is based in fear. Any choice made in fear will never bring harmony or balance in to your life. That is why these mega-rich people are no happier than the average person. By acquiring another $1 billion does not increase your happiness by another 1 billion. All of them, bar none, are in the Young Soul phase of their Soul's journey (see **Book I: Secrets of the Soul** for more details about Soul Ages). The average millionaire / billionaire is somewhere around the 5th -6th level. The Illuminati kingpins are usually at the 7th level of the Young Soul age. For that reason, they cannot really see anything wrong with what they do. They honestly believe that because they are filthy rich that they are smarter than we are, and therefore they deserve to run things. We are seen as "below" them – the unwashed masses – the useless eaters. These are terms they use for us.

The real control freaks will never run for office. They will happily pay to have a puppet run for them. That way they get to do what they want, for longer, and without being in the direct firing line when people are unhappy with your decisions. As soon as people realise, and I mean really realise, that we outnumber them by millions to one, that is when we will see a massive change.

How Putin Saved Russia

National Geographic's **Human Edge** TV Series presented a brilliant documentary which outlines the rise and fall of the Russian-Jewish oligarchs, after the fall of the Soviet Union (Human Edge, 2011). The reason why this period in history is important, is because it delivered to us, and into the political arena, **Vladimir Putin**, the now Russian President. Putin is the antidote to President Obama, who's serving on behalf of Rothschild Zionist and their total control of the United States of America.

Had this not taken place, the world we live in would now have been very different, with more wars and conflicts, and we would be further in the grip of International Rothschild Jewry, as per the *Protocols of Zion*.

Putin is truly remarkable because he, and he alone, thwarted Rothschild Zionist and the U.S. puppet President Obama, in their attempt to overthrow the Syrian government. They want to do this to change the geopolitical climate in the Middle East in favour of Israel, as was the US invasion of Iraq, and all for one purpose - the future invasion of Iran.

One need only to look at the countries and Presidents the U.S. boycotts and criticises to figure out who Rothschild Zionist Jewry are targeting and then everything will fall into place.

Putin has been compared to Hitler by the Western (Zionist owned) media for a variety of reasons. One is because he will not allow the West to meddle in Russian affairs and try to change the political and social climate. They try and bring in these changes through "democratic revolutions" or challenging authority through "human right campaigns," aimed at legalising homosexual Gay Pride parades for example. Of course, they are designed to outrage the people, distract, and create social unrest. But mostly because he revived his country out of the rubble that Jewish Bolshevism created, which even Putin himself admits was Jewish (JewishSoviets, 2015).

Of course the Ashkenazi Jews, as usual, claim Putin perpetuates this as an "anti-Semitic lie" (Yanover, 2013).

But what happened to the Jewish oligarchs after Putin became President? **Berezovsky** was exiled and allegedly committed suicide, **Khodorkovsky** rots in prison at this very moment, others fled to Israel or the West, but people like **Abramovich** stayed and were most likely forced to pledge allegiance, not to International Jewry, but to Russia as loyal, law-abiding citizens.

And as for the Jewish community in Russia, at some point in time it was made clear to them that there would be no conspiring with their tribal brethren in the West to meddle with the affairs in Russia. They had to declare their allegiance to the country (Berger, 2013).

We can only look to the future with hope and keep our eyes and ears open and most importantly, inform people on what's happening and why it's happening. Who knows, maybe one day we will also be able to put a President like Putin into the Whitehouse!

References:

Arthur, C. (2015). *Artificial intelligence: 'Homo sapiens will be split into a handful of gods and the rest of us'* [online] the Guardian. Available at: http://www.theguardian.com/business/2015/nov/07/artificial-intelligence-homo-sapiens-split-handful-gods [Accessed 9 Nov. 2015].

Ba, (2015). *Ancient Egyptian concept of the soul.* [online] Wikipedia. Available at: https://en.wikipedia.org/wiki/Ancient_Egyptian_concept_of_the_soul#Ba [Accessed 14 Dec. 2015].

Bennu, (2015). *Bennu.* [online] Wikipedia. Available at: https://en.wikipedia.org/wiki/Bennu [Accessed 14 Dec. 2015].

Berger, P. (2013). *Russian Chief Rabbi Tells Jews To Back Off on Criticizing Vladimir Putin.* [online] The Forward. Available at: http://forward.com/news/183459/russian-chief-rabbi-tells-jews-to-back-off-on-crit/?p=all [Accessed 14 Dec. 2015].

Chong, P. (2010). *Popular Japanese Capsule Accommodation Spreading Abroad.* [online] P21chong's Blog. Available at: http://paulchong.net/2010/04/16/popular-japanese-capsule-accommodation-spreading-abroad/ [Accessed 1 Dec. 2015].

Guidestones, (2015). *Georgia Guidestones.* [online] Wikipedia. Available at: https://en.wikipedia.org/wiki/Georgia_Guidestones [Accessed 13 Dec. 2015].

Gulag, (2015). *The Gulag Archipelago.* [online] Wikipedia. Available at: https://en.wikipedia.org/wiki/The_Gulag_Archipelago [Accessed 12 Dec. 2015].

Hillary, (2015). *The Violent Crimes and Shady Dealings of Hillary Clinton.* [online] infowars. Available at: http://www.prisonplanet.com/the-violent-crimes-and-shady-dealings-of-hillary-clinton.html [Accessed 13 Dec. 2015].

Human Edge, (2011). *Human Edge Rise and Fall (Oligarch) 1.* [online] YouTube. Available at: https://youtu.be/uDPrnckr82c [Accessed 14 Dec. 2015].

Huxley, A. (1998). *Brave new world.* New York: Perennial Classics.

JewishSoviets, (2015). *Russian President Vladimir Putin: First Soviet government was mostly Jewish - Jewish World News.* [online] Haaretz.com. Available at: http://www.haaretz.com/jewish/news/1.530857 [Accessed 14 Dec. 2015].

Message, (2015). *The Georgia Guidestones - Illuminati Ten Commandments?.* [online] Rense.com. Available at: http://www.rense.com/general16/georgiaguidestones.htm [Accessed 13 Dec. 2015].

Mims, C. (2015). *First-ever human head transplant is now possible, says neuroscientist.* [online] Quartz. Available at: http://qz.com/99413/first-ever-human-head-transplant-is-now-possible-says-neuroscientist/ [Accessed 1 Dec. 2015].

Morrow, M. (2015). *The world's first head transplant.* [online] NewsComAu. Available at: http://www.news.com.au/technology/science/terminally-ill-man-set-to-be-first-to-undergo-the-worlds-first-full-head-transplant/story-fn5fsgyc-1227301771920 [Accessed 1 Dec. 2015].

Morton, E. (2015). *Beware of Blucifer, the Demon Horse of Denver Airport.* [online] Slate Magazine. Available at: http://www.slate.com/blogs/atlas_obscura/2014/03/17/the_blue_mustang_is_part_of_several_conspiracy_theories_centered_on_denver.html [Accessed 9 Dec. 2015].

Movie, (1980). *Brave New World(1980)-Full Length Movie.mp4.* [online] YouTube. Available at: https://youtu.be/Wlb1bdU-G7o [Accessed 1 Dec. 2015].

Quotes, (1979). *Darth Vader (Character).* [online] IMDb. Available at: http://www.imdb.com/character/ch0000005/quotes [Accessed 1 Dec. 2015].

Singer, P. (2015). *Military robots and the future of war.* [online] Ted.com. Available at: https://www.ted.com/talks/pw_singer_on_robots_of_war#t-529904 [Accessed 1 Dec. 2015].

Solzhenitsyn, A.I. (1974). *The Gulag Archipelago, 1918-1956.* New York: Harper & Row.

Urmson, C. (2015). *How a driverless car sees the road.* [online] Ted.com. Available at: https://www.ted.com/talks/chris_urmson_how_a_driverless_car_sees_the_road?language=en [Accessed 1 Dec. 2015].

Yanover, Y. (2013). *Putin Perpetuates Antisemitic Lie of First Soviet 'Mostly Jewish'.* [online] The Jewish Press. Available at: http://www.jewishpress.com/news/breaking-news/putin-perpetuates-antisemitic-lie-of-first-soviet-mostly-jewish/2013/06/20/ [Accessed 14 Dec. 2015].

17

PREVIEW BOOK III: SECRETS OF THE MIND CONTROL

f I ask the question, "Finish this statement...Woodrow Wilson was the man that...". If you answered "sold America to the banksters", then you were right (and paying attention!). Every time I mentioned Woodrow Wilson, I used the (true) statement – the man that sold America to the banksters. I did this for two reasons. First, it is true, and people need to know this. Secondly, I wanted to use it as a means to demonstrate how easy it is for the media to control your thoughts. Yes, in a way, I used the main stream media's own technique to "brain wash" you, in a nice way! And that is what the next book is all about.

This book, **Book II: Secrets of the Illuminati** was originally going to include all of the information in **Book III: Secrets of the Mind Control**. However, when I was about 50% finished writing this book, I realised it was already as big as **Book I – Secrets of the Soul**! Therefore, due to space and size limitations, I had to halve this book into two books. That is why **Book III** will really go hand-in-hand with this one. You could say it is a companion book.

Whilst this book focused on the groups and individuals that run the world from behind the curtain, the next book will look at **how** the Illuminati control the world. It will explore the techniques and methods used by our rulers to control the masses, and control individuals. They do this via several "mind control" methods. We learnt about the Occult and Crowley in this book, because in **Book III**, I will expose the Satanic Ritual Abuse used to brain wash individuals. As well as that, I will be detailing how the main stream media is used to control the masses, plus so much more. The next book will touch on some dark subjects. Firstly, because no one else does, and for that reason, I feel it is very important that I do.

To fix a problem, you must first understand it, even if that means you must uncover some nasty stuff. Imagine you had a wound on your leg, and it was covered by a bandage. After a week or so, it began to bleed, and leak and smell awful. Would you remove the bandage, knowing it would not look or smell nice, but it meant you could clean it. Or would you ignore it until the leg had to be amputated because it went bad, as you were too scared to take the bandage off?

In **Book I**, I talk about the **Wise Mind**. The Wise Mind tells us that we can look at the wound, no matter how bad it is, because only then can we clean it, and heal it. The same can be said for the injustices and horrors that are allowed to go on in our world. Once we get the dark side of life out of the way, we can focus on the Light.

The subjects included in **Book III - Secrets of the Mind Control** include, but not limited to: Individual and mass mind control, Satanic Ritual Abuse, CIA mass media manipulation, Paedophiles in High Places, hyper-sexualisation of children, Exposed: Music Industry / Hollywood /Disney, Mind control drugs, weapons, public education system and GMO foods.

Plus, I will get into the not much talked about, biggest threat of all – **AI** (Artificial Intelligence). If you wonder why I think that is our greatest threat, then you will need to read my next book to find out why!

Thanks for reading this book. If you liked it, please tell your friends about it, or post it on Facebook or Twitter or whatever you do.

Love and Light

Danny

ANNEX 3.6.1

WHO WERE THE KNIGHTS TEMPLAR?

By Stephen Dafoe and Danny Searle

Within two decades of the victory of the First Crusade (1095-1099) a group of knights led by **Hugues (Hugh) de Payens** offered themselves to the Patriarch of Jerusalem to serve as a military force.

This group had the mandate of protecting Christian pilgrims who were en route to the Holy Land to visit the shrines sacred to their faith. Somewhere between the years of 1118 CE – 1120, **King Baldwin II** granted the group quarters in a wing of the Royal Palace on the **Temple Mount** (the Al Aqsa Mosque).

It has been generally accepted that, for the first nine years of their existence, the Templars – as they came to be known – consisted of nine members. Although it has been widely speculated that the Templars wished to keep it this way to cover their secret mission of digging for buried treasure on the Temple Mount, the simple fact remains that the lifestyle adopted by the Order was not to everyone's taste. As such, the Templars had difficulty in recruiting members to their cause in the early years.

In the year **1127** the Cistercian abbot, **Bernard of Clairvaux**, wrote a rule of order for the Templars that was based on his own Cistercian Order's rule of conduct. Additionally, Bernard did a great deal to promote the Templars. Perhaps Bernard's greatest contribution to the Order was a letter that he wrote to **Hugues de Payens**, entitled *De laude novae militae* (*In praise of the new knighthood.*)

This letter swept throughout Christendom drawing many men, of noble birth, who joined the ranks of the Templar Order. Those who were unable to join often gifted the Templars with land and other valuables. While it is true that the Templars were not permitted by their rule, to own much of anything personally, there was no such restriction on the Order as a whole. As such, the gifts of land were accepted and put to immediate use by the Templars, who farmed the land generating additional wealth.

Over the years the Templars rose from their humble beginnings to become the wealthiest of the Crusading Orders – eventually garnering the favour of the Church and the collective European monarchs. This wealth, generated in the West was put to immediate use in the East to buy arms and raise armies. Although the Templars are regarded as the greatest of the medieval military Orders, the record shows that they lost more battles than they won. Despite a brutal win/loss record, the Order did play an important role in the Holy Land.

However, after two centuries of defending the Christian faith, the Order met its demise when **Philip IV** – known as *Philip le Belle* (the Fair) – sought to destroy the Templars.

Historians are generally in agreement that Philip was motivated by greed rather than his belief that the Templars were corrupt. Regardless of his motivations, Philip had the Templars arrested on October [Friday] 13, 1307. [This is where the superstition about Friday 13th came from]

The Templars were tortured and confessions were given. These confessions included:

- Trampling and spitting on the cross
- Homosexuality
- Idolatry

Philip was successful in ridding the Templars of their power and wealth and urged all fellow Christian leaders to do the same thing. Phillip confiscated all of their lands, gold, and other treasures.

In **1312** the Templars were officially dissolved by **Pope Clement V** at the Council of Vienne. Although the Templars were not found guilty of the crimes they were charged with, it was felt that the reputation of the Order had fallen to so low a state as to warrant dissolving the Order.

On March 18th, 1314 the last Grand Master of the Knights Templar, **Jacques de Molay**, was burned at the stake, for having recanted his earlier confessions of guilt.

De Molay is said to have cursed King Philip and Pope Clement as he burned, asking both men to join him in death within a year. The story is an apocryphal legend; however, it is one that has come to be widely accepted. Although there is no historical truth to the de Molay curse story, both Pope Clement V and Philip IV followed de Molay to their graves within the year (Dafoe, 2015).

References:

AUTemplars, (2015). *The Templars.* [online] Thetemplars.com.au. Available at: http://thetemplars.com. au/ [Accessed 6 Dec. 2015].

Dafoe, S. (2015). *Templarhistory.com.* [online] Templarhistory.com. Available at: http://www. templarhistory.com/ [Accessed 6 Dec. 2015].

History, (2015). *History of the Knights Templar.* [online] Wikipedia. Available at: https://en.wikipedia. org/wiki/History_of_the_Knights_Templar [Accessed 6 Dec. 2015].

New Advent, (2015). *CATHOLIC ENCYCLOPEDIA: The Knights Templar.* [online] Newadvent.org. Available at: http://www.newadvent.org/cathen/14493a.htm [Accessed 6 Dec. 2015].

Templars, (2015). *Home.* [online] The Knights Templar. Available at: http://www.theknightstemplar.org/ [Accessed 6 Dec. 2015].

ANNEX 3.7.1

COMMITTEE OF 300 INSTITUTIONS AND MEMBERS

Some major world-wide *Committee of 300* institutions and organisations are as follows:

All democratic parties worldwide	All Fortune 500 countries
All Military Industrial Companies (Rand, Raytheon, Lockheed Martin etc.)	AOL-Time-Warner, Walt Disney, Viacom, News Corporation (Fox), Comcast, CBS, Sony
All Stock Exchanges	American Israel Public Affairs Committee
Anti-Defamation League (ADL)	All Reserve Banks
Biblical Archaeology Review	Bilderbergers
British Petroleum / BHP / Rio Tinto	Canadian Institute of Foreign Relations
Catholic Church/Vatican	Christian Fundamentalism
Council on Foreign Relations	Egyptian Exploration Society
Fabian Society	General Electric
Halliburton	Harvard, Yale University etc.
Imperial Chemical Industries	International Institute for Strategic Studies
Microsoft	Order of Skull and Bones
Palestine Exploration Fund	Poor Knights of the Templars
Royal Dutch Shell Company	Socialist International Wilton Park
South Africa Foundation	Tavistock Institute of Human Relations
Temple Mount Foundation	The Atheist Club
The Carlyle Group	The Fourth State of Consciousness Club
The Golden Dawn	The Milner Group
The Nasi Princes	The Order of Magna Mater
The Order of the Divine Disorder	The RIIA
The Round Table	Trilateral Commission
United Nations	Universal Freemasonry
Universal Zionism	Vickers Armament Company
Warren Commission	Westinghouse
World Council of Churches	World Health Organization

The Committee of 300: The Conspirator's Hierarchy by John Coleman

About The Committee of 300

The Committee of 300, who refer to themselves as **The Olympians**, is a product of the **British East India** Company's Council of 300 around **1727**. The East India Company was chartered by the British Royal family in 1600. It made vast fortunes in the opium drug trade with China and became the largest company on earth in its time. Today, through many powerful alliances, the Committee of 300 rules the world and is the driving force behind the criminal agenda to create a "New World Order," under a "Totalitarian Global Government."

The Committee of 300 with its "aristocracy," its ownership of the U.S. Federal Reserve banking system, insurance companies, giant corporations, foundations, communications networks, presided over by a hierarchy of conspirators-this is the enemy. Secret societies exist by deception.

Each is a hierarchy with an inner circle at the top, who deceives those below with lies, such as claiming a noble agenda; thus, duping them into following a web of compartmentalized complicity. The inner circle of the Committee of 300 is the **Order of the Garter**, headed by **Queen Elizabeth Windsor II** (Saxe-Coburg-Gotha).

The enemy is clearly identifiable as the Committee of 300 and its front organisations, such as the **Royal Institute for International Affairs** (Chatham House), the **Club of Rome, NATO, U.N., the Black Nobility**, the **Tavistock** Institute, **CFR** and all its affiliated organisations, the think tanks and research institutions controlled by Stanford and the Tavistock Institute of Human Relations and last, but certainly not least, the **military industrial complex.**

The Committee of 300 is the ultimate secret society made up of an untouchable ruling class, which includes the Queen of the United Kingdom (Elizabeth II), who still receives financial tribute from the US, and holds vast tracts of land there, the Queen of the Netherlands, the Queen of Denmark and the royal families of Europe. These aristocrats decided at the death of Queen Victoria, the matriarch of the Venetian Black Guelphs that, in order to gain world-wide control, it would be necessary for its aristocratic members to "go into business" with the non-aristocratic, but extremely powerful leaders of corporate business on a global scale, and so the doors to ultimate power were opened to what the Queen of England likes to refer to as "the commoners". Through their illicit banking cartel, they own the stock of the Federal

Reserve, which is a private for profit corporation that violates U.S. Constitution and is a root of the problem.

The decadent American families of the unholy partnership, thoroughly corrupted and wallowing in tainted opium money, went on to become what we know today as the **Eastern Liberal Establishment**. Its members, under the careful guidance and direction of the British Crown, and subsequently, its foreign policy executive arm, the Royal Institute for International Affairs (RIIA), ran the United States from top to bottom through their secret upper-level, parallel government, which is tightly meshed with the Committee of 300, the ultimate secret society. That secret, all-powerful government is now more in control of the United States than ever before.

Below is taken from John Coleman's book *Conspirator's Hierarchy-The Committee of 300*. It was first published in 1992, and it is remarkable in 2015 how many of these aims have come to pass, or are already well established.

Ten Top Aims:

1. A **One World Government**-New World Order with a unified church and monetary system under their direction. Not many people are aware that the One World Government began setting up its "church" in the 1920's/ 1930's, for they realised the need for a religious belief inherent in mankind to have an outlet and, therefore, set up a "church" body to channel that belief in the direction they desired.

2. The utter destruction of all **national identity** and national pride.

3. The **destruction of religion** and more especially the Christian religion, with the one exception, their own creation mentioned above.

4. **Control of each and every person** through means of mind control and what Brzezinski call *"technotronics"* which would create human-like robots and a system of terror beside which **Felix Dzerzinski's** Red Terror will look like children at play.

5. **An end to all industrialisation** and the production of nuclear generated electric power in what they call "the post-industrial zero-growth society." Exempted are the computer and service industries. United States industries that remain will be exported to countries such as Mexico where abundant slave labour is available. Unemployables in the wake of industrial destruction will either become opium-heroin and or cocaine addicts, or become statistics in the elimination process

we know today as **Global 2000** [Agenda 21].

6. Legalisation of drugs and pornography.

7. **Depopulation of large cities** according to the trial run carried out by the **Pol Pot** regime in Cambodia. It is interesting to note that Pol Pot's genocidal plans were drawn up in the United States by one of the **Club of Rome's** research foundations. It is also interesting that the Committee is presently seeking to reinstate the Pol Pot butchers in Cambodia.

8. **Suppression of all scientific development** except for those deemed beneficial by the Committee. Especially targeted is nuclear energy for peaceful purposes. Particularly hated are the Cold Fusion experiments presently being scorned and ridiculed by the Committee and its jackals of the press. Development of the fusion torch would blow the Committee's conception of *"limited natural resources"* right out of the window. A fusion torch properly used could create unlimited untapped natural resources from the most ordinary substances. Fusion torch uses are legion and would benefit mankind in a manner which is as yet not even remotely comprehended by the public.

9. **Cause by means of limited wars** in the advanced countries, and by means of starvation and diseases in Third World countries, the death of 3 billion people by the year 2000, people they call "useless eaters."

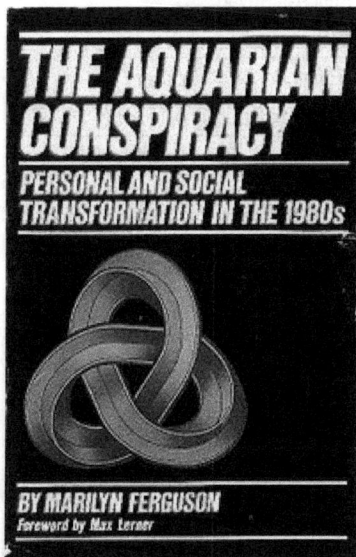

The Aquarian Conspiracy by Marilyn Ferguson

The Committee of 300 commissioned **Cyrus Vance** to write a paper on this subject of how best to bring about such genocide. The paper was produced under the title the "Global 2000 Report" and was accepted and approved for action by **President Carter**, for and on behalf of the U.S. Government, and accepted by **Edwin Muskie**, then Secretary of State. Under the terms of the Global 2000 Report, the population of the United States is to be reduced by 100 million by the year 2050.

10. **To weaken the moral fib e of the nation** and to demoralize workers in the labour class by creating mass unemployment. As jobs dwindle due to the post-industrial zero growth policies

introduced by the **Club of Rome**, demoralized and discouraged workers will resort to alcohol and drugs. The youth of the land will be encouraged by means of rock music and drugs to rebel against the status quo, thus undermining and eventually destroying the family unit. In this regard The Committee of 300 commissioned **Tavistock Institute** to prepare a blueprint as to how this could be achieved. Tavistock directed **Stanford Research** to undertake the work under the direction of **Professor Willis Harmon**. This work later became known as *The Aquarian Conspiracy*.

The Membership List as of 2010

(Type in name at Wikipedia to view more info)

Abdullah II of Jordan	Abramovich, Roman Arkadyevich
Ackermann, Josef	Adeane, Edward
Agius, Marcus Ambrose Paul	Ahtisaari, Martti Oiva Kalevi
Akerson, Daniel	Albert II of Belgium
Alexander - Crown Prince of Yugoslavia	Alexandra (Princess), The Honourable Lady Ogilvy
Alphonse, Louis, Duke of Anjou	Amato, Giuliano
Anderson, Carl A.	Andreotti, Giulio
Andrew (Prince) - Duke of York	Anne - Princess Royal
Anstee, Nick	Ash, Timothy Garton
Astor, William Waldorf, 4th Viscount Astor	August, Ernst, Prince of Hanover
Aven, Pyotr	Balkenende, Jan Peter
Ballmer, Steve	Balls, Ed
Barroso, José Manuel	Beatrix (Queen), Netherlands
Belka, Marek	Bergsten, C. Fred
Berlusconi, Silvio	Bernake, Ben
Bernhard (Prince) of Lippe-Biesterfeld	Bernstein, Nils
Berwick, Donald	Bildt, Carl
Bischoff, Sir Winfried Franz Wilhen "Win"	Blair, Tony
Blankfein, Lloyd	Blavatnik, Leonard
Bloomberg, Michael	Bolkestein, Frits
Bolkiah, Hassanal	Bonello, Michael C
Bonino, Emma	Boren, David L.
Borwin, Duke of Mecklenburg	Bronfman, Charles Rosner

Bronfman, Edgar Jr.	Bruton, John
Brzezinski, Zbigniew	Budenberg, Robin
Buffet, Warren	Bush, George HW
Cameron, David William Donald	Camilla, Duchess of Cornwall
Cardoso, Fernando Henrique	Carington, Peter - 6th Baron Carrington
Carlos, Duke of Parma	Carlos, Juan, King of Spain
Carney, Mark J.	Carroll, Cynthia
Caruana, Jaime	Castell, Sir William
Chan, Anson	Chan, Margaret
Chan, Norman	Charles, Prince of Wales
Chartres, Richard	Chiaie, Stefano Delle
Chipman, Dr John	Chodiev, Patokh
Christoph, Prince of Schleswig-Holstein	Cicchitto, Fabrizio
Clark, Wesley Kanne Sr. (General)	Clarke, Kenneth
Clegg, Nick	Clinton, Bill
Cohen, Abby Joseph	Cohen, Ronald
Cohn, Gary D.	Colonna, Marcantonio (di Paliano), Prince and Duke of Paliano
Constantijn (Prince) of the Netherlands	Constantine II Greece
Cooksey, David	Cowen, Brian
Craven, Sir John	Crockett, Andrew
Dadush, Uri	D'Aloisio, Tony
Darling, Alistair	Davies, Sir Howard
Davignon, Étienne	Davis, David
De Rothschild, Benjamin	De Rothschild, David René James
De Rothschild, Evelyn Robert	De Rothschild, Leopold David
Deiss, Joseph	Deripaska, Oleg
Dobson, Michael	Draghi, Mario
Du Plessis, Jan	Dudley, William C.
Duisenberg, Wim	Edward (Prince), Duke of Kent
Edward (The Prince), Earl of Wessex	Elkann, John
Emanuele, Vittorio, Prince of Naples, Crown Prince of Italy	Fabrizio (Prince), Massimo-Brancaccio
Feldstein, Martin Stuart "Marty"	Festing, Matthew
Fillon, François	Fischer, Heinz
Fischer, Joseph Martin	Fischer, Stanley
FitzGerald, Niall	Franz, Duke of Bavaria

Fridman, Mikhail	Friedrich, Georg, Prince of Prussia
Friso (Prince) of Orange-Nassau	Gates, Bill
Geidt, Christopher	Geithner, Timothy
Gibson-Smith, Dr Chris	Gorbachev, Mikhail
Gore, Al	Gotlieb, Allan
Green, Stephen	Greenspan, Alan
Grosvenor, Gerald, 6th Duke of Westminster	Gurría, José Ángel
Gustaf, Carl XVI of Sweden	Hague, William
Hampton, Sir Philip Roy	Hans-Adam II, Prince of Liechtenstein
Harald V Norway	Harper, Stephen
Heisbourg, François	Henri, Grand Duke of Luxembourg
Hildebrand, Philipp	Hills, Carla Anderson
Holbrooke, Richard	Honohan, Patrick
Howard, Alan	Ibragimov, Alijan
Ingves, Stefan Nils Magnus	Isaacson, Walter
Jacobs, Kenneth M.	Julius, DeAnne
Juncker, Jean-Claude	Kenen, Peter
Kerry, John Forbes	King, Mervyn
Kinnock, Glenys	Kissinger, Henry
Knight, Malcolm	Koon, William H. II
Krugman, Paul	Kufuor, John
Lajolo, Giovanni	Lake, Anthony
Lambert, Richard	Lamy, Pascal
Landau, Jean-Pierre	Laurence, Timothy James Hamilton
Leigh-Pemberton, James	Leka, Crown Prince of Albania
Leonard, Mark	Levene, Peter - Baron Levene of Portsoken
Leviev, Lev	Levitt, Arthur
Levy, Michael, Baron Levy	Lieberman, Joe
Livingston, Ian	Loong, Lee Hsien
Lorenz (Prince) of Belgium, Archduke of Austria-Este	Louis-Dreyfus, Gérard
Mabel (Princess) of Orange-Nassau	Mandelson, Peter Benjamin
Manning, Sir David Geoffrey	Margherita, Archduchess of Austria-Este
Margrethe II Denmark	Martínez, Guillermo Ortiz
Mashkevitch, Alexander	Massimo, Stefano (Prince), Prince of Rocca-secca dei Volsci
McDonough, William Joseph	McLarty, Mack

Mersch, Yves	Michael (Prince) of Kent
Michael of Romania	Miliband, David
Miliband, Ed	Mittal, Lakshmi
Moreno, Glen	Moritz - Prince and Landgrave of Hesse-Kassel
Murdoch, Rupert	Napoléon, Charles
Nasser, Jacques	Niblett, Robin
Nichols, Vincent	Nicolás, Adolfo
Noyer, Christian	Ofer, Sammy
Ogilvy, David, 13th Earl of Airlie	Ollila, Jorma Jaakko
Oppenheimer, Nicky	Osborne, George
Oudea, Frederic	Parker, Sir John
Patten, Chris	Pébereau, Michel
Penny, Gareth	Peres, Shimon
Philip (Prince), Duke of Edinburgh	Pio, Dom Duarte, Duke of Braganza
Pöhl, Karl Otto	Powell, Colin
Prokhorov, Mikhail	Quaden, Guy Baron
Rasmussen, Anders Fogh	Ratzinger, Joseph Alois (Pope Benedict XVI)
Reuben, David	Reuben, Simon
Rhodes, William R. "Bill"	Rice, Susan
Richard (Prince), Duke of Gloucester	Rifkind, Sir Malcolm Leslie
Ritblat, Sir John	Roach, Stephen S.
Robinson, Mary	Rockefeller, David Jr.
Rockefeller, David Sr.	Rockefeller, Nicholas
Rodríguez, Javier Echevarría	Rogoff, Kenneth Saul "Ken"
Roth, Jean-Pierre	Rothschild, Jacob, 4th Baron
Rubenstein, David	Rubin, Robert
Ruspoli, Francesco, 10th Prince of Cerveteri	Safra, Joseph
Safra, Moises	Sands, Peter A.
Sarkozy, Nicolas	Sassoon, Isaac S.D.
Sassoon, James Meyer,Baron Sassoon	Sawers, Sir Robert John
Scardino, Marjorie	Schwab, Klaus
Schwarzenberg, Karel	Schwarzman, Stephen A.
Shapiro, Sidney	Sheinwald, Nigel
Sigismund (Archduke), Grand Duke of Tuscany	Simeon of Saxe-Coburg and Gotha
Snowe, Olympia	Sofía (Queen) of Spain
Soros, George	Specter, Arlen

Stern, Ernest	Stevenson, Dennis, Baron Stevenson of Coddenham
Steyer, Tom	Stiglitz, Joseph E.
Strauss-Kahn, Dominique	Straw, Jack
Sutherland, Peter	Tanner, Mary
Tedeschi, Ettore Gotti	Thompson, Mark
Thomson, Dr. James A.	Tietmeyer, Hans
Trichet, Jean-Claude	Tucker, Paul
Van Rompuy, Herman	Vélez, Álvaro Uribe
Verplaetse, Alfons Vicomte	Villiger, Kaspar
Vladimirovna, Maria, Grand Duchess of Russia	Volcker, Paul
Von Habsburg, Otto	Waddaulah, Hassanal Bolkiah Mu'izzaddin
Walker, Sir David Alan	Wallenberg, Jacob
Walsh, John	Warburg, Max
Weber, Axel Alfred	Weill, Michael David
Wellink, Nout	Whitman, Marina von Neumann
Willem-Alexander, Prince of Orange	William (Prince) of Wales
Williams, Dr Rowan	Williams, Shirley, Baroness Williams of Crosby
Wilson, David, Baron Wilson of Tillyorn	Wolfensohn, James David
Wolin, Neal S.	Woolf, Harry, Baron Woolf
Woolsey, R. James Jr.	Worcester, Sir Robert Milton
Wu, Sarah	Zoellick, Robert Bruce

References:

Coleman, J. (1992). *Conspirators' hierarchy*. Carson City, NV: America West Publishers.

Coleman, J. (1993). *21 Goals of the Illuminati and The Committee of 300* by Dr. John Coleman (ca. 1993). [online] Educate-yourself.org. Available at: http://educate-yourself.org/cn/johncolemangoalsofIlluminati.shtml [Accessed 5 Dec. 2015].

Ferguson, M. (1980). *The Aquarian conspiracy*. Los Angeles: J.P. Tarcher.

Mosesman, (2012). *Current Membership List of The Illuminati "Committee of 300"!*. [online] Socio-Economics History Blog. Available at: https://socioecohistory.wordpress.com/2012/04/23/current-membership-list-of-the-illuminati-committee-of-300/ [Accessed 5 Dec. 2015].

ANNEX 3.9.1

THE CARBON TAX SCAM

*NOTE: This article was originally written in 2011 at the time of the events, however the spectre of Manmade Global Warming is still looming, therefore I have included it as is.

After what one Aussie columnist calls.

> *"...the dirtiest and most dishonest campaign ever waged before the Australian public"*

– then, with millions of dollars spent on media ads to convince the uneducated population that manmade global warming was a fact, then, overwhelming evidence that contradicts the government's claims - The Australia's **House of Representatives** finally voted on **October 12, 2011**, 74 to 72, to levy a tax on carbon pollution.

The proposal, which was pushed by then Prime Minister, **Julia Gillard** will impose a price of $23 on a ton of carbon pollution, starting in 2015. After 2015, an emissions-trading scheme will be introduced, with the goal of cutting total carbon pollution by **5 percent** by 2020. The legislation still needs to pass the Senate, but because Greens control the balance of power there, that is not likely to be a problem. Unless something dramatic happens, in a few months Australia will have taken a devastating first step toward tyranny and enslavement by the global elite.

To put it bluntly, **Anthropogenic** (manmade) **Global Warming** is a load of Rothschild-sponsored bovine excrement. Its purpose is to trick you out of your money and into obedience. And despite the shrill cries of those who insist that government would never conceive or let alone, execute such a monstrous fraud upon the people, the fact is that Anthropogenic Global Warming has a very long pedigree of deception behind it.

The recent exposures of fraud coming from the **Hadley Climate Research Unit**, then followed by similar exposures at **New Zealand's NWIA, Australia's Climate Centre**, and **NOAA** (National Oceanic and Atmospheric Administration), have only confirmed the doubts arising from the obviously non-scientific methods employed by the Anthropogenic Global Warming supporters.

Human Caused Global Warming is not being researched; it is being promoted. **Al Gore** and his fellow investors have spent over a hundred million dollars in creating a crisis of human-caused global warming out of (quite literally) thin air. They are not doing this out of the goodness of their hearts. They expect to reap billions in profits from the trading of Carbon Credits, a "license to pollute," available for a price and subject to brokerage fees. One of the people Al Gore relied on to create this scheme was **Ken Lay**, late of **ENRON**, aka the Crooked "E." Al Gore plans to use Carbon Dioxide to do to the world what Ken Lay did to California using electricity - loot the people!

Coupled with the desire to reap huge profits from the general population of the world is also the agenda to promote a global government. Currently, the push for a global government rests on three pillars, Global Warming is one of them, leading to a surrendering of national sovereignty which was attempted at the **Copenhagen Conference** December 7th, 2009 (but temporarily delayed when the conference was hit with a major snow blizzard!). The other two pillars exploited to create the "need" for a global government are a **global flu pandemic**, requiring a global health organisation, and a **global financial crisis**, requiring a global bank. The political power behind this push for global government is immense; enough to win Al Gore an **Academy Award** and a **Nobel Peace Prize** for his film, *An Inconvenient*

Truth, despite a court ruling pointing out the numerous provable lies and distortions in it.

To any real objective observer, the methods employed by the pro global warmers are not those of science and research, but of salesmanship and propaganda. Scare tactics are also well in evidence.

What science does Julia Gillard listen to?

Because the climate is chaotic, it is not predictable in the long term. However, all of the evidence the Australian government has relied on is "consensus" science.

Consensus is basically an uneducated guess. For example, let's say you are sitting around with your friends planning a picnic. You more or less all decide that the park you will go to will not be very busy, and that the weather will be fine. But none of you know for certain that it will all work out that way. You may get to the park and it is pouring rain, or 2 busloads of the CWA (Country Women's Association) have just arrived for their annual get together. If one of you had done some research you probably would have picked another weekend or a different park!

That is why every scientist from **Aristotle,** 4200 years ago, to **Ibn al-Haytham**, the founder of the scientific method in 11th century Iraq, to **Karl Popper** in 1934 in the celebrated book *The Logic of Scientific Discovery,* employs rigorous standards to research, rather than rely on consensus.

The government of Australia has been listening to the consensus science expressed in the documents produced by *Inter Governmental Panel on Climate Change* **(IPCC)**, produced by the **United Nations**. If your country has signed onto the UN, then your leaders are getting their data from the IPCC.

Economist on the other hand tend to raise the question of insurance principle, in other words, if the cost of the premium exceeds the cost of the risk, don't insure.

Simply put, the Carbon Tax is going to cost more than letting global warming take place in the first place, so we are best to do nothing in the foreseeable future.

One question we should be asking is how much will a 5% reduction in Australia's emissions (which represents 1.2% of global emissions) actually achieve?

Well here are the numbers, and the truth may shock you!

0.06% of world carbon emission will be remitted over the next 10 years. The amount of CO2 that would have been in the atmosphere, according to the IPPC, would fall from **412** to **411.987** parts per million. This would equate to **0.00007** degrees Celsius reduction in global warming.

This is what the consensus scientists agree on, and they use this mainstream calculation. This is **1/14,000 of Celsius degrees** which is a **700th** of the threshold below which no modern method or instrument can detect any change in global temperature at all! In other words, we could not even measure the decrease with the instruments we currently have because it is too small.

How much will it cost?

Around **$127 Billion** over the next 10 years and if you were to apply the Julia Gillard method all over the world, the method as cost in effect as her proposal, then it would take **$60,000** per head of the world population (just in the next 10 years) or 60% of global GDP just to forestall the **0.23** Celsius of global warming that the IPCC predicts will occur over the next 10 years. Consequently, this would also mean that no one could drive cars, fly planes, boats etc. No industry or household could use coal powered electricity. We would all have to go back to pre-industrial life for 10 years, at $60,000 each, just so we do not allow the increase 0.23 Celsius, never mind reducing what is already there!

It is clearly cheaper to do nothing about global warming, and to adapt a focused way to any consequences that are adverse that may occur from any warming that may occur, than to spend any money what so ever now. So if the data doesn't stack up, and it will cost way too much, why would Julia Gillard force this farce onto the Australian People?

Follow the money

If you want to learn the answer to that question – just follow the money! Trust me, I think stopping pollution is a great idea, but the carbon tax and global warming scam has nothing to do with reducing pollution. It is all about **money, power,** and **control** of the population.

The global warming movement says our planet is heading for disaster because factories and cars are heating up the atmosphere with

Carbon dioxide. But the fact is, it is all a **scam**. An industry that feeds off our fears, tricking us to buy billions of dollars' worth of green products, and making us lose sleep worrying about our carbon footprints.

It is all a polluter's **Ponzi scheme**[19]. Politicians say they want to set limits on CO2 emissions, and at the same time they allow corporations that want to pollute more to buy and trade carbon credits from companies that pollute less. In other words, permission to pollute – if they pay!

Thousands of scientists believe that global warming is not a problem at all. Global warming has occurred and climate change occurs all the time, however human production of CO2 is not the cause of the warming.

The sun is the cause of all global warming

The sun, as the root cause of global warming problem has been all but ignored by the authorities and in particular the IPCC from the United Nations that are pushing the human cause of CO2 and global warming.

Another interesting fact these people ignore is that CO2 is plant food! Yes, plants love CO2. In fact, studies show that plants grown in a 35% more carbon dioxide environment thrive, growing twice as fast and producing more fruits and seeds. On top of this, plants release oxygen (what humans need) back into the atmosphere at night! So if anything, we should allow a small increase in CO2 because ultimately plants and humans would thrive!

So if human made global warming is not the cause, why are they telling us it is?

Control!

They can now control every aspect of your life. From the amount of children you can have to the type of vehicle you can drive, to the type of food you can consume. In other words, get used to only eating meat on special occasions. Quite simply, if you can control carbon, you can control the planet.

---

[19] A Ponzi scheme is a fraudulent investment operation where the operator, an individual or organisation, pays returns to its investors from new capital paid to the operators by new investors, rather than from profit earned by the operator. Sometimes called a Pyramid scheme.

The cap and trade market is reported to be worth trillions of dollars. The USA has already spent over $70 billion on science funding over the last 10 years. The last thing anyone would want to do is to solve the problem.

One company that stands to make billions from a Carbon Tax is The **Hara Corporation**. It has staked its future on global warming. The Hara Corporation says it can help companies reduce their carbon footprint through the use of their software program they specifically created to combat global warming. It works out your carbon footprint and how you can reduce it to save on carbon taxes. By getting a tick from Hara's software program, companies can save millions of dollars in carbon tax. So who wouldn't want to use Hara's software? In fact, one Silicon Valley newspaper article claimed Hara will become the next Microsoft. Did I mention who the majority shareholder is? **Al Gore**!

Al Gore's Inconvenient Hypocrisy

The **Tennessee Center for Policy Research**, which said it used figures from the **Nashville Electric service** reported that Gore's house used a whopping 221,000 kWh of electricity in 2006, more than 20 times

Former Vice President Al Gore's Nashville House 2006. A 20-room mansion (not including 8 bathrooms) heated by natural gas. Add on a pool (and a pool house) and a separate guest house all heated by gas. In ONE MONTH ALONE this mansion consumes more energy than the average American household in an ENTIRE YEAR.

the national average of 10,656 kWh. The report says the natural gas usage of Gore's home is high as well, and that the Gores spent more than $30,000 in combined electricity and natural gas bills in 2006. But you couldn't really call it a "house." The average house in his area is 4,000-square-feet, however Gore's house is a massive 10,000 square feet mansion.

The Gores also bought new digs in 2009 — a $8.875 million ocean view villa in Montecito, Calif., according to the *Los Angeles Times*. The *Times* asked for comment on whether the 6,500-square-foot property was going to be environmentally retrofitted, but the newspaper did not get a response.

In August 2012, *The New York* Times reported that Al Gore lives in the **Nashville** mansion, while ex-wife **Tipper Gore** divides her time between the **Montecito** villa and a family home in **Arlington, Va**. Al Gore also owns his family's farm in **Carthage, Tenn**. To move from one house to another, the Gore's use their private **Gulfstream jet**. God only knows what that thing consumes in fossil fuel. Not to mention the running and upkeep of three massive mansions. Al Gore's hypocrisy is breathtaking.

Former Vice President Al Gore's new $9 million ocean-view villa property in Montecito, CA. 2009. The two-story Italian-esque villa boasts five bedrooms, nine bathrooms, and six fireplaces. Complete with high ceilings, a wine cellar, terraces, and an exquisite outdoor pool, the property itself is 1.5 acres. Other Montecito inhabitants include Oprah Winfrey, Michael Douglas, Christopher Lloyd, and golfer Fred Couples.

Perhaps now you will understand why Al and his buddies need this Global Warming scam to work. It is costing him a bomb to run three houses, countless cars, and a private jet!

Where it all began - The Man Behind the Curtain

The entire global warming scam can be traced to 1 man – **Maurice Strong**. "Sir" Maurice Strong is a Canadian born, senior official for the **United Nations**. Strong has been very vocal over the last 20 years about forming a one world government based at the UN. The UN one world government would supersede all other country governments who would be little more than local administrators (Vassals).

If Al Gore is the front man for global warming, Maurice Strong is the wizard behind the curtain. Maurice Strong was the secretary general of the UN's **1972** conference on the *Human Environment*, the one which launched the green movement. It was at this conference Strong first introduced the idea of taxing nations for pollution. He then became the UN's first **Director of the Environment Program** and organised the **Earth Summit in Rio in 1992** which set the stage for the **Kyoto treaty,** controlling the emission of greenhouse gases. But many say Maurice Strong is a wolf in sheep's clothing. He pretended to be green so he could get rich and take over the world.

You see, Maurice Strong just happens to be a billionaire – an oil billionaire. He is a director of the **Chicago Climate Exchange** which trades and sells Carbon Credits – the ones that give permission to pollute. He has also been linked to the United Nations "Oil for Food" scandal where he was stood down by the UN for his involvement. He had to run to avoid criminal charges and ended up in Beijing, China.

As of 2005, he has been working for the Chinese government, helping them trade their pollution for clean credits – remember - permission to pollute slips!

Strong was one of those who were instrumental in establishing the *Inter-Governmental Panel on Climate Change* (IPCC). The IPCC has produce 4 major assessments of the climate, each of them more absurd than the last and they have now got things to such a fever pitch that they manage to get the Australian government to agree on a carbon tax.

Falsifying the Data

It is now on record that the IPCC was caught red handed falsifying their data. The **Climate Gate** scandal is only one example. Another example includes **Dr. Benjamin Santer**, a climate scientist and right hand man of Maurice Strong. He has admitted to altering a crucial UN report (*IPCC Second Assessment Climate Change 1995*). He deleted at least 5 opinions by leading scientists that opposed the global warming theory. So in other words, after the world's leading climate scientists sent in their data and conclusions about climate change that basically said there was no basis to it, Santer took it on himself to "edit" those findings to support his own agenda. He makes no apologies either claiming he had to do it for the "benefit of the planet." No charges were laid.

The Final Piece of the Puzzle

George Hunt was an official at the **4th World Wilderness Congress** conference when he met Maurice Strong in 1987. The Congress is an international forum for discussing the environment. But Maurice Strong showed up to introduce a new player, the financier **Edmond de Rothschild** of the Rothschild banking dynasty, with a proposal for something he called a **World Conservation Bank**.

For those that are not familiar with the Rothschild family, they have amassed a conservative estimate of just over $500 Trillion in assets, effectively owning around ½ of the world. They have started and financed every major military conflict since the Napoleonic Wars. They have bankrupted nations, chose and assassinated presidents and political rivals. The Rothschilds brokered the 1947 deal to hand over the Palestinian land to Israel. In fact, the Rothschilds openly brag that they own 80% of Israel and that the Star of David flag is actually their own family flag that they convinced Israel to use as its national flag!

Hunt says that the aim of Strong and Rothschild was to create an anxiety about global warming to such a fevered pitch that people would be willing to accept **One World Bank** that would be willing to accept the responsibility of cleaning up the environment.

Through of all this, Maurice Strong has been the Rothschilds right hand man in the environmentalist movement. Through Strong, they were able to monetise environmentalism.

In fact, in the USA, green products sales went from $203 Billion in 2007 to **$400 Billion** in 2010.

Almost every aspect of your life is connected to energy use and carbon emissions. From your hot shower in the morning, blow drying your hair, driving to work, cooking dinner, and reading a book in bed using a bed side lamp (and your digital alarm clock). Therefore with the introduction of a carbon tax, everything in your life is going to go up in price.

The hardest hit will be pensioners and low or fixed income earners. That is why Gillard is trying to soften the blow by giving these people a so-called tax break of less than $10 per week. This will quickly be absorbed by the rising cost of living. By 2020, most pensioners and fixed income / low income earners will be destitute and begging on the streets. I would also like to go on record as predicting Australia will be getting "**Smart Meters**" soon to "save you money on power bills". I would urge you to research these so-called smart meters. They basically turn your house into a microwave oven. Side effects reported so far include migraine headaches, dizziness, and nausea.

This is going to be seen as the biggest tax ever imposed on humanity in the history of the world. In effect, it is a tax on breathing. So for every dollar you spend on day to day living, a proportion of your hard earned money is going to go directly into the coffers of the Rothschild banking family, and you have the Australian government to thank for it. Our politicians have sold us to the global ruling families. It doesn't matter if you vote Gillard out because there are another 10 puppets there to take her place.

© Danny Searle 2011

Update 2015

Since writing this article back in 2011, Australia has gone through several government changes. The current government, who were Gillard's opposition, took the carbon tax off the agenda for now, due to a public ground swell opposing it. However, Gillard's party are still pushing for it, because this is a **Fabian Socity** agenda. If they get back into power at the next election, they will reintroduce it. Even though I talk about Australia, this is a global plan, and it will come to every town, in every country sooner or later. So all the figures I have quoted are still good globally. It all ties into **Agenda 21**.

Something I should have mentioned in the original article is that Julia Gillard is a proud and vocal member of the **Fabian Society**. She often makes reference (glorifying their work) in her public speeches. If you remember back, the Fabians are all for global governance, but at a snail's pace, so they don't startle the sheeple. Hitler's Nazi's were all for quick change via military means, whereas the Fabians are about long term change through stealth.

NASA satellite data showing that Antarctica is gaining ice.

2 Nov, 2015 Antarctica has been accumulating more ice than it's been losing in recent decades, a new study by NASA has revealed, challenging existing theories on climate change and rises in sea levels. NASA's Goddard Space Flight Center, the University of Maryland, and Sigma Space Corporation, analysed satellite data showing that Antarctica gained 112 billion tons of ice annually (Zabarenko, 2015).

If I could summarise this whole issue, I would say:

> *"Climate change is real, but the Earth Is actually cooling, rapidly, and is caused by sun cycles, not man made activities."*
> *– Danny Searle (2011)*

References:

Climategate, (2015). *Climatic Research Unit email controversy*. [online] Wikipedia. Available at: https://en.wikipedia.org/wiki/Climatic_Research_Unit_email_controversy [Accessed 27 Nov. 2015].

Driessen, P. (2015). *PAUL DRIESSEN: Earth may be cooling, not warming*. [online] The Washington Times. Available at: http://www.washingtontimes.com/news/2015/may/17/paul-driessen-earth-may-be-cooling-no-warming/?page=all [Accessed 27 Nov. 2015].

Gleick, P. (2015). *Breaking News: Climate Change Is Real, But the Earth Is Actually Cooling Rapidly*. [online] The Huffington Post. Available at: http://www.huffingtonpost.com/peter-h-gleick/breaking-news-climate-cha_b_2994164.html?ir=Australia [Accessed 27 Nov. 2015].

Huff, E. (2015). *Global warming debunked: NASA report verifies carbon dioxide actually cools atmosphere*. [online] NaturalNews. Available at: http://www.naturalnews.com/040448_solar_radiation_global_warming_debunked.html [Accessed 27 Nov. 2015].

NASA, (2015). *NASA - The Ups and Downs of Global Warming*. [online] Nasa.gov. Available at: http://www.nasa.gov/topics/earth/features/upsDownsGlobalWarming.html [Accessed 27 Nov. 2015].

Taylor, J. (2015). *Forbes Welcome*. [online] Forbes.com. Available at: http://www.forbes.com/sites/jamestaylor/2015/05/19/updated-nasa-data-polar-ice-not-receding-after-all/ [Accessed 27 Nov. 2015].

Zabarenko, D. (2015). *Antarctica gaining more ice than losing - NASA*. [online] RT English. Available at: https://www.rt.com/usa/320554-antarctica-gaining-ice-nasa/ [Accessed 3 Nov. 2015].

ANNEX 3.9.2

63RD BILDERBERG CONFERENCE 2015

*T*he official Bilderberg Group website released the full attendee list and agenda for the 2015 conference. As ever, the list of topics to be discussed is so vague, as to almost be meaningless.

The 63rd Bilderberg conference took place from 11 – 14 June 2015 in Telfs-Buchen, Austria. A total of around 140 participants from 22 countries were in attendance. As usual, a diverse group of political leaders and experts from industry, finance, academia, and the media have been invited.

The key topics for discussion this year include:

Artificial Intelligence	Cybersecurity
Chemical Weapons Threats	Current Economic Issues
European Strategy	Globalisation
Greece	Iran
Middle East	NATO
Russia	Terrorism
United Kingdom	USA
US Elections	World Migration Agenda

Founded in 1954, the Bilderberg conference is an annual meeting by the most powerful group of the Roundtable Groups. Every year, between 120-150 political leaders and experts from industry, finance, academia and the media are invited to take part in the conference. The topics are chosen by the Committee of 300, and given to the Steering Committee of Bilderberg to discuss with participants.

About two thirds of the participants come from Europe and the rest from North America; approximately one third from politics and government and the rest from other fields including, royalty, finance (bankers), defence force, weapon sales, Oil barons, and media to name but a few. All are sworn to secrecy.

Telfs-Buchen, Austria 11 – 14 June 2015 – Final:

Castries, Henri de	Chairman and CEO, AXA Group	FRA
Achleitner, Paul M.	Chairman of the Supervisory Board, Deutsche Bank AG	DEU
Agius, Marcus	Non-Executive Chairman, PA Consulting Group	GBR
Ahrenkiel, Thomas	Director, Danish Intelligence Service (DDIS)	DNK
Allen, John R.	Special Presidential Envoy for the Global Coalition to Counter ISIL, US Department of State	USA
Altman, Roger C.	Executive Chairman, Evercore	USA
Applebaum, Anne	Director of Transitions Forum, Legatum Institute	POL
Apunen, Matti	Director, Finnish Business and Policy Forum EVA	FIN
Baird, Zoë	CEO and President, Markle Foundation	USA
Balls, Edward M.	Former Shadow Chancellor of the Exchequer	GBR
Balsemão, Francisco Pinto	Chairman, Impresa SGPS	PRT
Barroso, José M. Durão	Former President of the European Commission	PRT
Baverez, Nicolas	Partner, Gibson, Dunn & Crutcher LLP	FRA
Benko, René	Founder, SIGNA Holding GmbH	AUT
Bernabè, Franco	Chairman, FB Group SRL	ITA
Beurden, Ben van	CEO, Royal Dutch Shell plc	NLD
Bigorgne, Laurent	Director, Institut Montaigne	FRA
Boone, Laurence	Special Adviser on Financial and Economic Affairs to the President	FRA
Botín, Ana P.	Chairman, Banco Santander	ESP
Brandtzæg, Svein Richard	President and CEO, Norsk Hydro ASA	NOR
Bronner, Oscar	Publisher, Standard Verlagsgesellschaft	AUT

Burns, William	President, Carnegie Endowment for International Peace	USA
Calvar, Patrick	Director General, DGSI	FRA
Castries, Henri de	Chairman, Bilderberg Meetings; Chairman and CEO, AXA Group	FRA
Cebrián, Juan Luis	Executive Chairman, Grupo PRISA	ESP
Clark, W. Edmund	Retired Executive, TD Bank Group	CAN
Coeuré, Benoît	Member of the Executive Board, European Central Bank	INT
Coyne, Andrew	Editor, Editorials and Comment, National Post	CAN
Damberg, Mikael L.	Minister for Enterprise and Innovation	SWE
De Gucht, Karel	Former EU Trade Commissioner, State Minister	BEL
Dijsselbloem, Jeroen	Minister of Finance	NLD
Donilon, Thomas E.	Former U.S. National Security Advisor; Partner and Vice Chair, O'Melveny & Myers LLP	USA
Döpfner, Mathias	CEO, Axel Springer SE	DEU
Dowling, Ann	President, Royal Academy of Engineering	GBR
Dugan, Regina	Vice President for Engineering, Advanced Technology and Projects, Google	USA
Eilertsen, Trine	Political Editor, Aftenposten	NOR
Eldrup, Merete	CEO, TV 2 Danmark A/S	DNK
Elkann, John	Chairman and CEO, EXOR; Chairman, Fiat Chrysler Automobiles	ITA
Enders, Thomas	CEO, Airbus Group	DEU
Erdoes, Mary	CEO, JP Morgan Asset Management	USA
Fairhead, Rona	Chairman, BBC Trust	GBR
Federspiel, Ulrik	Executive Vice President, Haldor Topsøe A/S	DNK
Feldstein, Martin S.	President Emeritus, NBER; Professor of Economics, Harvard University	USA
Ferguson, Niall	Professor of History, Harvard University, Gunzberg Center for European Studies	USA
Fischer, Heinz	Federal President	AUT
Flint, Douglas J.	Group Chairman, HSBC Holdings plc	GBR
Franz, Christoph	Chairman of the Board, F. Hoffmann-La Roche Ltd	CHE
Fresco, Louise O.	President and Chairman Executive Board, Wageningen University and Research Centre	NLD

Griffin, Kenneth	Founder and CEO, Citadel Investment Group, LLC	USA
Gruber, Lilli	Executive Editor and Anchor "Otto e mezzo", La7 TV	ITA
Guriev, Sergei	Professor of Economics, Sciences Po	RUS
Gürkaynak, Gönenç	Managing Partner, ELIG Law Firm	TUR
Gusenbauer, Alfred	Former Chancellor of the Republic of Austria	AUT
Halberstadt, Victor	Professor of Economics, Leiden University	NLD
Hampel, Erich	Chairman, UniCredit Bank Austria AG	AUT
Hassabis, Demis	Vice President of Engineering, Google DeepMind	GBR
Hesoun, Wolfgang	CEO, Siemens Austria	AUT
Hildebrand, Philipp	Vice Chairman, BlackRock Inc.	CHE
Hoffman, Reid	Co-Founder and Executive Chairman, LinkedIn	USA
Ischinger, Wolfgang	Chairman, Munich Security Conference	INT
Jacobs, Kenneth M.	Chairman and CEO, Lazard	USA
Jäkel, Julia	CEO, Gruner + Jahr	DEU
Johnson, James A.	Chairman, Johnson Capital Partners	USA
Juppé, Alain	Mayor of Bordeaux, Former Prime Minister	FRA
Kaeser, Joe	President and CEO, Siemens AG	DEU
Karp, Alex	CEO, Palantir Technologies	USA
Kepel, Gilles	University Professor, Sciences Po	FRA
Kerr, John	Deputy Chairman, Scottish Power	GBR
Kesici, Ilhan	MP, Turkish Parliament	TUR
Kissinger, Henry A.	Chairman, Kissinger Associates, Inc.	USA
Kleinfeld, Klaus	Chairman and CEO, Alcoa	USA
Knot, Klaas H.W.	President, De Nederlandsche Bank	NLD
Koç, Mustafa V.	Chairman, Koç Holding A.S.	TUR
Kogler, Konrad	Director General, Directorate General for Public Security	AUT
Kravis, Henry R.	Co-Chairman and Co-CEO, Kohlberg Kravis Roberts & Co.	USA
Kravis, Marie-Josée	Senior Fellow and Vice Chair, Hudson Institute	USA
Kudelski, André	Chairman and CEO, Kudelski Group	CHE
Lauk, Kurt	President, Globe Capital Partners	DEU
Lemne, Carola	CEO, The Confederation of Swedish Enterprise	SWE
Levey, Stuart	Chief Legal Officer, HSBC Holdings plc	USA
Leyen, Ursula von der	Minister of Defence	DEU

Leysen, Thomas	Chairman of the Board of Directors, KBC Group	BEL
Maher, Shiraz	Senior Research Fellow, ICSR, King's College London	GBR
Markus Lassen, Christina	Head of Department, Ministry of Foreign Affairs, Security Policy and Stabilisation	DNK
Mathews, Jessica T.	Distinguished Fellow, Carnegie Endowment for International Peace	USA
Mattis, James	Distinguished Visiting Fellow, Hoover Institution, Stanford University	USA
Maudet, Pierre	Vice-President of the State Council, Department of Security, Police and the Economy of Geneva	CHE
McKay, David I.	President and CEO, Royal Bank of Canada	CAN
Mert, Nuray	Columnist, Professor of Political Science, Istanbul University	TUR
Messina, Jim	CEO, The Messina Group	USA
Michel, Charles	Prime Minister	BEL
Micklethwait, John	Editor-in-Chief, Bloomberg LP	USA
Minton Beddoes, Zanny	Editor-in-Chief, The Economist	GBR
Monti, Mario	Senator-for-life; President, Bocconi University	ITA
Mörttinen, Leena	Executive Director, The Finnish Family Firms Association	FIN
Mundie, Craig J.	Principal, Mundie & Associates	USA
Munroe-Blum, Heather	Chairperson, Canada Pension Plan Investment Board	CAN
Netherlands, H.R.H. Princess Beatrix of the		NLD
O'Leary, Michael	CEO, Ryanair Plc	IRL
Osborne, George	First Secretary of State and Chancellor of the Exchequer	GBR
Özel, Soli	Columnist, Haberturk Newspaper; Senior Lecturer, Kadir Has University	TUR
Papalexopoulos, Dimitri	Group CEO, Titan Cement Co.	GRC
Pégard, Catherine	President, Public Establishment of the Palace, Museum and National Estate of Versailles	FRA
Perle, Richard N.	Resident Fellow, American Enterprise Institute	USA
Petraeus, David H.	Chairman, KKR Global Institute	USA
Pikrammenos, Panagiotis	Honorary President of The Hellenic Council of State	GRC

Reisman, Heather M.	Chair and CEO, Indigo Books & Music Inc.	CAN
Rocca, Gianfelice	Chairman, Techint Group	ITA
Roiss, Gerhard	CEO, OMV Austria	AUT
Rubin, Robert E.	Co Chair, Council on Foreign Relations; Former Secretary of the Treasury	USA
Rutte, Mark	Prime Minister	NLD
Sadjadpour, Karim	Senior Associate, Carnegie Endowment for International Peace	USA
Sánchez Pérez-Castejón,Pedro	Leader, Partido Socialista Obrero Español PSOE	ESP
Swers, John	Chairman and Partner, Macro Advisory Partners	GBR
Sayek Böke, Selin	Vice President, Republican People's Party	TUR
Schmidt, Eric E.	Executive Chairman, Google Inc.	USA
Scholten, Rudolf	CEO, Oesterreichische Kontrollbank AG	AUT
Senard, Jean-Dominique	CEO, Michelin Group	FRA
Sevelda, Karl	CEO, Raiffeisen Bank International AG	AUT
Stoltenberg, Jens	Secretary General, NATO	INT
Stubb, Alexander	Prime Minister	FIN
Suder, Katrin	Deputy Minister of Defense	DEU
Sutherland, Peter D.	UN Special Representative; Chairman, Goldman Sachs International	IRL
Svanberg, Carl-Henric	Chairman, BP plc; Chairman, AB Volvo	SWE
Svarva, Olaug	CEO, The Government Pension Fund Norway	NOR
Thiel, Peter A.	President, Thiel Capital (co-founded PayPal)	USA
Tsoukalis, Loukas	President, Hellenic Foundation for European and Foreign Policy	GRC
Üzümcü, Ahmet	Director-General, Organisation for the Prohibition of Chemical Weapons	INT
Vitorino, António M.	Partner, Cuetrecasas, Concalves Pereira, RL	PRT
Wallenberg, Jacob	Chairman, Investor AB	SWE
Weber, Vin	Partner, Mercury LLC	USA
Wolf, Martin H.	Chief Economics Commentator, The Financial Times	GBR
Wolfensohn, James D.	Chairman and CEO, Wolfensohn and Company	USA
Zoellick, Robert B.	Chairman, Board of International Advisors, The Goldman Sachs Group	USA

Some of the Outcomes:

- Bilderberg backs Hillary for 2016 Presidency, but Obama is threatening to expose the Clinton's crimes, so Jeb Bush is the back-up in case Hillary goes to jail or has to drop out.
- Speech given by former **DARPA** director and now Google Executive **Regina Dugan**. She spoke about their development and promotion of an ingestible, identification microchip. She also spoke about how close they are getting to creating a true AI robot brain.
- More false flag terror attacks for Europe, and a big one for US in 2015/16. They need them to justify increase in military spending which is really for the build-up preparations for WWIII.
- A regime change for **Syria**, however Russia is blocking that.
- They want **WWIII** to start in late 2017/ early 2018 and hope Russia and/or China will be the "enemy." They are working out ways to provoke them into a full war.

References:

InfoWars, (2015). *Bilderberg 2015: Full Attendee List & Agenda*. [online] Infowars.com. Available at: http://www.infowars.com/bilderberg-2015-full-attendee-list-agenda [Accessed 26 Nov. 2015].

Official List, (2015). *Participants | Bilderberg Meetings*. [online] Bilderbergmeetings.org. Available at: http://www.bilderbergmeetings.org/participants2015.html [Accessed 26 Nov. 2015].

OTHER BOOKS IN THIS SERIES

THE TRUTH CHRONICLES BOOK I: Secrets of the Soul

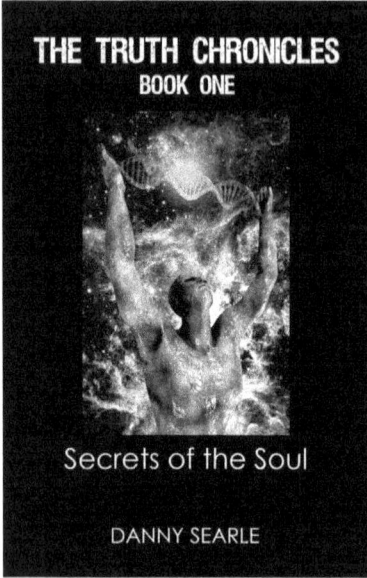

Your birth was not an accident. You chose your parents, your family, your friends, and your enemies. You also chose your gender, your race, and your appearance.

How is this possible?

In *The Truth Chronicles Book 1: Secrets of the Soul*, spiritual guidance counselor and YouTube sensation Danny Searle explains exactly what happens when we die, what our life in the spirit world is like, and what preparations our souls make before they return to the living world. Our souls grow through challenging experiences, and only life offers opportunity for such development.

Basing his explanations on a series of personal encounters with his spirit guide, Searle reveals how knowledge about the different soul ages can help us understand how people behave and why the world works as it does.

As Searle reveals the secrets of the spirit realm, he uncovers the hidden truth about humanity's origins—a secret locked within our DNA and recorded in ancient Sumerian texts.

Light-hearted, accessible, and entertaining, Searle's insights don't require previous experience in spiritual matters. But though this book is designed to be easily understandable, its consequences are profound.

Secrets of the Soul will change how you live and how you perceive death.

ISBN-13: 978-0992598105

ISBN-10: 0992598109

Availlbale on Amazon and Amazon Kindle.

www.ingramcontent.com/pod-product-compliance
Lightning Source LLC
Chambersburg PA
CBHW070612270326
41926CB00011B/1669